FIGURE 1.5

The U.S. Unemployment Rate Since World War II, the highest rate of unemployment has been the nearly 10 percent of 1982. Before World War II, peaks in unemployment were much higher, especially during the Great Depression of the 1930s.

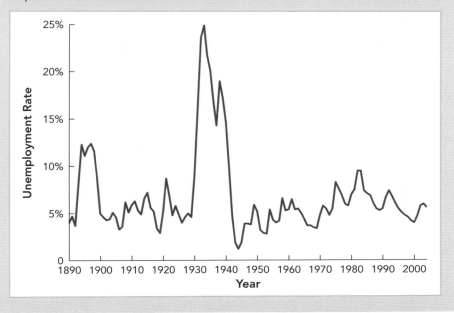

Source: Authors' calculations from the 2004 edition of *The Economic Report of the President* (Washington, DC: Government Printing Office) and from Christina Romer, "Spurious Volatility in Historical Unemployment Estimates," *Journal of Political Economy*, Vol. 94 (1986), 1, pp. 1–37.

FIGURE 1.6

Inflation in the United States Before 1970, periods when inflation rose above 10 percent were confined to major wars.

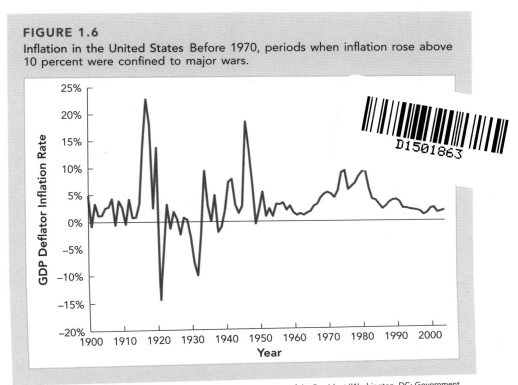

Source: Authors' calculations from the 2004 edition of *The Economic Report of the President* (Washington, DC: Government Printing Office) and from *Historical Statistics of the United States* (Washington, DC: Government Printing Office, 1975).

Macroeconomics

Second Edition

Macroeconomics

Second Edition

J. Bradford DeLong
University of California, Berkeley

Martha L. Olney
University of California, Berkeley

McGraw-Hill
Irwin

Boston   Burr Ridge, IL   Dubuque, IA   Madison, WI   New York   San Francisco   St. Louis
Bangkok   Bogotá   Caracas   Kuala Lumpur   Lisbon   London   Madrid   Mexico City
Milan   Montreal   New Delhi   Santiago   Seoul   Singapore   Sydney   Taipei   Toronto

McGraw-Hill
Irwin

MACROECONOMICS

Published by McGraw-Hill/Irwin, a business unit of The McGraw-Hill Companies, Inc., 1221 Avenue of the Americas, New York, NY, 10020. Copyright © 2006, 2002 by The McGraw-Hill Companies, Inc. All rights reserved. No part of this publication may be reproduced or distributed in any form or by any means, or stored in a database or retrieval system, without the prior written consent of The McGraw-Hill Companies, Inc., including, but not limited to, in any network or other electronic storage or transmission, or broadcast for distance learning.

Some ancillaries, including electronic and print components, may not be available to customers outside the United States.

This book is printed on acid-free paper.

1 2 3 4 5 6 7 8 9 0 WCK/WCK 0 9 8 7 6 5

ISBN 0-07-287758-8

Publisher: *Gary Burke*
Executive sponsoring editor: *Paul Shensa*
Senior developmental editor: *Tom Thompson*
Senior marketing manager: *Martin D. Quinn*
Lead producer, Media technology: *Kai Chiang*
Lead project manager: *Mary Conzachi*
Senior production supervisor: *Sesha Bolisetty*
Senior designer: *Adam Rooke*
Media project manager: *Matthew Perry*
Supplement producer: *Gina F. DiMartino*
Developer, Media technology: *Brian Nacik*
Cover and interior design: *Maureen McCutcheon*
Typeface: *10/12 Berkeley*
Compositor: *TechBooks/GTS, York, PA*
Printer: *Quebecor World Versailles Inc.*

Cover Image: Composition in Red, Blue and Yellow, 1930 Oil on canvas, 18 1/8″ × 18 1/8″ (46 × 46 cm) © 2004 Mondrian/Holtzman Trust c/o HCR International, Warrenton, VA

Library of Congress Cataloging-in-Publication Data

DeLong, J. Bradford.
    Macroeconomics. — 2nd ed. / J. Bradford DeLong, Martha L. Olney.
      p. cm.
    Various multi-media instructional materials are available to supplement the text.
    Includes index.
    ISBN 0-07-287758-8 (alk. paper)
    1. Macroeconomics. I. Olney, Martha L. II. Title.
  HB172.5.D435 2006
  339 — dc22   2005041667

www.mhhe.com

For Ann Marie Marciarille
and
For Esther Hargis

About the Authors

J. Bradford DeLong

J. Bradford DeLong is professor of economics at the University of California at Berkeley, where he has been teaching since 1995. Before starting to teach at Berkeley, he was deputy assistant secretary for economic policy in the United States Department of the Treasury (1993 to 1995), where an enormous range of issues crossed his desk — from what the Federal Reserve will do next week to whether the Uruguay Round of the GATT should be ratified to the macroeconomic implications of the (unsuccessful) health care reform. Before working at the Treasury he was an associate professor at Harvard University, where he was both an undergraduate student (B.A. 1982) and a graduate student (Ph.D. 1987). He has also taught at Boston University and MIT.

Professor DeLong is also a research associate of the National Bureau of Economic Research and a visiting scholar at the Federal Reserve Bank of San Francisco. And he is a former coeditor of the *Journal of Economic Perspectives*.

Professor DeLong's research interests range from the origins of the Great Depression to the effect of irrational speculation on stock market values; to whether there is a "new economy"; and, among other things, to the causes of long-run economic divergence across nations. He is a prolific writer and has contributed more than 100 articles to publications ranging from *The American Economic Review* to *Fortune* and *Foreign Affairs* to *The New York Times*. His own Web site contains an awesome amount of material — including reviews of books and scholarly articles and analyses of current events — and is widely considered to be one of the best academic economics Web sites available. Brad DeLong lives in Lafayette, California, with his wife and two children.

Martha L. Olney

Martha L. Olney received her B.S. in 1978 from the University of Redlands and Ph.D. in 1985 from the University of California, Berkeley. She is an adjunct professor of economics at U.C. Berkeley, where she has taught since 1992. Previously, she was a tenured member of the economics faculty at University of Massachusetts, Amherst. Professor Olney has also taught at Stanford University. Her research is in the areas of consumer spending and consumer indebtedness, focusing especially on the interwar years.

Professor Olney is the author of *Buy Now Pay Later: Advertising, Credit, and Consumer Durables* (University of North Carolina Press, 1991). Honored several times for her excellence in teaching, Professor Olney is the recipient of Distinguished Teaching Awards from the University of California, Berkeley and University of Massachusetts, Amherst. The Economic History Association awarded her the Jonathan Hughes Prize for Excellence in Teaching Economic History in 1997. Martha Olney lives in El Cerrito, California, with her partner and their son.

Brief Contents

Contents

PART 3
FLEXIBLE-PRICE MACROECONOMICS

CHAPTER 6
Building Blocks of the Flexible-Price Model   159

CHAPTER 7
Equilibrium in the Flexible-Price Model   193

PART 4
STICKY-PRICE MACROECONOMICS

PART 5
MACROECONOMIC POLICY

List of Boxes

Preface

Brad DeLong wrote the first edition of this book out of a sense that it was time for intermediate macroeconomics to spend some time in drydock and have the barnacles scraped off its hull. More than three-quarters of a century had elapsed since John Maynard Keynes wrote his *Tract on Monetary Reform,* which first linked inflation, production, employment, exchange rates, and policy together in a pattern that we today can recognize as "macroeconomics." Two-thirds of a century had elapsed since John Hicks and Alvin Hansen drew their IS and LM curves. More than one-third of a century had elapsed since Milton Friedman and Edward Phelps demolished the static Phillips curve, and since Robert Lucas, Thomas Sargent, and Robert Barro had taught us what rational expectations could mean. All this time, intermediate macroeconomics became more complicated, as new material was added while old material remained. It seemed to Brad that if he could successfully streamline the presentation of material, both traditional and modern, the result would be a more understandable and comprehensible book.

Martha Olney came on board for the second edition of this book out of a conviction that Brad had it right: The macro story of this book does move more smoothly through the water than its competitors. The focus is on what students need to know to understand our modern macroeconomy. Is a tax cut good or bad for the economy? Yes. If household saving increases, is that good or bad for the economy? Yes. By teaching both long-run growth and short-run fluctuations, and most important, in Martha's experience, by teaching the flexible-price flow of funds model, students clearly see the central dilemma policy makers face today: That what is good (or bad) for the macroeconomy in the short run may well be bad (or good) in the long run. Martha admits she was dragged into teaching long-run growth a decade or more ago when it cropped up in first one and then another textbook. She never liked the fact that the growth material seemed "crammed" into the book (and consequently into her lectures) without being part of a unifying story. But the treatment of growth in the first edition of *Macroeconomics,* and particularly the integration of Chapters 4 through 12 into one big story, have made her a full-fledged convert. Martha's best macro classes have been taught from this book.

The changes to the first edition focus almost entirely on pedagogy: What is the clearest way to teach a given concept? The second edition sticks with the five changes in the standard presentation of modern macroeconomics introduced in the first edition. Those five changes are not radical; rather they are shifts in emphasis and changes of focus. They do not require recasting of courses, but they are very important in bringing the organization of the book into line with what students learning macroeconomics today need to know.

MAJOR INNOVATIONS OF THE FIRST EDITION

The first two changes relate to *economic growth*.

◆ Provide a more student-friendly way of learning *growth theory*.

◆ Provide sufficient coverage of *growth facts* so that students learn the how and why of both growth over time and growth across countries.

Too often undergraduates find the standard presentation of growth theory — with concepts like "output per effective worker" — to be confusing. The more understandable and robust presentation of growth theory in this book focuses on the economy's balanced-growth capital-output ratio, which is itself a very simple function of the proximate determinants of accumulation: saving rates, depreciation rates, population growth, and labor-augmenting technical change. To make the links between the fundamental determinants of growth and the workings of the economy simpler and more transparent is more than half the battle.

Economic growth is worth much more than one or even two short chapters — here the growth chapters are among the longest in this book. Students have no business leaving macroeconomics courses without understanding broad cross-country and cross-time patterns: the Industrial Revolution, the spread of industrialization, the East Asian miracle, and the American century.

The third change, long overdue, has to do with the *open economy*.

◆ Treat the economy as open from the beginning of the book.

It is time to simply forget about the "closed-economy case" and ask students to analyze an open economy from the very beginning of the book. Even in the United States, virtually every economic policy issue and news event has an important international dimension. Presenting the closed-economy case first gives students a lot of wrong impressions — about the size of the Keynesian multiplier, about the freedom countries have to conduct independent monetary and fiscal policies, about the relationship between saving and investment — that then have to be unlearned in the "open-economy macro" chapters. Throughout the book, save in Chapter 15, the default assumption is that the exchange rate is freely floating. This assumption was not true in the past and may not be true in the distant future, but it is true now and for the foreseeable future and is thus a reasonable working assumption.

The fourth change, also long overdue, has to do with *monetary policy*.

◆ Deal with interest rates, not money stocks.

In today's world, where central banks set interest rates but not money stocks, the LM curve's underlying assumption that the nominal money stock is fixed is artificial. A major reason for giving the LM curve a central place is historical; it allows one to present the Keynesian–monetarist debate of the 1970s as a debate about the relative slopes of IS and LM curves. However, this debate has been dead for a generation, and conducting much of the discussion of the determination of real GDP in a framework in which the money stock is fixed gives students the wrong intuition. The LM curve cannot be eliminated: There are monetary regimes under which the central bank does not fix the interest rate. But it can be downplayed.

In our experience in the classroom, it is much better to downplay the LM curve and focus on the key factors of the position of the IS curve and the real interest rate that is determined by the term structure and central bank policy. This brings the presentation in the textbook much closer to what students will find when they open up *The Economist* or *The Wall Street Journal*. This makes our tasks as teachers much easier because there is no longer an artificial gap between the models taught and the actions seen in the world. And so we have made the presentation of the LM curve entirely optional by placing it in its own self-contained chapter. Instructors can easily choose to include — or exclude — coverage of the LM curve.

The fifth change has to do with the *Phillips curve* and *aggregate supply*.

◆ Focus on the Phillips curve and the Monetary Policy Reaction Function — not on the AS-AD diagram.

The variable on the vertical axis of the aggregate supply–aggregate demand (AS-AD) graph — the price level — is not the best price variable to use in analyzing economic policy. The best price variable is the one on the vertical axis of the Phillips curve, the inflation rate. We introduce the AS-AD graph in conjunction with IS-LM in optional Chapter 11, where the price level matters because it determines the real value of the fixed nominal money stock. But in Chapter 12 — the payoff chapter — we analyze the determination of inflation (not price level) and unemployment (not GDP). We do this by bringing together the Phillips curve on the supply side and the monetary policy reaction function (MPRF) on the demand side.

Our discussion of the expectations-augmented Phillips curve in Chapter 12 explains that rational, adaptive, and static expectations are not incompatible, but rather different strategies for dealing with the problems of inflation — each of which can be useful in the right economic environment. Students then have the full story in one comprehensive package: In the short run, with static or adaptive expectations, a tax cut can have the good effect of lowering unemployment while it alas generates inflationary pressure. Over time, our changing expectations of inflation will be met by the central bank's assault on inflation and gradually — or rapidly, depending on our expectations and the bank's hawkishness — the good effects of a tax cut will be supplanted by the bad effects of higher real interest rates and lower investment spending. It's a fireworks moment in teaching when everything from Chapter 4 through Chapter 12 comes together in one glorious finale.

PEDAGOGY

Much of the pedagogical work in this book is aimed at smoothing over what often turn out to be rough spots for the students. One important way that people learn is by watching other people solve problems, and then by repeating the process. Thus, students will note that this book contains a greater-than-usual number of worked examples. This will be especially helpful for those who hesitate before making conceptual leaps.

Boxes provided throughout the book try to reinforce the main narrative without disrupting it. They are an attempt to solve the perennial problem of how to provide additional depth and background to those who need (or want) it without boring or distracting those who wish to move on. *Macroeconomics* contains five kinds of boxes:

◆ *Tools* boxes remind students of some of the algebraic and conceptual tools economists use.

◆ *Data* boxes provide real-world information to support theoretical presentations.

- *Details* boxes provide for those who want to dig deeper into a particular subject.
- *Policy* boxes provide for those who want to know how the current thread of the book affects the making of economic policy.
- *Examples* boxes show how the concepts, ideas, and models of the current main thread of the book can be applied.

To keep students focused on the forest as well as the trees, each section ends with a Recap "box." These Recaps attempt to put the main ideas of the section into a nutshell. They are themselves recapitulated in the end-of-chapter summaries, which are also designed to review the most important concepts presented in the chapter.

The end-of-chapter exercises are divided into two sets, one that is tied to the theoretical material in the book — Analytical Exercises — and a second that is tied to recent events — Policy Exercises. And finally, an extended glossary provides fuller and deeper explanations of economics concepts than is typically found in other books. Terms in the glossary, when first encountered in the text, are italicized.

NEW TO THE SECOND EDITION

The story of the book has not changed but in several crucial points its presentation has. Chapters 4, 7, 11, and 12 were extensively revised, and the changes are noted below. Every chapter was rewritten to one degree or another, always with an eye to teachability. Definitions were inserted in the margins to aid learning. Data were updated, and a discussion of the policies of the administration of President George W. Bush (Bush 43) was incorporated.

Structure

While the treatment of many, if not all, topics is unique, the structure of the book follows a standard pattern that has served macroeconomists well. **Part 1** contains three chapters — Introduction to Macroeconomics, Measuring the Macroeconomy, and Thinking Like an Economist. **Chapter 1** begins with an overview of what macroeconomics is and then quickly focuses on six key variables that together allow one to gain a firm hold on the state of the macroeconomy. The chapter closes with a quick tour of recent macroeconomic events and policy dilemmas in the world, included both to pique students' interest and to give them a sense of the kinds of questions and issues that macroeconomics is supposed to help resolve.

Chapter 2 provides the standard review of national income accounting and other measurement issues, organized around the six key economic variables of Chapter 1.

Chapter 3, the most innovative material in this section, focuses on how economists view the world. It attempts to provide insight into the kind of "science" economics is, the dominance of the "circular flow" in how macroeconomists view the world, and how economists go about building the models they use to try to analyze the macroeconomy.

Part 2 focuses on long-run growth and contains two chapters — The Theory of Economic Growth and The Reality of Economic Growth: History and Prospect. **Chapter 4** focuses on the simple-to-understand capital-output ratio, how the economy converges to its balanced-growth equilibrium capital-output ratio, and the effect of technological progress on productivity. In the second edition, we begin with a more graphical and less algebraic approach, starting from the no-growth equilibrium and building to the punch line: While changes in the saving rate, depreciation rate, and labor-force growth rate can change the level of the standard of living, its growth from generation to generation depends upon the growth rate of technological and organizational progress.

Chapter 5 begins with a survey of very long run economic growth before the Industrial Revolution, moves on to the Industrial Revolution itself, and then covers the astonishing economic growth in the United States over the past century and a half that has made America a remarkably rich and productive society from the standpoint of any previous century. It then shifts its focus to patterns of growth and development the world over — including the East Asian miracle, stagnation in Africa, and the convergence of the Organisation for Economic Co-operation and Development (OECD) nations to common levels of productivity and industrial structure — before concluding with a discussion of economic policies and how they affect long-run growth. In a sense, Chapter 5 should be part of *everyone's* general education. It is, in summary and compressed form, an inquiry into the nature and causes of the wealth of nations.

Part 3 presents flexible-price, business-cycle macroeconomics with two real-side chapters — Building Blocks of the Flexible-Price Model and Equilibrium in the Flexible-Price Model — and one money and inflation chapter — Money, Prices, and Inflation. Since many of the functions are the same in the flexible-price full-employment model of Part 3 and the sticky-price model of Part 4, the real-side chapters are written with an eye toward making clear what changes and what doesn't when we move from flexible- to sticky-price models. **Chapter 6** covers the determination of potential output when wages and prices are flexible; the domestic components of aggregate demand — consumption, investment spending, and government purchases — and the determinants of the final component of aggregate demand, net exports.

Chapter 7 focuses on how the demand and supply for loanable funds in the flow of funds through financial markets pushes the real interest rate to the level at which investment demand equals saving supply, the economy is at full employment, and real GDP equals potential output. In the second edition, the algebra is saved for after the intuition has been developed graphically. Instructors who wish to skip the algebra altogether can readily do so — though we wouldn't — by skipping Section 7.5.

Chapter 8 moves from the real to the monetary side in the flexible-price framework. It focuses first on the utility of money and on the simple interest-inelastic quantity theory, and then moves on to consider the determinants of the price level and inflation when money demand is sensitive to the nominal interest rate.

Part 4 presents sticky-price macroeconomics and is divided into four chapters — The Sticky-Price Income-Expenditure Framework: Consumption and the Multiplier; Investment, Net Exports, and Interest Rates: The IS Curve; The Money Market and the LM Curve; and The Phillips Curve, Expectations, and Monetary Policy. This material not only rounds out the sticky-price business-cycle framework but also reaches back to the previous section to explain under what circumstances flexible-price and under what circumstances sticky-price modeling is likely to be appropriate. **Chapter 9** provides the standard treatment of the sticky-price income-expenditure inventory-adjustment model. Its innovative feature is that the model begins and ends with the open-economy case.

Chapter 10 then builds on Chapter 9 to construct the IS curve. An immediate payoff is that the last section of Chapter 10 uses the IS curve, along with changes in the Federal Reserve's interest rate targets, to help students understand why the state of the business cycle went as it did in post–World War II America.

Chapter 11 is in the second edition a truly optional chapter that considers the case when the central bank is following a policy of money-stock targeting. It explains that the interest rate and aggregate demand are jointly determined by money demand and the money stock — together summarized in the LM curve — and by the IS curve. It concludes with the concepts of aggregate demand and aggregate supply, again in the context of a central bank that targets the money stock.

Chapter 12 puts in place the keystone for Parts 3 and 4. In the second edition, we brought together here material that in the first edition had been scattered between Chapters 11 and 12, and added worked examples to aid understanding. The chapter presents the supply side using the Phillips curve, whose key determinants are the natural rate of unemployment on the one hand and the expected rate of inflation on the other. It develops the monetary policy reaction function (MPRF) — a demand-side summary of how the unemployment and inflation rates are generated when monetary policy reacts to inflation. The MPRF is itself a nifty summary of three relationships: Okun's law (introduced in Chapter 2), the IS curve (developed in Chapter 10), and the Taylor rule. The chapter then presents the three kinds of inflation expectations we expect to see — static, adaptive, and rational expectations of inflation — and the circumstances under which we expect to see each one. The MPRF and the expectations-augmented Phillips curve are combined to produce equilibrium inflation and unemployment rates and then used to illustrate the short-run and long-run effects of changes in economic policy or environment.

Part 5 begins with economic policy in three chapters — Chapter 13, Stabilization Policy; Chapter 14, Budget Balance, National Debt, and Investment; and Chapter 15, International Economic Policy. This material allows students to think through the issues and to understand the debates about proper macroeconomic management, both for stabilization and for enhancing economic growth. These policy chapters are then followed by three more discussions that emphasize the extent to which macroeconomics is an unfinished science. Chapter 16, Changes in the Macroeconomy and Changes in Macroeconomic Policy, deals with the fact that because the macroeconomy changes over time, macroeconomists are always aiming at a moving target. Chapter 17, The Future of Macroeconomics, focuses on where macroeconomists disagree and on how the science is evolving, even in the absence of structural change in the macroeconomy. Finally, the Epilogue sums up the lessons of the book and reminds readers of what we do not know.

Flexibility

The material in the first section can be compressed to the extent that it truly is review material. However, with the exception of omitting the economic growth material — Chapters 4 and 5, which would be a shame — this book does not lend itself to reordering especially well. The introductory chapters are there for good reasons, and the chain of logic and presentation from the start of the flexible-price model in Chapter 6 through the international economic policy discussion in Chapter 15 is a cumulative one.

In his classes of 30 or so students, Brad has occasionally shortchanged the chapters after 15, but doesn't recommend it. In her classes of 400 or so students, Martha has typically made it only to Chapter 13, but regrets having to stop there. While in government Brad had many conversations with smart people who could not see why the macroeconomics they had learned 35 years ago did not immediately apply. Teaching them that the world had changed and that the way macroeconomists thought about the world had changed proved remarkably hard. The historical perspectives provided in Chapters 16 and 17 and the Epilogue are (to our way of thinking, at least) worth the effort. If you won't have time to assign them, perhaps you can weave some of the perspectives offered there into your classes as you proceed through the term.

SUPPLEMENTS

For the Instructor

Instructor's Manual   Written by David DeJong at the University of Pittsburgh, this useful manual offers a number of general information elements — sample syllabi, Web resources, print resources, and some mathematical background (with some homework problems/solutions) — along with the following elements for each chapter: Overview, Annotated Outline, Mathematical Tools, Teaching Tips, Answers to Textbook Exercises, Additional Exercises (and Answers), and Additional Readings.

Test Bank   Written by Edward McNertney at Texas Christian University, this manual contains almost 1,400 multiple-choice questions categorized by objective, level, type, and source. The print test bank is also available in the latest test-generating software, ensuring maximum flexibility in test preparation, including the reconfiguring of graphing exercises. This software, EZTest, is the gold standard of testing programs.

PowerPoints   Prepared by Linda Ghent at Eastern Illinois University, these more than 1,000 slides contain all of the illustrations from the textbook, along with a detailed, chapter-by-chapter review of the important ideas presented in the book.

Web Site   Overseen by Scott Simkins at North Carolina A&T University, this site (www.mhhe.com/economics/delong2) contains a host of offerings helpful to teachers — Better Ways to Teach Macro (suggestions for presenting a new approach), a Career Center, Economics on the Web (an annotated list of URLs useful to macroeconomists), a Graphing Library (graphs that can be used to create exercises), some Supplemental Materials (information too timely for the textbook), the entire Instructor's Manual and all the PowerPoints, and finally a link to Brad DeLong's extremely rich and diverse site. To obtain an instructor login, contact your local sales representative.

For the Student

Study Guide   Prepared by co-author Martha Olney at the University of California, Berkeley, this guide takes students from development of an understanding of basic definitions through several steps to open-ended "real-world" problems. Two sets of exercises — Manipulation of Concepts and Models, and Applying the Concepts and Models — come with detailed answers. "To the

Chalkboard" boxes provide step-by-step derivations of complex graphs and all formulas plus explanations of difficult material.

Web Site   The site (www.mhhe.com/economics/delong2) contains a host of offerings helpful to students — Quizzes (questions written by the test bank preparer), Graphing exercises (graphs that can be manipulated to solve exercises like those in the textbook), In the News (links to current news articles), Applying the Theory (exercises that test textbook mastery), Working with Data (exercises that help students understand how economists use data), Career Center (job opportunities in economics), Economics on the Web (an annotated list of URLs useful to macroeconomics students), and finally a link to Brad DeLong's extremely rich and diverse site.

ACKNOWLEDGMENTS

I would like to thank, first of all, my students in intermediate macroeconomics — both those who took my courses in years when they were successful and, even more, those who took my courses in years when they were not: Thinking about what went wrong and about why large groups of students did not get it has been a principal spur to this book.

I was privileged to have Martin Feldstein, Olivier Blanchard, and Thomas Sargent as my teachers in the first three macroeconomics courses that I ever took. I thought they were awesome then, and I still think so. I was also lucky enough to have Lawrence Summers as my dissertation adviser. I have surely learned more about macroeconomics from him than from any single other person. Here at Berkeley, those who have had the greatest impact on my macroeconomics teaching are Christina Romer, David Romer, and Marty Olney — especially David, whose powerful arguments about how to teach macroeconomics better I have always found convincing.

Brad DeLong

I wish to thank Brad for his good cheer and most especially for his willingness to bring me aboard. We work well together, I learn a lot, and it's fun. My students — more than 5,000 of them in this course — and teaching assistants at UMass and Cal have kept me on my toes for over two decades now. Thank you for always pushing me to be a bit clearer and for laughing with me. I learn from each of you every day.

When I entered grad school in 1978, my aim was to become a macroeconomist. But at the time, it was an almost-exclusively male club. I shied away from what I envisioned would become a lifetime of battling for acceptance, and found my way to economic history, where by focusing on the Great Depression I could ask the questions that had driven me to macro in the first place. I'm grateful to all of the forces, big and small, in the intervening 25 years that have brought me back to where I began.

My biggest thanks go to my partner Esther and our son Jimmy. For your patience with my work schedule, your love, and, Jimmy, for sharing the computer with Momma, I thank you from the bottom of my heart. I owe you a year of bedtime stories, Jimmy K.

Martha Olney

We both would also like to thank the book team at McGraw-Hill for their professionalism, efficiency, and good humor. Paul Shensa, executive editor; Tom Thompson, development editor; Marty Quinn, marketing manager; Mary Conzachi, project manager; Sesha Bolisetty, production supervisor; Adam Rooke, designer; Gina DiMartino, supplements producer; Matthew Perry, media project manager; and Kai Chiang, media producer.

Kristy Piccinini at the University of California–Berkeley and John Nader at Grand Valley State University provided extremely helpful accuracy checks, and Ralph Husby at the University of Illinois contributed several in-depth reviews, for which we thank them profusely. Finally, we would like to thank the following reviewers of the first or second edition for their excellent suggestions:

Richard Ballman, *Augustana College*

Michael Brandl, *University of Texas–Austin*

James Campen, *University of Massachusetts–Boston*

Donald Coes, *University of New Mexico*

Linda Dobkins, *Emory and Henry College*

Robert Driskill, *Vanderbilt University*

Peter Frevert, *University of Kansas*

Barry Haworth, *University of Louisville*

Daniel Himarios, *University of Texas–Arlington*

Barney Hope, *California State University–Chico*

Murat Iyigun, *University of Colorado*

Garett Jones, *Southern Illinois University–Edwardsville*

Jinill Kim, *University of Virginia*

Ruby Kishan, *Southwest Texas State University*

Maria Kula, *Roger Williams University*

John Lapp, *North Carolina State University*

Anthony Lima, *California State University–Hayward*

Steven McCafferty, *The Ohio State University*

Roger McCain, *Drexel University*

Douglas McMillin, *Louisiana State University*

Starr McMullin, *Oregon State University*

Michael McPherson, *University of North Texas*

Chris Papageorgiou, *Louisiana State University*

Rowena Pecchenino, *Michigan State University*

Peter Pedroni, *Williams College*

Dennis Petruska, *Youngstown State University*

Uri Possen, *Cornell University*

Judy Ruha, *University of Washington*

Plutarchos Sakellaris, *University of Maryland*

Alden Shiers, *Cal Poly–San Luis Obispo*

David Spencer, *Brigham Young University*

David St. Clair, *California State University–Hayward*

Sheldon Stein, *Cleveland State University*

Philip Taylor, *Wesleyan University–Georgia*

Brian Trinque, *University of Texas–Austin*

Anne Villamil, *University of Illinois at Urbana-Champaign*

Charles Waldauer, *Widener University*

Ping Wang, *Vanderbilt University*

Charles Weise, *Gettysburg College*

Mark Wohar, *University of Nebraska–Omaha*

Robert Wright, *University of Sterling (UK)*

Jeffry Zax, *University of Colorado*

Preliminaries

What is intermediate macroeconomics? The first three chapters of this book provide an overview. Chapter 1 provides the basic guide to the major landmarks. It tells you that macroeconomics is the study not of individual markets but of the economy as a whole; that it studies total economic activity — how many people are employed, why the overall price level rises (and, rarely, falls) and at what rate, and what determines the level and rate of growth (and, sometimes, rate of decline) of total production.

Chapter 2 provides a brief survey of the major data used by macroeconomists. What indicators do macroeconomists focus on? How do they fit together? What are the national income and product accounts? These questions need to be answered before we can properly begin using macroeconomic data to understand the state of the economy.

Chapter 3 in this introductory section is "Thinking Like an Economist." Every subject has its own particular patterns of thought and fundamental assumptions that make it a separate discipline worth learning. Economists' patterns of thought, however, seem to be further from normal day-to-day experience than are those of many other disciplines. Economists have a very productive and insightful way of looking at the world, and it is different from common sense. To learn economics is to learn something genuinely new — and something instructive. Chapter 3 offers a brief introduction to the far-from-usual way that economists think: their use of graphs and equations, model building, and concepts like opportunity cost, equilibrium, and rational expectations.

CHAPTER 1

Introduction to Macroeconomics

QUESTIONS

How much richer are we than our parents were at our age?

How much richer will our children be than our grandparents were?

Will changing jobs be easy or hard in five years?

How many of us will have jobs in five years?

Will the businesses we work for vanish as demand for the products they make dries up?

Will inflation make us poor by destroying our savings or rich by eliminating our debts?

1.1 OVERVIEW

What Is Macroeconomics?

macroeconomics

The branch of economics that studies the economy as a whole: business cycles, the determinants of inflation and unemployment and long-run growth, and the effects of government fiscal and monetary policy.

What is macroeconomics? **Macroeconomics** is that subdiscipline of economics that tries to answer the six questions that begin this chapter. The answers to all these questions depend on what is happening to the economy as a whole, the economy in the large, the macroeconomy. "Macro" is, after all, nothing but a prefix meaning "large." Thus macroeconomics is the branch of economics related to the economy as a whole.

First, macroeconomists' principal task is to try to figure out why overall economic activity rises and falls. Why are measures like the total value of all production, the total income of workers and property owners, the total number of people employed, or the unemployment rate higher in some years than in others?

Second, macroeconomists also attempt to understand what determines the level and rate of change of overall prices. The proportional rate of change in the price level has a name: the inflation rate.

Third, along the way macroeconomists study other variables — such as interest rates, stock market values, and exchange rates — that play a major role in determining the overall levels of production, income, employment, and prices.

Why Macroeconomics Matters

Why does macroeconomics matter? Why should we care about the questions at the start of this chapter that are at the heart of macroeconomics? There are at least three reasons.

Cultural Literacy   First, macroeconomics is a matter of cultural literacy. Much discussion in newspapers, on television, and at parties concerns the macroeconomy. This should not be surprising: The twentieth-century U.S. economy was, all in all, extraordinarily successful. Today we are on average some 50 percent richer than our parents were when they were our age. If economic growth continues at its recent pace, our children may be five or more times as rich as our grandparents were.

Our modern industrial economy has delivered increases in material prosperity and living standards that no previous generation ever saw. (We discuss this topic at greater length in Chapter 5.) This increasing material prosperity means that the economy has a cultural salience today that it did not have in previous centuries, when productivity was stagnant and material standards of living improved only as fast as a glacier moves.

Thus, if you want to follow and participate in public debates and discussions, you need to know about macroeconomics. If you don't, you won't understand news reports on changes in the economy, such as those listed in Figure 1.1.

Self-Interest   A second (and more important) reason to care about macroeconomics is that the macroeconomy matters to you personally. Each of us is interested in particular issues in *micro*economics. Farmers and bakers are interested in the price of wheat; computer manufacturers and users are interested in the price of microprocessors; and economics professors are very interested in the price of economics professors. What happens in these individual markets — for wheat, for microprocessors, and for economics professors — shapes the lives of farmers, bakers, computer programmers, and economics professors.

Economics

Friday, February 18, 2005, 2:50 p.m.

Producer Prices Excluding Food, Energy Costs Climb the Most in Six Years . . .
Treasury Notes Drop as Measure of U.S. Inflation Rises More Than Forecast . . .
U.K. January Budget Surplus Widens to Three-Year High of $12.5 Billion . . .
Investors Seek Reassurance of U.K. Regulation for London Stock Exchange . . .
Shell and Exxon Tap "High Cost" Oil Sands, Gas as Other Reserves Dwindle . . .
U.K. Two-Year Gilts Decline for Fifth Straight Week Amid Signs of Growth . . .
Asian Stocks Advance as Ito-Yokado, Coles Myer Gain; Korea's Kospi Climbs . . .
Korea Electric Fourth-Quarter Net Rises Sixfold as Stronger Won Cuts Costs . . .
France Plans to Sell 50-Year Bond in 2005, First by Group of Seven Nation . . .
Ericsson, Nokia Foresee Takeovers in Saturated Market for Phone Equipment . . .
Norwegian 10-Year Notes Fall Most in World as Higher Interest Rates Loom . . .
Finland Raises $561 Million by Selling a Third of Its Stake in Sampo Bank . . .
Colombia's Peso Rises against Dollar for Fourth Week on Yield Advantage . . .
Mexican Supreme Court Orders Fox to Freeze $587 Million of Budget Spending . . .
Argentina's Merval Rises for Fourth Week, Led by Acindar; Bovespa Declines . . .
Colombia's Central Bank to Sell $1 Billion of Reserves to Help Prepay Debt . . .
Inflation Slows to Nine-Month Low in January as Cost of Vacations Declines . . .
Dollar Heads for Weekly Drop versus Euro as Greenspan Fails to Spur Buying . . .
Fuji TV May Cut Media Supply to Nippon Broadcasting if Takeover Bid Fails . . .
Japanese 10-Year Bonds Have Third Week of Declines on Stock Market Gain . . .

FIGURE 1.1
The Daily Flow of Economic News
Economic news flows past us constantly throughout the day. The total volume of information is overwhelming. Thus one of the major problems of macroeconomics is figuring out how to process all this information — how to make sense of it without drowning in information overload and without throwing valuable news away.

Source: http://www.bloomberg.com/news/index.html, February 18, 2005.

What happens in the *macro*economy shapes *everyone's* life. A rise in inflation is sure to enrich debtors (people who have borrowed) and impoverish creditors (people who have lent money to others). An expanding economy will make real incomes rise. A deep recession will increase unemployment and make those who lose their jobs have a hard time finding others. Your bargaining power vis-à-vis your employer (or, on the other side of the table, your bargaining power vis-à-vis your employees) depends on the phase of the business cycle.

Though you cannot control the macroeconomy, you can understand how it affects your opportunities. To some degree, forewarned is forearmed: Whether or not you understand your opportunities may depend on how much attention you pay in this course. The macroeconomy is not destiny: Some people do very well in their jobs and businesses in a recession, and many do badly in a boom. Nevertheless, it is a powerful influence on individual well-being. To paraphrase Russian revolutionary Leon Trotsky, you may not be interested in the macroeconomy, but the macroeconomy is interested in you.

Civic Responsibility   A third important reason to care about macroeconomics is that by working together we can improve the macroeconomy. Our right to vote is one of the most precious rights human beings have ever had. In electing our government, we indirectly make macroeconomic policy. As we will see in the next section, the government's macroeconomic policy matters because it can accelerate (or decelerate) long-run economic growth and stabilize (or destabilize) the short-run business cycle. In election after election, candidates will present themselves and seek your vote. Those who win will try to manage the macroeconomy. If you are not literate in macroeconomics, you won't be able to distinguish the candidates who might become effective macroeconomic managers from those who are clueless or cynical, promising more than they can deliver. And you need to, for many politicians cynically overpromise, and others seek to pursue economic policies that are bad for the economy in the long run but that promise to generate good short-run news — as Box 1.1 details.

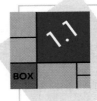

ECONOMIC POLICY AND POLITICAL POPULARITY: POLICY

Politicians believe strongly that their success at the polls depends on the state of the economy. They think that fairly *and* unfairly they get the credit when the economy does well and suffer the blame when the economy does badly. One of the most outspoken political leaders on this topic was mid-twentieth-century American politician Richard M. Nixon, who publicly blamed his defeat in the 1960 presidential election on the Eisenhower administration's unwillingness to take action against an economic slump:

"The matter was thoroughly discussed by the Cabinet. . . . [S]everal of the Administration's economic experts who attended the meeting did not share [the] bearish prognosis. . . . [T]here was strong sentiment against using the spending and credit powers of the Federal Government to affect the economy, unless and until conditions clearly indicated a major recession in prospect. . . . I must admit that I was more sensitive politically than some of the others around the cabinet table. I knew from bitter experience how, in both 1954 and 1958, slumps which hit bottom early in October contributed to substantial Republican losses in the House and Senate. . . . The bottom of the 1960 dip did come in October. . . the jobless rolls increased by 452,000. All the speeches, television broadcasts, and precinct work in the world could not counteract that one hard fact."

Economic historians continue to dispute the causes of the "stagflation" — a combination of relatively high inflation and relatively high unemployment — that struck the American economy in the early 1970s, after Richard Nixon finally became president. Was it the result of his manipulation of economic policy for political goals so that during his 1972 reelection campaign the economy would look better than it had in 1960? The evidence is contradictory. But no matter how much Nixon's policy contributed to stagflation, all observers agree that his major goal was not to create a healthier economy over the long term but to make the economy look good in 1972.

Source: Richard M. Nixon, *Six Crises* (Garden City, NY: Doubleday, 1962), pp. 309–311.

Macroeconomic Policy

Growth Policy

The government's growth policy — what it does to accelerate or decelerate long-run *economic growth* — is surely the most important aspect of macroeconomic policy. Nothing matters more in the long run for the quality of life in an economy than its long-run rate of economic growth.

Consider Argentina, which was once one of the most prosperous nations in the world. In 1929, for example, it was fifth in the world in the number of automobiles per capita. Yet today Argentina is classified as a "developing" country, and as Figure 1.2 shows, it has fallen far behind rich developed industrial economies like

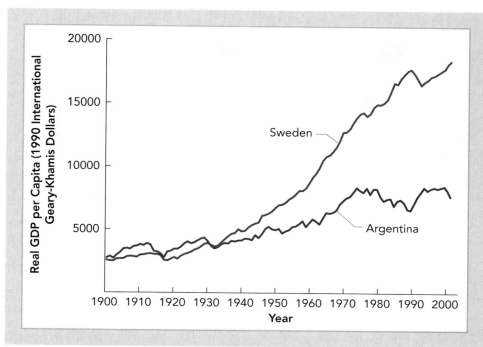

FIGURE 1.2

Long-Run Economic Growth: Sweden and Argentina, 1900–2001

At the start of the twentieth century, Argentina was richer — and seen as having a brighter future — than Sweden. But economic policies that were mostly bad for long-run growth left Argentina far behind Sweden.

Source: Angus Maddison, *The World Economy: Historical Statistics* (Paris: OECD, 2003).

Sweden. Why? Destructive economic policies have retarded Argentina's economic growth. Today Argentineans are richer than their predecessors were at the beginning of the twentieth century, but they are not nearly as well off as they might have been had Argentina's economic policies been as good and its economic growth as fast as those in Sweden.

In Scandinavian countries like Norway and Sweden, where throughout the twentieth century economic policies were supportive of growth, the past 100 years have led to extraordinary prosperity. Today economic output per person in Scandinavia is among the highest in the world. According to semiofficial estimates, Scandinavians today are more than six times as wealthy as their predecessors were at the start of the twentieth century.

In the long run, nothing a government can do does more good for the economy than adopting good policies for economic growth.

Stabilization Policy

The second major branch of macroeconomic policy is the government's *stabilization policy*. History does not show a steady, stable, smooth upward trend toward higher production and employment. Typically, levels of production and employment fluctuate above and below long-run growth trends. Production can easily rise several percentage points above the long-run trend or fall 5 percentage points or more below the trend (see Figure 1.3). Unemployment can fall so low that businesses become desperate for workers and will spend much time and money training them. Or it can rise to 10 percent of the labor force in a deep recession, as it did in 1982.

Such fluctuations in production and employment are commonly referred to as business cycles. Periods in which production grows and unemployment falls are

FIGURE 1.3

The American Business Cycle: Fluctuations in Total Production (Real GDP) Relative to the Long-Run Growth Trend

Since 1960 business-cycle fluctuations have caused the level of production in the United States to fluctuate as much as 5 percent below or 4 percent above the trend level of real GDP.

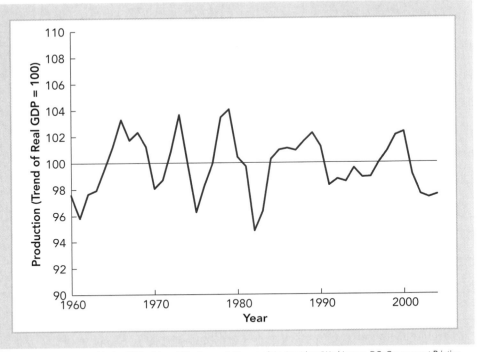

Source: Authors' calculations based on real GDP estimates contained in the 2004 edition of *The Economic Report of the President* (Washington, DC: Government Printing Office).

expansion

A period when real GDP is growing.

recession

A fall in the level of real GDP for at least six months, or two quarters of the year.

depression

A very severe recession.

deflation

The opposite of inflation: a decrease in the overall price level.

microeconomics

That field of economics that deals with the behavior of the individual elements in an economy with respect to the price of a single commodity and the behavior of individual households and businesses.

called booms, or macroeconomic **expansions**. Periods in which production falls and unemployment rises are called **recessions** or, worse, **depressions**. Booms are to be welcomed; recessions are to be feared.

Today's governments have powerful abilities to improve economic growth and to smooth out the business cycle by diminishing the depth of recessions and depressions. Good macroeconomic policy can make almost everyone's life better; bad macroeconomic policy can make almost everyone's life much worse (see Box 1.2). For example, policy makers' reliance on the gold standard as the international monetary system during the Great Depression was the source of macroeconomic catastrophe and human misery. Thus the stakes that are at risk in the study of macroeconomics are high.

Business-cycle fluctuations are felt not only in production and employment but also in the overall level of prices. Booms usually bring inflation, or rising prices. Recessions bring either a slowdown in the rate of inflation, or *disinflation* as it is called, or an absolute decline in the price level, called **deflation**. Interest rates, the level of the stock market, and other economic variables also rise and fall with the principal fluctuations of the business cycle.

Macroeconomics versus Microeconomics

By itself macroeconomics is only half of economics. For more than half a century economics has been divided into two branches, macroeconomics and microeconomics. Macroeconomists examine the economy in the large, focusing on feedback from one component of the economy to another and studying the total level of production and employment. In contrast, **microeconomics**, which was probably the subject of your

MACROECONOMIC POLICY AND YOUR QUALITY OF LIFE: DATA

At the end of 1982 the U.S. macroeconomy was in the worst shape since the Great Depression. The unemployment rate was more than 10 percent. In an average week in 1983, some 10.7 million Americans were unemployed — actively seeking work but unable to find a job that seemed worth taking. That year the average unemployed American had already been unemployed for more than 20 weeks. The average household income in the United States was 8 percent below its long-run trend.

By contrast, at the end of 2000 U.S. unemployment was just 4 percent, and average household income was 4 percent above trend. In which year would you rather have been trying to find a job?

Bad macroeconomic policy makes years like 1982 and 1983 much more common than years like 1999 and 2000. Although good macroeconomic policy cannot maintain the degree of relative prosperity seen in 2000 indefinitely, it can all but eliminate the prospect of years like 1982 and 1983.

last economics course, deals with the economy in the small. Microeconomists study the markets for single commodities, examining the behavior of individual households and businesses. They focus on how competitive markets allocate resources to create producer and consumer surplus, as well as on how markets can go wrong.

The two groups of economists also differ in their views of how markets work. Microeconomists assume that imbalances between demand and supply are resolved by changes in prices. Rises in prices bring forth additional supply, and falls in prices bring forth additional demand, until supply and demand are once again in balance. Macroeconomists consider the possibility that imbalances between supply and demand are resolved by changes in quantities rather than in prices. That is, businesses may be slow to change the prices they charge, preferring instead to expand or contract production until supply balances demand. Table 1.1 summarizes these differences in approach.

TABLE 1.1
The Two Branches of Economics

Macroeconomists	Microeconomists
Focus on the economy as a whole.	Focus on the markets for individual commodities and on the decisions of single economic agents.
Spend much time analyzing how total income changes and how changes in income cause changes in other modes of economic behavior.	Hold total income constant.
Spend a great deal of time and energy investigating how people form their expectations and change them over time.	Don't worry much about how decision makers form their expectations.
Consider the possibility that decision makers might change the quantities they produce before they change the prices they charge.	Assume that economic adjustment occurs first through prices that change to balance supply and demand and that only afterward do producers and consumers react to the changed prices by changing the quantities they make, buy, or sell.

In every generation, economists attempt to integrate microeconomics and macroeconomics by providing "microfoundations" for the macroeconomic topics of inflation, the business cycle, and *long-run growth*. But no one believes that the bridge between microeconomics and macroeconomics has yet been soundly built. Economists are divided roughly evenly between those who think that the failure to successfully integrate microeconomics and macroeconomics is a flaw that urgently needs to be corrected and those who think it is a regrettable but minor annoyance. Thus less knowledge may carry over from microeconomics to macroeconomics than one might expect or hope. Be careful in trying to apply the principles and conclusions of microeconomics to macroeconomic questions — and vice versa.

> **RECAP   OVERVIEW**
>
> Macroeconomics is that branch of economics related to not individual markets but the economy as a whole. The government's *growth policy* — what it does to accelerate or decelerate long-run economic growth — is surely the most important aspect of macroeconomic policy. Nothing matters more in the long run for the quality of life in an economy than its long-run rate of economic growth. The second major branch of macroeconomic policy is the government's *stabilization* policy. Typically, levels of production and employment fluctuate above and below long-run growth trends. Periods in which production grows and unemployment falls are called *booms*, or *macroeconomic expansions*. Periods in which production falls and unemployment rises are called *recessions*, or, worse, *depressions*.

1.2 TRACKING THE MACROECONOMY
Economic Statistics and Economic Activity

Macroeconomics could not exist without the economic statistics that are systematically collected and disseminated by governments. Estimates of the value and composition of economic activity, principally those contained in the *national income and product accounts (NIPA)* reported by the U.S. Commerce Department's *Bureau of Economic Analysis,* are the fundamental data of macroeconomics. We cannot try to explain fluctuations in economic activity unless we know what those fluctuations are. But what is economic activity?

Whenever you work for someone and get paid, that is economic activity. Whenever you buy something at a store, that is economic activity. Whenever the government taxes you and spends its money to build a bridge, that is economic activity. In general, if a flow of money is involved in a transaction, economists will count that transaction as economic activity. Overall, economic activity is the pattern of transactions in which things of real, useful value — resources, labor, goods, and services — are created, transformed, and exchanged. If a transaction does not involve something of useful value being exchanged for money, odds are that NIPA will not count it as part of economic activity.

In the United States, individual economic statistics are released month by month and quarter by quarter, a quarter being a three-month period: a quarter of a year. Thus you will often hear economists and other analysts talk about the "change in inventories in the second quarter." Table 1.2 shows a sample of the kinds of

TABLE 1.2
The Flow of Economic Data, 2003–2004

The items below are a representative selection of recent economic data, reported quarterly — that is, calculated four times a year, once for January through March, once for April through June, once for July through September, and once for October to December.

The Glossary will tell you much more about what these numbers mean.

	2003				2004		
	Q1	Q2	Q3	Q4	Q1	Q2	Q3
Percent changes at annual rates							
Production and Demand							
Gross domestic product	1.9	4.1	7.4	4.2	4.5	3.3	4.0
Personal consumption expenditures	2.7	3.9	5.0	3.6	4.1	1.6	5.1
Nonresidential fixed investment	−0.1	11.8	15.7	11.0	4.2	12.5	13.0
Residential investment	7.5	9.1	22.4	9.6	5.0	16.5	1.6
Exports of goods and services	−1.5	−1.6	11.3	17.5	7.3	7.3	6.0
Imports of goods and services	−2.0	2.5	2.8	17.1	10.6	12.6	4.6
Government purchases	0.2	7.2	0.1	1.6	2.5	2.2	0.7
Inflation							
Gross domestic purchases	3.9	0.4	1.6	1.2	3.4	3.5	2.0
Personal consumption expenditures	3.2	0.7	1.6	1.2	3.3	3.1	1.3
Gross domestic product	2.9	1.1	1.3	1.4	2.7	3.2	1.4
Billions of dollars, seasonally adjusted annual rates							
Federal Government Finances:							
Receipts	1,888.6	1,902.5	1,816.4	1,900.6	1,915.3	1,949.1	1,956.7
Current expenditures	2,170.2	2,266.9	2,249.4	2,279.8	2,306.3	2,329.1	2,340.8
Surplus or Deficit (−)	−281.6	−364.4	−433.0	−379.2	−391.0	−380.0	−384.1
Inventories:							
Change in private inventories	10.6	−15.3	−3.7	3.5	36.2	59.0	31.6
Ratio, Inventories to final sales	2.55	2.51	2.45	2.42	2.42	2.43	2.40
Balance of payments:							
Current account	−553	−536	−527	−508	−589	−658	−659
Various							
Labor Market							
Unemployment rate (percent)	5.8	6.1	6.1	5.9	5.7	5.6	5.4
Payroll growth (thousands)	−254	−53	99	302	531	693	401
Stock Market							
S&P 500 (index)	847	988	1,019	1,081	1,124	1,133	1,118
NASDAQ (index)	1,349	1,632	1,856	1,957	1,979	2,001	1,885
Nominal Interest Rates							
3-month (percent per year)	1.13	0.92	0.94	0.90	0.94	1.27	1.65
10-year (percent per year)	3.81	3.33	4.27	4.27	3.83	4.73	4.13
BAA (percent per year)	6.95	6.19	6.79	6.60	6.11	6.78	6.27
Exchange Rate							
Value of 100 yen ($)	0.84	0.84	0.85	0.92	0.93	0.91	0.91
Value of 1 euro ($)	1.07	1.14	1.13	1.19	1.25	1.20	1.22

Source: 2005 *Economic Report of the President.*

economic data that economists, politicians, and others, including investors in the stock and bond markets, use to assess the course of the economy. The sheer number of statistics is confusing at first glance, but all the statistics either (1) are direct measures of six key economic indicators that together tell most of the story or (2) are primarily useful as partial forecasts of or as factors that help determine the six key indicators of economic activity.

Six Key Variables

You can get a good idea of the pulse of recent economic activity by simply looking at the six key economic variables. Together they summarize the state of the macroeconomy. If you want to be able to say more than "the economy is good" or "the economy is not so good," you need to understand and be able to analyze these six variables:

- Real gross domestic product.
- The unemployment rate.
- The inflation rate.
- The interest rate.
- The level of the stock market.
- The exchange rate.

The first two are the most important: They are directly and immediately connected to people's material well-being. The other four are indicators and controls that are not directly and immediately connected to people's current material well-being, but they profoundly influence the economy's direction. Let's look at each of these indicators more closely.

Real GDP

real GDP

Inflation-adjusted gross domestic product; the most commonly used measure of national product, output, and income earned through domestically produced goods and services.

The first key variable is the level of real gross domestic product, called **real GDP** or often just GDP for short. "Real" means that this measure corrects for changes in the overall level of prices. If total spending doubles because the average level of prices doubles but the total flow of commodities does not change, then real GDP does not change. Economic variables are either *real* — that is, they have been adjusted for changes in the price level and inflation — or *nominal* — that is, they have not been adjusted for changes in the price level and inflation. "Gross" means that this measure includes the replacement of worn-out and obsolete equipment and structures as well as completely new investment. (Gross measures contrast with net measures, which include only investment that adds to the capital stock — not investment that merely replaces worn-out and obsolete capital stock. Net measures are better than gross measures, but the information needed to construct them is not as reliable.)

"Domestic" means that this measure counts economic activity that happens in the United States, whether or not the workers are legal residents and whether or not the factories are owned by American companies. (Domestic measures contrast with national measures, which count all the economic activity conducted by U.S. citizens and other permanent residents and by the companies they own.) Finally, "product" means that real GDP represents the production of *final goods and services.* It includes both consumption goods (things that consumers buy, take home or take out, and consume) and investment goods (things like machine tools, office equipment, and newly constructed houses and office buildings, which boost the country's capital stock and productive capacity). It also includes government purchases, things that the government (acting as our collective agent) buys and uses.

Real GDP divided by the number of workers in the economy is the most frequently used summary index of the economy (see Box 1.3). It is a measure of how well the economy produces goods and services that people find useful — the necessities, conveniences, and luxuries of life. It is, however, a flawed and imperfect index. It says nothing, for instance, about the relative distribution of the nation's economic product. And because it measures market prices, not user satisfaction, it is an imperfect measure of material well-being. Nevertheless, **real GDP per worker** remains the best readily available economic index.

The Unemployment Rate

The second key variable is the **unemployment rate.** The unemployed are people who want to work and are actively looking for jobs but have not yet found one (or have not yet found one that they consider attractive enough to take rather than continue to look for a still better job). The unemployment rate is equal to the number of unemployed people divided by the total labor force, which is the sum of the number of unemployed people and the number of people who have jobs. The U.S. Labor Department's *Bureau of Labor Statistics* conducts the *Current Population Survey,* a random survey of 60,000 of America's households, every month. The estimated number of unemployed workers obtained from the survey is then divided by the estimated total labor force, also obtained from the survey. The result is that month's unemployment rate. It is released to the public on the first Friday of the next month.

Most people consider unemployment to be a bad thing, and it usually is. Yet it is important to notice that an economy with no unemployment at all would probably be a badly working economy. Just as an economy needs inventories of goods — goods in transit, goods in process, goods in warehouses and sitting on store shelves — in order to function smoothly, it needs "inventories" of jobs looking for workers (vacancies) and workers looking for jobs (the unemployed). An economy in which each business grabbed the first person who walked through the door to fill a newly open job and in which each worker took the first job offered would be a less productive economy. Workers should be somewhat choosy about what jobs they take. They should decline jobs when they think that "this job pays too little" or "this job would be too unpleasant." Likewise, employers should be choosy about which workers they hire. Such *frictional unemployment* is an inevitable part of the process that makes good matches between workers and firms — matches that pair qualified workers with jobs that use their qualifications.

During recessions and depressions, however, unemployment is definitely not frictional. In these downturns in the business cycle the unemployment rate can rise far above the level resulting from a normal and healthy process of job search. The market economy breaks down, failing to match workers willing and able to work with businesses that could put their skills and labor power to making useful goods and services. Economists call this type of unemployment *cyclical unemployment.* In the United States during the Great Depression the unemployment rate rose to 25 percent (see Box 1.4). In Germany during the same period, the rate rose to 33 percent.

When the unemployment rate is high, the market economy is not functioning well. The unemployment rate is the best indicator of how well the economy is doing relative to its productive potential. In recent years, however, some economists have worried that the unemployment rate is becoming less useful as an indicator of the amount of "slack" in the economy — the gap between production and

real GDP per worker

One of the best available measures of long-term economic growth: real GDP divided by the number of workers (or, alternatively, by the total number of hours worked).

unemployment rate

The share of the labor force who are looking for but have not found an acceptable job.

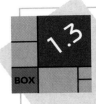

U.S. REAL GDP PER WORKER: DATA

In the year 2000, calculated using 2000 prices, officially measured U.S. real GDP per worker — the total value of all final goods and services produced in the United States divided by the number of workers in the labor force — reached $73,000. The measured productivity of the average American worker had more than sextupled since 1890, when the standard estimate of 2000-price real GDP per worker was some $12,000. Amazingly, this upward leap in economic well-being was accomplished in a little over four generations.

Figure 1.4 shows this upward trend in real GDP per worker. Despite temporary setbacks in recessions and depressions — of which the Great Depression of the 1930s was by far the largest — the principal event of the twentieth century was this sextupling of measured real GDP per worker. Other macroeconomic events visible in the figure include the World War II boom, the 1974–1975 and the 1980–1983 major recessions, the 1990–1991 minor recession, the two-decade-long period of stagnation from the early 1970s to the early 1990s — a period that saw the 1973 and 1979 sharp oil price increases by OPEC and the large investment-reducing government budget deficits of the 1980s — and the pre-1973 and post-1995 decade-long booms.

Note that this figure says nothing at all about how economic growth was distributed. In fact, the years between 1930 and 1970 saw the middle and working classes diminish the relative income gap between themselves and the rich. The years between 1970 and the present have seen this gap open wider once again.

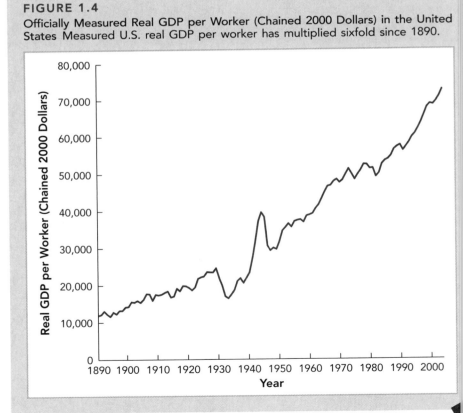

FIGURE 1.4
Officially Measured Real GDP per Worker (Chained 2000 Dollars) in the United States Measured U.S. real GDP per worker has multiplied sixfold since 1890.

Source: Angus Maddison, *Monitoring the World Economy* (Paris: OECD, 1995), as updated by the authors.

THE U.S. UNEMPLOYMENT RATE IN THE TWENTIETH CENTURY: DATA

In the twentieth century the U.S. unemployment rate dipped as low as 1.5 percent during World War II and reached as high as 25 percent during the Great Depression, the principal macroeconomic catastrophe of the past century. No other recession or depression in the nation's history, not even the depression of the early 1890s, came close to having the Great Depression's devastating impact (see Figure 1.5).

Since World War II, the U.S. unemployment rate has fluctuated between 3 and 10 percent, with the highest rates occurring in the decades of the 1970s and 1980s.

FIGURE 1.5

The U.S. Unemployment Rate Since World War II, the highest rate of unemployment has been the nearly 10 percent of 1982. Before World War II, peaks in unemployment were much higher, especially during the Great Depression of the 1930s.

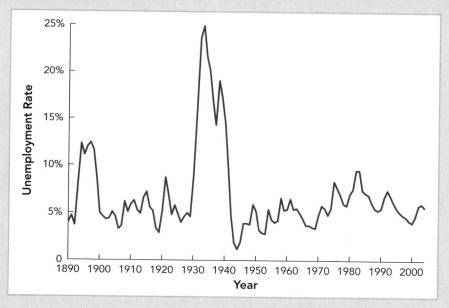

Source: Authors' calculations from the 2004 edition of *The Economic Report of the President* (Washington, DC: Government Printing Office) and from Christina Romer, "Spurious Volatility in Historical Unemployment Estimates," *Journal of Political Economy*, Vol. 94 (1986), 1, pp. 1–37.

the economy's potential. Employment fell sharply in the early 2000s, but the unemployment rate did not rise by much. This raised the possibility that many adults who were calling themselves "out of the labor force" were in fact discouraged workers — people who would be looking for (and finding) jobs if the macroeconomic news were better — and thus should be taken into account in calculating the economy's productive potential.

The Inflation Rate

A third key economic indicator is the **inflation rate**, a measure of how fast the overall price level is rising. If the inflation rate this year is 5 percent, that means that in general things cost 5 percent more this year than they cost last year in money

inflation rate

The annual rate of change of the overall level of prices in the economy.

terms, in terms of the symbols printed on dollar bills. A very high inflation rate —
more than 20 percent a month, say — can cause massive economic destruction, as
the price system breaks down and the possibility of using profit-and-loss calculations to make rational business decisions vanishes. Such episodes of *hyperinflation*
are among the worst economic disasters that can befall an economy. But not since
the Revolutionary War has the United States experienced hyperinflation. Box 1.5
tracks the inflation rate in the United States over the past century.

U.S. INFLATION RATES IN THE TWENTIETH CENTURY: DATA

In the United States in the twentieth century significant peaks of inflation occurred
during World Wars I and II, when overall rates of price increase peaked at more
than 20 percent per year (see Figure 1.6). Before World War II, deep recessions
like the Great Depression of the 1930s were accompanied by *deflation:* a decline in
the level of overall prices that bankrupted businesses and banks, exacerbating the
fall in output and employment.

FIGURE 1.6
Inflation in the United States Before 1970, periods when inflation rose above
10 percent were confined to major wars.

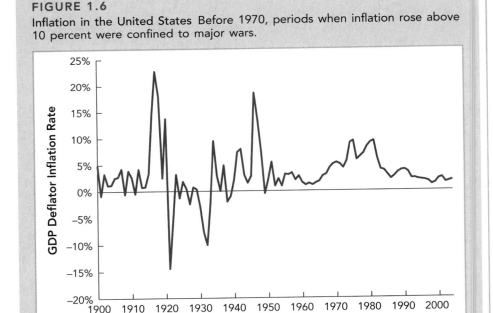

Source: Authors' calculations from the 2004 edition of *The Economic Report of the President* (Washington, DC: Government
Printing Office) and from *Historical Statistics of the United States* (Washington, DC: Government Printing Office, 1975).

Strangely, moderate inflation rates — a little more than 10 percent a year, say —
are highly unsettling to consumers and business managers. Moderate inflation
should not seriously compromise consumers', investors', and managers' ability to
determine the best use of their financial resources or to calculate profitability. Yet
all these groups are strongly averse to it. Politicians in the industrialized economies
have discovered that if they fail to preside over low and stable inflation rates then
they are likely to lose the next election.

Since World War II there has been only one single year — in the late 1940s — during which the price level declined. Otherwise, there has been inflation. Post–World War II inflation has come in two varieties: the "creeping" inflation of the 1950s, early and mid-1960s, and 1990s, too small and slow for anyone to pay much attention to it; and the "trotting" inflation of the late 1960s, 1970s, and 1980s — too high to ignore and too tempting a political football for politicians to resist blaming the current government.

The steep decline in inflation that occurred in the early 1980s is called the "Volcker disinflation," after then–Federal Reserve Chair Paul Volcker. Alarmed by the accelerating inflation of the late 1970s and early 1980s, Volcker decided to raise interest rates in order to decrease *aggregate demand*. In doing so, he risked a deep recession, which came in 1982–1983. But his action did stop the rise in inflation and reduce it back to the "creeping" range.

The Interest Rate

The fourth key economic indicator is the **interest rate**. Though economists speak of "the" interest rate, there are actually many different interest rates applying to loans of different durations and different degrees of risk. (After all, the person or business entity to whom you lend your money may be unable to pay it back; that is a risk you accept when you make a loan.) The different interest rates often move up or down together, so economists speak of "the" interest rate, referring to the entire complex of different rates. But interest rates do not move in concert all the time. The causes of variations in the *yield curve*, which describes the pattern of interest rates, are an important part of macroeconomics.

The interest rate is important because it governs the redistribution of purchasing power across time. Those people or business enterprises who think they can make good use of additional financial resources borrow, promising to return the purchasing power they use today with *interest* in the future. Those business enterprises or people who have no immediate use for their financial resources lend, hoping to profit when the borrower returns the borrowed sum — what financiers call the principal — with interest.

When economists think about interest rates, they almost always prefer to focus on the real interest rate rather than the nominal interest rate. The *nominal interest rate* is the interest rate in terms of money — for example, how many dollars' worth of interest a borrower must pay to borrow a given sum of money for one year. The *real interest rate* is the interest rate in terms of goods and services — for example, how much purchasing power over goods and services a borrower must pay in order to borrow a given amount of purchasing power for one year. The difference between the two is that nominal interest rates do not take proper account of the effect of inflation; real interest rates do.

Whenever interest rates are low — that is, when money is "cheap" — investment tends to be high, because businesses find that a wide range of possible investment projects will generate enough cash to pay the interest on borrowed money, repay the principal of the loan, and still produce a profit. Whenever interest rates are high — that is, when money is "dear" — investment tends to be low, because businesses find that most possible investment projects will not generate enough cash flow to repay the principal and the high interest. Box 1.6 shows changes in real interest rates in the United States since 1960.

interest rate

The price, measured in percent per year, paid for borrowing money. Conversely, the return earned by saving.

REAL INTEREST RATES: DATA

Interest rates on long-term debt, like the 10-year notes issued by the U.S. Treasury, are usually higher than interest rates on short-term debt, like the 3-month Treasury bills. Whenever long-term interest rates are lower than short-term interest rates, the yield curve is said to be "inverted." An inverted yield curve is one of the signals of a possible coming recession.

Interest rates have fluctuated widely in the United States since 1960 (see Figure 1.7). Real interest rates — that is, interest rates adjusted for inflation — have even been negative at times. During the 1970s nominal — money — interest rates were so low and inflation was so high that the interest and principal on a short-term loan bought fewer commodities when the loan was repaid than the original principal could have purchased when the loan was made. In the early 1980s — the Volcker years — interest rates increased radically. They remained higher than their levels in the 1950s and 1960s until 2001 when the Federal Reserve, led by Alan Greenspan, lowered nominal rates eleven times to stimulate the macroeconomy.

FIGURE 1.7

U.S. Real Interest Rates, 1960–2004 Between the Volcker disinflation of the early 1980s and the Greenspan rapid-fire cuts of nominal interest rates in 2001, real interest rates in the United States were markedly higher than they had been during the 1970s and even the 1960s. Since the early 1980s the yield curve has also been relatively steeply sloped; that is, the gap between long-term interest rates (like the interest rate on the 10-year U.S. Treasury note) and short-term interest rates (like the interest rate on the three-month U.S. Treasury bill) has been relatively large.

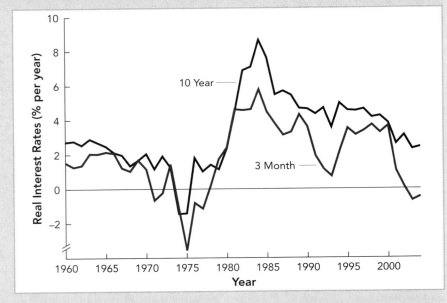

Source: Authors' calculations from the 2004 edition of *The Economic Report of the President* (Washington, DC: Government Printing Office) and from *Historical Statistics of the United States* (Washington, DC: Government Printing Office, 1975).

The Stock Market

The level of the **stock market** is the key economic indicator you hear about most often — you hear about it every single day unless you try hard to avoid the news. The level of the stock market is an index of expectations for the future. When the stock market is high, investors expect economic growth to be rapid, profits to be high, and unemployment to be relatively low. (Note, however, that there is an element of tail chasing in the stock market. Perhaps it would be more accurate to say that the stock market is high when average opinion expects that average opinion will expect that future economic growth will be rapid.) Conversely, when the stock market is low, investors expect the economic future to be relatively gloomy.

At times, such as the end of the 1960s or the end of the 1990s, the stock market appears significantly overvalued compared to its standard historical patterns. During such episodes investors are implicitly forecasting a major boom and continued rapid productivity growth. When their forecasts turn out to be wrong, these investors are severely disappointed with their stock market investments. Box 1.7 shows the course of the U.S. stock market over the past century.

stock market

The market in which the shares of common stock that carry ownership of companies are bought and sold.

THE STOCK MARKET: DATA

For more than a century and a quarter, the United States has had a thick market in equities — the "stocks" of a corporation, pieces of paper that indicate ownership of its shares. One of the major indexes that track the performance of the stock market as a whole is Standard and Poor's composite index, the S&P 500. Figure 1.8

FIGURE 1.8

Real Stock Index Prices Since 1997 real stock index prices have far exceeded their standard, conventional valuation of 15 times earnings.

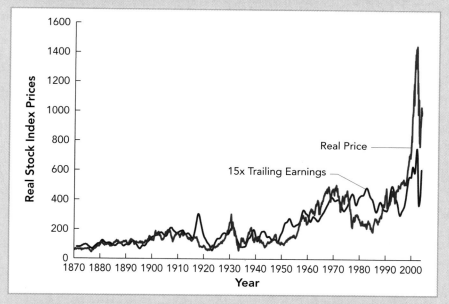

Source: Authors' calculations from data in Robert Shiller, *Market Volatility* (Cambridge, MA: MIT Press, 1987), as subsequently extended by Shiller, www.yale.edu/~rshiller/.

plots the real value — that is, the value adjusted for inflation — of this stock market index over time.

Over the past century, on average, a share of stock has traded for about 15 times its past year's, or "trailing," earnings per share. Earnings per share are calculated by dividing a corporation's annual profits by the number of shares of stock the corporation has outstanding. The 15-times-earnings figure is only an average: Companies with good prospects for growth sell for more than 15 times their earnings, and corporations seen as being in decline sell for less.

In some years expectations of the future of the economy are relatively depressed, and stock indexes like the S&P 500 sell for much less than the 15 times earnings rule of thumb. Consider 1982, when the stock market as a whole was worth 40 percent less than 15 times earnings.

Since 1997 real stock index prices have far exceeded their standard, conventional valuation of 15 times earnings. A large part of this was the result of the speculative mania — the "irrational exuberance" — of the dot-com bubble of the late 1990s. But a large gap between the stock market and conventional valuations remains even after the collapse of the dot-com bubble. Economists differ over how much of this phenomenon is due to (1) a continued irrational speculative mania that has outlasted even the stock market crash of 2000–2001, (2) an increased tolerance for risk, (3) a reflection of low interest rates, or (4) expectations of more rapid future economic growth.

The Exchange Rate

nominal exchange rate

The rate at which one country's money can be turned into another's; the price of one unit of foreign currency in terms of the home currency.

real exchange rate

The rate at which goods produced in a foreign country can be bought or sold for goods produced in the home country; the price of foreign-produced goods relative to domestic-produced goods.

The sixth and last key economic quantity is the *exchange rate*. The **nominal exchange rate** is the rate at which the moneys of different countries can be exchanged for one another. The **real exchange rate** is the rate at which the goods and services produced in different countries can be exchanged for one another. The exchange rate governs the terms on which international trade and investment take place. When the domestic currency is appreciated, its value in terms of other currencies is high. Foreign-produced goods are relatively cheap for domestic buyers, but domestic-made goods are relatively expensive for foreigners. In these circumstances imports are likely to be high; exports are likely to be low. When the domestic currency is depreciated, the opposite is the case. Domestically made goods are cheap for foreign buyers. Thus exports are likely to be high. But domestic consumers' and investors' power to purchase foreign-made goods is limited. Thus imports are likely to be low. Box 1.8 details the effects of changes in the U.S. exchange rate since 1977.

THE EXCHANGE RATE: DETAILS

The terms on which people in one country can buy goods and services made in other countries and sell the goods and services they make themselves are summarized in the exchange rate. The nominal exchange rate tells how many units of domestic currency it takes to buy 1 unit of foreign currency; it is the value of a foreign currency. The real exchange rate adjusts for differences in the rate of inflation between countries. Thus it measures the relative price of tradeable goods: how much in the way of foreign-produced goods can be bought with 1 unit of domestically produced goods.

FIGURE 1.9

The U.S. Real Exchange Rate: The Dollar against a Composite Index of Foreign Currencies The most significant fluctuation in the U.S. exchange rate came during the large depreciation of foreign currencies in the early and mid-1980s. By 1985 foreign-made goods were less than two-thirds as expensive relative to U.S.-made goods as they had been at the start of the decade.

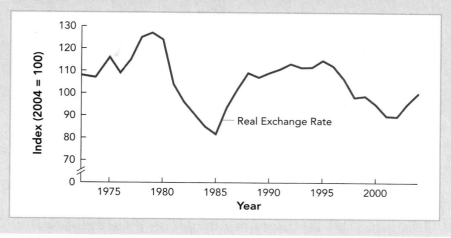

Source: Authors' calculations from the 2004 edition of *The Economic Report of the President* (Washington, DC: Government Printing Office).

Before the early 1970s, the U.S. exchange rate was *fixed* vis-à-vis other major currencies in the Bretton Woods system. The U.S. Treasury stood ready to buy or sell dollars in exchange for other currencies at fixed parities determined by each country's posted valuation of its currency in terms of gold.

Since the early 1970s the U.S. exchange rate has been *floating* — free to move up or down in response to the market forces of supply and demand (see Figure 1.9). When U.S. interest rates are relatively high compared to those of other countries — as in the early 1980s — the dollar *appreciates.* In such a case the dollar becomes much more valuable, as many people try to invest in America to capture the high interest rates. We then say that the value of the exchange rate is relatively low. The exchange rate is defined as the value (in terms of dollars) of foreign currency: When the relative value of the dollar rises, the value in dollars of foreign currency falls.

When U.S. interest rates fall relative to those in other countries, the dollar tends to *depreciate,* to fall in value, so U.S. goods are cheap to buy and easy to sell. When the dollar's value is low and the dollar has depreciated, the exchange rate — the value in dollars of foreign currency — is relatively high.

Real GDP, the unemployment rate, the inflation rate, the interest rate, the stock market, and the exchange rate — these are the six key economic indicators. Know the values of these key variables in context — both their relative levels today and their recent trends — and you have a remarkably complete picture of the current state of the macroeconomy.

RECAP   **TRACKING THE MACROECONOMY**

Know and understand six key variables, and you understand most of what there is to know about the state of the macroeconomy. The first key variable is the level of real GDP — the real inflation-adjusted value of goods and services. The second key variable is the unemployment rate — the fraction of the labor force that is out of work. The third key variable is the inflation rate — a measure of how rapidly the overall price level is changing. The fourth key variable is the interest rate. When economists think about interest rates, they almost always prefer to focus on the real interest rate rather than the nominal interest rate. The fifth key variable is the level of the stock market. The level of the stock market is a good indicator of investor confidence and of the likely future pace of investment spending. The sixth and last key variable is the exchange rate — the price at which goods made here at home are exchanged for goods made abroad.

1.3 THE CURRENT MACROECONOMIC SITUATION

The United States

As of the end of 2004, the U.S. macroeconomy was enjoying a moderately strong but uneven recovery. The collapse of the dot-com stock market bubble in 2000 and the September 11, 2001, terrorist destruction of the World Trade Center and attack on the Pentagon triggered a decline in economic activity — a recession — as businesses that were more pessimistic about the prospect of future profits and scared of the uncertainty produced by terrorism cut back their investment spending, and production and employment fell. Between the beginning of the recession and the end of 2001, the U.S. economy lost 0.9 million jobs. In response to these adverse shocks, the *Federal Reserve* reduced interest rates far and fast to try to encourage businesses to invest more: The three-month money-market nominal interest rate that had been 6.74 percent per year in the summer of 2000 had been cut to 1.75 percent per year by the late fall of 2001 and to 1 percent by the middle of 2003. And the Bush tax cuts directed more money into the hands of consumers, who increased their spending, which reduced the magnitude of the recession's spending shortfall.

Thus slowly in 2002 and more rapidly in 2003, the economy began to recover. Demand and production began to grow again. However, demand and production growth in 2003 and 2004 was, in everyone's estimation, insufficient. Because of rapid underlying productivity growth in the American economy, the renewed economic expansion did little to expand employment. With a relatively disappointing job market, wages did not rise by much. The recovery of 2003 and 2004 did enormous amounts to boost productivity and profits, substantial amounts to boost production, but little to boost employment or wages.

By the end of 2004 there were renewed worries among economists. One set of worries was that the United States could not afford the large tax cuts of the Bush administration — that they would produce very large budget deficits that would retard economic growth in the future. The Bush tax cuts, in combination with the extra defense spending authorized after September 11, eliminated the government budget surplus that had been painfully created during the 1990s. Given our low private saving rate, the elimination of public saving was likely in the medium run to reduce investment, and thus to slow growth. And the tax cuts were not designed in a way that would produce many significant supply-side production benefits. The principal long-run impact of the tax cuts would be a further reduction in America's already low national saving rate and a slowing of economic growth.

Moreover, by the end of 2004 there were worries that a forthcoming sharp decline in the value of the dollar would provide a further adverse and contractionary shock to the United States and to the world economy. Should foreign exchange speculators lose confidence in the dollar, the value of foreign currency could rise far and fast, possibly causing macroeconomic problems. Economists are very good at pointing out economic situations that are inconsistent with fundamental values — policies, imbalances, or balance sheet problems that cannot possibly last and are bound to end, perhaps in a crisis. But they are bad at forecasting when and how such imbalances will end.

The recession of 2001 had been preceded by a remarkable decade-long economic boom. Policy makers and economists advocating the Clinton administration's economic programs — deficit reduction and the lowering of trade barriers — had done so in the interest of accelerating long-run growth. Reduced trade barriers would allow for closer international integration, a finer international division of labor, and increased productivity. Deficit reduction would make possible high-investment economic expansion, which would then become high-productivity growth expansion.

Until 1996 there were few signs that high investment was leading to high productivity growth, but then the pace of economic growth exploded. Perhaps the political claims in the early 1990s that deficit reduction would ignite a high-investment and high-productivity growth recovery were coming true. Perhaps the U.S. economy was simply benefiting from the sudden wave of rapid productivity growth driven by the technological revolutions in data processing and data communications. The most likely possibility was and is that both were true. This was confirmed by the continuation of rapid growth in American labor productivity through the recession of 2001 and into the recovery that followed. The "new economy" of the 1990s that optimists had seen as the result of technological revolutions in information technology was indeed a reality, and the principal beneficiaries were consumers who found themselves able to buy at low prices and businesses that found that computerization greatly increased productivity.

Europe

In the early 2000s 11 western European countries adopted the euro as their common currency. The adoption of the euro was followed not by strong growth, but by stagnation and recession. European unemployment rates mounted toward 10 percent between 2000 and 2004, and real GDP growth for the euro zone was rarely above 2 percent per year. There was certainly room for economic expansion in Europe: Consumer prices were rising at less than 2 percent per year. The challenge for European economic policy remains one of avoiding rises in inflation while attempting to reduce western Europe's distressingly high and stubborn rate of unemployment, yet interpreting the European Central Bank's actions as part of any policy intended to try to meet that challenge remains difficult.

However, for the first time in decades Europeans were hopeful that the next decade would bring a reduction, not an increase, in unemployment. Changes in policy are making the European labor market more flexible and in the long run should make it easier for firms to change the number of workers they employ, which should make it easier for workers to find jobs and thus lower unemployment. Most of western Europe is perhaps half a decade behind the United States in its adoption of data processing and data communications technology. Thus there is good reason to hope that the information-technology-driven productivity growth acceleration experienced by the United States in the late 1990s should be visible in western Europe in the late 2000s.

And in eastern Europe, economies continue to grow, as the long and slow process of "transition" away from communism has continued.

Japan

As of the end of 2004, Japanese interest rates remained astonishingly low — 0.03 percent per year in the three-month money market — and were expected to remain low for the foreseeable future. Japan was still undergoing deflation, with consumer prices expected to fall by 1.0 percent in the next year.

Fortunately, Japan was no longer in recession: The country had experienced six straight quarters of positive growth in real GDP. Although unemployment in Japan remained above 5 percent — an astonishingly high level for Japan — it was no longer increasing. There was good reason to believe that Japan's decade-long experience with stagnation and recession was over, and that Japanese economic growth had resumed.

The start of the 1990s saw the collapse of the Japanese stock and real estate markets, the end of the so-called *bubble economy*. The 1990s as a whole saw the breakdown of the Japanese model of economic growth, as the economy stagnated for much of the decade. Now there is a general recognition that Japan faces a structural economic crisis. But there is no political consensus as to what is to be done, and the major political steps that need to be taken to restore growth — restructuring the Japanese financial system and deregulating transportation and distribution — have been long delayed.

The Bank of Japan is now pursuing a policy of making *short-term safe nominal interest rates* as close to zero as it can. But what matters for investment spending is not a low short-term safe nominal interest rate but a low long-term risky real interest rate, and that will remain high as long as bond traders fear that (1) the low-interest rate policy may be temporary, (2) many companies may go bankrupt and never repay the money they borrow, and (3) prices may decline more rapidly, turning low nominal interest rates into high inflation-adjusted real interest rates. For most of the 1990s and into the early 2000s, even interest rates near zero proved insufficient to boost investment.

Emerging Markets

Elsewhere in the world, the big economic news is the enormous growth booms in China and in India. Together their populations make up 40 percent of the human race, and their economies were expected to grow at 8 percent and 6 percent in 2005, respectively. The pace of investment in China is blistering as its exports continue to expand: China consumes more than a quarter of the world's steel and cement. China's boom is driven by its manufacturing exports. India's boom is driven by investment for the internal market and by growing exports of business and other services to the world's industrial core.

In the case of China, the boom is further driven by an undervalued exchange rate. The Chinese government would rather sell its workers' products cheaply than watch the value of its currency rise and risk high unemployment in its major cities. The Bank of China (along with other Asian central banks) buys up huge amounts of dollar-denominated assets every month in order to keep the value of the U.S. dollar from falling and the value of the Chinese yuan from rising. The U.S. government does not strongly object: Purchases by the Bank of China keep U.S. interest rates from rising and allow the funding of the U.S. government budget deficit and of much U.S. private investment that could not be covered by America's own small national saving.

As of the end of 2004, the financial crisis in East Asia of the past decade was only a distant memory. The panic that started in 1997 on the part of investors in New York, Frankfurt, London, and Tokyo, and the consequent withdrawal of their money from emerging market economies, imposed very high costs: massive bankruptcies, high interest rates, increases in unemployment, falls in production. But foreign investors appear to have regained confidence in East Asian economies.

However, the destabilizing factors in the world economy that made for the East Asian crisis of 1997–1998 are still present, as can be seen by the crash of the Argentinean economy at the end of 2001. Many argued that a critical cause of the East Asian crisis and, before it, the Mexican financial crisis was that the governments retained the ability to devalue and depreciate the currency and that that was a key source of the capital flight that rippled through their economies and set off the crises. Argentina, however, handed authority over its exchange rate to an independent organization — a "currency board." Yet that did not help. When in 2001 investors in New York, Frankfurt, London, Tokyo, and elsewhere became worried that the Argentine government's failure to balance its budget heralded a future of more rapid money printing and inflation, the same factors came into play. And the fact of Argentina's currency board only meant that the crisis became more convoluted and difficult to resolve — it was still not resolved three years after its beginning.

Elsewhere in Latin America as of 2005 growth continued to be positive, but disappointing. The Mexican government continued to wrestle with the problem of fixing its still-insolvent banking system. Brazil struggled under the burden of its large national debt and attempted to fulfill the hopes of growth with equity raised by the election of left-of-center president Luis Ignacio da Silva.

The most disappointing areas of the world as far as economic growth was concerned continued to be the Middle East and Africa.

Chapter Summary

1. Macroeconomics is the study of the economy in the large — the determination of the economywide levels of production, employment and unemployment, and inflation or deflation.

2. There are three key reasons to study macroeconomics: to gain cultural literacy, to understand how economic trends affect you personally, and to exercise your responsibility as a voter and citizen.

3. The six key variables in macroeconomics are real GDP, the unemployment rate, the inflation rate, the interest rate, the level of the stock market, and the exchange rate.

Key Terms

macroeconomics (p. 4)

expansion (p. 8)

recession (p. 8)

depression (p. 8)

deflation (p. 8)

microeconomics (p. 8)

real GDP (p. 12)

real GDP per worker (p. 13)

unemployment rate (p. 13)

inflation rate (p. 15)

interest rate (p. 17)

stock market (p. 19)

nominal exchange rate (p. 20)

real exchange rate (p. 20)

Analytical Exercises

1. What are the key differences between microeconomics and macroeconomics?

2. Why are real GDP and the unemployment rate important macroeconomic variables?

3. Why are the interest rate and the level of the stock market important economic variables?

4. Roughly, what was the highest level that the U.S. inflation rate reached in the twentieth century? What was the highest peacetime unemployment rate?

5. Roughly, how much higher is measured real GDP per worker today than it was in 1973?

Policy Exercises

1. What was the rate of real GDP growth in the United States in 2004?

2. What is the current unemployment rate?

3. What is the current inflation rate? If you find more than one inflation rate listed, are the rates consistent with each other?

4. What is the current level of the stock market? How does it compare to the level of the stock market at the beginning of 2000?

5. How does the current level of the stock market compare with the historical average, roughly 15 times a stock market index's trailing earnings?

CHAPTER 2

Measuring the Macroeconomy

QUESTIONS

What key data do macroeconomists look at?

How are key macroeconomic data estimated and calculated?

What is the difference between nominal and real values?

How are stock market values related to interest rates?

How are interest rates related to the price level and the inflation rate?

How is unemployment related to total production?

What is right — and what is wrong — with the key measure of economic activity, real GDP?

2.1 MACROECONOMIC DATA

Economics is a social science: It is about us, about what we do. Thus it shares with other social sciences one important source of information: introspection. We can ask ourselves "Why did I do that?" or "If I had done that, what would I have been thinking?" We can ask other people, and listen to their answers ("I did that because . . ."). In most of the other social sciences, however, the overwhelming source of information is introspection, either our own or other people's.

Economists are in a better position than most other social scientists as far as their sources of information are concerned. Everything that passes through the economy is priced and sold. Thus economists have quantitative data to work with: prices, quantities, and values. Having quantitative data allows economists to do more than many other social scientists. They can use theories to make not just qualitative but quantitative forecasts ("The change from Carter- to Reagan-era fiscal policy reduced the growth rate of the U.S. economy by 0.3 percent per year"). With data they can test theories, comparing what was actually the case to what various theories would have predicted.

The most important macroeconomic data are, of course, the six key variables introduced in Chapter 1:

- Real GDP (gross domestic product).
- The unemployment rate.
- The inflation rate.
- The interest rate.
- The level of the stock market.
- The exchange rate.

Learn about these six measurements of the economy — what their current values are, what their trends have been over time, what their future values are projected to be, how they are calculated, and what they mean — and you will have an excellent knowledge of the state of the economy. Table 2.1 summarizes the major features of these key economic variables. Let's see in more detail what they are and how they are calculated, but in reverse order — starting with the exchange rate and ending with real GDP.

RECAP   THE IMPORTANCE OF DATA

In most of the other social sciences, the overwhelming source of information is introspection — either our own or other people's. Economists share this source, but they have the advantage that everything that passes through the economy is priced and sold. Thus economists have quantitative data to work with: prices, quantities, and values. Having quantitative data allows economists to do more than many other social scientists. Especially important is the ability to measure the six key variables — real GDP, the unemployment rate, the inflation rate, the interest rate, the stock market, and the exchange rate.

TABLE 2.1
The Six Key Economic Variables

Variable	Details	Importance
Real GDP	Rough synonyms include GNP, NNP, NDP, national income, aggregate demand, and total production.	The principal measure of material well-being and economic productivity.
Unemployment rate	As reported, omits "discouraged workers" who would like to work but have stopped looking for jobs.	The principal measure of how far production is falling short of potential output; a measure of the relative distribution of economic well-being.
Inflation rate	Most economists think officially reported statistics overstate the true increase in the nominal cost of living by 0.5 to 1 percent per year.	The proportional rate of change of the price level. Central banks today view their principal mission as ensuring price stability — keeping the rate of inflation low enough that nobody worries about it much.
Interest rate	The most important interest rates are "real" — those that control for the effects of inflation — and long-term.	The real long-term interest rate is the principal determinant of the level of investment and a principal determinant of future production growth.
Stock market	A broad index like the S&P is better than a narrow index like the Dow-Jones.	The stock market summarizes into one single index a large number of influences on investment, including investors' optimism, expected future profits, and the real interest rate.
Exchange rate	Once again, the most important rate is the real rate.	The exchange rate determines the relative price of foreign-made goods in terms of home-produced goods. Economists usually work with an index of the value of the dollar against an average of all other currencies and call it the exchange rate.

2.2   THE EXCHANGE RATE

Nominal versus Real Exchange Rates

We define the **nominal exchange rate**, which we will call *e* for "exchange," to be the value of *foreign currency* in terms of the home currency — in the case of the United States, the dollar. The nominal exchange rate is thus the relative price of two different kinds of money. It is set in the *foreign exchange market*.

What is the foreign exchange market, and how does it work? Domestic exporters earn foreign currency when they export. They sell their goods to people abroad, who have foreign currency — yen or yuan or euros or pounds or pesos — to pay them. Foreign producers earn domestic currency when they sell us imports. They sell their goods to people here, who have home currency — in the case of the United States, dollars — to pay them.

nominal exchange rate

The rate at which one country's money can be turned into another's; the price of one unit of foreign currency in terms of the home currency.

Both domestic exporters and foreign producers have a problem. Domestic exporters can't pay their own domestic workers with foreign currency — their workers expect to be paid in the home currency, dollars. Foreign producers can't pay their own workers with domestic currency — their workers expect to be paid in the foreign currency, yen or yuan or euros or pounds or pesos. Foreign producers need to trade the dollars they have earned from selling us imports for money that is useful to them; domestic exporters need to trade the foreign currency they have earned by selling exports for dollars that they can use.

How do foreign producers and domestic exporters solve this problem? They turn to the foreign exchange market, where those who have foreign currency — say, euros € — but want dollars exchange it for dollars, and those who have dollars but want foreign currency exchange dollars for other currencies. Those with foreign currency who want dollars include not only domestic exporters but also foreigners wishing to invest in the United States. Those with dollars who want foreign currency include not only foreigners who have sold Americans imports but also American residents who wish to invest abroad. (See Figure 2.1.)

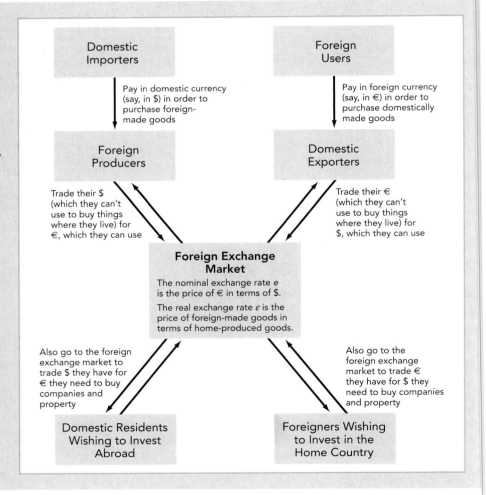

FIGURE 2.1

The Market for Foreign Exchange

In the foreign exchange market, domestic exporters and foreigners wishing to travel or to invest trade their foreign currency for domestic currency. Conversely, those who want foreign currency trade domestic currency for it.

If the dollar (the currency of the United States) and the euro (€, the currency of the European Union) trade on the foreign exchange market for \$1.20 = €1.00, then a single euro costs \$1.20 in U.S. currency. It takes less than one euro — €0.83 and change — to buy a single dollar. And 1.20 is the value of the dollar–euro exchange rate: It is the value of the euro in terms of the dollar.

Economists are less interested in the nominal exchange rate than in what we will call ε, the **real exchange rate**: the nominal rate adjusted for changes in the value of the currency. The nominal — the money — exchange rate can change without affecting the pattern of cross-national trade. When the real exchange rate — the rate in terms of goods and services — changes, the pattern of cross-national trade will change as well. The nominal exchange rate tells us the value of foreign currencies in terms of the home currency. The real exchange rate tells us the value of foreign-produced goods in terms of home-produced goods.

Suppose a burst of inflation doubled the price level in the United States, so everything that once cost \$1 in the United States now costs \$2, everything that used to cost \$2 now costs \$4, and so on. Suppose also that the nominal exchange rate changed from \$1.20 = €1.00 to \$2.40 = €1.00. Before the burst of inflation you could sell goods in Europe for €0.83, turn the euros into \$1.00, and buy American goods. After the burst of inflation you could sell goods in Europe for €0.83, turn the euros into \$2.00, and buy exactly the same American goods as before. The change in the nominal exchange rate has offset the change in the U.S. price level. In this case the real exchange rate — the rate at which goods trade for goods — has not changed. The terms at which the goods of one country are traded for the goods of another are the same.

Now suppose that a burst of inflation doubled the price level in the United States but that \$1.20 still exchanges for €1.00 on the foreign exchange market. Has the exchange rate changed? The nominal exchange rate has not changed: €0.83 will still get you a paper dollar; \$1.20 will still get you a euro. However, that paper dollar will buy only as many goods in the United States as 50 cents would have bought before. The doubling of the U.S. price level, coupled with the unchanged nominal exchange rate, means that the same quantity of U.S.-made goods will buy twice as many European-made goods. Flip it over: From the U.S. perspective, the cost of internationally produced goods has halved: The real exchange rate has halved.

Of course, if the price levels in different countries do not change, then there is no distinction between a change in the nominal exchange rate and a change in the real exchange rate. If the nominal exchange rate doubled — changed from \$1.20 = €1.00 to \$2.40 = €1.00 — but the price levels in the United States and Europe remained the same, then investors would need twice as many dollars to buy the same amount of foreign currency. Thus it would cost twice as many U.S.-made goods to buy the same amount of foreign-made goods. From the U.S. perspective, the real exchange rate would have doubled.

real exchange rate

The real exchange rate is the rate at which goods produced in a foreign country can be bought or sold for goods produced in the home country; the price of foreign-produced goods relative to domestic-produced goods.

The Real Exchange Rate

Calculating the Real Exchange Rate

Thus to calculate the real exchange rate ε, you need to know three pieces of information. First, you need to know the price level in the home country — call it P, for price. Second, you need to know the price level abroad — call it P^f: P for price, f for foreign. Third, you need to know the nominal exchange rate, e.

You can then calculate the value of the real exchange rate by multiplying the nominal exchange rate by the ratio of the foreign price level to the home price level:

$$\varepsilon = \frac{e \cdot P^f}{P}$$

Box 2.1 illustrates how the process works.

CALCULATING THE REAL EXCHANGE RATE: AN EXAMPLE

Suppose that the index of the U.S. price level is 120, the index of the euro-zone price level is 83.33, and the nominal exchange rate — the value of a euro in dollars — is 1.20: $1.20 = €1.00$. Then the real exchange rate would be

$$\varepsilon = \frac{e \cdot P^f}{P} = \frac{1.20 \cdot 83.33}{120} = 0.83$$

Now suppose that the U.S. price level were to rise to 150, the foreign price level were to rise to 120, and the nominal value of the euro were to fall to parity: $1.00 = €1.00$. Then the real exchange rate would become

$$\varepsilon = \frac{e \cdot P^f}{P} = \frac{1.00 \cdot 120}{150} = 0.80$$

The price of foreign goods in terms of domestic goods — the real exchange rate — has fallen. That is all there is to calculating real exchange rates.

- Holding the nominal exchange rate — the dollar cost of foreign currency — fixed, increases in the domestic price level lower the real exchange rate, which is the real value of foreign-produced goods in terms of home-produced goods.
- Holding the nominal exchange rate — the dollar cost of foreign currency — fixed, increases in the foreign price level raise the real exchange rate, which is the real value of foreign-produced goods in terms of home-produced goods.
- Holding the domestic and foreign price levels fixed, increases in the nominal exchange rate — in the dollar cost of foreign currency — raise the real exchange rate, which is the real value of foreign-produced goods in terms of home-produced goods.

Calculating the Overall Exchange Rate: Index Numbers

If you open up a newspaper in search of the exchange rate for the dollar, you will not find it. Instead, you will find a list of rates similar to the one in Table 2.2 but with many more entries — one line for almost every country.

An exchange rate for the dollar is listed against each and every other currency — a dollar–Swiss franc exchange rate, a dollar–yen exchange rate, a dollar–euro exchange rate, a dollar–pound exchange rate, a dollar–Canadian dollar exchange rate, a dollar–Mexican peso exchange rate, and more than 100 more for all the other currencies. Which of these is *the* exchange rate?

TABLE 2.2
Sample Exchange Rates

Currency	Value
Australian dollar*	0.7582
British pound*	1.8768
Canadian dollar	1.2219
Chinese yuan	8.2765
The euro*	1.3084
Japanese yen	104.17
New Zealand dr*	0.6945
Swiss franc	1.1815

*U.S. dollars per currency unit; otherwise, currency units per U.S. dollar.

In this situation economists do what they usually do when they are confronted with too much variety. They take an average and hope that deviations from the average will cancel each other out. In other words, they construct an **index number** to stand in place of the more than 100 exchange rates of the U.S. dollar against other currencies. The usual approach is to take a trade-weighted average, in which each currency receives a weight equal to its share of total U.S. trade: multiply the change in the real exchange rate vis-à-vis each other country by that country's share of U.S. trade, and add up all the results. Figure 2.2 presents the exchange rate index from 1983 to 2004.

index number

A number that isn't a set sum, value, or quantity in well-defined units (like dollars, people, or percent) but that is a quantity relative to a base year given an arbitrary index value of 100.

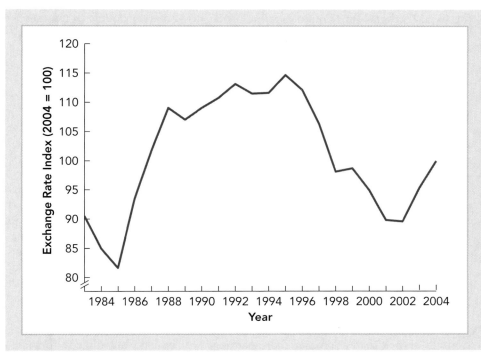

FIGURE 2.2
The Exchange Rate Index, 1983–2004

In 2002 — a year when the dollar was strong — the real exchange rate for the U.S. dollar was some 20 percent below its level in 1992 — a year when the dollar was weak. In 2002 a given amount of foreign-made goods could be used to purchase only 80 percent as many U.S.-made goods as it could have purchased in 1992. Since 2002, the dollar has weakened.

Source: Authors' calculations from the 2004 edition of *The Economic Report of the President* (Washington, DC: Government Printing Office).

RECAP   THE EXCHANGE RATE

Domestic exporters earn foreign currency when they export — sell goods to people abroad. Foreign producers earn domestic currency when they sell us imports — sell their goods to people here. Both then have a problem. Domestic exporters can't pay domestic workers with foreign currency. Foreign producers can't pay foreign workers with domestic currency. Domestic producers need to trade the foreign currency they have earned for dollars they can use. They turn to the foreign exchange market, where those who have foreign currency but want dollars exchange it for dollars, and those who have dollars but want foreign currency exchange dollars for other currencies.

2.3 THE STOCK MARKET AND INTEREST RATES

The Stock Market

stock market

The market on which the shares of common stock that carry ownership of companies are bought and sold.

We don't have to calculate the value of an index for the **stock market** because news agencies perform that task for the public. The best — the most representative — index of the U.S. stock market is probably Standard and Poor's composite index, usually called the S&P 500. The index you will hear about most, however, is the Dow-Jones Industrial Average (DJIA). But if the DJIA tells a different story from the S&P, ignore it; it is less representative of the market than is the S&P 500.

Although we don't have to assemble and calculate a stock market index, we do have to divide the numbers reported in the news by some measure of the price level — usually either the GDP deflator or the consumer price index (CPI). If both the price level and the (nominal) value of the stock market double, a representative share of stock is worth no more in real terms. To arrive at real magnitudes, economists deflate nominal magnitudes like a stock index by some measure of the price level. In this case we are most interested in the real value of the stock market.

The Utility of Knowledge about the Stock Market

Current stock market indexes are the easiest economic statistics to get. But what good is knowing the real value of the stock market to a macroeconomist? The stock market is a sensitive indicator of the relative optimism or pessimism of investors, and therefore it is a good forecaster of future investment spending.

To see why, we need to think about the mechanisms underlying the stock market. Most investors in the stock market face a choice between holding stocks and holding bonds. **Stocks** are shares of ownership of a corporation, and they give you ownership of that corporation's profits or earnings. **Bonds** are debts that the corporation owes you. A bond is a piece of paper that gives you periodic interest payments and, at the bond's *maturity*, returns to you the principal amount of the bond.

stock

A tradable financial instrument that is a share of ownership of a corporation.

bond

A tradable financial instrument that is a promise by a business or a government to repay money that it has borrowed.

The rate of return on money invested in bonds is simply the interest payment the bond issuer makes divided by the price of the bond. Call this real rate of interest in the economy r. If you invest in shares of stock, what is your rate of return? You paid a price P^s (P for price, s for stock) for each share. The corporation reports earnings E^s per share. Some of those earnings will be paid out directly to *shareholders* in the form of *dividends*. Others will be retained and reinvested, boosting the corporation's fundamental value. Both components increase shareholder wealth, and together they are the return on the investment in stocks. Thus an investor in stocks gets a return on each dollar invested of

$$\frac{E^s}{P^s}$$

Which will the investor prefer to hold, stocks or bonds? Saying that investors will prefer stocks if E^s/P^s is greater than r is not quite right. Investments in stocks are widely perceived to be risky. The company might go bankrupt, its reported earnings might be rigged, or the market might go down. As compensation for this risk, investors in stocks demand an extra return called the *risk premium,* or σ^s (the Greek lowercase letter sigma, with s for stocks as a superscript). So investors will want to hold only stocks if

$$\frac{E^s}{P^s} > r + \sigma^s$$

Investors will want to hold safer bonds if

$$\frac{E^s}{P^s} < r + \sigma^s$$

And investors will be willing to hold either stocks or bonds if

$$\frac{E^s}{P^s} = r + \sigma^s$$

Since in the world outside the classroom we see investors holding both stocks and bonds — some holding one, some holding the other, and some holding both — it is this last equation that must be true: This is our *equilibrium condition.* If it does not hold, investors as a group will be either frantically selling stocks (and so pushing the prices of stocks down) or frantically buying stocks (and so pushing the prices of stocks up).

If we turn this equation around, the value of stocks is equal to corporate earnings divided by the sum of the real interest rate on bonds and the risk premium:

$$P^s = \frac{E^s}{r + \sigma^s}$$

However, there is one more complication. The accounting earnings reported in the financial press — call them E^a — are not the earnings E^s that belong in the numerator of the stock valuation equation. The financial press reports what the firm's accountants have calculated, but investors are interested in some long-run average of expected future earnings. To apply the stock-price valuation formula, you also need an estimate of the relationship between the current earnings E^a that you see in the newspaper and "permanent" earnings E^s. (See Figure 2.3.)

The Stock Market Summarizes a Lot of Information
The real value of the stock market sums up, in one number that is reported every day,
- The current level of accounting earnings: reported corporate profits.
- Whether investors are optimistic (expecting long-run earnings to be above today's level) or pessimistic (expecting long-run earnings to be below today's level), and how optimistic or pessimistic they are.

FIGURE 2.3
Calculating the Value
of a Basket of Stocks

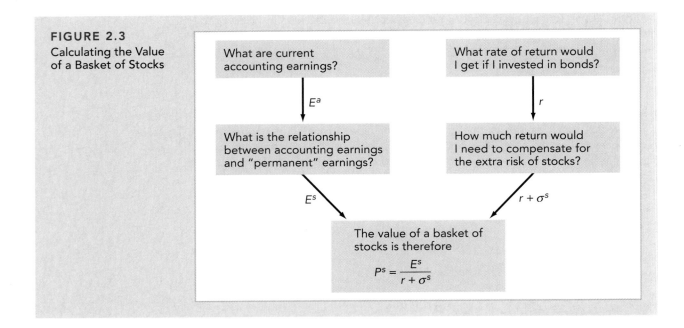

- The current cost of capital — whether money is cheap and easy to borrow (in which case r is low) or expensive (in which case r is high).
- Attitudes toward risk — whether people are strongly averse to the risks involved in entrepreneurship (in which case σ^s is high) or willing to gamble on new industries and new businesses (in which case σ^s is low).

These are the factors that determine whether corporate managers are willing to undertake investments to boost their companies' capital stocks. Thus the stock market summarizes all the information relevant to the economywide level of investment spending. Its usefulness as a summary of all the information relevant to determining investment spending is the reason it is one of the six key variables of macroeconomics.

Interest Rates

The interest rate is the price at which purchasing power can be shifted from the future into the present — borrowed today with a promise to pay it back with interest in the future. Interest is not a single lump sum but an ongoing stream of payments made over time. Thus it is what economists call a *flow variable*. A flow variable cannot be measured simply as a quantity; it must be measured as a quantity per unit of time. In the case of the interest rate, it is measured not just as a percentage of the amount borrowed, the principal, but as a percentage *per year.*

Economists like to talk about "the" interest rate in the same way that they like to talk about "the" exchange rate. But just as there are a large number of different exchange rates, there are a large number of interest rates. Loans of higher risk carry higher interest rates: Whomever you lent your money to might not pay it back — that is a risk you accepted when you lent in the first place. Loans of

TABLE 2.3
U.S. Treasury Bond Market

Term	Coupon	Maturity	Price	Yield	Change
3-month	—	5/26/2005	2.66%	2.71%	+0.030
6-month	—	8/25/2005	2.86%	2.95%	+0.015
2-year	3.375	2/28/2007	99 $^{22}/_{32}$	3.53%	+0.000
5-year	3.500	2/15/2010	98 $^{5}/_{32}$	3.91%	+0.006
10-year	4.000	2/15/2015	97 $^{27}/_{32}$	4.27%	−0.020
30-year	5.375	2/15/2031	111 $^{1}/_{32}$	4.64%	−0.030

Source: *Bloomberg Business News*, February 25, 2005.

different duration carry different interest rates as well. Moreover, differences in tax treatment — whether and when you have to pay taxes on interest earned from bonds — also lead to differences in interest rates. Thus even U.S. government bonds — the ultimate in safe investments — have no single interest rate. Table 2.3 shows a small sample of the interest rates — the column labeled "yield" — quoted on U.S. Treasury securities with maturities between a few months and 30 years.

Moreover, the interest rates published in the newspaper are nominal rates: They tell how much money you earn in interest per year if you lend out a sum of dollars now and collect the principal at the loan's maturity. You will not be surprised to learn that economists are interested instead in the real interest rate: how much purchasing power over goods and services you get in the future in return for trading away your purchasing power over goods and services today.

When we calculate real exchange rates, or real stock values, or real GDP, we divide the nominal exchange rate or stock index value or nominal GDP level by the price level, but that is not what we do to calculate real interest rates. Instead of *dividing* the nominal interest rate by the price level, we *subtract* the inflation rate — the percentage rate of change in the price level — from the nominal interest rate to get the real interest rate. Box 2.2 explains how.

CALCULATING REAL INTEREST RATES: AN EXAMPLE
Why subtract the inflation rate from the nominal interest rate? Suppose you borrow $10 million for one year at a nominal interest rate of 8 percent per year. Suppose further that the annual inflation rate is also 8 percent, so the price level will rise by 8 percent between now and next year. Thus whatever goods you want to buy will be more expensive. Let's say you want to buy television sets priced at $200 a set this year; they will cost $216 a set by next year.

Right now when you borrow, you get $10 million. Next year you will have to pay back $10.8 million — $10 million principal and $800,000 interest. You borrow enough now to buy 50,000 TV sets. Next year, when you pay back your loan with interest, you will pay the lender $10.8 million, just enough money to buy 50,000 TV sets. Thus you will return the same purchasing power over

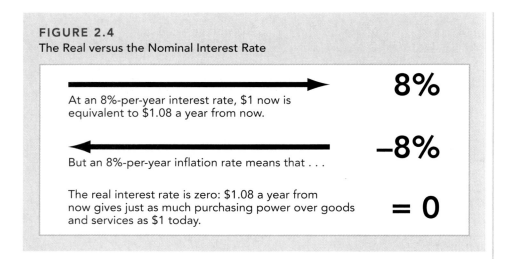

FIGURE 2.4
The Real versus the Nominal Interest Rate

At an 8%-per-year interest rate, $1 now is equivalent to $1.08 a year from now.   **8%**

But an 8%-per-year inflation rate means that . . .   **–8%**

The real interest rate is zero: $1.08 a year from now gives just as much purchasing power over goods and services as $1 today.   **= 0**

goods and services as what you borrowed, making a real interest rate of zero (see Figure 2.4).

Suppose the inflation rate had been 4 percent, so the price of a standard basket of goods and services, and of the TV sets you are buying, will rise from $200 to $208 next year. You borrow $10 million, enough to buy 50,000 TV sets. Next year, when you pay back your loan with its 8 percent annual interest, you will pay the lender $10.8 million, enough money to buy 51,923 TV sets. The extra 1,923 TV sets are a 3.846 percent increase in purchasing power over goods and services. Thus you will return 3.846 percent more purchasing power than you borrowed. However, to keep things simple, economists round the percentage off and call it a 4 percent real interest rate. (You will find that economists often round off numbers, drop small terms from equations, and generally do whatever they can to make things simpler.)

Thus the rule: To calculate a *real* interest rate, subtract the inflation rate from the *nominal* interest rate.

RECAP   THE STOCK MARKET AND INTEREST RATES

We don't have to calculate an index for the stock market because news agencies perform that task for the public already. We do, however, have to divide the numbers reported in the news by some measure of the price level in order to adjust for inflation and determine the real value of the stock market. To arrive at real magnitudes, economists *divide* nominal magnitudes like a stock index by some measure of the price level in order to arrive at *real* magnitudes. In this case we are most interested in the real value of the stock market. Note that when we calculate real interest rates, we do not divide the nominal interest rate by the price level. Instead we *subtract* the inflation rate — the percentage rate of change in the price level — from the nominal interest rate to get the real interest rate.

2.4 THE PRICE LEVEL AND INFLATION

The Consumer Price Index

The idea that economists need to measure the price level and to use it to calculate real quantities has come up several times already. Estimating the **price level** and its proportional rate of change — the inflation rate — is at the heart of macroeconomics.

The most frequently seen measure of the overall price level is the **consumer price index**, or **CPI**. (Other measures of prices include the producer price index of prices paid not by consumers but by companies, the economywide **GDP deflator**, and the domestic purchases deflator.) The CPI is calculated and reported once a month by the Bureau of Labor Statistics. It is an expenditure-weighted index, in which each good or service receives a weight equal to its share in total expenditure in the *base year.* (See Box 2.3 for a sample calculation.)

price level

The average level of nominal prices in the economy.

consumer price index (CPI)

The most frequently used measure of the cost of living; it measures the cost of a basket of consumer goods.

GDP deflator

The ratio of nominal GDP to real GDP.

CALCULATING PRICE INDEXES: AN EXAMPLE

BOX 2.3

One standard example economists use to illustrate how a price index is calculated is an index for consumers of fruit (perhaps because calculating indexes allows economists to really add apples and oranges). Suppose that in the base year a consumer buys $4.50 worth of oranges at a price of $0.75 a pound, $4.20 worth of apples at $1.20 a pound, $0.90 worth of pears at $0.90 a pound, and $0.40 worth of bananas at $0.40 a pound. Then, with a total of $10 spent on fruit in the base year, the price index for fruit will be given by

$$\text{Price index for fruit} = \left(\frac{\text{price of oranges today}}{\text{price of oranges in base year}} \times \text{orange index weight}\right)$$

$$+ \left(\frac{\text{price of apples today}}{\text{price of apples in base year}} \times \text{apple index weight}\right)$$

$$+ \left(\frac{\text{price of pears today}}{\text{price of pears in base year}} \times \text{pear index weight}\right)$$

$$+ \left(\frac{\text{price of bananas today}}{\text{price of bananas in base year}} \times \text{banana index weight}\right)$$

$$= \left(\frac{\text{price of oranges today}}{\$0.75} \times 45\right) + \left(\frac{\text{price of apples today}}{\$1.20} \times 42\right)$$

$$+ \left(\frac{\text{price of pears today}}{\$0.90} \times 9\right) + \left(\frac{\text{price of bananas today}}{\$0.40} \times 4\right)$$

We multiply the shares of total annual expenditure on each fruit by 100 so that in the base year the price index will be equal to 100, as is customary for economists to do.

Now consider a year in which, as shown in Table 2.4 on page 40, the price of oranges has risen to $1.50, the price of apples has fallen to $1.00, and the prices of pears and bananas have not changed. The overall fruit price index will be

$$\text{Price index for fruit} =$$

$$\left(\frac{\$1.50}{\$0.75} \times 45\right) + \left(\frac{\$1.00}{\$1.20} \times 42\right) + \left(\frac{\$0.90}{\$0.90} \times 9\right) + \left(\frac{\$0.40}{\$0.40} \times 4\right) = 138$$

TABLE 2.4
Calculating a Price Index for Fruit: An Example

Fruit	Base-Year Expenditure	Base-Year Price (per Pound)	Subsequent-Year Price (per Pound)
Oranges	$4.50	$0.75	$1.50
Apples	4.20	1.20	1.00
Pears	0.90	0.90	0.90
Bananas	0.40	0.40	0.40

Bureau of Labor Statistics

A bureau of the U.S. Department of Labor that calculates the unemployment rate and the consumer price index (CPI).

The **Bureau of Labor Statistics** changes the basket of goods and services used in constructing the CPI on a somewhat irregular basis. It updates the basket every five years if it has the money in its budget to do so; if not, it updates the basket every 10 years. Statisticians try to keep the weighted "market basket" of goods and services used in calculating the index reasonably close to the goods and services consumers are currently buying. If it were not, the CPI would be of doubtful relevance. Who would care about the rate of change in the price of a statistical market basket that didn't represent what consumers were really buying?

Kinds of Index Numbers

Using relative expenditure levels in a fixed base year as the weights in a price index produces a kind of index that economists call a Laspeyres index. The CPI is a Laspeyres price index. Another type of index, a Paasche index, is in a sense the opposite of a Laspeyres index. The expenditure weights in a Laspeyres index are fixed: A Laspeyres index of production or consumption counts up the current dollar value of what is produced or consumed and divides by what the value of what is produced or consumed would have been if all commodities had sold for their prices in the base year. The expenditure weights in a Paasche index are variable: If expenditures on a particular good rise this year and make it a large part of the current dollar value, then that good's weight in the price index will rise too. The second most-often-seen indicator of the price level, the GDP deflator, is a Paasche index. Box 2.4 compares the pluses and minuses of these two kinds of price indexes.

In general, a Laspeyres index overstates price increases. In the real world, when some items become expensive, consumers substitute and buy other items that remain

BOX 2.4

LASPEYRES AND PAASCHE INDEX NUMBERS: DETAILS
To see the difference between a Laspeyres and a Paasche index, return to our fruit example in Box 2.3. Suppose the prices of apples, pears, and bananas remain at their base-year levels, but surprise frosts destroy the orange crops in both Florida and California. The price of oranges skyrockets to $8.25 a pound (see Table 2.5), so no one buys any oranges — instead, consumers double their purchases of apples, pears, and bananas to 7 pounds of apples, 2 pounds of pears, and 2 pounds of bananas.

The CPI for fruit, a Laspeyres index, would then be

Price index for fruit =

$$\left(\frac{\$8.25}{\$0.75}\times 45\right)+\left(\frac{\$1.20}{\$1.20}\times 42\right)+\left(\frac{\$0.90}{\$0.90}\times 9\right)+\left(\frac{\$0.40}{\$0.40}\times 4\right)=550$$

According to this index, the price of fruit is five and a half times as high as that in the base year.

The deflator for fruit, a Paasche index, will be

- Total nominal expenditure on fruit in the frost year: $11
- Cost of buying those pieces of fruit in the base year: $11
- Dividing the first number by the second and following the standard practice of multiplying by 100, we discover that the price of fruit has not changed from its base-year value, 100.

TABLE 2.5
Two Different Kinds of Indexes: An Index Number Example

Fruit	Base-Year Expenditure	Base-Year Price (per Pound)	Subsequent-Year Price (per Pound)	Subsequent-Year Expenditure
Oranges	$4.50	$0.75	$8.25	$0.00
Apples	4.20	1.20	1.00	8.40
Pears	0.90	0.90	0.90	1.80
Bananas	0.40	0.40	0.40	0.80

cheap. But a Laspeyres index, because it is based on a fixed market basket of goods and services, does not take account of this substitution. Thus it suffers from what economists call substitution bias, and it tends to overstate changes. A Paasche index, on the other hand, understates the increase in fruit prices. It calculates the difference between the price today of the fruit you bought and the price back in the base year. The Paasche index takes account of substitution. But it doesn't take account of the fact that the substituted items are less valued than the items they replace. The Paasche index reports, in the example of Box 2.4, that the skyrocketing price of oranges has no effect on fruit prices. Yet it makes no sense to say that a frost that makes oranges completely unaffordable has no effect on the price of fruit.

So which is the "correct" price index? Neither: There is no final and definitive resolution to this "index number problem." All price indexes are imperfect. All try to summarize in a single number what is inherently a multidimensional reality of many prices changing in different directions and different proportions.

To strike a balance between the two types of indexes and their two types of biases, the Commerce Department's **Bureau of Economic Analysis** and the Labor Department's Bureau of Labor Statistics have begun to move toward hybrid indexes. To reduce substitution bias, the Bureau of Labor Statistics has begun using geometric averages — multiply two numbers together and take the square root — instead of

Bureau of Economic Analysis

A bureau in the U.S. Department of Commerce that maintains the national income and product accounts, the NIPA.

arithmetic averages. And the Bureau of Economic Analysis has begun using a procedure called *chain weighting* to construct its indexes.

With chain weighting, each year's proportional change in the index is calculated using a different base year. For instance, the percentage change in the index from 1999 to 2000 is calculated using the average of 1999 and 2000 as the base; the change from 2000 to 2001 is calculated using the average of 2000 and 2001 as the base; and the change from 2001 to 2002 is calculated using the average of 2001 and 2002 as the base. The results of these calculations are then "chained" together to make up the index.

The Inflation Rate

The CPI is reported once a month in the form of the percentage change in consumer prices over the preceding month. "Consumer prices in November rose 0.3 percent above their level in October," a newscaster will say. Eventually, 12 monthly changes in consumer prices over the course of the year are added up and become that year's **inflation rate.** "The consumer price inflation rate in 2004 was 2.3 percent," the newscaster will say.

Because the inflation rate is a measure of the rate of change in prices over time, it is a flow variable. When we speak of the inflation rate, we speak of it as such-and-such percent *per year.* Speaking of the inflation rate without reference to a measure of time is incomplete. But people do, and we always assume that when the time measure is omitted, the inflation percentage is an annual rate.

What the inflation rate is at any moment depends on which price level it is based on. The CPI-based inflation rate will not be exactly the same as the GDP-deflator-based inflation rate. Figure 2.5 plots three different measures of inflation in the

inflation rate

The annual rate of change of the overall level of prices in the economy.

FIGURE 2.5
Different Measurements of U.S. Inflation, 1960–2004

Different measures of inflation tell slightly different stories about inflation. But all tell the same broad story: Differences are small relative to the large swings in the inflation rate from one decade to another.

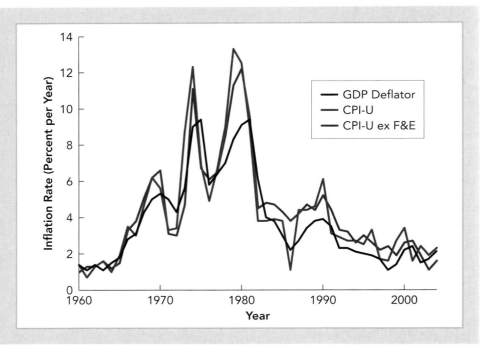

United States: the GDP deflator, a CPI for all urban consumers (the CPI-U), and a CPI that omits the volatile prices of food and energy, which can cause severe transitory fluctuations in the overall index (the CPI-U ex F&E).

RECAP **THE PRICE LEVEL AND INFLATION**

Already the idea that economists need to measure the price level and to use it to calculate real quantities has come up several times. Estimating the price level and its proportional rate of change — the inflation rate — is at the heart of macroeconomics. The most frequently seen measure of the overall price level is the consumer price index, or CPI. It is a fixed weight — a Laspeyres — index of prices. Each good or service receives a weight equal to its share in total expenditure in the base year. And periodically the base year is moved forward in time.

2.5 UNEMPLOYMENT

Calculating the Unemployment Rate

The **unemployment rate** is a key indicator of economic performance. An economy with persistent high unemployment is wasting its productive resources: Its level of output is below its productive potential. Such an economy surely has a lower level of social welfare than otherwise might easily be attained. Being unemployed is not pleasant, and neither is fearing unemployment for no other reason than the turning of the wheel of the business cycle.

unemployment rate

The share of the labor force who are looking for but have not found an acceptable job.

Keeping unemployment low is one of the chief goals of macroeconomic policy. Yet in the course of the business cycle unemployment rises and falls. Figure 2.6 shows the annual unemployment rate in the United States since 1950. It shows the large variation in unemployment. Even though the second half of the twentieth century saw nothing like the extraordinary peaks of unemployment in the *Great Depression*, the unemployment rate still varied from a low of less than 4 percent of the labor force to a high of almost 10 percent of the labor force.

Every month the Labor Department's Bureau of Labor Statistics (BLS) sends interviewers to talk to 60,000 households in a nationwide survey called the Current Population Survey (CPS). The BLS uses the CPS data to estimate the unemployment rate — the fraction of people who (1) wanted a job, (2) looked for a job, but (3) could not find an acceptable job. Statisticians classify the people who are interviewed into four categories:

1. Those who were employed in some sort of job when interviewed.

2. Those who were out of the labor force and did not want a job immediately.

3. Those who did want a job immediately but had not been looking for one because they did not think they could find one.

4. Those who did want a job immediately, had been looking, but had not found a job they would take.

According to the BLS definition of the unemployment rate, the *labor force* is group 1 plus group 4 — those who had jobs plus those who were looking for jobs:

$$\text{Labor force} = \text{employed} + \text{looking for work}$$

FIGURE 2.6

The U.S. Unemployment Rate since 1950

On average, the unemployment rate was relatively low in the 1950s — about 4.5 percent. It then rose to an average of nearly 6 percent in the 1970s and 7 percent in the 1980s before falling back to near 4 percent in the second half of the 1990s. In addition to these slow decade-to-decade swings, we also see the ups and downs of the business cycle — the boom of the late 1960s, the deep recession of 1982–1983, the smaller recession of 1990–1992, and the recession that began in 2001, among others.

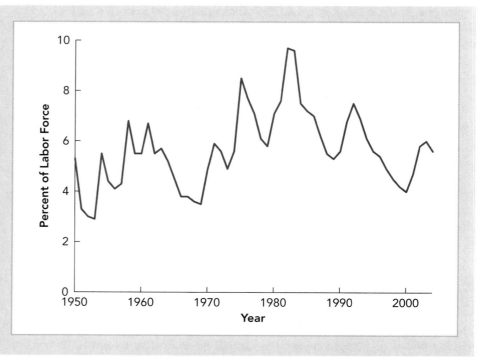

Source: 2004 edition of *The Economic Report of the President* (Washington, DC: Government Printing Office).

The unemployment rate is the number of unemployed — those in group 4 — divided by the total labor force:

$$\text{Unemployment rate} = \frac{\text{looking for work}}{\text{employed} + \text{looking for work}}$$

In contrast to the inflation rate, which is a flow variable, the unemployment rate is a *stock variable*. Saying that the current unemployment rate is 5 percent, with no reference to a measure of time, makes perfect sense.

The official unemployment rate may well underestimate the real experience of unemployment. Someone in group 3, who wants a job but has given up looking, certainly feels unemployed and may well feel as unemployed as someone in group 4. Perhaps these *discouraged workers* should be included in the unemployment rate. Furthermore, some people in group 1 have part-time jobs but want full-time jobs. Perhaps these part-timers for economic reasons should be counted as unemployed, or as half-unemployed.

Economists have noted striking and persistent variations in unemployment by demographic group and class. Teenagers age 16 to 19 have higher unemployment rates than adults, African-Americans have higher unemployment rates than whites, and high school dropouts have higher unemployment rates than those who have postgraduate degrees. For most of the post–World War II period (but not recently) women have had higher unemployment rates than men. Significantly, recessions don't just raise the unemployment rate; they disproportionately raise the unemployment rate among these high-unemployment groups. Figure 2.7 contrasts the unemployment rates of various groups of workers.

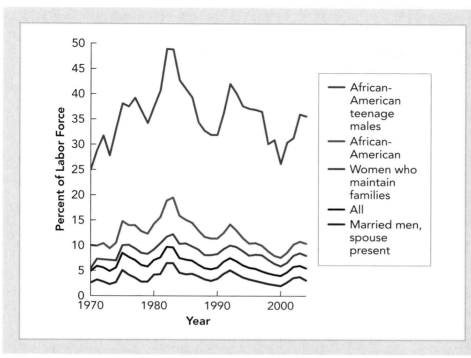

FIGURE 2.7
U.S. Unemployment Rates by Demographic Group, 1970–2004
The higher a group's average unemployment rate, the more the group's unemployment rate rises in recessions (and falls in booms). Recessions — times of high and rising unemployment — are unusually difficult for teenage and adult African-American workers.

Source: 2005 edition of *The Economic Report of the President* (Washington, DC: Government Printing Office).

The question "How long is the typical person who loses his or her job unemployed?" is hard to answer because it is ambiguous. Most people who become unemployed on any one day — say, July 16, 2005 — remain unemployed for only a short time; more than half find a job within a month. Yet of all the people who are unemployed on July 16, 2005, some three-quarters will be unemployed for more than two months before they find another job.

Okun's Law

For most of the time in the United States since World War II, the unemployment rate has been tightly coupled with the rate of growth of real GDP in a relationship called **Okun's law** (see Figure 2.8). From any one year to the next, the very simple equation

$$\text{Percentage change in real GDP} = \text{percentage growth in potential output} - (2.5)(\text{percentage-point change in unemployment rate})$$

fits the data well. According to Okun's law, unemployment falls (rises) when real GDP grows faster (slower) than *potential output*. Specifically, in the United States a 1-percentage-point fall in the unemployment rate is associated with an extra 2.5 percentage points of growth in real GDP relative to potential output. For example, in a year in which potential output grew 2 percent and the unemployment rate fell by 1 percentage point, real GDP would grow by fully 4.5 percent.

Because of Okun's law, if you know what is happening to real GDP relative to potential output, you have a good idea of what is happening to the unemployment rate, and vice versa. Box 2.5 explains the details of Okun's law.

Okun's law

The association between unemployment and real GDP: Periods of high (or low) unemployment are the same as periods of low (or high) growth of real GDP relative to potential output.

FIGURE 2.8
Okun's Law

An extra 2.5 percent of growth in a year's real GDP is associated with a 1-percentage-point decline in the unemployment rate. Note that before 1974 the real GDP growth rate that kept unemployment constant was about 4 percent per year. Between 1974 and 1995, the unemployment rate was constant when real GDP growth was about 2.8 percent per year. Since 1995 there have been signs that the old pre-1974 relationship is reemerging. We call the rate of growth at which the unemployment rate is constant the rate of growth of potential output. The fall in the rate of growth of potential output after 1973 — the so-called productivity growth slowdown — is one of the most important features of recent American economic history.

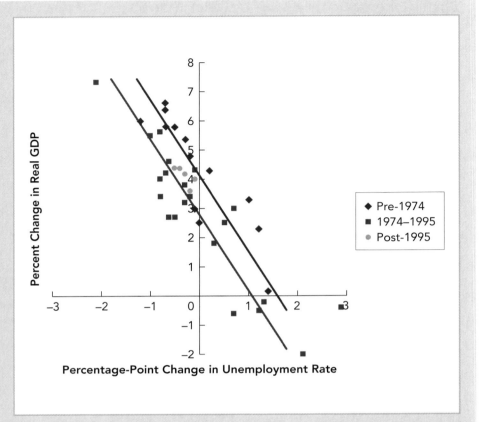

Percentage-Point Change in Unemployment Rate

Source: Authors' calculations from the 2001 edition of *The Economic Report of the President* (Washington, DC: Government Printing Office).

BOX

FORMS OF OKUN'S LAW: DETAILS

Okun's law sees not a 1-to-1 relation but a 2.5-to-1 relationship between real GDP growth and the unemployment rate. That is, a 1-percentage-point fall in the unemployment rate is associated not with a 1 but a 2.5 percent boost in the level of production.

Why is the Okun's law coefficient so large? Why isn't it the case that a 1-percentage-point fall in unemployment produces a 1 percent rise in output, or even less? Part of the answer is that the unemployment rate, as officially measured, does not count discouraged workers. In a recession, the number of people at work falls, the number of people looking for work rises, and the number of people who are not looking for work because they doubt they could find jobs — but who would be working if business conditions were better — rises. When conditions improve, many of these discouraged workers return to the labor force. Because the conventionally measured unemployment rate does not include these discouraged workers, more than a 1 percent rise in real GDP is needed to reduce the unemployment rate by 1 percentage point.

In addition, when business returns to normal, firms' initial response is not to hire more employees but to ask existing employees to work longer hours. So average hours of work per week go up, and the unemployment rate falls by less than one would otherwise expect.

Finally, in some industries, employing more workers increases production by more than a proportional amount: Product design and setup need to be done only once, no matter how much is produced. Thus businesses that have economies of scale do not need twice as many workers to produce twice as much output.

Since 2000 the quantitative form of Okun's law has shifted: The Okun's law coefficient appears to have grown even larger than 2.5. More than 2.5 percent growth of real GDP relative to potential output is now needed to lower the unemployment rate by 1 percentage point. We are not yet sure whether Okun's law will return to its old pattern or, if it does not, what the new quantitative relationship between unemployment and the output gap is. Many economists think that the relatively stagnant employment levels seen between 2000 and 2005 led a great many people who would seek jobs in normal times to temporarily drop out of the labor force, and so artificially lowered the unemployment rate. We must wait a few years to learn whether the change in the Okun's law coefficient is permanent, temporary, or — allowing for measurement error — even nonexistent!

> **RECAP   THE UNEMPLOYMENT RATE**
>
> The unemployment rate is a key indicator of economic performance. An economy with persistent high unemployment is wasting its productive resources: its level of output is below its productive potential. Moreover, the official unemployment rate may well underestimate the real experience of unemployment in the American economy.

2.6 REAL GDP

Sixth and last of the key economic variables is **real GDP,** the most frequently used measure of economic performance. You will see other measures of total production and total income as well. All of them are close cousins of real GDP: GNP (*gross national product*), NNP (*net national product*), NDP (*net domestic product*), and NI (*national income*). And you will hear commentators refer to "total output," "total production," "national product," "total income," and "national income." Except when you are focusing explicitly on the details of the national income and product accounts (**NIPA**), treat all these terms as synonyms for real GDP.

real GDP

Inflation-adjusted gross domestic product; the most commonly used measure of national product, output, and income. Equal as well to total expenditure on domestically produced goods and services.

NIPA

National income and product accounts; the system that government statisticians use to measure, estimate, and check data on the flow of economic activity.

Calculating Real GDP

Real GDP is calculated by adding up the value of all final goods and services produced in the economy. Because it measures the rate at which goods and services are produced, real GDP is a flow variable; it is usually expressed as an annual amount. Often, however, you will not hear the phrase "per year." But when you hear that real GDP in the fourth quarter of 2002 was such and such, remember that such a statement means that the flow of production in the fourth quarter was such and such *per year.* And when you hear that real GDP in the fourth quarter of 2002 grew at so-and-so percent, remember that such a statement means that real GDP in the fourth quarter grew at so-and-so percent *per year* — the difference between real GDP in the third quarter and real GDP in the fourth quarter is only one-quarter of the reported annual growth rate.

What are the final goods and services that make up GDP? A final good or service is something that is not used further in production during the course of the year. Thus final goods and services include

- Everything bought by consumers.
- Everything bought by businesses not as an input for further production but as an investment to increase the business's capital stock and expand its future production capacity.
- Everything bought by the government.

Because GDP measures *product* and not *spending,* it includes a balancing item, *exports* minus *imports.* Because exported goods bought by foreigners were made in the United States, they are part of GDP and need to be added to the total. Because imported goods bought by consumers, installed as pieces of investment, or bought by the government were not made in the United States, they are not part of gross domestic product, so imports need to be subtracted from GDP.

Real and Nominal GDP

When economists add up final goods and services produced in the year to calculate GDP, how do they weight each good or service? The answer is that they use market value — what people paid for a good or service — in the calculation of *nominal GDP.* Box 2.6 presents a stylized, hypothetical example of how this is done.

WEIGHTING GOODS AND SERVICES BY THEIR MARKET VALUES: AN EXAMPLE

How do economists weight goods and services by their market values? Recall the discussion of the CPI in Box 2.3 in which the representative consumer bought 11.5 pounds of fruit:

Fruit	Quantity (Pounds)	Price (per Pound)
Oranges	6	$0.75
Apples	3.5	1.20
Pears	1	0.90
Bananas	1	0.40

If these quantities were the final goods and services produced in a particular year — let's call it year 1 — and we then wanted to measure the GDP of fruit, we simply multiply the quantities produced by their market prices:

$$GDP = (6 \text{ lbs. oranges} \times \$0.75/\text{lb.}) + (3.5 \text{ lbs. apples} \times \$1.20/\text{lb.})$$
$$+ (1 \text{ lb. pears} \times \$0.90/\text{lb.}) + (1 \text{ lb. bananas} \times \$0.40/\text{lb.})$$

$$= \$10.00$$

The nominal GDP of fruit in year 1 is $10.

In 2003 nominal GDP (that is, GDP measured at 2003 prices) was $11.00 trillion; in 2002 nominal GDP (that is, measured at 2002 prices) was $10.49 trillion. Thus the growth rate of nominal GDP between 2002 and 2003 was 4.9 percent. But this nominal measure of GDP, in which current-year prices are used to weight the final goods and services produced and to calculate growth rates, is clearly not a good measure of *productivity* or material output. It confuses changes in the overall price level — inflation or deflation — with changes in total production. Suppose production in the next year stayed unchanged but prices doubled; nominal GDP would double. Suppose production doubled but prices stayed the same; nominal GDP would also double. Although nominal GDP does not distinguish between these two sources of increase in total expenditure, we need to distinguish between them. Hence economists favor real GDP — the value of final goods and services weighted by the prices of some particular base year. Box 2.7 illustrates the weighting of goods and services in terms of base-year prices.

WEIGHTING GOODS AND SERVICES BY THEIR BASE-YEAR VALUES: AN EXAMPLE

Recall the hypothetical example in Box 2.6. Assume that in the year following year 1 — year 2 — the prices and quantities of fruit produced are as follows:

BOX 2.7

Fruit	Quantity (Pounds)	Price (per Pound)
Oranges	8	$1.00
Apples	3.5	1.20
Pears	1	0.50
Bananas	1	0.40

Now we can calculate nominal GDP of fruit in both year 1 and year 2 and real GDP of fruit (at year 1 prices) in both year 1 and year 2:

- Nominal GDP of fruit in year 1: $10.00
- Real GDP of fruit in year 1 (at year 1 prices): $10.00
- Nominal GDP of fruit in year 2: $13.10
- Real GDP of fruit in year 2 (at year 1 prices): $11.50

The nominal quantity grows by 31 percent between year 1 and year 2. The real quantity grows by only 15 percent between year 1 and year 2. The difference is inflation, the change in the price level.

Whenever you hear a statement such as "Real GDP in 2002 was 10.07 trillion 2000 dollars," remember that "2000 dollars" means that 2000 is the base year of the calculation. When measured using 2000 prices, GDP in 2002 — real GDP — was not $10.49 trillion but only $10.07 trillion. The difference, the gap between $10.49 trillion and $10.07 trillion, was due to price inflation between 2000 and 2002. Real GDP between 2002 and 2003 rose by only 3.0 percent, not 4.9 percent.

As has been noted, economists construct an alternative index number for the rate of inflation, the GDP deflator, from nominal GDP and real GDP. The procedure is

1. Calculate nominal GDP.
2. Calculate real GDP.
3. Divide the first number by the second; the quotient is the GDP deflator.

The GDP deflator is a Paasche index — the kind of index that tends to understate the effect on the price level of a rise in the price of a particular good. While the GDP deflator takes account of purchasers' ability to substitute away from items that have increased prices, it does not take account of the reduction in utility — the implicit cost to consumers — of settling for second best.

Intermediate Goods, Inventories, and Imputations

Intermediate Goods

GDP is defined as the market value of final goods and services produced. Thus so-called *intermediate goods* — goods sold to another business for use in further production — are excluded from GDP. A product made by one business and sold to another will eventually show up in the national income and product accounts and be counted as part of GDP. It will show up when the second business sells its product (which will by then embody the value added by the first producer) to a consumer, an investor, a foreign purchaser, or the government. Meanwhile, because the value of an intermediate good is included in the price of the final good that the intermediate good is used to make, its value must be excluded from GDP.

For example, if a builder buys wood from a lumber mill to build a house, the value of the wood becomes part of the value of the house. To count the sale of the wood to the home builder as well as the sale of the newly built house to its purchaser would be to count the wood twice. And what would happen if the builder bought the lumber mill and thus no longer had to buy finished wood? GDP should not go down just because two businesses have merged.

One way to think about intermediate goods is that GDP represents the economic value added at every stage of production. The *value added* by any one business is equal to the total value of the firm's products minus the value of the materials and intermediate goods the firm purchases. In computing value added from start to finish, each intermediate good and service enters the calculation twice: once with a plus sign, when the value added of the business that made the good is calculated, and once with a minus sign, when the value added of the business that uses the good is calculated. Using this value-added approach, every good and service in the economy cancels out except those that are not sold to other businesses for use in the production process. The goods whose values do not cancel out are the final goods and services — consumption goods, goods purchased by the government, goods purchased as part of investment, and net exports.

Inventories

What happens if the production process is not finished when the end of the year rolls around and the Commerce Department's Bureau of Economic Analysis (BEA) closes the books on that year's GDP calculation? Some intermediate goods will not have been used to produce goods for final sale. The value has already been added in making the intermediate good, but no final good that embodies that value has yet been sold. The NIPA finesses this problem by treating inventories at the end of a period as a special kind of final good, a form of investment. A business that produces intermediate goods or final goods and doesn't sell them by the end of the year is treated as having "purchased" those goods for itself as part of its capital stock. The general rule is that whenever a business increases its end-of-period inventory, that increase is counted as a component of investment and of final demand.

What happens the next year when the final goods are finished and sold? The value of those final goods sold becomes part of the next period's GDP. But the intermediate goods that went into them are counted as a negative investment, a disinvestment, in inventory. Thus the intermediate goods left over from this year and used next year are subtracted from next year's GDP.

Imputations

What about goods and services that are produced and consumed but not sold in the marketplace? Such goods and services lack prices and market values; how are they counted in GDP? In some cases national income accounts estimate — they guess, really — what goods or services would have sold for on the market if there had been a market.

The largest such "imputation" in the NIPA is found in housing. When somebody rents an apartment or a house, the rent he or she pays to the landlord becomes part of GDP as the purchase of "housing services" by the renter. When a landlord rents a house to a tenant, the landlord is selling a service — the usefulness of having a roof over the renter's head — just as a barber is selling a service when a customer gets a haircut. Thus rent is one item in consumer spending on services.

However, about 60 percent of all Americans own their own houses and are their own landlords. These homeowners do not write a monthly rent check to themselves. Counting renter-occupied housing as part of GDP but ignoring owner-occupied housing would not be consistent. Therefore GDP includes the *imputed rent* on owner-occupied dwellings — the amount the BEA thinks that owner-occupied apartments and houses would rent for if they were rented out.

The inclusion of the cost of goods and services bought by the government may also be understood as an imputation. Since citizens do not directly pay firefighters, police officers, judges, and other government employees, the value of what the government spends on firefighting — in wages, insurance, materials, and so forth — is counted in GDP.

Components of Real GDP

How does the Bureau of Economic Analysis construct its measure of real GDP? The BEA includes in its measure of real GDP, which we will always denote by Y in equations and diagrams, the values of the following:

- Goods and services that are ultimately bought and used by households (except for newly constructed buildings); these goods and services are termed **consumption spending** (denoted C).
- Goods and services (including newly constructed buildings) that become part of society's business or residential *capital stock;* these goods and services are termed **investment spending** (denoted I). *Gross investment* spending is divided into two parts: the capital consumption allowance, or the *depreciation* of worn-out or obsolete capital; and *net investment,* which increases the total capital stock. Investment can be divided into four components: houses and apartments (residential *structures*), other buildings and infrastructure (nonresidential structures), machines (*producers' durable equipment*), and, as noted above, the change in business inventories (see Table 2.6).

consumption spending

Spending on goods and services purchased and used by consumers.

investment spending

That portion of total spending devoted to increasing business capacity and the economy's capital stock.

TABLE 2.6
Components of Investment, Third Quarter of 2003

Category of Investment	Annual Rate (Billions of chained 2000 dollars)
Total private gross investment spending	$1,656
Residential structures	517
Nonresidential structures	238
Producers' durable equipment	908
Change in business inventories	−9

Source: 2004 edition of *The Economic Report of the President* (Washington, DC: Government Printing Office).

government purchases

Government spending on goods or services (including the wages of government employees).

net exports

The difference between exports and imports.

- **Government purchases** (denoted *G*). Note that government purchases do not include any payments the government makes that are not payment for a good or service provided to the government.
- **Net exports** (denoted *NX*) are a balancing item included in GDP: The GDP total needs to be adjusted for the difference between exports and imports to make the national income and product accounts consistent.

Accountants add up all these components to arrive at GDP (see Table 2.7). This definition of GDP, the *national income identity,* is one of the most fundamental bases of macroeconomics:

$$Y = C + I + G + NX$$

This is the equation that you will write down more than any other during any macroeconomics course.

Goods (and services) produced abroad but consumed or used in the United States are imports. Goods (and services) produced in the United States and shipped abroad to be consumed or used there are *gross exports.* The distinction between gross exports and net exports is similar to the distinction between gross investment and net investment. Gross exports are exports before the counterbalancing factor of imports has been subtracted. Most often gross exports are less important than net exports — the difference between gross exports and imports, the net flow of goods into or out of the United States.

TABLE 2.7
Components of Real GDP, Third Quarter of 2003

Category of Spending	Annual Rate (Billions of chained 2000 dollars)
Total GDP	$10,493
Consumption spending	7,427
Investment spending	1,656
Government purchases	1,911
Net exports	−505

Source: 2004 edition of *The Economic Report of the President* (Washington, DC: Government Printing Office).

The final component of the national income identity, net exports, has been growing in relative size and importance. In the years just after World War II, imports into and exports from the United States were about 5 percent of GDP. The United States was then more or less a *closed economy*. Macroeconomics textbooks gave short shrift to international trade and finance; it was not very important. Today imports into and exports from the United States are about 15 percent of GDP, three times as large a share as the percentage 50 years ago. The American economy is now more an *open economy*, and so international economics issues can no longer be downplayed.

What Is and Is Not in GDP

Depreciation and Net Output

Real GDP is a very imperfect measure of total economic activity, or material well-being. Some things that are included in GDP should not be, and some things that are not included in GDP should be. For example, every year a portion of the nation's capital stock loses value. It wears out or becomes obsolete, so keeping it operating is no longer worthwhile because the cost of doing so is higher than the value of the goods the capital produces. Replacing such worn-out or obsolete capital is as much a cost of production to a business (or a government) as is meeting the business's payroll. Such replacement is surely not an increase in the nation's capital stock. Yet GDP counts all investment — including this replacement investment — in its measure of total economic activity, for the measure of investment included in real GDP is gross investment.

Why is replacement investment included in real GDP? Why is it seen not as a cost of doing business but as the near-equivalent of building a new factory to expand the business's productive capacity? Depreciation expenditures are counted in real GDP because the statisticians who compile the NIPA have no confidence in their estimates of economywide depreciation. A better measure of economic activity is net domestic product (NDP), which includes only net investment and excludes depreciation. However, the national income accountants prefer to focus attention on measures that they think are reasonably accurate, and so they downplay the (poorly measured) NDP and play up the GDP estimate.

Government Purchases

Government purchases of goods and services are also counted in GDP. The government uses the goods and services it purchases: It builds roads, provides police protection and courts, runs schools, issues weather reports, maintains the national parks, maintains the armed services, and so on.

Many of these services, if they were provided by private businesses, would be counted as intermediate goods — things that are not of final value themselves but are aids to private-sector production. As such, they would be excluded from the GDP. Think about it. Suppose two companies made a contract that a certain arbitrator would be the judge of any disputes that arose between them, and suppose they paid the arbitrator a retainer. The services of the private judge that they hired would be classified in the NIPA as an intermediate good and would not be included in the final goods and services added up to calculate GDP.

Nevertheless, all government purchases of goods and services are counted as part of GDP, including the money the government collects in taxes and then pays to its own judges, bailiffs, and clerks, many of whom decide business-to-business disputes. A large number of government purchases fall into this category. They are counted as part of GDP, but they would not be counted had they been made for analogous substantive purposes by private businesses.

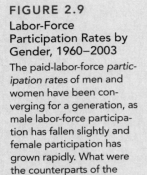

FIGURE 2.9
Labor-Force Participation Rates by Gender, 1960–2003

The paid-labor-force *participation rates* of men and women have been converging for a generation, as male labor-force participation has fallen slightly and female participation has grown rapidly. What were the counterparts of the women who worked for wages in 2003 doing back in 1960? They were working, but not for wages. And their work then wasn't counted as part of GDP.

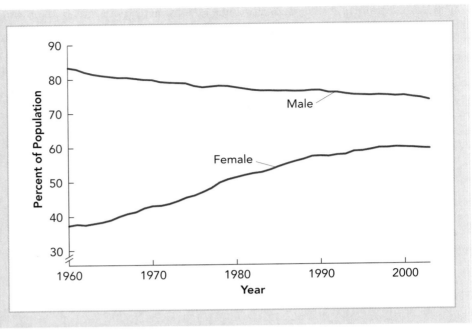

Source: 2004 edition of *The Economic Report of the President* (Washington, DC: Government Printing Office).

What Isn't in GDP but Should Be

Moreover, many expenditures excluded from the NIPA, and thus from GDP, probably should not be. Production that takes place within the household is excluded from GDP. That is, the work family members do to keep their own households going, for which they are not paid, is excluded from GDP. This exclusion warps our picture of the U.S. economy. In 2000 some 129 million Americans, male and female, worked a total of about 206 billion paid hours (and some 7 million Americans spent a total of 5 billion hours looking for jobs). But many Americans — most of them adult women — also spent at least 100 billion hours performing services such as cooking, cleaning, shopping, and chauffeuring that would count as employment and would count in GDP if they were receiving pay for them rather than doing them for their own families. As Figure 2.9 shows, less than 40 percent of American women were counted in the labor force in 1960, even though most of them would have said that they worked full days. Within-the-household production has never been counted as part of GDP. When the NIPA system was set up, economists believed that obtaining reasonable, credible, defensible estimates of the economic value of within-the-household production would be difficult or impossible.

Yet the exclusion of within-the-household production makes a difference not just for the level of national product but for its rate of growth. Over time the border between paid market and unpaid nonmarket, within-the-household work has shifted. Be suspicious of economic growth rates based on total GDP, GDP per capita, or GDP per adult, because they are distorted by the shifting dividing line between what people do and how they arrange their work. A meal cooked is a meal cooked whether it is part of the market-paid work of a restaurant chef or part of the unpaid work of a homemaker. Over time the share of meals prepared in the first way has grown, while the share of meals prepared in the second way has shrunk.

This shift in the dividing line between home cooking and dining out has raised measured GDP, but the shift by itself is not an increase in society's wealth.

Depletion, Pollution, and "Bads"

The NIPA system makes no allowance for the depletion of scarce natural resources. To the extent that an economy produces a high income in the act of using up valuable natural resources, that income is not true GDP at all but the depletion of natural resources. Kuwait, Qatar, and Saudi Arabia have high levels of measured real GDP per worker, but much of their income arises not out of sustainable production but out of the sale of limited and depletable natural resources. A better system would have a category for the depletion of natural resources.

Moreover, the NIPA contains no category for the production of **bads** — things that you would rather not have. Producing more smog does not diminish GDP. The extra cases of lung cancer produced by cigarette smoking do not diminish GDP (indeed, they raise the medical care sector's contribution to GDP). If the demand for locks and alarm systems rises because crime increases, GDP increases. As noted before, GDP is a measure only of the economy's level of productive effort, not of well-being.

"bads"

Elements produced by an economy that diminish consumers' welfare and that would constitute a subtraction from GDP in some better, future system of social accounts to measure economic welfare.

RECAP REAL GDP

Real GDP is calculated by adding up the value of all final goods and services produced in the economy. Because it measures the rate at which goods and services are produced, real GDP is a flow variable: Remember that real GDP is measured as the value of goods and services produced *per year.* Real GDP has four components: (1) consumer spending for final goods and services, (2) investment spending by firms to increase their capital stock, (3) purchases of goods and services by the government (including the time of bureaucrats), and (4) net exports.

Chapter Summary

1. Because economics studies goods and services that flow through the market and are bought and sold with prices attached, economists have a lot of quantitative data to work with.

2. The real exchange rate is the relative price at which two countries' goods exchange for each other. You calculate it by adjusting the nominal exchange rate for changes in the price levels in the two countries.

3. The level of the stock market is a valuable summary index of a range of factors that affect investment: the current level of profits, investors' optimism or pessimism, the real rate of interest, and attitudes toward risk.

4. Real interest rates are much more important variables to keep track of than are nominal interest rates. Calculate the real interest rate by subtracting the rate of inflation from nominal interest rates.

5. The most commonly seen measure of the price level is the consumer price index (CPI). The proportional rate of change of the price level is called the inflation rate.

6. Unemployment and total output are linked through Okun's law: A 1-percentage-point change in the unemployment rate comes with a 2.5 percent change in the opposite direction in the level of output relative to potential output.

7. Real GDP is the most frequently seen measure of the overall level of economic activity. It is the value — calculated using market prices in some chosen base year — of all final goods and services produced in a year.

8. The line between what's in GDP and what's not in GDP is principally the result of economists' beliefs in the 1940s and 1950s about what could be readily measured. It is not the result of a set of principled decisions about what kinds of activities should and should not be included in a measure of material welfare.

Key Terms

nominal exchange rate (p. 29)

real exchange rate (p. 31)

index number (p. 33)

stock market (p. 34)

stock (p. 34)

bond (p. 34)

price level (p. 39)

consumer price index (CPI) (p. 39)

GDP deflator (p. 39)

Bureau of Labor Statistics (p. 40)

Bureau of Economic Analysis (p. 41)

inflation rate (p. 42)

unemployment rate (p. 43)

Okun's law (p. 45)

real GDP (p. 47)

NIPA (p. 47)

consumption spending (p. 51)

investment spending (p. 51)

government purchases (p. 52)

net exports (p. 52)

"bads" (p. 55)

Analytical Exercises

1. Are capital goods — large turbine generators, jet airliners, bay-spanning bridges — intermediate goods or final goods? How are they included in GDP?

2. How do the labor and other factors of production that go into producing intermediate goods ultimately get counted in GDP?

3. Explain whether or not and why the following items are included in the calculation of GDP:
   a. Increases in business inventories.
   b. Sales of existing homes.
   c. Fees earned by real estate agents on selling existing homes.
   d. Income earned by Americans living and working abroad.
   e. Purchases of IBM stock by your brother.
   f. Purchase of a new tank by the Department of Defense.
   g. Rent that you pay to your landlord.

4. Which interest rate concept — the nominal interest rate or the real interest rate — do lenders and borrowers care more about? Why?

5. Which is the more important measure for assessing an economy's performance, real GDP or nominal GDP?

Policy Exercises

1. In 1979 the (short-term) nominal interest rate on three-month Treasury bills averaged 10 percent, and the GDP deflator rose from 50.88 to 55.22.
   a. What was the annual rate of inflation in 1979? What was the real interest rate in 1979?
   b. Were real interest rates higher in 1979 or in 2003, when the (short-term) nominal interest rate on three-month Treasury bills was 1.0 percent and the inflation rate was 1.7 percent?

2. In 1992 the implicit GDP deflator (in 1992 dollars) was equal to 100; in 1993 it was equal to 102.64. What was the annual rate of inflation between 1992 and 1993? In 1993 the implicit GDP deflator (in 1992 dollars) was equal to 102.64; in 1994 it was 105.09. What was the annual rate of inflation between 1993 and 1994?

3. In 1992 both nominal GDP and real GDP (measured in 1992 dollars) were equal to $6.244 trillion. By 1997 nominal GDP had risen to $8.111 trillion, and the implicit GDP deflator had risen to 111.57. What was real GDP in 1997? What was the average rate of real GDP growth between 1992 and 1997?

4. In 1997 nominal GDP was $8.111 trillion, and the implicit GDP deflator (measured in 2000 dollars) was 93.85. By 2003 nominal GDP had risen to $10.977 trillion, and the implicit GDP deflator had risen to 105.64. What was real GDP in 2003? What was the average rate of real GDP growth between 1997 and 2003?

3

Thinking Like an Economist

QUESTIONS

In what way and to what degree can we say that economics is a science?

What do economists mean by a "model"?

Why are economists so attracted to formal, mathematical models?

What patterns and habits of thought do you need to learn in order to be able to think like an economist?

3.1 UNDERSTANDING MACROECONOMICS

Every new subject that you learn requires that you learn not just new facts but also new patterns of thought. Every intellectual discipline has its own way of thinking about the world, which you need to learn. That is, after all, what makes a subject a discipline: A discipline allows (and forces) people to think about a slice of the world in some new way.

Economics is no exception. Think of it this way: There is a sense in which learning a new intellectual discipline like macroeconomics is similar to learning a new language. Economists' way of thinking allows us to see the economy more sharply and clearly than if we were limited to thinking like a sociologist, or a political scientist, or a business reporter. (Of course, restricting yourself to one mode of thought can also have costs. Thinking only like an economist can also cause us to miss certain relationships that are hard to quantify or hard to think of as purchases and sales. That is why economics is not the only social science, and we need sociologists, political scientists, historians, psychologists, and anthropologists as well.)

In this chapter we will survey the intellectual landmarks of economists' system of thought. The idea is to help you orient yourself in the mental landscape of macroeconomics. For some of you this chapter will seem pointless and obvious. But for some of you it will be like a lightbulb being turned on: "So that's what's going on!" you will think.

Economics: How Is It Like a Science?

If you are coming to economics from a background in the natural sciences, you probably expect economics to be something like a natural science, only less so: To the extent that it works, it works more or less like chemistry, though it does not work as well. Economic theories are unsettled and poorly described. Economists' predictions are often wrong.

If you hold these opinions, you are half-right. While economics is like a science in many respects, it is not and cannot be identical to a natural science. It is a *social* science. Its subject is not electrons or elements but human beings: people and how they behave. This subject matter has several important consequences. Some of them make economics easier than a natural science, some of them make economics harder than a natural science, and some of them just make it different.

First, because economics is a social science, debates within economics last a lot longer and are much less likely to end in a clear consensus than are debates in the natural sciences. The major reason is that different people have different views of what makes a free, a good, a just, or a well-ordered society. They look for an economy that harmonizes with their vision of what a society should be. They ignore or explain away facts that turn out to be inconvenient for their particular political views. People are, after all, only human.

Economists try to approach the objectivity that characterizes most work in the natural sciences. After all, what is is, and what is not is not. Even if wishful thinking or predispositions contaminate the results of a single study, later studies can correct the error. But economists never approach the unanimity with which physicists embraced the theory of relativity, chemists embraced the oxygen theory of combustion, and biologists rejected the Lamarckian inheritance of acquired characteristics. Biology departments do not have Lamarckians. Chemistry departments do not have phlogistonists. But economics departments do have a wide variety of points of view and schools of thought. Because economists never approach unanimity, maintaining a diversified intellectual portfolio is important in economics.

Second, the fact that economics is about people means that economists cannot ethically undertake large-scale experiments. Economists cannot set up special situations in which potential sources of disturbance are reduced to a minimum, then observe what happens, and generalize from the results of the experiment (where sources of disturbance are absent) to what happens in the world (where sources of disturbance are common). Thus the experimental method, the driver of rapid progress in many of the natural sciences, is largely lacking in economics. This flaw makes economics harder to analyze, and it makes economists' conclusions much more tentative and subject to dispute than is the case with natural sciences.

Third, the subjects economists study — people — have minds of their own. They observe what is going on around them, plan for the future, and take steps to avoid future consequences that they foresee and fear will be unpleasant. At times they simply do what they want, just because they feel like doing it. Thus in economists' analyses the present often depends not just on the past but on the future as well — or on what people expect the future to be. Box 3.1 presents one example of this: how people's **expectations** of the future and particularly their fear that there might be a depression contributed to the coming of the Great Depression of the 1930s.

expectations

What investors, consumers, employers, and workers think the future will be like.

EXPECTATIONS AND THE COMING OF THE GREAT DEPRESSION: AN EXAMPLE

An important example of how people's expectations can change the course of economic events comes from the stock market crash of 1929. The crash changed what Americans expected about the future of the economy, and the shifts in spending caused by their changed expectations played a key role in causing the greatest economic depression in American history, the Great Depression.

On October 29, 1929, the price of shares traded on the New York Stock Exchange suffered their largest one-day percentage drop in history. Stock values bounced back a bit initially, but by the end of the week they were down by more than a quarter (see Figure 3.1 on page 60). Gloom fell over Wall Street. Many people had lost a lot of money.

At that time stock ownership was confined to the rich. Middle-class Americans owned little stock. Nonetheless, the crash affected their perceptions of the economy: Bad times were coming. Because people expected the economic future to be dimmer, many cut back on spending, especially on big-ticket consumer durables. The 1920s had been the first decade in which consumer credit was widely available to finance purchases of cars, refrigerators, stoves, and washing machines. With the economic future uncertain, spending on consumer durables collapsed. It made sense to borrow to buy a consumer durable only if you were confident that you could make the payments and pay off the loan. If you thought the economic future might be bad, you had a powerful incentive to avoid debt. And in the short run the easiest way to avoid debt is to refrain from purchasing large consumer durables on credit.

You can probably guess what happened in the months after the crash. Most people simply stopped buying big-ticket items like cars and furniture. This massive drop in demand reduced new orders for goods. The drop in output generated layoffs

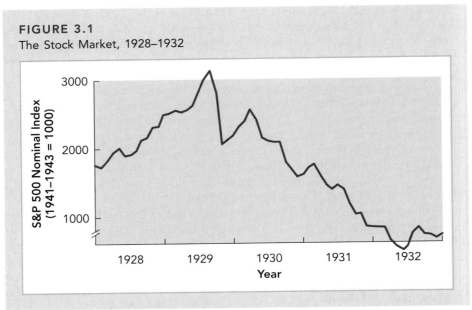

FIGURE 3.1
The Stock Market, 1928–1932

Source: J. Bradford DeLong and Andrei Shleifer, "Closed End Fund Discounts: A Yardstick of Small-Investor Sentiment," *Journal of Portfolio Management* 18:2 (Winter 1992), pp. 46–53.

in many industries. Even though most people's incomes had not yet changed, their expectations of their future income had.

The drop in demand produced by this shift in expectations helped bring on what people feared; it put America on the path to the Great Depression. The Great Depression happened in large part because people expected something bad to happen. Without that pessimistic shift in expectations triggered by the crash of 1929, there would have been no Great Depression.

This third wrinkle is the thing that does the most to make economics very hard. Natural scientists can always assume the arrow of causality points from the past to the future. In economics people's expectations of the future mean that the arrow of causality often points the other way, from the (anticipated) future back to the present. This means that sometimes in economics things will happen just because they are expected to happen — and that if they weren't expected to happen, they would not.

Reliance on Quantitative Models

In spite of the political complications, the nonexperimental nature, and the peculiar problems of cause and effect in economics, the discipline of economics remains very quantitative. Economists are lucky in that almost everything that they study comes to us already labeled, measured, and quantified: prices, values, transactions all come with numbers attached or are numbers. Thus economics makes heavy use of arithmetic and algebra, whereas most of political science, sociology, and history do not. Economics makes heavy use of arithmetic to measure economic variables of interest. Economics makes heavy use of algebra in building the simplified, stripped-down mathematical models that economists use to try to understand the relationships between these economic variables.

The American economy is complex: 140 million workers, 10 million firms, and 100 million households buying and selling some $30 trillion worth of final and intermediate goods and services per year. Economists must simplify it. You can't talk about 140 million individuals and expect to understand everything. So you simplify. You restrict your attention to a very few simple **behavioral relationships** — cause-and-effect links between economic quantities — and a handful of **equilibrium conditions** — conditions that must be satisfied for economic activity to be stable and for supply and demand to be in balance.

What is a behavioral relationship? It's something like a rule that relates the number of workers and the value of the capital stock to the total amount of goods and services produced in the economy. It's something like a rule that tells us how consumer spending changes when household income changes. What's an equlibrium condition? It's something like supply equals demand. Economists attempt to capture these behavioral relationships and equilibrium conditions in simple algebraic equations and geometric diagrams. Then they try to apply their equations and graphs to the real world, while hoping that their simplifications have not made the model a distorted and faulty guide to how the real-world economy works.

Among economists, the process of reducing the complexity and variation of the real-world economy to a handful of equations is known as "building a **model**." Using models to understand what is going on in the complex real-world economy has been a fruitful intellectual strategy. But model building tends to focus on the variables and relationships that fit easily into the algebraic model. It overlooks other factors.

An Emphasis on the Abstract

Economics might have developed as a descriptive science, like sociology or political science. If it had, courses in economics would concentrate on economic institutions and practices and the institutional structure of the economy as a whole. But economics has instead become a more abstract science that emphasizes general principles applicable to a variety of situations. Thus a large part of economics involves a particular set of tools. Economics is a unique way of thinking about the world that is closely linked with these analytical tools and is couched in a particular technical language and relies on a particular set of data. While you can get a lot out of sociology and political science courses without learning to think like a sociologist or a political scientist (because of their focus on institutional description), you cannot get much out of an economics course without learning to think like an economist.

Introducing the Rhetoric of Economics

Surrounding the models, economists build a special rhetoric: a set of analogies and metaphors that economists use to help laypeople grasp the functioning of the macroeconomy. Metaphors and analogies are the basic stuff of human thought. To understand something we do not know, we will often compare it to something we do know.

Economics is no exception. In economics, curves "shift" and money has a "velocity." When the *central bank* raises interest rates and throws people out of work, economists say that this "pushes the economy down the Phillips curve." Conversely, when the central bank lowers interest rates and the economy booms, economists say that this "pushes the economy up the Phillips curve" — as if the

---

behavioral relationship

A connection between economic variables that is the result of people's actions.

equilibrium condition

A relationship between two economic quantities that holds because the operation of the system as a whole pushes the economy to a state in which the relationship holds.

model

A construct that aims to establish relationships — usually quantitative — between and among economic variables.

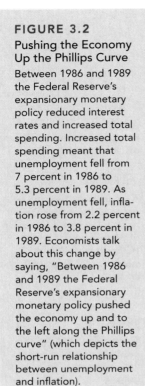

FIGURE 3.2

Pushing the Economy Up the Phillips Curve

Between 1986 and 1989 the Federal Reserve's expansionary monetary policy reduced interest rates and increased total spending. Increased total spending meant that unemployment fell from 7 percent in 1986 to 5.3 percent in 1989. As unemployment fell, inflation rose from 2.2 percent in 1986 to 3.8 percent in 1989. Economists talk about this change by saying, "Between 1986 and 1989 the Federal Reserve's expansionary monetary policy pushed the economy up and to the left along the Phillips curve" (which depicts the short-run relationship between unemployment and inflation).

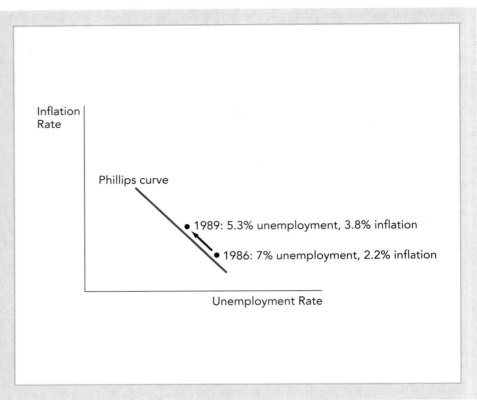

Source: 2004 edition of *The Economic Report of the President* (Washington, DC: Government Printing Office).

economy were a dot on a diagram drawn on a piece of paper, constrained to move along a particular curve called the *Phillips curve,* and monetary policy really did push the dot up and to the left (see Figure 3.2).

As a student you should be conscious of (and a little critical of) the rhetoric of economics. If you don't understand the metaphors, much of economics may simply be incomprehensible. All will become clear, or at least clearer, if you are conscious of the metaphors. For example, there is a central dominant metaphor in macroeconomics, the circular flow metaphor, without which discussions of the "velocity" of money are simply incomprehensible. The circular flow metaphor compares the process of spending throughout the economy to the flow of a liquid. Thus if the total amount of spending increases but the quantity of money does not, the money must be "flowing" faster than it did in the past, since a fixed quantity of pieces of money are changing hands more often. Hence money must have a higher speed or velocity. Without the concept of spending as a circular flow of purchasing power, references to the velocity of money will make no sense.

Much of the rhetoric of economics can be reduced to four dominant concepts:

circular flow

The central, dominant metaphor in macroeconomics which states that purchasing power flows from businesses to households and back in a circular fashion.

- The image of the **circular flow** of purchasing power through the economy — the circular flow of economic activity.
- The use of the word "market" to describe intricate and decentralized processes of exchange, as if all the workers and all the jobs in the economy really were being matched in a single open-air market.

- The idea of **equilibrium:** that economic processes tend to move the economy into some sort of balance and to keep the economy at this point of balance.

- The use of graphs and diagrams as an alternative to arithmetic and equations as tools to express economic relationships. Economists identify equations with geometric curves; situations of equilibrium with points where curves cross; and changes in the economic environment or in economic policy with shifts in the positions of particular curves.

We will look next at the circular flow of economic activity. The market, equilibrium, and the relationship between graphs and equations will be covered in later sections.

equilibrium

A state of balance in a particular market or in the economy as a whole.

RECAP   UNDERSTANDING MACROECONOMICS

While economics is a science, it is not a *natural* science. It is a *social* science. The subjects economists study — people — have minds of their own, and think ahead. Thus in economics it is common for the (expected) future to influence the past, and chains of causation can get very tangled. Economics might have developed as a descriptive science, like sociology or political science. It didn't. Economics, instead, developed as an abstract, simplifying, model-oriented discipline.

3.2 THE CIRCULAR FLOW OF ECONOMIC ACTIVITY

When economists speak of the "circular flow" of economic activity, they have a definite picture in mind. They see patterns of spending, income, and production as liquid flowing through various sets of pipes. In this extended metaphor, categories of agents in the economy — all businesses, the government, all households — are the pools into and out of which the fluid of purchasing power (i.e., money) flows. Thus economists think of economic activity — the pattern of production and spending in the economy — as a circular flow of purchasing power through the economy.

The circular flow metaphor allows them confidently to predict that changes in one part of the economy will affect the whole and to explain what the likely effects will be. It allows them to simplify economic behavior, to understand a great deal about the entire set of decisions made by all different agents in different parts of the economy by thinking of just a few typical decisions made by just a few abstract agents whose decisions nevertheless represent the decisions made by all the households, businesses, investors, consumers, and workers in the economy.

The Circular Flow Diagram

Figure 3.3 shows a simplified diagram of the circular flow. It omits the government and international trade. Nevertheless, it is a good starting point for our discussion. In this figure, money payments flow from firms to households as businesses pay their workers and their owners for their labor and capital. This is the *income side* of the circular flow: Firms buy the factors of production, capital and labor, from the households that own them. Money payments then flow from households to firms as households buy goods. This is the *expenditure side* of the circular flow: Households buy final goods and services from businesses. Note that these flows

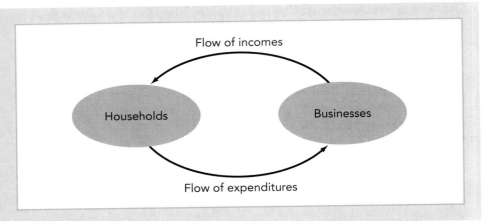

FIGURE 3.3

The Circular Flow Diagram

Households spend money buying the products made by businesses, and businesses turn around and spend the same money buying factors of production — workers' time and attention, finance, the use of land and other property — from households.

balance: The purchasing power that firms earn by selling their goods is the same as the purchasing power that firms spend by buying factors of production, and the incomes of households are equal to their total expenditures.

This simplified diagram is expanded in Figure 3.4 to take account of the roles of the government, *financial markets,* and international trade and investment. But the core idea of a balanced circular flow of purchasing power is still present. Along the top of the diagram there is still the flow of incomes to households from businesses as businesses purchase labor and other factors of production from the households that own them. All these components of business expenditure — rent, wages, salaries, benefits, interest, and profits — become the components of household income.

At the bottom of the diagram are the uses of household incomes — consumption spending, *taxes,* and *household saving.* Consumption spending flows directly to businesses as households purchase consumption goods. Total taxes flow to the government, which uses some of this revenue to make *transfer payments* — classified here as negative taxes — back to households, uses most of it for government purchases, and borrows the resulting *government budget deficit* from financial markets as the government funds its budget deficit by issuing bonds.

Households save the portion of their incomes that is left over after taxes and consumption spending. This saving flows into financial markets as it is put into banks and mutual funds. Businesses seeking to invest draw on the pool of saving to gain financing for purchasing capital goods to expand their productive capacity. Exports serve as an addition to (and imports a subtraction from) total demand for domestically made products.

At the right of Figure 3.4 we have the components of planned expenditure or *aggregate demand:* consumption spending, government purchases, investment spending, and net exports (which are, in the United States today, net imports, a subtraction from GDP, because imports are greater than gross exports).

Within the business sector, businesses buy and sell intermediate goods from each other as they strive to produce goods and services and make profits. Within the household sector, households buy and sell assets from and to one another. These within-the-business-sector and within-the-household-sector transactions are important components of the economy. But because they net out to zero within the business sector or within the household sector, they are not counted as part of the circular flow of economic activity. And so the circular flow diagram pays little attention to them, and

FIGURE 3.4

The Circular Flow of Economic Activity

This version of the circular flow is complicated by the addition of the government and financial markets to the diagram. Not all final goods and services are bought by households. Some are bought by the government, which taxes to raise resources to finance itself. Some are bought by businesses seeking to invest, which raise the needed resources by issuing stock, issuing bonds, and borrowing — all of which take place in *financial markets*. This version is also complicated by its recognizing that there is a world outside, a world that buys the products of domestic businesses and that invests through domestic financial markets.

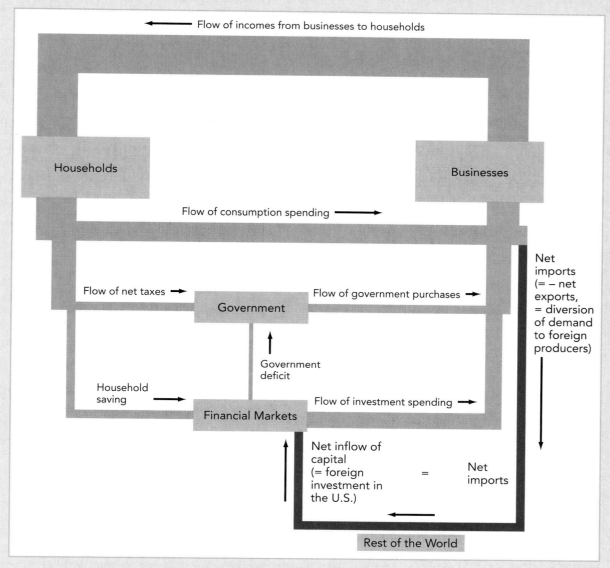

macroeconomics as a discipline does not focus on the exchange of intermediate goods between businesses or on the exchange of used goods between households.

Is the circular flow still a little unclear? Let's try to get a better grasp of it. Let's take a closer look at one particular part of the circular flow: a dollar paid out by a business as a dividend to a shareholder who is a member of a household. The dollar is partial payment for a factor of production owned by the household — the capital that has been invested in the business by the shareholder. When the dividend check is deposited, it becomes part of the shareholder's household income. Three things happen to household income: Some of it is spent on consumption goods and services, some of it is paid to the government in taxes, and some of it is not spent but saved.

Suppose the household doesn't spend this particular dollar but simply keeps the money in the bank, thus saving it for future use. The bank will notice that it has an extra dollar on deposit and will loan that dollar out to a business in need of cash to build up its inventory. That business will then spend the dollar buying goods and services as it builds up its inventory. As soon as the dollar shows up as a component of business investment spending, the circular flow is complete. The dollar's worth of purchasing power has flowed from the business sector to the household sector, then flowed as part of the flow of savings into the financial markets, and finally flowed out of the financial markets and back to the business sector as part of business investment spending.

Different Measures of the Circular Flow

Income, production, and expenditure can be measured at three different points in the circular flow:

1. At the point where consumers, exporters, the government, and firms that are making investments purchase goods and services from businesses. This measurement is *real GDP*, or total output. It is the total economywide production of final goods and services. It is the expenditure-side measure of the circular flow.

2. At the point in the circular flow where businesses pay households for the factors of production. Businesses need labor, capital, and natural resources, all factors of production owned directly or indirectly by households. When businesses buy factors of production, they provide households with incomes. This measurement is called total income, or *national income*. It is the income-side measure of the circular flow.

3. At the point where households decide how to use their income. How much do they save? How much do they pay in taxes? How much do they spend on consumption goods? This measure of the circular flow of economic activity is the *uses-of-income* measure.

The measure used most frequently is the expenditure-side measure: the gross domestic product produced by firms and demanded by purchasers. It is estimated by summing the four components of spending (and sales) — consumption, government purchases, investment, and net exports. If we compare the expenditure-side measure of GDP with the income-side or uses-of-income measure, we will find that, aside from differences created by different accounting conventions, they are equal (see Box 3.2). They are equal because the circular flow principle is designed into the national income and product accounts (NIPA). Every expenditure on a final good or service is accounted for as a payment to a business. Every dollar payment that flows into a business is then accounted for as paid out

ACCOUNTING DEFINITIONS AND STATISTICAL DISCREPANCIES: TOOLS

Because of the technical details of national income accounting, the different measures of the circular flow do not exactly balance. The gap is the *statistical discrepancy*. All pieces of GDP reported by the Commerce Department are estimates. All estimates are imperfect. It is not unusual for $90 billion a year to go "missing" in the circular flow; as Table 3.1 shows, this happened in the third quarter of 2004.

TABLE 3.1

Measures of the U.S. Circular Flow (in Billions of Dollars per Year), Third Quarter of 2004

Gross domestic product	$11,815
Minus: Depreciation	−1,498
Equals: Net domestic product	$10,317
Plus: Net factor incomes from abroad	+38
Equals: Net national product	$10,355
Minus: Statistical discrepancy	−90
Equals: National income	$10,265

Source: Authors' calculations from the 2005 edition of *The Economic Report of the President* (Washington, DC: Government Printing Office).

to somebody. It can be paid out as income — wages, fringe benefits, profits, interest, or rent — or as an expenditure on goods or services of another business that then, in turn, purchases factors of production.

What if you want to withdraw your income from the circular flow? Suppose, for instance, that you simply take the dollar bills you receive and use them to buy something old and precious from another household — a bar of gold, say. And suppose you keep the bar of gold in your basement. Doesn't that break the circular flow? The answer is that it does not. You no longer have your income, but the household that you bought the gold bar from does. That household will then spend it on consumption goods, save it, or have it taxed away.

What if you decided not to spend your dollar bills, not to pay them in taxes, and not to save them in the bank? Suppose you decided to hide the dollar bills in your basement? Doesn't that break the circular flow? The answer, again, is that it does not. When you hide the dollar bills in the basement, the Bureau of Engraving and Printing will notice that the total number of dollar bills circulating in the economy has dropped. It will print up more dollar bills and hand them to the Treasury. The government will spend these extra dollar bills, and thus replace the ones you hid. The net effect is the same as it would be if you had saved the dollar bills by lending them out to the government through the purchase of a Treasury bond. There are only two differences between buying a Treasury bond and your basement storage scheme:

1. You have a stack of dollar bills in your basement rather than a piece of paper with the words "Treasury bond" written on it.

2. The government does not pay interest on the dollar bills stacked in your basement, but it does pay interest on its bonds. In the circular flow diagram, you saved your income, but you saved it in a relatively pointless way by making the government an interest-free loan.

RECAP   THE CIRCULAR FLOW OF ECONOMIC ACTIVITY

Money flows from households to firms as households buy goods. This is the "expenditure side" of the circular flow: Households buy *final goods and services* from businesses. Businesses then turn around and buy factors of production from households. These payments make up household income. This is the "income side" of the circular flow. The circular flow principle is that the two flows must match: In the economy as a whole, expenditure must equal income.

3.3 PATTERNS OF ECONOMISTS' THOUGHT

Besides the circular flow of economic activity, three other sets of concepts, not obvious to outsiders, dominate the patterns of economists' thought: the idea of markets, the idea of equilibrium, and the use of math in the form of graphs and equations. Let's look at each of these in turn — the first two briefly, and the last at much greater length.

Markets

Economists often speak as if all economic activity took place in great open-air marketplaces like those of medieval merchant cities. Contracts between workers and bosses are made in the "labor market." All the borrowing of money from and the depositing of money into banks take place in the "money market." Supply and demand balance in the *"goods market."* Indeed, in the market squares of preindustrial trading cities you could survey the buyers and sellers and form a good idea of what was being sold and for how much.

In using the open-air markets of centuries past as a metaphor for the complex processes of matching and exchange that take place in today's modern industrial economy, economists are assuming that information travels fast enough and buyers and sellers are well enough informed for prevailing prices and quantities to be as they would be if we actually could walk around the perimeter of a marketplace and examine all buyers and sellers in an hour. In most cases this bet that a decentralized matching process is like an open-air market will be a good intellectual bet to make. But sometimes (for example, in situations of so-called *structural unemployment*, where people who could work effectively at some of the jobs in the economy find that those jobs are not open) it may not be.

Equilibrium

Economists spend most of their time searching for the state of equilibrium — a point or points of balance at which some economic quantity is neither rising nor falling because the different economic forces pushing or pulling it up or down exactly counteract each other. The dominant metaphor is that of an old-fashioned scale whose two pans are in balance.

The search for equilibrium is an attempt to simplify the problem of understanding how the economy will behave. Economists' questions are much easier to analyze if we can identify "points of rest" where the pressures for economic quantities to rise and fall are evenly balanced. Once the potential points of rest have been identified, economists can figure out how fast economic forces will push the economy to those points of equilibrium. The search for points of equilibrium, followed by an analysis of the speed of adjustment to equilibrium, is the most common way of proceeding in any economic analysis.

Do not forget, however, that this pattern of thought is merely an aid to understanding economic theories and principles. It is not the theories and principles themselves. The theories and principles, in turn, are just aids to understanding the reality; they are not themselves the reality.

Graphs and Equations

In the seventeenth century, the French philosopher and mathematician René Descartes spent much of his life demonstrating that graphs and equations can be thought of as two different ways of representing the same underlying concepts. An algebraic equation relating two variables x and y can also be seen as a curve drawn on a graph where the value of x is marked on the horizontal axis and the value of y is marked on the vertical axis. Thus each of the variables in the equation can be thought of as one of the axes of the graph. The set of points whose x-axis value is the first variable and whose y-axis value is the second — that is, the set of points for which the equation holds — makes up a line or curve on the graph. That line or curve is the equation (see Figure 3.5). Thus the solution to a set of two equations is the point on the graph where the two curves that represent the equations intersect. Moreover, you can just as easily move back in the other direction, by thinking of a curve in terms of the equation that generates it. Today economists make very extensive use of these ideas from Descartes's **analytic geometry.**

Just after the end of World War II Professor *Paul Samuelson* of MIT discovered that many of his students were much more comfortable manipulating diagrams than solving algebraic equations. With diagrams, they could see what was going on in a hypothetical economy. Thinking of how a particular curve would shift was often easier than thinking of the consequences of changing the value of the constant term in an equation.

When economists translate their algebraic equations into analytical geometric diagrams, they do things that may annoy you. Economists (like mathematicians) think

analytic geometry

The idea that graphs and equations are two different ways of expressing the same concepts.

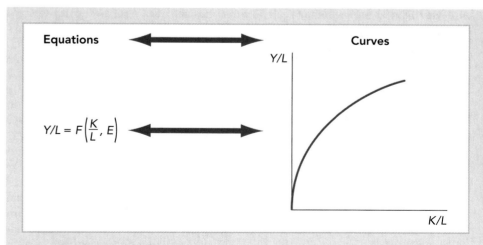

Equations　　**Curves**

$$Y/L = F\left(\frac{K}{L}, E\right)$$

FIGURE 3.5
Two Forms of the Production Function
Economists build their arguments by moving back and forth between equations and diagrams representing the same relationship. The graph on the right is the geometric representation of the algebraic equation on the left.

of a "line" as a special kind of "curve" (and it is: It is a curve with zero curvature). So you may find words — in this book, in your lecture, or in your section — referring to a "Phillips curve," but when you look at the accompanying diagram, you see that it is a straight line. Do not let this bother you. Economists use the word "curve" to preserve a little generality.

If you find analytic geometry easy and intuitive, then Samuelson's intellectual innovation will make macroeconomics more accessible to you. Behavioral relationships become curves that shift about on a graph. Conditions of economic equilibrium become dots where curves describing two behavioral relationships cross (and thus both behavioral relationships are satisfied). Changes in the state of the economy become movements of a dot. Understanding economic theories and arguments becomes as simple as moving lines and curves around on a graph and looking for the place where the correct two curves intersect. And solving systems of equations becomes easy, as does changing the presuppositions of the problem and noting the results.

If you are not comfortable with analytic geometry, then you need to find other tools to help you think like an economist. Remember that the graphs are merely tools to aid your understanding. If they don't, then you need to concentrate on understanding and manipulating the algebra, or understanding and using the verbal descriptions of a problem. Use whatever method feels most comfortable. Grab hold of what makes most sense to you, and recognize that all of these approaches are ways of reaching the same conclusions.

RECAP   PATTERNS OF ECONOMISTS' THOUGHT

Three concepts in addition to the circular flow dominate the patterns of economists' thoughts. Understand these three concepts and their role in economic analysis and you will be well on your way to being an economist. The three concepts are *markets* — where trades take place; *equilibrium* — points where economic forces are in balance; and *mathematical expression* through graphs and equations.

3.4 MODEL BUILDING

Economists use their graphs and equations to build their mathematical models. The first thing to remember about their models is that they are simple: Simplification is at the core of economists' model building. Economists build simple models for two reasons. First, no one really understands excessively complicated models. A model is of little use if economists cannot understand the logic behind its prediction. Second, the predictions generated by simple models are nearly as good as the ones generated by more complex models. While the economic models used by the Federal Reserve or the *Congressional Budget Office* are more complicated than the models presented in this textbook, in essence they are cousins of the models used here.

You may have heard that economics is more of an art than a science. This means that the rules for effective and useful model building — for omitting unnecessary detail and complexity while retaining the necessary and important relationships — are nowhere written down. In this important respect, economists tend to learn by doing or by example. But almost every successful construction of a macroeconomic model follows certain fundamental steps. These include the use of representative agents, a focus on opportunity costs in understanding agents' decisions, and careful attention to the effect of people's expectations on events.

Representative Agents

One simplification that macroeconomists, but not microeconomists, invoke constantly is that all participants in the economy are the same or, rather, that the differences between businesses and workers do not matter much for the issues macroeconomists study. Thus macroeconomists analyze a situation by examining the decision making of a single **representative agent** — be it a business, a worker, or a saver. They then generalize to the economy as a whole from what would be the rational decisions of that single representative agent.

> **representative agents**
>
> A simplification often made in macroeconomics that assumes all participants in the economy are the same.

The use of representative agents makes macroeconomics simpler, yet it also makes some questions very hard to analyze. Consider unemployment: The key concept is that some workers have jobs but others do not. If one has adopted the simplifying assumption of a single representative worker, how can one worker represent both those who are employed and those who are not?

The assumption of a representative agent is also useless when the relative distribution of income and wealth among people in the economy is the important question. Consider an economy in which everyone works equally hard, but 1 million lucky people receive $10,000,000 a year in income and 99 million receive $10,000 a year in income. Now consider an economy in which all 100 million people work equally hard and each receives $80,000 a year in income. Almost all of us would think that the second was a happier and fairer economy, even though total income in the first economy amounts to $10.99 trillion and total income in the second economy amounts to only $8 trillion. As noted earlier, every discipline sees some things clearly and some things fuzzily. Distribution and its impact on social welfare are an area that macroeconomics has trouble bringing into focus.

Opportunity Cost

Perhaps the most fundamental principle that economists use in modeling the decisions individuals make is the principle that there is always a choice. You could always have chosen to do something else. And the very act of making a choice excludes your ability to have done its alternatives instead: It forecloses your opportunities.

If you keep your wealth in the form of easily spendable cash, you pass up the chance to keep it earning interest in the form of bonds. If you keep your wealth in the form of interest-earning bonds, you pass up the capability of immediately spending it on something that suddenly strikes your fancy. If you spend it on consumption goods, you pass up the opportunity to save. Economists use the term **opportunity cost** to refer to the value of the best alternative that you forgo in making any particular choice.

> **opportunity cost**
>
> The next best opportunity forgone in order to do something else.

At the root of every behavioral relationship is somebody's decision. In analyzing such decisions, economists always think about the decision maker's opportunity costs. What else could the decision maker do? What opportunities and choices does the decision maker foreclose by taking one particular course of action? Many students make economics a lot harder than it has to be by not remembering that this opportunity-cost way of thinking is at the heart of every behavioral relationship in an economic model.

The Focus on Expectations

Many times the opportunity cost of taking some action today is not an alternative use of the same resources today but a forgone opportunity to save one's resources for the future. A worker trying to decide whether to quit a job and search for another will be thinking about future wages after a successful search. A consumer trying to decide whether to spend or save will be thinking about what interest rate savings will earn in the future.

No one, however, knows the future. At best people can form rational and reasonable expectations of what the future might be. Hence nearly every behavioral relationship in macroeconomic models depends on expectations of the future. Expectations formation is a central, perhaps *the* central, piece of macroeconomics. Every macroeconomic model must explain the amount of time people can spend thinking about the future, the information they have available, and the rules of thumb they use to turn information into expectations.

As we will see in Chapter 12, economists tend to consider three types of expectations:

- *Static expectations*, in which decision makers simply don't think about the future.
- *Adaptive expectations*, in which decision makers assume that the future is going to be like the recent past.
- *Rational expectations*, in which decision makers spend as much time as they can thinking about the future and know as much (or more) about the structure and behavior of the economy as the model builder does.

The behavior of an economic model will differ profoundly depending on what kind of expectations economists build into the model.

Solving Economic Models: Behavioral Relationships and Equilibrium Conditions

When economists are trying to analyze the implications of how people act — say, how the overall level of production would change with a larger capital stock — they almost always write an equation that represents a behavioral relationship. This behavioral relationship states how the effect (the total level of production) is related to the cause (the available capital stock). The economist usually draws a diagram to help visualize the relationship and writes it down verbally. For example, an economist trying to relate an economy's productive resources to the level of economic output would reason: "A larger capital stock means that the average employee will have more machines and equipment to work with, and this will increase total production per worker. But increases in capital will probably be subject to *diminishing returns*, so the gain in production from increasing the capital stock per worker from $40,000 to $80,000 will be less than the gain in production from increasing the capital stock per worker from $0 to $40,000." Box 3.3 fleshes out this example of a behavioral relationship — in this case, the *production function*. This particular behavioral relationship, the production function, is a very important part of the next chapter.

**THE PRODUCTION FUNCTION: AN EXAMPLE
OF A BEHAVIORAL RELATIONSHIP**

One of the key behavioral relationships in macroeconomics is the *production function,* which specifies the relationship between the economy's productive resources. The production function relates:

- The economy's capital-labor ratio (how many machines, tools, and structures are available to the average worker), written *K/L* (*K* for *capital* and *L* for labor, the number of workers in the economy).
- The level of technology or efficiency of the labor force, written *E*.
- The level of real GDP per worker, written *Y/L* (*Y* for real GDP or total output and *L* for the number of workers in the economy).

An economist could write the production function in this general, abstract form:

$$\frac{Y}{L} = F\left(\frac{K}{L}, E\right)$$

This formula states that the level of output per worker is some *function, F,* of *K/L* and *E;* that is, the level of output per worker depends in a systematic and predictable way on the capital-labor ratio and the *efficiency of labor* in the current year. But this abstract form does not specify the particular form of this systematic and predictable relationship.

Alternatively, an economist could write the production function in a particular algebraic form, for example, the Cobb-Douglas form, which is convenient to use (Box 3.4 explains why):

$$\frac{Y}{L} = \left(\frac{K}{L}\right)^{\alpha} \times E^{1-\alpha}$$

This equation states: "Take the capital-labor ratio, raise it to the exponential power α, and multiply the result by the efficiency of labor *E* raised to the exponential power $(1 - \alpha)$. The result is the level of output per worker that the economy can produce." While this equation is more particular than the abstract form $Y/L = F(K/L, E)$, it remains flexible: The parameter α could have any of a wide range of different values, and the efficiency of labor *E* could have any value. This Cobb-Douglas algebraic form still stands for a whole family of possible production functions. The values chosen for *E* and α will tell us exactly which production function is the real one and thus what the behavioral relationship is between the economy's resources and its output. Once we know the values of *E* and α, we can calculate what the output per worker will be for every possible value of capital per worker.

Why do economists choose to write the production function in this particular algebraic form? Ease of use is the key reason. This form of the production function makes a lot of calculations *much* simpler and more straightforward than other forms.

In addition to analyzing behavioral relationships, economists consider equilibrium conditions — conditions that must be true if the economy is to be in balance. If an equilibrium condition does not hold, then the state of the economy must be changing rapidly, moving toward a state of affairs in which the equilibrium condition does hold. In microeconomics the principal equilibrium condition

WORKING WITH EXPONENTS: SOME TOOLS

What is the point behind the use of the Cobb-Douglas production function, with all its exponents?

$$\frac{Y}{L} = \left(\frac{K}{L}\right)^{\alpha} \times E^{1-\alpha}$$

Recall that exponents greater than 1 are a means of repeated multiplication. Thus 2^1 is 2 multiplied by itself once, that is, 2; 2^2 is 2 times itself twice, that is, $2 \times 2 = 4$; 2^3 is 2 times itself three times, that is, $2 \times 2 \times 2 = 8$. Recall that exponents between 1 and zero are a way of taking roots. Thus $2^{0.5}$ is the square root of 2, and $2^{1/3}$ is the cube root of 2.

Whenever the Cobb-Douglas production function is used, the *parameters* that are the exponents will be between zero and 1. In fact, in most applications of this production function the parameter α will be something like $\frac{1}{2}$. Raising the capital-labor ratio to the α power is something like taking the square root of the capital-labor ratio. So the production function will state that output per worker is proportional to the square root of the capital-labor ratio. This function (a) is easy to calculate or look up for particular cases, (b) is one with which we have a lot of experience, (c) is an increasing function (so it fits the intuitive requirement that more capital is useful), and (d) is a function with diminishing returns — the higher the capital stock, the less valuable is the next investment in expanding the capital stock still further. Thus a lot of features that economists would like a sensible behavioral relationship between the capital-labor ratio and output per worker to have are already built into the Cobb-Douglas production function.

Moreover, using the Cobb-Douglas production function offers an additional advantage. It makes calculating *growth rates* easy. Output per worker is proportional to the capital-labor ratio raised to the power α. Thus if nothing else is changing, the growth rate of output per worker equals α times the growth rate of the capital-labor ratio. If α is $\frac{1}{2}$ and if the capital-labor ratio is growing at 4 percent per year and if efficiency of labor is not changing, then output per worker is growing at

$$\frac{1}{2} \times 4\% = 2\% \text{ per year.}$$

is that supply must equal demand. If it does not, then buyers who find themselves short are frantically raising their bids (and prices are rising) or sellers who find themselves with excess inventory are frantically trying to shed it (and prices are falling). Only if supply equals demand can the price in a market be stable. In macroeconomics, the supply-must-equal-demand equilibrium condition is the most important, but there are other important equilibrium conditions too. Box 3.5 provides an example of one that will be very important in Chapter 4: the equilibrium condition required for balanced economic growth.

If the equilibrium conditions are not satisfied, then the economy cannot be stable. Someone's expectations must turn out to be false, or someone's plans for what to buy and sell must be unsatisfied. If the behavioral relationships are not satisfied, the relationships are not adequately describing our behavior. So the behavioral

A SAMPLE EQUILIBRIUM CONDITION — THE CAPITAL-OUTPUT RATIO: AN EXAMPLE

An important equilibrium condition that is not of the supply-must-equal-demand form is the equilibrium condition for *balanced growth,* which plays a big part in Chapter 4. This equilibrium condition relates the following economic variables:

- The share of total income in the economy that is saved and invested, written s.
- The proportional rate of growth of the labor force, written n.
- The proportional rate of growth of the efficiency of the labor force, written g.
- The *depreciation rate* — the rate at which capital wears out — written δ (Greek lowercase letter delta).

Growth will be *balanced* if, and only if, the ratio of the economy's stock of capital K to its level of output Y is constant. This equilibrium condition holds if, and only if, the capital-to-output ratio K/Y is equal to

$$\frac{K}{Y} = \frac{s}{n + g + \delta}$$

The capital-output ratio must be equal to the economy's saving rate s divided by the sum of the population growth rate n, the labor efficiency growth rate g, and the depreciation rate δ.

If the capital-output ratio is lower than this value, it will grow because net investment will be high relative to the capital stock. If the capital-output ratio is higher than this value, it will shrink because net investment will be low relative to the capital stock. In either case, the capital-output ratio will converge to its *balanced-growth equilibrium* level over time.

Thus this balanced-growth capital-output-ratio equation satisfies the two requirements for being an equilibrium condition. If the economy does not satisfy the equilibrium condition, it will be heading toward it. If the economy satisfies the equilibrium condition, it will remain in the same place.

relationships must be satisfied as well; they tell us what choices people make given the situations in which they find themselves.

Economists hope that the simplified behavioral relationships of models are a good enough match to actual behavior. And they hope that the actual economy moves to equilibrium rapidly enough that the only situations they need to consider are those in which the equilibrium conditions hold. If both of these hopes are fulfilled, then economists' models are powerful ways of analyzing what's going on in the real economy out there in the world.

Why Do Economists Use So Much Algebra?

Algebraic equations turn out to be a remarkably good way to summarize cause-and-effect behavioral relationships in economics, so economists use a lot of them.

You can understand why economists might use a lot of arithmetic. After all, so many economic concepts are already or can be easily quantified. But arithmetic has its limits. It restricts you to one case, and one case only. Algebra — because it has variables that can take on any of an uncountable number of values — allows you to think, at least implicitly, about many different cases at once.

You may be able to pass — even do well in — a macroeconomics course without feeling comfortable with all the algebra. In this book we generally go through each topic three times: once in words, stating the logic of the argument and telling which quantities influence which others; once in algebra; and once in diagrams that represent the algebraic and verbal relationships. If you don't understand a concept the first time it is presented, you have two more chances. Recognize, however, that words, equations, and diagrams are simply three ways of presenting the same material. They should agree. So a discrepancy between your understanding of the algebra, the diagrams, and the words is a sign that something has gone wrong.

For many students, economists' heavy use of algebra is a very useful tool that helps them understand. For others, it is a stumbling block. If algebra does not sing to you, there are ways to compensate: focus on the words and the diagrams, and realize that the algebra is just another way of saying the same things that the verbal descriptions say and to show the same things that the diagrams show. Or work through the equations for sample values of variables — assume that real GDP is $10 trillion, for example, and solve the abstract equations with specific numerical values. That algebra is one of the primary languages that economists use for their models does not mean that it is ever the only way to think about the economy.

RECAP MODEL BUILDING

Economists use models, and stress simple models, for no one really understands excessively complicated models and a model is of little use if you cannot understand the logic behind it. Economists consider two types of relationships between variables in building their models, *behavioral relationships* and *equilibrium conditions* — conditions that must be true if the economy is to be in balance. They base their behavioral relationships on an analysis of representative agents' *opportunity costs*. And they use algebraic equations to describe both kinds of relationships between variables.

Chapter Summary

1. Economists' ways of thinking are strange — peculiar to their intellectual discipline.

2. Economics is abstract. Today's economics courses focus more on analytic tools and chains of reasoning and less on institutional descriptions.

3. Economics is a relatively mathematical subject because so much of what it analyzes can be measured. Thus economists use arithmetic to count things and use algebra because it is the best way to analyze and understand arithmetic.

4. When macroeconomists build models, they usually follow four key strategies:

- Strip down a complicated process to a few economy-wide behavioral relationships and equilibrium conditions.

- Simplify — ignore differences between people in the economy.

- Look at opportunity costs as ways to understand behavioral relationships.

- Focus on expectations of the future, and how such expectations affect the present.

Key Terms

expectations (p. 59)

behavioral relationship (p. 61)

equilibrium condition (p. 61)

model (p. 61)

circular flow (p. 62)

equilibrium (p. 63)

analytic geometry (p. 69)

representative agents (p. 71)

opportunity cost (p. 71)

Analytical Exercises

1. What do you think a science is? List five characteristics that you think a science must have. Which of these does economics satisfy?

2. List five characteristics that you think a science must not have. Which of these does economics satisfy?

3. Why does the fact that economic agents take actions today that depend on their expectations of the future make economics an extra-hard subject?

4. What do economists mean when they say that it is time to "build a model" of a situation or a problem?

5. List four metaphors that you have heard people use in talking about the economy that are now, or were at the time, obscure to you.

6. In what sense can a line on a graph be an equation?

7. What advantage do models with symbolic parameters (which can later be varied or specified) have over models in which the parameters are specific numbers hardwired into the equations of the model?

8. What are behavioral relationships? List five behavioral relationships that you have encountered in previous economics courses.

9. What are equilibrium conditions? List some equilibrium conditions that you have encountered in previous economics courses.

10. Which do you think is the best measure of the circular flow of economic activity: GDP, NDP, NNP, or national income? Why?

Long-Run Economic Growth

Long-run economic growth is the subject of this two-chapter part of the book. Chapter 4 covers the theory of growth, and Chapter 5 covers the worldwide pattern of economic growth. Long-run economic growth is the most important topic in macroeconomics. Standards of living in the United States today are at least seven times what they were at the end of the nineteenth century. Successful economic growth has meant that almost all citizens of the United States today live better, and we hope happier, lives than even the rich elite of a century ago. The study of long-run economic growth aims at understanding its sources and causes and at determining what government policies will promote or retard long-run economic growth.

Long-run growth is a module that is not very closely connected to the study of business cycles, recessions, unemployment, inflation, and stabilization policy that makes up the bulk of this book. The models used and the conclusions reached in Part 2 will by and large not be central to subsequent parts, for starting in Chapter 6 we turn to business cycles.

Why, then, include this two-chapter part? The principal reason is that long-run economic growth is such an important topic.

CHAPTER 4

The Theory of
Economic Growth

QUESTIONS

What are the causes of long-run economic growth — that is, of sustained and significant growth in an economy's level of output per worker?

What is the "efficiency of labor"?

What is an economy's "capital intensity"?

What is an economy's "balanced-growth path"?

How important is faster labor-force growth as a drag on economic growth?

How important is a high saving rate as a cause of economic growth?

How important is technological and organizational progress for economic growth?

4.1 SOURCES OF LONG-RUN GROWTH

Step back and take a broad, sweeping view of the economy. Look at it, but do not focus on the "short run" of calendar-year quarters or even of a year or two in which shifts in investment spending and other shocks push the unemployment rate up or down — that's what we will do in Chapters 9 through 12. Look at it, but do not focus on the "long run" period of 3 to 10 years or so, in which prices have time to adjust to return the economy to a full-employment equilibrium but in which the economy's productive resources do not change much — that's what we will look at in Chapters 6 through 8. What do we do here in Chapters 4 and 5? We take that step back and focus on the very long run of decades and generations — a period over which everything else dwindles into insignificance except the sustained and significant increases in standards of living that we call long-run **economic growth**.

When we take this broad, sweeping view, it is clear that what we are calling economic growth is the only truly important factor. As Table 4.1 shows, material

economic growth

The process by which productivity, living standards, and output increase.

TABLE 4.1

Current GDP per Capita Levels for Countries with More than 50 Million People

The World Bank's latest estimates of GDP per capita levels, measured at purchasing power parities. (That is, currencies are converted into dollars at a rate that gives approximately the same purchasing power both before conversion in the other country and after conversion in the United States.) The final column shows how far the country's GDP per capita is "behind" the United States — when the United States's level of GDP per capita was last below that of the country's current value.

Country	GDP per Capita	Matches U.S. Level in . . .
United States	$35,060	2004
Germany	26,220	1988
France	26,180	1988
Japan	26,070	1988
United Kingdom	25,870	1987
Italy	25,320	1987
Mexico	8,540	1940
Russia	7,820	1940
Brazil	7,250	1939
Thailand	6,680	1928
Iran	6,340	1925
Turkey	6,120	1924
China	4,390	1900
Philippines	4,380	1900
Egypt	3,710	1897
Indonesia	2,990	1879
India	2,570	1874
Vietnam	2,240	1854
Pakistan	1,940	1849
Bangladesh	1,720	1836
Nigeria	780	—
Ethiopia	720	—
Congo	580	—

Source: World Bank.

standards of living and levels of economic productivity today in the United States are more than four times what they are in, say, Mexico (and more than nine times those of Egypt, and more than 40 times those of Nigeria). Only a trivial part of these differences is due to whether unemployment in a country is currently above or below its average level or whether various bad macroeconomic policies are currently disrupting the functioning of the price system. The overwhelming bulk of these differences is the result of differences in economies' productive potentials and in the factors that determine productive potential — the skills of the **labor force**, the value of the **capital stock**, and the level of technology and organization currently used in production.

These enormous gaps between the productive potentials of different nations spring from favorable initial conditions and successful growth-promoting economic policies in the United States — and from less favorable initial conditions and less successful policies in Mexico and downright unsuccessful policies in Egypt and Nigeria. As Figure 4.1 shows, material standards of living and levels of economic productivity in the United States today are at least seven times what they were at the end of the nineteenth century (and more than 30 times what they were at the founding of the republic). The bulk of today's gap between living standards and productivity levels in the United States and Mexico (and Egypt

labor force

The sum of those who are employed and those who are actively looking for work.

capital stock

The economy's total accumulated stock of buildings, roads, other infrastructure, machines, and inventories.

FIGURE 4.1

American Real GDP per Capita, 1800–2004 (in 2000 Dollars) The pace of modern economic growth in the United States has been astonishing. Economic historians estimate — and if anything, their estimates are underestimates — economic product per person in the United States measured in 2000 prices has grown from $1,200 at the time of the writing of the Constitution to over $36,000 in 2004.

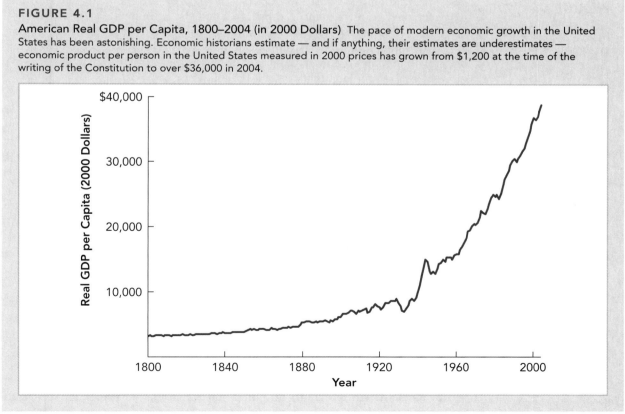

Source: Louis Johnston and Samuel H. Williamson (2004), "The Annual Real and Nominal GDP for the United States, 1789–Present." Economic History Services, March 2004, http://www.eh.net/hmit/gdp/.

and Nigeria) opened up in the past century; the bulk of success (or failure) at boosting an economy's productive potential is thus — to a historian at least — of relatively recent origin.

Successful economic growth means that nearly all citizens of the United States today live better — along almost every dimension of material life — than did even the rich elites of preindustrial times. If good policies and good circumstances accelerate economic growth, bad policies and bad circumstances cripple long-run economic growth. Argentineans were richer than Swedes before World War I, but Swedes today have four times the standard of living and the productivity level of Argentineans.

We classify the factors that generate differences in economies' productive potentials into two broad groups:

- First, differences in the economy's *efficiency of labor* — how technology is deployed and organization is used to increase the amount of output a worker can produce, even with the same amount of capital.

- Second, differences in the economy's *capital intensity* — how large a multiple of current production has been set aside in the form of useful machines, buildings, and infrastructure to boost the productivity of workers, even with the same technology or organization.

Economists have spent much time over the past two generations dividing economic growth into that part due to improvements in technology and in social and business organization that boost the efficiency of labor, on the one hand, and into that part generated by investment in capital to boost the economy's capital intensity — the ratio of the capital stock to output — on the other. A very important finding is that investment that boosts capital intensity plays a substantial role in generating growth. But an even more important finding is that the lion's share of economic growth comes from factors that affect the efficiency of labor.

In this two-chapter section on economic growth, this first chapter, Chapter 4, sets out economists' basic theory of economic growth. It presents the concepts and models economists use to organize their thinking about the causes of long-run economic growth and stagnation. Chapter 5 then sketches the facts of economic growth over time and across the world. Chapter 4 is a tour of how economists think about economic growth. Chapter 5 is a tour of how economic growth is progressing or not progressing around the world.

Now let's begin our tour of how economists think by looking in more detail at the two broad groups into which economists divide factors affecting long-run economic growth: the efficiency of labor, on the one hand, and capital intensity, on the other.

The Efficiency of Labor

efficiency of labor

The skills and education of the labor force, the ability of the labor force to handle modern technologies, and the efficiency with which the economy's businesses and markets function.

The biggest reason that Americans today are vastly richer and more productive than their predecessors of a century ago is that they have enjoyed an extraordinary amplification of the **efficiency of labor**. Efficiency has risen for two reasons: advances in technology and in organization. We now know how to make electric motors, dope semiconductors, transmit signals over fiber optics, fly jet airplanes, machine internal combustion engines, build tall and durable structures out of concrete and steel, record entertainment programs on DVDs, make hybrid seeds, fertilize crops with nutrients, organize assembly lines, and do a host of other things our predecessors did not know how to do. These technological advances allow American workers to easily perform value-generating tasks that were unimaginable, or at least extremely difficult to accomplish, a century ago.

Moreover, the American economy is equipped to make use of all these technological capabilities. It has the forms of business organization, it has the stability and honesty of government, it has the schools to educate its population, and it has the other socioeconomic institutions needed to successfully utilize modern technology. So it is both better technology and advances in organization that have led to vast increases in the efficiency of labor and thus to American standards of living.

We have to admit that we economists know less than we should about the processes by which this better technology and these advances in organization come to be. Economists are good at analyzing the consequences of advances in technology and improvements in organization and other factors that make for a high efficiency of labor, but they have less to say about their sources.

Capital Intensity

A secondary but still large part of America's very long run economic growth — and a secondary but still large component of differences in material standards of living across countries today — has been generated by the second source of growth: **capital intensity**. Does the economy have a low ratio of capital per unit of output, that is, relatively little in the way of machines, buildings, roads, bridges, and so on? Then it is likely to be poor. The higher is the economy's capital intensity, the more prosperous the economy will be: A more capital-intensive economy will be a richer and a more productive economy.

capital intensity
The ratio of the capital stock to total potential output, K/Y, which describes the extent to which capital, as opposed to labor, is used to produce goods and services.

Fitting the Two Together

The task of the rest of Chapter 4 is to build economists' standard model of long-run economic growth, a model into which we can fit these two broad groups of factors. This standard model is called the *Solow growth model,* after Nobel Prize–winning MIT economist Robert Solow. The Solow growth model is a dynamic model of the economy: It describes how the economy changes and grows over time as saving and investment, labor-force growth, and progress in advancing technology and improving social organization raise the economy's level of output per worker and thus its material standard of living. Saving and investment are the drivers leading to increases in capital intensity. Progress in technology and organization are the drivers leading to increases in the efficiency of labor.

RECAP SOURCES OF LONG-RUN GROWTH

In the very long run, economic growth is the most important aspect of economic performance. Two major factors determine economic growth: growth in the efficiency of labor — a product of advances in technology on the one hand and improvements in economic and social organization on the other — and the economy's capital intensity. Policies that accelerate innovation or improve institutions and so boost the efficiency of labor accelerate economic growth and create prosperity, as do policies that boost investment and raise the economy's capital intensity to a higher level.

4.2 THE SOLOW GROWTH MODEL

As is the case for all economic models, the Solow growth model consists of

- *Variables:* economic quantities of interest that we can measure.
- *Behavioral relationships:* relationships that (1) describe how humans, making economic decisions given their opportunities and opportunity costs, decide what to do and (2) determine the values of the variables.
- *Equilibrium conditions:* conditions that tell us when the economy is in a position of balance, when the variables we are focusing on are "stable" — that is, when the variables are changing in simple and predictable ways.

Almost every economic model has a single key economic variable at its heart. We will be most interested in that one variable — the one the model is organized around.

In the case of the Solow growth model, the key variable is *labor productivity:* output per worker, how much the average worker in the economy is able to produce. We calculate output per worker by simply taking the economy's level of real GDP or output *Y*, and dividing it by the economy's labor force *L*. This quantity, output per worker, *Y/L*, is our best simple proxy for the standard of living and level of prosperity of the economy.

In every economic model — and the Solow growth model is no exception — economists analyze the model by looking for an *equilibrium:* a point of balance, a condition of rest, a state of the system toward which the model will converge over time. Economists look for equilibrium for a simple reason: either an economy is at its (or one of its) equilibrium position(s), or it is moving — and probably moving rapidly — to an equilibrium position.

Once you have found the equilibrium position toward which the economy tends to move, you can use it to understand how the model will behave. If you have built the right model, it will tell you in broad strokes how the economy will behave. *In economic growth, the equilibrium economists look for is an equilibrium in which the economy's capital stock per worker, its level of real GDP per worker, and its efficiency of labor are all three growing at exactly the same proportional rate.*

The equilibrium economists look for in the case of the Solow growth model is thus a *balanced-growth equilibrium.* In this growth equilibrium the capital intensity of the economy — its capital stock divided by its total output, *K/Y* — remains constant as the rest of the variables in the economy grow. The amount of capital that the economy uses to produce each unit of output remains constant over time, as both the capital stock and output grow at the same proportional rate, and thus capital intensity does not change.

balanced-growth path

The path toward which total output per worker tends to converge as the capital-output ratio converges to its equilibrium value.

For each balanced-growth equilibrium, there is a **balanced-growth path:** this is a growing economy and so the economy's variables of interest change over time. We need to know how fast it is growing: at what rate output per worker, *Y/L*, is increasing. So, after finding the balanced-growth equilibrium, we calculate this balanced-growth path. Forecasting then becomes straightforward. If the economy is on its balanced-growth path, the present value of output per worker is on and future values of output per worker will continue to follow the balanced-growth path. If the economy is not yet on its balanced-growth path, it will head toward it: Over time, the economy will converge to its balanced-growth path.

We will see how this works later on. First we need to set out the pieces of the Solow growth model.

The Production Function

Let's start with the average worker, a worker whose productivity is simply Y/L, the economywide average. This average worker uses the economy's current level of technology and organization. These are captured by the current value of the efficiency of labor E. This average worker also uses an average share of the economy's capital stock: He or she has K/L worth of capital to amplify his or her productivity. We want to analyze how these two — efficiency of labor E and the capital-to-labor ratio K/L — affect the average worker's productivity Y/L.

To do this, we write down a behavioral relationship that tells us how the average worker's productivity Y/L is related to the efficiency of labor E and the amount of capital K/L at the average worker's disposal. We give this behavioral relationship a name: the **production function**. Tell the production function what resources the economy's average worker has available, and it will tell you how much output the typical worker can produce. In an abstract form we write the production function as

$$\frac{Y}{L} = F\left(\frac{K}{L}, E\right)$$

This says just that there is a systematic relationship between **output per worker** Y/L — real GDP divided by the number of workers — and the economy's available resources: the capital stock per worker K/L and the efficiency of labor E. The pattern of this relationship is prescribed by the form of the function $F(\ )$.

As long as all we know about the production function is that we write it with the symbols $F(\ )$ — one capital letter and one set of parentheses — it is not of much use. We know that there is a relationship between resources and production, but we don't know what that relationship is. We cannot calculate much of anything; we cannot give quantitative answers to any questions we are asked about the effects of changes in economic policy and the economic environment on economic growth.

To make our model more useful, we will give a simple algebraic form to our production function: the Cobb-Douglas form, which we choose primarily because using it makes lots of formulas later in the chapter simpler than they would otherwise be. We write the Cobb-Douglas production function as

$$\frac{Y}{L} = \left(\frac{K}{L}\right)^{\alpha}(E)^{1-\alpha}$$

where α is a parameter between zero and 1. The economy's level of output per worker Y/L is equal to the capital stock per worker K/L raised to the power of a parameter α, and then multiplied by the current efficiency of labor E itself raised to the power $(1 - \alpha)$.[1]

The value of α in the Cobb-Douglas production function tells us how rapidly the economic usefulness of additional *investment* in buildings and machines declines as the economy accumulates more and more of them. That is, α measures how fast diminishing returns to investment set in, in the economy. A value of α near zero means that the extra amount of output made possible by an additional unit of capital declines very quickly as the capital stock rises. A value of α near 1

production function

The relationship between the national product per worker and the resources used to produce it: the quantity of capital per worker, and the efficiency of labor. Equivalently, the relationship between the national product and capital, labor, and the efficiency of labor.

output per worker

The average amount of output produced in a year per worker, Y/L. Equal to the average labor productivity. Used as a proxy for the material standard of living.

---

[1]When we are interested not in the level of output per worker but in the total level of output Y in the economy, we simply multiply both the left- and right-hand sides of the equation above by the labor force L to get the total output form of the production function $Y = (K)^{\alpha}(LE)^{1-\alpha}$.

FIGURE 4.2

The Cobb-Douglas Production Function for Different Values of α As the exponent α in the Cobb-Douglas production function changes, the speed with which diminishing returns to investment set in — and thus the curvature of the production function — changes. With a high value of α near 1, output per worker Y/L increases nearly one-for-one with the capital stock per worker K/L. With a low value of α near zero, the economy quickly reaches the point where additional capital accumulation raises output by only a little. For each of the values of α plotted in this figure, the value of the efficiency of labor E has been adjusted so that output per worker Y/L is equal to $40,000 a year when the capital stock per worker K/L is equal to $100,000.

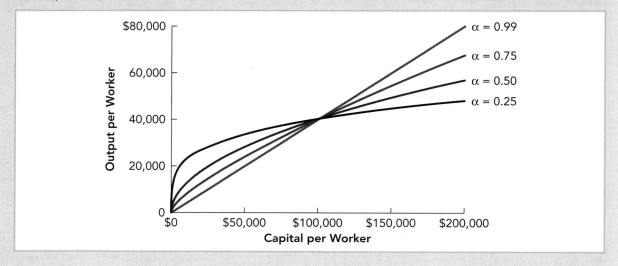

means that each additional unit of capital makes possible almost as large an increase in output as the last additional unit. As α varies from a high number near 1 to a low number near 0, the force of diminishing returns to investment gets stronger, as Figure 4.2 shows.[2]

The value of α determines how quickly the Cobb-Douglas production function flattens out when output per worker is plotted on the vertical axis and capital per worker is plotted on the horizontal axis. The value of the efficiency of labor E tells us how high the production function rises: A higher level of E means that more output per worker is produced for each possible value of the capital stock per worker, as Figure 4.3 shows.

The Cobb-Douglas production function is flexible. It can be "tuned" to fit any of a wide variety of different economic situations. Are we studying an economy in which productivity is high? Use the Cobb-Douglas production function with a high value of the efficiency of labor E. Does the economy rapidly hit the wall as investment proceeds, with little increase in the level of production? Use the Cobb-Douglas function with a low value — near zero — of α. Is the speed

---

[2]One way of illustrating this point in algebra is to use a little calculus to calculate the *marginal product of capital*, the MPK — how much total output increases as a result of a one-unit increase in the capital stock. For the Cobb-Douglas production function, MPK = $\alpha/(K/Y)$. The higher the current capital-to-output ratio, the lower is the marginal product of capital. And the lower the parameter α, the lower is the marginal product of capital.

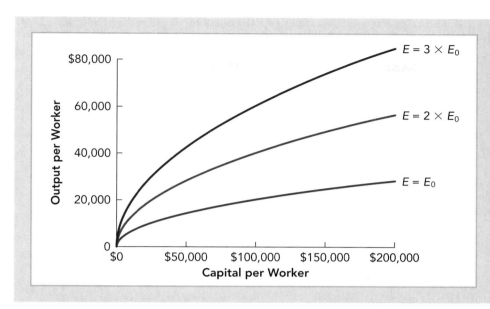

FIGURE 4.3

The Cobb-Douglas Production Function for Different Values of E

As the parameter E in the Cobb-Douglas production function increases, the curve representing the function moves upward. With a higher value of E, each possible value of capital per worker produces a larger value for output per worker.

with which diminishing returns to investment set in moderate? Pick a middle value of α. The Cobb-Douglas function will once again fit.

Given values for the diminishing-returns-to-investment parameter α, the efficiency of labor E, the economy's capital stock K, and the labor force L, we can calculate the level of output per worker Y/L in the economy. Box 4.1 shows how to use the production function.

USING THE PRODUCTION FUNCTION: AN EXAMPLE

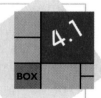

Suppose we know that the current value of the efficiency of labor E is \$10,000 a year and that the diminishing-returns-to-investment parameter α is 0.3. Then determining how the level of output per worker Y/L depends on the capital stock per worker K/L is straightforward.

Let's start with the case in which the capital stock per worker is \$125,000. The Cobb-Douglas production function is

$$\frac{Y}{L} = \left(\frac{K}{L}\right)^{\alpha}(E)^{1-\alpha}$$

Substitute in the known values of K/L, E, and α to get

$$\frac{Y}{L} = (125{,}000)^{0.3}(10{,}000)^{0.7}$$

Use your calculator to evaluate the effect of raising numbers to these exponents to get

$$\frac{Y}{L} = (33.812)(630.957)$$

And then multiply to get

$$\frac{Y}{L} = \$21{,}334 \text{ per year}$$

If we are interested in a capital stock per worker level of $250,000, the calculations are

$$\frac{Y}{L} = (250{,}000)^{0.3}(10{,}000)^{0.7}$$

And, using your calculator,

$$\frac{Y}{L} = (41.628)(630.957)$$

$$\frac{Y}{L} = \$26{,}265 \text{ per year}$$

Note that the first $125,000 of capital per worker boosted output per worker from $0 to $21,334, while the second $125,000 of capital per worker boosted output per worker only from $21,334 to $26,265 — by less than one-quarter as much. These substantial diminishing returns to investment should come as no surprise: The value of α is quite low at 0.3, and low values of α produce rapidly diminishing returns to capital accumulation.

This example offers another important lesson: Keep your calculator or computer's spreadsheet handy! Nobody expects anyone to raise $250,000 to the 0.3 power in her or his head and come up with 41.628. The Cobb-Douglas form of the production function, with its fractional exponents, carries the drawback that students (or professors) can do problems in their heads or with just pencil and paper only if the problems have been carefully rigged beforehand.

Nevertheless, we use the Cobb-Douglas production function because of its extraordinary convenience: By varying just two parameters we can fit the model to an enormous variety of potential economic situations.

Saving, Investment, and Capital Accumulation

In Chapter 6 we will talk in detail about the circular-flow relationship you learned in your Principles of Economics class: The amount of output an economy produces (real GDP, or Y) equals total spending, with total spending divided into four parts, consumption spending C, investment spending I, government purchases G, and net exports NX, which equal gross exports minus imports, $NX = GX - IM$.

Here we want to use this relationship to understand how investment spending is equal to *total saving*. The answer is that they are very closely related: The net flow of saving — household saving, plus *foreign saving* invested in our country, minus the *government's budget deficit* — is equal to the amount of investment. In the end, there is no place that net saving can go but to finance investment. If you save it, and it gets into the hands of a bank, then unless some other household borrows it (and so offsets your positive saving with its negative saving) the bank will lend it out, and it will be spent on business investment.

To see this more formally, a little bit of easy algebra is all we need. Start from the national income identity: Consumption C plus investment I plus government purchases G plus net exports $GX - IM$ equals real GDP Y:

$$C + I + G + GX - IM = Y$$

First subtract *net taxes* T from both sides:

$$C + I + (G - T) + GX - IM = Y - T$$

Next subtract consumption spending C, the government budget deficit $G - T$, and net exports $GX - IM$, from both sides:

$$I = (Y - T - C) + (T - G) + (IM - GX)$$

The right-hand side is the three pieces of total saving: household saving, government saving, and foreign saving. $Y - T - C$, real GDP minus net taxes minus consumption spending, is household saving. Call it S^H, S for saving and H for household.

When government purchases are less than net taxes, $T - G$ is positive, the government is running a *surplus* and is saving. Call this S^G, S for saving and G for government. But with the exception of a few years at the end of the 1990s, the U.S. government has run *deficits*. Then the government is "dissaving" — borrowing by running a deficit. $G - T$, government purchases minus net taxes, is the government's deficit. When the government runs a deficit, its saving S^G is negative.

$IM - GX$ is simply the excess of imports over exports, which equals the net flow of saving that foreigners invest here. Call it S^F, S for saving and F for foreign. With these new symbols, our equation above tells us that investment is equal to saving:

$$I = S^H + S^G + S^F$$

The right-hand term, $S^H + S^G + S^F$, is the total saving flowing into the economy. The equation says that businesses take all this saving and use it to invest — to buy and install the machines and build the buildings that make up our capital stock.[3]

Now, let's assume that total saving $S^H + S^G + S^F$ is a constant fraction s of real GDP Y:

$$s = \frac{S^H + S^G + S^F}{Y}$$

Multiply both sides by Y and you get $sY = S^H + S^G + S^F$. Thus investment spending I is equal to saving sY:

$$I = S^H + S^G + S^F = sY$$

In this chapter we will assume that s is almost always constant. We may think about the consequences of its taking an upward or downward jump or two at some particular moment of time, but the background assumption (made because it makes formulas much simpler) will be that s will remain at its current value as far as we look into the future. We call s the economy's **saving rate** or, more completely, its *saving-investment rate* to remind us that s is measuring both the flow of saving into the economy's financial markets and also the share of total production that is invested and used to build up and increase the economy's capital stock.

saving rate

The share of total GDP that an economy saves, s, equal to the sum of household, government, and foreign saving divided by total output.

---

[3]With more time, pages, and patience, we would develop this relationship further, by taking into account the differences between the government's investment that builds up publicly owned capital such as roads and bridges, and the remainder of government purchases. But here we will follow economists' custom of ruthless simplification, and say that all investment is captured in I.

FIGURE 4.4
Investment and
Depreciation
Gross investment adds to
and depreciation subtracts
from the capital stock.

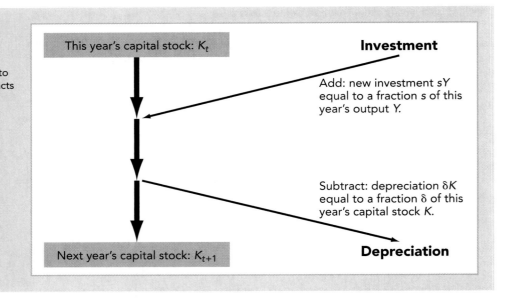

depreciation

The difference between gross
and net investment in capital;
the amount by which capital
stock wears out, becomes
obsolete, or is scrapped over
a year.

We assume the saving-investment rate s is constant, but we can't make the same assumption about the capital stock. The economy's capital stock K is not constant. It changes from year to year. Let's adopt the convention of using a subscript when we need to identify the year to which we are referring. K_0 denotes the capital stock at some initial year, usually the year at which we begin the analysis; K_{2003} means the capital stock in 2003; K_t denotes the capital stock in the current year; K_{t+1} means the capital stock next year; and K_{t-1} means the capital stock last year.

Over time investment makes the capital stock tend to grow. But over time **depreciation** makes the capital stock tend to shrink — old capital becomes obsolete, or breaks, or simply wears out. We make a simple assumption for depreciation: The amount of capital that wears out, breaks, and becomes obsolete in any year is simply a constant parameter δ (lowercase Greek delta, the depreciation rate) times the current capital stock. Thus we can write that next year's capital stock will be[4]

$$K_{t+1} = K_t + \text{Investment} - \text{Depreciation}$$

$$K_{t+1} = K_t + sY_t - \delta K_t$$

as illustrated in Figure 4.4. From these definitions, we can see that the capital stock is constant — that this year's capital stock K_t is equal to next year's K_{t+1} — when

$$sY_t = \delta K_t$$

capital-output ratio

The economy's capital
stock divided by potential
output, K/Y.

And this is true when the **capital-output ratio** is

$$\frac{K_t}{Y_t} = \frac{s}{\delta}$$

---

[4]Sometimes you will hear people refer to the change in the capital stock as *net investment* — investment net of depreciation — and refer to the amount of plant and equipment purchased and installed as *gross investment*. In this book "investment" will mean *gross investment*, and we will use "investment minus depreciation" in place of *net investment*.

Now suppose for a page or two that our economy has no labor-force growth and no growth in the efficiency of labor. (We will immediately drop this assumption when we leave this subsection, and we include it here only because understanding a more complex case later will be easier if we understand the simpler case now.) The labor force is constant at its initial value L_0. The efficiency of labor is constant at its value E_0.

If the capital-output ratio K/Y is lower than s/δ, then depreciation (δK) is less than investment (sY) so the capital stock and the capital-output ratio will grow. They will keep growing until K/Y reaches s/δ. If the capital-output ratio K/Y is greater than s/δ, then depreciation (δK) is more than investment (sY), so the capital stock and the capital-output ratio will shrink. They will keep shrinking until K/Y falls to s/δ. In the very long run, the capital-output ratio will be s/δ. The requirement

$$\frac{K_t}{Y_t} = \frac{s}{\delta}$$

is the equilibrium condition in this particular simple case of the Solow growth model — the case in which there is neither growth in the labor force nor growth in the efficiency of labor.

What is that equilibrium value of output per worker? A little algebra detailed in Box 4.2 shows us that we can move back and forth between the capital-per-worker

---

THE TWO FORMS OF THE PRODUCTION FUNCTION: SOME DETAILS

How do we transform our production function from one that focuses on the capital-labor ratio to one that focuses on the capital-output ratio? Through a little bit of simple algebra. Begin with our capital-per-worker form of the Cobb-Douglas production function:

$$\frac{Y}{L} = \left(\frac{K}{L}\right)^\alpha (E)^{1-\alpha}$$

Rewrite K/L as (K/Y) times (Y/L):

$$\frac{Y}{L} = \left(\frac{K}{Y}\frac{Y}{L}\right)^\alpha (E)^{1-\alpha}$$

Regroup:

$$\frac{Y}{L} = \left(\frac{K}{Y}\right)^\alpha \left(\frac{Y}{L}\right)^\alpha (E)^{1-\alpha}$$

Divide both sides by $(Y/L)^\alpha$:

$$\left(\frac{Y}{L}\right)^{1-\alpha} = \left(\frac{K}{Y}\right)^\alpha (E)^{1-\alpha}$$

Finally, raise both sides to the $1/(1-\alpha)$ power in order to get Y/L by itself on the left-hand side:

$$\frac{Y}{L} = \left(\frac{K}{Y}\right)^{\frac{\alpha}{1-\alpha}} (E)$$

This is the capital-output ratio form of the production function.

form of the production function that we have already seen,

$$\frac{Y}{L} = \left(\frac{K}{L}\right)^{\alpha}(E)^{1-\alpha}$$

and a different (but more convenient) form, the capital-output ratio form of the production function:

$$\frac{Y}{L} = \left(\frac{K}{Y}\right)^{\frac{\alpha}{1-\alpha}}(E)$$

Both forms of the production function contain the same information. But for our purposes the capital-output ratio form is more convenient to work with, so work with it we shall.

What, then, is the equilibrium value of output per worker? We know the value of the diminishing-returns-to-investment parameter α. We know the value of the efficiency of labor E. And we know that in equilibrium K/Y will be equal to s/δ. So just substitute s/δ in for K/Y where it appears, and calculate. Box 4.3 shows how.

CALCULATING OUTPUT PER WORKER: AN EXAMPLE
Suppose we know that the current value of the efficiency of labor E is $10,000 a year, and that the diminishing-returns-to-investment parameter α is 0.5. Then — in this special case in which both the labor force and the efficiency of labor are constant — we can calculate what the long-run value of output per worker will be once we know the saving-investment rate s and the depreciation rate δ.

Suppose the economy's saving-investment rate s is 16 percent, and the depreciation rate δ is 4 percent. Then substituting the parameters into the capital-output ratio form of the production function is straightforward:

$$\frac{Y}{L} = \left(\frac{K}{Y}\right)^{\frac{\alpha}{1-\alpha}}(E)$$

$$\frac{Y}{L} = \left(\frac{K}{Y}\right)^{\frac{0.5}{1-0.5}}(10,000)$$

And we know that in the very long run the capital-output ratio K/Y will be $s/\delta = .16/.04 = 4$. Thus

$$\frac{Y}{L} = (4)^{\frac{0.5}{1-0.5}}(10,000)$$

Output per worker will be $40,000 per year.

We can reach the same conclusion by a different, graphical, approach — an approach that is more friendly to those who prefer lines and curves on graphs to Greek variables and exponents in equations. Recall Figure 4.2, which showed how to draw the production function at any one moment in time (for a fixed and known level of the efficiency of labor E). Plot output per worker Y/L on the

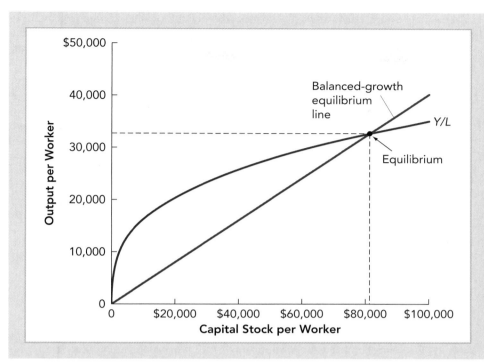

FIGURE 4.5

Equilibrium with Just Investment and Depreciation

The blue line shows output per worker as a function of the capital stock per worker for the known, constant values of the diminishing returns to investment parameter α and the efficiency of labor E. The red line shows the reciprocal of the equilibrium capital-output ratio, δ/s. If the economy is to the left of where the lines cross, the capital stock is growing. If the economy is to the right, the capital stock is shrinking. Where the lines cross is the equilibrium value of output per worker and capital per worker.

vertical axis, and capital per worker K/L on the horizontal axis. This curve tells you the relationship between levels of capital per worker and what the economy can produce.

Which of the many points on this production function curve is the economy's equilibrium? Recall our equilibrium condition: In equilibrium the economy's capital intensity, its capital-output ratio K/Y, is equal to s/δ. We can think of this equilibrium condition $K/Y = s/\delta$ as another line on the figure. It is a straight line starting at the bottom left (0,0) origin point and climbing to the upper right, with its slope Y/K equal to δ/s. Figure 4.5 shows that only one point satisfies both (1) this equilibrium condition for the economy's capital intensity and (2) the behavioral relationship relating output per worker to capital per worker, that is, the production function. This point is where the curves in Figure 4.5 cross.

We can use either the algebra or the graphical method to think about the long-run consequences of, say, changes in a government's fiscal policy. Before the 2000 presidential election the U.S. federal budget was in surplus and was expected to remain in surplus for decades. In the following few years, however, the George W. Bush administration pushed hard for significant increases in spending (which drove conservative small-government Republicans up the wall) and significant decreases in taxes (which drove liberal pro–government-program Democrats around the bend), with the result being a large downward shift in government saving S^G and thus in the economy's saving-investment rate s. Such a shift is going to mean that the equilibrium line rotates counterclockwise, and so the intersection point moves to a lower equilibrium value of output per worker. The economy's equilibrium condition $K/Y = s/\delta$ will be satisfied at a lower capital intensity, and so the economy will be poorer.

This depressing effect of rising government deficits on the standard of living is one important reason that international agencies like the International Monetary Fund (IMF) and the World Bank and almost all economists advise governments to avoid large and prolonged deficits.

Note that in this particular, restricted case the economy's labor force is constant. Its capital stock is constant. There are no changes in the efficiency of labor. Thus equilibrium output per worker is constant. There is — in this particular, restricted case — no growth of output per worker when the economy is in equilibrium. If we are to have a model in which economic growth continues, then we need to have growth in the labor force and, more important, growth in the efficiency of labor — which is why we have to move on to the next subsection, and think about a more complicated model.

Adding in Labor-Force and Labor-Efficiency Growth

If labor forces were constant and technological and organizational progress non-existent, we could stop the chapter here. But the economy's labor force continues to grow as more people turn 16 and join the labor force than retire and as immigrants continue to arrive. And the efficiency of labor rises as science and technology progress and people keep thinking of new and more efficient forms of business organization.

We assume — once again making a simplifying leap — that the economy's *labor force L* is growing at a constant proportional rate *n* every year. (Note that *n* is not the same across countries and can shift over time in any one country, but our background assumption will be that *n* is constant as far as we can see into the future.) Thus between this year and the next the labor force grows according to the formula

$$L_{t+1} = (1 + n)L_t$$

Next year's labor force will be *n* percent higher than this year's labor force, as Figure 4.6 shows. If this year's labor force is 10 million and its growth rate *n* is 2 percent per year, then next year's labor force will be

$$L_{t+1} = (1 + n)L_t$$
$$L_{t+1} = (1 + 2\%)(10,000,000)$$
$$L_{t+1} = (1.02)(10,000,000)$$
$$L_{t+1} = 10,200,000$$

We assume that the rate of growth of the labor force is constant not because we believe that labor-force growth is unchanging, but because the assumption makes the analysis of the model simpler. The trade-off between realism in the model's description of the world and simplicity as a way to make the model easier to analyze is one that economists always face, and economists have a strong bias toward resolving this trade-off in favor of simplicity.

We also assume that the efficiency of labor *E* grows at a constant proportional rate *g*:

$$E_{t+1} = (1 + g) E_t$$

Next year's level of the efficiency of labor will be *g* percent higher than this year's level, as Figure 4.7 shows. If this year the efficiency of labor is $10,000 per worker,

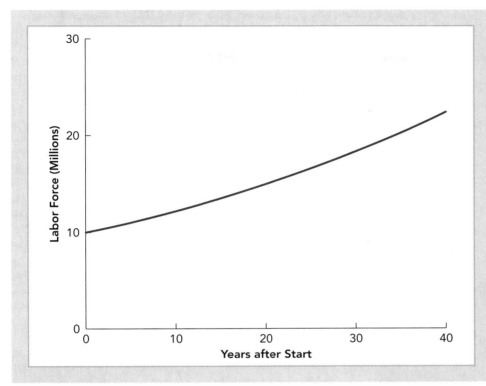

FIGURE 4.6
Constant Labor-Force Growth at *n* = 2 Percent per Year

The labor force growing at 2 percent per year. A labor force increasing at 2 percent per year will double roughly every 35 years.

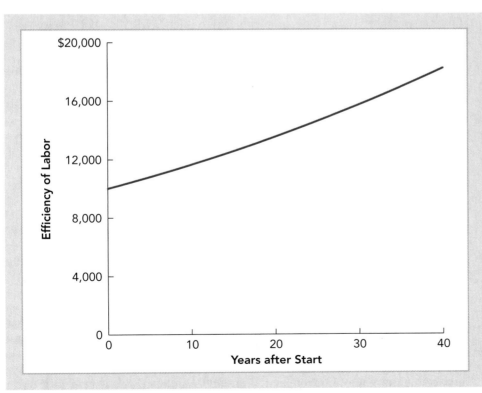

FIGURE 4.7
Efficiency-of-Labor Growth at *g* = 1.5 Percent per Year

Labor efficiency growing at 1.5 percent per year. If the efficiency of labor grows at 1.5 percent per year, it will take roughly 47 years for it to double.

and if g is 1.5 percent per year, then next year the efficiency of labor will be

$$E_{t+1} = (1 + g)E_t$$

$$E_{t+1} = (1 + 0.015)(\$10,000)$$

$$E_{t+1} = \$10,150$$

The Balanced-Growth Capital-Output Ratio

Earlier, when we had assumed that labor force and efficiency were both constant, and thus that n and g were both equal to 0, our equilibrium condition was $K/Y = s/\delta$. Since the saving-investment rate s and the depreciation rate δ are both constant, our equilibrium condition required that the capital-output ratio K/Y be constant. Now we've added realism to our model by allowing the labor force and efficiency to both increase over time at constant rates n and g. What effect does this added realism — allowing n and g to take on values other than 0 — have on our equilibrium condition?

In an important sense, none! Once again, our equilibrium condition is that the capital-output ratio be constant. When the capital-output ratio is constant, we say that the economy is in **balanced growth**: Output per worker is then growing at the same rate as the capital stock per worker. The two variables are in balance, and they are also both growing at the same rate as the efficiency of labor.

But at what *value* will the economy's capital-output ratio be constant? Here is where allowing n and g to take on values other than 0 matters. The capital-output ratio will be constant — and therefore we'll be in balanced-growth equilibrium — when $K/Y = s/(n + g + \delta)$. Add up the economy's labor-force growth rate, efficiency-of-labor growth rate, and depreciation rate; divide the saving-investment rate by that sum; and that is your **balanced-growth equilibrium capital-output ratio**.

Why is $s/(n + g + \delta)$ the capital-output ratio in equilibrium? Think of it this way: Suppose the economy is in balanced growth. How much is it investing? There must be investment equal to δK to replace depreciated capital. There must be investment equal to nK to provide the labor force which is expanding at rate n with the capital it will need. And since the efficiency of labor is growing at rate g, there must be investment equal to gK in order for the capital stock to keep up with increasing efficiency of labor. Adding these three parts of required investment together and setting the sum equal to the investment sY actually going on,

$$(n + g + \delta)K = sY$$

shows clearly that the economy's *investment requirements* for balanced growth equal the actual flow of investment when

$$\frac{K}{Y} = \frac{s}{(n + g + \delta)}$$

This is the balanced-growth equilibrium condition. It is constant because s, n, g, and δ are all constant. So when there is balanced growth — when output per worker Y/L and capital per worker K/L are growing at the same rate — the capital-output ratio K/Y will be constant.

To see more formally that $K/Y = s/(n + g + \delta)$ is the balanced-growth equilibrium condition requires a short march through simple algebra. Take a look again

balanced growth

When output per worker Y/L and capital per worker K/L are growing at the same rate.

balanced-growth equilibrium capital-output ratio

The value of the capital-output ratio to which an economy with constant saving rate, depreciation rate, labor-force growth rate, and efficiency growth rate converges over time. Equal to $s/(n + g + \delta)$.

at the capital-output ratio form of the production function:

$$\frac{Y}{L} = \left(\frac{K}{Y}\right)^{\frac{\alpha}{1-\alpha}} (E)$$

Recall that the efficiency of labor E is growing at the constant proportional rate g. With the capital-output ratio K/Y constant, output per worker must be growing at the rate g as well. Recall also that the labor force is growing at a constant proportional rate n. With output per worker growing at rate g and the number of workers growing at rate n, total output is growing at the constant rate $n + g$.[5] For the capital-output ratio K/Y to be constant, the capital stock also has to be growing at rate $n + g$. This means that the year-over-year change ΔK_{t+1} in the capital stock must be

$$\Delta K_{t+1} = (n + g)K_t$$

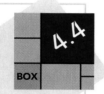

SOME MATHEMATICAL RULES OF THUMB: TOOLS

This is a good place to introduce four mathematical rules of thumb to make life easier throughout this book. They are all only *approximations*. But they are good enough for our purposes. They are:

1. *The growth-of-a-product rule:* The growth rate of a *product* is equal to the *sum* of the growth rates of its components. Since total output Y is equal to output per worker Y/L times the number of workers L, the growth rate of total output Y will be equal to the growth rate of Y/L plus the growth rate of L.

2. *The growth-of-a-quotient rule:* The proportional change of a *quotient* is equal to the *difference* between the proportional changes of its components. Since output per worker Y/L is equal to the quotient of output Y and the number of workers L, its growth rate will be the difference between their growth rates.

3. *The growth-of-a-power rule:* The proportional change of a *quantity raised to a power* is equal to the *proportional change in the quantity times the power* to which it is raised. For example, suppose that we have a situation in which output Y is equal to the capital stock K raised to the power α: $Y = K^\alpha$. Then the growth rate of Y will be equal to α times the growth rate of K.

4. *The rule of 72:* A quantity growing at k percent per year doubles in $72/k$ years. A quantity shrinking at k percent per year halves itself in $72/k$ years.

You may hear people say that a background in calculus is needed to understand intermediate macroeconomics. That is not true. These four mathematical rules of thumb contain 95 percent of what calculus is used for in intermediate macroeconomics. (Of course, you do need calculus if you want to do more than just take them on faith, and instead have a deep understanding of just *why* these rules of thumb work.)

---

[5]The fact that the growth rate of a product, Y/L times L, is equal to the sum of the growth rates, growth rate of Y/L plus the growth rate of L, is one of the handy mathematical rules of thumb contained in Box 4.4.

Since next year's capital stock equals this year's plus investment minus depreciation, the year-over-year change in the capital stock is also equal to

$$\Delta K_{t+1} = sY_t - \delta K_t$$

Setting our two expressions for the change in the capital stock equal to each other,

$$(n + g)K_t = sY_t - \delta K_t$$

collecting the terms with the capital stock on the left-hand side,

$$(n + g + \delta)K_t = sY_t$$

and then dividing,

$$\frac{K_t}{Y_t} = \frac{s}{n + g + \delta}$$

gives us the Solow growth model's equilibrium condition: $K/Y = s/(n + g + \delta)$. The balanced-growth equilibrium capital-output ratio is equal to the share of production that is saved and invested for the future — the economy's saving-investment rate s — divided by the sum of three things:

- The growth rate of the labor force n.
- The growth rate of the efficiency of labor g.
- The depreciation rate δ at which capital breaks down and wears out.

We'll sometimes call $s/(n + g + \delta)$ the *"equilibrium" capital-output ratio,* and we'll sometimes call it the "balanced-growth" capital-output ratio. To be always saying "balanced-growth equilibrium" is too much of a mouthful.

How do we know $K/Y = s/(n + g + \delta)$ gives us balanced growth, where capital per worker K/L and output per worker Y/L grow at the same rate? Suppose the current capital-output ratio is lower than $s/(n + g + \delta)$. Then $(n + g + \delta) K$ will be less than the economy's total investment which is equal to sY, the saving rate s times the level of output Y. Thus saving and investment will more than provide new workers with the capital they need to be fully productive, more than cover the increase in output due to the increase in labor efficiency, and more than compensate for the wearing out of capital through depreciation. The capital stock will grow faster than $n + g$. Since $n + g$ is the rate at which output grows, the capital-output ratio will rise.

Suppose instead the current capital-output ratio is above $s/(n + g + \delta)$. Then sY will be less than $(n + g + \delta) K$ — the economy's total investment sY will be insufficient to keep the capital stock growing at rate $n + g$. And since $n + g$ is the rate at which output grows, the capital-output ratio will fall.

Thus a capital-output ratio greater than $s/(n + g + \delta)$ makes the capital-output ratio fall. And a capital-output ratio less than $s/(n + g + \delta)$ makes the capital-output ratio rise. So a capital-output ratio equal to $s/(n + g + \delta)$ is indeed the balanced-growth equilibrium condition.

We now have our Solow growth model. It consists of one equilibrium condition telling us that the stable capital-output ratio will be $K/Y = s/(n + g + \delta)$. It consists of a production function. And it consists of four assumptions:

- The rate of labor-force growth equals n.
- The rate of increase in the efficiency of labor equals g.
- The rate of depreciation equals δ.
- The saving-investment rate equals s.

"Robert Solow got the Nobel Prize for that?!" you may ask. Ah, but what he got the Nobel Prize for was taking a complicated subject and making a useful model of it that was very simple indeed. The model is simple to write down. But it is powerful. As we unfold its implications and use it to understand very long run economic growth, we will see that it generates many insights.

RECAP   THE SOLOW GROWTH MODEL

When the economy's capital stock and its level of real GDP are growing at the same proportional rate, its capital-output ratio — the ratio of the economy's capital stock K to annual real GDP Y — is constant, and the economy is in balanced-growth equilibrium. In equilibrium, the capital-output ratio K/Y will equal the constant ratio $s/(n + g + \delta)$. The standard growth model analyzes how this balanced-growth equilibrium is determined by four factors: the economy's saving-investment rate s, the economy's labor-force growth rate n, the growth rate of the efficiency of labor g, and the capital stock depreciation rate δ.

4.3 UNDERSTANDING THE GROWTH MODEL

Balanced-Growth Output per Worker

Suppose that the capital-output ratio is equal to its balanced-growth equilibrium value: The economy is on its *balanced-growth path*. What does an economy on its balanced-growth path look like? The first and most important thing to look at is output per worker Y/L — what it is now, and how it grows. Y/L is, after all, our best simple proxy for the economy's overall level of prosperity: for material standards of living and for the possession by the economy of the resources needed to diminish poverty. Let's calculate the level of output per worker Y/L along the balanced-growth path (paying close attention to the time subscripts, for we are interested in where the economy is, where it was, and where it will be).

Begin with the capital-output ratio version of the production function:

$$\frac{Y_t}{L_t} = \left(\frac{K_t}{Y_t}\right)^{\frac{\alpha}{1-\alpha}}(E_t)$$

Since the economy is on its balanced-growth path, it satisfies the equilibrium condition $K/Y = s/(n + g + \delta)$. Substitute that in:

$$\frac{Y_t}{L_t} = \left(\frac{s}{n + g + \delta}\right)^{\frac{\alpha}{1-\alpha}}(E_t)$$

But s, n, g, δ, and α are all constants, and so $[s/(n + g + \delta)]^{\alpha/1-\alpha}$ is a constant. This tells us that along the balanced-growth path, output per worker is simply a constant multiple of the efficiency of labor, with the multiple equal to

$$\left(\frac{s}{n + g + \delta}\right)^{\frac{\alpha}{1-\alpha}}$$

Over time, the efficiency of labor grows. Each year it is g percent higher than the last year. Since along the balanced-growth path output per worker Y/L is just a

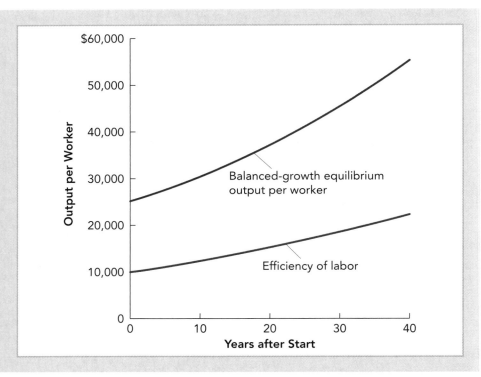

FIGURE 4.8

Balanced Growth: Output per Worker and the Efficiency of Labor

Along its balanced-growth path, the level of output per worker is a constant multiple of the efficiency of labor. What that multiple is depends on all the parameters of the growth model: the saving rate s, the labor-force growth rate n, the efficiency-of-labor growth rate g, the depreciation rate δ, and the diminishing-returns-to-investment parameter α.

constant multiple of the efficiency of labor, it too must be growing at the same proportional rate g. Figure 4.8 shows the pattern of balanced-growth output per worker and the efficiency of labor.

We now see how capital intensity and technological and organizational progress drive economic growth. Capital intensity — the economy's capital-output ratio — determines what multiple output per worker Y/L is of the current efficiency of labor E. Things that increase capital intensity — raise the capital-output ratio — make balanced-growth output per worker a higher multiple of the efficiency of labor, and so make the economy richer. Things that reduce capital intensity make balanced-growth output per worker a lower multiple of the efficiency of labor, and so make the economy poorer.

Suppose that α is 1/2, so that $\alpha/(1-\alpha)$ is 1, and that $s = n + g + \delta$, so that the balanced-growth capital-output ratio is 1. Then balanced-growth output per worker is simply equal to the efficiency of labor. But if we consider another economy with twice the saving rate s, its balanced-growth capital-output ratio is 2, and its balanced-growth level of output per worker is twice the level of the efficiency of labor.

The higher is the parameter α — that is, the slower diminishing returns to investment set in — the stronger is the effect of changes in the economy's balanced-growth capital intensity on the level of output per worker.

- Suppose that the balanced-growth capital-output ratio is 4. Then if α is 1/3, $\alpha/(1-\alpha)$ is 1/2, and the level of output per worker is twice the level of the efficiency of labor. Economists think that 1/3 is a reasonable parameter value for the United States today.

- By contrast, if α is 1/2, $\alpha/(1 - \alpha)$ is equal to 1, and again with a balanced-growth capital-output ratio of 4, the level of output per worker is fully four times the level of the efficiency of labor. Economists think that 1/2 is a reasonable parameter value for the United States a century ago or for relatively poor countries today.

Note — this is important — that changes in the economy's capital intensity shift the balanced-growth path up or down to a different multiple of the efficiency of labor, but the growth rate of Y/L along the balanced-growth path is simply the rate of growth g of the efficiency of labor E. The material standard of living grows at the same rate as labor efficiency. To change the very long run growth rate of the economy you need to change how fast the efficiency of labor grows. Changes in the economy that merely alter the capital-output ratio will not do it.

This is what tells us that technology, organization, worker skills — all those things that increase the efficiency of labor and keep on increasing it — are ultimately more important to growth in output per worker than saving and investment. The U.S. economy experienced a large increase in its capital-output ratio in the late nineteenth century. It may be experiencing a similar increase now, as we invest more and more in computers. But the Gilded Age industrialization came to an end, and the information technology revolution will run its course. Aside from these episodes, it is growth in the efficiency of labor E that sustains and accounts for the lion's share of long-run economic growth.

We are now finished with our analysis of the economy's balanced-growth path. We see that calculating output per worker when the economy is on its balanced-growth path is a straightforward three-step procedure:

1. Calculate the balanced-growth equilibrium capital-output ratio $s/(n + g + \delta)$, the saving rate divided by the sum of the labor-force growth rate, the efficiency of labor growth rate, and the depreciation rate.

2. Raise the balanced-growth capital-output ratio to the $\alpha/(1 - \alpha)$ power, where α is the diminishing-returns-to-investment parameter in the production function.

3. Multiply the result by the current value of the efficiency of labor E.

The result is the value of output per worker:

$$\frac{Y_t}{L_t} = \left(\frac{s}{n + g + \delta}\right)^{\frac{\alpha}{1-\alpha}}(E_t)$$

An example is given in Box 4.5.

CALCULATING EQUILIBRIUM OUTPUT PER WORKER: AN EXAMPLE

To see how to use the expression for output per worker when the economy is on its balanced-growth path,

$$\frac{Y_t}{L_t} = \left(\frac{s}{n + g + \delta}\right)^{\frac{\alpha}{1-\alpha}}(E_t)$$

let's work through an example. Suppose that the economy's labor-force growth rate n is 1 percent per year, the efficiency-of-labor growth rate g is 2 percent per year, and the depreciation rate δ is 3 percent per year. Suppose further that the diminishing-returns-to-investment parameter α is 1/2, and the economy's saving-investment rate s is 18 percent.

Then the balanced-growth equilibrium capital-output ratio $s/(n + g + \delta)$ equals 3, and $\alpha/(1 - \alpha)$ equals 1. Substituting these values into the equation above,

$$\frac{Y_t}{L_t} = (3)^1 (E_t)$$

$$\frac{Y_t}{L_t} = 3E_t$$

For these parameter values, balanced-growth output per worker is simply three times the efficiency of labor, whatever the value of the efficiency of labor is. When the efficiency of labor is $10,000 per year, balanced-growth output per worker is $30,000 per year. When the efficiency of labor rises to $20,000 per year, balanced-growth output per worker rises to $60,000 per year.

Over time, because balanced-growth output per worker is a constant multiple of the efficiency of labor, its growth rate is the same as g, the growth rate of the efficiency of labor, 2 percent per year.

The implications of the balanced-growth capital-output ratio for the balanced-growth level of output per worker, and how that level changes over time, can be seen in an alternative, diagrammatic way. Take a look at Figure 4.9. As in Figure 4.5, draw the production-function curve that shows output per worker Y/L as a function of capital per worker K/L for the current level of the efficiency of labor E_t. In addition, as in Figure 4.5, draw the line that shows where the capital-output ratio

FIGURE 4.9
Calculating Balanced-Growth Output per Worker

The economy is on its balanced-growth path at that level of capital per worker and output per worker at which the capital-output ratio is equal to its equilibrium value.

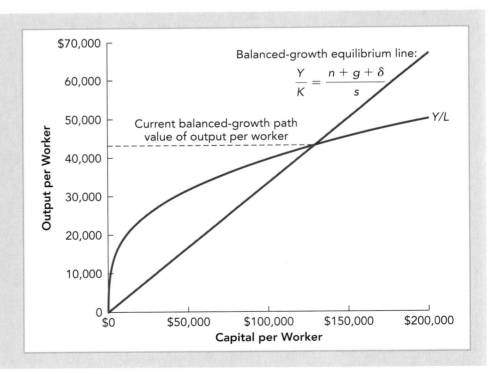

is equal to its balanced-growth equilibrium value, $K/Y = s/(n + g + \delta)$. This line starts at the bottom left origin point $(0, 0)$ and climbs toward the upper right. Because K/L is on the horizontal axis and Y/L is on the vertical axis, the slope of the line is not K/Y but instead Y/K or $(n + g + \delta)/s$.

Look once again at where the curves cross. That point shows the current level of output per worker along the balanced-growth path. Output per worker is given by the production function for the current levels of capital per worker and the efficiency of labor. And the capital-output ratio is at its balanced-growth path level. Anything that increases the balanced-growth capital-output ratio will lower Y/K so rotate the equilibrium line clockwise raising the balanced-growth path level of output per worker. Anything that decreases the balanced-growth capital output ratio rotates the equilibrium line counterclockwise. It thus lowers the level of output per worker for the given value of the efficiency of labor E.

Over time the efficiency of labor increases. As the efficiency of labor increases, the production-function curve in Figure 4.9 will shift up and out to the right. Over time, therefore, the balanced-growth path equilibrium levels of output per worker and capital per worker levels will rise as the economy climbs up and to the right along the constant balanced-growth equilibrium line.

Off the Balanced-Growth Path

What if the economy is not on its balanced-growth path? How can we use a model which assumes that the economy is on its balanced-growth path to analyze a situation in which the economy is *not* on that path? We still can use the model — and this is an important part of the magic of economics — because being on the balanced-growth path is an *equilibrium condition*. In an economic model, the thing to do if an equilibrium condition is not satisfied is to wait and, after a while, look again. When we look again, it will be satisfied.

Whenever the capital-output ratio K/Y is above its balanced-growth equilibrium value $s/(n + g + \delta)$, K/Y is falling: Investment is insufficient to keep the capital stock growing as fast as output. Whenever K/Y is below its balanced-growth equilibrium value, K/Y is rising: Capital stock growth outruns output. Figure 4.10 on page 106 gives an indication of how this process of **convergence** to the balanced-growth value proceeds. And as the capital-output ratio converges to its balanced-growth value, so does the economy's level of output per worker converge to its balanced-growth path.

The fact that an economy converges to its balanced-growth path makes analyzing the long-run growth of an economy not on its balanced-growth path relatively easy as well:

1. Calculate the balanced-growth path.
2. From the balanced-growth path, forecast the future of the economy: If the economy is on its balanced-growth path today, it will stay on that path in the future (unless some of the parameters — n, g, δ, s, and α — change). If the economy is not on its balanced-growth path today, it is heading for that path and will get there eventually. But as Figure 4.10 points out, decades may pass before an economy finally gets on that balanced-growth path.

Thus economic forecasting becomes simple. All you have to do is predict that the economy will head for its balanced-growth path, and calculate what the balanced-growth path is.

convergence

The tendency for a country to approach its balanced-growth path with a constant capital-output ratio.

FIGURE 4.10

Convergence to a Balanced-Growth Capital-Output Ratio of 4

Suppose the balanced-growth equilibrium capital-output ratio is 4. Whether the capital-output ratio starts above or below its balanced-growth equilibrium value, it converges to the level equal to $s/(n + g + \delta)$.

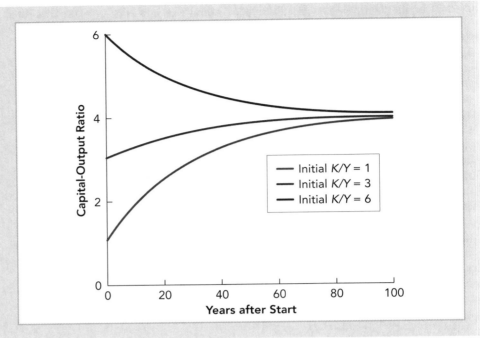

How Fast the Economy Heads for Its Balanced-Growth Path

How fast does an economy head for its balanced-growth path? We assert — but will not derive — that a fraction $(1 - \alpha)(n + g + \delta)$ of the gap between its current position and the balanced-growth path will be closed each year. If $(1 - \alpha)(n + g + \delta)$ turns out to be equal to 0.04, the capital-output ratio will close approximately 4 percent of the gap between its current level and its balanced-growth value in a year. According to the *rule of 72* (see Box 4.4) an economy closing 4 percent of the gap between its current and its equilibrium value each year will move halfway to equilibrium in 72/4, or 18, years. An example is given in Box 4.6. The convergence of an economy following the Solow growth model to its balanced-growth path does not happen overnight or in a year. It is a matter of decades. The Solow growth model is definitely a long-run model.

BOX

4.6

CONVERGING TO THE BALANCED-GROWTH PATH: AN EXAMPLE

Consider an economy in which the rate of labor-force growth $n = 1$ percent per year, in which the efficiency of labor grows at a rate $g = 2$ percent per year, in which the depreciation rate $\delta = 5$ percent per year, and in which the diminishing-returns-to-investment parameter $\alpha = 1/2$.

This economy will, according to the Solow growth model, each year close a fraction of the gap between its current capital-output ratio and its balanced-growth capital-output ratio equal to

$$(1 - \alpha)(n + g + \delta) = (1 - 1/2)(0.01 + 0.02 + 0.05) = 0.04$$

or 4 percent per year. According to the rule of 72, the economy will close half of the gap to its balanced-growth path in 18 years.

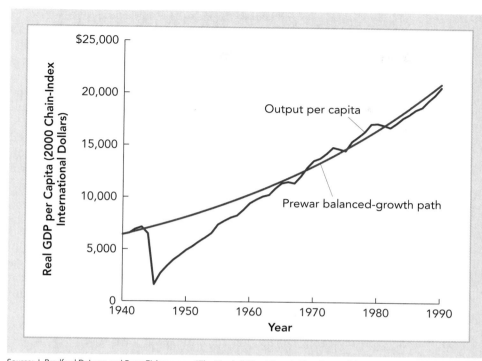

FIGURE 4.11
The Return of the West German Economy to Its Balanced-Growth Path
Economies do converge to and then remain on their balanced-growth paths. The West German economy after World War II is a case in point.

Source: J. Bradford DeLong and Barry Eichengreen, "The Marshall Plan: History's Most Successful Structural Adjustment Programme," in Rüdiger Dornbusch, Willhelm Nolling, and Richard Layard, eds., *Postwar Economic Reconstruction and Lessons for the East Today* (Cambridge, MA: MIT Press, 1993), pp. 189–230.

We can see such convergence in action in many places and times. For example, consider the post–World War II history of West Germany. The defeat of the Nazis left the German economy at the end of World War II in ruins. Output per worker was less than one-third of its prewar level. The economy's capital stock had been wrecked and devastated by three years of American and British bombing and then by the ground campaigns of the last six months of the war. But in the years immediately after the war, the West German economy's capital-output ratio rapidly grew and converged back to its prewar value. As Figure 4.11 shows, within 12 years the West German economy had closed half the gap back to its pre–World War II growth path. And within 30 years the West German economy had effectively closed the entire gap between where it had started at the end of World War II and its balanced-growth path.

RECAP UNDERSTANDING THE GROWTH MODEL

According to the Solow growth model, capital intensity and growth in the efficiency of labor together determine the destiny of an economy. The value of the balanced-growth equilibrium capital-output ratio and the economy's diminishing-returns-to-investment parameter determine the multiple that balanced-growth output per worker is of the current efficiency of labor. The growth rate of output per worker along the economy's balanced-growth path is equal to the growth rate of the efficiency of labor. And if the economy is not on its balanced-growth path, the Solow growth model tells us that it is converging to it — although this convergence takes decades, not years.

4.4 USING THE SOLOW GROWTH MODEL

Up until now we have assumed that all the parameters of the Solow growth model are unchanging. But what if one or more of them were to shift? What if the labor-force growth rate were to rise, or the rate of technological progress to fall? The principal use of the Solow growth model is to analyze questions like these: how changes in the economic environment and in economic policy will affect an economy's long-run levels and growth path of output per worker *Y/L*.

Let's consider, as examples, several such shifts: an increase in the growth rate of the labor force *n*, a change in the economy's saving-investment rate *s*, and a change in the growth rate of labor efficiency *g*. All of these will have effects on the balanced-growth path level of output per worker. But only one — the change in the growth rate of labor efficiency — will permanently affect the growth rate of the economy.

The Labor-Force Growth Rate

Real-world economies exhibit profound shifts in labor-force growth. The average woman in India today has only half the number of children that the average woman in India had only half a century ago. The U.S. labor force in the early eighteenth century grew at nearly 3 percent per year, doubling every 24 years. Today the U.S. labor force grows at 1 percent per year. Changes in the level of prosperity, changes in the freedom of migration, changes in the status of women that open up new categories of jobs to them (Supreme Court Justice Sandra Day O'Connor could not get a private-sector legal job in San Francisco when she graduated from Stanford Law School even with her amazingly high class rank), changes in the average age of marriage or the availability of birth control that change fertility — all of these have powerful effects on economies' rates of labor-force growth.

What effects do such changes have on output per worker *Y/L* — on our measure of material prosperity? The faster the growth rate of the labor force *n*, the lower will be the economy's balanced-growth capital-output ratio $s/(n + g + \delta)$. Why? Because each new worker who joins the labor force must be equipped with enough capital to be productive and to, on average, match the productivity of his or her peers. The faster the rate of growth of the labor force, the larger the share of current investment that must go to equip new members of the labor force with the capital they need to be productive. Thus the lower will be the amount of investment that can be devoted to building up the average ratio of capital to output.

A sudden and permanent increase in the rate of growth of the labor force will lower the level of output per worker on the balanced-growth path. How large will the long-run change in the level of output be, relative to what would have happened had labor-force growth not increased? It is straightforward to calculate if we know the other parameter values, as is shown in Box 4.7.

How important is all this in the real world? Does a high rate of labor-force growth play a role in making countries relatively poor not just in economists' models but in reality? It turns out that it is important, as Figure 4.12 on page 110 shows. Of the 22 countries in the world with output-per-worker levels at least half of the U.S. level, 18 have labor-force growth rates of less than 2 percent per year, and 12 have labor-force growth rates of less than 1 percent per year. The additional investment requirements imposed by rapid labor-force growth are a powerful reducer of capital intensity and a powerful obstacle to rapid economic growth.

AN INCREASE IN THE LABOR-FORCE GROWTH RATE: AN EXAMPLE

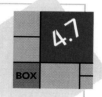

Consider an economy in which the parameter α is 1/2, the efficiency of labor growth rate g is 1.5 percent per year, the depreciation rate δ is 3.5 percent per year, and the saving rate s is 21 percent. Suppose that the labor-force growth rate suddenly and permanently increases from 1 to 2 percent per year.

BOX

Before the increase in the labor-force growth rate, the balanced-growth equilibrium capital-output ratio was

$$\frac{s}{n + g + \delta} = \frac{0.21}{0.01 + 0.015 + 0.035} = \frac{0.21}{0.06} = 3.5$$

After the increase in the labor-force growth rate, the new balanced-growth equilibrium capital-output ratio will be

$$\frac{s}{n + g + \delta} = \frac{0.21}{0.02 + 0.015 + 0.035} = \frac{0.21}{0.07} = 3$$

Before the increase in labor-force growth, the level of output per worker along the balanced-growth path was equal to

$$\frac{Y_t}{L_t} = \left(\frac{s}{n + g + \delta}\right)^{\left(\frac{\alpha}{1 - \alpha}\right)}(E_t) = (3.5)^{\left(\frac{1/2}{1 - 1/2}\right)}(E_t) = (3.5)^1(E_t) = 3.5\, E_t$$

After the increase in labor-force growth, the level of output per worker along the balanced-growth path will be equal to

$$\frac{Y_t}{L_t} = \left(\frac{s}{n + g + \delta}\right)^{\left(\frac{\alpha}{1 - \alpha}\right)}(E_t) = (3)^{\left(\frac{1/2}{1 - 1/2}\right)}(E_t) = (3)^1(E_t) = 3\, E_t$$

This fall in the balanced-growth path level of output per worker means that in the very long run — after the economy has converged to its new balanced-growth path — one-seventh of its economic prosperity has been lost because of the increase in the rate of labor-force growth.

In the short run of a year or two, however, such an increase in the labor-force growth rate has little effect on output per worker. In the months and years after labor-force growth increases, the increased rate of labor-force growth has had no time to affect the economy's capital-output ratio. But over decades and generations, the capital-output ratio will fall as it converges to its new balanced-growth equilibrium level.

A sudden and permanent change in the rate of growth of the labor force will immediately and substantially change the level of output per worker along the economy's balanced-growth path: It will shift the balanced-growth path for output per worker up (if labor-force growth falls) or down (if labor-force growth rises). But there is no corresponding immediate jump in the actual level of output per worker in the economy. Output per worker doesn't immediately jump — it is just that the shift in the balanced-growth path means that the economy is no longer in its Solow growth model long-run equilibrium.

It takes time, decades and generations, for the economy to converge to its new balanced-growth path equilibrium, and thus for the shift in labor-force

FIGURE 4.12

The Labor-Force Growth Rate Matters

The average country with a labor-force growth rate of less than 1 percent per year has an output-per-worker level that is nearly 60 percent of the U.S. level. The average country with a labor-force growth rate of more than 3 percent per year has an output-per-worker level that is only 20 percent of the U.S. level. To some degree poor countries have fast labor-force growth rates because they are poor: Causation runs both ways. Nevertheless, high labor-force growth rates are a powerful cause of low capital intensity and relative poverty in the world today.

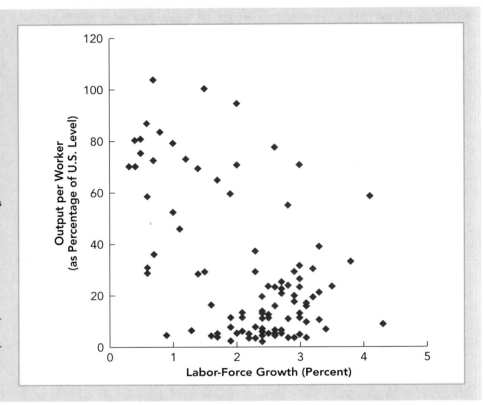

Source: Authors' calculations from Alan Heston, Robert Summers, and Bettina Aten, Penn World Table Version 6.1, Center for International Comparisons at the University of Pennsylvania (CICUP), October 2002, www.nber.org.

growth to affect average prosperity and living standards. But the time needed is reason for governments that value their countries' long-run prosperity to take steps now (or even sooner) to start assisting the demographic transition to low levels of population growth. Female education, social changes that provide women with more opportunities than being a housewife, inexpensive birth control — all these pay large long-run dividends as far as national prosperity levels are concerned.

U.S. President John F. Kennedy used to tell a story of a retired French general, Marshal Lyautey, "who once asked his gardener to plant a tree. The gardener objected that the tree was slow-growing and would not reach maturity for a hundred years. The Marshal replied, 'In that case, there is no time to lose, plant it this afternoon.'"

The Saving Rate and the Price of Capital Goods

The most frequent sources of shifts in the parameters of the Solow growth model are shifts in the economy's saving-investment rate. The rise of politicians eager to promise goodies — whether new spending programs or tax cuts — to voters induces large government budget deficits, which can be a persistent drag on an economy's saving rate and its rate of capital accumulation. Foreigners become alternately overoptimistic and overpessimistic about the value of investing in our country, and so either foreign saving adds to or foreign *capital flight* reduces our own saving-investment rate. And changes in households' fears of future economic disaster, in households' access to credit, or in any of numerous other factors change the share of household income that is saved and invested as well.

What effects do changes in saving rates have on the balanced-growth path levels of Y/L? The higher the share of national product devoted to saving and gross investment — the higher is s — the higher will be the economy's balanced-growth capital-output ratio s/(n + g + δ). Why? Because more investment increases the amount of new capital that can be devoted to building up the average ratio of capital to output. Double the share of national product spent on gross investment, and you will find that you have doubled the economy's capital intensity, or its average ratio of capital to output.

One way to think about this is that the equilibrium is the point at which the economy's investment effort and its investment requirements are in balance. Investment effort is simply s, the share of total output devoted to saving and investment. Investment requirements are the amount of new capital needed to replace depreciated and worn-out machines and buildings, plus the amount needed to equip new workers who increase the labor force, plus the amount needed to keep the stock of tools and machines at the disposal of workers increasing at the same rate as the efficiency of their labor. So double the saving rate and you double the balanced-growth capital-output ratio, as seen in Box 4.8.

AN INCREASE IN THE SAVING-INVESTMENT RATE: AN EXAMPLE

BOX 4.8

To see how an increase in the economy's saving rate s changes the balanced-growth path for output per worker, consider an economy in which the parameter α is 2/3, the rate of labor-force growth n is 1 percent per year, the rate of labor efficiency growth g is 1.5 percent per year, and the depreciation rate δ is 3.5 percent per year. Suppose that the saving rate s, which was 18 percent, suddenly and permanently jumped to 24 percent of output.

Before the increase in the saving rate, when s was 18 percent, the balanced-growth equilibrium capital-output ratio was

$$\frac{s}{n + g + \delta} = \frac{0.18}{0.01 + 0.015 + 0.035} = 3$$

After the increase in the saving rate, the new balanced-growth equilibrium capital-output ratio will be

$$\frac{s}{n + g + \delta} = \frac{0.24}{0.01 + 0.015 + 0.035} = 4$$

Before the increase in saving, the balanced-growth path for output per worker was

$$\frac{Y_t}{L_t} = \left(\frac{s}{n + g + \delta}\right)^{\left(\frac{\alpha}{1 - \alpha}\right)}(E_t) = (3)^{\left(\frac{2/3}{1 - 2/3}\right)}(E_t) = (3)^2(E_t) = 9E_t$$

After the increase in saving, the balanced-growth path for output per worker will be

$$\frac{Y_t}{L_t} = \left(\frac{s}{n + g + \delta}\right)^{\left(\frac{\alpha}{1 - \alpha}\right)}(E_t) = (4)^{\left(\frac{2/3}{1 - 2/3}\right)}(E_t) = (4)^2(E_t) = 16E_t$$

Divide the second equation by the first. We see that balanced-growth path output per worker after the jump in the saving rate is higher by a factor of 16/9, or fully 78 percent higher.

Just after the increase in saving has taken place, the economy is still on its old, balanced-growth path. But as decades and generations pass the economy converges to its new balanced-growth path, where output per worker is not 9 but 16 times the efficiency of labor. The jump in capital intensity makes an enormous difference for the economy's relative prosperity.

Note that this example has been constructed to make the effects of capital intensity on relative prosperity large: The high value for the diminishing-returns-to-investment parameter α means that differences in capital intensity have large and powerful effects on output-per-worker levels.

But even here, the shift in saving and investment does not *permanently* raise the economy's growth rate. After the economy has settled onto its new balanced-growth path, the growth rate of output per worker returns to the same 1.5 percent per year that is g, the growth rate of the efficiency of labor.

The same consequences as a low saving rate — a lower balanced-growth capital-output ratio — would follow from a country that makes the purchase of capital goods expensive. An abnormally high price of capital goods can translate a reasonably high saving effort into a remarkably low outcome in terms of actual gross additions to the real capital stock. The late economist Carlos Diaz-Alejandro placed the blame for much of Argentina's poor growth performance since World War II on trade policies that restricted imports and artificially boosted the price of capital goods. Economist Charles Jones reached the same conclusion for India. And economists Peter Klenow and Chang-Tai Hsieh argued that the world structure of prices that makes capital goods relatively expensive in poor countries plays a major role in blocking development.

How important is all this in the real world? Does a high rate of saving and investment play a role in making countries relatively rich not just in economists' models but in reality? It turns out that it is important indeed, as Figure 4.13 shows. Of the 22 countries in the world with output-per-worker levels at least half of the U.S. level, 19 have investment that is more than 20 percent of output. The high capital-output ratios generated by high investment efforts are a very powerful source of relative prosperity in the world today.

Growth Rate of the Efficiency of Labor

By far the most important impact on an economy's balanced-growth path values of output per worker, however, is from shifts in the growth rate of the efficiency of labor g. We already know that growth in the efficiency of labor is absolutely essential for sustained growth in output per worker and that changes in g are the only things that cause permanent changes in growth rates that cumulate indefinitely.

Recall yet one more time the capital-output ratio form of the production function:

$$\frac{Y_t}{L_t} = \left(\frac{K_t}{Y_t}\right)^{\frac{\alpha}{1-\alpha}} (E_t)$$

The capital-output ratio K/Y is constant along the balanced-growth path. The returns-to-investment parameter α is constant. And so the balanced-growth path level of output per worker Y/L grows only if and only as fast as the efficiency of labor E grows.

FIGURE 4.13

Investment Shares of Output and Relative Prosperity The average country with an investment share of output of more than 25 percent has an output-per-worker level that is more than 70 percent of the U.S. level. The average country with an investment share of output of less than 15 percent has an output-per-worker level that is less than 15 percent of the U.S. level. This is not entirely due to a one-way relationship from a high investment effort to a high balanced-growth capital-output ratio: Countries are poor not just because they invest little; to some degree they invest little because they are poor. But much of the relationship is due to investment's effect on prosperity. High saving and investment rates are a very powerful cause of relative wealth in the world today.

Where is the United States on this graph? For these data it has an investment rate of 21 percent of GDP and an output-per-worker level equal (not surprisingly) to 100 percent of the U.S. level.

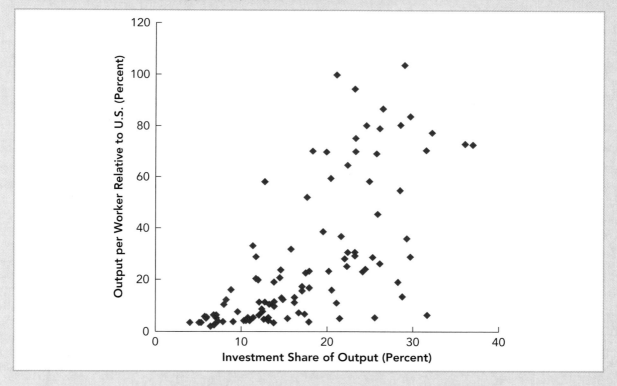

Source: Authors' calculations from the Penn World Table data constructed by Alan Heston, Robert Summers, and Bettina Aten, www.nber.org.

Increases or decreases in the rate of growth of the efficiency of labor g have effects on capital intensity that are in one sense just like changes in the rate of labor-force growth. An increase in the efficiency of labor growth rate g reduces the balanced-growth equilibrium capital-output ratio, just as an increase in labor-force growth did. And, as with a shift in labor-force growth, the level of output per worker after such a change in the labor efficiency growth rate begins the process of converging to its new balanced-growth path.

You might think that this means that an increase in g lowers output per worker Y/L — it lowers the capital-output ratio, after all. But you would be wrong. The effect on the capital-output ratio K/Y is only a small part of the story.

Changes in the efficiency of labor change the growth rate of output per worker along the balanced-growth path. In the very long run, no matter how large the

TABLE 4.2
Effects of Increases in Parameters on the Solow Growth Model

When there is an increase in the parameter . . .	The effect on . . .				
	Equilibrium K/Y	Level of Y	Level of Y/L	Permanent Growth Rate of Y	Permanent Growth Rate of Y/L
s saving-investment rate	Increases	Increases	Increases	No change	No change
n labor-force growth rate	Decreases	Increases	Decreases	Increases	No change
δ depreciation rate	Decreases	Decreases	Decreases	No change	No change
g efficiency of labor growth rate	Decreases	Increases	Increases	Increases	Increases

effects of a shift in efficiency of labor growth g on the economy's capital-output ratio, these effects are overwhelmed by the direct effect of g on output per worker. It is the economy with a high rate of efficiency of labor force growth g that becomes by far the richest over time.

This is our most important conclusion. The growth rate of the standard of living — of output per worker — can change if and only if the growth rate of labor efficiency changes. Other factors — a higher saving-investment rate, lower labor-force growth rate, or lower depreciation rate — can shift output per worker up as noted in Table 4.2, but they do not permanently change the growth rate of output per worker. Only a change in the growth rate of labor efficiency can permanently change the growth rate of output per worker. If we are to increase the rate of growth of the standard of living, we must pursue policies that increase the rate at which labor efficiency grows — policies that enhance technological or organizational progress. Chapter 5 looks at centuries of economic history for examples of just those all-important changes in the growth rate of labor efficiency.

RECAP   USING THE SOLOW GROWTH MODEL

Changes in the economic environment and in economic policy can have powerful effects on the economy's long-run economic growth path. In the Solow model we analyze the effects of such changes by looking at their effects on capital intensity and on the efficiency of labor. Shifts in the growth rate of the efficiency of labor have the most powerful effects: They change the long-run growth rate of the economy. Shifts in other parameters affect the economy's capital intensity, affect what multiple of the efficiency of labor the balanced-growth path of output per worker follows, and make the economy richer or poorer as it converges to a new, different balanced-growth path. But only a change in the growth rate of labor efficiency can produce a permanent change in the growth rate of output per worker.

Chapter Summary

1. One principal force driving long-run growth in output per worker is the set of improvements in the efficiency of labor springing from technological progress and advances in organization.

2. A second principal force driving long-run growth in output per worker is the increases in capital intensity, the ratio of the capital stock to output.

3. The balanced-growth equilibrium in the Solow growth model occurs when the capital output ratio K/Y is constant. When K/Y is constant, the capital stock and real output are growing at the same rate.

4. The Cobb-Douglas production function we use is

$$\frac{Y}{L} = \left(\frac{K}{L}\right)^{\alpha} E^{(1-\alpha)}$$

This function is equivalent to

$$\frac{Y}{L} = \left(\frac{K}{Y}\right)^{\frac{\alpha}{1-\alpha}} (E)$$

An increase in the returns-to-investment parameter α makes the production function steeper. An increase in labor efficiency E makes the production function shift up.

5. In equilibrium, investment equals saving: $I = S = S^H + S^G + S^F$. We assume S/Y, the saving-investment rate s, is constant.

6. The balanced-growth equilibrium value of the capital output ratio K/Y is a constant equal to the saving rate s divided by the sum of the labor-force growth rate n, the labor efficiency growth rate g, and the depreciation rate δ: in balanced-growth equilibrium, $K/Y = s/(n + g + \delta)$.

7. If the economy's actual value of K/Y is initially greater than $s/(n + g + \delta)$, then K/Y will fall until it reaches its equilibrium value. If the economy's actual value of K/Y is initially less than $s/(n + g + \delta)$, then K/Y will rise until it reaches its equilibrium value. It can take decades or generations for K/Y to reach its balanced-growth equilibrium value.

8. An increase in the saving rate s, a decrease in the labor-force growth rate n, or a decrease in the depreciation rate δ increases output per worker Y/L. The growth rate of Y/L will accelerate as the economy moves to its new higher balanced-growth path. But once the economy is on its new balanced-growth path, output per worker will grow at the same rate as it did initially.

9. In balanced-growth equilibrium, the growth rate of output per worker equals the growth rate of labor efficiency g. So only an increase in the rate at which labor efficiency grows can produce a lasting increase in the rate of growth of output per worker.

Key Terms

economic growth (p. 82)

labor force (p. 83)

capital stock (p. 83)

efficiency of labor (p. 84)

capital intensity (p. 85)

balanced-growth path (p. 86)

production function (p. 87)

output per worker (p. 87)

saving rate (p. 91)

depreciation (p. 92)

capital-output ratio (p. 92)

balanced growth (p. 98)

balanced-growth equilibrium capital-output ratio (p. 98)

convergence (p. 105)

Analytical Exercises

1. Consider an economy in which the depreciation rate is 3 percent per year, the rate of population increase is 1 percent per year, the rate of technological progress is 1 percent per year, and the sum of household and foreign saving rates is 16 percent of GDP. Suppose that the government increases its budget deficit, which had been at 1 percent of GDP for a long time, to 3.5 percent of GDP and keeps it there indefinitely.
   a. What will be the effect of this shift in policy on the economy's equilibrium capital-output ratio?
   b. What will be the effect of this shift in policy on the economy's equilibrium balanced-growth path for

output per worker? How does your answer depend on the value of the diminishing-returns-to-investment parameter α?

c. Suppose that your forecast of output per worker 20 years in the future had been $100,000. What is your new forecast of output per worker 20 years hence?

2. Suppose that a country has the production function

$$Y = K^{0.5}(LE)^{0.5}$$

a. Express output Y as a function of the level of the efficiency of labor E, the size of the labor force L, and the capital-output ratio K/Y.
b. What is the expression for output per worker Y/L?

3. Suppose that with the production function

$$Y = K^{0.5}(LE)^{0.5}$$

the depreciation rate on capital is 3 percent per year, the rate of population growth is 1 percent per year, and the rate of growth of the efficiency of labor is 1 percent per year.

a. Suppose that the saving rate is 10 percent of GDP. What is the equilibrium capital-output ratio? What is the value of output per worker on the balanced-growth path written as a function of the level of the efficiency of labor?
b. Suppose that the saving rate is 15 percent of GDP. What is the equilibrium capital-output ratio? What is the value of output per worker on the balanced-growth path?
c. Suppose that the saving rate is 20 percent of GDP. What is the equilibrium capital-output ratio? What is the value of output per worker on the balanced-growth path?

4. What happens to the equilibrium capital-output ratio if the rate of technological progress increases? Would the balanced-growth path of output per worker for the economy shift upward, shift downward, or remain in the same position?

5. Discuss the following proposition: "An increase in the saving rate will increase the equilibrium capital-output ratio and so increase both output per worker and the rate of economic growth in both the short run and the long run."

6. Would the balanced-growth path of output per worker for the economy shift upward, shift downward, or remain the same if capital were to become more durable — if the rate of depreciation on capital were to fall?

7. Suppose that a sudden disaster — an epidemic, say — reduces a country's population and labor force but does not affect its capital stock. Suppose further that the economy was on its equilibrium balanced-growth path before the epidemic.
a. What is the immediate effect of the epidemic on output per worker? On the total economywide level of output?
b. What happens subsequently?

8. According to the marginal productivity theory of distribution, in a competitive economy the real rate of return on a dollar's worth of capital — its profits or interest — is equal to capital's marginal productivity. With the production function

$$\frac{Y}{L} = \left(\frac{K}{L}\right)^{\alpha} E^{(1-\alpha)}$$

what is the marginal product of capital? That is, how much is total output (Y, not Y/L) boosted by the addition of an extra unit to the capital stock?

9. According to the marginal productivity theory of distribution, in a competitive economy the real rate of return on a dollar's worth of capital — its profits or interest — is equal to capital's marginal productivity. If this theory holds and the marginal productivity of capital is indeed

$$\frac{dY}{dK} = \alpha \frac{Y}{K}$$

how large are the total earnings received by capital? What share of total output will be received by the owners of capital as their income?

10. Suppose that environmental regulations lead to a slowdown in the rate of growth of the efficiency of labor in the production function but also lead to better environmental quality. Should we think of this as a "slowdown" in economic growth or not?

Policy Exercises

1. In the mid-1990s during the Clinton presidency the United States eliminated its federal budget deficit. The national saving rate was thus boosted by 4 percent of GDP, from 16 percent to 20 percent of real GDP. In the mid-1990s, the nation's rate of labor-force growth was 1 percent per year, the depreciation rate was 3 percent per year, the rate of increase of the efficiency of labor was 1 percent per year, and the diminishing-returns-to-investment parameter α was 1/3. Then when George W. Bush took office, the fiscal reforms of the Clinton administration were reversed, leading to deficits of 4 percent of GDP once again.

a. Suppose that the federal budget deficit remains at 4 percent indefinitely. What will the U.S. economy's equilibrium capital-output ratio be? If the efficiency of labor in 2000 was $30,000 per year, what would be your forecast of output per worker in 2040?

b. Suppose that George W. Bush had not taken office, and that Clinton's successor, Al Gore, and his successors had continued to run a balanced budget. What would be your calculation of the U.S. economy's balanced-growth equilibrium capital-output ratio? If the efficiency of labor in 2000 was $30,000 per year, what would be your forecast of output per worker in 2040?

2. How would your answers to question 1 change if your estimate of the diminishing-returns-to-investment parameter α was not 1/3 but 1/2 and if your estimate of the efficiency of labor in 2000 was not $30,000 but $15,000 a year?

3. How would your answers to question 1 change if your estimate of the diminishing-returns-to-investment parameter α was not 1/3 but 2/3?

4. What are the long-run costs as far as economic growth is concerned of a policy of taking money that could reduce the national debt — and thus add to national saving — and distributing it as tax cuts instead? What are the long-run benefits of such a policy? How can we decide whether such a policy is a good thing or not?

5. At the end of the 1990s it appeared that because of the computer revolution the rate of growth of the efficiency of labor in the United States had doubled, from 1 percent per year to 2 percent per year. Suppose this increase is permanent. And suppose the rate of labor-force growth remains constant at 1 percent per year, the depreciation rate remains constant at 3 percent per year, and the American saving rate (plus foreign capital invested in America) remains constant at 20 percent per year. Assume that the efficiency of labor in the United States in 2000 was $15,000 per year and that the diminishing-returns-to-investment parameter α was 1/3.

a. What is the change in the balanced-growth equilibrium capital-output ratio? What is the new capital-output ratio?

b. Would such a permanent acceleration in the rate of growth of the efficiency of labor change your forecast of the level of output per worker in 2040?

6. How would your answers to question 5 change if your estimate of the diminishing-returns-to-investment parameter α was not 1/3 but 1/2 and if your estimate of the efficiency of labor in 2000 was not $30,000 but $15,000 a year?

7. How would your answers to question 5 change if your estimate of the diminishing-returns-to-investment parameter α was not 1/3 but 2/3?

8. Output per worker in Mexico in the year 2000 was about $10,000 per year. Labor-force growth was 2.5 percent per year. The depreciation rate was 3 percent per year, the rate of growth of the efficiency of labor was 2.5 percent per year, and the saving rate was 16 percent of GDP. The diminishing-returns-to-investment parameter α is 0.5.

a. What is Mexico's equilibrium capital-output ratio?

b. Suppose that Mexico today is on its balanced-growth path. What is the current level of the efficiency of labor E?

c. What is your forecast of output per worker in Mexico in 2040?

9. In the framework of question 8, how much does your forecast of output per worker in Mexico in 2040 increase if:

a. Mexico's domestic saving rate remains unchanged but the nation is able to finance extra investment equal to 4 percent of GDP every year by borrowing from abroad?

b. The labor-force growth rate immediately falls to 1 percent per year?

c. Both *a* and *b* happen?

10. Consider an economy with a labor-force growth rate of 2 percent per year, a depreciation rate of 4 percent per year, a rate of growth of the efficiency of labor of 2 percent per year, and a saving rate of 16 percent of GDP. If the saving rate increases from 16 to 17 percent, what is the proportional increase in the equilibrium level of output per worker if the diminishing-returns-to-investment parameter α is 1/3? 1/2? 2/3? 3/4?

5

The Reality of Economic Growth: History and Prospect

QUESTIONS

What is modern economic growth?

What was the post-1973 productivity growth slowdown? What were its causes?

Why has American growth been so rapid since 1995?

Why are some nations so (relatively) rich and other nations so (relatively) poor?

What policies can speed up economic growth? What policy mistakes can slow it down?

What are the prospects for successful and rapid economic development in tomorrow's world?

We are used to modern economic growth. We are used to having production rise by 3 percent to 4 percent each year and productivity rise by 2 percent to 3 percent each year. In our time, a year in which production stagnates or falls is unusual. In the United States, only 6 of the last 50 years have seen real GDP lower than that of the year before.

For most of human history, however, things have been very different. Since the invention of agriculture roughly 10,000 years ago (and, as far as we know, before that), economic progress was generally glacial or nonexistent. The transition to our modern era of growth took place about two centuries ago, with what is called the Industrial Revolution.

This chapter surveys the history of economic growth — especially of modern economic growth — and also attempts to peer into the future. It is informed by the models of economic growth set out in Chapter 4, but it does not depend on them; the theory tells us what questions to ask, but the questions and answers stand on their own.

The chapter opens with a survey of what the economy looked like before the Industrial Revolution, before the transition to the age of modern economic growth. It continues with the story of the Industrial Revolution and modern economic growth in the United States, before widening its view to take a look at modern economic growth all over the world. It concludes with a brief sketch of the relationship between economic policies and economic growth.

5.1 BEFORE MODERN ECONOMIC GROWTH
Before the Industrial Revolution

Taking what we know and what we guess about the economy from back in the deep mists of time up to today produces a picture like that of Table 5.1. The numbers in Table 5.1 are — save for the past century — guesses, and they are — save for the past three centuries — extremely shaky guesses. Nevertheless, they do tell a coherent and consistent story.

Industrial Revolution

The transformation of the British economy between 1750 and 1850 when, due to technological advances, largely handmade production was replaced by machine-made production.

Until the **Industrial Revolution** of the late eighteenth century began in Britain — until 1800 or so — the human population of the world grew only as rapidly as a glacier moves. Population growth between 5000 BC and AD 1800 averaged less than one-tenth of a percent per year. Nevertheless, the cumulative magnitude of population growth was impressive; over a long-enough time span even glaciers can move very far, and 7,000 years is a long time indeed. Preindustrial population growth carried the number of human beings alive on this planet from perhaps 5 million in 5000 BC to 900 million in AD 1800.

The glacial pace of human population growth before the Industrial Revolution was accompanied by complete or near-complete stagnation in median standards of living. Up until 1500, as best we can tell, there had been next to no growth in the material standard of living of the typical human for millennia. Even in 1800 the average human had a material standard of living (and an economic productivity level) at best twice that of the average human in the year 1.

The problem was not that there was no *technological progress*. There was. Humans have long been ingenious. Warrior, priestly, and bureaucratic elites in 1500 or 1800 lived much better than their counterparts in previous millennia had lived. But just because the ruling elite lived better does not mean that other people lived any better. From 4000 BC to at least AD 1500, the typical life expectancy at birth

TABLE 5.1
Economic Growth through Deep Time

Year	Population*	Real GDP per Capita†
5000 BC	5	$ 130
1000 BC	50	160
1 AD	170	135
1000	265	165
1500	425	175
1800	900	250
1900	1,625	850
1950	2,515	2,030
1975	4,080	4,640
2000	6,120	8,175

*World population in millions.

†Guesstimates of real GDP per capita measured in year-2000 international dollars.

Source: Joel Cohen, *How Many People Can the Earth Support?* (New York: Norton, 1995), plus authors' estimates.

was low (less than 30 years), and the typical adult human was short (5 feet, 4 inches or less, due to chronic undernutrition), lost his or her teeth early (although for him sugar was still a great luxury, George Washington needed false teeth because he was calcium-deprived and his body sacrificed the teeth to maintain the bones), and ate a remarkably monotonous diet (rations for the Roman legions in AD 1 consisted of two pounds of bread per soldier per day, plus salt, plus a pint or two of wine, plus "garnishes"; rations for the British navy in 1800 were worse — save that the liquor was stronger, and the diet was supplemented by weevils in the crackers and enough fruit and vegetables to fight off scurvy).

Only after 1800 do we see large, sustained increases in worldwide standards of living. Worldwide, output per capita grew at perhaps 0.15 percent per year between 1500 and 1800. It grew at roughly 1 percent per year worldwide between 1800 and 1900. And, as Table 5.1 implies, material output per capita has grown at an average pace of roughly 2 percent per year, worldwide, since 1900.

It is after 1800 that we also see extraordinary growth in human numbers, as the population explosion depicted in Figure 5.1 took hold. The population explosion carried the total world population to 6 billion before the year 2000. Population growth on a world scale accelerated from a rate of 0.2 percent per year between 1500 and 1800, to 0.6 percent per year between 1800 and 1900, to 0.9 percent per year between 1900 and 1950, and 1.9 percent per year between 1950 and 1975 before the first slowing of the global rate of population growth — 1.6 percent per year from 1975 to 2000.

Premodern Economies

Why did no sustained increases in the material productivity of human labor occur before 1500? The principal reasons are two. Improvements in human technology quickly ran aground on a combination of (1) resource scarcity and (2) expanding populations.

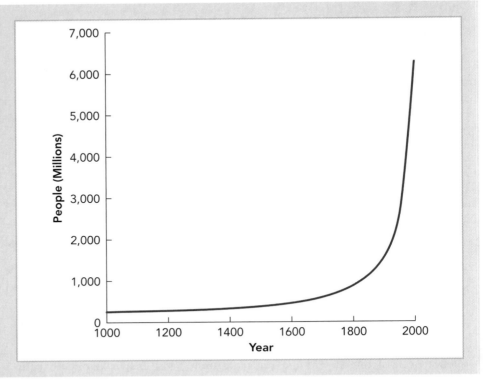

FIGURE 5.1
World Population Growth since 1000

The growth of human population was very slow until approximately 1800. The boom in population since 1800 is called, not surprisingly, the population explosion.

Source: Joel Cohen, *How Many People Can the Earth Support?* (New York: Norton, 1995).

In Chapter 4 we saw that output-per-worker levels depended on two factors: the economy's capital intensity K/Y and the efficiency of labor E. Understand the determinants of these two factors, and you understand the level of output per worker Y/L through the equation

$$\frac{Y}{L} = \left(\frac{K}{Y}\right)^{\frac{\alpha}{1-\alpha}} E$$

where, you recall, α is a parameter that tells us how fast diminishing returns to investment set in.

We also saw that in the long run each economy's capital intensity K/Y tended to approach some equilibrium value and then stay there. Sustained growth in output per worker must be driven by sustained increases in the efficiency of labor. So the question, "Why no sustained increases in productivity?" is the same as the question, "Why didn't the efficiency of labor grow?"

The answer is that the efficiency of labor depends not just on the storehouse of physical and organizational technologies at workers' disposal, but also on the natural resources available to the average worker. In modern times our skills at handling materials are so great that natural resources play only a small role: Soil bad? Dump some nitrogen on it. Plants too dry? Pipe water in from 300 miles away to irrigate them. Technology and capital make natural **resource scarcity** a much less important phenomenon now than in the past. But back before the Industrial Revolution natural resources and their scarcity played a very important

resource scarcity

Shortage in natural resources such as fertile land and water, relative to population.

role. It is no accident that for most of recorded history humanity has lived primarily in the great river valleys of the Nile, the Tigris and Euphrates, the Indus, the Ganges, the Yangtze, and the Yellow River — good silt and regular supplies of water were that important.

Before the Industrial Revolution, as human populations grew, the stocks of known natural resources had to be divided among more and more people. Miners had to exploit lower quality metal ores, and farmers had to farm lesser quality agricultural land. Over time, overcut forests vanished. Where today are the cedars of Lebanon? Over time, land that had been irrigated too long and seen too much water evaporate in the hot summer sun became poisoned with salt. What we call the northern deserts of the Middle East were once called the "Fertile Crescent" and were the home to at least a third of humanity's farmers. The net effect of resource scarcity and human fertility was that, in spite of technological progress, the world average efficiency of labor was little, if any, greater in AD 1500 than in 1500 BC.

The idea that increases in technological capability induce increases in fertility that inevitably run into natural resource scarcity is one of the oldest ideas in economics. It was introduced early, before the end of the eighteenth century, by Thomas R. Malthus, who became the first academic professor of economics ever (Adam Smith had been a professor of moral philosophy) at the East India Company's Haileybury College.

Malthus saw a world in which inventions and higher living standards led to increases in the rate of population growth. With higher living standards there were more pregnancies and more pregnancies were successfully carried to term. Better nourished children (and adults) had a better chance of resisting diseases. Moreover, when incomes were high, new farmsteads were relatively plentiful, and getting the permission of one's father or elder brother to marry was easier. For these reasons — both social and biological — before 1800 a higher standard of living inevitably led to a faster rate of population growth. The faster rate of population growth increased the scarcity of natural resources, and so lowered productivity. After a burst of invention, population would rise and resource scarcity increase until once again people were so poor and malnourished that population growth was back at roughly zero — to less than one-tenth of one percent per year characteristic of the preindustrial age.

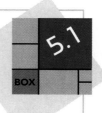

UNDERSTANDING THE ECONOMY BEFORE THE INDUSTRIAL REVOLUTION: DETAILS

In the models of Chapter 4, we identified the efficiency of labor with "technology" broadly understood: the storehouse of techniques for manipulating matter and forms of social organization that we can use to boost the productivity of the average worker. Before the Industrial Revolution humans were certainly inventive. "Technology" broadly understood improved to a remarkable degree in the millennia before 1800. So why were there no improvements in the efficiency of labor?

Because the model of Chapter 4 made a shortcut. We lumped the effect of natural resources on production into the efficiency of labor E. And before the Industrial Revolution, depletion of natural resources typically offset the beneficial effects of technological improvement. So the net effect was no improvement in the efficiency of labor: a constant value of E.

The End of the Malthusian Age

Malthusian age

A period in which natural-resource scarcity limits any gains from increases in technology; a larger population becomes poor and malnourished, lowering their standard of living, and ultimately lowering population growth to zero.

Whether Malthus saw clearly what was in the past or not, he would have been astonished by what we have seen of his future. We do not live in a **Malthusian age.** For at least 200 years improvements in the efficiency of labor made possible by new technologies and better organizations have not been neutralized by natural resource scarcity.

However, a Malthusian age may return. Suppose that population in the twenty-first and twenty-second centuries grows as fast as population did in the twentieth century, when it grew at an average rate of 1.33 percent per year. The rule of 72 tells us that a population growing at 1.33 percent per year doubles in $72/1.33 = 54$ years. Two hundred years is time for 3.7 doublings, enough time to multiply population about 14-fold. Take the year-2000 estimated population of 6.125 billion, multiply it by 14, and get about 86. If population grows at its twentieth-century average rate for the next two centuries, there will be nearly 90 billion people on Earth in 2200.

Surely, should such a population increase come to pass, resource scarcity would once again be a dominant feature of our world. For the past two centuries we economists have been justified in writing down production functions in which the limited supply of natural resources plays only a small part in the determination of productivity and production on a global scale. In a world with a population of 90 billion, we would probably not be justified in doing so. We would have to place more stress on the insights of Malthus.

However, it is much more likely that the age of the population explosion is almost over. Current United Nations projections forecast a rise in world population from a bit over 6 billion today to around 10 billion by 2050, and there population increase may well stop. Even in a country like India today, fertility is only a little above two children per potential mother. And in a wide section of the rich world from Japan to Italy, the average woman has fewer than two children in her lifetime.

What caused the end of the Malthusian age? How did humanity escape from the trap in which invention and ingenuity increased the numbers but not the material well-being of humans?

The key is that even in the Malthusian age the pace at which inventions occurred increased steadily. First of all, the population grew. Inventions made communication easier; especially after the invention of printing, knowledge could spread widely and quickly. More people meant more inventions: Two heads are better than one. The rate of technological progress slowly increased over the millennia. By about 1500 technological progress passed the point at which it could offset increased scarcity of natural resources due to population growth. Sustained increases not just in population but in the productivity of labor followed. As real incomes and standards of living showed sustained growth, what we call the **demographic transition** began.

The Demographic Transition

demographic transition

A period in history which sees first a rise and then a fall in birth rates and a sharp fall in death rates as material standards of living increase above "subsistence" levels.

At first the rise in material standards of living brought sharp increases in the rate of population growth: the population explosion. But as material standards of living rose far above subsistence, countries began to undergo the demographic transition, sketched out in Figure 5.2. Birth control meant that those who did not wish to have more children could exercise their choice. Parents began to find more satisfaction in having a few children and paying a great deal of attention to each. The resources of the average household continued to increase, but the number of children born fell. The long-run relationship between levels of productivity and

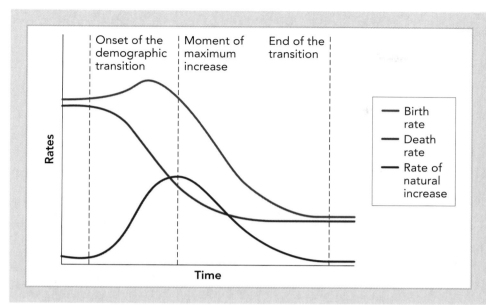

FIGURE 5.2

Stylized Picture of the Demographic Transition

The demographic transition sees, first, a rise in birth rates and a sharp fall in death rates as material standards of living increase above subsistence levels. But after a while birth rates start to decline rapidly too. The end of the demographic transition sees both birth and death rates at a relatively low level and the population nearly stable.

population growth rates was not — as Malthus thought — a spiral of ever-faster population growth rates as material standards of living increased. Instead, population growth rates peaked and began to decline.

In the world today not all countries have gone through their demographic transitions. Many countries are not rich enough to have begun the population growth declines seen in the second half of the demographic transition. Countries such as Nigeria, Iraq, Pakistan, and the Congo are currently projected to have population growth rates in excess of 2 percent per year over the next generation, as Figure 5.3 shows. But in a large group of developing countries like Thailand, China, Korea, and South Africa, population growth over the next generation is projected to be less than 1 percent per year. And in the industrialized countries like Japan, Italy, and Germany, populations are projected to stay nearly the same over the next generation.

The Industrial Revolution

The century after 1750 saw the Industrial Revolution proper: the invention of the steam engine, the spinning jenny, the power loom, the hydraulic press, the railroad locomotive, the water turbine, and the electric motor, as well as the hot-air balloon, gas lighting, photography, and the sewing machine. But the Industrial Revolution was not just a burst of inventions. It was an economic transformation that revolutionized the process of invention as well. Since 1850 the pace of invention and innovation has further accelerated: steel making, the internal combustion engine, pasteurization, the typewriter, the cash register, the telephone, the automobile, the radio, the airplane, the tank, the limited-access highway, the photocopier, the computer, the pacemaker, nuclear weapons, superconductivity, genetic fingerprinting, and the human genome map. The coming of the Industrial Revolution marked the beginning of the era of modern economic growth in which new technological leaps routinely revolutionized industries and generated major improvements in living standards.

FIGURE 5.3
Expected Population Growth Rates, Present–2020

The population of India is projected to grow at 1.3 percent and that of China at 0.7 percent per year over the next generation. Demographers today believe that the world population has at most one more doubling to undergo before the demographic transition will have taken hold throughout the world.

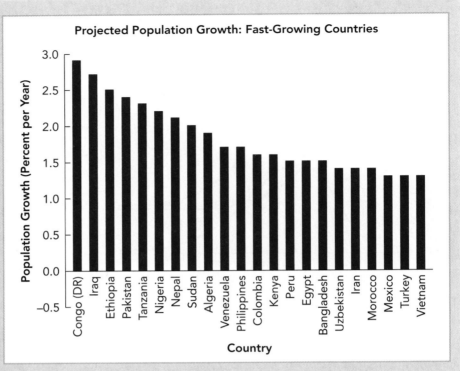

Projected Population Growth: Fast-Growing Countries

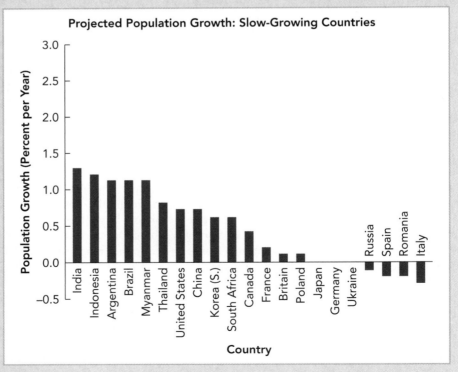

Projected Population Growth: Slow-Growing Countries

Source: United Nations.

Yet it is important to recognize that the gulf that separates us in the world economy's industrial core from the citizens of Industrial Revolution Britain is much greater than the gulf that separated Britain in 1800 from medieval or ancient peasants and nobles. Economic historian N. F. R. Crafts calculated that 10 modern-day automobiles have more horsepower than all the steam engines of Britain in 1800, and the vehicles of Berkeley, California, today have more horsepower than the steam power of Britain in 1870. Growth during the Industrial Revolution was, by our standards, very slow. And the people who lived through the Industrial Revolution were very poor. Consider the standard of living portrayed in Charles Dickens's *Oliver Twist* — or Karl Marx's *Capital*.

The fact that Britain was the center of the Industrial Revolution meant that for a century, from 1800 to 1900, British levels of industrial productivity and British standards of living were the highest in the world. It also meant that English (rather than Hindi, Mandarin, French, or Spanish) became the world's de facto second language. But the technologies of the Industrial Revolution did not remain narrowly confined to Britain. Their spread was rapid to western Europe and the United States. It was less rapid — but still relatively thorough and complete — to southern and eastern Europe and, most interesting perhaps, Japan, as shown in Figure 5.4.

Why the Industrial Revolution took place in Britain and why it took place in the years around 1800 have long been and will long remain among the knottiest and most important puzzles in world economic history. The standard explanation sees two largely independent strands coming together: secure property rights for commercial and manufacturing property on the one hand, and modern science and technology on the other. The establishment of limited government, security of property, and freedom of contract in Britain after the Glorious Revolution of 1688 played a huge role. The creation of modern science and of the technological

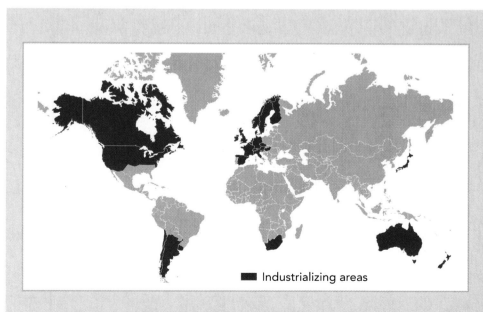

FIGURE 5.4

Industrializing Areas of the World, 1900

Perhaps the most important lesson to draw from this short look at economic history is that economists' standard growth models apply to a relatively narrow slice of time. For instance, the Solow growth model discussed in Chapter 4 does not illuminate very much regarding the period before 1800, yet it is very useful in analyzing what has happened over the past two centuries, as well as what is going on today with respect to the growth of different national economies.

Industrializing areas

Source: Steven Dorwick and J. Bradford DeLong, "Globalization and Convergence," in Michael D. Bordo, Alan M. Taylor, and Jeffrey G. Williamson, eds., *Globalization in Historical Perspective* (Chicago: University of Chicago Press, 2003).

tradition of sustained inquiry into how the world worked — free of constraints from theology — was the other.

Medieval China under the Sung Dynasty had a market economy and security of property, and Sung China did indeed produce more iron than Britain was to produce until the very end of the eighteenth century. Sung China was the heir of much technological innovation — printing, gunpowder, the compass, greatly improved forms of rice, river barges that in conjunction with the great civil engineering works like the Grand Canal made transport extraordinarily cheap — but no Scientific Revolution. Classical and Hellenistic Greece had the tradition of inquiry into how the world worked — but it would have been beneath the gentlemen who created Greek mathematics and science for them to devote themselves to improving processes of manufacture.

> **RECAP   BEFORE MODERN ECONOMIC GROWTH**
>
> Up until 1800 human populations grew very slowly, and human living standards were stagnant. After 1800 we see sustained rises in living standards. And after 1800 human numbers grew as the population explosion took hold and carried our total population to 6 billion in 2004. At first the rise in material standards of living brought sharp increases in the rate of population growth: the population explosion. But as material standards of living rose far above subsistence, countries began to undergo the demographic transition, as population growth rates peaked and began to decline toward stability.

5.2 MODERN AMERICAN ECONOMIC GROWTH

Before 1500 human material standards of living and productivity levels rose at perhaps 0.01 percent per year. Between 1500 and 1800 they rose faster in the areas that were to become the industrial core of the modern world economy — first northwestern Europe and then northwestern Europe's settler colonies in North America — rising at a rate of perhaps 0.2 percent per year. The first half of the nineteenth century saw leading-edge economies' levels of productivity rise at about 0.5 percent per year, and the second half of the century saw productivity accelerate still further.

American Long-Run Growth, 1800–1973

The Pace of Economic Growth

Let us focus on the pace of long-run growth in what has been the world's leading-edge economy for the past 100 years: the United States. Growth in the years before and after the Civil War was faster than it had been in the first half of the nineteenth century. It accelerated still further as a second wave of industrialization took hold, fueled by new inventions and innovations such as steel making, organic chemicals manufacture, oil extraction, the internal combustion engine, pasteurization, the typewriter, the cash register, and the telephone. The accelerated pace of invention and economic growth has been maintained ever since.

Late-nineteenth-century *total factor productivity* growth was, by our standards, relatively slow: at most 1 percent per year. But the capital-output ratio increased mightily as America ceased being a country of riverboats and blacksmiths and became a country of railroads and steel mills. Once the railroads were built, the possibility of supplying an entire continental market from a large factory induced the entrepreneurs and robber barons (or is that "industrial statesmen"?) of what Mark Twain called America's Gilded Age to borrow and invest. On the other side of the capital market three important factors greased the skids and made it easy for Americans to boost their savings: the development of larger and better banks, the growing use and acceptability of bonds and other securities as forms of wealth, and the development of investment banking houses like Peabody-Morgan and then J. P. Morgan to make a market by assuring business investors that the financing for expansion would be there and assuring savers that their money would not be stolen.[1] Similar patterns of growth in labor productivity driven for a couple of generations by the mobilization of savings and a resulting increase in the capital-output ratio have been seen in other times and places: Germany before World Wars I and II, Japan from 1900 to 1970, and the rest of east Asia in the years since World War II.

But, as Chapter 4 argued, eventually the capital-output ratio reaches an equilibrium value, no matter how large the boost to the national saving-investment rate. And further growth depends not on increasing capital intensity but on increases in the efficiency of labor: education, invention, and reorganization.

Throughout the nineteenth century and the first three-quarters of the twentieth century the measured pace of **productivity growth** continued to accelerate. The measured growth rate of output per worker rose from perhaps 0.5 percent per year between 1800 and 1870 to about 1.5 percent per year between 1870 and today. Growth has not been steady over that 135-year period. The growth rate was about 1.6 percent per year between 1870 and 1929 (the eve of the Great Depression), as is shown in Figure 5.5. Growth slowed slightly during the Great Depression and World War II decades — a measured growth rate of 1.4 percent per year from 1929 to 1950. But then it accelerated: The growth rate of output per worker between 1950 and 1973 in the United States was 2.1 percent per year. Next to none of the growth since 1929 was the result of increases in K/Y. Almost all of it was the result of increases in the efficiency of labor E. At least, that is what our best estimates of long-run economic growth tell us.

But should we believe what our best official and semiofficial estimates tell us? Perhaps not. Many economists believe that official estimates overstate inflation and understate real economic growth by 1 percent per year, in large part because national income accountants have a very hard time valuing the boost to productivity and standards of living generated by the invention of new goods and services. This was the conclusion reached by a blue-ribbon commission on consumer price measurement in the 1990s that was chaired by Stanford economist Michael Boskin. It is indeed very likely that true output-per-worker growth since 1870 has been even faster than our official statistics tell us. So for the average rate of output-per-worker growth in the United States since 1870, perhaps we should be thinking not of 1.5 percent per year, but rather of 2 to 2.5 percent per year.

Small differences in growth rates compounded over long periods of time make a huge difference. If Michael Boskin and his committee members are right (as we believe that they are), then those of us living in the United States today have a level of productivity — a material standard of living — somewhere between 14 and

productivity growth

The rate at which the economy's full-employment productivity expands from year to year as technology advances, as human capital increases, and as investment increases the economy's physical capital stock.

---

[1]As it sometimes was. Every student of American history should read Charles Francis Adams's *Chapters of Erie*, if only to marvel at the variety of financial frauds perpetrated by the executives of the Erie Railroad.

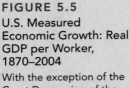

FIGURE 5.5
U.S. Measured Economic Growth: Real GDP per Worker, 1870–2004

With the exception of the Great Depression of the 1930s and the productivity growth slowdown period of the 1970s and 1980s, measured real GDP per worker in the United States has grown steadily with only minor interruptions.

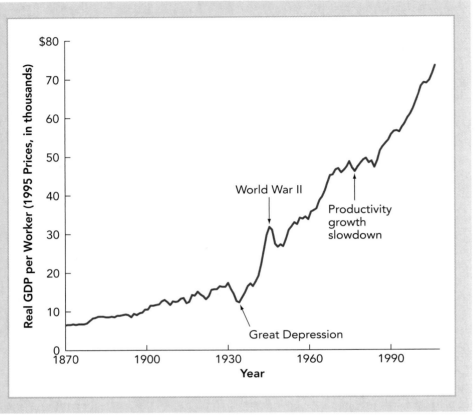

Source: Authors' calculations from the 2004 edition of *The Economic Report of the President* (Washington, DC: Government Printing Office) and from *Historical Statistics of the United States* (Washington, DC: Government Printing Office, 1975).

25 times that of our counterparts in the late nineteenth century. For middle-class and richer consumers today such an estimate does not seem at all unreasonable. It takes only one-eighth as much time to earn the money to buy a hairbrush, one-twelfth as much time to earn the money to buy a chair, and one-thirty-fifth as much time to earn the money to buy a book today as it did in 1895 (see Table 5.2). And in 1895, no matter how long you worked, you couldn't earn enough money to buy a plane ticket, a TV, an iPod, a laptop computer, an automatic washing machine, an electric blender, or a microwave oven.

Consider that Nathan Meyer Rothschild — the richest man in the world in the first half of the nineteenth century — died in his fifties of an infected abscess in his back. Who is really richer, Nathan Meyer Rothschild in his day or a working-class American today who can go to a Kaiser Permanente clinic and get some penicillin? Who has a higher standard of living: a nineteenth-century robber baron with box seats to the theater to see *The Importance of Being Earnest* or a twenty-first-century American teenager ordering DVDs online from Netflix? Thinking about truly long run economic growth leads you to ask such questions, and the benefit is not in getting a single number as an answer but in thinking about what an answer might mean.

However, for the relatively poor of the world, or even of the United States, it is not reasonable to say that their incomes and material standards of living have multiplied to nearly as great an extent as those of America's great middle class. An

TABLE 5.2
Labor-Time Costs of Commodities, 1895 and 1997

Commodity	Time to Earn (Hours)* 1895	1997	Productivity Multiple
Horatio Alger books (6 vols.)	21.0	0.6	35.0
One-speed bicycle	260.0	7.2	36.1
Cushioned office chair	24.0	2.0	12.0
100-piece dinner set	44.0	3.6	12.2
Hairbrush	16.0	2.0	8.0
Cane rocking chair	8.0	1.6	5.0
Solid gold locket	28.0	6.0	4.7
Encyclopaedia Britannica	140.0	4.0	35.0
Steinway piano	2,400.0	1,107.6	2.2
Sterling silver teaspoon	26.0	34.0	0.8
Oranges (dozen)	2.0	0.1	20.0
Ground beef (1 lb.)	0.8	0.2	4.0
Milk (1 gal.)	2.0	0.25	8.0
Television	∞	15.0	∞
Plane ticket: SFO–BOS	∞	20.0	∞
Antibiotic strep-throat cure	∞	1.0	∞
Dental X-ray	∞	2.0	∞
Laptop computer	∞	70.0	∞

*Time needed for an average worker to earn the purchase price of the commodity.

Source: 1895 Montgomery Ward catalogue and authors' calculations.

invention or innovation has no effect on people's material standard of living if they cannot afford to acquire it. The ability to fly from Minneapolis to Cancun in the middle of the winter is a very valuable thing, but only if you can afford to fly to Cancun.

Structural Change

Modern economic growth is also a shift in the kinds of things we do at work and play — in the way that we live. In the immediate aftermath of the Civil War perhaps half of all Americans were farmers. Today less than 2 percent of American workers are farmers and farm laborers; there are more gardeners, groundskeepers, and growers and maintainers of ornamental plants in the United States today than there are food-growing farmers and farm laborers. In the second half of the nineteenth century Americans traveled by foot, horse, wagon, train, and riverboat; at the end of the twentieth century, they traveled by foot (rarely), bicycle (rarely), automobile, bus, train, boat, and plane. Most Americans in the second half of the nineteenth century were literate, but very few had finished anything equivalent to today's high school. Modern economic growth is the large-scale shift of employment from agriculture to manufacturing and now to services. And it is the creation of large business organizations. At the start of the nineteenth century, a business with 100 people was a very large organization for its time.

America's Edge

Between approximately 1890 and 1930, or perhaps 1890 and 1950, a host of innovative technologies and business practices were adopted in the United States. Europeans speak of "Fordism": taking the part — Henry Ford's assembly lines in Detroit and his mass production of the Model-T Ford — for the whole. The fact that other industrial economies were unable to fully adopt American technologies of mass production and mass distribution in the first half of the twentieth century gave the United States a unique level of industrial dominance and technological leadership in the years after 1950.

This acceleration in American economic growth that placed America ahead of the rest of the industrialized countries seems, in the framework of Chapter 4, to have had two components. The first was a rise in America's investment effort propelled in part by the fact that more capital-intensive production processes — processes with a higher capital-output ratio — seemed more likely to be profitable in America, where you were serving a continent-sized market, than in Europe, where tariffs, language barriers, and other impediments to trade kept most production local and national. At some point in the late nineteenth and early twentieth centuries the American economy underwent what the late Stanford economist Moses Abramovitz and his colleague Paul David called a "great traverse" to a more capital-intensive growth path. This drive to a more capital-intensive growth path was also propelled, as Gavin Wright (yet a third Stanford economist) pointed out, by the extraordinary richness of the natural resource deposits discovered as the American continent was surveyed in the late nineteenth century.

The second component is the turn-of-the-last century acceleration in the rate of growth of the efficiency of labor, which in turn comes from two sources: the creation of the managerial and organizational structure of the modern corporation, on the one hand, and the routinization and industrialization of science and technology, on the other. When businesses began to spend serious money on their own research and development laboratories, the pace of technological innovation and thus of growth in the efficiency of labor sped up.

Why couldn't Great Britain, or the other industrial countries, maintain their lead or even keep up? Why was the twentieth century economically — and therefore also politically — an American century? Why didn't western Europe have its own Henry Ford, its own industrial R&D labs, and so forth?

Four factors appear to explain America's position at the leading edge of technology in the world economy throughout the twentieth century:

- The United States had an exceptional commitment to education — to schooling everyone (everyone who was white, that is; and boys more than girls) even in the largely rural economy of the nineteenth century and to making the achievement of a high school diploma the rule rather than the exception in the cities of the early twentieth century. An exceptionally educated workforce was the source of new ideas about how to make a better mousetrap, and it could quickly copy and adapt others' ideas as well.

- The United States was of extraordinarily large size — the largest market in the world. Thus the nation could take advantage of potential economies of scale in ways that other, smaller economies could not match. And this mattered for capital intensity.

- The United States was extraordinarily rich in natural resources, particularly energy. To the extent that energy-intensive and natural resource–intensive industries were at the heart of early-twentieth-century industrial growth, the United States was again well positioned. By contrast, western Europe had been mined over and logged for at least a millennium.

- The United States avoided fratricide. Europeans killed each other and destroyed each other's buildings and factories (and we helped) at a historically unprecedented rate in the first half of the twentieth century. Your chances of meeting a violent or unnatural death in Europe between 1914 and 1945 were greater than in any other generation we know of except perhaps for those in the paths of the armies of Genghis Khan.

In the long run, however, western Europe did catch up to the United States. There is little difference in standards of living and productivity levels between western Europe and the United States today. Americans have somewhat more things and bigger houses but work longer hours and have fewer public services; Europeans have longer vacations and better public transportation but fewer opportunities to work and a harder time living in the suburbs.

Up until 1973, with the important exception of the Great Depression, the picture of American economic growth since the Industrial Revolution seemed to be one of increasing progress at an increasing rate. The rate of increase in the efficiency of labor had jumped upward with the original Industrial Revolution, and it had jumped upward again with the coming of modern science and technology and the industrial R&D laboratory. The capital intensity of the economy had increased as businesses had sought to exploit the continent-sized market by grasping for economies of scale.

But then came 1973, and American economic growth hit a large speed bump.

American Economic Growth 1973–1995: The Productivity Growth Slowdown

In 1973 the steady trend of climbing rates of productivity growth stopped cold. Between 1950 and 1973 the rate of labor productivity growth in the United States was 2.1 percent per year. Between 1973 and 1995 measured growth in output per worker in the U.S. economy grew at only 0.6 percent per year. The slowdown did not affect the U.S. economy alone: It hit — to different degrees and with different effects — the other major economies of the world's industrial core in western Europe, Japan, and Canada as well (see Table 5.3 on page 134).

What caused the **productivity growth slowdown**? Various observers at different times have attributed this slowdown in the growth rate of productivity to four different factors: increased problems of economic measurement, environmental protection expenditures, the baby boom, and oil prices.

The first two of these are really the same thing. The argument that the productivity growth slowdown can be explained by expenditures on environmental protection is a branch of the "problems-of-measurement" argument, and it is by far the most important branch of that argument. When the price of electricity goes up because power companies switch to burning higher priced low-sulfur coal or install sulfur-removing scrubbers in their chimneys, they are producing not just electric power but electric power plus cleaner air. But the NIPA does not count pollution reduction as a valued economic output. America has spent a fortune on environmental protection in the past generation, and it has received big benefits from this investment. But these gains aren't included in measured GDP.

The surge in investment in environmental protection in the United States started just about when the productivity growth slowdown did. Nevertheless, the argument

productivity growth slowdown

The period from 1973 to about 1995 when the rate of productivity growth in the United States and other economies suddenly slowed, for still mysterious reasons.

TABLE 5.3
The Magnitude of the Post-1973 Productivity Growth Slowdown
in the G-7 Economies

Country	Output-per-Worker Annual Growth (%)	
	1950–1973	1973–1995
United States	2.1	0.6
Canada	2.7	1.6
Japan	7.4	2.6
Britain	2.4	1.8
Germany (West)	5.7	2.0
France	4.4	1.5
Italy	4.9	2.3

Source: Authors' calculations from the 2004 edition of *The Economic Report of the President* (Washington, DC: Government Printing Office).

that this can be the full rather than a partial and relatively small part of the explanation is difficult to win. The math doesn't seem to add up: The productivity growth slowdown we have experienced seems to be multiple times the size of the one that would have been expected from the redirection of investment from increasing productive capacity to environmental protection.

Aside from the failure to measure the benefits of pollution control, the rest of the argument that the productivity growth slowdown can be explained by problems of economic measurement is a bit too subtle to work. Few doubt that economic measurement entails big problems. These problems can reasonably be assumed to lead to significant understatements of the rate of economic growth. But to account for the productivity growth slowdown, the problems of measurement must have gotten worse. They must be much worse now than they were five decades ago. And how that can be true is not clear.

The third proposed explanation of the productivity growth slowdown is that in the 1970s the baby-boom generation of Americans began to enter the labor force. This generation is very large. We should know: Brad was born in 1960, the year in which more Americans were born than in any year either before or since. The relatively young labor force had many more workers with little experience than did the labor force of the 1960s and 1950s. Some economists argue that this fall in the average level of labor-force experience generated the productivity growth slowdown. Others point out that the baby-boom generation had little experience but a lot of education, and that in the past education had been a powerful booster of productivity. The average level of education in the labor force increased quite rapidly as the baby-boom generation entered the economy. Once again, this is an unlikely full explanation: Entry of the baby boomers into the labor force may be part of the answer, but the combination of their low experience and their high education makes it hard to sell the entry of the baby-boom generation as a large net reduction in labor-force quality.

The last explanation of the productivity growth slowdown is the tripling of world oil prices by the OPEC cartel in 1973, in the wake of the third Arab-Israeli war. Productivity growth slowed at almost exactly the same time that oil prices skyrocketed. Economists hypothesized that in response to the tripling of world oil prices firms began redirecting their capital expenditures from capital that produced more output to capital that used less energy; firms retired a large share of their most energy-intensive capital and began to substitute workers for energy use wherever possible.

The problem with this explanation is twofold. First, since 1986 real oil prices have been lower than they were before 1973; hence the productivity growth slowdown should have ended in the late 1980s, but it didn't. Second, energy costs are not that large a share of the typical business's costs. By the start of the 1990s the productivity growth slowdown had left America with real GDP levels about a quarter lower than they would have been had productivity growth continued at its pre-1973 rate. How could even the tripling of the price of a commodity that accounts for less than 4 percent of costs lead to a more than 25 percent reduction in output? Thus it is hard to see the oil price increases of the 1970s as a full accounting.

That an event as important as the productivity growth slowdown that started in the early 1970s remains so mysterious is extremely frustrating to economists. The causes of the productivity growth slowdown remain uncertain. The best theory combines all the others — the "a lot of different bad things happening all at once" theory. But it remains unsatisfactory.

Effects of the Productivity Growth Slowdown

At a productivity growth rate of 2.1 percent per year — the rate the United States enjoyed from 1950 to 1973 — output per worker doubles every 34 years. At the 1973–1995 growth rate of 0.6 percent per year, output per worker takes 120 years to double — three and a half times as long. Social psychologists tell us that 40-year-olds feel happiest not when their incomes are high but when their incomes are high relative to those of their households when they were growing up. Before 1973, when growth in output per worker was more rapid, most American voters felt much richer than their parents and hence were more willing to invest in social welfare programs and other liberal political initiatives. Between 1973 and 1995, slower growth made Americans feel much less well off than they had expected they would be.

Economic growth slowed sharply as a result of the productivity growth slowdown. But whether economic growth stopped for large numbers of Americans is not clear. Box 5.2 analyzes what we know about the "true" pace of economic growth during the productivity growth slowdown. The consequences of this are uncertain: Former president Jimmy Carter saw it as the origin of a national "malaise." Liberals have blamed it for a rightward shift in politics. American conservatives have blamed it for a rush to security and an unwillingness to undertake bold libertarian experiments. All have seen it as a cause of more (not necessarily unjustified) skepticism toward the government and its programs.

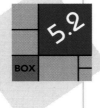

DID REAL STANDARDS OF LIVING DECLINE DURING THE SLOWDOWN PERIOD? THE DETAILS

For some categories of workers (e.g., males in their twenties with less than a high-school diploma), the productivity growth slowdown of roughly 1973 to 1995 was accompanied by stagnant or declining measured real wages. Yet offsetting this are many improvements in quality of life — from cleaner air to the convenience of automated teller machines — that the national income accounting system cannot measure.

If we accept the estimates of the mid-1980s Boskin Commission (chaired by economist Michael Boskin), we conclude that unmeasured growth in material well-being is greatly uncertain but somewhere around 1 percent per year. If this is correct, then true total product-per-worker growth in the United States has slowed not to the 0.6 percent per year recorded in official statistics for 1973–1995 but to 1.6 percent per year. This is still a substantial drop from the estimated 3.1 percent per year that the same adjustment produces for growth before 1973.

And increased income inequality has produced declines in real income or near stagnation for some groups (see Figure 5.6). But it is not true that America's output per worker stagnated for all workers over the two decades before 1995. Whether we as a society have distributed the gains in productivity to persons and households and to private and public uses wisely and appropriately — that is another question.

FIGURE 5.6
Measured Real Mean Household Income, by Quintile The era of the productivity growth slowdown saw not just slow economic growth but a widening of the American distribution of income.

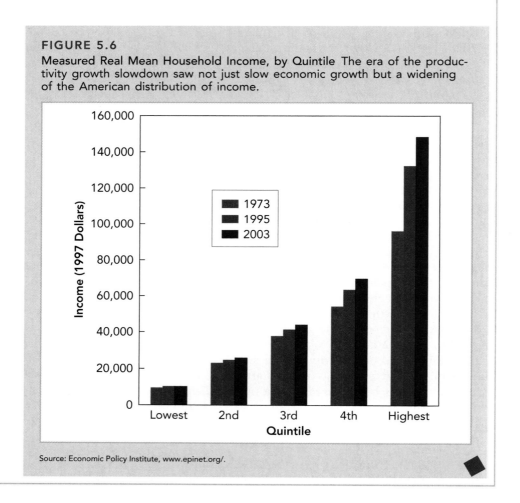

Source: Economic Policy Institute, www.epinet.org/.

Productivity Growth Speedup: The New Economy

As computers improved and spread throughout the U.S. economy in the 1970s and 1980s, economists kept waiting to see the wonders of computing show through in national productivity. But that didn't happen. The productivity growth slowdown continued throughout the 1970s and 1980s. This surprising phenomenon came to be called the "computer paradox" after Robert Solow's famous 1987 observation: "We see the computer age everywhere except in the productivity statistics." Since

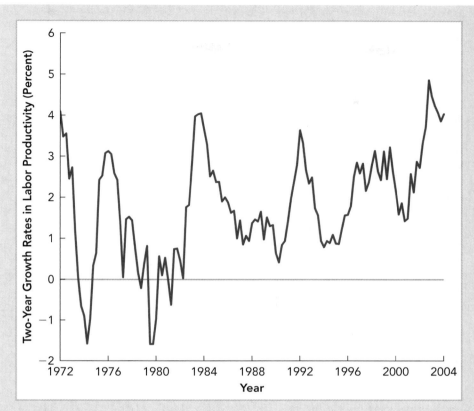

FIGURE 5.7
Two-Year Growth Rates in Labor Productivity
Trend productivity growth was low throughout the late 1970s, 1980s, and early 1990s, with the only hopeful news about productivity coming in the early stages of business-cycle recoveries. By contrast, in the late 1990s and early 2000s the news about labor productivity was good no matter what the phase of the business cycle.

Source: Authors' calculations from data available at www.bls.gov.

1995, however, labor productivity growth in the American economy has accelerated once again, first to a pace of 2.1 percent per year in the second half of the 1990s, and now to a pace of 3.5 percent per year so far in the first half of the 2000s.

The U.S. economy has benefited from a stunning investment boom since 1992. Between 1992 and 1998 real GDP rose by an average of 3.6 percent per year, and business fixed investment soared at a 10.1 percent average rate, almost three times as fast. As a consequence, the share of business fixed investment in GDP jumped from 9.2 percent to 13.2 percent, with much of the additional investment going into computers and related equipment. The consensus among economists is that the recent acceleration in productivity growth resulted from this boom in real investment, a huge share of which was driven by the rapidly falling price of computers. According to the Commerce Department's Bureau of Economic Analysis, the price of computing equipment fell by an average of 19 percent per year between 1990 and 2003. Each year the same nominal expenditure on computers bought 19 percent more in terms of real computer equipment.

Consensus opinion was tipped into believing that the post-1995 reversal of the productivity growth slowdown was a durable phenomenon by the fact that productivity growth in America despite falling somewhat during the short business-cycle recession of 2001, continued to be quite rapid throughout the period of uneven business-cycle recovery that followed in 2002, and the faster period of recovery in 2003 and 2004 as shown in Figure 5.7. The normal business cycle pattern is for productivity growth to be slow — not fast — during a recession. This normal pattern did not hold, as businesses used investment in high-tech equipment to continue to boost their productivity even when the labor market was a buyer's market.

A rapidly falling price of capital goods has the same effect on total investment as a rapidly rising saving rate. We know that the higher is the share of national product devoted to saving and gross investment — the higher is s — the higher will be the economy's balanced-growth capital-output ratio $s/(n + g + \delta)$. The same thing applies to falling prices of capital goods — in this case, the falling prices of information technology and communications equipment. Halve the price of capital goods, and you will find that in the long run you have doubled the economy's capital intensity — doubled its average ratio of capital to output — with important consequences for the level of output per worker.

One way to think about it is that, as long as the technological revolution in information technology continues and the price of computers and related goods keeps falling at an astronomical rate, the United States is undergoing a new "great traverse" — only this time it is not to a growth path with a higher ratio of industrial capital like steel mills to output, but to a growth path with a higher ratio of information capital like computer chips to output.

There is every reason to expect that technological progress in the computer and communications sectors will continue, and there is every reason to expect that these useful technologies will continue to diffuse throughout the economy. The best bet in forecasting future productivity growth is to make future projections on the basis of what has happened in the past half-decade. The productivity growth slowdown has been brought to an end by the technological revolution in computers and communications. But that is a subject to be explored further toward the end of this book, in Chapter 16.

RECAP   MODERN AMERICAN ECONOMIC GROWTH

Over the past two centuries measured economic growth in the United States has raised output per worker at an average pace of between 1.5 and 2.0 percent per year. Moreover, it is likely that true output-per-worker growth since 1890 has been even faster. Many economists believe that official estimates overstate inflation and understate real economic growth by 1.0 percent per year, in large part because national income accountants have a very hard time valuing the boost to productivity and standards of living generated by the invention of new goods and services, and new types of goods and services.

Accompanying this increase in productivity and living standards is structural change: the move from the country to the city, the large-scale shift of employment from agriculture to manufacturing and now to services, and the creation of large business organizations. Starting in 1973 the steady trend of climbing rates of productivity growth stopped cold: Between 1973 and 1995 measured growth in output per worker in the U.S. economy grew at only 0.6 percent per year. Since 1995, however, productivity growth in the American economy has accelerated once again to a pace of 2.7 percent per year, the result of an investment boom, the rapidly falling prices of computers and communications equipment, and technological advances.

5.3 MODERN ECONOMIC GROWTH AROUND THE WORLD

Divergence, Big Time

The industrial core of the world economy saw its level of material productivity and standard of living explode in the nineteenth and twentieth centuries. Elsewhere the growth of productivity levels and standards of living and the spread of industrial technologies were slower. As the industrialized economies grew while industrial technologies spread slowly elsewhere, the world became a more and more unequal place. As development economist Lant Pritchett puts it, the dominant feature of world economic history from the Industrial Revolution up until 1980 or so is "**divergence**, big time." In terms of relative incomes and productivity levels, the world today is very unequal and very divergent, as Figure 5.8 shows.

Those who live in relatively poor regions of the world today have higher material living standards than did their predecessors who lived in those regions a century ago. But the relative gap vis-à-vis the industrial core has grown extraordinarily and extravagantly. In the first half of the nineteenth century the average inhabitant of an average country had perhaps one-half the material standard of living of a citizen of the world's leading industrial economy. Although the difficulties of making such comparisons are overwhelming (and Box 5.3 provides some insight into the difficulties of making such comparisons), our best estimate is that the average inhabitant of an average country has only one-sixth the material standard of living and productivity level of a leading nation like the United States today.

divergence

The tendency for a per capita measurement such as income or standard of living in various countries to become less equal over a period of time.

The Exception: OECD Economies

Such divergence is not inevitable. The United States, with its perhaps 14- to 25-fold increase in output per worker over the years since 1870, has not been the fastest growing economy in the world. A number of other economies at different levels of industrialization, development, and material productivity a century ago have now converged, and their levels of productivity, economic structures, and standards of living today are very close to those of the United States (see Box 5.4). The six largest of these converging economies and the United States make up the so-called Group of Seven (G-7) economies. The six non-U.S. members' steady process of convergence to the U.S. level from 1950 until about 2000 is shown in Figure 5.9 on page 142.

Most of these economies were much poorer than the United States in 1870. Most were significantly poorer in 1950. The Japanese economy, for example, went from a level of output per capita equal to 16 percent of the U.S. level in 1950 to 84 percent of the U.S. level in 1992 — before falling steeply backward during Japan's recent recession. Italian levels of GDP per capita have gone from 30 to 65 percent of the U.S. level; German levels, from 40 to 75 percent; Canadian levels, from 70 to 85 percent; and British levels, from 60 to 70 percent in the past half-century.

Moreover, much of the remaining differential between the United States and western Europe is the result of different institutions and tastes for leisure; for example, western Europeans take what many Americans would regard as extravagant vacations. Much of today's differential between the United States and Japan is the result of deliberate political choice: Japan's politicians have decided to keep their agriculture-based industries and their wholesale and retail distribution systems protected from competition, small scale, and thus — from an American standpoint — inefficient.

FIGURE 5.8
World Distribution of Income, Selected Countries

In some places modern economic growth has taken hold and propelled levels of productivity and living standards upward. In other places people on average live little, if any, better than their ancestors did. The world is a more unequal place, in relative income terms, than it has been since there were some human tribes that had fire and others that did not.

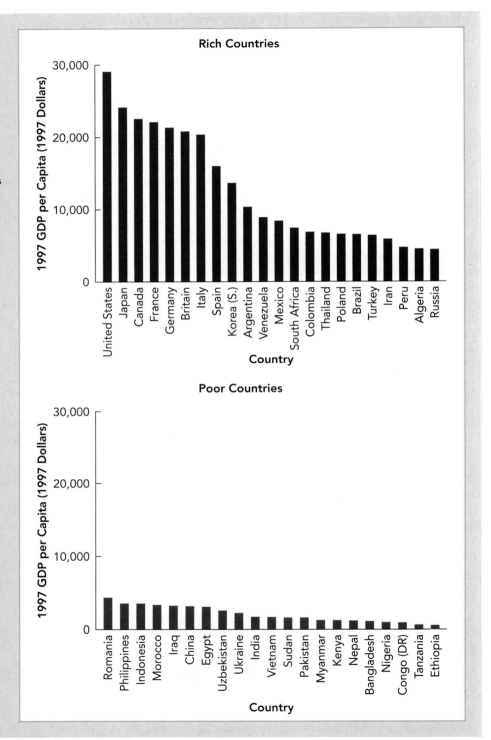

Source: Authors' calculations from Alan Heston, Robert Summers, and Bettina Aten's Penn World Table, www.nber.org.

PURCHASING-POWER-PARITY AND REAL EXCHANGE RATE COMPARISONS: SOME TOOLS

When our focus is on comparing standards of living, either across time or across countries, we get much more meaningful figures by correcting current (and even average trend) exchange rates for differences in *purchasing power parity (PPP)*. The differences between estimates of relative income levels based on current exchange rates and estimates based on PPP calculations can be very large. On a purchasing-power-parity basis GDP per worker in the United States today is some 13 times GDP per worker in India; by contrast, on an average exchange rate basis GDP per worker in the United States today is more than 70 times the level in India.

PPP-based calculations attempt (as the name implies) to translate one currency into another at a rate that preserves average purchasing power. But current exchange rates do not preserve purchasing power. If you exchange your dollars in the United States for rupees in India you will find that your rupees in India will buy about the same amount of internationally traded manufactured goods as your dollars would have bought in the United States. (Unless, of course, you try to buy something that the Indian government has decided to put up a trade barrier against.) But your rupees in India will buy you vastly more in the way of personal services, the products of skilled craftspeople, and any other labor-intensive goods and services.

Why? International *arbitrage* keeps the exchange rate at the level that makes easily traded manufactured goods roughly equally expensive. If they weren't, someone could make an easy fortune by shipping them from where they were cheap to where they were dear. But how — in this world of stringent immigration restrictions — can a cook in Bangalore take advantage of the fact that there is fierce demand in Marin County, north of San Francisco, for caterers who can prepare a good curry? Because relative productivity levels in labor services are much more equal than relative productivity levels in manufacturing, living standards throughout the world are more equal than exchange rate–based calculations suggest.

WHY HAVE THESE ECONOMIES CONVERGED? A POLICY

By and large the economies that have converged are those that belong to the *Organization for Economic Cooperation and Development (OECD)*, which was started shortly after World War II, in the days of the Marshall Plan, as a group of countries that received (or gave) Marshall Plan aid to help rebuild and reconstruct after the war. Countries that received Marshall Plan aid adopted a common set of economic policies: large private sectors freed of government regulation of prices, investment with its direction determined by profit-seeking businesses, large social insurance systems to redistribute income, and governments committed to avoiding mass unemployment.

The original OECD members all wound up with *mixed economies*. In these, markets direct the flow of resources, while governments stabilize the economy, provide social insurance safety nets, and encourage entrepreneurship and enterprise. The member nations arrived at this setup largely due to good luck, partly due to the Cold War, and partly as a result of post–World War II institutional reforms.

This configuration was essentially the price countries had to pay for receiving Marshall Plan aid. The U.S. executive branch was unwilling to send much aid to countries that it thought were likely to engage in destructive economic policies, largely because it did not believe that it could win funding from the Republican-dominated Congress for a Marshall Plan that did not impose such strict conditionality upon recipients. By contrast, countries that were relatively rich after World War II but did not adopt OECD-style institutional arrangements — such as Argentina and Venezuela — lost relative ground.

As the OECD economies became richer, they completed their demographic transitions: Population growth rates fell. The policy emphasis on entrepreneurship and enterprise boosted national investment rates, so the OECD economies all had healthy investment rates as well. These factors boosted their equilibrium capital-output ratios. And the diffusion of technology from the United States did the rest of the job in bringing OECD standards of economic productivity close to the U.S. level.

The G-7 economies have not been the only ones to buck the global trend. As Box 5.5 shows, the east Asian economies have also "converged."

The Rule: Divergence behind the Iron Curtain

But convergence is the exception. Divergence is the rule. And perhaps the most important driving force behind divergence is communism: Being unlucky enough

FIGURE 5.9

Convergence among the G-7 Economies: Output per Capita as a Share of U.S. Level

In 1950 GDP per capita levels in the six nations that now are America's partners in the G-7 varied from 20 percent of the U.S. level (Japan) to 70 percent of the U.S. level (Canada). Today estimates of GDP per capita place levels in all six at more than 65 percent of the U.S. level — and they would be even closer to the U.S. level if the measurements took account of the shorter average work year abroad.

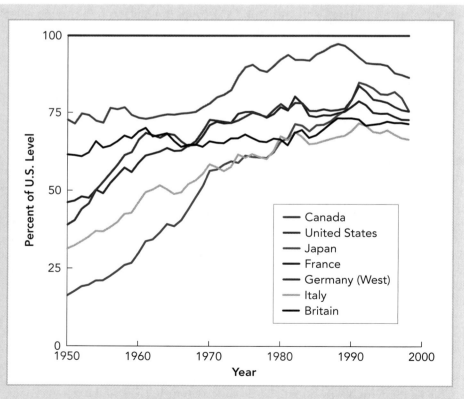

Source: Authors' calculations from Alan Heston, Robert Summers, and Bettina Aten's Penn World Table, www.nber.org.

THE EAST ASIAN MIRACLE: POLICY

The story of extraordinarily successful economies goes beyond the original OECD nations. The economies of the *"east Asian miracle"* have over the past two generations exhibited stronger growth than has ever before been seen anywhere in the world. They have not yet converged to the standards of living and levels of economic productivity found in the world economy's industrial core, but they are converging.

Immediately before World War II the regions that are now South Korea, Hong Kong, Singapore, and Taiwan had output-per-worker levels less than one-tenth the level of the United States. Today Singapore's GDP per capita is 90 percent, Hong Kong's is 70 percent, Taiwan's is 50 percent, and South Korea's is 45 percent of the U.S. level. A second wave of east Asian economies — Malaysia and Thailand — now average more than one-quarter of the U.S. level of GDP per capita.

The successful east Asian economies share a number of similarities with the OECD economies in terms of economic policy and structure. Resource allocation decisions are by and large left to the market. Governments regard the encouragement of entrepreneurship and enterprise as a major goal. And high saving and investment rates are encouraged by a number of different government policies.

Yet there are also a number of differences vis-à-vis the OECD. Governments in east Asia have been more aggressive in pursuing industrial policy and somewhat less aggressive in establishing social insurance systems than have the OECD economies. However, they have also had more egalitarian income distributions and hence less need for redistribution and social insurance. They have subsidized corporations that they believe are strategic for economic development, thinking that their bureaucrats know better than the market — heresy to economists. (However, it is worth noting that they have focused subsidies on the companies that have proved successful at exporting goods to other countries, so their bureaucrats have in a sense been rewarding the judgment of *foreign* markets.) The examples of successful catching up suggest that growth could have been faster in the world economy. Economies — even very poor ones — *can* rapidly adopt modern machine technologies and move their productivity levels close to first-world leading-edge standards.

to have been ruled by communists in the twentieth century is a virtual guarantee of relative poverty.

Winston Churchill once labeled a snaky geographic line across Eurasia the "Iron Curtain." On one side were regimes that owed their allegiance to Karl Marx and to Marx's viceroys on Earth. On the other side were regimes that claimed, in the 1946–1989 Cold War, to be of the "free world" — regimes that were, if not good, at least less bad. Walk this geographic line from Poland to Korea and then hop over to the only Western hemisphere communist satellite, Cuba, looking first at the level of material welfare in the communist countries and then at the level of material welfare in the noncommunist countries. The location of the Iron Curtain is a historical accident: It is where Stalin's Russian armies stopped after World War II, where Mao's Chinese armies stopped in the early 1950s, and where Giap's Vietnamese armies stopped in the mid-1970s.

TABLE 5.4
The Iron Curtain: GDP-per-Capita Levels of Matched Pairs of Countries

East-Bloc Country	GDP per Capita	Matched West-Bloc Country	GDP per Capita	Relative Gap (%)
North Korea	$ 700	South Korea	$13,590	94
China	3,130	Taiwan	14,170	78
Vietnam	1,630	Philippines	3,520	54
Cambodia	1,290	Thailand	6,690	81
FSR Georgia	1,960	Turkey	6,350	69
Russia	4,370	Finland	20,150	78
Bulgaria	4,010	Greece	12,769	69
Slovenia	11,800	Italy	20,290	42
Hungary	7,200	Austria	22,070	67
Czech Republic	10,510	Germany	21,260	51
Poland	6,520	Sweden	19,790	67
Cuba	3,100	Mexico	8,370	63

Source: Authors' calculations from Alan Heston, Robert Summers, and Bettina Aten's Penn World Table, www.nber.org.

Notice as you walk that outside the Iron Curtain, the countries are far better off in terms of GDP per capita (see Table 5.4). They are not necessarily better off in education, health care, or the degree of income inequality. If you were in the poorer half of the population, you probably received a better education and had access to better medical care in Cuba than in Mexico. But the countries fortunate enough to lie outside what was the Iron Curtain were and are vastly more prosperous. Depending on how you count and how unlucky you are, between 40 and 94 percent of the potential material prosperity of a country was annihilated if it happened to fall under communist rule in the twentieth century. The fact that a large part of the globe was under communist rule in the twentieth century is one major reason for the world's divergence. A failure to successfully aid postcommunist economies in their transition would be a further blow, and, as Box 5.6 discusses, "transition" is not going well.

The Rule: Divergence in General

Even if attention is confined to non–communist-ruled economies, there still has been enormous divergence in relative output-per-worker levels over the past 100 years. Since 1870, the ratio of richest to poorest economies has increased sixfold. In 1870 two-thirds of all countries had GDP-per-capita levels between 60 and 160 percent of the average. Today the range that includes two-thirds of all countries extends from 35 to 280 percent of the average.

There is reason to hope that the era of widening world income and productivity gaps is over. China for the past 25 and India for the past 20 years have begun to grow much faster than before, and to begin the process of catching up to the world's industrial leaders. Together they are home to nearly 40 percent of the human race.

POSTCOMMUNISM: POLICY

The demolition of the Berlin Wall and the elimination of the Iron Curtain have not significantly improved the situation in what are euphemistically and optimistically called "economies in transition" (from socialism to capitalism, that is). Figuring out how to move from a stagnant, ex-communist economy to a dynamic, growing one is very difficult, and no one has ever done it before.

A few of the economies in transition appear to be on the path toward rapid convergence with western Europe: Slovenia, Hungary, the Czech Republic, and Poland have already successfully maneuvered through enough of the transition phase to have advanced their economies beyond the point reached before 1989. It seems clear that their economic destiny is to become, effectively, part of western Europe. Slovakia, Lithuania, Latvia, and Estonia appear to have good prospects of following their example.

Elsewhere, however, the news is bad. Whether reforms have taken place step-by-step or all at once, whether ex-communists have been excluded from or have dominated the government, and whether governments have been nationalist or internationalist, the results have been similar. Output has fallen, corruption has been rife, and growth has not resumed. Material standards of living in Ukraine today are less than half of what they were when General Secretary Gorbachev ruled from Moscow.

Economists debate ferociously the appropriate economic strategy for unwinding the inefficient centrally planned Soviet-style economy. The fact that such a transition has never been undertaken before should make advice givers cautious. And one other observation should make advice givers depressed: The best predictor of whether an eastern European country's transition will be rapid and successful or not appears to be its distance from western European political and financial capitals like Vienna, Frankfurt, and Stockholm.

Sources of Divergence

The principal cause of the extraordinary variation in output per worker between countries today is differences in their respective equilibrium capital-output ratios. Two secondary causes are, first, openness to creating and adapting the technologies that enhance the efficiency of labor as measured by levels of development two generations ago and, second, the level of education today.

Productivity two generations ago is a good indicator of the level of technological knowledge that had been acquired as of a half-century ago. The level of education today captures the country's ability to invent and acquire further technological expertise today. Without education, inventing new and adopting foreign technological knowledge are simply not possible.

Global Patterns

Together these factors — the determinants of capital intensity (the capital-output ratio) and the two determinants of access to technology — account for the bulk of the differences between countries in their relative productivity levels.

The determinants of the equilibrium capital-output ratio play a very powerful role. A higher share of investment in national product is powerfully correlated with relative levels of output per worker. No country with an investment rate of less than 10 percent has an output-per-worker level even 20 percent that of the United

States. No country with an investment share of less than 20 percent has an output-per-worker level greater than 75 percent of the U.S. level.

A high level of labor-force growth is correlated, albeit less powerfully, with a low level of output per worker. The average country with a labor-force growth rate of more than 3 percent per year has an output-per-worker level of less than 20 percent of the U.S. level. The average country with a labor-force growth rate of less than 1 percent has an output-per-worker level that is greater than 60 percent of the U.S. level.

Together these determinants of the equilibrium capital-output ratio can, statistically, account for up to half of the variation in national economies' levels of productivity per worker in the world today. The power of these factors is central to the theoretical model of economic growth presented in Chapter 4 and should not be underestimated. Indeed, their power is the reason we spent so much space on the standard growth model in Chapter 4.

But the factors stressed in Chapter 4 are not the only major determinants of relative wealth and poverty in the world today. Differences in the efficiency of labor are as important as differences in equilibrium capital-output ratios. Differences in the efficiency of labor arise from the differential ability of workers to handle and utilize modern technologies. The efficiency of labor is high where education levels are high — so workers can use the modern technologies they are exposed to — and where economic contact with the industrial core is high — so workers and managers are exposed to the modern technologies invented in the world's R&D laboratories.

Schooling is the variable that has the strongest correlation with output per worker. Countries that have an average of four to six years of schooling have output-per-worker levels that average 20 percent of the U.S. level. Those with an average level of schooling of more than 10 years have output-per-worker levels of 65 percent of the U.S. level, as Figure 5.10 shows.

No single best indicator exists of a country's exposure to — and thus ability to adopt and adapt — the technologies invented in the industrial core that amplify the efficiency of labor. Some economists focus on trade and foreign investment as the main sources of increased efficiency and technological capability. Others focus on geographic and climatic factors that have influenced migration and still influence trade and intellectual exchange. Still others focus on institutions of governance and their effect on entrepreneurship as the key variable. But as much as economists dispute which variables are most important as determinants of *technology transfer* and the efficiency of labor, all agree that all these variables are important indeed to understanding why our world today is the way it is.

Cause and Effect, Effect and Cause

All the factors discussed are both causes and effects. High population growth and low levels of output per worker go together both because rapid population growth reduces the equilibrium capital-output ratio and because poor countries have not yet undergone their demographic transitions. This interaction — in which a high rate of population growth reduces the equilibrium capital-output ratio and a low equilibrium capital-output ratio means that the demographic transition is not far advanced — creates a vicious spiral that reinforces relative poverty.

Moreover, demography is not the only vicious spiral potentially present. A poor country must pay a high relative price for the capital equipment it needs to acquire in order to turn its saving into productive additions to its capital stock. This should

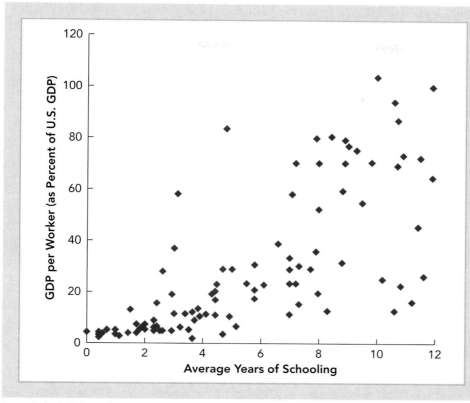

FIGURE 5.10

GDP-per-Worker Levels and Average Years of Schooling

Countries with a high number of average years of schooling have a better chance of being relatively well off. Education opens the door to acquiring the technologies of the Industrial Revolution.

Source: Authors' calculations from Alan Heston, Robert Summers, and Bettina Aten's Penn World Table, www.nber.org.

come as no surprise. The world's most industrialized and prosperous economies are the most industrialized and prosperous because they have attained very high levels of manufacturing productivity: Their productivity advantage in unskilled service industries is much lower than that in capital- and technology-intensive manufactured goods. The higher relative price of machinery in developing countries means that poor countries get less investment — a smaller share of total investment in real GDP — out of any given effort at saving some fixed share of their incomes.

Moreover, to the extent that education is an important kind of investment, a good education is much harder to provide in a poorer country. Even primary education requires at its base a teacher, some books, and a classroom — things that are relatively cheap and easy for a rich country to provide but expensive for a poor country. In western Kenya today the average primary school classroom has 0.4 book per pupil.

But virtuous circles are also possible. Anything that increases productivity and sets the demographic transition in motion will reduce the rate of growth of the labor force, increase the amount of investment bought by any given amount of saving, and make education easier.

How important are these vicious spirals and virtuous circles? It is hard to look at the cross-country pattern of growth over the past century without thinking that such vicious spirals and virtuous circles must have been very important. Otherwise, the massive divergence in relative productivity levels seems inexplicable.

> ### RECAP   MODERN ECONOMIC GROWTH AROUND THE WORLD
>
> The industrial core of the world economy saw its level of material productivity and standards of living explode in the nineteenth and twentieth centuries. Elsewhere the growth of productivity levels and standards of living and the spread of industrial technologies were slower, and the gap between rich and poor countries has widened enormously over the past century.
>
> High population growth and low levels of output per worker go together both because rapid population growth reduces the equilibrium capital-output ratio and because poor countries have not yet undergone their demographic transitions, which lower population growth. Low investment rates and low levels of output per worker go together both because low investment reduces the equilibrium capital-output ratio and because poor countries face adverse terms of trade and high prices for capital goods, which make investment difficult and expensive. Thus the obstacles to rapid growth in many poor countries in the world today are overwhelming.

5.4 POLICIES AND LONG-RUN GROWTH

Hopes for Convergence

Relative and Absolute Stagnation

Always keep in mind that in the context of economic growth "stagnation" and "failure" are relative terms. Consider Argentina once again, for it has been one of the world's most disappointing performers in terms of economic growth in the twentieth century. Argentina has experienced substantial economic growth. Officially measured labor productivity or national product per capita in Argentina today is perhaps three times what it was in 1900. True productivity, taking adequate account of the value of new commodities, is higher. But the much more smoothly running engine of capitalist development in Norway — no more, and probably less, rich and productive than Argentina in 1900 — has multiplied measured national product per capita there by a factor of 9.

A pattern of productivity growth like Argentina's is heartbreakingly slow when compared to what, reasonably, might have been and was achieved by the world's industrial leaders. What is bad about falling behind, or falling further behind, is not that second place is a bad place to be — it is false to think that the only thing that matters is to be top nation and that it is better to be poor but first than rich but second. What is bad about falling behind is that the world's industrial leaders provide an easily viewable benchmark of how things might have been different and of how much better things might have been. There was no destiny keeping Buenos Aires today from looking like and having its people as rich as those of Paris, Toronto, or Sydney.

Half Empty and Half Full

In many respects, it is decidedly odd that the world distribution of output per worker is as unequal as it is. World trade, migration, and flows of capital should all work to move resources and consumption goods from where they are cheap to where they are dear. As they travel with increasing speed and increasing volume as transportation and communication costs fall, these commodity and factor-of-production flows should erode differences in productivity and living standards between national economies. Moreover, most of the edge in standards of living and productivity levels held by the industrial core is no one's private property but, instead, is the common intellectual and scientific heritage of humankind. Hence every poor economy has an excellent opportunity to catch up with the rich by adopting and adapting from this open storehouse of modern machine technology.

We can view this particular glass either as half empty or as half full. Half full is that much of the world has already made the transition to sustained economic growth. Most people today live in economies that, while far poorer than the leading-edge postindustrial nations of the world's economic core, have successfully climbed onto the escalator of economic growth and thus the escalator to modernity. The economic transformation of most of the world is less than a century behind that of the leading-edge economies — only an eyeblink behind from the perspective of the six millennia since the spread of agriculture out of the Middle East's fertile crescent.

Moreover, perhaps we can look forward to a future in which convergence of relative income levels will finally begin to take place. The bulk of humanity is now achieving material standards of living at which the demographic transition takes hold. As population growth rates in developing countries fall, their capital-output ratios will begin to rise quickly. With tolerable government, reasonable security of property, and better ways of achieving an education, their output-per-worker levels and material standards of living will converge to the world's leading edge.

Half empty is that we live today in the most unequal age — in terms of the divergence in the life prospects of children born into different economies — that the world has ever seen. One and a half billion people today live in economies that have not made the transition to intensive economic growth and have not climbed onto the escalator to modernity. It is very hard to argue that the median inhabitant of Africa is any better off in material terms than his or her counterpart of a generation ago.

Policies for Saving, Investment, and Education

Any government can adopt policies that boost *national saving*, improve the ability to translate saving into productive investment, and accelerate the demographic transition.

Saving and Investment

Policies that ensure savers get reasonable rates of return on their savings have the potential to boost the saving rate. By contrast, systems of economic governance in which profits are diverted into the hands of the politically powerful through restrictions on entrepreneurship tend over time to diminish saving, as do economic policies that divert the real returns to savings into the hands of financiers or the government through inflation. Government deficits also have the potential to reduce the saving rate: Unless consumers and investors are farsighted enough to recognize that a government deficit now means a tax increase later, a government that spends more than it raises in revenue must borrow — and the amount borrowed is not a contribution to total national saving because it is not available to fund investment.

A number of potential policies work to boost investment for a given amount of saving. Policies that welcome foreign investors' money have the potential to cut a decade or a generation off the time needed to industrialize — if the foreign-funded capital is used wisely. Free-trade policies that allow businesses to freely earn and spend the foreign exchange they need to purchase new generations of machinery and equipment are an effective way of boosting investment. Policies that impose heavy tariffs or require scarce import licenses in order to purchase foreign-made capital equipment are a sure sign that a country will not get its money's worth out of a given nominal savings share but will, instead, find that real investment remains low. Indeed, many of the most successful developing states have done the opposite. They have provided large subsidies to fund investment and expansion by businesses that have demonstrated their competence and productivity by successfully exporting and thus competing in the world market.

Education

Universal education, especially of girls, pays a twofold benefit. Investments are more likely to be productive with a better educated workforce to draw on; hence investments are more likely to be made. Educated women are likely to want at least as much education for their children as they had, and they are likely to have relatively attractive opportunities outside the home, so the birthrate is likely to fall.

The developing countries of the world appear, for the most part, to be going through the demographic transition faster than the economies of today's industrial core did in the past three centuries. Thus current estimates of the world's population in 2050 are markedly lower than the estimates of a decade ago. Ten years ago the projected global population in 2050 was 16 billion or more; today it is 12 billion or less. This is due, in part at least, to rapid expansions in educational attainment in today's developing economies.

A high level of educational attainment also raises the efficiency of labor both by teaching skills directly and by making it easier to advance the general level of technological expertise. A leading-edge economy with a high level of educational attainment is likely to have more inventions. A follower economy with a high level of educational attainment is likely to have a more successful time at adapting to local conditions the inventions and innovations from the industrial core of the world economy. How large these effects are at the macroeconomic level is uncertain, but that they are there nobody doubts.

The east Asian economies, especially, provide examples of how uncorrupt and well-managed developing states can follow macroeconomic policies that accelerate economic growth and convergence. These economies, which have provided incentives to accelerate the demographic transition and boost saving and investment, have managed to close the gap vis-à-vis the world economy's industrial core faster than anyone would have believed possible.

Policies for Technological Advance

Without better technology, increases in capital stock produced by investment rapidly run into diminishing returns. And without improvements in the "technologies" of organization, government, and education, productivity stagnates.

Somewhat surprisingly, economists have relatively little to say about what governs technological progress. Why did better technology raise living standards by 2 percent annually two generations ago but by less than 1 percent during the subsequent two decades? Why did technology progress by only 0.25 percent per year in the early 1800s? Improving literacy, communications, and research and development may help explain faster progress since the Industrial Revolution than before it and faster progress in the twentieth than in the nineteenth century. Yet, as noted above, as important a feature of recent economic history as the 1973–1995 productivity growth slowdown remains largely a mystery.

Invention and Innovation

Economists note that technological progress has two components: science (solid-state physics and the invention of the transistor, the mapping of the human genome, the discovery that potassium nitrate, sulfur, and charcoal when mixed together and exposed to heat have interesting properties) and research and development that lead to successful innovation. About pure science economists have almost nothing to say. About research and development, and the innovations it generates, economists have rather more to say.

Economists note that perhaps 75 percent of all U.S. scientists and engineers work on research and development for private firms. R&D spending amounts to about 3 percent of GDP in the United States and other advanced industrial economies. One-fifth of total gross investment is research and development. More than half of net investment is research and development — investments in knowledge, as opposed to investments in machinery, equipment, structures, and infrastructure.

Businesses conduct investments in R&D to increase their profits. Firms spend money on R&D for reasons analogous to those that lead them to expand their capacity or improve their factories. If the expected present value of profits from an R&D project at the prevailing rate is greater than the costs of the project, then the business will spend money on the project. If not, then it will not.

Rivalry and Excludability

But some features of technology make thinking about the R&D process more complicated than thinking about other types of investment. First and most important, research and development is a public good. A firm that has discovered something — a new and more profitable process, a new and better way of organizing the factory, a new type of commodity that can be produced — will not reap the entire social benefit from its discovery. Other businesses can examine the innovation — the product, the process, the method of organization — and copy it. They can probably do so for a much lower cost than was needed to research and develop the innovation in the first place.

By contrast, a firm that has just spent a large sum to buy and move into a new building does not have to worry that any other firm will use that building as well. As a commodity, a building — or a machine, or even the skills and experience inside a worker's head — is both rival and excludable. To say that a commodity is rival means that if one firm is using it, another firm cannot do so: I cannot use that hammer to pound this nail if you are now using it to pound that other nail. To say that a commodity is excludable means that the "owner" of the commodity can easily monitor who is using it and can easily keep those whom he or she does not authorize from using it.

Most physical commodities are (or, with the assistance of the legal system, can easily be made) both rival and excludable. But by their nature ideas are not. Ideas are definitely not rival — nothing in the physical universe makes it impossible for me to use the same idea you are using. And ideas are hard to make excludable as well: How can you keep me from thinking what I want to think?

Patents and Copyrights

patent laws and copyrights

Laws designed to encourage invention and innovation by providing the right to exclude anyone else from using a discovery (patent) or intellectual property (copyright) for a period of years.

To protect ideas and intellectual property in general, countries have **patent laws and copyrights.** In fact, one of the few enumerated powers that the U.S. Constitution gives Congress is the power to set up limited-term patent and copyright laws. Patents give a firm that has discovered something new the right to exclude anyone else from using that discovery for a period of years. But even the strictest patent and copyright laws are incomplete. Often the most valuable part of the R&D process is figuring out not how to do something but whether it (or something very close to it) can be done at all. Once a patent has been granted, other firms can and do search for alternative ways of making it or ways of making something close to it that are not covered by the patent.

Governments seeking to establish patent laws face a difficult dilemma. If their patent laws are strong, then much of the modern technology in the economy will be restricted in use. Technology may be restricted to being used only by the inventor or restricted because the inventor is allowed to charge other firms high licensing fees to use it (or to not let them use it at all). Letting everyone use the idea or the process or the innovation, once it is discovered, entails no social cost. Information, after all, wants to be free. Thus a government that enacts strict patent laws is pushing the average level of technology used in its factories and businesses at some particular moment far below the level that could be achieved at that particular moment.

On the other hand, if the patent laws are weak and thus provide little protection to inventors and innovators, then the profits that inventors and innovators earn will be low. Why then should businesses devote money and resources to research and development? They will not. And the pace of innovation, and thus of technological improvement, will slow to a crawl.

This dilemma cannot be evaded. The profits from innovation derive from the innovator's monopoly right to the innovation — and hence the rest of the economy is excluded from using that item of technology. Reduce the degree of exclusion to lower the deadweight loss from using less-than-best-practice technology, and you will find that you have reduced the rewards to research and development (and thus presumably the pace of R&D as well). Increase the strength of the patent system to raise the rewards to research and development, and you will find that you have increased the gap between the average technology used in the economy and the feasible best practice.

Moreover, technological progress depends on more than the appropriability of research — the extent to which the increased productivity made possible by innovation boosts the profits of the innovating firm. It also depends on the productivity of research: How much in the way of new productivity-enhancing inventions is produced by a given investment in R&D? Economists don't know much about the interactions among product development, applied research, and basic research, so they have little to say about how to improve the productivity of research and the pace of productivity growth.

Government Failure

That governments can assist in growth and development does not mean that governments will. The broad experience of growth in developing economies — outside the Asian Pacific Rim, outside the OECD — has been that governments often won't.

Over the past two decades many have argued that typical systems of regulation in developing countries have retarded development by

- Embarking on "prestige" industrialization programs that keep resources from shifting to activities in which the country has a long-run comparative advantage.
- Inducing firms and entrepreneurs to devote their energies to seeking rents by lobbying governments, instead of seeking profits by lowering costs.
- Creating systems of regulation and project approval that have degenerated into extortion machines for manufacturing bribes for the bureaucrats.

Many governments — particularly unelected governments — are not that interested in economic development. Giving valuable industrial franchises to the nephews of the dictator; making sure that members of your ethnic group are in key places to extort bribes; or taking the foreign exchange that would have been spent importing productive machinery and equipment and using it instead to buy more modern weapons for the army — these can seem more attractive options. In the absence of political democracy, the checks on a government that does not seek economic development are few.

Moreover, checks on government that do exist may not be helpful. In a nondemocracy, or a shaky semidemocracy, government faces two possible sources of pressure: riots in the capital and coups by the soldiers. Even a government that seeks only the best for its people in terms of economic growth will have to deal with these sources of pressure and will have to avoid riots in the capital and coups by the soldiers.

Riots in the capital are best avoided by making sure that the price of food is low and that influential opinion leaders in the capital are relatively happy with their material standards of living. Coups by the soldiers are best avoided by spending money on the military. Thus governments find themselves driven to policies that redistribute income from the farms to the cities, from exporting businesses to urban consumers of imported goods, from those who have the power to invest and make the economy grow to those who have the power to overthrow the government.

If the rulers have the worst of motives, government degenerates into kleptocracy: rule by the thieves. If government has the best of motives, it is still hard to avoid policies that diminish saving and retard the ability to translate saving into productive investment. W. W. Rostow recounts a visit by President Kennedy to Indonesia in the early 1960s; Kennedy talked about economic development and a South Asian Development Bank to provide capital for Indonesia's economic growth. Indonesia's then-dictator, Sukarno, responded, "Mr. President, development takes too long. Give me West Irian [province, the western half of the island of New Guinea, to annex] instead."

Taken as a group, the poor countries of the world have not closed any of the gap relative to the world's industrial leaders since World War II.

Neoliberalism

Much thinking about the proper role of government in economic growth over the past two decades has led to conclusions that are today called neoliberal. The government has a sphere of core competencies — administration of justice, maintenance of macroeconomic stability, avoidance of deep recessions, some infrastructure development, provision of social insurance — at which it is effective. But there is a large area of potential activities in which governments (or, at least, governments that do not have the bureaucratic honesty and efficiency needed for a successful developing state) are more likely to be destructive than constructive, hence the neoliberal recommendation that governments attempt to shrink their role back to their core competencies and thus to deregulate industries and privatize public enterprises. Whether such policies will in fact lead to convergence rather than continued divergence is still an open question.

RECAP   POLICIES AND LONG-RUN GROWTH

Most people today live in economies that, while far poorer than the leading-edge postindustrial nations of the world's economic core, have successfully climbed onto the escalator of economic growth and thus the escalator to modernity. A follower economy with a higher level of educational attainment is likely to have a much more successful time at adapting to local conditions inventions and innovations from the industrial core of the world economy. Thus education appears to be a key policy for successful economic growth outside the industrial core. Inside the industrial core, without better technology increases in the capital stock produced by investment rapidly run into diminishing returns. One-fifth of total gross investment is research and development. More than half of net investment is research and development — investment in knowledge, as opposed to investment in machinery, equipment, structures, and infrastructure.

That governments *can* assist in growth and development does not mean that governments *will*. Many governments — particularly unelected governments — are not that interested in economic development. In the absence of political democracy, the checks on a government that does not seek economic development are few.

Chapter Summary

1. Before the commercial revolution (1500 or so) economic growth was very slow. Populations grew at a glacial pace. And as best we can tell there were no significant increases in standards of living for millennia before 1500: Humanity was caught in a Malthusian trap.

2. The way out of the Malthusian trap opened about 1500. Thereafter populations grew, and standards of living and levels of material productivity grew as well.

3. The Industrial Revolution was the start of the current epoch: the epoch of modern economic growth. Beginning in the mid-eighteenth century the pace of invention and innovation ratcheted up. Key inventions

replaced muscle with machine power, and material productivity levels boomed.

4. Modern economic growth is well described by the growth model in Chapter 4, which is why we spent so much time on it. Output per worker and capital per worker increase at a pace measured in percent per year, a pace that is extraordinarily rapid in long-term historical perspective.

5. Productivity growth rates slowed down worldwide after 1973, causing living standards to rise more slowly in the 1970s and 1980s than they otherwise would have. Several explanations have been offered for the productivity growth slowdown, but economists generally agree the causes remain a mystery.

6. Productivity growth rates sped up after 1995 and continue at this higher pace. The acceleration was due to a boom in real investment in computers and related equipment, driven largely by the decline in prices of computers.

7. Looked at across nations, the world today is an astonishingly unequal place in relative terms. The relative gap between rich and poor nations in material productivity is much greater than it has ever been before.

8. Combining the determinants of the balanced-growth capital-output ratio with the proximate determinants —

the level of technological knowledge in a country after World War II and its average level of educational attainment — accounts for the overwhelming bulk of variation in the relative wealth and poverty of nations today.

9. Macro policies to increase economic growth are policies to accelerate the demographic transition (through education), to boost saving rates, to boost the amount of real investment that a country gets for a given saving rate, and (again through education) to boost the rate of invention or of technology transfer.

Key Terms

Industrial Revolution (p. 120)

resource scarcity (p. 122)

Malthusian age (p. 124)

demographic transition (p. 124)

productivity growth (p. 129)

productivity growth slowdown (p. 133)

divergence (p. 139)

patent laws and copyrights (p. 152)

Analytical Exercises

1. Why do many economists think that the consumer price index overstates the true rate of inflation?

2. Would an increase in the saving and investment share of U.S. total output raise productivity growth and living standards?

3. Many observers project that by the end of the twenty-first century the population of the United States will be stable. Using the Solow growth model, what would such a downward shift in the growth rate of the labor force do to the growth of output per worker and to the growth of total output? Consider both the effect on the balanced-growth equilibrium path *and* the transition from the "old" positive population growth to the "new" zero population growth balanced-growth path.

4. What are the arguments for having a strong patent system to boost economic growth? What are the arguments for having a weak system of protections of intellectual property? Under what systems do you think that the first will outweigh the second? Under what circumstances do you think that the second will outweigh the first?

5. What steps do you think that international organizations — the U.N., the World Bank, or the IMF — could

take to improve political leaders' incentives to follow growth-promoting policies?

6. Suppose somebody who hasn't taken any economics courses asks you why humanity escaped from the Malthusian trap of very low standards of living and slow population growth rates, which nevertheless put pressure on available natural resources and kept output per worker from rising, in which humanity found itself between 8000 BC and AD 1800. What answer would you give?

7. Suppose somebody who hasn't taken any economics courses asks you why some countries are so very, very much poorer than others in the world today. What answer would you give?

8. The endogenous growth theorists, led by Stanford's Paul Romer, argue that separating the determinants of the efficiency of labor from investment is a mistake, because investment both raises the capital-worker ratio and increases the efficiency of labor as workers learn about the new technology installed with the purchase of new, modern capital goods. If the endogenous growth theorists are correct, is the case for government policies to boost national saving and investment rates strengthened or weakened? Why?

Policy Exercises

1. Look in the back of this book, after page 554, at the rate of growth of real GDP per worker in the United States over the past 10 years. Guess what the average magnitude of annual fluctuations in growth about its trend rate are. How large was the "trend" component of growth in the past year? How large was the "cycle" component of growth in the past year?

2. Take a look at the first three columns of the "U.S. Macroeconomic Data" table at the back of the book, after page 554. Identify the years that are business cycle peaks — years that are followed by a decline in real GDP or real GDP per worker. Are the two possible sets of business cycle peaks the same? Calculate economic growth rates between business cycle peaks, and make a table of these annual peak-to-peak growth rates. Is this a good way of looking for and estimating changes in long-run economic growth trends in the United States? Why or why not?

3. Look at the relative purchasing-power-parity levels of GDP per worker for the G-7 economies (Germany, France, Britain, Italy, Canada, Japan, and the United States). Have the nations drawn closer together in levels of GDP per worker in the past five years?

4. What items of news have you read about in the past week that you would classify as shifts in macro policies that encourage growth?

5. What items of news have you read about in the past week that you would classify as shifts in macro policies that discourage growth?

6. What items of news have you read about in the past week that you would classify as shifts in micro policies that encourage growth?

7. What items of news have you read about in the past week that you would classify as shifts in micro policies that discourage growth?

8. Do you believe that over the next three decades the lower income countries of the world will catch up to — or at least draw nearer in relative terms to — the high-income countries? Why or why not?

9. What are the prospects for successful rapid development in tomorrow's world? Do you see the glass as half empty or half full?

Flexible-Price Macroeconomics

In this part we shift our point of view and take a "snapshot" of the economy, looking at it over such a short period that its productive resources are fixed but such a long period that wages and prices are fully flexible. In this analysis, the key questions are: What are the economic forces that keep real GDP at its equilibrium value? And in an economy with flexible wages and prices what determines the division of real GDP among consumption spending, investment spending, government purchases, and net exports?

Part 3 contains three chapters. Chapter 6 assembles the building blocks. It analyzes the determinants of the components of spending that make up GDP. The answers to the questions above are the same whether prices are flexible (Part 3) or sticky (as they will be in Part 4). So our building blocks form the basis for both our long-run and our short-run stories. In Chapter 7 these building blocks are put together. Chapter 7 demonstrates how to use the flexible-price model to analyze the composition of real GDP and how a flexible-price macroeconomy reacts to disturbances and shocks. Chapter 8 turns the focus of attention from production to the price level. It performs the straightforward task of analyzing the determinants of the price level and inflation in the flexible-price model.

6

Building Blocks of the Flexible-Price Model

QUESTIONS

What is a full-employment analysis?

What keeps the economy at full employment when wages and prices are flexible?

What determines the level of consumption spending?

What determines the level of investment spending?

What determines the level of net exports?

What determines the level of the real exchange rate?

In the previous two chapters we looked at long-run growth — at how the economy develops and evolves over periods as long as generations. In this chapter we look at the economy over such a short period that its productive resources are fixed but such a long period that wages and prices are fully flexible.

This chapter, Chapter 6, first answers the question: What are the economic forces that keep real GDP at its equilibrium value? In Section 6.1 we show that if wages and prices are flexible enough (as we assume they are here in Part 3), then markets clear: Quantities demanded are equal to quantities supplied. In particular, the labor market clears: Employment is equal to the labor force (save for some "frictional" unemployment), and production is equal to potential output. Should production not be equal to potential output, rising or falling real wages will quickly lower or raise firms' demands for labor and bring the economy back to equilibrium at full employment.

Then this chapter assembles the building blocks we need for nearly every remaining chapter in the book. How do consumers decide on consumption spending — how much to spend on themselves and their households? How do businesses decide on the level of investment spending? How are net exports determined? The answers to these questions are the same whether prices are flexible (Part 3) or sticky (as they will be in Part 4 of this book). So our building blocks form the basis for both our long-run and short-run stories.

A word is needed about the *flexible price assumption* made in this part. Part 3 answers the first question above in the case where wages and prices are flexible, in which the market system works well, in which markets clear — every buyer finds a willing seller and every seller finds a willing buyer. This means, most important, that labor supply equals demand: No firms wanting to hire workers are left unsatisfied, and no workers willing to work are left permanently unemployed. (In Part 4 we analyze the case in which prices are sticky, the market system does not work perfectly, real GDP is not always equal to potential output, and unemployment can rise high enough to become a critical economic problem.)

6.1   POTENTIAL OUTPUT AND REAL WAGES

potential output

The level at which national product would be if all resources were fully employed.

In the *flexible-price* model of the macroeconomy, two sets of factors determine the levels of potential output and of real wages: the production function and the balance of supply and demand in the labor market. Once we have determined **potential output** — the economy's full-employment productive potential — we then know what its actual level of output is, for in the flexible-price model potential output and actual output are the same. Why are they the same? We'll see shortly that it is the flexibility of prices and wages that guarantees that potential output and the actual level of output are equal.

The Production Function

production function

The relationship between the total amount of output produced in an economy and the quantities of labor and capital and the levels of technology and organization used to produce it.

Chapter 4 introduced the **production function**, the rule that tells us how much the economy can produce given its available productive resources. In the Cobb-Douglas form of the production function, as we learned, potential output Y^* is determined by the size of the labor force L, the economy's capital stock K, the efficiency of labor E, and a parameter α that tells us how fast returns to investment

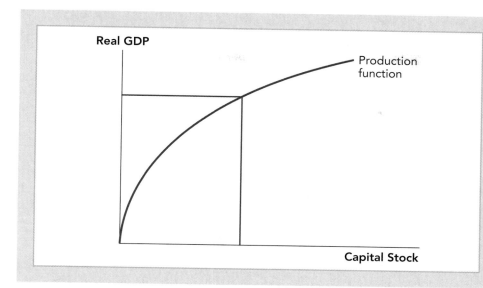

FIGURE 6.1

The Production Function

Holding the labor force and the efficiency of labor constant, real GDP increases as the capital stock increases. Because each successive addition to the capital stock produces a smaller increase in output, the production function is curved. The smaller the level of α, the greater the curvature and the more rapidly the returns to investment diminish.

diminish. The production function tells us that potential output is[1]

$$Y^* = K^\alpha (LE)^{1-\alpha}$$

The graph in Figure 6.1 shows us, once again, just one slice of this production function — the relationship between the capital stock K and potential output Y^*, holding the supply of labor L and the efficiency of labor E fixed. In Chapters 4 and 5, we were looking at changes over time. In this chapter we are looking at the economy at one instant, not over time.

The assumption that wages and prices are flexible was commonly made by the classical economists, who wrote before World War II. Thus this assumption is also called the **classical assumption**. The classical assumption guarantees that markets work — that prices adjust rapidly to eliminate gaps between the quantities demanded and the quantities supplied. No businesses find their inventories of unsold goods piling up, and there is full employment: Everyone who wants a job (at the market-clearing level of wages) can get a job. Every business that wants to hire a worker (at the market-clearing level of wages) can hire a worker. Thus actual output is equal to potential output: There is no gap between the economy's productive potential and the level of output the economy produces.

This classical assumption that we make in this part of the book — in Chapters 6, 7, and 8 — means that Part 3 is devoted to full-employment flexible-price macroeconomics. However, the flexible-price assumption is not always a good one. Experience has shown that a market economy does not always have flexible prices. Sometimes prices and wages turn out to be sticky, or sluggish, or stuck. Thus the economy does not always work well, and does not always provide full employment.

In Part 4 we will drop the classical flexible-price full-employment assumption. From Part 4 on, we will instead make the "Keynesian" assumption that wages

classical assumption

The assumption that wages and prices are flexible.

---

[1] In Chapter 4, the production function we worked with was usually expressed as $Y/L = (K/L)^\alpha E^{1-\alpha}$. Multiplying both sides of that equation by L and rearranging terms gives us the equation in the text. We did not distinguish between actual output Y and potential output Y^* in Chapter 4 but need to do so here.

TABLE 6.1
Classical Flexible-Price versus Keynesian Sticky-Price Analyses

Issue	Classical	Keynesian
Wages and prices	Fully flexible	Can be "sticky" or fixed
Expectations	Consistent with full employment	Volatile — can take a number of forms
Labor market	Always in equilibrium with full employment	Can be out of equilibrium, causing involuntary unemployment
Effect of shocks to aggregate demand	Change in the composition but not the level of GDP	Change in the composition and the level of GDP

and prices are sticky and that markets do not work perfectly. This leads to a number of important differences in the analysis, some of which are briefly noted in Table 6.1.

If the classical flexible-price assumption is not always a good one to make, why make it at all? First, it can be a very good assumption if conditions are right. It is a good assumption if wages and prices are relatively flexible, and if we are looking at processes that take enough time for prices in all of the economy's markets to adjust in order to balance supply and demand. Second, starting with the classical assumption makes this course easier. It simplifies the analysis of several issues and facilitates an understanding of how the macroeconomy works in the long run. One habit of economists is to start with the simpler cases, and only after they are well understood, to look at more complicated ones.

Moreover, the way an economy functions under the flexible-price assumption provides a useful baseline against which to assess economic performance. If we want to assess the costs to society of sticky prices and periods of high unemployment, we need a benchmark against which to make comparisons, and the behavior of the economy in the flexible-price model provides such a benchmark.

Nevertheless, we must remember that Part 3 presents only one model of the economy. The Keynesian sticky-price model behaves very differently in a number of ways. So Part 3 does not tell the full story.

The Labor Market

When markets work well, what keeps the economy at full employment and actual production equal to potential output? One way to look at this issue is that the answer lies in the adjustment of prices and supply and demand in the **labor market**. When the supply of and demand for labor balance, real GDP will equal potential output.

labor market

The market in which workers are hired by firms.

Labor Demand

Economists try to suppress every detail and difference that does not matter for the overall result in order to simplify the analysis and focus it on the important factors — the ones that really count. Because differences between businesses will not matter, let's think about an economy with K typical — identical — representative firms, each of which owns 1 unit of the economy's capital stock.

Each of these firms hires a number of workers — let's call the number of workers each firm hires L_{firm}. Each firm in the economy pays each worker the same nominal wage W. Each firm sells Y_{firm} units of its product at a per-unit price P. The typical firm does not control either the wages it must pay or the prices it receives; those are determined by the market, and each firm takes the wages and prices it is offered. And each firm tries to make as much profit as it can.

Thus we have a very simple and standard model of a typical firm. The firm's *profits* are simply its revenues minus its costs, and its only costs are the wages it pays to workers:

$$\text{Profits} = \text{Revenues} - \text{Costs}$$

$$= P \times (Y_{firm}) - W \times (L_{firm})$$

To figure out how many workers to hire in order to maximize its profits, the firm must:

1. Hire workers in order to boost output.
2. Stop hiring workers when the extra revenue from selling the output produced by the last worker hired just equals the value of the last worker's wage.

The value of the output produced by the last worker hired is the product's price times what economists call the **marginal product of labor (MPL)**. What is the marginal product of labor? The marginal product of labor is the difference for some time period between what the firm can produce with its current labor force L_{firm} and what it would produce if it hired one more worker, as Figure 6.2 shows for the benefit of those of you who like graphs rather than sentences with subclauses.

marginal product of labor (MPL)

The increase in potential output from a 1-unit increase in the quantity of labor employed by the firm.

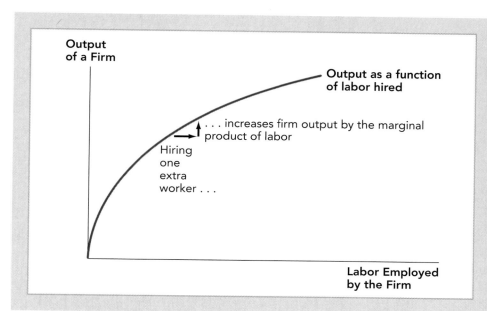

Output of a Firm

Output as a function of labor hired

... increases firm output by the marginal product of labor

Hiring one extra worker ...

Labor Employed by the Firm

FIGURE 6.2

The Firm's Output as a Function of the Firm's Employment

Holding the capital stock of the typical firm constant, each extra worker the firm employs produces smaller and smaller increases in total output. As the level of employment increases, this marginal product of labor (MPL) decreases.

Since a typical firm owns 1 unit of capital, its output is what can be produced using that single unit of capital and the firm's workers, according to the production function

$$Y_{firm} = F(\text{Capital, Labor}) = F(1, L_{firm})$$

And so the marginal product of labor (MPL) is

$$MPL_{firm} = F(1, L_{firm} + 1) - F(1, L_{firm})$$

The MPL for the representative firm with a Cobb-Douglas production function, where $K = 1$, is just the derivative with regard to labor L of the production function:

$$MPL = \frac{K^{\alpha}(1 - \alpha)E^{1-\alpha}}{(L_{firm})^{\alpha}} = \frac{(1 - \alpha)E^{1-\alpha}}{(L_{firm})^{\alpha}}$$

There is nothing deep in this math. Indeed, the Cobb-Douglas function was tweaked so that it would yield such simple forms for quantities like the MPL. That is why economists use it so often.

Now that we know the MPL, determining how many workers this representative firm will hire is straightforward. It will keep hiring workers as long as doing so remains profitable. As Figure 6.3 shows, the firm hires workers up to the point where the product of the price it sells its goods for and the marginal product of labor has fallen so that it equals the wage

$$P \times (MPL) - W = 0$$

For the Cobb-Douglas production function, this profit-maximizing level of labor demand for the firm is

$$L_{firm} = \left[\frac{(1 - \alpha)E^{1-\alpha}}{\frac{W}{P}} \right]^{(1/\alpha)}$$

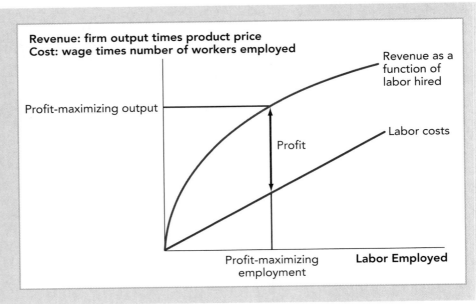

FIGURE 6.3

The Typical Firm's Hiring Policy

The typical firm chooses to hire the number of workers that make marginal revenue product — the MPL times the product price P — equal to the wage W. At that point the revenue and cost curves are parallel, and profit is maximized.

Revenue: firm output times product price
Cost: wage times number of workers employed

Revenue as a function of labor hired

Profit-maximizing output

Profit

Labor costs

Profit-maximizing employment

Labor Employed

An example is provided in Box 6.1. And since there are K firms in the economy — one for each unit of capital — this gives us an economywide demand for labor by firms L^d equal to

$$L^d = K\left[\frac{(1 - \alpha)E^{1-\alpha}}{\dfrac{W}{P}}\right]^{1/\alpha}$$

FIRM LABOR DEMAND: AN EXAMPLE

Suppose that we have a specific Cobb-Douglas production function — suppose that for the firm the value of labor efficiency E equals 1, the parameter α equals 1/2, and so the production function is

$$Y_{firm} = K_{firm}^{1/2}(L_{firm} \cdot 1)^{1/2} = (\sqrt{K_{firm}})(\sqrt{L_{firm}})$$

The annual output of the firm is equal to the square root of the firm's capital stock times the square root of the firm's labor force. This — since the typical firm has only 1 unit of capital — immediately simplifies to

$$Y_{firm} = \sqrt{L_{firm}}$$

Suppose further that the wage the firm pays each of its workers is $25,000 a year, that output is measured in millions of gallons, and that each gallon of output sells for $1. (Let's not ask gallons of what.)

Now let's think about how many workers the firm should hire. Raising employment from 0 to 1 increases production from 0 to 1 million-gallon-unit per year and raises the firm's total sales by $1,000,000. Since the first worker has to be paid only $25,000, this looks like a very good deal. Raising employment from 100 to 101 would increase output from 10 million-gallon-units to 10.050 units (that's the square root of 101). That amounts to an extra $50,000 in annual revenue at an extra wage cost of $25,000. This still looks like a very good deal.

How about raising employment from 400 to 401? That raises output from 20 million-gallon-units to 20.02498 million-gallon-units. That's an extra $24,980 in extra revenue, but at an extra wage cost of $25,000. The 401st worker lowers profits. So at 400 workers it is time to stop.

Should the firm have stopped earlier? Suppose that you cut employment from 400 to 399. You save $25,000 a year in reduced wage costs. But you also cut your output from 20 million-gallon-units to 19.97498 units: $20 - 19.97498 = 0.02502$. So you lose $25,020 in revenue. The 400th worker earns his or her keep, and the firm should not cut employment below 400.

Labor Market Equilibrium

Economywide labor demand is only half of the labor market. To understand what is going on in the labor market we also need to know what is going on with the **labor supply.** The answer is simple: The labor supply is the number of workers who want to work. The labor market will be in equilibrium when firms' total demand for workers is equal to the economy's labor force L.

Can the labor market be out of equilibrium if wages and prices are flexible? No. Think about what happens when wages and prices are flexible if labor supply is not equal to demand. Suppose there are more workers who want to work than the

labor supply

The number of workers who want to work.

number of workers that firms want to hire at current wages and prices. Some of the workers will find themselves unemployed. Then some of the unemployed will underbid the employed workers, offering to take their jobs and work for less. The workers who are employed will respond by offering to accept lower wages to keep their jobs.

The wage W will decline relative to the price level P, and the **real wage** W/P will fall. Unless the firm changes its labor demand, the marginal product of the last worker hired will now exceed the real wage. To maximize profit, the firm should change its labor demand until the MPL falls to the point where it equals the new lower real wage. But the firm knows that the marginal product of the last worker hired will fall as it hires more workers, something we economists call *diminishing returns*. So as this real wage falls, firms wishing to profit maximize will hire more workers.

Suppose, on the other hand, that firms want to hire more workers than there are people in the labor force. Some firms will try to bid workers away from other firms by offering higher wages. The real wage W/P will rise. As the real wage rises, other employers will reduce the quantity of labor they demand. Thus, as Figure 6.4 shows, in **labor market equilibrium**, labor demand L^d will equal the labor force L:

$$L = L^d = K\left[\frac{(1-\alpha)E^{1-\alpha}}{\dfrac{W}{P}}\right]^{1/\alpha}$$

We can rearrange this equation and solve for the real wage W/P to see that labor demand is equal to the labor force when the real wage W/P is

$$\frac{W}{P} = \left[(1-\alpha)E^{1-\alpha}\right]\left(\frac{K}{L}\right)^{\alpha} = (1-\alpha)\left(\frac{Y}{L}\right)$$

real wage

The wage paid to the average worker divided by the price level.

labor market equilibrium

When, save for those in the process of changing jobs, the economy is at full employment.

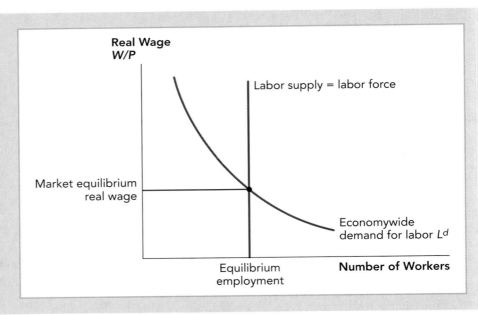

FIGURE 6.4
Equilibrium in the Labor Market

The equilibrium level of employment is equal to the labor force. At the equilibrium level of the real wage, there is neither excess demand for nor excess supply of labor.

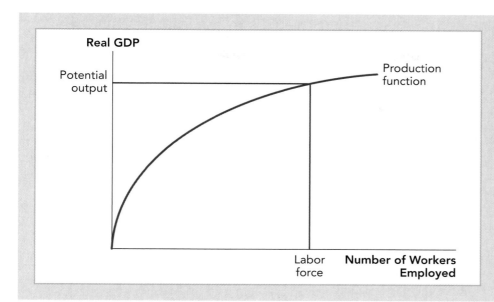

FIGURE 6.5

In a Full-Employment Economy, Real GDP Equals Potential Output

When the economy is at full employment, the level of employment is equal to the labor force and real GDP is equal to potential output.

because we already know from Chapter 4 that $(E^{1-\alpha})(K/L)^{\alpha}$ is equal to output per worker Y/L. As long as wages and prices are flexible enough for this adjustment process to work and for the real wage to converge to this, its equilibrium level, the economy will be at and will remain at full employment.[2]

The conclusion is clear: If markets work well — if wages and prices are flexible and adjust to balance supply and demand, and if markets are competitive so that firms take wages and prices as given rather than controlling them — then we can expect the labor market to be at full employment, and the actual level of production in the economy Y to be equal to the economy's potential output Y^*, as Figure 6.5 shows.

As long as we are looking at a short enough interval of time that the labor force, the capital stock, and the efficiency of labor do not change, in the flexible-price model the answer to a great many questions is simple and straightforward. If somebody asks you what is the effect on real GDP of a change in government spending or an increase in interest rates overseas or of a stock market boom or pretty much anything else, the answer will always be the same: Real GDP doesn't change, because the economy's output is equal to its productive potential. In the flexible-price model the questions that have more complicated answers are those that relate to the *division* of real GDP among its various main components: consumption, investment, government spending, and net exports.

---

[2]Note that this full-employment economy is not necessarily the best or even a good economy. The real incomes of people who don't own chunks of the capital stock are their real wages: $W/P = (1 - \alpha)(Y/L)$. If α is large, their real incomes will be small, and social welfare may be low.

RECAP   POTENTIAL OUTPUT AND REAL WAGES

A flexible-price economy is a full-employment economy: Wages are flexible enough to keep supply and demand in balance in the labor market. Because there are enough jobs for all the workers who want to work at the prevailing market-clearing wage, real GDP in a flexible-price economy is always equal to potential output and unemployment is not a problem. This classical model of the macroeconomy is the polar opposite of the Keynesian model, where prices and wages are sticky, markets do not always clear with supply and demand in balance, high unemployment is possible, and there are gaps between real GDP and potential output.

6.2 DOMESTIC SPENDING

In Chapters 2 and 3 we saw, through the national income identity, that total spending for goods and services is divided into four components:

- Consumption spending C
- Investment spending I
- Government purchases G
- Net exports NX

Every dollar spent on final goods and services, whether spent by households on their own consumption (C), spent by businesses in maintaining or expanding their capital stock (I), purchased by the government (G), or purchased by foreigners (GX), flows to firms as revenue — except for that part of the spending flows C, I, and G that is spent buying imported goods IM. So total receipts by business firms — canceling out payments one firm makes to another — are equal to the four components of spending $C + I + G + GX - IM$, which we find more convenient to write as $C + I + G + NX$. Every dollar that firms receive is counted as somebody's income, whether paid out to workers or retained to become the property of the firm's owners or shareholders. So national income is equal to $C + I + G + NX$.

And the circular flow principle tells us that total spending and national income are essentially the same thing as real GDP, for the value of income is the same as the value of what is sold and produced. Thus

$$C + I + G + NX = Y = \text{real GDP}$$

In this section of Chapter 6 we look at the determinants of the three domestic components of spending: C, I, and G. International trade and net exports will be deferred for the moment until the next section.

Note that the rest of this chapter offers no big payoff, no single lesson to be learned at the end. The big lesson comes at the end of Chapter 7. The rest of this chapter simply sets out the factors that determine the components of spending; it does not show how all the pieces fit together.

Consumption Spending

The spending and saving decisions that determine the magnitude of the flow of consumption spending are made by households, so this subsection lays out how households make their big decisions. The decisions we focus on are those that determine how households divide their income up among taxes, saving, and consumption spending.

Household Decisions

The circular flow principle tells us that the wages of workers plus the profits of property owners (rent, interest, dividends, and retained earnings) add up to national income, which is — because at this level of analysis we are uninterested in picky accounting distinctions — essentially the same as real GDP. So for simplicity let's use Y for both income and total output.

Households pay some of their income to the government in net taxes — *taxes less transfer payments* from the government — which we write as T. To keep the analysis simple, throughout this book we will assume that net taxes are equal to the constant average tax rate t multiplied by national income Y:

$$T = tY$$

In the real world taxes are not proportional to income. Our tax system is somewhat progressive, which means that richer taxpayers on average pay more of their income in taxes than do the relatively poor. Once again, however, the complications introduced by the fact that our tax system is not proportional to income are not central to the analysis, so we follow economists' standard practice of simplifying wherever possible.

The amount left after households pay their net taxes is their **disposable income**, written Y^D:

$$Y^D = Y - T = (1 - t)Y$$

Households also save some of their income to boost their wealth and future spending. We represent private household saving by S^H — S for "saving" and H for "household." (Note that household saving includes the retained earnings of corporations: The NIPA treats undistributed corporate earnings that are retained by the corporation as if they were distributed to the shareholding households and then immediately reinvested back into the corporation.) As Figure 6.6 shows, households spend the rest of their income — everything that is not saved or paid to the

disposable income

What is left of income after taxes have been paid and transfer payments received.

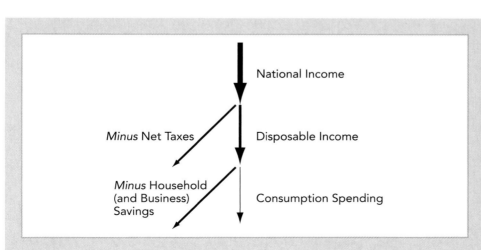

FIGURE 6.6

From National Income to Consumption Spending

To get disposable income, subtract taxes from and add transfers to national income. To get consumption spending, subtract household saving (including the retained earnings of businesses) from disposable income.

government in net taxes — buying consumption goods:

$$C = Y^D - S^H = Y - T - S^H$$

In the United States today, consumption spending — purchases by households for their own use, from pine nuts and flour to washing machines and automobiles, from Big Macs and haircuts to rent and financial consulting — accounts for roughly two-thirds of GDP.

We will break consumption spending down into a baseline level of consumption (which we define as a parameter C_0) and a fraction (which we define as a parameter C_y) of disposable income Y^D, or a fraction $C_y(1 - t)$ of total income Y:

$$C = C_0 + C_y Y^D = C_0 + C_y(1 - t)Y$$

marginal propensity to consume (MPC)

The increase in consumption spending resulting from a one-dollar increase in disposable income.

The fraction C_y is more commonly known as the **marginal propensity to consume** (**MPC**). It tells us the change in consumption spending when disposable income changes by one dollar:

$$C_y = \frac{\Delta C}{\Delta Y^D}$$

Thus we assume that consumption spending C is a simple linear function of real GDP Y: If we plot consumption on the vertical axis and real GDP on the horizontal axis of a graph, the **consumption function** will be a straight line.

consumption function

The relationship between baseline consumption C_0, the marginal propensity to consume C_y, and disposable income Y^D.

Notice that in writing this particular consumption function, we again follow the economists' principle (or vice) of ruthless simplification. In our more complicated world, consumption spending does not depend on disposable income alone. As Figure 6.7 shows, other factors affecting consumption include changes in the real interest rate, household total stock market and real estate wealth, the demographic structure of the population, income distribution, consumers' relative optimism,

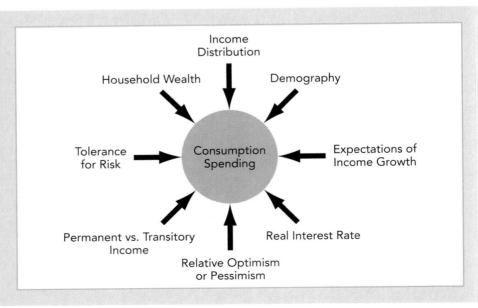

FIGURE 6.7
Other Determinants of Consumption Spending
Other factors besides taxes and saving affect consumption spending. Each of these factors can change baseline consumption C_0.

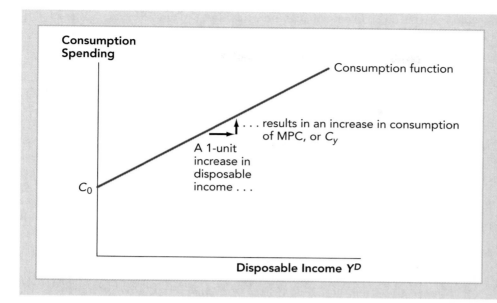

FIGURE 6.8

The Consumption Function

Consumption spending depends on the level of disposable income and two parameters: C_y (the marginal propensity to consume, or MPC) and C_0 (the baseline level of consumption). If we know both these parameters and the value of disposable income Y^D, we can plot the level of consumption spending at each possible level of disposable income.

expected future income growth, tolerance for risk, and whether consumers see changes in disposable income as *transitory* or *permanent*. (If consumers expect an income increase to be transitory, they will save most of it and spend only a little; if they expect an income increase to be permanent, they will spend most of it.) But here and throughout the book we will sweep these complications under the rug. We will think only about baseline consumption C_0, the marginal propensity to consume C_y, and disposable income Y^D as the determinants of consumption spending and allow all these other factors in by saying that they change baseline consumption C_0.

The Marginal Propensity to Consume

The marginal propensity to consume (MPC), the parameter C_y in the consumption function, is the amount by which consumption spending rises in response to a \$1 increase in disposable income (see Figure 6.8). We are sure that C_y is greater than zero: If disposable incomes rise, households will use some of their extra income to boost their consumption spending. We are also sure that C_y is less than 1: As disposable incomes rise, households will increase their saving as well; they will not spend all their extra disposable income on consumption goods.

The value of the marginal propensity to consume also depends on how long people expect the change in disposable income to last. As discussed in Appendix 6a, if people expect the change in disposable income to be permanent, then the MPC is likely to be relatively large. If they expect the change in disposable income to be transitory — and think their disposable income next year will revert back to its normal pattern — the MPC is likely to be relatively small.

Baseline Consumption

Although sometimes we say the baseline level of consumption, the parameter C_0, is the amount households would spend on consumption goods if they had no income at all, that's somewhat misleading. Such a definition invites you to (incorrectly!) think of the consumption function as some sort of individual consumption function for an individual household. But it's not. The consumption function tells us, for the economy as a whole, how consumption varies with changes in real GDP and total national income.

The baseline level of consumption spending, the parameter C_0, tells us where the aggregate consumption function hits the vertical axis. If wealth increases, the consumption function shifts up; C_0, the baseline level of consumption, increases. But would this economy truly consume C_0 if the entire economy produced not one single good or service and its real GDP was zero? No one knows. And because knowing requires observing a completely devastated economy, we hope no one ever will!

With these two parameters, C_0 and C_y, we can calculate what the total level of consumption spending will be for each possible level of disposable income Y^D (see Box 6.2).

BOX 6.2

CALCULATING CONSUMPTION FROM INCOME: AN EXAMPLE

If we know the parameters C_0 (the baseline level of consumption), C_y (the marginal propensity to consume, or MPC), and t (the tax rate), we can calculate the level of consumption spending C for any level of total national income Y using the equation

$$C = C_0 + C_y Y^D = C_0 + C_y(1 - t)Y$$

Suppose the tax rate t is 25 percent, the total national income Y is $10 trillion, the baseline level of consumption C_0 is $2 trillion, and the marginal propensity to consume C_y is 0.6. We first calculate disposable income — how much households have left after paying their taxes. Disposable income is equal to $(1 - t)Y$, which for these parameter values and this level of national income is

$$Y^D = (1 - 0.25)(\$10 \text{ trillion}) = \$7.5 \text{ trillion}$$

We can then calculate consumption:

$$C = C_0 + C_y (\$7.5 \text{ trillion})$$
$$= \$2 \text{ trillion} + 0.6\,(\$7.5 \text{ trillion})$$
$$= \$6.5 \text{ trillion}$$

What will happen if disposable income rises from $7.5 trillion to $8 trillion? Consumption spending will rise from $6.5 trillion to $6.8 trillion — a change in consumption spending equal to the marginal propensity to consume, 0.6, times the change in disposable income, $0.5 trillion.

Investment Spending

In the United States today investment spending averages only about 15 percent of GDP. But investment spending is the most volatile and variable component of GDP. When economists use the term "investment," they mean something different from what most people mean by the word. Most people use it to mean activity such as buying a stock or bond, a *certificate of deposit,* or *commodity futures.* But such purchases do not directly increase the economy's capital stock or have any place in the national income and product accounts.

When economists use the term "investment" or "investment spending," they are talking about transactions that replace depreciated machinery and equipment, or add to the capital stock and increase potential output. Such transactions include the purchase and installation of new business machinery and equipment, the construction and purchase of new buildings or residential structures (or the repair of old ones), and a change in business inventories. Box 6.3 highlights two different ways economists break down total investment spending.

KINDS OF INVESTMENT: SOME DETAILS

Economists categorize investment in two different ways. The first distinction they draw is between gross investment and net investment. Gross investment is the total sum of spending on machines, construction (houses, factories, office buildings, privately owned roads, dams, and bridges), and additions to inventories.

Some of gross investment adds to the capital stock of machines, goods in process, buildings, and other structures. The rest of gross investment replaces worn-out and obsolete pieces of capital. The amount of gross investment spending that increases the capital stock is called net investment. The amount of investment spending that replaces obsolete and worn-out capital is called depreciation or capital consumption.

Economists also categorize investment according to use, as follows:

1. *Residential construction*
2. Nonresidential construction
3. Equipment investment
4. *Inventory investment*

To some degree, these four subcategories of investment have different determinants and different consequences. But in order to simplify and construct a useful model, we ignore those differences.

Fluctuations in economywide investment spending have two sources. First is the interest rate: The higher the **real interest rate**, the lower is investment spending. A higher real interest rate makes investment projects more expensive for firms to undertake, so they undertake fewer of them. Second is business managers' and investors' confidence — what John Maynard Keynes called their "*animal spirits*." The higher their confidence, the higher is investment spending. Optimistic managers and investors are more willing than pessimistic ones to bet their careers and fortunes on the belief that an expansion of productive capacity or some other investment will pay off.

real interest rate

The nominal interest rate minus the inflation rate.

Why Firms Invest

Interest Rates   A business invests because its managers believe that the investment project will be profitable. One way managers decide if a project is profitable is by comparing the appropriately discounted return on the investment with the investment's cost. Their rule: Undertake the investment project only if the return is at least as great as the investment's cost. The higher the interest rate, the lower is the appropriately discounted return on the investment project. And so the higher the interest rate, the smaller is the number of potential investment projects that will be profitable. Thus a higher interest rate leads to lower investment spending.

present value

The value in today's dollars of a sum of money to be received in the future.

Why does the discounted return fall when interest rates rise? The answer uses the economists' concept of **present value** — the amount of wealth that you would have to set aside today and put into financial assets earning the real interest rate to generate some particular amount of purchasing power in the future. If the real interest rate is 5 percent per year, to have $130 million of inflation-adjusted purchasing power in five years you would have to take $101.85 million today, put it aside, and let it compound in the bond market: $101.85 \times (1.05)^5 = $130 million. Thus the present value of $130 million in five years at an interest rate of 5 percent is $101.85 million.

To calculate the present value $PV of a sum of inflation-adjusted purchasing power $SUM to be received n years in the future at an interest rate of r percent per year, you *discount* the future sum back to the present at the rate r using the formula

$$\$PV = \frac{\$SUM}{(1 + r)^n}$$

because $PV in the bond market at an interest rate of r for n years will compound to $SUM. (If whether or not the $SUM will actually be paid in the future is subject to more than the usual amount of risk found in the bond market, the present value will be lower: You can either risk-adjust the $SUM to a lower value or risk-adjust the discount rate r by adding a risk premium σ^s and discounting at $r + \sigma^s$.)

At a real interest rate of 6 percent, the present value of $130 million received in five years is $130 million/$(1.06)^5 = $97.14 million. When we used an interest rate of 6 percent rather than 5 percent, the present value of $130 million received in five years fell from $101.85 million to $97.14 million. What's true in our example is true in general: The higher the real interest rate, the lower the discounted value — the present value — of an investment project that will generate revenue in the future.

With present value, the decisions of business managers become easier. One investment project will be a better use of resources than another only if the first has a higher present value than the second.

Most investment projects don't yield returns in the shape of a single, lump-sum payment n years into the future. Most yield a stream of profits each year for a prolonged period. Thus more useful than the formula for the present value of a $SUM n years in the future is the $STREAM formula for the present value of a stream of payments each year from now into the indefinite future:

$$\$PV = \frac{\$STREAM}{r}$$

Think of how much a flow of real purchasing power of $1 million per year each year into the indefinite future is worth. If you wanted to receive such an annual flow, how much would you have to put into the bond market today? $1/$r$ million invested in the bond market yields an annual flow of real purchasing power of $1 million per year. Thus an investment project that you expect to yield a cash flow of $STREAM in real purchasing power per year each year has a present value of $STREAM/$r$.

You can see from these financial formulas how important the real interest rate is for determining whether investments are worthwhile or not. If an investment project promises a long-running stream of returns — as in the example above — a small change in the real interest rate can have an enormous impact on present value.

How many investment projects will a higher interest rate discourage? How much lower will investment be if the interest rate is higher? The answer is captured by a parameter we call "investment's response to a change in the interest rate," or I_r. The greater is I_r, the greater is the change in investment spending in response to a change in the real interest rate.

The interest rate most relevant to determining investment is the long-term, real, risky interest rate. The relevant interest rate is *long-term* because investment projects affect the business's profits and costs for a long time to come. The relevant interest rate is *real* — that is, inflation-adjusted — because an investment project gives the business that undertakes it a real, physical asset, not a financial claim denominated in dollars. The relevant interest rate is *risky* because investment projects are risky. In calculating whether investment projects are worthwhile, be sure to compare apples to apples. Discount the long-term, real, risky profits anticipated from undertaking an investment project by the long-term, real, risky interest rate.

Animal Spirits   A number of factors other than changes in interest rates can affect investment spending; we capture all these other factors in what Keynes called "animal spirits." When businesspeople's optimism soars, their expected return from an investment project soars too. More projects become profitable at every interest rate. Investment spending rises.

When businesspeople's perception of risk increases — when their certainty about the future return on an investment project becomes, well, less certain — then they tend to become more cautious in committing large quantities of money to a long-term investment project. At every interest rate, investment spending falls.

The Investment Function

To model the inverse relationship between the level of investment spending and the long-term, real, risky interest rate, set investment spending I equal to the baseline level of investment (the value of the parameter I_0) minus the real interest rate r times the slope of the **investment function**, parameter I_r (see Figure 6.9):

$$I = I_0 - I_r r$$

investment function

The relationship between the real interest rate r and investment spending.

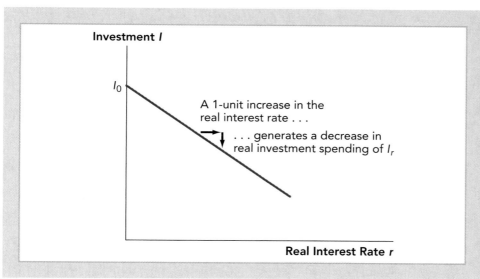

Investment *I*

I_0

A 1-unit increase in the real interest rate . . .

. . . generates a decrease in real investment spending of I_r

Real Interest Rate *r*

FIGURE 6.9
The Investment Function

Investment spending increases as the real interest rate decreases. How much investment spending changes is measured by I_r. Changes in baseline investment spending shift the investment function.

HOW INVESTMENT RESPONDS TO A CHANGE IN INTEREST RATES: AN EXAMPLE

From the parameters I_0 (the baseline level of investment) and I_r (the responsiveness of investment to a change in real interest rates) we can calculate the level of investment spending for each possible value of the real interest rate r.

For example, suppose that I_0 is $2 trillion and that I_r is $10,000 billion. Then we can use the equation

$$I = I_0 - I_r r$$

to calculate that if the real interest rate is 5 percent ($r = 0.05$), then the level of investment spending is $1.5 trillion:

$$I = \$2 \text{ trillion} - (\$10,000 \text{ billion} \cdot 0.05) = \$1.5 \text{ trillion}$$

If the real interest rate is 10 percent ($r = 0.10$), the level of investment spending is $1 trillion:

$$I = \$2 \text{ trillion} - (\$10,000 \text{ billion} \cdot 0.10) = \$1 \text{ trillion}$$

And if the real interest rate is 0 percent, the level of investment spending is $2 trillion:

$$I = \$2 \text{ trillion} - (\$10,000 \text{ billion} \cdot 0) = \$2 \text{ trillion}$$

Box 6.4 shows how to use this investment function equation to calculate the level of investment spending at a particular interest rate. Box 6.5 presents an alternative way of thinking about the investment function — one that focuses on the stock market, not on interest rates.

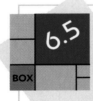

THE STOCK MARKET: SOME DETAILS

An alternative way of looking at investment — one that would complicate our models too much for us to use here — sees the level of investment spending as a function of the level of the stock market. Think about what determines stock market values. Most investors in the stock market face a choice between holding stocks — shares of ownership of a corporation that also give you ownership of that corporation's profits or earnings — or holding bonds: pieces of paper that represent loans that pay interest. If you hold your wealth in bonds, you earn the real interest rate r. If you buy shares of stock, your return is equal to your share of the profits of the companies whose stock you own.

When expected future profits are high, investors find stocks more attractive than bonds and thus bid up stock prices. When the real interest rate falls, investors also find stocks more attractive than bonds and bid up stock prices. In either case, the stock market will rise. However, when expected future profits are high, businesses invest more. When the real interest rate falls, businesses find investment projects cheaper and also invest more. The same things that determine the value of the stock market also determine the level of investment spending. The stock market and investment move together: What raises or lowers one raises or lowers the other.

The only significant difference is that causes of fluctuations in investment affect the stock market first and investment spending second. The stock market is thus a very useful leading indicator of investment spending. Keep a close watch on the stock market if you want to forecast the level of investment spending.

Notice the regular pattern used for parameters so far: C_0, C_y, I_0, I_r. This regular pattern is an attempt to make the names of parameters used in algebraic equations clearer and easier to remember. In general, the capital letter in the name of each parameter tells you what variable is on the left-hand side of the equation in which the parameter appears. A C means that the parameter is part of an equation determining the level of consumption spending C; an I means it is part of an equation determining the level of investment spending I; and so forth. The subscript tells you the variable by which the parameter is multiplied in that equation. For example, I_r is the amount by which investment spending I changes in response to a change in the real interest rate r.

Like the consumption function, the investment function is an enormous simplification of real-world investment patterns. In the real world, firms' investment decisions depend not only on the real interest rate but also on how much money the firms have available. Total profits are also an important determinant of investment. In the real world, some components of investment — construction, for example — are very sensitive to changes in the real interest rate. Other components of investment — for example, inventory investment by small firms with little access to outside sources of funding — are not. Box 6.6 discusses two tools government policy makers sometimes have at their disposal to change the level of investment.

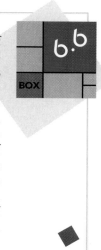

HOW TO BOOST INVESTMENT: A POLICY ISSUE

As we saw in Chapters 4 and 5, a high level of saving and investment is one of the keys to a prosperous economy. The higher the share of GDP devoted to investment spending, the higher is the equilibrium capital-output ratio and the richer is the economy.

Governments seeking to boost investment have two major tools at their disposal. First, they can induce the central bank to lower real interest rates. If real interest rates are lowered, more investment projects will be undertaken and investment spending will rise. Second, governments can try to raise the baseline level of investment by encouraging private decision makers. They can exhort and reassure them — although the tactic sometimes backfires, as in President Herbert Hoover's repeated declaration during the Great Depression that "prosperity is just around the corner." More important, policy makers can try to reduce or eliminate sources of risk. Instilling confidence that the economy will be stable and risks will be managed is perhaps the best way to boost investment by encouraging optimism.

Government Purchases

The federal government buys the labor of government employees — judges, air traffic controllers, customs inspectors, FBI agents, National Oceanic and Atmospheric Administration researchers, and others — as well as military hardware, sections of the interstate highway system, and other goods and services. All these expenditures plus those of state and local governments make up the **government purchases** component of GDP. Such government purchases of goods and services add up to about 20 percent of GDP.

Note that government *spending* is larger than government *purchases*. In addition to buying goods and services (including the work time of its employees), the

government purchases

Government spending on goods or services (including the wages of government employees).

FIGURE 6.10
Government Purchases, Transfer Payments, and Taxes

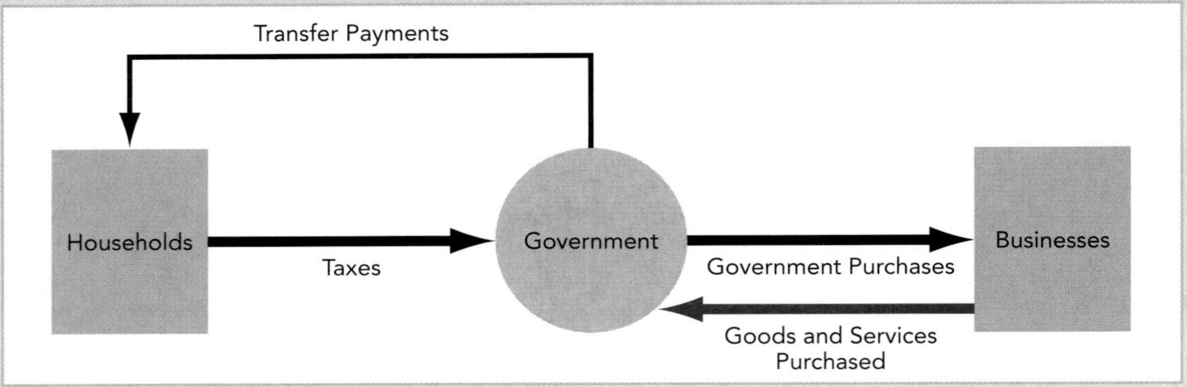

transfer payments

Spending by the government
that is not a purchase of
goods or services but instead
simply a transfer of income
from taxpayers to program
recipients.

net taxes

The difference between taxes
collected by the government
and transfer payments
received by households and
businesses.

government also spends by transferring money to citizens through Social Security
and other programs, disability benefits, food stamps, and other **transfer payments**.
Because transfer payments do not themselves represent demand for final goods and
services, they do not show up directly as a portion of GDP in government purchases G. Rather, transfer payments show up in the NIPA as negative taxes. The
variable T represents **net taxes**, taxes less transfer payments. It is the net amount
by which the government's tax and transfer system reduces disposable income. (See
Figure 6.10.)

As noted previously, in this book we assume net taxes T, taxes less transfers,
are equal to the average tax rate t times income Y:

$$T = tY$$

We do not inquire into what determines either government purchases G or the
average tax rate t. We leave that for the political scientists. We will look at what
happens when government spending G or the tax rate t changes.

RECAP   DOMESTIC SPENDING

Consumption spending C depends on four factors: the baseline level of consumption C_0, the marginal propensity to consume (MPC) C_y, the tax rate t, and
the level of real GDP (or national income) Y:

$$C = C_0 + C_y (1 - t)Y$$

Investment spending I depends on three things: the baseline level of investment I_0, the interest sensitivity of investment I_r, and the real interest rate r:

$$I = I_0 - I_r r$$

We leave the determinants of government purchases G to the political scientists.

6.3 INTERNATIONAL TRADE

The final component of GDP is **net exports** — the difference between gross exports and imports. **Gross exports** are made up of goods and services that are produced in the home country and then sold abroad. GDP is a measure of production, and since gross exports are part of production, they need to be counted in GDP. But first **imports** need to be subtracted from GDP. Not all the goods and services that make up consumption, investment, and government purchases are produced domestically. Consumption, for instance, includes spending on Chinese toys, Irish computers, Brazilian coffee, and Scottish tweeds as well as on domestically made goods. Investment includes spending on British airplanes and Italian machinery. Federal, state, and local government purchases include German buses and Japanese subway cars. So adding up C, I, and G overestimates domestic demand for U.S.-made products. By adding net rather than gross exports to $C + I + G$, economists (1) take account of goods made domestically that are sold to foreigners and don't show up in $C + I + G$ and (2) correct $C + I + G$ for the amount of foreign-made goods it counts.

net exports

The difference between exports and imports.

gross exports

Total goods and services produced at home and sold to purchasers in foreign countries.

imports

Goods and services produced in other countries and purchased by residents of our country.

Gross Exports

The volume of gross exports from the United States depends on two variables. The first is the real GDP of our trading partners — call it Y^f, for "foreign GDP." The second is the real exchange rate — call it ε. The higher the value of the real exchange rate — the more expensive the foreign currency — the cheaper are U.S.-made goods to foreigners, and the more of them they buy, as Figure 6.11 shows.

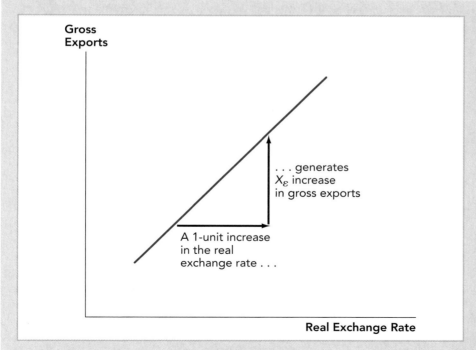

Gross Exports

. . . generates X_ε increase in gross exports

A 1-unit increase in the real exchange rate . . .

Real Exchange Rate

FIGURE 6.11

Gross Exports and the Real Exchange Rate

Gross exports of goods and services to the rest of the world increase as the real exchange rate increases. How much gross exports change is measured by X_ε.

Thus the function for gross exports GX is

$$GX = X_f Y^f + X_\varepsilon \varepsilon$$

Here, just as in the investment and consumption equations, X_ε and X_f are parameters that help determine gross exports. X_f is the increase in exports generated by an increase in foreign GDP. It measures the change in our exports as foreign GDP changes. X_ε measures the increase in exports produced by a rise in the real exchange rate ε.

In the real world, the relationship between the real exchange rate and exports is not as simple as shown in Figure 6.11. Many determinants of gross exports are suppressed in order to keep the model simple. Moreover, the process entails substantial lags. A change in the real exchange rate has little or no effect on gross exports this year but will have effects on gross exports one, two, and three years into the future, as Box 6.7 explains. But as we move forward we again follow the economist's pattern of simplifying whenever doing so doesn't alter our essential story, and simply assume gross exports GX respond to changes in foreign income Y^f and the real exchange rate ε.

Imports and Net Exports

The value of demand for imports — for products produced abroad — depends on domestic real GDP: The higher the real GDP, the more money consumers and businesses and government agencies spend on imported goods and services. The higher, that is, the *value* of imports IM.

The quantity of imports demanded depends as well on the real exchange rate ε. The higher the real exchange rate — the higher the purchasing power of foreign currency — the more expensive are foreign-made goods and the fewer of them do domestic consumers and investors buy. However, we are interested not in the *quantity* but in the *value* of imports. When the quantity of imports falls as the real exchange rate rises, the real dollar value of imports is about the same. So the value of imports IM is largely independent of the real exchange rate.

Therefore, we simplify and model gross imports IM as a constant share — a share that is the propensity to import IM_y — of real GDP Y:

$$IM = IM_y Y$$

Net exports NX are the difference between gross exports and imports. Thus they depend on the real exchange rate ε; on real GDP abroad Y^f; and on real GDP here at home Y:

$$NX = GX - IM = (X_f Y^f + X_\varepsilon \varepsilon) - (IM_y Y)$$

The Exchange Rate

We have seen that the real exchange rate is an important determinant of net exports. And in Chapter 2 we had the *definition* of the real exchange rate: $\varepsilon = e \cdot P^f/P$, the real exchange rate is the product of the nominal exchange rate and the price ratio between the foreign and domestic economies. But what *determines* the nominal and real exchange rates? What is the behavioral story?

THE J-CURVE: SOME DETAILS

Trade links across countries take time to create, time to modify, and time to destroy. So while an increase of the U.S. real exchange rate causes an increase in foreign purchases of U.S. goods, a year or more will pass before we see the change in the volume of trade. In the short run, a rise in the real exchange rate — an increase in the purchasing power of foreign currency — may generate a fall, not a rise, in exports. Economists call this the *J curve*, because the plot of exports over time after a rise in the exchange rate looks a little like a "J." The real exchange rate began to rise very steeply in 1986, but as Figure 6.12 shows, real exports in 1986 were flat. It was not until 1987 and 1988 that the increased competitiveness of U.S. exporters led to an export boom.

BOX

FIGURE 6.12

The J Curve in the 1980s During the 1980s the U.S. real exchange rate, the purchasing power of foreign currency, fell from 20 percent above its 1973 level to 25 percent below its 1973 level and then reversed itself. As the real exchange rate fell, U.S.-made goods became more expensive to foreigners, and exports fell. As the real exchange rate rose in the late 1980s, U.S.-made goods became cheaper to foreign purchasers, and exports ultimately rose but changes in export volumes lagged behind changes in the real exchange rate by a year or more.

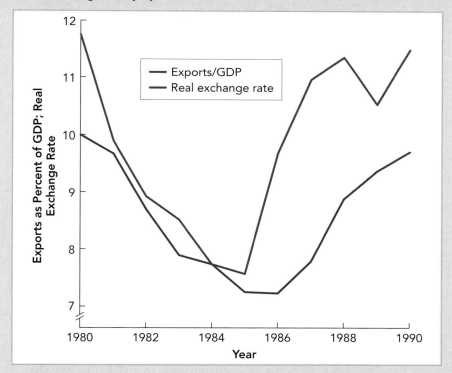

Source: The 2004 edition of *The Economic Report of the President* (Washington, DC: Government Printing Office).

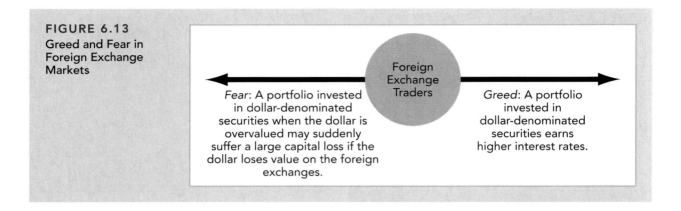

FIGURE 6.13
Greed and Fear in
Foreign Exchange
Markets

Consider foreign exchange speculators whose job is to trade currencies and make money. They spend their days glued to computer terminals, watching the prices of bonds denominated in different currencies flash across the screen. They buy and sell bonds and stocks of different countries and governments denominated in different currencies — dollars, euros, pounds, yen, pesos, ringgit, and more than 100 others. Their lives are ruled by greed and fear, as sketched out in Figure 6.13:

• *Greed:* Suppose a trader sees higher interest rates paid on the dollar-denominated bonds of U.S. companies than on the euro-denominated bonds of German companies. In this case, there is money to be made by selling ("going short on") German companies' bonds, buying ("going long on") U.S. companies' bonds, and pocketing the extra interest.

• *Fear:* Suppose that the trader is long on dollar-denominated bonds (owns many of them) and short on euro-denominated bonds (owns few of them) and the U.S. exchange rate then rises. At a higher real exchange rate, each dollar will be worth fewer euros; whatever profits were expected from the interest rate spread are wiped out by the loss caused by the exchange rate movement. So if today's value of the exchange rate is below long-run historical trends, the fear that exchange rates will soon rise to their normal relationships and impose large foreign exchange losses will be immense. Traders will shy away from dollar-denominated bonds if they fear an imminent depreciation of the dollar.

The greater the difference in interest rates in favor of dollar-denominated securities, the higher is the greed factor. Foreign exchange traders demand more dollar-denominated assets and demand fewer assets denominated in other currencies. They thus need less foreign currency and so they decrease their demand for foreign currency. By the laws of supply and demand, this lowers the price of foreign currency which is the nominal exchange rate e, which makes the real exchange rate ε drop also. So when the gap between domestic and foreign real interest rates increases, the greed factor leads to a lower real exchange rate.

But at this lower real exchange rate, fear is heightened. Foreign exchange traders worry that a future exchange rate movement might wipe out their gains. So not all traders rush to fill their portfolios with dollar-denominated assets, despite the more favorable domestic interest rates. The enormously liquid, enormously high-volume, enormously volatile foreign exchange markets settle at the point where greed and fear balance. Thus we say the real exchange rate ε is equal to the average foreign exchange trader's opinion ε_0 of what the exchange rate should be if there were no interest rate differentials, minus a parameter ε_r times the interest rate differential between domestic real interest rates r and foreign real interest rates r^f:

$$\varepsilon = \varepsilon_0 - \varepsilon_r(r - r^f)$$

The longer that interest rate differentials are expected to continue, and the more slowly that real exchange rates are expected to revert to trend, the higher ε_r will be and the larger will be the effect of a given interest rate differential on the exchange rate.

Remember: The exchange rate is the value of foreign currency. If foreign currency becomes more valuable, the exchange rate rises; if domestic currency becomes more valuable, the exchange rate falls. Often you will hear people talk of an appreciation or revaluation of the dollar or of a depreciation or devaluation of the dollar. An *appreciation* or *revaluation* of the dollar is a fall in the value of the exchange rate. A *depreciation* or *devaluation* of the dollar is a rise in the value of the exchange rate.

Our equations for net exports

$$NX = GX - IM = (X_f Y^f + X_\varepsilon \varepsilon) - (IM_y Y)$$

and for the exchange rate

$$\varepsilon = \varepsilon_0 - \varepsilon_r(r - r^f)$$

are the last of the building blocks of the flexible-price model.

RECAP   INTERNATIONAL TRADE

Gross exports depend positively on foreign real GDP and on the real exchange rate. Imports depend positively on domestic real GDP. The difference between gross exports and imports is net exports, which is the fourth and last component of aggregate demand.

In turn, the exchange rate depends on a number of factors, the most important of which is the difference between domestic and foreign real interest rates. The higher the domestic real interest rate or the lower foreign real interest rates, the lower are the nominal and real exchange rates. The most important of the other factors that affect the real exchange rate is foreign currency speculators' confidence.

6.4 CONCLUSION

This chapter has focused only on the building blocks of the analysis. Putting the blocks together and determining the division of real GDP between its four components are tasks reserved for the next chapter. Moreover, recall that this chapter has presented only a snapshot view of the flexible-price economy. It has not discussed the impact of changes in policy and in the economic environment on economic growth. That was done in Chapters 4 and 5 (refer to them to analyze how changes in investment spending ultimately affect productivity). This chapter has ignored the nominal financial side of the economy — money, prices, and inflation — entirely. That topic will be covered in Chapter 8.

Last, but not least, the flexible-price analysis of this part, Part 3, is itself not a complete analysis of even the real side of the economy. It needs to be supplemented by the analysis of what happens in the short run when prices are sticky. That analysis is carried out in Part 4.

Chapter Summary

1. This chapter has begun the analysis of a flexible-price, full-employment economy in a period short enough that potential output is fixed, but long enough for flexible wages and prices to bring supply and demand into balance and thus markets into equilibrium.

2. When the economy is at full employment, the level of real GDP is equal to potential output, which is the level of output generated by the production function of Chapter 4 from the current stocks of labor and capital and the current efficiency of labor.

3. When wages and prices are flexible, the working of the labor market keeps the economy at full employment. If labor demand is less than the size of the labor force, falling wages raise employment; if labor demand is greater than the size of the labor force, rising wages lower employment.

4. The level of consumption spending is determined by many things, but the most important of them are four: real GDP (or national income) Y, the average tax rate t, the baseline level of consumption C_0, and households' marginal propensity to consume C_y. National income and the tax rate together determine disposable income Y^D:

$$Y^D = (1 - t)Y$$

Disposable income, the baseline level of consumption, and the MPC together determine the level of consumption according to the consumption function:

$$C = C_0 + C_y Y^D$$

or

$$C = C_0 + C_y(1 - t)Y$$

5. The level of investment spending is primarily determined by two factors: business managers' degree of optimism, which powerfully affects the baseline level of investment spending I_0, and the real interest rate r, for the higher is the real interest rate the lower is investment spending. The simple investment function is

$$I = I_0 - I_r r$$

6. The real exchange rate is determined largely by foreign exchange traders' reactions to the differential between domestic and foreign real interest rates.

7. Net exports are determined by the level of the real exchange rate, the level of real GDP abroad (which affects the level of exports), and the level of real GDP (which determines the level of imports).

Key Terms

potential output (p. 160)

production function (p. 160)

classical assumption (p. 161)

labor market (p. 162)

marginal product of labor (MPL) (p. 163)

labor supply (p. 165)

real wage (p. 166)

labor market equilibrium (p. 166)

disposable income (p. 169)

marginal propensity to consume (MPC) (p. 170)

consumption function (p. 170)

real interest rate (p. 173)

present value (p. 174)

investment function (p. 175)

government purchases (p. 177)

transfer payments (p. 178)

net taxes (p. 178)

net exports (p. 179)

gross exports (p. 179)

imports (p. 179)

Analytical Exercises

1. In the full-employment model, what determines the level of real GDP?

2. In the economy as a whole, what makes labor demand equal to the labor force?

3. What happens if the parameter C_0 in the consumption function rises?

4. What happens to net exports if foreign exchange speculators become more optimistic about the long-run real value of the domestic currency?

5. What happens to net exports if interest rates abroad rise?

Policy Exercises

1. Suppose an economy with the standard Cobb-Douglas production function

$$Y^* = K^\alpha(LE)^{1-\alpha}$$

has a diminishing-returns-to-investment parameter α equal to $\frac{1}{3}$, a value of the labor force L equal to 100 million workers, a value of the capital stock K equal to $40 trillion, and an efficiency of the labor force E equal to $50,000. What is the value of potential output Y^*? What is the value of potential output per worker Y^*/L? What is the market-clearing real wage (in dollars per year) at which the economy is at full employment, with neither unemployed workers nor excess demand for labor?

2. In an economy at full employment with an unchanging diminishing-returns-to-investment parameter α and output per worker growing at 3 percent per year, at what rate must the real wage be growing in order to maintain full employment?

3. What would you expect happened to real investment in the United States in 1996–2001 given that the real value of the stock market doubled during that time?

4. During the 1990s foreign exchange speculators became much more confident in the long-run value of the dollar. What would you suspect happened to net exports over that period?

5. Consumers whose stock market wealth multiplied over the 1990s pulled money out of the stock market to enhance their standard of living. What kind of shift in which parameter of the consumption function could be used to model this phenomenon?

A Closer Look at Consumption

APPENDIX

6a.1 PERMANENT AND TRANSITORY INCOME

One of the most important factors omitted from our consumption function is the distinction between permanent and transitory income. Your *permanent income* is the average level that you expect your level of income to be in the future. Your *transitory income* is the difference between your income now and your permanent income. *Milton Friedman* was the very first to point out that not this year's income but permanent income is likely to be the main determinant of consumption.

The Budget Constraint

Think of a consumer trying to decide how much to spend in two periods only — now and the future. Suppose that he or she can save (or borrow) in the present for the future at a real interest rate r. And suppose that the "now" and the "future" are not necessarily the same length of time: The future period is some parameter θ times the length of the present period. In the present the typical consumer decides how much to spend and how much to save. Income Y_{now}, consumption C_{now}, and saving S are linked by

$$S = Y_{\text{now}} - C_{\text{now}}$$

In the future, the consumer adds his or her future income to savings — which have in the meantime grown because they have earned real interest at rate r — and spends the total (you can't take it with you, after all!):

$$\theta(C_{\text{future}}) = \theta(Y_{\text{future}}) + (1 + r)S$$

Combining these two equations produces what economists call the *present value* form of the *consumer's budget constraint*:

$$C_{\text{now}} + \frac{\theta C_{\text{future}}}{(1 + r)} = Y_{\text{now}} + \frac{\theta Y_{\text{future}}}{(1 + r)}$$

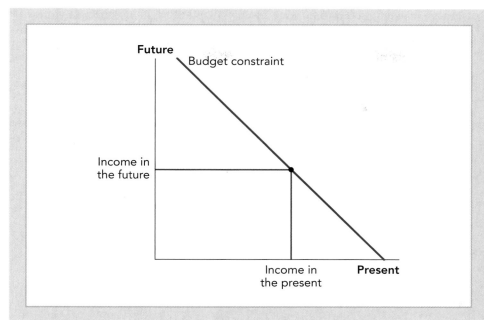

FIGURE 6a.1
The Budget Constraint
You can read off income in the present and the future from the diagram showing the consumer's income in both periods. By borrowing and lending, the consumer is free to choose levels of consumption in the present and the future corresponding to any point along the budget-constraint line. The slope of the budget line corresponds to the real interest rate. The higher the real interest rate, the steeper is the line — the more you can boost consumption in the future by cutting back and saving today.

Total consumption spending now and in the future must equal total income in the two periods. Future income and consumption count a little bit less — are "discounted" by the real interest rate — in order to turn them into "present values" before adding them to current consumption. Because savings earn interest, you must put aside only $1/(1 + r)$ dollars today in order to be able to spend 1 dollar on consumption in the future. Hence 1 dollar of consumption — or income — in the future has a "present value" of only $1/(1 + r)$ dollars today.

We can show this budget constraint on a diagram that plots the present on the horizontal axis and the future on the vertical axis (see Figure 6a.1). By borrowing or saving the consumer can redistribute consumption across time.

The Marginal Utility of Consumption

A representative consumer modeled by an economist will try to arrange his or her consumption now and in the future to maximize his or her utility. And any representative consumer in a model built by an economist will have a very simple utility function to maximize, such as

$$U = C_{\text{now}}{}^{\gamma} \times C_{\text{future}}{}^{(1-\gamma)}$$

where γ — the Greek letter "gamma" — is the parameter of the utility function. It governs how much the consumer values consumption now as opposed to consumption in the future.

If the marginal utility of per unit of time consumption (MUC) today is more than $(1 + r)/\theta$ times the MUC in the future, the consumer can increase his or her total utility a bit by cutting consumption in the future by an average of $(1 + r)/\theta$ dollars, reducing saving now by 1 dollar and increasing consumption now by 1 dollar. If the marginal utility of consumption today is less than $(1 + r)/\theta$ times the MUC in the future, the consumer can increase his or her total utility a bit by boosting consumption in the future by $(1 + r)/\theta$ dollars, increasing saving now by 1 dollar and cutting consumption now by 1 dollar. Thus if the consumer is behaving like a proper agent in an economist's model, it must be that

$$\frac{\text{MUC}_{\text{now}}}{\text{MUC}_{\text{future}}} = \frac{1 + r}{\theta}$$

What is the marginal utility of consumption now? Just as with the marginal product of labor, it is the change in utility produced by adding 1 more unit of consumption now:

$$\text{MUC}_{\text{now}} = [(C_{\text{now}} + 1)^{\gamma}](C_{\text{future}}^{1-\gamma}) - (C_{\text{now}}^{\gamma})(C_{\text{future}}^{1-\gamma})$$

which can be simplified to

$$\text{MUC}_{\text{now}} = [(C_{\text{now}} + 1)^{\gamma} - C_{\text{now}}^{\gamma}](C_{\text{future}}^{1-\gamma})$$

We can evaluate the marginal utility of consumption now by taking the derivative with regard to C_{now} of the utility function. It is

$$\text{MUC}_{\text{now}} = [\gamma(C_{\text{now}})^{\gamma-1}](C_{\text{future}}^{1-\gamma})$$

Similarly, the marginal utility of consumption in the future is

$$\text{MUC}_{\text{future}} = C_{\text{now}}^{\gamma}[(1 - \gamma)C_{\text{future}}^{1-\gamma}]$$

Thus if the consumer is behaving as expected,

$$\frac{1 + r}{\theta} = \frac{[\gamma(C_{\text{now}})^{\gamma-1}]C_{\text{future}}^{1-\gamma}}{C_{\text{now}}^{\gamma}[(1 - \gamma)C_{\text{future}}^{1-\gamma}]} = \frac{\gamma C_{\text{future}}}{(1 - \gamma)C_{\text{now}}}$$

or

$$C_{\text{future}} = \left[\frac{(1 + r)(1 - \gamma)}{\theta\gamma}\right]C_{\text{now}}$$

This equation tells us that the consumer spends a fraction γ of the present value of his or her total income on current consumption:

$$C_{\text{now}} = \gamma\left(Y_{\text{now}} + \frac{\theta Y_{\text{future}}}{1 + r}\right)$$

He or she spends the rest on future consumption. Once again, there is nothing especially "deep" in this simple result. Economists use this particular utility function often because it produces simple results.

Note that using this equation, a \$1 increase in transitory income — in Y_{now} but not in Y_{future} — would lead to a γ dollar increase in consumption today. But a \$1 increase in permanent income — in both Y_{now} and Y_{future} — would generate an increase in consumption in the present of

$$\Delta C_{\text{now}} = \gamma\left(1 + \frac{\theta}{1 + r}\right)$$

Thus the marginal propensity to consume is much larger if a change in income is permanent than if it is transitory. When an increase is transitory, consumers tend to smooth out their consumption over time by saving the bulk of the windfall, as shown in Figures 6a.2 and 6a.3. If consumers do not believe a change in income will be permanent, they will not adjust their spending now by very much.

For example, in the late 1960s President Lyndon Johnson proposed and Congress passed the Vietnam War income surtax. The surtax, a 10 percent increase in federal taxes, was imposed in an attempt to reduce consumption spending and so reduce

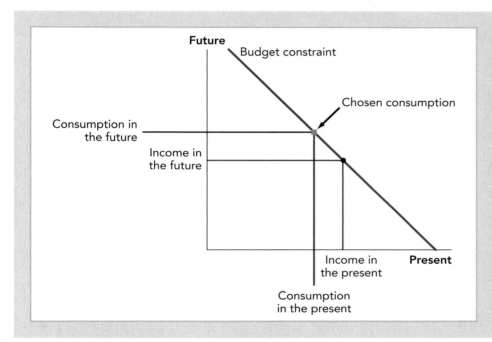

FIGURE 6a.2
Consumption Smoothing
Consumers try to smooth consumption over time. If their income is unusually high in the present, they will spend little of the excess and save most of it.

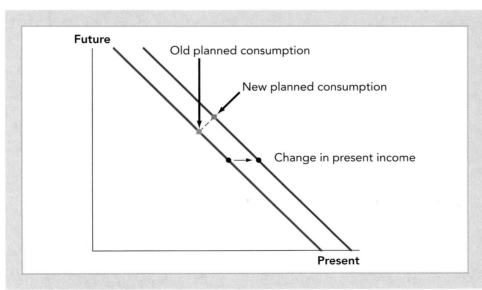

FIGURE 6a.3
The Effect of an Increase in Transitory Income
A change in transitory income — a change in income in the present but not the future — leads to a change in consumption in the present that is only a small fraction of the change in today's income.

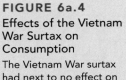

FIGURE 6a.4

Effects of the Vietnam War Surtax on Consumption

The Vietnam War surtax had next to no effect on consumption because it was broadly seen as a *transitory* change in tax policy.

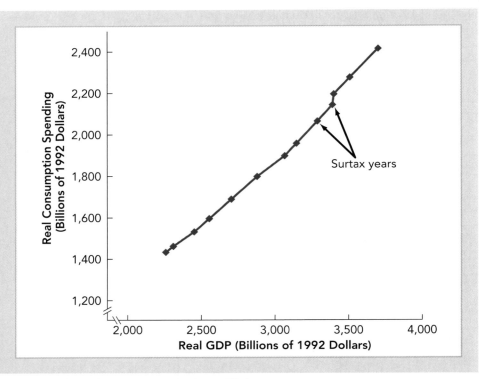

Source: The 1999 edition of *Economic Report of the President* (Washington, DC: Government Printing Office).

inflationary pressures during the Vietnam War. But President Johnson sold the surtax to Congress (and to the public) by promising that it would be a short-term, temporary measure with no permanent effects. He was convincing. Because everyone believed that the tax increase was short-term and temporary, it had no effect on consumers' beliefs about their permanent income. Everyone saw it as a change in transitory income only. And so it had next to no effect on consumption spending, as you can see in Figure 6a.4.

6a.2 CONSUMPTION AND THE REAL INTEREST RATE

An increase in the real interest rate makes saving more profitable: It means a higher rate of return earned on wealth saved and invested. Consumer saving is equal to after-tax income minus consumption. Does this mean that consumption spending is powerfully affected by the real interest rate and that an increase in the real interest rate decreases consumption spending? Probably not. An increase in the real interest rate does increase the rate of return on savings, and this induces a consumer to *substitute* saving for consumption in the present. But return to the expression for consumption spending now — C_{now} — derived earlier in this appendix:

$$C_{now} = \gamma \left(Y_{now} + \frac{\theta Y_{future}}{1 + r} \right)$$

If current income is large relative to future income — as it is if we are thinking of people saving for their retirement — then a change in the real interest rate r has no effect on current consumption spending. Thus it has no effect on current saving — the difference between current income and current consumption.

Why not? Because an increase in saving doesn't just make it more attractive to substitute saving for consumption today. An increase in the real interest rate also increases consumers' total lifetime wealth: Their permanent income is boosted because they earn higher returns on the money that they do save. This higher *permanent income* increases consumption in the present — and so reduces current saving. Which effect dominates? Is the income effect stronger, or is the substitution effect stronger? For consumers with low future incomes, the two effects almost cancel out. For consumers with high future incomes, they do indeed save more. But consumers with high future incomes had little reason to save to begin with, so even a large proportional increase in their saving has little effect on total economywide saving.

As a result, most economists think that these two effects roughly balance each other. They believe that changes in real interest rates have a small negative effect on consumption spending and a small positive effect on saving. But the effect of the real interest rate on consumption spending is not large enough to be worth the extra complication it would add to our models here.

7

Equilibrium in the Flexible-Price Model

QUESTIONS

In the flexible-price model, what keeps aggregate demand and the level of production equal to potential output?

In the flexible-price model, what makes the supply of funds — saving — equal to the demand for funds — investment — in financial markets?

When saving or investment demand changes, what happens in the flexible-price model to the real interest rate, and why?

As government policies, the international economic environment, or other features of policy or the economic environment change, what happens in the flexible-price model to consumption, investment, government, and net export spending?

7.1 FULL-EMPLOYMENT EQUILIBRIUM

Chapter 6 set out the determinants of the components of total spending. But knowing what determines consumption spending C, investment spending I, and net exports NX is not enough for understanding the macroeconomy. The macroeconomy is a system. The determinants of net exports are affected indirectly by the level of investment spending. Investment spending cannot be analyzed without knowing what has happened to consumption spending. But consumption spending depends on income, which in turn depends on the levels of net exports and investment spending.

We need a way of analyzing the macroeconomy as an interdependent system, rather than as a collection of parts we stack next to each other. What are the forces in the economy that make aggregate demand equal output? This question has two answers. One answer is correct when we assume prices are fully flexible. A second — different — answer is correct when we assume prices are sticky. Starting in Chapter 9, we will look at the sticky-price model of the macroeconomy. In this chapter, we assume prices are fully flexible.

When prices are fully flexible, the amount of output the economy produces Y is always equal to its potential output Y^*. So what guarantees that in a flexible-price economy, this full-employment level of output will also be an equilibrium level of output, where output equals aggregate demand? The real interest rate r ensures equilibrium in a flexible-price macroeconomy. We saw in Chapter 6 that the real interest rate determines investment spending. Also, the real interest rate determines the real exchange rate ε, and this real exchange rate determines net exports. What you will learn in this chapter is that changes in the real interest rate are what make the demand for output equal to the available output — which in this flexible-price economy is the potential output Y^*. We will call this the *flow-of-output* approach to understanding macroeconomic equilibrium in a flexible-price economy.

The Flow-of-Funds Approach

What you will also learn is that an equivalent approach is to start with the supply of funds — saving — and the demand for funds — investment: the flow-of-funds approach to understanding macroeconomic equilibrium in a flexible-price economy. The *flow-of-funds* through **financial markets** is key to understanding why the real interest rate brings the macroeconomy to equilibrium.

financial markets

The stock market, the bond market, the short-term borrowing market, plus firms' borrowings from banks.

What is the real interest rate that plays this role? The real interest rate is simultaneously the price the lender charges and the price of borrowing money. Money flows through financial markets. Savers try to find a productive, profitable, and interest-earning place to put their savings. Businesses try to find cheap financing for the investment projects they hope will be profitable.

Why do people lend money? Because they have no immediate spending use for it, and receiving some interest is better than having it sit under the mattress. Why do businesses borrow money? They borrow money because they hope to make a profit by using the funds they borrow to invest in new plant and equipment in order to expand their operations.

Thus the saving of households and others flows into financial markets, and the borrowing of businesses seeking to finance investment flows out of financial markets. This flow of funds through financial markets is a key set of economic transactions. The real interest rate is the price charged and received in this market for *loanable funds*. When the interest rate is at its long-run equilibrium level, the supply of loanable funds equals the demand for loanable funds. Financial markets are in balance.

Assumption of Price Flexibility

The key assumption that separates how we analyze equilibrium in this chapter from our analysis that begins in Chapter 9 is the assumption of price flexibility. In this chapter, we assume prices are fully flexible. (See Box 7.1 for an example of what it means for prices to be fully flexible.) We must confess: This assumption is not a realistic description of the short run. We use it because assuming prices are flexible is very helpful for analyzing the economy in the long run.

IF PRICES WERE TRULY FLEXIBLE ... : SOME DETAILS

What does it mean for prices to be flexible? The authors work in Berkeley, where sometimes it seems every student in a morning class arrives with a paper coffee cup in hand. The lines at one of the most popular cafés, Caffé Strada, typically go out the door just before the 10:00 a.m. classes begin. Everyone in line *needs* to have their cappuccino, latte, or espresso if they're going to make it through class. This is especially the case on our foggy, chilly mornings in late spring.

If prices were fully flexible, the price of the coffee drinks would rise between the time the last student got in line and the time she reached the counter. The chill in the air increased demand. The time (morning) increased demand. In a world of fully flexible prices, the price of the product would respond by rising *immediately*. As you stood there, waiting to reach the counter, you'd see the price of your coffee drink rise. But 45 minutes later, when the sun had burned off the fog so the chill in the air was gone, and when everyone was already in class, the subsequent fall in demand would lead to falling prices. That swing in prices in immediate response to changes in demand would be an example of *fully flexible* prices.

This is, of course, an example on a micro scale. When the same story applies in industry after industry, then you have a macro story.

The long-run model we already studied was Chapter 4's model of economic growth. Remember — or review — that when the saving rate increases in the long run, the capital-labor ratio and the capital-output ratio both increase. More saving produces a higher standard of living. But in Chapter 4, we had no story about *how* an increase in saving produces a higher capital-labor ratio. What is the mechanism? Chapter 7 provides the answer to that question: the real interest rate. You will learn in this chapter that when saving increases, real interest rates decline, and so investment spending increases. And more investment in plant and equipment produces a larger capital stock, which in the very long run increases the capital-labor ratio, the capital-output ratio, and output per worker.

Note that there will be a certain tension in this chapter. Prices are flexible; the time scale of the analysis must be long enough for prices to adjust so that there is no excess demand or excess supply in any of the economy's markets. So this analysis of Chapter 7 applies to changes in the economy only if they take significantly longer than a month or a quarter. On the other hand, we are going to assume that potential output Y^* does not change, which means that the analysis of Chapter 7 applies to changes in the economy only if they take significantly less than a decade. The usefulness of the flexible-price model thus tends to get squeezed between the sticky-price fluctuations model covered in later chapters and the long-run growth model covered earlier.

But before we get too far ahead of ourselves, let's build the model.

RECAP FULL-EMPLOYMENT EQUILIBRIUM

In a flexible-price economy, real output Y always equals potential output Y^*. At equilibrium in output markets, this potential output will equal aggregate demand; this is the flow-of-output approach. We can also look at equilibrium with the flow-of-funds approach; saving equals investment in equilibrium. Changes in the real interest rate will take the economy to equilibrium.

7.2 TWO APPROACHES, ONE MODEL

The goal of this chapter is to show how the real interest rate ensures full-employment equilibrium in an economy with flexible prices. At equilibrium, two statements will be true: The supply of funds will equal the demand for funds, and aggregate demand for output will equal potential output. Both statements are true because there are two approaches to this one flexible-price model. In this section, we will show that these two approaches — the flow-of-funds approach and the flow-of-output approach — are mathematically equivalent.

Why, if the two approaches to this one model are equivalent mathematically, do we bother with two approaches? The answer is worth remembering, because this will not be the last time in your studies of economics that a second, mathematically equivalent, approach is suddenly substituted for an approach you have already figured out. There are times in economics — and this is one of them — when a mathematically equivalent approach has much better economic intuition than the original approach you already mastered. And the best economics is always the most intuitive story.

We can show that the flow-of-funds approach and the flow-of-output approach are equivalent ways of modeling the flexible-price economy in two ways. We can show the equivalence with algebra. And we can show the equivalence using the drawing introduced in Chapter 2 of the economy's circular flow. Let's start with the circular flow, depicted in Figure 7.1.

Using the Circular Flow Diagram

Goods and services — output — are produced in businesses, generating income (the blue flow) for households. Household income includes not just wage and salary income, but interest income, rent income, retained business earnings, and more. Households can do three things with this income (the green flows): consume goods and services that are produced by businesses, pay net taxes to government, or save — household saving — in financial markets. With the net tax revenues,

FIGURE 7.1

The Circular Flow Diagram This version of the circular flow is complicated by the addition of the government and financial markets to the diagram. Not all final goods and services are bought by households. Some are bought by the government, which taxes to raise resources to finance itself. Some are bought by businesses seeking to invest, which raise the needed resources by issuing stock, issuing bonds, and borrowing — all of which take place in *financial markets*. This version is also complicated by its recognizing that there is a world outside, a world that buys the products of domestic businesses and that invests through domestic financial markets.

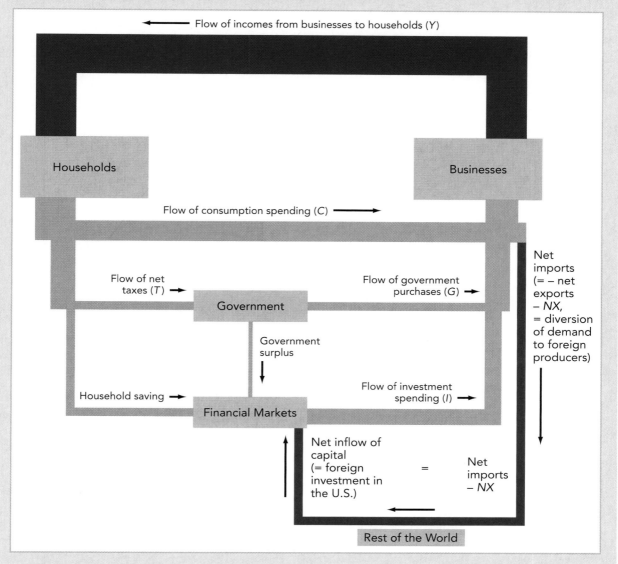

government can buy goods and services from businesses (the pink flow) or accumulate a surplus (green flow) which it saves in financial markets. Some goods and services are imported from other countries, so not all of the spending for goods and services flows back to domestic businesses; some of it flows to the rest of the world. Imports are at least partially offset by our exports of goods and services to other countries. The difference — imports less exports — represents funds from our economy that accumulate in the rest of the world. This net inflow of financial capital from the rest of the world (red flow) is saved in financial markets.

The financial markets lend the funds saved by households, government, and the rest of the world to businesses, which use the funds to invest in plant and equipment (pink flow). **Total saving** S is the sum of household saving S^H, government saving S^G, and foreign saving by the rest of the world S^F. So through the financial markets, total saving S equals investment I. This is the *flow-of-funds* approach to equilibrium.

The sum of consumption spending (pink flow from households), government spending (pink flow from government), investment spending (pink flow from financial markets), less the net imports (red flow to rest of the world) flows into businesses. This is aggregate demand. Businesses produce output in response to this aggregate demand. So through the output markets, aggregate demand equals output. This is the *flow-of-output* approach to equilibrium.

And the output produced by businesses generates income for households. Off we go on another round through the circular flow.

The circular flow diagram is one way to understand that the flow-of-funds and flow-of-output approaches to the macroeconomy are equivalent. We can also demonstrate that equivalence a second way: algebra.

Using Some Algebra

We start from the familiar flow-of-output equilibrium condition, and derive the flow-of-funds equilibrium condition. Begin with the definition of aggregate demand AD:

$$AD = C + I + G + NX$$

Under the flow-of-output approach, aggregate demand AD and output Y are equal in macroeconomic equilibrium. When wages and prices are flexible, then output Y equals the economy's potential productive output Y^*. So in flow-of-output equilibrium, potential output Y^* will equal aggregate demand AD. We have

$$Y^* = C + I + G + NX$$

Now a few steps will take us to the equivalent flow-of-funds equilibrium statement. Subtract consumption C, government purchases G, and net exports NX from both sides in order to move everything except investment spending I to the left-hand side:

$$Y^* - C - G - NX = I$$

And then a little math trick will give us economically meaningful concepts: Subtract *and* add net taxes T on the left-hand side by subtracting it from income Y^* and adding it to $-G$. Add some parentheses so we can group terms by economic concepts:

$$(Y^* - T - C) + (T - G) + (-NX) = I$$

Now let's step back and look at what this flow-of-funds equation means.

Unpacking the Flow-of-Funds Equation

The right-hand side of this equation is simply investment spending I. Under the flow-of-output approach, investment spending is simply spending by firms to build factories and structures and boost their productive capacity. But under the flow-of-funds

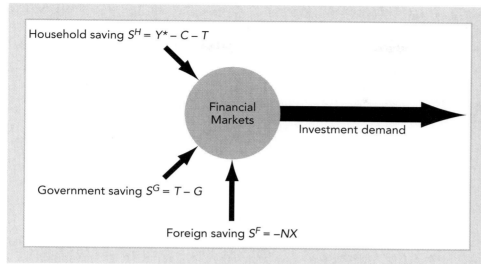

FIGURE 7.2

The Flow of Funds through Financial Markets

Household saving, government saving, and foreign saving flow into financial markets. These funds flow out of financial markets to businesses, which use the funds to finance investment demand — the purchase of new plant and equipment.

approach, we think of investment I not as the *output* that businesses buy, but as the *funds* that businesses allocate to buying these investment goods. Investment spending I is the flow of funds out of financial markets to businesses, which then use the funds to undertake investment. It is the demand for loanable funds.

The left-hand side of the equation measures the total saving flowing into financial markets from three different groups — households (which, remember, include not only the workers but also the owners of businesses), the government, and the rest of the world (see Figure 7.2).

The first term $Y^* - T - C$ is equal to **household saving** S^H. In this flexible-price model, potential output Y^* is equal to real output. Output and household income are always equal. So Y^* is just household income. Subtract net taxes T and consumption spending C from household income Y^* and what is left? What is left is household saving — the flow of funds from households into financial markets — because saving is the only thing that households do with income other than pay it to the government as taxes and spend it on consumption goods.

The second term $T - G$ is equal to **government saving** S^G. T is simply the taxes the government collects minus the transfer payments it makes to individuals. G is government purchases. So $T - G$ is the difference between the taxes that the government collects and the transfer payments and purchases the government makes. When $T - G$ is positive, the government is running a *budget surplus*. The surplus is government saving S^G. When $T - G$ is negative, the government is running a deficit (as it is today). Then S^G will be less than zero.

The last term — the opposite of net exports, $-NX$ — is **foreign saving** S^F, saving by foreigners directed into the United States. It is the **capital inflow**, the net flow of funds that the rest of the world channels into domestic financial markets. As Figure 7.3 illustrates, net exports are the difference between the dollars foreigners spend buying our exports and the dollars earned by foreigners selling us imports. If net exports are less than zero — which they typically are for America — foreigners have dollars left over after they buy all our exports they want. These internationally owned dollars flow into financial markets. They aren't spent buying our exports, and the only other useful thing the rest of the world can do with them

household saving

Equal to households' disposable incomes (which include earnings retained by corporations and then reinvested) minus their consumption spending. Household saving includes both saving done directly by households and saving done on their behalf by firms whose stock they own.

government saving

The government's budget surplus. Government saving is negative when the government runs a budget deficit.

foreign saving

The net amount of money that foreigners are committing to buying up property and assets in the home country. Equal to minus net exports.

capital inflow

Net investment by the citizens of one country in another — the "flow" of financial capital from one country to another.

FIGURE 7.3

Imports Minus Exports Equals Foreign Saving

Dollars earned by foreigners from selling us imported goods and services return to the United States either as payments for goods and services we export or as foreign saving that flows into U.S. financial markets.

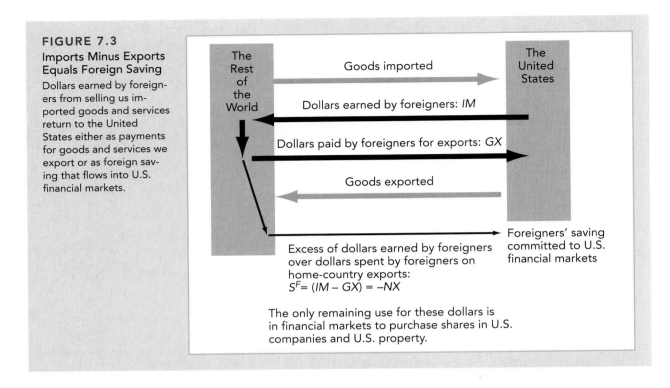

is save them. (When net exports are positive, this term has a different interpretation. It is the net amount of domestic saving that is diverted into international financial markets — the amount of saving that does not show up as loanable funds available to finance investment at home, but instead finances investment abroad.)

We have derived the flow-of-funds equilibrium equation. The three left-hand side terms of

$$(Y^* - T - C) + (T - G) + (-NX) = I$$

are the three flows of purchasing power into the financial markets: household saving S^H, government saving S^G, and foreign saving S^F. Added together they make up total saving S, which is the supply of loanable funds. The demand for loanable funds is simply investment spending I, the right-hand side of the equation above. So the flow-of-funds equilibrium equation can also be written

$$S^H + S^G + S^F = I$$

What we have shown is that the flow-of-output equilibrium condition — output equals aggregate demand — is equivalent to the flow-of-funds equilibrium condition — saving equals investment. When one statement is true, the other must also be true. When one is false, the other must also be false. If supply equals demand in the market for loanable funds

$$S^H + S^G + S^F = I$$

then aggregate demand in the flexible-price economy is equal to full-employment output. And if output equals aggregate demand in the markets for goods and services

$$Y^* = C + I + G + NX$$

FINANCIAL TRANSACTIONS AND THE FLOW OF FUNDS: SOME DETAILS

The relationship between the funds that flow into and the funds that flow out of financial markets is indirect. When the government runs a surplus, it does not directly lend money to a business that wants to build a new factory. Instead, the government uses the surplus to buy back some of the bonds that it previously issued. The bank that owned those bonds then takes the cash it received from the government and uses it to buy some other financial asset — perhaps bonds issued by a corporation.

Similarly, households or foreigners using financial markets to save rarely buy newly issued corporate bonds. Moreover, they rarely buy shares of stock that are part of an initial public offering. On the rare occasion when they do, they are directly transferring purchasing power to a company undertaking investment. Instead, households and foreigners usually save by purchasing already-existing securities or simply depositing their wealth in a bank.

The relationship between the flows of funds into and out of financial markets is indirect, but it is very real.

then the supply and demand in the flow of funds through financial markets balances as well. (Although, as Box 7.2 points out, the relationship between the supply and demand for funds is not direct.)

RECAP TWO APPROACHES, ONE MODEL

We can approach equilibrium in two ways. One is the flow-of-output approach: In equilibrium, output equals aggregate demand. The other is the flow-of-funds approach: In equilibrium, saving equals investment. We can show that these two approaches are equivalent using the circular flow diagram. We can also show they are equivalent algebraically, by starting with one equilibrium condition, $Y = AD$, and deriving from it the other, $S = I$.

7.3 THE REAL INTEREST RATE ADJUSTS TO ENSURE EQUILIBRIUM

In a flexible-price economy, equilibrium exists when aggregate demand equals potential output. But what economic forces will make aggregate demand equal potential output? The determinants of C, I, G, and NX are things like consumers' optimism, interest rates, the sensitivity of exports to exchange rates, and so on. These determinants seem to have nothing at all to do with the determinants of Y^*. It is the form of the production function and the available resources on the supply side that determine the level of potential output Y^*. So what will make the sum of C, I, G, and NX equal potential output?

The answer is: The real interest rate r plays the key role. If government policy, the international economic environment, or domestic conditions change, then the real interest rate changes in response. In turn, the change in the real interest rate causes changes in investment spending, the exchange rate, and net exports. The real interest rate will continue to change until the economy is again at equilibrium. It is these changes in the real interest rate that ensure that in the long run a flexible-price macroeconomy reaches and stays at equilibrium where aggregate demand equals potential output.

But how could a disequilibrium between aggregate demand and output lead to a change in the real interest rate? Here is where the flow-of-funds approach comes in. Equilibrium with aggregate demand equal to potential output is equivalent to equilibrium with the supply of funds — saving — equal to the demand for funds — investment. When aggregate demand is less than potential output, saving is greater than investment. And when aggregate demand is greater than potential output, investment is greater than saving.

When the supply of funds — saving — is greater than the demand for funds — investment — what will happen? The price of funds — the real interest rate r — will fall. Some financial institutions — banks, mutual funds, venture capitalists, insurance companies, whatever — will find purchasing power piling up as more money flows into their accounts than they can find good projects to commit to. They will try to underbid their competitors. How do they underbid? They underbid by saying that they will accept a lower interest rate than the current real interest rate.

As the real interest rate falls, two things happen. The number and value of investment projects that are profitable rise. Investment spending rises, closing the gap between saving and investment (and, not coincidentally, closing the gap between aggregate demand and potential output). And net exports rise, decreasing foreign saving and further closing the gap between saving and investment (and, again not coincidentally, further closing the gap between aggregate demand and potential output). The process will stop when the interest rate has fallen just enough to make the flow of saving into the financial markets equal to investment. So that's the big bottom line: The real interest rate ensures equilibrium in the flexible-price model because both investment and saving respond to changes in the real interest rate.

Graphing the Saving-Investment Relationship

We can depict these relationships graphically. Investment spending is the demand for loanable funds. As the real interest rate r falls, investment spending I rises. The graph in Figure 7.4 should remind you of Figure 6.9, though we have switched the horizontal and vertical axes.

Total saving is the supply of loanable funds. It has three components: household saving S^H, government saving S^G (which is usually negative), and foreign saving S^F. Let's start with foreign saving. As the real interest rate r falls, foreign saving S^F falls. The intuition is a bit roundabout. As the real domestic interest rate falls, the nominal and real exchange rates rise. (If you want to review why this is so, see Section 6.3.) When the real exchange rate ε rises, gross exports GX rise. When gross exports rise, net exports NX rise, which is the same thing as saying net imports $(-NX)$ fall. When net imports fall, net foreign inflow of financial capital falls. And net foreign inflow of financial capital is just a long phrase for foreign saving S^F.

The relationship is depicted in Figure 7.5. It is important to remember that foreign saving can be either negative or positive. When a country runs a *trade surplus,* foreign saving is negative. When it runs a *trade deficit,* as the United States

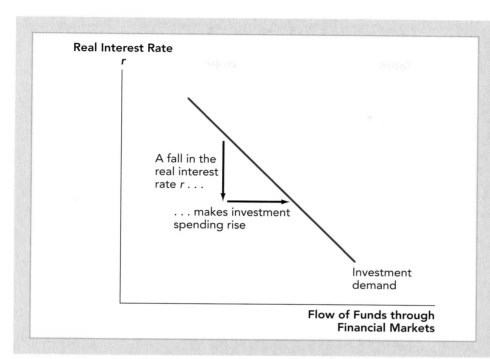

FIGURE 7.4
The Demand for Loanable Funds
The demand for loanable funds is investment demand. When the real interest rate falls, the number and value of profitable investment projects rise, increasing businesses' demand for loanable funds to finance investment.

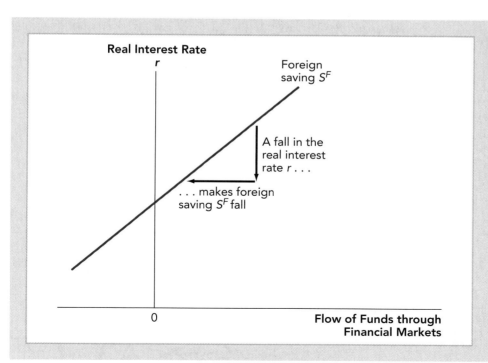

FIGURE 7.5
Foreign Saving: The Supply of Loanable Funds from Foreigners
The supply of loanable funds from foreigners is foreign saving. When the domestic real interest rate falls, foreigners will move some funds out of dollar-denominated assets and into assets denominated in other currencies, decreasing foreign saving as nominal and real exchange rates rise.

has been doing for many years, foreign saving is positive. To remind ourselves that foreign saving can be negative or positive, we draw the foreign saving curve crossing the vertical axis, as in Figure 7.5.

Household saving is another component of total saving. Household saving S^H is what's left over after net taxes T and consumption C have been subtracted from household income. Consumption spending depends on income, as do net taxes. But as we noted in Appendix 6a, real interest rates do not affect consumption. And because we are assuming that household income is always equal to potential output Y^*, which depends on the supplies of inputs and the production function, then income is not dependent on the real interest rate. And since neither the tax rate nor income depends on the real interest rate, net taxes don't change when the real interest rate changes. So household saving S^H does not change when the real interest rate changes. We show the relationship between household saving and the real interest rate as a vertical line, as in panel (*a*) of Figure 7.6.

Government saving S^G is the final component of total saving. But its value also does not depend on the value of the real interest rate. So here again, we would show

---

FIGURE 7.6
Household and Government Supply of Loanable Funds

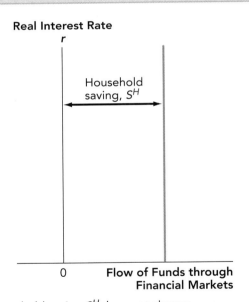
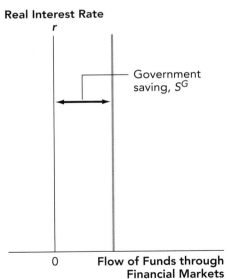

(*a*) Household saving S^H does not change when the real interest rate *r* changes. The distance from the vertical axis to the household saving line measures the amount of funds that flow into financial markets from households. If households dissave, so that S^H is negative, the household saving line is to the left of zero.

(*b*) Government saving S^G also does not change when the real interest rate *r* changes. The distance from the vertical axis to the government saving line would measure the amount of funds that flow from financial markets to the government. If the government runs a deficit, so that S^G is negative, the government saving line is to the left of zero.

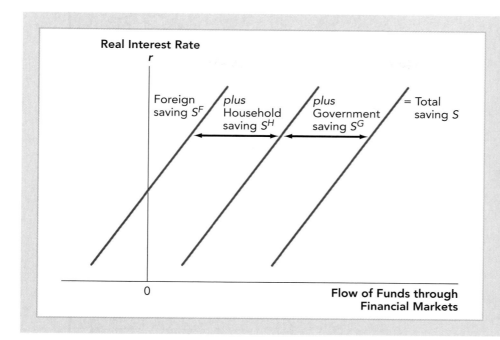

FIGURE 7.7

Total Saving: The Supply of Loanable Funds

Total saving is the sum of foreign, household, and government saving. Total saving increases as the real interest rate rises because of the relationship between the real interest rate and foreign saving.

the relationship between government saving and the real interest rate as a vertical line, as shown in panel (*b*) of Figure 7.6. If government saving was negative — if the government was running a deficit — then the government saving line would be to the left of zero.

Total saving is the sum of foreign, household, and government saving. Graphically, we take the foreign saving line, shift it over by the amount of household saving, and shift it over again — or in the case of a government budget deficit shift it *back* — by the amount of government saving. This gives us the relationship between total saving *S* and the real interest rate. We do this in Figure 7.7.

We now have the two sides of the loanable funds market. The demand for loanable funds is investment spending, depicted in Figure 7.4. The supply of loanable funds is total saving, depicted in Figure 7.7. Bring them together to see the market for loanable funds, as we have done in Figure 7.8 on page 206. When total saving *S* equals investment demand *I*, the market for loanable funds is in equilibrium.

The Adjustment to Flow-of-Funds Equilibrium

Suppose that the real interest rate is initially greater than the equilibrium real interest rate, as shown in Figure 7.9. Saving will exceed investment by the amount labeled "excess saving." Some lenders will offer to accept a lower interest rate. As interest rates fall, investment spending will increase, moving along the investment demand curve. And as interest rates fall, foreign saving will fall, moving along the total saving curve. The macroeconomy will move to the equilibrium interest rate, where saving equals investment. And, as we showed above, when saving equals investment, aggregate demand equals potential output. When prices are fully flexible, the real interest rate adjusts to ensure full employment.

FIGURE 7.8

Equilibrium in the Flow of Loanable Funds

The market for loanable funds is in equilibrium when the supply of loanable funds — total saving *S* — equals the demand for loanable funds — investment demand *I*.

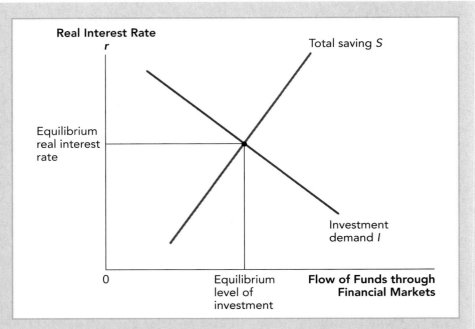

FIGURE 7.9

Excess Saving in the Market for Loanable Funds

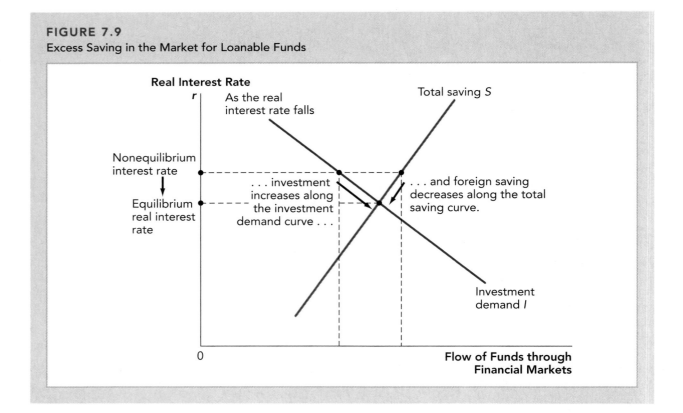

7.4 USING THE MODEL: WHAT MAKES THE REAL INTEREST RATE CHANGE?

We can use this graphical way of looking at the flow of funds to figure out what happens to the equilibrium real interest rate when there is some change in the economic environment or in economic policy. Some changes make either the saving or the investment curve shift. Other changes also affect the slope of the saving or investment curve. When one or both of the curves shift or change slope, there will be a new equilibrium real interest rate. Let's take a look.

The Effect of a Change in Saving

Total saving S is the sum of household, government, and foreign saving. So a decrease in any of those components of S will decrease total saving. It could be a decrease in household saving, decreasing S^H. It could be an increase in government spending, which decreases government saving S^G. It could be a decrease in our imports, which decreases foreign saving S^F. Any of these changes would be shown by a shift to the left of the total saving S curve, as shown in Figure 7.10.

As an example, let's suppose the economy is in equilibrium when policy makers decide to increase annual government purchases by the amount ΔG. More government purchases mean less government saving. Less government saving means that the supply of saving in the loanable funds market is shifted to the left: At each possible interest rate, total saving flowing into the loanable funds market is decreased.

At the original real interest rate, investment demand will now exceed total saving. This shortfall in saving will cause the real interest rate r to rise; some borrowers bid up interest rates in an attempt to obtain funding for their investment projects. But the rising interest rate squeezes other borrowers out of the market; the total quantity of funds demanded for investment falls, moving us up and to the left along the investment demand curve. The rising domestic real interest rate also lowers the real exchange rate ε and increases foreign saving flowing into domestic financial markets, moving us along the second total saving curve. The real interest rate will rise until saving again equals investment. In the end, the flow-of-funds market settles down to equilibrium at a new, higher equilibrium interest rate r with a new, lower level of investment.

When the supply of loanable funds S decreases, the real interest rate r rises, investment spending falls, and (not surprisingly) the amount of saving falls. But

FIGURE 7.10

A Decrease in Saving Increases the Real Interest Rate

When government purchases rise or taxes are cut, government saving is lowered. The drop in total saving leads to higher real interest rates, increased financing of investment by foreigners, and a fall in investment spending by businesses. Economists worry about the long-run effects of rising government deficits because of their effect on capital accumulation.

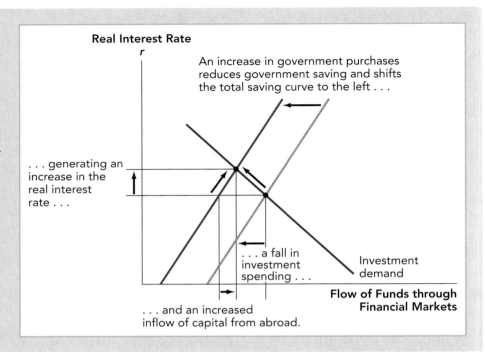

notice what has happened. The final change in investment and saving, shown along the horizontal axis, is smaller than the change in saving that threw the flow-of-funds markets out of equilibrium. How could that be? The final change in saving is smaller than the initial change in saving because foreign saving rose when the real interest rate rose. But this rise in foreign saving is relatively small so, overall, saving still falls.

A drop in household saving S^H would be analyzed the same way, as would a drop in foreign saving S^F that occurred at every interest rate. In both of these cases, the total saving curve shifts to the left, raising the real interest rate, increasing foreign saving slightly to offset part but not all of the initial drop in saving, and decreasing investment demand.

A tax cut has a slightly different effect. It is very like the effect of a government purchases increase. But because a tax cut increases disposable income and the marginal propensity to consume is less than 1, there is one difference. The difference is that a portion of the addition to household income from the tax cut shows up as household saving. So the initial shift to the left of the total saving curve is smaller than the drop in government saving by the amount of this change in household saving. Otherwise the effects are very similar: Like a government purchases increase, a tax cut leads to an increase in the interest rate, a rise in foreign saving, and a fall in investment spending.

Why do economists make such a big deal out of a decrease in government saving — whether it's due to a decrease in taxes or an increase in government purchases? Because as Figure 7.10 illustrates, in the long run, a decrease in government saving — an increase in the budget deficit — makes interest rates rise, which reduces investment spending. And remember one of the lessons of Chapter 4: Investment spending increases the capital stock, which ultimately increases

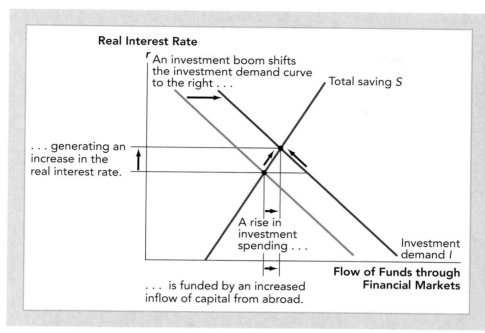

FIGURE 7.11

An Increase in Investment Also Increases the Real Interest Rate

Increased investment demand leads to higher real interest rates, which dampen business enthusiasm for new investment projects while increasing financing of investment by foreigners.

the standard of living. In the long run, increases in government borrowing "crowd out" — reduce — investment spending, which, all else equal, slows the country's rate of economic growth while the economy adjusts to a lower balanced-growth path.

The Effect of a Change in Investment Demand

We can also use the flow-of-funds graph to see the effect of an increase in investment I. Suppose that businesses suddenly become more optimistic about the future and increase the amount they wish to spend on new plant and equipment (as they did in the late 1990s). What would be the effect of such a domestic investment boom?

Investment — the demand-for-loanable-funds curve — *shifts* to the right, as Figure 7.11 shows. At the initial interest rate, investment demand now exceeds saving. Firms that wish to increase their investment spending will bid up interest rates as they compete for scarce loans. As interest rates rise, two things simultaneously happen. One, other firms will decrease their investment spending because their planned investment projects are no longer profitable at these now-higher interest rates — a *movement along* the new investment demand curve. Two, the higher real interest rate leads to a fall in the real exchange rate, to a fall in net exports, and thus to an increase in foreign saving flowing into domestic financial markets — a *movement along* the saving curve. In the end, the loanable funds market settles at a higher interest rate with an increased level of saving and investment.

Notice what happened: The higher interest rates due to the first shift in investment led to a subsequent decrease in investment that partly — but not entirely — offset the initial shift. But investment did increase. What made the increase in investment possible? The increase in foreign saving. If saving had not increased in reaction to the higher interest rates, investment could not increase. Without an increase in saving, the shift in investment demand would make interest rates rise so much that investment spending would fall right back to its initial position.

Instead, when foreign saving increases with real interest rates, both saving and investment increase in response to increased business optimism.

> **RECAP   USING THE MODEL: WHAT MAKES THE REAL INTEREST RATE CHANGE?**
>
> We can use the graphical approach to flow-of-funds equilibrium to see that an increase in saving or a decrease in investment — shifts to the right in the saving curve or to the left in the investment demand curve — would lead to a fall in the real interest rate. And a decrease in saving or an increase in investment would make the real interest rate rise. When the supply of saving shifts, the ultimate change in saving will be smaller than the initial change in saving. When investment demand shifts, the ultimate change in investment will be smaller than the initial change in investment. In both cases, this is due to changes in the real interest rate which induce movements along the saving and investment curves that partly offset the initial shifts.

7.5 CALCULATING THE EQUILIBRIUM REAL INTEREST RATE: ALGEBRA

The flow-of-funds graphs let us figure out whether interest rates rise or fall in reaction to a change in policy or economic environment that affects investment demand or total saving. But what if we are policy makers who want to know the precise value of the real interest rate at equilibrium, and by how much the interest rate will change if we implement some policy? To figure out the value of the interest rate and *how much* it changes in reaction to a change in policy or economic environment, we need to do some algebra.

What we need are the equations for total saving S and for investment demand I. Equilibrium occurs when saving S equals investment I, so we will just set the equations equal to each other. Then we solve for the real interest rate.

This sounds straightforward — and it is. But the equations can get quite messy. Don't get discouraged. If the notation and the algebra get to be a bit much, remember that all we're doing is setting saving equal to investment and solving for r.

The Formula for the Equilibrium Real Interest Rate

Start with total saving, which is the sum of household saving S^H, government saving S^G, and foreign saving S^F:

$$S = S^H + S^G + S^F$$

Household saving is equal to total income Y minus net taxes T minus consumption spending C. But since we are in a world of flexible prices (that's our assumption in this chapter, remember), total income Y is always equal to potential output Y^*. Consumption spending depends on baseline consumption C_0, the marginal propensity to consume C_y, the tax rate t, and potential income Y^* (peek back at Section 6.2 to refresh your memory). Thus

$$S^H = Y^* - T - C = Y^* - tY^* - [C_0 + C_y(1 - t)Y^*]$$

Government saving is equal to net taxes T minus government purchases G. As in Chapter 6, let net taxes be a constant proportion of income: $T = tY$. Government saving then equals

$$S^G = T - G = tY^* - G$$

Notice that neither household saving nor government saving depends on the real interest rate. That is why we graphed household saving S^H and government saving S^G as vertical lines in Figure 7.6.

What about foreign saving S^F? Here the real interest rate plays a role. (Section 6.3 laid out the details.) Foreign saving is imports minus exports. The determinants of foreign saving are three parameters — the propensity to import IM_y, foreigners' propensity to buy exports X_f, and the sensitivity of exports to the exchange rate X_ε — and three variables — foreign incomes Y^f, domestic total income Y^*, and the exchange rate ε:

$$S^F = -NX = IM_y Y^* - X_f Y^f - X_\varepsilon \varepsilon$$

And it is the exchange rate that changes when the real interest rate r changes:

$$\varepsilon = \varepsilon_0 - \varepsilon_r(r - r^f)$$

where the real exchange rate ε depends on the baseline value of the real exchange rate ε_0, the sensitivity of the real exchange rate to changes in interest rates ε_r, the domestic real interest rate r, and the foreign real interest rate r^f.

So, because foreign saving depends on the exchange rate, and because the exchange rate depends on the interest rate, foreign saving S^F depends on the real interest rate r. When the real interest rate rises, the total saving flow increases. Why? Because an increase in the real interest rate attracts foreign capital into domestic financial markets and increases foreign saving. We can write this as

$$S^F = IM_y Y^* - X_f Y^f - X_\varepsilon \varepsilon_0 + X_\varepsilon \varepsilon_r r - X_\varepsilon \varepsilon_r r^f$$

In the fourth term of this equation we see that foreign saving depends on the real interest rate.

On the other side, demand for funds is simply investment spending. Use the investment equation from Section 6.2. When the real interest rate r rises, investment spending I falls:

$$I = I_0 - I_r r$$

The level of investment spending depends on the real interest rate.

The flow-of-funds equilibrium is where supply and demand balance — where total saving is equal to investment spending:

$$\text{At equilibrium, } S^H + S^G + S^F = I$$

So now we solve this equation for r, the equilibrium real interest rate. The details of the derivation are given in Box 7.3. In equilibrium, the real interest rate r will equal

$$r = \frac{I_0 - [Y^* - C_0 - C_y(1 - t)Y^*] + G - (IM_y Y^* - X_f Y^f - X_\varepsilon \varepsilon_0 - X_\varepsilon \varepsilon_r r^f)}{I_r + X_\varepsilon \varepsilon_r}$$

Interpreting the Equilibrium Real Interest Rate Equation

What does that equation say? First look at the numerator. When I_0 increases — when business people become more optimistic — the real interest rate will increase.

7.3 BOX

DERIVING THE EQUILIBRIUM INTEREST RATE EQUATION: DETAILS

To derive the equation for the equilibrium real interest rate, we start from either the flow-of-output or the flow-of-funds equilibrium statement:

$$Y = C + I + G + NX \quad \text{or} \quad S^H + S^G + S^F = I$$

Because one equilibrium statement leads to the other (see Section 7.2), many students like to start from the more familiar statement $Y = C + I + G + NX$. If you do so, you'll follow the same "plug-and-chug" steps that we use here. But here, let's use the flow-of-funds approach, so we begin with the flow-of-funds equilibrium statement $S^H + S^G + S^F = I$.

First, we need the expression for household saving:

$$S^H = Y^* - T - C$$

Substituting the equations for taxes and for consumption gives us

$$S^H = Y^* - tY^* - C_0 - C_y(1 - t)Y^*$$

Next, we need the expression for government saving, into which we substitute the equation for taxes

$$S^G = T - G = tY^* - G$$

Finally, we need the expression for foreign saving

$$S^F = -NX = IM - GX$$

First we substitute the equations for imports and for exports

$$S^F = IM_y Y^* - (X_f Y^f + X_\varepsilon \varepsilon)$$

and then we substitute the equation for the real exchange rate

$$S^F = IM_y Y^* - X_f Y^f - X_\varepsilon[\varepsilon_0 - \varepsilon_r(r - r^f)] = IM_y Y^* - X_f Y^f - X_\varepsilon \varepsilon_0 + X_\varepsilon \varepsilon_r r - X_\varepsilon \varepsilon_r r^f$$

Remember the equation for investment

$$I = I_0 - I_r r$$

Now "plug and chug": Set saving — the sum of household, government, and foreign saving — equal to investment:

$$[Y^* - tY^* - C_0 - C_y(1 - t)Y^*] + (tY^* - G) +$$
$$(IM_y Y^* - X_f Y^f - X_\varepsilon \varepsilon_0 + X_\varepsilon \varepsilon_r r - X_\varepsilon \varepsilon_r r^f) = I_0 - I_r r$$

Notice that tY^* cancels out. Make that cancellation and also move every term that includes the real interest rate to the left-hand side and every other term to the right-hand side of the equation:

$$I_r r + X_\varepsilon \varepsilon_r r = I_0 - [Y^* - C_0 - C_y(1 - t)Y^*] -$$
$$(-G) - (IM_y Y^* - X_f Y^f - X_\varepsilon \varepsilon_0 - X_\varepsilon \varepsilon_r r^f)$$

Isolate the real interest rate on the left-hand side, and we're done:

$$r = \frac{I_0 - [Y^* - C_0 - C_y(1 - t)Y^*] + G - (IM_y Y^* - X_f Y^f - X_\varepsilon \varepsilon_0 - X_\varepsilon \varepsilon_r r^f)}{I_r + X_\varepsilon \varepsilon_r}$$

That is what we found in Figure 7.11. When G increases — when the government runs a larger deficit, decreasing its saving — the real interest rate will rise. That is what we found in Figure 7.10.

But now we can figure out by how much the real interest rate will increase. The answer comes from looking at the denominator: $I_r + X_\varepsilon \varepsilon_r$. The larger the denominator, the smaller the change in r when investors' optimism rises. Why? The first term I_r captures the change in investment due to a change in the real interest rate. The larger the sensitivity of investment to interest rates I_r, the flatter the investment demand curve; the more quickly investment spending will fall in response to a rise in interest rates (the *movement along* the now flatter investment curve). And the faster investment falls when interest rates rise, the smaller the rise in interest rates needed to restore equilibrium in the flow of funds.

The second term $X_\varepsilon \varepsilon_r$ captures the change in foreign saving due to a change in the real interest rate. The larger is foreigners' sensitivity to the exchange rate X_ε or the larger the sensitivity of the real exchange rate to changes in interest rates ε_r, the flatter is the total saving curve; the larger is the change in foreign saving when the real interest rate rises (the *movement along* the now flatter S curve). And the larger the change in foreign saving, the less interest rates will be pulled up by a rise in investment demand.

Figure 7.12 gives two examples. In panel (*a*), the sensitivity of investment to changes in the real interest rate is very low. In panel (*b*), it is very high. Notice

FIGURE 7.12

The Slope of the Investment Curve Affects the Size of Changes in the Real Interest Rate

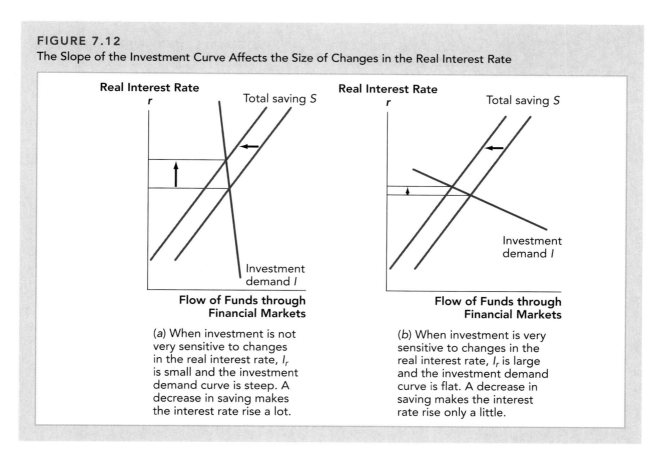

(*a*) When investment is not very sensitive to changes in the real interest rate, I_r is small and the investment demand curve is steep. A decrease in saving makes the interest rate rise a lot.

(*b*) When investment is very sensitive to changes in the real interest rate, I_r is large and the investment demand curve is flat. A decrease in saving makes the interest rate rise only a little.

how a decrease in saving has a much larger effect on the real interest rate when I_r is small (panel *a*) than when it is large (panel *b*).

With the algebraic equations, we can calculate the equilibrium value of the real interest rate. To do so requires the value of all of those constants in the equilibrium equation above. Often, however, the information is given to us not as a list of values of parameters such as the marginal propensity to consume C_y and so on, but as equations for the four components of aggregate demand. Here again, we can calculate the equilibrium value of the real interest rate. We just remember that equilibrium occurs when saving S equals investment I, *which is the same thing as* aggregate demand AD equals output Y. Box 7.4 is an example of substituting in values of the parameters. Box 7.5 starts from the equations for aggregate demand and calculates the value of the equilibrium real interest rate.

Determining the Effect of a Change in Policy on Aggregate Demand

With the graphs of saving and investment, we were able to figure out whether the interest rate would increase or decrease. Now we can figure out the effect of a change in policy on the real interest rate and on the values of consumption, investment, government purchases, and net exports. Let's use a familiar example: an increase in government purchases G.

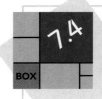

CALCULATING THE EQUILIBRIUM REAL INTEREST RATE FROM PARAMETER VALUES: AN EXAMPLE

Assume that the parameters of the model are:

$I_0 = 12,000$	Baseline investment spending is $12,000 billion per year.
$Y^* = 21,000$	Potential output is $21,000 billion per year.
$C_0 = 0$	Baseline consumption spending.
$C_y = 0.8$	The marginal propensity to consume is 80 percent.
$t = 0.375$	Tax rate is 37.5 percent of income.
$G = 2,000$	Government spending is $2,000 billion per year.
$IM_y = 0.3$	Imports are 30 percent of total spending.
$X_f = 0.1$	A $1 billion increase in foreign income increases our exports by $0.1 billion.
$Y^f = 1,000$	Foreign income is $1,000 billion per year.
$X_\varepsilon = 600$	A 1-point increase in the real exchange rate increases exports by $600 billion.
$\varepsilon_0 = 5$	Baseline value of the real exchange rate is 5.
$\varepsilon_r = 10$	A 1-percentage-point increase in the difference between domestic and foreign interest rates ($\Delta r = +0.01$ or $\Delta r^f = -0.01$) decreases the real exchange rate by 0.1.
$r^f = 0.05$	The foreign real interest rate is 5 percent.
$I_r = 9,000$	A 1-percentage-point fall in the interest rate ($\Delta r = -0.01$) increases investment spending by $90 billion a year.

To find the equilibrium real interest rate, we substitute these values into the equation for the real interest rate and then simplify.

$$r = \frac{I_0 - [Y^* - C_0 - C_y(1-t)Y^*] + G - (IM_yY^* - X_fY^f - X_\varepsilon\varepsilon_0 - X_\varepsilon\varepsilon_r r^f)}{I_r + X_\varepsilon\varepsilon_r}$$

$$r = \frac{12{,}000 - [21{,}000 - 0 - 0.8(1 - 0.375)21{,}000] + 2{,}000 - [0.3(21{,}000) - 0.1(1{,}000) - 600(5) - 600(10)(0.05)]}{9{,}000 + 600(10)}$$

$$r = \frac{600}{15{,}000} = 0.04$$

When the economy is in equilibrium, the real interest rate will be 0.04, or 4 percent.

CALCULATING THE EQUILIBRIUM REAL INTEREST RATE FROM AGGREGATE DEMAND EQUATIONS: AN EXAMPLE

BOX 7.5

Suppose that we had the same economy that was described in Box 7.4, but instead of being given the values of the parameters, we were given the aggregate demand equations themselves:

$$Y^* = 21{,}000$$

$$C = 0 + 0.8(1 - 0.375)21{,}000 = 10{,}500$$

$$I = 12{,}000 - 9{,}000r$$

$$G = 2{,}000$$

$$GX = 0.1(1{,}000) + 600[5 - 10(r - 0.05)]$$

$$IM = 0.3(21{,}000)$$

First, combine the expressions for gross exports and imports to get

$$NX = -2{,}900 - 6{,}000r$$

Now how do we find the equilibrium real interest rate? We can't exactly look at the equation $C = 10{,}500$ and pick out the values of C_0, C_y, t, and Y^*. In this case, we start from the flow-of-output equilibrium statement, and then solve for the equilibrium real interest rate. In equilibrium, output Y^* equals aggregate demand AD, which is the sum of consumption C, investment I, government G, and net exports NX. Thus

$$21{,}000 = 10{,}500 + (12{,}000 - 9{,}000r) + 2{,}000 + (-2{,}900 - 6{,}000r)$$

$$-600 = -15{,}000r$$

$$0.04 = r$$

When the economy is in equilibrium, the real interest rate will be 0.04, or 4 percent.

Because the equilibrium real interest rate is

$$r = \frac{I_0 - [Y^* - C_0 - C_y(1 - t)Y^*] + G - (IM_y Y^* - X_f Y^f - X_\varepsilon \varepsilon_0 - X_\varepsilon \varepsilon_r r^f)}{I_r + X_\varepsilon \varepsilon_r}$$

a change in government spending ΔG will change the real interest rate by

$$\Delta r = \frac{\Delta G}{I_r + X_\varepsilon \varepsilon_r}$$

The size of the change in the real interest rate depends on the sensitivity of investment to changes in the real interest rate, the sensitivity of exports to a change in the real exchange rate, and the sensitivity of the real exchange rate to a change in domestic real interest rates. That is, it depends on how much investment and saving change when interest rates change.

When government spending rises, what happens to the components of aggregate demand? The change in government purchases has no effect on consumption. Because potential output does not change, national income does not change. National income, baseline consumption, the tax rate, and the marginal propensity to consume do not shift, so there is no effect on the consumption function

$$C = C_0 + C_y(1 - t)Y^*$$

Thus the change in consumption spending is zero:

$$\Delta C = 0$$

The shift in government purchases has an indirect effect on investment. Investment depends on the interest rate, and the interest rate will change as a result of the change in government purchases. So from the investment equation

$$I = I_0 - I_r r$$

we see that investment spending will change by

$$\Delta I = -I_r \Delta r$$

Substituting the expression for the change in the real interest rate gives us

$$\Delta I = -I_r \left(\frac{\Delta G}{I_r + X_\varepsilon \varepsilon_r} \right)$$

crowding out

Decreases in investment spending caused by a drop in government saving that leads to higher real interest rates.

Investment spending will fall when government spending rises. This is what we call **crowding out**: The rise in government purchases increases real interest rates, which "crowds out" private investment spending. The change in investment spending will be equal to the sensitivity of investment to the interest rate times the change in the equilibrium real interest rate.

Nothing in the international economic environment — our propensity to import, foreigners' propensity to export — changes when domestic fiscal policy changes. Nor does the level of potential output change. But the interest rate does change. Look back at our exchange rate equation

$$\varepsilon = \varepsilon_0 - \varepsilon_r(r - r^f)$$

A change Δr in the domestic real interest rate will change the exchange rate by an amount $-\varepsilon_r \Delta r$. Looking back at our export equation, a change in the exchange rate of $-\varepsilon_r \Delta r$ will in turn change exports by an amount $-X_\varepsilon \varepsilon_r \Delta r$. So net exports will shift too:

$$\Delta NX = \Delta GX - \Delta IM = -X_\varepsilon \varepsilon_r \Delta r - 0$$

Substituting the expression for the change in the real interest rate gives us

$$\Delta NX = -X_\varepsilon \varepsilon_r \left(\frac{\Delta G}{I_r + X_\varepsilon \varepsilon_r} \right)$$

Last, real GDP does not change because potential output does not change, and this is a long-run full-employment model, with real GDP always equal to potential output:

$$\Delta Y = \Delta Y^* = 0$$

The change in aggregate demand is the sum of the changes in consumption, investment, government purchases, and net exports, so substituting we get

$$\Delta AD = \Delta C + \Delta I + \Delta G + \Delta NX = 0 + \left[-I_r \left(\frac{\Delta G}{I_r + X_\varepsilon \varepsilon_r} \right) \right] + \Delta G$$

$$+ \left[-X_\varepsilon \varepsilon_r \left(\frac{\Delta G}{I_r + X_\varepsilon \varepsilon_r} \right) \right] = 0$$

The change in aggregate demand is 0! The increase in government spending ΔG is just offset by the decreases in investment spending and net exports. Aggregate demand does not change when government spending changes because this is a *long-run model* in which we have assumed that real GDP is always equal to its potential value Y^*. In the long run, a change in one of the components of aggregate demand leads to a reallocation of aggregate demand but doesn't change the overall value of aggregate demand.

Determining the Effect of a Change in Policy on Saving

What effect does an increase in government purchases have on total saving S? Since neither household income nor consumption changes, household saving does not change:

$$\Delta S^H = 0$$

Government purchases, however, do change. Since government saving is taxes minus government purchases, and since government purchases have gone up, the change in government saving is

$$\Delta S^G = -\Delta G$$

Foreign saving is the opposite of net exports, so foreign saving changes by

$$\Delta S^F = X_\varepsilon \varepsilon_r \left(\frac{\Delta G}{I_r + X_\varepsilon \varepsilon_r} \right)$$

Put all these pieces together and we get

$$\Delta S = \Delta S^H + \Delta S^G + \Delta S^F = 0 + (-\Delta G) + X_\varepsilon \varepsilon_r \left(\frac{\Delta G}{I_r + X_\varepsilon \varepsilon_r} \right) = -I_r \left(\frac{\Delta G}{I_r + X_\varepsilon \varepsilon_r} \right)$$

The change in total saving just equals the change in investment. This is precisely what Figure 7.10 led us to expect. The increase in government purchases reduces the flow of saving into financial markets. The interest rate rises. The higher interest rate reduces businesses' plans for investment spending but also calls forth additional saving from foreigners. And so the higher interest rate has returned the flow of funds to balance.

Note that the falls in investment and in total saving are not as large as the rise in government purchases. This is also what Figure 7.10 led us to expect. The increase in government purchases reduced the flow of domestic saving into financial markets, but the increased flow of foreign-owned capital into the market partially offset this reduction. The extra foreign saving kept the decline in investment from being as large as the rise in government purchases, as Figure 7.10 showed.

What is the point of the march through the algebra? It allows us to calculate quantitative effects: to know not just that the interest rate will go up, but by how much the interest rate will go up. An example of how to actually calculate the change in the interest rate is provided in Box 7.6.

BOX 7.6

A GOVERNMENT PURCHASES BOOM: AN EXAMPLE

Start with the same economy that was described in Boxes 7.4 and 7.5. We have

$C_y = 0.8$ The marginal propensity to consume is 80 percent.

$t = 0.375$ Tax rate is 37.5 percent of income.

$X_\varepsilon = 600$ A 1-point increase in the real exchange rate increases exports by $600 billion.

$\varepsilon_r = 10$ A 1-percentage-point increase in the difference between domestic and foreign interest rates ($\Delta r = +0.01$ or $\Delta r^f = -0.01$) decreases the real exchange rate by 0.1.

$I_r = 9,000$ A 1-percentage-point fall in the interest rate ($\Delta r = -0.01$) increases investment spending by $90 billion a year.

Initially we had an equilibrium real interest rate of 4 percent, $r = 0.04$.

Suppose that there is a sudden but sustained increase in government purchases of $150 billion a year. This sustained boom in spending increases the equilibrium real interest rate by 1 percentage point:

$$\Delta r = \frac{\Delta G}{I_r + X_\varepsilon \varepsilon_r} = \frac{150}{9,000 + 600(10)} = \frac{150}{15,000} = 0.01 = 1\%$$

The new interest rate will be $r = 0.05$, or 5 percent. As a result, the equilibrium values of the components of aggregate demand will change by

$\Delta C = 0$

$$\Delta I = -I_r \left(\frac{\Delta G}{I_r + X_\varepsilon \varepsilon_r} \right) = -9,000 \left[\frac{\$150 \text{ billion}}{9,000 + 600(10)} \right] = -\$90 \text{ billion}$$

$\Delta G = +\$150 \text{ billion}$

$$\Delta NX = -X_\varepsilon \varepsilon_r \left(\frac{\Delta G}{I_r + X_\varepsilon \varepsilon_r} \right) = -600(10) \left[\frac{\$150 \text{ billion}}{9,000 + 600(10)} \right] = -\$60 \text{ billion}$$

And total saving will change by

$$\Delta S = \Delta S^H + \Delta S^G + \Delta S^F = 0 + (-150 \text{ billion}) + (60 \text{ billion}) = -\$90 \text{ billion}$$

Figure 7.13 illustrates the change in the real interest rate, investment, and saving.

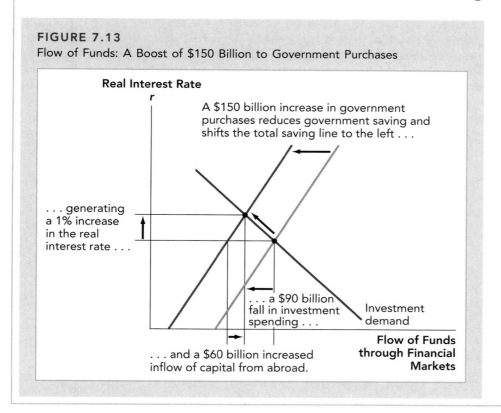

FIGURE 7.13
Flow of Funds: A Boost of $150 Billion to Government Purchases

Real Interest Rate
r

A $150 billion increase in government purchases reduces government saving and shifts the total saving line to the left . . .

. . . generating a 1% increase in the real interest rate . . .

. . . a $90 billion fall in investment spending . . .

Investment demand

Flow of Funds through Financial Markets

. . . and a $60 billion increased inflow of capital from abroad.

We can use this same approach to analyze any change to economic policy or the economic environment. Suppose business people become optimistic and increase their investment spending. The change in autonomous investment ΔI_0 will generate an increase in the interest rate equal to $\dfrac{\Delta I_0}{(I_r + X_\varepsilon \varepsilon_r)}$. Suppose the foreign real interest rate r^f rises. The increase in r^f will generate an increase in the domestic real interest rate equal to $\dfrac{X_\varepsilon \varepsilon_r \Delta r^f}{(I_r + X_\varepsilon \varepsilon_r)}$. Suppose consumers become wealthier due to a stock market boom and so increase their baseline consumption by ΔC_0. The change in C_0 will generate an increase in the real interest rate equal to $\dfrac{\Delta C_0}{(I_r + X_\varepsilon \varepsilon_r)}$. Suppose the government cuts the tax rate by Δt. The tax cut will generate an increase in the real interest rate equal to $\dfrac{-C_y Y^* \Delta t}{(I_r + X_\varepsilon \varepsilon_r)}$.

Notice the appearance, over and over again, of the expression $I_r + X_\varepsilon \varepsilon_r$. This is the sum of two terms: I_r, the amount by which an increase in interest rates reduces investment spending; and $X_\varepsilon \varepsilon_r$, the amount by which an increase in interest rates raises the inflow of capital from abroad. The sum of these two terms is a measure of how powerful changes in the interest rate are in stabilizing the loanable funds market, of how big a gap between supply and demand is closed by each change in the interest rate. If these two terms add up to a large number, shocks to the economy will have little effect on interest rates because only a small change in interest rates will be needed to powerfully affect both demand for funds to finance investment and the supply of saving. If these two terms add up to a small number, shocks to the economy will have large effects on interest rates, because big changes in interest rates will be needed to restore equilibrium.

> **RECAP   CALCULATING THE EQUILIBRIUM REAL INTEREST RATE**
>
> We can use the flexible-price model to calculate the equilibrium real interest rate. With equations for the components of aggregate demand and the value of potential output, we would use the flow-of-output equilibrium condition — set aggregate demand equal to output — and solve for equilibrium r. Or we can use the flow-of-funds equilibrium condition — set total saving equal to investment — and solve for equilibrium r. Either approach gives the same result. We can then use the equilibrium real interest rate and our knowledge of the economic environment to calculate the equilibrium values of the components of aggregate demand and total saving. We can also use the model to calculate how the economy's equilibrium will change in response to changes in the environment or in policy.

7.6 CONCLUSION

This chapter has analyzed a flexible-price macroeconomy in the short run — a time span in which neither labor nor capital stocks have an opportunity to change enough to materially affect the level of potential output. It has taken a snapshot of the economy in equilibrium at a point in time. It has asked how the equilibrium would be different if the economic environment or economic policy were different. It has at times implicitly talked about the dynamic evolution of the economy in the short run by describing the economy as shifting from one equilibrium to another in response to a change in policy or in the environment.

Remember that there was a tension: Prices are flexible so output always adjusts to its potential, but potential output does not change. We are caught between the long-run model of Chapter 4 and the upcoming short-run model of Chapters 9 to 12. Nevertheless, the flexible-price model presented here is powerful. It allows us to say a great deal about the way various kinds of shocks will affect the economy and the composition of total spending and output as long as full employment is maintained. And we have been able to resolve the big mystery of Chapter 4: How does a change in consumption spending or government purchases cause the standard of living to fall?

In the flexible-price model, the interest rate plays the key role in keeping the economy in balance: keeping aggregate demand equal to potential output and the economy at full employment. Changes in economic policy and the economic environment induce changes in the mix of spending. They shift the proportions of aggregate demand between consumption, investment, government purchases, and net exports. But they do not affect the *level* of aggregate demand. Things that reduce saving — whether they reduce household saving, government saving, or the capital inflow — raise interest rates and reduce investment. Changes in economic policy and in the economic environment that increase saving lower interest rates and increase investment.

Think back to Chapters 4 and 5, where long-run growth depended on the economy's saving-investment rate. Here we have seen how a great many changes in economic policy and in the economic environment affect saving and investment. There are powerful links in the long run between shifts that change equilibrium interest rates and the economy's long-run growth path. Drawing those links explicitly would be too hard and too complicated. Nevertheless, when doing analyses using this chapter's flexible-price model remember that this chapter's assumption that the level of potential output is not changed by different levels of investment spending is just a "snapshot" simplifying assumption. In the long run of Chapters 4 and 5, changes in investment have powerful effects on production and prosperity.

We have covered a lot of ground in this chapter. However, it is worth emphasizing what this chapter has not done:

- As the paragraphs above stressed, this chapter has not dealt with the impact of changes in policy and the economic environment on economic growth, which was done in Chapters 4 and 5. Refer to those chapters to analyze how changes in saving and investment ultimately affect productivity and material standards of living in the long run.

- It has ignored the nominal financial side of the economy — money, prices, and inflation — completely. That topic will be covered in Chapter 8.

- It has maintained the full-employment assumption — that notion will be relaxed in the chapters starting with Chapter 9.

Chapter Summary

1. When the economy is at full employment, real GDP is equal to potential output.

2. In a flexible-price full-employment economy, the real interest rate shifts in response to changes in policy or the economic environment to keep real GDP equal to potential output.

3. The real interest rate balances the supply of loanable funds committed to financial markets by savers — total saving — with the demand for funds to finance investments — investment demand. The circular flow principle guarantees that when the saving equals investment, aggregate demand will equal potential output.

4. An increase in saving will make the real interest rate fall. An increase in investment makes the real interest rate rise. How much the interest rate changes depends on the sensitivity of investment demand to real interest rates, the sensitivity of exports to the real exchange rate, and the sensitivity of the real exchange rate to the real domestic interest rate.

5. In a flexible-price full-employment economy, an increase in aggregate demand leads to a reallocation of output among the components of aggregate demand — consumption, investment, government, and net export spending — but not to a change in the level of aggregate demand.

6. In analyzing the effects of changes in economic policy or the economic environment on the macroeconomy, we can use the equations for flow-of-funds equilibrium.

Key Terms

financial markets (p. 194)

total saving (p. 198)

household saving (p. 199)

government saving (p. 199)

foreign saving (p. 199)

capital inflow (p. 199)

crowding out (p. 216)

Analytical Exercises

1. Suppose that in the flexible-price full-employment model, the government increases taxes and government purchases by equal amounts. The tax increase reduces consumption spending. What happens qualitatively to investment, net exports, the real exchange rate, the real interest rate, and potential output? (State the direction of change only.)

2. What happens according to the flexible-price full-employment model if the intercept C_0 of the consumption function rises? Explain qualitatively what happens to consumption, investment, net exports, the real exchange rate, the real interest rate, and potential output. (State the direction of change only.)

3. Explain qualitatively the direction in which consumption, investment, net exports, the real exchange rate, the real interest rate, and potential output move in the flexible-price full-employment model if the government cuts taxes.

4. Give three examples of changes in economic policy or in the economic environment that would shift the total saving curve on the flow-of-funds diagram to the left.

5. Give three examples of changes in the economic environment or in economic policy that would increase the equilibrium real interest rate.

Policy Exercises

1. Suppose that the relevant parameters of the economy are

$t = 0.33$	Tax rate of one-third.
$I_r = 9{,}000$	A 1-percentage-point fall in the interest rate raises investment spending by $90 billion a year.
$C_y = 0.75$	A marginal propensity to consume of three-quarters.
$\varepsilon_r = 10$	A 1-percentage-point increase in the gap between domestic and foreign real interest rates decreases the real exchange rate by 0.10.
$X_\varepsilon = 600$	A 1-point increase in the real exchange rate leads to a $600 billion-a-year increase in gross exports.

   And suppose that irrational exuberance causes a stock market boom that leads consumers to increase their spending by $200 billion at a constant level of disposable income. What would be the increase in interest rates in response to such an exuberance-driven consumption boom?

2. In the economy presented in question 1, suppose that total GDP is $10 trillion and that the government does not want real interest rates to rise and investment to fall in response to the stock market–generated consumption boom. What kinds of policies can the government undertake? How successful will they be?

3. When President Bill Clinton took office, he spent essentially all his political capital on his first-year effort to raise taxes and cut spending by $300 billion a year in an economy with an annual GDP of $6 trillion. What, qualitatively and quantitatively, does the flexible-price full-employment model say should have been the consequences of these policies if the relevant parameters of the economy are those given in question 1?

4. When President George W. Bush took office, he cut taxes by $300 billion and raised spending by $200 billion a year in an economy with an annual GDP of $9 trillion. What, qualitatively and quantitatively, does the flexible-price full-employment model say should have been the long-run consequences of these policies if the relevant parameters of the economy are those given in question 1?

5. Consider two economies. In one, the relevant parameters are

$Y^* = \$10,000$ In billions; potential output equals $10 trillion.

$t = 0.33$ Tax rate is one-third.

$I_r = 9,000$ A 1-percentage-point fall in the interest rate raises investment spending by $90 billion a year.

$C_y = 0.75$ The marginal propensity to consume is three-quarters.

$\varepsilon_r = 10$ A 1-percentage-point increase in the gap between domestic and foreign real interest rates decreases the real exchange rate by 0.10.

$X_\varepsilon = 600$ A 1-point increase in the real exchange rate leads to a $600 billion-a-year increase in gross exports.

In the other, the relevant parameters are the same except

$C_y = 0.5$ The marginal propensity to consume is one-half.

Compare the effects of a $100 billion increase in government purchases on these two economies. What effect does the drop in the marginal propensity to consume have on the size of change in the real interest rate? On the size of the change in investment demand? Are the levels of the real interest rate and investment spending the same in both economies?

6. From an economic theory point of view, one of the most interesting policies of the current Bush administration is the idea of replacing some of the Social Security system by private accounts. In terms of our model, this policy involves (*a*) a reduction in government tax revenues and (*b*) an increase in private after-tax incomes but (*c*) the government requires that the increase in after-tax income be saved. Qualitatively, how would you think that the consumption function would change as a result of this policy? What would happen in equilibrium to the interest rate? To the exchange rate? To total saving?

7. Most economists at the start of 2005 were anticipating a rise in ε_0, in foreign exchange speculators' assessments of the underlying fundamental value of foreign currency, as they began to focus on the long-run implications of America's foreign trade deficit. Qualitatively, what would you expect to happen to the economy if ε_0 were to suddenly rise?

CHAPTER

8

Money, Prices, and Inflation

QUESTIONS

What do economists mean when they say "money"?

Why is money useful?

What is a "unit of account"?

What determines the demand for and supply of money?

What determines the price level and the inflation rate?

Why is inflation best avoided?

Why would a government ever generate hyperinflation — a condition in which prices rise by more than 20 percent a *month*?

8.1 MONEY

price level

The average level of prices in an economy.

Economists believe strongly that price stability is a good thing. The prices of individual commodities need to rise and fall with supply and demand. But average prices — the overall **price level** — need to be stable. A stable average price level is beneficial because only then can the price system work effectively at a microeconomic level: If nobody is certain whether a rise in the price of oranges reflects a shortage of oranges relative to demand or is part of a general overall rise in prices, the price signal that the market system sends to consumers (to cut back, because oranges are now more expensive relative to other commodities) and to producers (to expand production, because oranges have become more valuable relative to other commodities) will not be understood. As British economist John Maynard Keynes put it in his 1924 *Tract on Monetary Reform,* in order to function well at a microeconomic level, "the Individualistic Capitalism of today . . . *presumes a stable measuring-rod of value, and cannot be efficient* — perhaps cannot survive — without one."

inflation

An increase in the overall price level in an economy, usually measured as the annual percentage change in its consumer price index or its GDP price index.

In today's world, much of the economic news reported in newspapers and on television concerns the rate of **inflation** — the rate of change of the overall price level. (Fortunately, we have not had experience with **deflation** — falling prices in general — since the Great Depression of the 1930s.) A price level that is unstable — moving either up through inflation or down through deflation — has a number of damaging consequences in addition to the damage it does to the ability of businesses, consumers, and investors to understand the microeconomic price signals that the market system sends to guide resource allocation. To quote Keynes again:

deflation

The opposite of inflation: a decrease in the overall price level in an economy.

> Inflation . . . means Injustice to individuals and to classes — particularly to investors; and is therefore unfavorable to saving. . . . Deflation which causes falling prices means Impoverishment to labor and to enterprise by leading entrepreneurs to restrict production, in their endeavor to avoid loss to themselves; and is therefore disastrous to employment. . . . Inflation is unjust and Deflation is inexpedient. . . . [B]oth are evils to be shunned. . . . Those who are not in favor of drastic changes in the existing organization of society believe that [our current economic] arrangements, being in accord with human nature, have great advantages. But they cannot work properly if the money, which they assume as a stable measuring-rod, is undependable. Unemployment, the precarious life of the worker, the disappointment of expectation, the sudden loss of savings, the excessive windfalls to individuals, the speculator, the profiteer — all proceed, in large measure, from the instability of the standard of value.

To avoid inflation and deflation, especially large and unexpected inflation and deflation, is therefore one of the chief economic policy tasks of the government. Moreover, the government also has the task of avoiding even the *expectation* of inflation or deflation, for even when inflation is absent, fear that it will emerge has a powerful effect on the economy. Central banks — in the United States, the Federal Reserve — have as their principal tasks the maintenance of stable prices and the preservation of the expectation that prices will be stable.

The Federal Reserve does not always succeed. As Figure 8.1 shows, the United States experienced an episode of relatively mild inflation — prices rising at between 5 and 13 percent per year — in the 1970s. Although relatively mild, that inflation was large enough to cause significant economic and political trauma. Avoiding a repeat of the inflation of the 1970s remains a major goal of economic policy even today, three decades later.

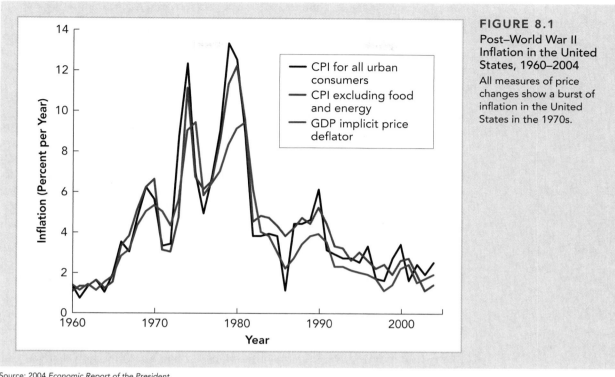

Source: 2004 *Economic Report of the President.*

FIGURE 8.1
Post–World War II Inflation in the United States, 1960–2004
All measures of price changes show a burst of inflation in the United States in the 1970s.

Many countries have experienced inflations that are not mild. In Russia in 1998 the price level rose at an annual rate of 60 percent. In Germany in 1923 prices rose at a rate of 60 percent *per week.* So-called **hyperinflations** appeared in many other countries in the twentieth century, from Argentina to Ukraine, from Hungary to China. They are extremely destructive, inflicting severe damage on the ability of money to grease the wheels of the social mechanism of exchange that is the market economy. The system of prices and market exchange breaks down, and production can fall to a small fraction of potential output.

hyperinflation

Extremely high inflation. One rule of thumb is that inflation of more than 20 percent per month is hyperinflation.

What causes inflation and deflation? How must the Federal Reserve act in order to keep prices stable? Chapters 6 and 7 did not tell us. They did not discuss the determination of the level of prices and the inflation rate. They did not have to. It was perfectly possible to figure out the real interest and exchange rates, the level of real GDP, and the division of real GDP into its components without mentioning the overall price level or the rate of inflation. And there was no feedback from production and output back to the price level.

The power to analyze real variables without referring to the price level is a special feature of the flexible-price full-employment model of the economy. Economists call it the **classical dichotomy**: Real variables (such as real GDP, real investment spending, or the real exchange rate) can be analyzed and calculated without thinking of nominal variables such as the price level. Economists also speak of it as the property whereby money is neutral or is a veil, a covering that does not affect the shape of the face underneath. Starting in Chapter 9 the classical dichotomy will not hold. Money will not be neutral; the determination of

classical dichotomy

When real variables can be analyzed and calculated without thinking about nominal variables.

the price level and its changes will be intimately tied up with fluctuations in production and employment. This is because Chapter 9 introduces prices that are sluggish, or sticky, or that are fixed. Hence they cannot adjust smoothly and instantaneously to changes in nominal variables like the money stock and the price level. But here in Part 3 prices are flexible, and the classical dichotomy holds.

This chapter explores what determines the overall level of prices and the rate of inflation (or deflation) in our flexible-price full-employment model of the macro-economy. This topic is worth examining for three reasons. First, it provides a useful baseline analysis against which to contrast the conclusions of future chapters. Second, whenever we look over relatively long spans of time — decades, perhaps — wages and prices are effectively flexible, they have time to move in response to shocks, and the flexible-price assumption is a fruitful and useful one. Third, as we stressed above, the maintenance of price stability and of the expectation of price stability is one of the things the government needs to do if the market economy is to function well.

Money: Liquid Wealth That Can Be Used to Buy Things

money

Wealth in the form of readily spendable purchasing power.

When noneconomists use the word "money," they may mean a number of things: "She has a lot of money" usually means that she is wealthy; "He makes a lot of money" usually means that he has a high income. When economists use the word "money," however, they mean something special. To economists, money is wealth that is held in a readily spendable form. **Money** is that kind of wealth that you can use immediately to buy things because others will accept it as payment. Today the economy's stock of money is made up of:

- Coins and *currency* that are transferred by handing the cash over to a seller (almost everyone will accept cash as payment for goods and services).
- *Checking account balances* that are transferred by electronic debit or by writing a check (which most people will accept as payment for goods and services).
- Other assets, like savings account balances, that can be turned into cash or *demand deposits* nearly instantaneously, risklessly, and costlessly.

Why do economists adopt this special definition of money? We do not know. Giving everyday words special definitions is in general a bad thing to do: It causes confusion and misunderstanding. But economists do it, and they do it not only for "money" but also for terms such as "investment" and "rational" and "utility."

Whether assets that can be quickly and cheaply turned into cash (savings account balances, money market mutual funds, liquid Treasury securities, and so on) are included in the money stock is a matter of taste and judgment. At what level of cost and inconvenience is an asset no longer "readily spendable"? There is no clear answer. Thus economists have a number of different measures of the money stock — identified by symbols like H, $M1$, $M2$, and $M3$ — each of which draws the line around a different set of assets that it counts as wealth readily enough spent to be "money."

The Usefulness of Money

In our world all you need to carry out a market transaction — whether you want to buy or sell some good or service — is either to have money yourself (if you

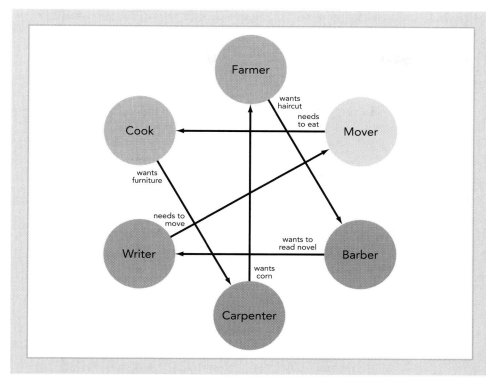

FIGURE 8.2
Coincidence of Wants
Without money, how is the carpenter to persuade the farmer to give him corn when the farmer wants a haircut but doesn't need furniture — which the cook wants? How is the mover going to persuade the cook to feed him when the cook doesn't need the moving truck — the writer does? With money, all can sell what they have for cash and have confidence that they can then turn around and use the cash to buy what they need.

want to buy) or to deal with a purchaser who has money (if you want to sell). In a barter economy, an economy without the social convention of money, market exchange would require the so-called coincidence of wants: You would have to have, physically in your possession, some particular good or service that another person wants, and that person would have to have in his or her possession some good or service that you want. As Figure 8.2 shows, finding consumption goods to satisfy the coincidence of wants would get remarkably complicated very quickly. Without money, an extraordinary amount of time and energy would be spent simply arranging the goods one needed to trade.

Units of Account

There is one other feature worth noting. The same assets that serve as the most common form of readily spendable purchasing power also serve as units of account. Dollars or euros or yen are not only what we use to settle transactions but also what we use to quote prices to one another. At some times and places the functions of money as a **medium of exchange** and as a **unit of account** have been separated, but today they almost invariably go together.

This is a potential cause of trouble. Anything that alters the real value of the domestic money in terms of its purchasing power over goods and services will also alter the real terms of existing contracts that use money as the unit of account. The effect of changes in the price level on contracts that have used the domestic money as a unit of account is a principal source of the social costs of inflation and deflation. The effect of changes in the exchange rate on contracts

medium of exchange

A commodity or an asset that almost everyone will accept as payment for a transaction.

unit of account

Money is a unit of account when a great many contracts are written promising to exchange a good or service for a number of units of money.

that have used foreign moneys as units of account is a principal source of the social costs of *currency crises*.

RECAP MONEY

To an economist, "money" is wealth that is held in a readily spendable form. Money is that kind of wealth that you can use immediately to buy things because others will accept it as payment. Money is useful because in its absence we would have a barter economy and market exchange would require the so-called coincidence of wants. Without money, an extraordinary amount of time and energy would be spent simply arranging the goods one needed to trade.

The same assets that serve as the most common form of readily spendable purchasing power also serve as *units of account*. Dollars or euros or yen are not only what we use to settle transactions but also what we use to quote prices to one another. This is a potential cause of trouble. The effect of changes in the price level on contracts that have used the domestic money as a unit of account is a principal source of the social costs of inflation and deflation. The effect of changes in the exchange rate on contracts that have used foreign moneys as units of account is a principal source of the social costs of currency crises.

8.2 THE QUANTITY THEORY OF MONEY

The Demand for Money

money demand

How much wealth in the form of readily spendable purchasing power — money — households and businesses wish to hold at the given levels of national income and nominal interest rates.

People have a **demand for money** just as they have a demand for any other good. They want to hold a certain amount of wealth in the form of readily spendable purchasing power because the stuff is useful. The more money in your portfolio, the easier it is to buy things. Too little money makes life pointlessly difficult. You have to waste time running to the bank for extra cash or waste energy and time liquidating pieces of your portfolio before you can carry out your normal daily transactions.

Nevertheless, you don't want to have too much of your wealth in the form of readily spendable purchasing power. Cash sitting in your pocket is not earning interest at the bank. Wealth you do not want to spend for five years could earn a higher return as a certificate of deposit or as an investment in the stock market than as cash in your checking account.

Figure 8.3 summarizes the reasons for and opportunity cost of holding money. The higher the flow of spending, the more money the households and businesses in the economy will want to hold. How much more? That depends on the transactions technology of the economy: what businesses will take credit cards, how easy it is to get checks approved, how long the float is, and so forth. In this section of the chapter, however, we ignore all other determinants of money demand and focus on the flow of spending as the principal determinant of money demand.

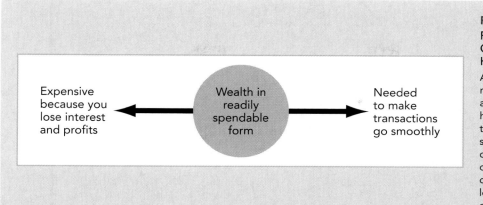

FIGURE 8.3

Reasons for and Opportunity Cost of Holding Money

As with every other economic decision, the amount of wealth households and businesses want to hold in the readily spendable form of money depends on the benefits of holding money and the opportunity cost — the lost interest and profits — of doing so.

The Quantity Equation

The theory that the only important determinant of the demand for money is the flow of spending is called the **quantity theory of money**. It is summarized in the quantity equation

$$MV = PY$$

M is the money stock. PY represents the total nominal flow of spending: Y is, by the circular flow principle, both national income and total national spending; and P is the average price in dollars for which goods sell. The parameter V — a constant, or perhaps growing slowly and predictably — is the **velocity** of money. It tells you how often a given unit of money is spent and changes hands over the course of a year. (Or, alternatively, you can think of $1/V$ as the amount of dollars' worth of money that households and businesses want to hold for each dollar of annual spending on goods and services.) The velocity of money is a measure of how fast money moves through the economy.

quantity theory of money

The theory that money demand is insensitive to changes in interest rates and that the velocity of money is nearly constant. Summarized in the equation $MV = PY$.

velocity

A measure of how often the average monetary asset is used as a means of payment over the course of a year, equal to nominal expenditure or income PY divided by the money stock M.

Money and Prices

The Price Level

Together, the quantity theory of money and the full-employment assumption allow us to determine the price level in the flexible-price model of the macroeconomy. Real GDP Y is equal to potential output: $Y = Y^*$. The velocity of money V is determined by the sophistication of the banking system and the social conventions that govern payment and settlement. For the "M1" concept of money — currency plus checking account deposits — the current velocity V is about 8.6: Businesses and households want to hold about $1 of their wealth in the form of M1 for every $8.60 of real GDP produced. Changes in financial sophistication have increased velocity over time. In the years immediately after World War II, the M1 velocity of money was only 3. For the M2 concept, velocity is considerably lower (see Figure 8.4).

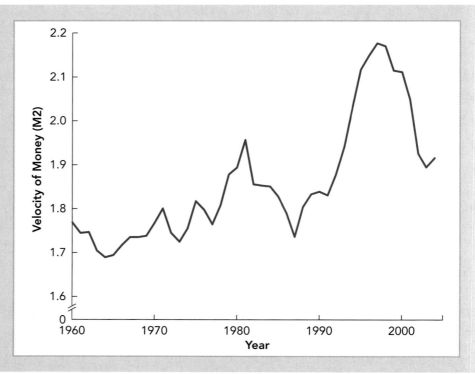

FIGURE 8.4

The Velocity of Money

Between 1960 and 1980 it looked as though the velocity of money was slowly and steadily increasing as the banking system improved its efficiency and the technology available for conducting transactions. But after 1980 the velocity of money fell far short of its pre-1980 trend. Economists attribute this to lower inflation rates in the last quarter century, which diminished incentives to economize on cash and checking account balances.

Source: Authors' calculations from 2004 *Economic Report of the President.*

Thus if we know real GDP Y, the velocity of money V, and the money stock M, we can calculate that the price level is

$$P = \left(\frac{V}{Y}\right)M$$

Box 8.1 presents an example of such a quantity-theory calculation.

Should the price level be momentarily higher than the quantity equation predicts, households and businesses will notice that they have less wealth in the form of readily spendable purchasing power than they want. They will cut back on purchases for a little while to build up their *liquidity.* As they cut back on purchases, sellers will note that demand is weak and will cut their prices, so the price level will fall. Should the price level be momentarily lower than the quantity equation value, households and businesses will note that they have more wealth in the form of money than they want, so they will accelerate their purchases to reduce their money balances. Sellers will note that demand is strong and will raise their prices, so the price level will rise.

As long as prices are flexible, the economy's price level will remain at its quantity-theory equilibrium. Transitory fluctuations in the velocity of money mean that day-to-day or even year-to-year changes in the money stock are not mirrored in equivalent proportional changes in the price level. But on a decade-to-decade time scale the quantity theory of money is a very reliable guide to and predictor of large movements in prices.

CALCULATING THE PRICE LEVEL FROM THE QUANTITY EQUATION: AN EXAMPLE

It is straightforward to use the quantity theory of money

$$P = \left(\frac{V}{Y}\right)M$$

to calculate the price level. For example, in the third quarter of 1998 real GDP (in chained 1992 dollars) was equal to $7,566 billion, the M1 measure of the money stock was equal to $1,072 billion, and the velocity of money was equal to 7.964. Therefore,

$$P = \left(\frac{7.964}{\$7,566}\right)(\$1,072) = 1.1284$$

In the third quarter of 1998 the price level was equal to 112.84 percent of its 1992 level, which works out to an average rate of inflation of about 2.03 percent per year from 1992 to 1998.

Had velocity grown an additional 10 percent between 1992 and 1998, the price level would have grown an additional 10 percent as well if the money stock and real GDP were unchanged from their historical values. Had the money stock grown by an additional 10 percent between 1992 and 1998, the price level would have grown by an additional 10 percent as well if velocity and real GDP were unchanged from their historical values. And had real GDP grown by an additional 10 percent between 1992 and 1998, this would have reduced the 1998 price level by 10 percent relative to its historical value if velocity and the money stock were unchanged from their historical values.

From this perspective, the economic policy task of maintaining stable prices is relatively straightforward. Since

$$P = \left(\frac{V}{Y}\right)M$$

the economy will have a stable price level P if the **central bank** — in the United States, the **Federal Reserve**, or simply the Fed — allows the nominal money stock M to increase and decrease to offset fluctuations in V/Y, the ratio of the velocity of money V to the level of output Y.

But using the quantity theory in this way requires that we know the level of the money stock, and know how to change the level of the money stock. What determines the level of the money stock? And how does the Federal Reserve change the level of the money stock?

The Money Stock

The central bank directly determines what economists call the **monetary base**, the sum of currency in circulation and of deposits at the Federal Reserve's 12 branches. When the central bank wants to reduce the monetary base, it sells short-term government bonds and accepts as payment either currency or, as an alternative, deposits that banks already hold at the Fed's regional branches. Why do banks have funds on deposit at the regional branches of the Federal Reserve? Because of the

central bank

The arm of a national government that controls the money supply and the credit pattern of an economy and usually oversees and regulates the banking system as well.

Federal Reserve

The United States' central bank, consisting of a Board of Governors (seven, one of whom is chair) and 12 regional Federal Reserve banks.

monetary base

The sum total of currency and of bank reserves on deposit at the Federal Reserve; also often called "high-powered money."

FIGURE 8.5
Open-Market
Operations
The Federal Reserve controls the money supply through open-market operations: purchases and sales of bonds on the open market. A purchase of bonds increases the economy's money stock. A sale of bonds sucks cash out of the economy and reduces the money stock.

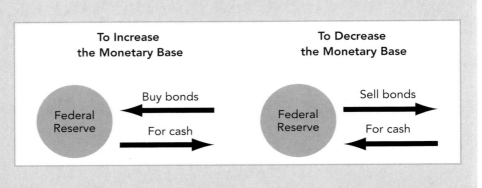

open-market operations

The principal way that central banks affect interest rates; the purchase (or sale) of short-term government bonds to increase (or decrease) the money supply, and push interest rates down (or up).

money stock

The equilibrium of money supply and money demand. The amount of money the Federal Reserve has allowed the banking system to create.

reserve requirements

The amount of money — usually expressed as a share of total deposits — that the central bank requires banks to maintain either as cash in their vaults or as deposits at the central bank.

excess reserves

Bank reserves held over and above those mandated by the central bank.

law: The Federal Reserve requires that national banks deposit funds in its branches so the Fed can have additional confidence that the bank is not being stripped of assets by fraud, and that the resources to pay depositors' demands to withdraw money from the bank will be met.

When the Federal Reserve sells bonds for currency, the currency it accepts as payment is then removed from circulation, no longer part of the money stock. When the Federal Reserve sells bonds and accepts as payment deposits that national banks hold at the Fed's regional branches, these deposits are then erased from its books. Thus the monetary base declines. When the Federal Reserve wants to increase the monetary base, it buys short-term government bonds, paying for them with currency, or by crediting the seller with an enlarged deposit at the Federal Reserve. These transactions are called **open-market operations**, because the Federal Reserve buys or sells bonds on the open market. (See Figure 8.5.) When and how the U.S. central bank, the Federal Reserve, undertakes open-market transactions are decided at periodic meetings of the *Federal Open Market Committee (FOMC)*, which meets eight times a year.

The Federal Reserve directly controls the monetary base. But the monetary base is not the entire **money stock**. "Money" includes many other things than just currency and reserve deposits held at the 12 regional *Federal Reserve banks:* checking account deposits, savings account deposits, small-denomination certificates of deposit, and a number of other assets that are sometimes included and sometimes excluded in various alternative measures of the money stock.

However, changes in the monetary base indirectly induce changes in these other components of the money stock as well. For example, national banks accept checking and savings account deposits. They lend out the purchasing power deposited in the bank, earn interest, and provide the depositor with a claim to wealth in readily spendable form. How much of the deposits they take in do banks then turn around and lend out? The Federal Reserve limits national banks' ability to accept deposits, and limits the proportion of the deposits they do accept that national banks can then lend out.

The Federal Reserve requires that national banks redeposit at the local regional branch of the Federal Reserve a certain proportion of their total deposits — a proportion called the **reserve requirement**. In addition, financial institutions find it prudent to hold liquid **excess reserves** in case an unexpectedly large number of depositors seek to withdraw their money. For a financial institution, nothing is

DIFFERENT DEFINITIONS OF THE MONEY STOCK: SOME DETAILS

The different definitions of the money stock all draw the line separating "money" from "not-money" in different places. Economists' definition of "money" considers any wealth held in the form of readily spendable purchasing power to be money. But ready spendability is, to some degree at least, a thing found in the eye of the beholder.

The narrowest definition of money — called "H" for "*high-powered money*," or sometimes "B" for "monetary *base*" — includes only cash and deposits at branches of the Federal Reserve. The assets that make up the monetary base are special because only they can serve as reserves to satisfy the Federal Reserve's requirement that institutions that accept deposits also maintain funds to cover any emergency spike in withdrawals.

The narrowest commonly used definition of money is M1, which consists of currency plus checking account deposits, traveler's checks, and any other deposits at institutions from which the depositor can demand his or her money back and get it instantaneously. Almost anyone will accept M1-type money as a means of payment for almost any purchase. M2 adds to M1 wealth held in the form of savings accounts, wealth held in relatively small term deposits, and money held in money market mutual funds. Some of the money included in M2 cannot be spent without paying a penalty for early withdrawal. Moreover, if the bank wants, it has the legal right to delay a withdrawal for a period of time. M2-type money is a little bit less spendable than M1-type money. The broadest definition of money, M3, includes large term deposits and institutional money market fund balances.

worse than being unable to meet depositors' demands for money. Broader measures of the money stock listed in Box 8.2 are also limited in their size by the amount of the monetary base, the regulatory reserve requirements imposed on banks and other financial institutions, and financial institutions' extremely powerful incentive never to get caught without enough cash to satisfy depositors' demands.

In this chapter (and later chapters too) we sweep these complications under the rug. We assume that the central bank can easily set the money stock at whatever level it wishes. (Although these subjects are given short shrift in this book, they are explored in great depth in money and banking textbooks by authors such as Rick Mishkin, Glenn Hubbard, and Steve Cecchetti.)

What, then, is the actual level of the money stock? This is one thing that economists argue over, because they construct different alternative measures and definitions. Table 8.1 summarizes some of these alternative definitions of the money stock.

The Rate of Inflation

The quantity equation

$$MV = PY$$

leads immediately to an equation for the **inflation rate**, which we will call π — the proportional rate of change of the price level. Recall our rule from Chapter 4 about how to calculate the proportional growth rates of products: The proportional growth rate of a product is the sum of the growth rates of the terms multiplied together. Thus

Inflation = Money growth rate + Velocity growth rate − Real GDP growth rate

inflation rate

The annual rate of change of the overall level of prices in the economy.

TABLE 8.1
Measures of the Money Stock

Concept of Money	Assets Included in Concept	Amount, 2003 (in Billions)
C	Currency	$ 664
H	Monetary base: assets that can serve as reserves for banks; equals currency plus reserve deposits at Federal Reserve banks	721
M1	Currency plus checking account deposits and traveler's checks	1,287
M2	M1 plus savings account deposits, small time deposits, and household money market funds	6,045
M3	M2 plus institutional money market funds, eurodollar accounts, large time deposits, and repurchase agreements	8,807

Source: The 2004 edition of the *Economic Report of the President* (Washington, DC: Government Printing Office).

To write this relationship in more compact form, use a lowercase m and v for the proportional growth rates of the money stock and velocity, respectively, and use a lowercase y for the growth rate of real GDP. Then

$$\pi = m + v - y$$

If the proportional growth rate of real GDP is 4 percent per year, the velocity of money V increases at a proportional rate of 2 percent per year, and the money stock M grows at 5 percent per year, then

$$\pi = 5\% + 2\% - 4\% = 3\%$$

The inflation rate is 3 percent per year.

In actual empirical fact, most changes in the rate of inflation in the medium run of years and the long run of a decade or more are due to changes in the rate of growth of the money stock. Substantial and persistent changes in y, the rate of growth of real GDP, are rare. The variable v — the rate of growth of the velocity of money — is determined by the slow pace of institutional and technological change in the banking system.[1] But m, the rate of growth of the money stock, can change quickly and substantially. Thus if you see a large and persistent change in inflation, odds are that it is due to a change in the rate of growth of the money stock. It is this fact that led Chicago economist Milton Friedman to pronounce that "inflation is always and everywhere a monetary phenomenon."

If the Federal Reserve keeps the money stock relatively stable, prices will be relatively stable and inflation will be low. If the Federal Reserve lets the money stock grow more quickly, then prices will be unstable and inflation will be relatively high. But on a year-to-year time scale, the relationship is not close: in the short run, fluctuations in y and v have a powerful role to play as well.

On a decade-to-decade scale, however, the relationship between money growth and inflation is strong. Consider what has happened in the United States in the past half century decade-by-decade, as shown in Table 8.2. The acceleration in the

---

[1]And also, in a complication deferred to this chapter's appendix, by the level of nominal interest rates.

TABLE 8.2
American Inflation and Money Growth by Decade, 1955–2004

Period	Average Inflation Rate (CPI)	Average Money Growth Rate (M2)
1955–1965	1.7%	4.7%
1965–1975	5.8	7.5
1975–1985	7.1	9.4
1985–1995	3.5	4.1
1995–2004	2.3	6.1

Source: 2004 *Economic Report of the President* and Macroeconomic Associates forecasts.

average rate of money growth from 4.7 percent for the period 1955–1965 to 9.4 percent for the period 1975–1985, an increase of 4.7 percentage points, is almost matched by the increase of 5.4 percentage points in the rate of inflation. The only recent decade in which money growth and inflation moved in opposite directions is the one we just finished, 1995–2004.

When one looks across countries, some of which have astonishingly high rates of money growth, the correlations between money growth and inflation are even stronger, as Figure 8.6 shows: The higher the rate of money growth, the higher the rate of inflation.

You should note that this section has greatly simplified money demand — most important, it has ignored how money demand depends on the interest rate. The appendix at the end of this chapter analyzes how changing interest rates affect money demand.

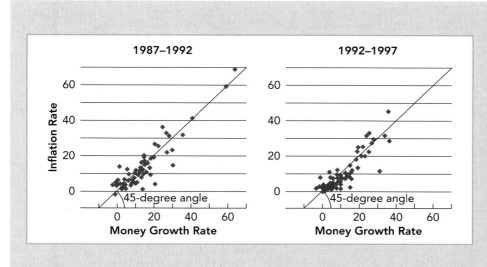

FIGURE 8.6
Money Growth and Inflation across Countries

For each country, one point shows the growth rate of money and the inflation rate for five-year periods, 1987–1992 (left) and 1992–1997 (right). Points on the 45-degree angle line have money growth rate equal to the inflation rate. Almost all countries are clustered close to that 45-degree line; the higher the money growth rate, the higher the inflation rate.

Source: Gerald P. Dwyer and R. W. Hafer, "Are Money Growth and Inflation Still Related?" *Federal Reserve Bank of Atlanta Monthly Review*, Second Quarter 1999, pp. 32–43.

Inflation and the Nominal Interest Rate

It was Yale University economist Irving Fisher who, early in the last century, pointed out that we would expect higher inflation to be accompanied by higher nominal interest rates. Households wanting to save and businesses wanting to borrow funds to use for investment bargain in financial markets over the terms of loans and debts. The market equilibrium real reward to saving and the real cost of borrowing is the real interest rate r. Changes in the rate of inflation shouldn't, in the long run, affect the terms of savers' and borrowers' bargains and the market equilibrium real interest rate, as long as they recognize the change in inflation and expect it to continue.

The interest rate we see on the evening news, however, is not the real interest rate r, but the nominal interest rate i:

$$i = r + \pi^e$$

Thus when the expected inflation rate rises, we would expect in the long run to see the nominal interest rate rise with it, point-for-point. This theoretical prediction — and rough empirical regularity — is called the **Fisher effect.**

Fisher effect

An empirical regularity whereby nominal interest rates typically rise roughly point-for-point with the expected inflation rate.

> **RECAP   THE QUANTITY THEORY OF MONEY**
>
> People want to hold a certain amount of wealth in the form of readily spendable purchasing power because the stuff is useful. The more money in your portfolio, the easier it is to buy things. However, you don't want to have too much of your wealth in the form of readily spendable purchasing power. Cash sitting in your pocket is not earning interest at the bank. Wealth you do not want to spend for five years could earn a higher return as a certificate of deposit or as an investment in the stock market than as cash in your checking account.
>
> The theory that the only important determinant of the demand for money is the flow of spending is the quantity theory of money, $MV = PY$, where PY represents the total nominal flow of spending. For each dollar of spending on goods and services, households want to hold $1/V$ dollars' worth of money. The parameter V, a constant, or perhaps growing slowly and predictably, is the velocity of money. The velocity of money is a measure of how "fast" money moves through the economy: how many times a year the average unit of money shows up in someone's income and is then used to buy a final good or service that counts in GDP.

8.3 THE COSTS OF INFLATION

Why should we care whether the central bank controls the money supply so that inflation is low and stable or lets the money supply expand rapidly and produce high and unpredictable inflation? One reason *not* to care about inflation is the fear that inflation makes us directly and significantly poorer. Any claim by a politician that inflation is the "cruelest tax" because its higher prices rob Americans of the benefits of their wages is not coherent. Inflation raises all nominal prices and wages in the economy. The higher nominal prices that a worker has to pay because of inflation are, on average (but only on average), offset by the higher *nominal wages* that his or her employer can pay because of inflation. Higher living standards come from better technology and more capital-intensive production processes, not from reduced inflation.

Inflation does have costs, but they are subtle. For the most part, the costs of moderate inflation appear to be relatively small, perhaps smaller than one would guess given the strength of today's political consensus that price stability is a very desirable goal.

The Costs of Moderate Expected Inflation

A rise in the **expected inflation rate** raises the nominal interest rate, which you will recall is equal to the real interest rate plus the expected rate of inflation. If the nominal interest rate did not rise when inflation rose, borrowers would recognize that borrowing had suddenly become a very good deal: Borrow now at the same nominal interest rate, and pay back later. But because inflation will increase prices and wages, fewer goods and services will be forgone in order to make the loan payment. For this reason we expect to see nominal interest rates rise roughly point-for-point with the expected inflation rate — the *Fisher effect,* as noted earlier.

Since the nominal interest rate is the opportunity cost of holding money balances, when the rate is high, you devote more time and energy to managing your cash balances. From the viewpoint of the economy as a whole, this extra time and energy is just wasted. Nothing useful is produced, and valuable resources that could be used to add to output or be simply spent on enjoying yourself are used up.

Expected inflation wastes time and energy in other ways as well. Firms find that they must spend resources changing their prices not because of any change in their business but simply because of inflation. Households find that it is harder to figure out what is a good buy and what is a bad one as inflation pushes prices away from what they had perceived normal prices to be. The most serious costs of expected inflation surely come from the fact that our tax laws are not designed to deal well with inflation. Lots of productive activities are penalized, and lots of unproductive ones rewarded, simply because of the interaction of inflation with the tax system. The fact that debt interest is treated as a cost means that in times of high inflation, financing businesses by issuing bonds or borrowing at the bank is artificially cheap, and so businesses adopt debt-heavy capital structures that may make the economy more vulnerable to financial crises and that certainly increase the amount of resources wasted paying bankruptcy lawyers, as businesses with lots of debt tend to go bankrupt relatively easily.

And, as was stressed at the start of the chapter, inflation fuzzes up the price signals about relative scarcities, values, and opportunities that the market system sends to businesses, investors, and consumers. Stable prices make the market system work better in a microeconomic sense as a social resource-allocation calculation mechanism.

Nevertheless, when the rate of inflation is low — perhaps less than 10 percent per year, probably less than 5 percent per year, and certainly less than 2 percent per year — these costs are too small to worry about because they are counterbalanced by benefits. Suppose the central bank wants to push the real interest rate below zero in some economic crisis? It cannot do so unless there is some inflation in the economy, because nominal interest rates cannot be less than zero

expected inflation rate

A hunch, formed today, of what the inflation rate will be at some time in the future. Economists usually collapse the range of different and conflicting expectations held by people into a single average number.

and the real interest rate is the difference between the nominal interest rate and the inflation rate. Moreover, many economists and psychologists have speculated that worker morale is greatly harmed if worker wages are clearly and unambiguously cut. A small amount of inflation may then grease the wheels of the labor market, allowing for wage adjustment without the damaging effect on morale of explicit wage cuts. These considerations have led the Federal Reserve's policy makers to adopt a rather odd definition of "price stability"; as far as they are concerned, an inflation rate of about 2 percent per year is price stability, and many members of today's FOMC become alarmed if the rate of inflation threatens to fall below that level.

The Costs of Moderate Unexpected Inflation

Unexpected inflation has significantly larger and more worrisome costs, for unexpected inflation redistributes wealth from creditors to debtors. Creditors receive much less purchasing power than they had anticipated if a loan falls due during a time of significant inflation. Debtors find the payments they must make much less burdensome if they borrow over a period of significant inflation. The process works in reverse as well: If inflation is less than had been expected, creditors receive a windfall and debtors go bankrupt. Most people are averse to risk. We buy insurance, after all. People who are averse to risk dislike uncertainty and unpredictability — and unexpected inflation certainly creates uncertainty and unpredictability.

Yet perhaps the economic costs of moderate unexpected inflation are relatively low. Why don't debtors and creditors want to insure themselves against inflation risk by indexing their contracts and using some alternative, more stable unit of account? In economies with high and variable inflation, we do see such indexation. The fact that we do not see it in countries with moderate and low inflation suggests that the costs of inflation to individual debtors and creditors (though perhaps not to society as a whole) must be relatively low, as long as changes in the inflation rate are low and are not too sudden.

Nevertheless, a powerful political argument holds that the costs of moderate inflation are high. Voters do not like moderate inflation. The 1970s saw government after government in the industrialized world voted out of office. Polls showed that voters interpreted the rising rates of inflation as signs that the political parties in power were incompetent at managing the economy. Since the end of the 1970s, no major political party in the industrialized world has dared run on a platform of less price stability and more inflation.

Hyperinflation and Its Costs

The costs of inflation mount to economy-destroying levels during episodes of hyperinflation, when inflation rises by more than 20 percent a month or so. Hyperinflations arise when governments attempt to obtain extra revenue by printing money but overestimate how much revenue they can raise. For some governments, printing money is an important source of revenue. Most governments tax their citizens or borrow from people who think that the government will pay them back. But if a government finds that it does not have the administrative reach to increase its explicit tax take and that no one will lend to it, it can simply print money and use the bills hot off the press to purchase goods and services.

Where do the resources — the power to buy goods and services — that the government acquires by printing money come from? A government that finances its spending by printing money is actually financing its spending by levying a tax on holdings of cash. Suppose I have $500 in cash in my pocket when the government suddenly announces it has printed up enough extra dollar bills to double the economy's cash supply. With Y and V unchanged, doubling the money supply doubles the price level. The $500 in my pocket will buy only as much after the government's money-printing spree as $250 would have bought before. The situation is as if the government levied a special one-time 50 percent tax on cash holdings.

Where did the 250 real dollars in my pocket go? The government has them: It now has 500 newly printed dollars, even if each of them is worth half a preinflation dollar in real terms. (See Figure 8.7.) Clearly, printing money can be easier than imposing a 50 percent explicit tax. To collect an explicit tax, a government needs an entire wealth-tracking, money-collecting, compliance-monitoring bureaucracy. To print money, all the government needs is a printing press, some ink, some paper, and a working connection to the electric power grid.

Almost everyone agrees that this **inflation tax** — also called *seigniorage* because the right to coin money was originally a right reserved to certain feudal lords, certain seigneurs — is very bad policy. One of the first principles of public finance is that taxes should be broad-based and lie relatively lightly on economic activity. The inflation tax is a heavy tax on a narrow base of economic activity, the activity of holding money. Moreover, the inflation tax is a heavy tax on one small slice of money holding: cash and deposits at the central bank.

inflation tax

The tax implicitly levied on an economy's private sector by the government's exercise of its power to print more money; also called *seigniorage*.

Households and businesses have $500 billion in cash and reserves.

The government prints an extra $500 billion in cash.

The price doubles, and so household and business cash and reserves lose half their real value: They're now worth only $250 billion in preinflation terms.

Where did the other $250 billion in real purchasing power go? The government now has it, having raised it through the "inflation tax."

FIGURE 8.7
The Inflation Tax
The "inflation tax" is a way for the government to get command over goods and services just as much as is any other tax. Those who pay the inflation tax are those who hold assets that lose value in the event of inflation.

Other components of the money stock — your checking account, say — are not a potential source of purchasing power for the government through the inflation tax. Suppose that you deposited your money in your checking account and the bank then took that purchasing power and used it to buy an office building. If the price level doubles, you have lost half the real value of your checking account, but the gainer in real terms is not the government. The gainer in real terms is the bank, which now finds the value of the office building it owns is twice as large relative to the value of the money it owes to its depositors. Not only is an inflation tax a bad tax, but its operation disrupts the rest of the financial system as well.

For these reasons, the inflation tax is resorted to only by a government that is falling apart and lacks the administrative capacity to raise money in any other way. Even so, such a government usually finds out afterward that the costs of the inflation tax and hyperinflation outweigh the benefits. Eventually prices rise so rapidly that the monetary system breaks down. People would rather deal with each other in barter terms than use a form of cash whose value is shrinking measurably every day. GDP starts to fall as the economy begins to lose the benefits of the division of labor. In the end the government finds that its currency is next to worthless. It runs the printing presses faster and faster and yet finds that the money it prints buys less and less. At the end of the German hyperinflation of the 1920s, 1 trillion marks were needed to buy what 1 mark had bought less than 10 years before.

Writing in the immediate aftermath of World War I, early-twentieth-century British economist *John Maynard Keynes* in his *Tract on Monetary Reform* put the case against this kind of inflation more eloquently than anybody else we have ever read:

> [Soviet Russia's dictator Vladimir] Lenin is said to have declared that the best way to destroy the capitalist system was to debauch the currency. By a continuing process of inflation, governments can confiscate, secretly and unobserved, an important part of the wealth of their citizens. By this method they not only confiscate, but they confiscate arbitrarily; and, while the process impoverishes many, it actually enriches some. The sight of this arbitrary rearrangement of riches strikes not only at security, but at confidence in the equity of the existing distribution of wealth. Those to whom the system brings windfalls, beyond their desserts and even beyond their expectations or desires, become "profiteers," who are the object of the hatred of the bourgeoisie, whom the inflationism has impoverished, not less than of the proletariat.
>
> As the inflation proceeds and the real value of the currency fluctuates wildly from month to month, all permanent relations between debtors and creditors, which form the ultimate foundation of capitalism, become so utterly disordered as to be almost meaningless; and the process of wealth-getting degenerates into a gamble and a lottery.
>
> Lenin was certainly right. There is no subtler, no surer means of overturning the existing basis of society than to debauch the currency. The process engages all the hidden forces of economic law on the side of destruction, and does it in a manner which not one man in a million is able to diagnose. In the latter stages of the war all the belligerent governments practiced, from necessity or incompetence, what a Bolshevist might have done from design. Even now, when the war is over, most of them continue out of weakness the same malpractices.

> **RECAP** **THE COSTS OF INFLATION**
>
> The economic costs of expected moderate inflation are small. They are largely the costs of extra trips to the bank and of time and resources wasted in the socially unproductive activity of keeping one's money balance near its target level. The economic costs of moderate unexpected inflation are larger. It redistributes wealth unexpectedly between debtors and creditors and increases risk. Largest, however, are the political costs of moderate inflation: Voters seem to use inflation as a sign that the government's economic policy is not sound.
>
> If you look for high economic costs of inflation, you must turn your attention to episodes of hyperinflation. In a hyperinflation a government without the ability to tax or borrow resorts to printing money to buy goods and services. The inflation rate rises to 20 percent per month or more. The price mechanism breaks down as people resort to barter. And production falls.

Chapter Summary

1. By "money" economists mean something special: wealth in the form of readily spendable purchasing power.

2. Without money it is hard to imagine how our economy could successfully function. The fact that everyone will accept money as payment for goods and services is necessary for the market economy to function.

3. Money is not only a medium of exchange, but also a unit of account — a yardstick that we use to measure values and to specify contracts.

4. Money demand is determined by (a) businesses' and households' desire to hold wealth in the form of readily spendable purchasing power in order to carry out transactions, and (b) businesses' and households' recognition that there is a cost to holding money — wealth in the form of readily spendable purchasing power pays little or no interest.

5. The velocity of money is how many transactions a given piece of money manages to facilitate in a year. The principal determinant of the velocity of money is the economy's "transactions technology": the organization of its financial system.

6. The stock of money is determined by the central bank.

7. The price level is equal to the money stock times the velocity of money divided by the level of real GDP.

8. The inflation rate is equal to the proportional growth rate of the money stock plus the proportional growth rate of velocity minus the proportional growth rate of real GDP.

9. Governments cause hyperinflations because printing money is a way of taxing the public, and a government that cannot tax any other way will be strongly tempted to resort to it.

Key Terms

price level (p. 226)

inflation (p. 226)

deflation (p. 226)

hyperinflation (p. 227)

classical dichotomy (p. 227)

money (p. 228)

medium of exchange (p. 229)

unit of account (p. 229)

money demand (p. 230)

quantity theory of money (p. 231)

velocity (p. 231)

central bank (p. 233)

Federal Reserve (p. 233)

monetary base (p. 233)

open-market operations (p. 234)

money stock (p. 234)

reserve requirements (p. 234)

excess reserves (p. 234)

inflation rate (p. 235)

Fisher effect (p. 238)

expected inflation rate (p. 239)

inflation tax (p. 241)

Analytical Exercises

1. Economists say that a government can raise real revenue — real power to buy goods and services — through the "inflation tax." Who is it that pays this tax? How is it that the government collects it?

2. Suppose that real GDP is $10,000 billion, the velocity of money is 5, and the money stock is $2,500 billion. What is the price level?

3. Suppose that the rate of labor-force growth is 1 percent per year, the rate of growth of the efficiency of labor is 3 percent per year, the economy is on its balanced-growth path, and the velocity of money is increasing at 1 percent per year. Suppose that the Chair of the Federal Reserve calls you into her office and asks how fast money growth should be to achieve a constant price level. What answer do you give?

4. Suppose that the rate of labor-force growth is 3 percent per year, the efficiency of labor is stable, and the economy is on its balanced-growth path. Suppose also that the rate of growth of the nominal money stock is 10 percent per year. Do you think that it is likely that the inflation rate is less than 5 percent per year? Why or why not?

5. What would the Federal Reserve have to do if it wanted to raise the monetary base today by $10 billion? What do you think would happen to the price of short-term government bonds if the Federal Reserve did this? Why?

6. Suppose that the nominal interest rate i is 4 percent, and that the rate of inflation π is 2 percent. Suppose the rate of inflation jumps to 6 percent and remains at that new higher level indefinitely. What do you think will happen to the nominal interest rate i in the long run?

Policy Exercises

1. At the end of December 2003 the U.S. monetary base was $720 billion. Suppose that the U.S. government decided to raise $360 billion in real purchasing power (in the dollars of December 2003) through the inflation tax. What do you think would happen to the price level?

2. In the third quarter of 1998 nominal GDP was $8,574 billion. The monetary base H was $494 billion; M1 was $1,072 billion; and M2 was $4,210 billion. Calculate the velocities of the monetary base, M1, and M2.

3. By the third quarter of 2003 nominal GDP was $11,107 billion. The monetary base H was $709 billion; M1 was $1,286 billion; M2 was $6,144 billion; and M3 was $8,956 billion. Calculate the velocities of the monetary base, M1, and M2.

4. Between 1990 and 2004 M1 increased from $792 billion to $1,287 billion, while nominal GDP increased from $5,744 billion to a projected $11,650 billion. What was the average annual rate of increase of the M1 money stock? Of nominal GDP? Of M1 velocity?

5. Between 1980 and 1990, and between 1990 and 2000, M1 increased from $409 billion to $826 billion to $1,084 billion; M2 rose from $1,601 billion to $3,280 billion to $4,932 billion; and M3 rose from $1,992 billion to $4,066 billion to $7,100 billion. During these same periods nominal GDP rose from $2,784 billion to $5,744 billion to $9,817 billion. Calculate the average annual rates of increase of M1, M2, M3, and nominal GDP between 1980 and 1990 and between 1990 and 2000. Calculate the average annual rates of increase of the velocity of M1, M2, and M3 between 1980 and 1990 and between 1990 and 1998. How constant do these velocity trends appear to be both across time and across different measures of the money stock?

6. Suppose that you were told that the rate of inflation was about to decline significantly over the next decade. Would you expect the velocity of money to rise unusually fast, behave normally, or fall over the course of the decade? Why?

The Interest Rate and Money Demand

APPENDIX 8a

8a.1 A MORE SYSTEMATIC LOOK AT MONEY DEMAND

In the main body of Chapter 8, we talked of the velocity of money as a constant (or as a slowly moving steady trend). The real world is more complicated. Velocity changes over time, in not always predictable ways, and so inflation is not always proportional to money growth.

As Figure 8a.1 on page 246 shows, in the 1980s in the United States the inflation rate fell sharply, but the money growth rate stayed relatively high until nearly the end of the decade. In the late 1990s the rate of money growth accelerated, but the inflation rate did not. In both cases shifts in velocity made money growth rates, for a while, not good guides to what inflation was about to be.

One important determinant of velocity is the inflation rate itself, working through the nominal interest rate. When inflation rises, we see the nominal interest rate rise as well. And a higher nominal interest rate reduces demand for money — and so increases the velocity of money.

Why? Money demand reflects the choice households and businesses make about how much of their wealth to hold in readily spendable liquid form (money) versus in other assets. The readily spendable cash in your purse or wallet does not earn interest. Your checking account balances earn little or no interest as well. As a result, their purchasing power over real goods and services erodes at the rate of inflation. The expected real return on keeping your money in readily spendable form is $-\pi^e$, the negative of the expected inflation rate π^e.

By contrast, were you to take a dollar out of your checking account and purchase a financial asset such as a bond, its real return would be the real interest rate r. The difference between the rate of return on other assets and the rate of return on *money balances* is the opportunity cost of holding money. This opportunity cost is the sum of the real interest rate r and the expected inflation rate π^e, that is, the nominal interest rate i. The higher the opportunity cost of holding

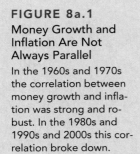

FIGURE 8a.1

Money Growth and Inflation Are Not Always Parallel

In the 1960s and 1970s the correlation between money growth and inflation was strong and robust. In the 1980s and 1990s and 2000s this correlation broke down.

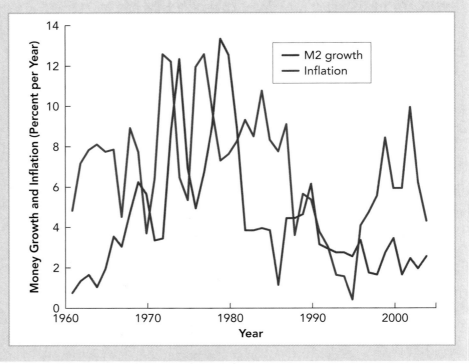

Source: The 2004 edition of *The Economic Report of the President* (Washington, DC: Government Printing Office).

money, the lower is the demand for money balances likely to be, as Figure 8a.2 shows.

Economists try to fit these insights into their model by writing down a demand-for-money function:

$$\frac{M^d}{P} = M_y Y - M_i i$$

where M^d is the nominal quantity of money that households and businesses want to hold. It is divided by the overall price level P because what households and businesses really care about is not how many pieces of paper with George Washington's face they have, but how much in the way of goods and services their money holdings can buy. M/P is called "*real money balances.*"

The parameter M_y tells how much in the way of extra real money balances people demand when total income Y goes up. Remember from Chapter 7, the circular flow principle tells us we can also think of income Y as total spending or GDP, so money demand is related to our total spending. Over long periods of time M_y tends to fall as the financial system becomes more sophisticated, the time it takes checks to clear falls, and credit card balance limits rise.

The parameter M_i tells how much households and businesses reduce the amount of wealth they want to hold in the liquid form of money when the nominal interest rate i goes up.

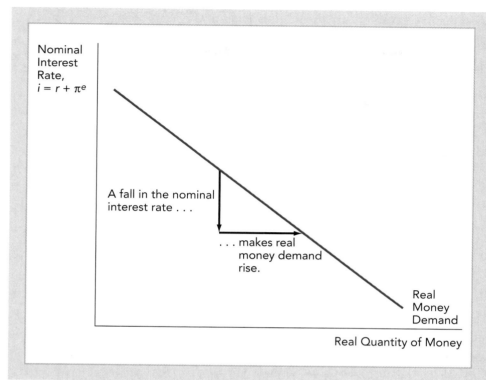

FIGURE 8a.2
The Nominal Interest Rate and Money Demand
When the nominal interest rate falls, the opportunity cost of holding wealth in readily spendable form falls, increasing the real demand for money. The amount by which real money demand rises depends on the size of the parameter M_i.

8a.2 MONEY, PRICES, AND INFLATION

Because the level of money demand depends on the current rate of inflation working through the nominal interest rate, we need to keep track of two equations to determine the behavior of money, prices, and inflation. The first equation comes directly from the money-demand function above. Simply set money demand M^d equal to the money stock M, and solve the equation for P to get

$$P = \frac{M}{M_y Y - M_i i}$$

Then recognize that the nominal interest rate i is equal to the real interest rate r plus the expected inflation rate π^e, and substitute in $r + \pi^e$ for i to get our first equation:

$$P = \frac{M}{M_y Y - M_i r - M_i \pi^e}$$

This tells us that a jump in the expected inflation rate π^e — in the rate at which prices are expected to increase — will cause an immediate and sudden upward jump in the price level P as well.

The second equation we pick up directly from the body of Chapter 8. If inflation is constant at some rate π, and if the proportional change in velocity is constant at some rate v, then

$$\pi = m + v - y$$

FIGURE 8a.3

Effects of an Increase in Money Growth

An increase in the rate of growth of the money stock leads to an immediate jump in the price level, a step-up of the inflation rate, and a fall in the quantity of money demanded as a fraction of nominal GDP. Prices initially increase by 3 percent per year when the money growth rate is 6 percent and the inflation rate is 3 percent. But when the money growth rate jumps to 8.5 percent, the inflation rate jumps to 5.5 percent (middle) so the price level (top) rises more rapidly. As expectations rise to the new higher inflation rate, nominal interest rates rise, decreasing money demand M^d relative to nominal spending PY (bottom) and thus increasing velocity.

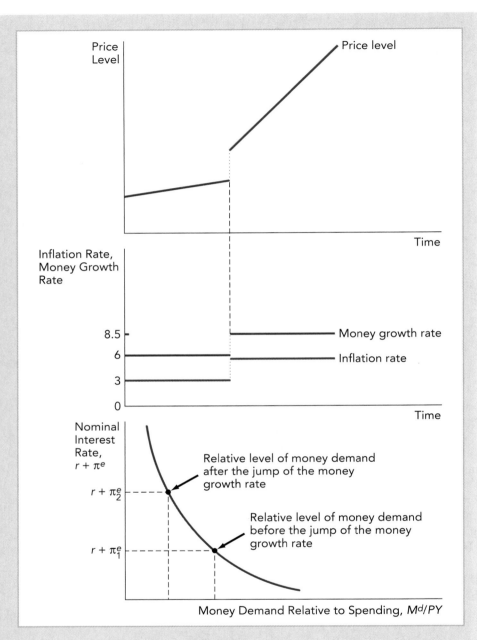

Thus if the rate of growth of the money stock is 6 percent per year, the velocity trend is 1 percent per year, and real GDP growth is 4 percent per year, inflation is 3 percent per year.

Suppose that the rate of growth of the money stock suddenly increases permanently from 6 to 8.5 percent per year. When the economy settles down, the new inflation rate will be 2.5 percent per year higher, or 5.5 percent instead of 3 percent per year. But at an inflation rate of 5.5 percent per year, the opportunity cost of holding money is higher. If the real interest rate is stable at 3 percent per year, then the opportunity cost of holding money has just jumped from 6 to 8.5 percent per year.

This higher opportunity cost of holding money — the higher nominal interest rate — will tend to raise the price level suddenly and instantly. That's what our first equation for the price level tells us.

$$P = \frac{M}{M_y Y - M_i r - M_i \pi^e}$$

Now at the moment that the rate of growth of the money stock jumps, the *level* of the money stock does not jump. It is growing faster, but the faster growth has not yet had time to take effect. Our equation thus tells us that the price level will jump suddenly and discontinuously, as is shown in Figure 8a.3! By how much will the price level jump? That depends on how sensitive money demand is to changes in the nominal interest rate — on the parameter M_i. The more sensitive is money demand to the nominal interest rate, the larger will be the sudden jump in the price level.

This sensitivity of the demand for money to the interest rate creates the possibility of expectational instability in the price level and the inflation rate. If a given rate of money growth is thought to be consistent with low inflation, then money demand will be relatively high — and inflation may well be low. But if that rate of money growth is thought for some reason to be a signal of high future inflation, money demand will fall — in which case inflation will be high.

Sticky-Price Macroeconomics

Chapters 4 through 8 do not give a complete picture of the macroeconomy. In Chapters 4 through 8, growth is smooth from year to year. But in the real world growth is not. In Chapters 4 through 8, supply and demand in the labor market are always in balance. But in the real world the labor market is not always in equilibrium.

To understand these business-cycle fluctuations in economic growth and unemployment, we need a model that does not require that employment be full and real GDP be equal to potential output. The full-employment model of Part 3 is not of help because its flexible-price assumption guarantees full employment. Here in Part 4, therefore, we need to break this flexible-price assumption to build a useful model of the business cycle.

From this point forward, prices will be "sticky": They will not move freely and instantaneously in response to changes in demand and supply. We will use this sticky-price model to account for business-cycle fluctuations.

Building this sticky-price model of the macroeconomy is the task of Part 4. Chapter 9 focuses on how, when prices are sticky, the inventory adjustment process is the key to understanding how GDP can fall below or rise above potential output. Chapter 10 analyzes how changes in the interest rate affect investment, exports, and GDP. Chapter 11 focuses on equilibrium in the money market and the balance of aggregate demand and aggregate supply. Chapter 12 focuses on monetary policy, expectations, and inflation. It links the sticky-price model of Part 4 back to the flexible-price model of Part 3 by analyzing which model is most useful in which sets of circumstances.

9

The Sticky-Price Income-Expenditure Framework: Consumption and the Multiplier

QUESTIONS

What are "sticky" prices?

What factors might make prices sticky in the short run?

In the short run when prices are sticky, what determines the level of real GDP?

When prices are sticky, what happens to real GDP if some component of planned total expenditure rises or falls?

What is the spending multiplier? What factors determine its size?

Over the past decade real GDP in the American economy has grown at an average rate of 3.3 percent per year. At the same time, the American unemployment rate has fluctuated around an average level consistent with stable inflation — a *natural rate of unemployment* — of roughly 5.0 percent.[1] During the past decade, the inflation rate in the United States has been low: an average of about 1.8 percent per year as measured by the price index associated with GDP, the GDP deflator.[2]

If Chapters 4 through 8 gave a complete picture of the macroeconomy, this economic growth would have been smooth. Real GDP would have grown 3.4 percent — the CBO's estimate of the current rate of growth of potential GDP — year after year, not just on average. The unemployment rate would have remained steady at its natural rate of approximately 5.0 percent. And inflation would have been steady as well, determined by the rates of growth of potential output and the money stock and the velocity of money.

And if this were the case, the analysis in Chapters 4 and 5 would provide a complete picture of how potential output grew over time. The analysis in Chapters 6 and 7 would explain why real GDP equals potential output and how national income is divided among the different components of total expenditure. The analysis in Chapter 8 would detail how the price level and the inflation rate are determined. It would be the last chapter in this textbook. Your survey of macroeconomics would be finished now.

But it isn't. This is not the case. Chapters 4 through 8 do not give a complete picture of the macroeconomy. Growth is not at all smooth; on a year-to-year time scale, it is not even guaranteed. In 1982 real GDP was not 3.4 percent more but 1.9 percent less than it was in 1981 (see Figure 9.1). Between 1979 and 1982 the unemployment rate rose by 3.9 percentage points, and it rose again by 2.2 percentage points between 1989 and 1992. Unemployment may have been only 4 percent at the end of 2000, but it was 7.6 percent in the middle of 1992. Inflation at the end of 2000 may have been only 2.2 percent per year, but in 1981 it was 9.4 percent.

These fluctuations are called *business cycles*. A business cycle has two phases: an expansion or boom phase as production, employment, and prices all grow rapidly, and a subsequent recession or depression phase during which inflation falls or prices slump, unemployment rises, and production falls. During booms, output grows faster than trend, investment spending amounts to a higher-than-average share of GDP, unemployment falls, and inflation usually accelerates. During recessions, output falls, investment spending is a low share of real GDP, unemployment rises, and inflation usually decelerates. Compared to the overall upward trend of long-run growth, these short-run fluctuations (with the exception of the Great Depression) appear relatively small. But, as we noted in Chapter 1, they have a large impact on the lives of those unlucky enough to lose their jobs or to fail to find jobs when a recession hits.

---

[1]This natural rate of unemployment is not a constant; it moves slowly over time. And we are never sure what it was until after the fact.

[2]As measured by the Consumer Price Index — the CPI — the average rate of inflation has been higher: 2.4 percent. This difference exists because the prices of capital goods, chiefly computers and communications equipment, have been falling in nominal terms over the past decade. Capital goods are by and large not bought by households, and so do not make it into the CPI.

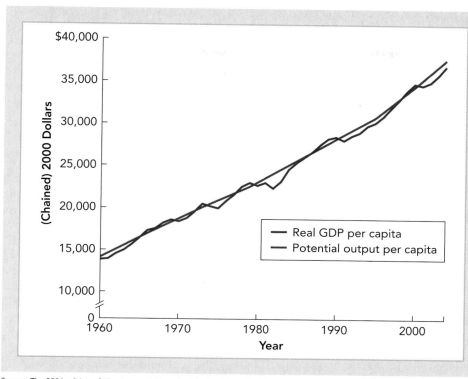

FIGURE 9.1
Real GDP and Potential Output per Capita 1960–2004

From year to year real GDP per capita fluctuates around potential output. The flexible-price full-employment classical model of Chapters 6 and 7 cannot account for these fluctuations in real GDP per capita relative to potential output per capita.

Source: The 2004 edition of *The Economic Report of the President* (Washington, DC: Government Printing Office).

9.1 STICKY PRICES

Sticky Prices

To understand business cycles, we need a model that does not guarantee full employment and in which real GDP does not always equal potential output. Business cycles are not fluctuations in potential output. They are fluctuations of actual production around potential output — above potential output when the economy is "overheated," and below potential output when the economy possesses substantial "slack." Thus the full-employment model of Chapters 6 through 8 is of no help here. Its assumption that prices are flexible guarantees full employment. The **flexible-price** assumption allowed us to start our analysis in a simple and straightforward way, by noting that the labor market would clear, that as a result firms would fully employ workers who wanted to work, and thus that real GDP and household income would be equal to potential output. (And the flexible-price assumption is not a bad one to make if employment is nearly full, either because there have been no large disturbances to demand in a while so that wages and prices in labor and product markets have had time to adjust, or because the Federal Reserve has done a good job of neutralizing disturbances to total expenditure.)

But we cannot afford to keep the flexible-price assumption. We need to break it if we are to build a more useful model of the business cycle. Thus from this point on wages and prices will be "sticky": They will not move freely and instantaneously in response to changes in demand and supply. Instead, prices will remain fixed at predetermined levels as businesses expand or contract production in response to changes in demand and costs. As you will see, such sticky prices make a big

flexible prices

When wages and prices in an economy are not sticky but move smoothly and rapidly to keep supply equal to demand in the labor market and in the goods market.

sticky prices

When wages and prices do not move smoothly and immediately to keep supply equal to demand in the labor and goods markets.

difference in economic analysis; they will drive a wedge between real GDP and potential output and between the supply of workers and the demand for labor. We will then be able to use this sticky-price model to account for business-cycle fluctuations.

Building this **sticky-price** model of the macroeconomy will take up all of Part 4. In this chapter, we will focus on how, when prices are sticky, firms hire or fire workers and expand or cut back production on the basis of whether their inventories are falling or rising. Inventory adjustment is the key to understanding how the level of real GDP can fluctuate around potential output. Chapter 10 focuses on how changes in the interest rate affect the levels of investment, exports, and real GDP in the sticky-price model.

Chapter 11 takes a deeper look at equilibrium in the money market: How are interest rates in the short run really determined? It is an optional chapter. You can simply say that the Federal Reserve — the Fed — sets interest rates, not inquire into how, and skip Chapter 11. But if you want to understand what happens when there is no interest rate–pegging central bank around, or how the Federal Reserve pegs interest rates, or what happens if the Federal Reserve pegs not interest rates but the money stock, then you need to study Chapter 11.

The last chapter of Part 4, Chapter 12, takes up the topics of expectations and inflation in an environment in which the Fed sets interest rates. By the end of Chapter 12 we will have linked up the sticky-price model of Part 4 with the flexible-price model of Part 3. We will understand the sorts of situations for which the sticky-price model is appropriate. And we will understand under what sets of circumstances wages and prices are flexible enough and have enough time to adjust for the flexible-price model to be the most useful way of analyzing the macroeconomy.

At each stage in the building of our sticky-price macroeconomic model, the preceding topic serves as a necessary foundation. The analysis of inflation and expectations in Chapter 12 rests on the analysis of how changes in interest rates affect investment, exports, and real GDP in Chapter 10. And the analysis of Chapter 10 in turn rests on the analysis of income, expenditure, and equilibrium in a sticky-price economy carried out here in Chapter 9. Chapter 11 also rests on Chapters 9 and 10, and it provides a fuller foundation for Chapter 12.

Up to this point, this book has not been cumulative. You could understand the long-run growth analysis in Chapters 4 and 5 without a firm grasp of the introductory material in Chapters 1 through 3. You could understand the flexible-price analysis in Chapters 6 and 7 without a firm grasp of either the introductory or the long-run-growth chapters. And you could understand Chapter 8 without having read anything earlier in the book. But from this point on, the chapters of this book become interdependent and very cumulative indeed.

Consequences of Sticky Prices

Flexible-Price Logic

To preview the difference between the flexible-price and the sticky-price models, let us analyze a decline in consumers' propensity to spend under both sets of assumptions. Suppose there is a sudden fall in the parameter C_0 that determines the baseline level of consumption in the consumption function

$$C = C_0 + C_y(1 - t)Y$$

where Y is GDP or national income, t is the tax rate, C is consumption spending, and C_0 and C_y are the parameters of the consumption function that determine

(1) the baseline level of consumption and (2) how much consumption increases for a $1 increase in national income, respectively. When C_0 falls, then at any given level of national income Y, consumers wish to save more and spend less.

To make this concrete, consider what happens when baseline consumption spending falls. Suppose that the function for annual consumption spending (in billions of dollars) declines from

$$C = 2,000 + 0.5(1 - t)Y$$

to

$$C = 1,800 + 0.5(1 - t)Y$$

In the full-employment model of Chapters 6 through 8, such a $200 billion fall in annual baseline consumption spending would have no impact on the level of real GDP. No matter what the flow of total expenditure, the labor market would still reach its full-employment equilibrium shown in Figure 9.2 because nominal wages and prices are flexible. And because the economy remains at full employment, real GDP would equal potential output.

The fall in consumption spending would have an effect on the economy — just not on the level of real GDP. As we saw in Chapters 6 and 7, a fall in consumption spending means an increase in saving. As consumption falls, the total saving curve shifts rightward on the flow-of-funds diagram, as Figure 9.3 on page 258 shows. The fall in consumption spending reduces the equilibrium real interest rate. The fall in the interest rate then leads to increases in the equilibrium level of investment and net exports. By how much does investment plus net exports increase? By $200 billion, the amount necessary to offset the fall in consumption spending and keep real GDP equal to potential output.

Thus these are the flexible-price-model consequences of a fall in households' desired baseline consumption spending:

- Consumption falls.
- Household saving rises.

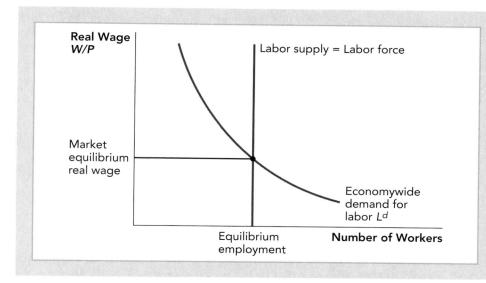

Real Wage W/P

Labor supply = Labor force

Market equilibrium real wage

Economywide demand for labor L^d

Equilibrium employment

Number of Workers

FIGURE 9.2

Flexible-Price Logic: Labor-Market Equilibrium

No matter what the flow of planned expenditure, flexible wages and prices mean that employment remains at full employment and the level of real GDP produced remains at potential output.

FIGURE 9.3

Flexible-Price Logic: The Effect on Saving of a Fall in Consumption Spending

With flexible prices, a fall in consumption spending means a rise in household saving and an increase in the flow of saving through financial markets. Thus the real interest rate falls, and more investment projects are undertaken. The fall in the real interest rate also raises the value of the exchange rate and boosts net exports.

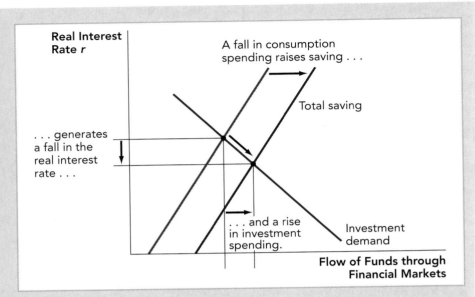

- The real interest rate falls.
- Investment rises.
- The value of foreign currency — the exchange rate — rises.
- Net exports rise; foreign saving falls.

Sticky-Price Logic

If wages and prices are sticky, the analysis is different. The first consequence of consumers' cutting back their spending will be a fall in expenditure for goods. Consumer spending has fallen, yet nothing has happened to change the flow of spending on investment goods, the flow of net exports, or the flow of government purchases.

As businesses see spending on their products begin to fall, they will not cut their nominal prices (remember, prices are sticky). Instead, they will respond to the fall in the quantity of their products demanded by reducing their production. They want to avoid accumulating unsold and unsellable inventory. As they reduce production, they will fire some of their workers, and the income of the fired workers will drop. By how much will total national income drop? Initially, it will fall by the amount of the fall in baseline consumption spending: $200 billion a year. (Moreover, because the decline in income leads to a further decline in consumption as households that have lost income cut back on their spending, national income and real GDP will fall by more than the decline in C_0. This *multiplier* process is discussed later on in the chapter.)

Thus the consequences of a fall in consumption spending under the sticky-price assumption are

- Consumption falls.
- Production and employment decline.
- National income declines.

In the flexible-price model, when consumption falls, investment and net exports rise. Why doesn't the same thing happen in the sticky-price model? Why doesn't a rise

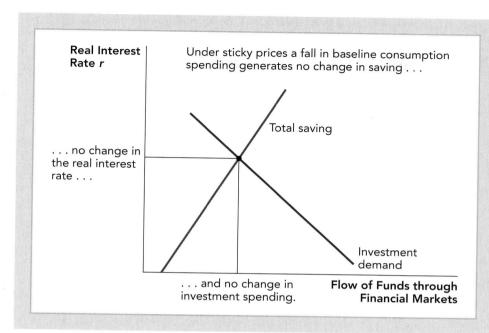

FIGURE 9.4
Sticky-Price Logic: The Effect on Saving of a Fall in Consumption Spending

With sticky prices, a fall in baseline consumption spending carries with it a fall in income. Because both total consumption spending and ultimately income decline by the same amount, there is no change in total saving through financial markets. Thus the real interest rate remains unchanged. There is no change in investment spending or gross exports.

in investment spending keep GDP equal to potential output and keep employment full? What goes wrong with the flexible-price logic, according to which a fall in consumption spending generates an increase in saving that then boosts both investment spending and net exports?

The answer hinges on the fact that in the sticky-price model, firms respond to falling demand not by cutting prices but by cutting back production and employment, and so total income falls. A fall in total income reduces saving (if consumption is held constant) just as a fall in consumption raises saving (if income is held constant). Under the sticky-price assumption, the effect on total saving of the fall in consumption and the fall in income cancel each other out; there is no change in the flow of saving. Thus there is no rightward shift in the position of the total saving curve on the flow-of-funds diagram in Figure 9.4. There is no fall in interest rates to trigger higher investment (and a higher value of the exchange rate and expanded net exports). There is nothing to offset the fall in consumption spending and keep GDP from falling below potential output.

Why doesn't this sticky-price unemployment-generating logic work when prices are flexible? The answer is that when flexible-price firms see a fall in total spending, they respond not by cutting production and employment but by cutting the prices they charge and the wages they pay. Since prices and wages both fall, the real income households earn remains constant. Thus with flexible prices a fall in consumption spending does induce a rise in saving — hence a fall in the real interest rate, a rise in investment spending, an increase in the value of the exchange rate, and a rise in net exports.

Expectations and Price Stickiness

If managers, workers, consumers, and investors had time to foresee a fall in consumption and gradually adjust their wages and prices to it in advance, even considerable stickiness in prices would not be a problem. With sufficient advance notice unions and businesses would strike wage bargains, and businesses could adjust their selling prices to make sure demand matched productive capacity. Both the stickiness of prices and the failure to accurately foresee changes far enough ahead to adjust to them in advance are needed if the sticky-price framework is to create business cycles in employment and output like the ones we see.

One way to think about this is that the analysis in Part 4 is a short-run analysis, and the analysis in Part 3 is a longer run analysis (although still not as long run as the truly long-run growth analysis of Part 2). In the Part 4 short run, prices are sticky; shifts in policy or in the economic environment that affect the components of planned total expenditure will affect real GDP and employment. In the Part 3 long run, prices are flexible and workers, bosses, and consumers have time to react and adjust to changes in policy or the economic environment. Thus in the long run, such shifts do not affect real GDP or employment.

Why do we need a sticky-price short-run model as well as the long-run flexible-price model? Why don't economists simply say that once wages and prices have fully adjusted (however long that takes), employment will be full and real GDP will be equal to potential output? The most famous and effective criticism of such let's-look-only-at-the-long-run analyses was made by John Maynard Keynes in his 1924 *Tract on Monetary Reform*. Criticizing one such long-run-only analysis, Keynes wrote:

> In the long run [this] is probably true. . . . But this long run is a misleading guide to current affairs. In the long run we are all dead. Economists set themselves too easy, too useless a task if in tempestuous seasons they can only tell us that when the storm is long past the ocean will be flat once more.

Where is the line that divides the short run from the long run? Do we switch from living in the short run of Part 4 to the long run of Part 3 on June 19, 2006? No, we do not. The "long run" is an analytical construct. A change can be considered long run if enough people see it coming far enough in advance and have had time to adjust to it — to renegotiate their contracts and change their standard operating procedures accordingly. The length of the long run, and thus how many of us will be dead before it comes, depends in turn on the degree of price stickiness and the process by which people form their expectations — both hot topics for academic research in modern macroeconomics.

Why Are Prices Sticky?

Why don't prices adjust quickly and smoothly to maintain full employment? Why do businesses respond to fluctuations in demand first by hiring or firing workers and accelerating or shutting down their production lines? Why don't they respond first by raising or lowering their prices?

Economists have identified any number of reasons that prices could be sticky, but they are uncertain which are most important. Some likely explanations are:

- Managers and workers find that changing prices or renegotiating wages is costly and hence best delayed as long as possible.
- Managers and workers lack information and so confuse changes in total economywide spending with changes in demand for their specific products.
- The level of prices is as much a sociological as an economic variable — determined as much by what levels people think are "fair" as by the balance of supply and demand. Workers take a cut in their wages as an indication

that their employer does not value them; hence managers avoid wage cuts because they fear the consequences for worker morale.

- Managers and workers suffer from simple "money illusion"; they overlook the effect of price-level changes when assessing the impact of changes in wages or prices on their real income or sales.

Let's look more closely at each of these likely explanations. Economists call the costs associated with changing prices **menu costs**, a shorthand reference to the fact that when a restaurant changes its prices, it must print up a new menu. In general, changing prices or wages may be costly for any of a large number of reasons. Perhaps people want to stabilize their commercial relationships by signing long-term contracts. Perhaps reprinting a catalog is expensive. Perhaps customers find frequent price changes annoying. Perhaps other firms are not changing their prices and what matters most to a firm is its price relative to the prices of competitors. Hence managers and workers prefer to keep their prices and wages stable as long as the shocks that affect the economy are relatively small — or, rather, as long as the change they might want to make in their prices and wages is small.

A second source of price stickiness is **imperfect information**: a misperception of real and nominal price changes. If managers and workers lack full information about the state of the economy, they may be unsure whether a change in the flow of spending on their products reflects a change in overall aggregate demand or a change in demand for their particular products. If it is the latter, they should respond by changing how much they produce, not necessarily by changing the price. If it is the former, they should respond by changing their price in accord with overall inflation, not by changing how much they produce. If managers are uncertain which it is, they will split the difference. Hence firms will lower their prices less in response to a downward shift in total nominal demand than the flexible-price macroeconomic model would predict. If they keep their prices too high, they will have to fire workers and cut back production. Imperfect information is a possible source of sticky prices.

Yet a third reason why prices and wages are sticky is that workers and managers are really not the flinty-eyed rational maximizers of economic theories. In real life, work effort and work intensity depend on whether workers believe they are being treated fairly. A cut in nominal wages is almost universally perceived as unfair; wages depend on social norms that evolve slowly. Thus wages are by nature sticky. And if wages are sticky, firms will find that their best response to shifts in demand is to hire and fire workers rather than to change prices.

Last, workers, consumers, and managers suffer from **money illusion**: They confuse changes in nominal prices with changes in real (that is, inflation-adjusted) prices. Firms react to higher nominal prices by thinking falsely that it is more profitable to produce more — even though it isn't because their costs have risen in proportion. Workers react to higher nominal wages by searching more intensively for jobs and working more overtime hours, even though rises in prices have erased any increase in the real purchasing power of the wage paid for an hour's work. Such money illusion is a powerful generator of price stickiness and business-cycle fluctuations.

All these factors are potential sources of price stickiness. Your professor may have strong views about which is most important. We find ourselves more confused and agnostic. Our reading is that economists' knowledge is more limited. We are not sure the evidence is strong enough to provide clear and convincing support for any particular single explanation as the most important one. A safer

menu costs

The costs to a firm of changing the price(s) of a good(s) or service(s).

imperfect information

The information workers or managers have for decision making when they lack full information about the state of the economy.

money illusion

When managers, workers, and others fail to recognize that some of the change in their nominal income and revenue is a result of inflation and is not a change in their real income and revenue.

position is to remain agnostic about the causes of sticky wages and prices, and so in this book we will focus on analyzing not their causes but their effects.

> **RECAP   STICKY PRICES**
>
> The full-employment model of Chapters 6 through 8 does not help explain business cycles because its assumption that prices are flexible guarantees that real GDP is always equal to potential output. To build a more useful model of the business cycle, we need to assume that prices are sticky. If prices are sticky, the first consequence of a shock like consumers cutting back their spending will be a reduction in production, not a cut in prices. Prices might be sticky for a number of reasons: menu costs, imperfect information, concerns of fairness, or simply money illusion. All seem plausible but no one explanation indisputably dominates the others.

9.2 INCOME AND EXPENDITURE

If prices are sticky, higher planned expenditure boosts production, and this boosts income. Higher income gives a further boost to consumption, and this in turn boosts planned expenditure some more. Thus any shift in a component of planned expenditure upward or downward leads to an amplified shift in total production because of the induced shift in consumption, as Figure 9.5 shows. The early-twentieth-century British economist John Maynard Keynes was one of the first to stress the importance of this multiplier process.

Whereas in booms the multiplier process induces an upward spiral in production, in bad times it is a source of misery. The downward shock is amplified as those who have been thrown out of work cut back on their consumption spending in turn.

Because consumption spending is more than two-thirds of planned expenditure, this multiplier effect can be significant because the positive-feedback loop is so large — if the tax system has not been designed to provide the economy with so-called "*automatic stabilizers*," and if the government does not take active steps to cushion the effects of shocks to planned expenditure.

Building Up Planned Total Expenditure

The rest of this chapter shows how the level of planned total expenditure, which we called *PE* back in Chapter 6, is determined in the sticky-price macroeconomic

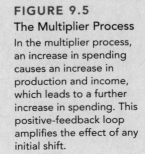

FIGURE 9.5
The Multiplier Process
In the multiplier process, an increase in spending causes an increase in production and income, which leads to a further increase in spending. This positive-feedback loop amplifies the effect of any initial shift.

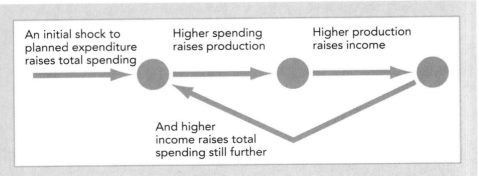

An initial shock to planned expenditure raises total spending

Higher spending raises production

Higher production raises income

And higher income raises total spending still further

model. We will use a bottom-up approach, building planned total expenditure PE on domestically produced products up from the determinants of each of its components, consumption spending C, investment spending I, government purchases G, and net exports NX. The circular flow principle tells us that PE is the sum of C, I, G, and NX:

$$PE = C + I + G + NX$$

As long as prices are sticky, the level of real GDP is determined by the level of planned total expenditure

$$Y = PE$$

and not by the level of potential output Y^*.

Why? Recall our sticky-price assumption: Firms respond to falling spending by cutting back production and firing workers (and respond to rising spending by increasing production and hiring workers).

The Consumption Function

The two-thirds of GDP that is consumption spending is spending by households on things they find useful: *services* such as haircuts, nondurable goods such as food, and durable goods such as washing machines. As Figure 9.6 shows, when income rises consumption spending rises with it, increasing planned total expenditure and setting the multiplier process in motion. As we saw in Chapter 6, consumption spending does not rise dollar for dollar with total income. Economists call the share of an extra dollar of disposable income that is added to consumption spending the **marginal propensity to consume (MPC)**, which is the parameter C_y in the **consumption function** equation that we saw in Chapter 6:

$$C = C_0 + C_y(1 - t)Y$$

The share of an extra dollar of national income that shows up as additional consumption spending is equal to the marginal propensity to consume times the share of income that escapes taxes: $C_y(1 - t)$.

marginal propensity to consume (MPC)

The increase in consumption spending resulting from a one-dollar increase in disposable income, C_y.

consumption function

The relationship between baseline consumption C_0; the marginal propensity to consume C_y; and disposable income Y^D. $C = C_0 + C_y(Y^D) = C_0 + C_y(1 - t)Y$.

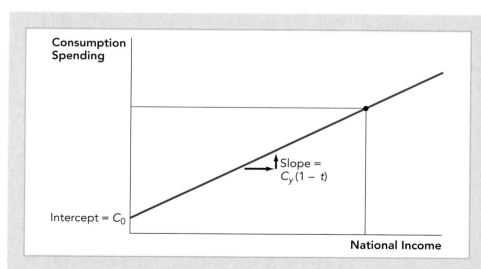

FIGURE 9.6

The Consumption Function and the Marginal Propensity to Consume

When drawn on a graph with economywide income on the horizontal axis and consumption spending on the vertical axis, the slope of the consumption function is the marginal propensity to consume times $(1 - t)$.

If changes in income are considered permanent, the MPC will be high: A $1 increase in income will lead to an increase in consumption of as much as 80 cents. But if changes in income are considered transitory, the MPC will be low: A $1 increase in income will lead to an increase in consumption of only 30 cents or so. Transitory increases in income have only a small effect on consumption because as we discussed in Appendix 6a people seek to smooth out their consumption spending over time.

For reasonably long-lasting shifts in the level of income, the MPC is roughly 0.6. That is, 60 cents of every extra dollar of disposable income shows up as higher consumption. Figure 9.7 shows how we get from the total flow of GDP down to the flow of consumption spending, which is GDP's largest component.

FIGURE 9.7

Consumption as a Function of After-Tax Disposable Income Three different factors drive the wedge between GDP and consumption spending. The first is depreciation: goods produced that merely replace obsolete and worn-out capital and so are a component of total cost rather than total income. The second is the tax system — both direct and indirect taxes. The third is household saving.

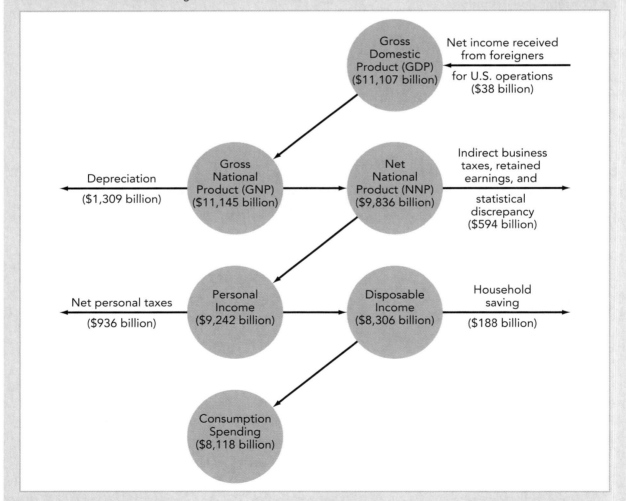

Source: The 2004 edition of *The Economic Report of the President* (Washington, DC: Government Printing Office).

Box 9.1 shows how to use the consumption function and its parameters — baseline spending C_0, the MPC C_y, and the tax rate t — to calculate consumption spending.

CALCULATING THE CONSUMPTION FUNCTION: AN EXAMPLE

Suppose statistical evidence tells us that the marginal propensity to consume out of disposable income C_y is 0.75. Suppose further that taxes amount to 40 percent of national income and that when real GDP — total national income — equals $8 trillion, consumption equals $5.5 trillion.

The fact that C_y is 0.75 and that the average tax rate t is 0.4 allows us to fill in some of the parameters in the consumption function:

$$C = C_0 + C_y(1 - t)Y$$
$$= C_0 + 0.75(1 - 0.4)Y$$
$$= C_0 + 0.45Y$$

We also know that when national income Y equals $8 trillion, consumption C equals $5.5 trillion:

$$\$5.5 \text{ trillion} = C_0 + 0.45(\$8 \text{ trillion})$$
$$\$5.5 \text{ trillion} = C_0 + \$3.6 \text{ trillion}$$
$$\$1.9 \text{ trillion} = C_0$$

So the numerical form of the consumption function is

$$C = \$1.9 \text{ trillion} + 0.45\, Y$$

Other Components of Total Expenditure

The determinants of the other components of planned total expenditure — investment spending, government purchases, and net exports — are familiar from Chapter 6. The level of investment spending is determined by the real interest rate and assessments of profitability made by business investment committees. In our model we represent these determinants by making investment spending I a function of the real interest rate r and of the parameters I_0 and I_r, the baseline level of investment spending and the interest sensitivity of investment.

$$I = I_0 - I_r r$$

The level of government purchases G is set by politics.

Net exports are equal to gross exports GX (a function of the real exchange rate ε and the level of foreign real GDP Y^f) minus imports. Imports IM are a function of national income Y:

$$NX = GX - IM = (X_f Y^f + X_\varepsilon \varepsilon) - IM_y Y$$

Figure 9.8 on page 266 shows the relative sizes of these four components of total expenditure.

FIGURE 9.8

Components of Total Expenditure By far the largest component of GDP is made up of consumption spending. Government purchases come second, and gross investment comes third. For the past two decades the United States has imported more than it has exported; hence net exports have been negative, not a contribution to but a subtraction from GDP.

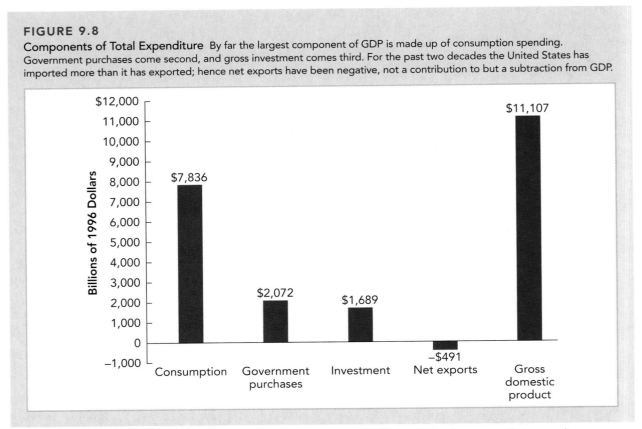

Source: The 2004 edition of *The Economic Report of the President* (Washington, DC: Government Printing Office). Values do not sum exactly due to rounding.

Autonomous Spending and the Marginal Propensity to Expend

Let's take the equation for planned total expenditure

$$PE = C + I + G + NX$$

then separate net exports into its gross exports and imports components:

$$PE = C + I + G + (GX - IM)$$

and replace the two components of total expenditure that depend directly on national income Y — consumption spending C and imports IM — with their determinants:

$$PE = [C_0 + C_y(1 - t)Y] + I + G + (GX - IM_yY)$$

We can now classify the components of planned total expenditure into two groups. The first group is so-called **autonomous spending**, which we will call A. Autonomous spending is made up of the components of planned total expenditure that do not depend directly on national income Y. Baseline consumption C_0, investment spending I, government spending G, and gross exports GX are the components of autonomous spending A:

$$A = C_0 + I + G + GX$$

autonomous spending

Those components of planned expenditure that are independent of the level of national income.

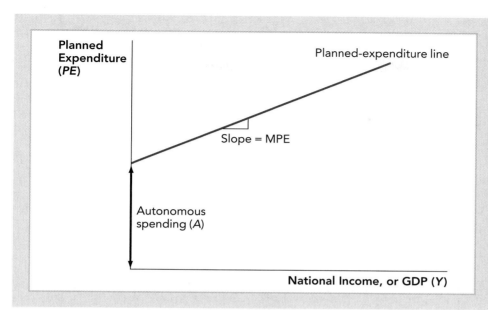

FIGURE 9.9

The Income-Expenditure Diagram

On the income-expenditure diagram, the line showing the relationship between total economy-wide income and total planned expenditure — the planned-expenditure line — is determined by two things: autonomous spending, the level at which the planned-expenditure line intercepts the vertical axis; and the marginal propensity to expend, the slope of the planned-expenditure line.

The second group includes the other two components of total expenditure — non–baseline consumption $C_y(1-t)Y$ and a negative contribution from imports IM_yY:

$$C_y(1-t)Y - IM_yY$$

Factor out income from this expression to get

$$[C_y(1-t) - IM_y]Y$$

and let's call $C_y(1-t) - IM_y$ the **marginal propensity to expend** on domestic goods: the MPE. Then we can write planned total expenditure PE in the simple form

$$PE = A + (MPE)(Y)$$

which Figure 9.9 shows, plotting planned total expenditure on the vertical axis and national income or real GDP on the horizontal axis of this version of what is called the **income-expenditure diagram.**

The vertical intercept of the **planned-expenditure line** is the level of autonomous spending A. The planned-expenditure line's slope is the marginal propensity to expend MPE. A change in the value of any determinant of any component of autonomous spending — the baseline levels of consumption C_0, investment I_0, or government purchases G; the real interest rate r; and foreign-determined variables that affect exports directly or indirectly (like foreign interest rates r^f, foreign levels of real income Y^f, or speculators' view of exchange rate fundamentals ε_0) — will shift the planned total expenditure line up or down. The higher the autonomous spending, the further from the horizontal axis the planned total expenditure line will be (see Figure 9.10 on page 268).

Changes in the marginal propensity to consume C_y, the tax rate t, or the propensity to spend on imports IM_y will change the MPE and the slope of the planned expenditure line. The higher the MPE, the steeper is the slope of the planned-expenditure line (see Figure 9.11 on page 268). Box 9.2 on page 269 provides an example of how to calculate the MPE.

marginal propensity to expend (MPE)

The increase in total spending — on consumption goods through the marginal propensity to consume and on net exports — from a one-dollar increase in national income.

income-expenditure diagram

The tool for figuring out what the equilibrium level of planned expenditure and gross domestic product is. Also known as the *Keynesian cross diagram.*

planned-expenditure line

Found on the income-expenditure (or Keynesian cross) diagram that shows planned expenditure on the vertical axis and national income on the horizontal axis. The planned-expenditure line shows planned total expenditure, $PE = C + I + G + NX$, as a function of the level of national income.

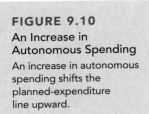

FIGURE 9.10

An Increase in Autonomous Spending

An increase in autonomous spending shifts the planned-expenditure line upward.

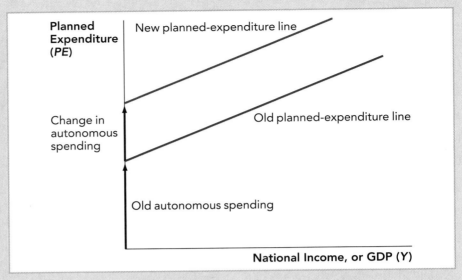

FIGURE 9.11

An Increase in the Marginal Propensity to Expend

A change in the marginal propensity to expend changes the slope of the planned-expenditure line.

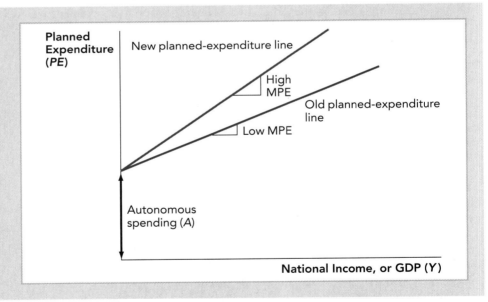

Sticky-Price Equilibrium

The economy will be in equilibrium when planned total expenditure equals real GDP — which is, according to the circular-flow principle, the same as national income. Under these conditions there will be no short-run forces pushing for an immediate expansion or contraction of national income, real GDP, or total expenditure.

On the income-expenditure diagram, the points at which planned total expenditure equals national income are a line running up and to the right at a 45-degree angle with respect to the horizontal axis, as Figure 9.12 on page 270 shows. This

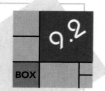

CALCULATING THE MPE: AN EXAMPLE

In the planned-expenditure function

$$PE = A + (MPE)(Y)$$

the marginal propensity to expend (MPE) will be less than the slope of the consumption function $C_y(1 - t)$ because of the effect on the economy of imports.

Thus if the marginal propensity to consume C_y is 0.75 and the tax rate is 40 percent, the 0.45 slope of the consumption function is an upper bound to the MPE. If imports are 15 percent of real GDP, then

$$MPE = \left[C_y(1 - t) - IM_y\right]$$
$$= [0.75\,(1 - 0.4) - 0.15]$$
$$= 0.45 - 0.15 = 0.30$$

Such relatively small values of the MPE are typical for modern industrialized economies, which have substantial amounts of international trade (that is, relatively high values for IM_y), large social-democratic social-insurance states (that is, relatively high values for t), and deep and well-developed financial systems that provide ample room for household borrowing and lending to smooth out consumption (that is, relatively small values for C_y as well). However, in the past, in relatively closed economies, or in economies with undeveloped financial systems, the MPE can be significantly higher.

45-degree line shows all the possible points of equilibrium: all the points where planned expenditure equals national income. The actual equilibrium the economy will find in the sticky-price short run will be that point at which planned total expenditure is equal to actual national income; the point where this planned-expenditure line intersects the 45-degree equilibrium-condition line is the economy's equilibrium.

In algebra, the equilibrium values of planned total expenditure PE and real GDP or national income Y must satisfy both the **planned-expenditure function:**

$$PE = A + (MPE)(Y)$$

and the equilibrium condition

$$PE = Y$$

Substituting Y for PE in the first of these equations and regrouping, the solution is

$$Y = \frac{A}{1 - MPE}$$

If the numerical values of the parameters of the planned-expenditure function are $A = \$5,600$ billion and $MPE = 0.3$, then planned total expenditure as a function of real GDP is

$$PE = 5,600 + 0.3(Y)$$

The equilibrium level of real GDP and total expenditure is then

$$Y = \$8,000 \text{ billion}$$

What forces drive the economy to its short-run sticky-price *goods market equilibrium*? If the economy is not on the 45-degree line, then planned expenditure PE does not equal real GDP Y. If Y is greater than PE, there is excess supply of goods.

planned-expenditure function

The relationship $PE = C + I + G + NX$ used to build planned expenditure for domestically produced products from the determinants of each of its components: consumption spending C, investment spending I, government purchases G, and net exports NX.

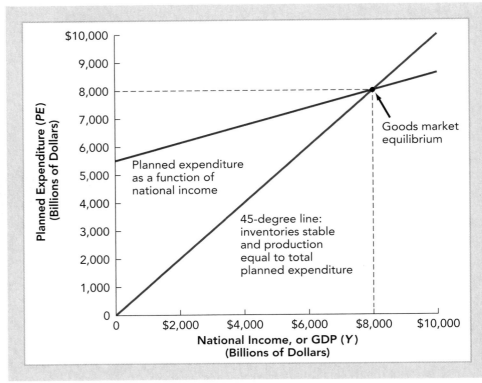

FIGURE 9.12

Equilibrium on the Income-Expenditure Diagram

On the income-expenditure diagram, the equilibrium point of the economy is that point where planned expenditure (as a function of national income) is equal to total product.

If *PE* is greater than *Y*, there is excess demand for goods. In neither case is the economy in equilibrium.

In the first case, in which production exceeds planned expenditure, inventories are rising rapidly, and firms unwilling to accumulate unsold and unsellable inventories are about to cut production and fire workers (see Figure 9.13). In the second case, in which planned expenditure exceeds production, inventories are falling rapidly. Businesses are selling more than they are making. Some businesses will respond to the fall in inventories by boosting prices, trying to earn more profit per good sold. But the bulk of businesses will respond to the fall in inventories by expanding production to match planned expenditure. They are about to hire more workers. Real GDP and national income are about to expand.

Now suppose that businesses see their inventories falling and respond by boosting their production to equal last month's planned expenditure. Will such an increase bring the economy into goods market equilibrium, with planned expenditure equal to total income and real GDP? The answer is that it will not. To boost production, firms must hire workers, paying more in wages and causing household income to rise. But when income rises, total spending rises as well. Thus the increase in production and income generates a further expansion in planned expenditure.

Even after production has increased to close the initial gap between planned expenditure and national income, the economy will still not be in equilibrium, as Figure 9.14 shows. Inventories will be falling even though hiring more workers has increased production. Because hiring more workers has also boosted total income and further increased planned expenditure, production will have to

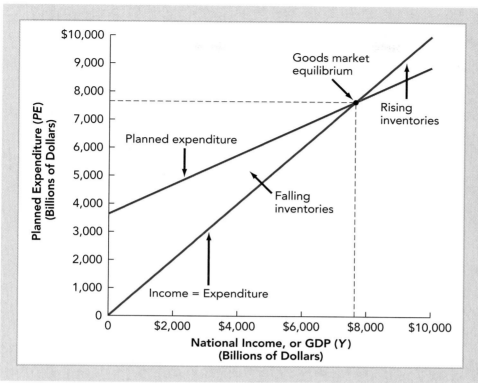

FIGURE 9.13

Inventory Adjustment and Equilibrium: The Income-Expenditure Diagram

If the economy is not at its equilibrium point, then either actual production exceeds planned expenditure (in which case inventories are rising) or planned expenditure exceeds actual production (in which case inventories are falling).

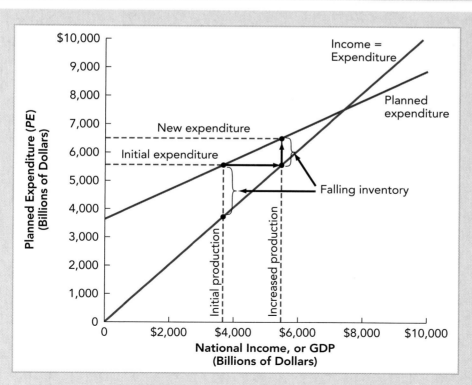

FIGURE 9.14

The Inventory-Adjustment Process

If planned expenditure is greater than total production, inventories are falling. Businesses will hire more workers and increase production. But increasing production just by the fall in inventory won't bring the economy to equilibrium because planned expenditure rises with production and income.

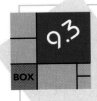

HOW FAST DOES THE ECONOMY MOVE TO EQUILIBRIUM? SOME DETAILS

At any one particular moment the economy does not have to be in short-run equilibrium. Planned expenditure can exceed real GDP and national income, and inventories can fall, for periods as long as a year. Strong forces are pushing the economy toward short-run equilibrium. Businesses do not like to lose money by producing things that they cannot sell or by not having things on hand that they could sell. But it takes at least months, usually quarters, and possibly more time for businesses to expand or cut back production.

For example, between the summer of 1990 and the summer of 1991 inventories fell for five straight quarters. Real GDP was less than planned expenditure as businesses decided that their high levels of inventories were too large given the economic uncertainties created by the Iraqi invasion of Kuwait and the subsequent recession. Between the winter of 1994 and the summer of 1995, for six quarters, inventories rose. For a year and a half GDP was greater than planned expenditure. (See Figure 9.15.)

FIGURE 9.15
Inventories as the Balancing Item: Inventory Investment in the Early and Mid-1990s

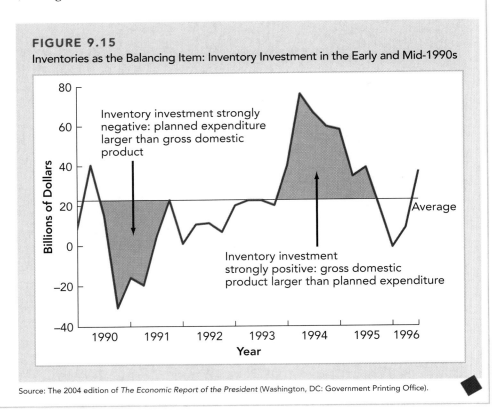

Source: The 2004 edition of *The Economic Report of the President* (Washington, DC: Government Printing Office).

expand by a multiple of the initial gap in order to stabilize inventories. The process will come to an end, with planned expenditure equal to national income, only when both have risen to the level at which the planned-expenditure line crosses the 45-degree income-equals-expenditure line. Box 9.5 provides a worked example. And the process works in reverse to lower production and expenditure if planned expenditure is initially below national income.

THE SEPTEMBER 11 TERRORIST ATTACK ON THE WORLD TRADE CENTER: AN EXAMPLE

BOX 9.4

The U.S. economy was already in recession in the summer of 2001 when the terrorist attack on the World Trade Center sent it into a further downward spiral. The attack on September 11, 2001, reduced autonomous spending through two different channels. First, the attack shook *consumer confidence:* The Conference Board's index fell from 114 in August 2001 to 85 in November. Baseline consumption spending, the parameter C_0 in the consumption function, is closely linked to consumer confidence. Second, the attack increased uncertainty. Would there be further attacks? What would the U.S. military response be? How would U.S. government spending shift in response to the attack?

The first rule of planning for the future is that whenever uncertainty is unusually high, you are better off delaying whatever decisions you can until some of this uncertainty is resolved. Thus businesses undertaking investment projects adopted a wait-and-see approach. The result was that autonomous spending fell.

Had the terrorist attack been the only major shock to the U.S. economy, the recession would have been longer and deeper than turned out to be the case. However, three countervailing forces boosted planned expenditure. First, the Federal Reserve greatly reduced interest rates, and so stimulated investment. Second, the Bush tax cut of 2001 boosted consumers' incomes in 2002 by some $80 billion

FIGURE 9.16

Month-to-Month Changes in U.S. Industrial Production, 2000–2002 Industrial production in the United States had been declining since late 2000 but was showing signs of recovery when the attack on the World Trade Center on September 11, 2001, shook consumer and business confidence. As consumers cut back on spending and as businesses adopted a wait-and-see attitude, U.S. industrial production dropped an additional 2.2 percent in the four months before recovery began.

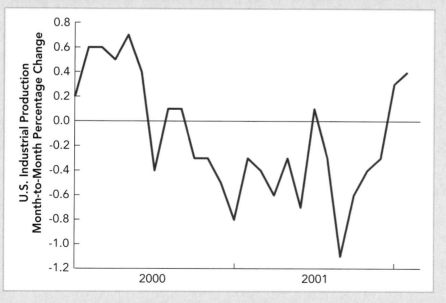

Source: Authors' calculations from the 2004 edition of the *Economic Report of the President* (Washington, DC: Government Printing Office).

and so boosted consumption spending. Most of this money went to high-income consumers with relatively low marginal propensities to consume, so it was not the most effective stimulus, but it was still welcome at the time. Third, the mobilization for the War against Terror boosted government purchases G.

Thus the economy began to rebound in 2002. But because the downward shock had been large and because the tax cut was not well designed to be the most effective employment-generating stimulus, the recovery from September 11 was slower than average as far as employment growth was concerned.

BOX

9.5

CALCULATING THE DIFFERENCE BETWEEN PLANNED EXPENDITURE AND REAL GDP: AN EXAMPLE

Suppose that our planned-expenditure function has numerical values for its coefficients, so that in trillions

$$PE = A + (MPE)(Y)$$

$$= \$5.6 + 0.3Y$$

Suppose first that the current level of real GDP Y is $7.5 trillion. Then *planned* total expenditure is

$$PE = \$5.6 + (0.3)(\$7.5)$$

$$= \$7.85 \text{ trillion}$$

and business inventories are being drawn down at a rate

$$\frac{\Delta \ inventories}{\Delta \ time} = Y - PE = -\$0.35 \text{ trillion per year}$$

Suppose, instead, that the current level of total real GDP Y is $8.5 trillion. Then planned total expenditure is

$$PE = \$5.6 + (0.3)(\$8.5)$$

$$= \$8.15 \text{ trillion}$$

and business inventories are being added to at a rate

$$\frac{\Delta \ inventories}{\Delta \ time} = \$0.35 \text{ trillion per year}$$

However, if the current level of total national income (and of real GDP) Y is $8.0 trillion, then total planned expenditure is

$$PE = \$5.6 + (0.3)(\$8.0)$$

$$= \$8.0 \text{ trillion}$$

and business inventories are stable

$$\frac{\Delta \ inventories}{\Delta \ time} = \$0$$

> **RECAP   INCOME AND EXPENDITURE**
>
> The force that pushes real GDP Y to equal planned total expenditure PE is the inventory-adjustment process. If real GDP exceeds planned expenditure, inventories are rising rapidly. Firms are unwilling to accumulate unsold and unsellable inventories, so they are about to cut production and fire workers to reduce real GDP. If real GDP is less than planned expenditure, inventories are falling rapidly as businesses are selling more than they are making. Businesses are about to expand production, hire more workers, and thus raise real GDP.

9.3 THE MULTIPLIER

Determining the Size of the Multiplier

Suppose something happens to change the level of planned total expenditure at every possible level of national income. Anything that affects the level of autonomous spending will do. What would then happen to the equilibrium level of total income and real GDP?

An upward shift in the planned-expenditure line would increase the equilibrium level of national income. At the prevailing level of national income, planned total expenditure would be larger than real GDP. Businesses would find themselves selling more than they were making, and their inventories would fall. In response, businesses would boost production to try to keep inventories from being exhausted, and production would expand.

How much production would expand depends on the magnitude of the change in autonomous spending and the value of the **spending multiplier.**

The value of this spending multiplier depends on the slope of the planned-expenditure line, the marginal propensity to expend (MPE). The higher the MPE, the steeper is the planned expenditure line and the greater is the multiplier. A large multiplier can amplify small shocks to spending patterns into large changes in total production and income, as Figure 9.17 on page 276 shows.

To calculate the multiplier, recall the equation for the short-run sticky-price equilibrium level of real GDP,

$$Y = \frac{A}{1 - MPE}$$

Suppose autonomous spending changes by an amount ΔA. Then the change ΔY in the equilibrium level of real GDP is

$$\Delta Y = \left(\frac{1}{1 - MPE} \right) \Delta A$$

The factor $1/(1 - MPE)$ is the multiplier: It multiplies the upward shift in the planned-expenditure line as a result of the increase in autonomous spending into a change in the equilibrium level of real GDP, total income, and total expenditure.

Why the factor $1/(1 - MPE)$? Think of it this way: The MPE — the marginal propensity to expend — is the slope of the total-expenditure line. A $1 increase in national income raises the equilibrium level of planned expenditure by $1, because

spending multiplier

The change in national income and total expenditure that follows from a one-dollar change in any component of autonomous spending. Also known as the *Keynesian multiplier.*

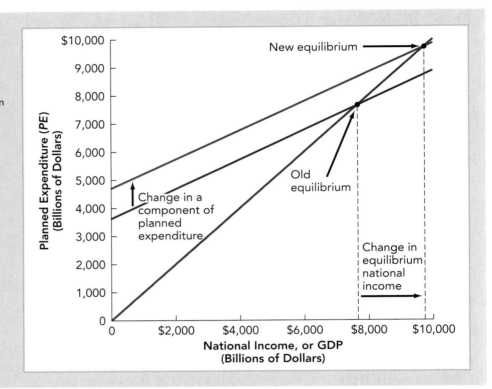

FIGURE 9.17
The Multiplier Effect

An increase in autonomous spending will generate an amplified increase in the equilibrium level of national income. Why? Because planned expenditure will rise not just by the increase in autonomous spending but by the increase in autonomous spending plus the marginal propensity to expend times the increase in the equilibrium level of national income.

expenditure has to go $1 higher to balance income and production. It also raises the level of planned expenditure by $MPE. Thus a $1 increase in the level of total income closes $(1 − MPE) of the gap between planned expenditure and total income as Figure 9.17 shows. To close a full initial gap of ΔA between planned expenditure and national income, the equilibrium level of national income must increase by $\Delta A/(1 − MPE)$.

Because autonomous spending is influenced by a great many factors,

$$A = C_0 + (I_0 − I_r r) + G + (X_f Y^f + X_\varepsilon \varepsilon_0 − X_\varepsilon \varepsilon_r r + X_\varepsilon \varepsilon_r r^f)$$

almost every change in economic policy or the economic environment will set this multiplier process in motion.

Changing the Size of the Multiplier

One factor that tends to minimize the multiplier is the tax system: whether the tax system has been designed to provide the government with *fiscal automatic stabilizers*. The government doesn't levy a total lump-sum tax independent of the state of the economy. Instead the government imposes roughly proportional (actually slightly progressive) taxes on the economy, so government tax collections are equal to a tax rate t times the level of GDP Y: the total tax take equals tY.

This means that when GDP is relatively high the government collects more in tax revenue than it would with a lump-sum tax. The collection of extra revenue

THE VALUE OF THE MULTIPLIER: AN EXAMPLE

Suppose that the planned-expenditure function has values for its parameters of $A = \$5.6$ trillion and MPE $= 0.3$, so that

$$PE = A + (MPE)(Y)$$

$$= \$5.6 \text{ trillion} + 0.3Y$$

Then the equilibrium value of total income (and of real GDP) Y is $8 trillion, for only at $Y = \$8$ trillion is planned expenditure equal to real GDP.

Now suppose that autonomous spending A increases by an amount of $100 billion, or $0.1 trillion:

$$\Delta A = \$0.1$$

Then the planned-expenditure function is

$$PE = \$5.7 + 0.3Y$$

and the equilibrium value of total income (and real GDP) Y is $8.143.

The change in Y divided by the change in autonomous spending is

$$\frac{\Delta Y}{\Delta A} = 1.43$$

This is equal to

$$1.43 = \frac{1}{1 - 0.3} = \frac{1}{1 - MPE}$$

which we saw above is the definition of the multiplier.

---

dampens swings in after-tax income and thus reduces consumption. Similarly, the government collects less in tax revenue when GDP is relatively low; thus after-tax income is higher than that under lump-sum taxes, and this higher income boosts consumption. Because the fall in consumption is smaller with a proportional rather than a lump-sum tax, the multiplier is smaller. Disturbances to spending are not amplified as much as they would be with a lump-sum tax, and so shocks to the economy tend to cause smaller business cycles. The automatic working of the government's tax system (and, to a lesser extent, its social welfare programs) functions as an automatic stabilizer, reducing the magnitude of fluctuations in real GDP and unemployment.

Substituting our detailed expression for calculating the MPE,

$$MPE = C_y(1 - t) - IM_y$$

into our definition of the multiplier,

$$\text{Multiplier} = \frac{1}{1 - MPE}$$

tells us that under a proportional tax system the multiplier is

$$\frac{\Delta Y}{\Delta A} = \frac{1}{1 - MPE} = \frac{1}{1 - \left[C_y(1 - t) - IM_y\right]}$$

If the government levied lump-sum taxes, the multiplier would be

$$\frac{\Delta Y}{\Delta A} = \frac{1}{1 - MPE} = \frac{1}{1 - (C_y - IM_y)}$$

The difference is the $(1 - t)$ term that is missing from the denominator of the last expression in the equation above.

How important is this $(1 - t)$ term? How large are fiscal automatic stabilizers in the United States today? When national product and national income drop by a dollar, income tax and social security tax collections fall automatically by at least one-third of a dollar. Thus the fall in consumers' disposable income is only two-thirds as great as the fall in national income, and the fall in consumption is only two-thirds as large as it would be without fiscal automatic stabilizers.

A more globalized economy will also have a smaller multiplier. An economy that is more open to world trade will have a smaller multiplier than will a less open economy. The more open the economy, the greater is the marginal propensity to expend on imports. The more of every extra dollar of income spent on imports, the less is left to be devoted to planned expenditure on domestic products — and therefore the smaller is the multiplier. If the share of imports in GDP is large, the potential change in the multiplier from an *open economy*,

$$\frac{\Delta Y}{\Delta A} = \frac{1}{1 - MPE} = \frac{1}{1 - \left[C_y(1 - t) - IM_y\right]}$$

to that for a *closed economy*,

$$\frac{\Delta Y}{\Delta A} = \frac{1}{1 - MPE} = \frac{1}{1 - \left[C_y(1 - t)\right]}$$

can be considerable. The difference is the missing IM_y term in the denominator of the equation above. In modern industrialized economies where the share of imports in real GDP is certainly more than 10 percent, any calculation of the multiplier will be significantly off unless it takes account of the effects of world trade.

RECAP   THE MULTIPLIER

If prices are sticky, higher planned expenditure boosts production, and this boosts income. Higher income gives a further boost to consumption, and this in turn boosts aggregate demand some more. Thus any shift in a component of planned expenditure upward or downward leads to a multiplied shift in total production. The early-twentieth-century British economist John Maynard Keynes was one of the first to stress the importance of this multiplier process. The multiplier arises because planned expenditure PE is equal to autonomous spending A plus the marginal propensity to expend MPE times national income Y: $PE = A + (MPE)(Y)$.

In equilibrium, planned expenditure PE equals national income Y, which is true if and only if $Y = A[1/(1 - MPE)]$. The term $1/(1 - MPE)$ is the value of the multiplier.

Chapter Summary

1. Business-cycle fluctuations can push real GDP away from potential output and push unemployment far away from its average rate.

2. If prices were perfectly and instantaneously flexible, there would be no such thing as business-cycle fluctuations. Hence macroeconomics must consist in large part of models in which prices are not flexible but sticky.

3. Prices might be sticky for a number of reasons: menu costs, imperfect information, concerns of fairness, or simple money illusion. All seem plausible. None has overwhelming evidence of importance vis-à-vis the others.

4. In the short run, while prices are sticky, the level of real GDP is determined by the level of planned total expenditure.

5. The short-run equilibrium level of real GDP is that level at which planned total expenditure as a function of national income is equal to the level of national income, or real GDP, itself.

6. Two quantities summarize planned total expenditure as a function of total income: the level of autonomous spending and the marginal propensity to expend (MPE).

7. The level of autonomous spending is the intercept of the planned-expenditure function on the income-expenditure diagram. It tells us what the level of planned expenditure would be if national income were zero.

8. The MPE is the slope of the planned-expenditure function on the income-expenditure diagram. It tells us how much planned expenditure increases for each $1 increase in national income.

9. The value of the MPE depends on the tax rate t, the marginal propensity to consume C_y, and the share of spending on imports IM_y. Algebraically, $MPE = C_y(1 - t) - IM_y$.

10. In the simple macro models, an increase in any component of autonomous spending causes a more-than-proportional increase in real GDP. This is the result of the multiplier process.

11. The size of the multiplier depends on the marginal propensity to expend (MPE): the higher the MPE, the higher is the multiplier. The value of the multiplier is
$$\frac{\Delta Y}{\Delta A} = \frac{1}{(1 - MPE)}.$$

Key Terms

flexible prices (p. 255)

sticky prices (p. 256)

menu costs (p. 261)

imperfect information (p. 261)

money illusion (p. 261)

marginal propensity to consume (MPC) (p. 263)

consumption function (p. 263)

autonomous spending (p. 266)

marginal propensity to expend (MPE) (p. 267)

income-expenditure diagram (p. 267)

planned expenditure line (p. 267)

planned-expenditure function (p. 269)

spending multiplier (p. 275)

Analytical Exercises

1. Describe, in your own words, the factors that determine the slope of the planned-expenditure line.

2. Suppose that government purchases increase by $100 billion but there are no other changes in economic policy or the economic environment.
   a. What effect does this increase in government purchases have on the location of the planned-expenditure line?

   b. What effect does this increase in government purchases have on the planned-expenditure function?
   c. What effect does this increase in government purchases have on the equilibrium level of total expenditure, national income, and real GDP?

3. Consider an economy in which prices are sticky, the marginal propensity to consume out of disposable

income C_y is 0.6, the tax rate t is 0.25, and the share of national income spent on imports IM_y is 20 percent.
a. Suppose that total autonomous spending is $6 trillion. Graph planned expenditure as a function of total national income.
b. Determine the equilibrium level of national income and real GDP.
c. What is the value of the multiplier?
d. Suppose that total autonomous spending increases by $100 billion to $6.1 trillion. What happens to the equilibrium level of national income and real GDP Y?

4. Suppose that prices are sticky; the marginal propensity to consume out of disposable income C_y is 0.9. Suppose further that the economy is closed — the share of national income spent on imports is zero — and that the tax rate is 12.5 percent.
a. What is the marginal propensity to expend?
b. What is the value of the multiplier?

c. What level of autonomous spending would be needed to attain a level of equilibrium total expenditure equal to $10 trillion?

5. Classify the following changes into two groups: those that increase equilibrium real GDP and those that decrease real GDP.
a. An increase in consumers' desire to spend today.
b. An increase in interest rates overseas.
c. A decline in foreign exchange speculators' confidence in the value of the home currency.
d. A fall in real GDP overseas.
e. An increase in government purchases.
f. An increase in managers' expectations of the future profitability of investments.
g. An increase in the tax rate.

Policy Exercises

1. Suppose that the economy is at its full-employment level of output of $8 trillion, with government purchases equal to $1.6 trillion, the net tax rate equal to 20 percent, and the budget in balance.
a. Suppose that adverse shocks to consumption and investment lead real GDP to fall to $7.5 trillion. What is the level of taxes collected? What is the government's budget deficit?
b. Suppose that favorable shocks to consumption and investment lead real GDP to rise to $9.5 trillion. What is the level of taxes collected? What is the government's budget balance?
c. Most economists like to calculate a "full-employment budget balance," equal to government purchases minus what tax collections would be if the economy were at full employment, and to take that balance as their summary measure of the short-run effect of government taxes and spending on the level of real GDP. What advantages does such a full-employment budget measure have over the actual budget as a measure of economic policy? What disadvantages does it have?

2. Suppose that the economy is short of its full-employment level of GDP, $8 trillion, by $500 billion, with the MPC out of disposable income equal to 0.6, the import share IM_y equal to 0.2, and the tax rate t equal to 25 percent.
a. Suppose the government wants to boost real GDP up to full employment by cutting taxes. How large a cut

in the tax rate is required to do so? How large a cut in total tax collections is produced by this cut in the tax rate?
b. Suppose the government wants to boost real GDP up to full employment by increasing government spending. How large an increase in government spending is required to do so?
c. Can you account for any asymmetry between the answers to a and b?

3. Think about the four possible sources of price stickiness mentioned in this chapter: money illusion, fairness considerations, imperfect information, and menu costs. What have you read or seen in the past two months that strike you as examples of any of these four phenomena? In your opinion, which of the four sources seems most likely to be the most important?

4. What changes in the economy's institutions can you think of that would diminish price stickiness and increase price flexibility? What advantage in terms of the size of the business cycle would you expect to follow from such changes in institutions? What disadvantages do you think that such institutional changes might have?

5. Suppose the government wants to increase real GDP by $500 billion. How would you suggest the government go about accomplishing this goal?

CHAPTER 10

Investment, Net Exports, and Interest Rates: The IS Curve

QUESTIONS

How do the determinants of investment and net exports in the sticky-price model differ from those of the flexible-price model?

How do changes in interest rates affect the equilibrium level of real GDP and national income in the sticky-price model?

What is the IS curve? How do we use it?

How do we calculate the equilibrium level of real GDP in the sticky-price model when the central bank's policy is to peg the real interest rate?

If we can understand the causes and consequences of changes in investment spending, we will understand much of what we need to know in order to understand the causes of America's business cycles. We do so in this chapter by building an analytical tool called the *IS curve*, where "IS" stands for "investment-saving." The IS curve tells us the relationship between total expenditure or real GDP on the one hand and the long-term risky real interest rate on the other. Changes in the interest rate increase or depress investment and gross exports and so move the economy down or up along the IS curve. Changes in businesses' optimism or pessimism cause increases or decreases in investment unrelated to changes in interest rates, and so shift the entire IS curve itself either out or in.

10.1 INTEREST RATES AND PLANNED TOTAL EXPENDITURE

The Importance of Investment

The changes in investment spending shown in Figure 10.1 are the principal driving force behind the business cycle. Without exception, reductions in investment have played a powerful role in every single recession and depression. Falls in investment spending played an important role in generating the recessions of 1970, of 1974–1975, of 1979–1982, of 1990–1991, and of 2001–2002. Increases in investment have spurred every single *boom* — whether the late 1960s, the early 1970s, the late 1970s, the mid-1980s, or the late 1990s. Because of the multiplier, the swings in real GDP have invariably been larger than the swings in investment spending themselves.

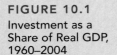

FIGURE 10.1

Investment as a Share of Real GDP, 1960–2004

The substantial year-to-year swings in investment are one of the principal drivers of the business cycle. When investment booms, the economy as a whole booms too.

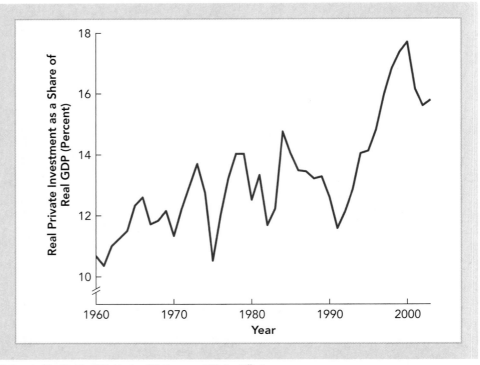

Source: The 2005 edition of *The Economic Report of the President* (Washington, DC: Government Printing Office).

The Role of Investment

From this point our analysis of the role of investment spending will be the same but also different from the analysis carried out in the flexible-price model of Chapters 6 and 7. The determinants of investment are the same in both models: In both cases, investment is determined by (1) a baseline level of investment I_0, (2) a sensitivity of investment to the real interest rate I_r, and (3) the level of the real interest rate r. But the kind of equilibrium the economy reaches and the process by which the economy reaches equilibrium are different. Hence the investment function plays a very different role in the two models.

In the flexible-price model in Chapters 6 and 7, the real interest rate was the market-clearing price. It was pushed up or down by supply and demand to equate the flow of saving into financial markets (from households and businesses, the government, and foreigners) to the flow of investment funding out of financial markets (to finance replacement of depreciated capital and increases in the capital stock). Supply and demand in the loanable funds market determined the interest rate. In the flexible-price model, the level of saving determined the level of investment, and the strength of investment demand determined the interest rate.

In the sticky-price model, the interest rate is not set in the loanable funds market. Instead, it is set directly by the central bank or indirectly by the combination of the stock of money and the liquidity preferences of households and businesses. The interest rate then determines the level of investment, which then plays a key role in autonomous spending. Together, autonomous spending and the multiplier determine the level of output.

"What happened to equilibrium in the loanable funds market?" you may ask. In a sticky-price model the fact that businesses match the quantity they produce to planned total expenditure automatically creates balance in the financial market, no matter what the interest rate. Any interest rate can be an equilibrium interest rate because the inventory-adjustment process has already made saving equal to investment.

Sources of Fluctuations in Investment

Fluctuations in investment have two sources. Some are triggered by changes in the real interest rate r. A lower real interest rate means higher investment spending, and a higher real interest rate means lower investment spending. Other fluctuations are triggered by shifts in investors' expectations about future growth, profits, and risk. These two sources of fluctuations in investment correspond, respectively, to changes in investment spending I produced by (1) the interest sensitivity of investment parameter I_r times changes in r, and (2) changes in the baseline level of investment I_0 in the investment function:

$$I = I_0 - I_r r$$

Both sources of fluctuation are important. Neither is clearly dominant.

Investment and the Real Interest Rate

A business that undertakes an investment project always has alternative uses for the money. One alternative would be to take the money that would have been spent building the factory or buying the machines and place it instead in the financial markets — that is, lending it out at the market real rate of interest. Thus the opportunity cost of an investment project is the real interest rate. The higher the interest rate, the fewer the number and the smaller the value of investment projects that will return more than their current cost, and the lower the level of investment spending. But which interest rate is the relevant one? There are many different interest rates.

The Long-Term Interest Rate

long-term interest rate

The interest rate required if you are going to borrow money not for a short term of months but for a long term of decades.

The interest rate that is relevant for determining investment spending is a **long-term interest rate**. Investments are durable and long-lasting. Whenever a manager considers undertaking an investment project, he or she must compare the potential profits from the project to the opportunity to make money from a long-term alternative commitment of the funds elsewhere. The interest rate that is the opportunity cost of undertaking an investment project with a life length of a decade or more is the interest rate on a long-term loan for a period of a decade or more: the long-term interest rate.

short-term interest rate

The interest rate paid to borrow money for the short term — three to six months.

This distinction matters because long- and **short-term interest rates** are different and do not always move in step. Figure 10.2 shows a standard yield curve chart, the *term structure* of interest rates, that plots the interest rate on safe U.S. government bonds of three different maturities — 3-month *Treasury bills,* 3-year *Treasury notes,* and 10-year *Treasury bonds* — at three different moments — 1992, 1996, and 2003. Looking at the shifts over time in such a yield curve chart shows that different interest rates do not always fluctuate together. The variable premium in the interest rate that the market charges on long-term loans vis-à-vis short-term loans is called the term premium. This creates the potential for problems for the Federal Reserve: What if it wants to lower interest rates to stimulate investment, and so buys three-month Treasury bills for cash to reduce the short-term interest

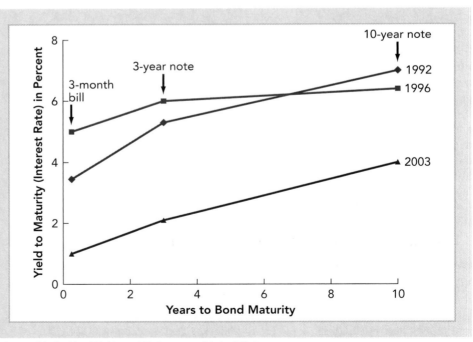

FIGURE 10.2
Bond Yield Curves
The interest rate the U.S. government must pay to borrow money depends on how long it wants to borrow the money. The same applies to private borrowers as well: Usually, the longer the term for which one wishes to borrow, the higher the interest rate one must pay.

Source: The 2004 edition of *The Economic Report of the President* (Washington, DC: Government Printing Office).

rate, but finds the term premium rising and thus the long-term interest rate that matters for investment unchanged?

Long-term interest rates are usually higher than short-term rates because long-term assets are riskier, and investors demand a higher average return to compensate them for bearing this extra risk. As this chapter's appendix explains, when Wall Street bond traders expect short-term interest rates to rise in the future, the term premium is large. When they expect short-term interest rates to fall steeply, the term premium is negative, but such an inverted term premium is rare — the term structure of interest rates or yield curve is almost always upward sloping.

In 1992 and 2003 the yield curve was steep: long-term loans carried significantly higher interest rates than short-term loans; the term premium was high.[1] In 1996 the yield curve was nearly flat; the term premium was low. In 1992 and 1996 the general levels of interest rates were about the same. By 2003 the general level of interest rates had fallen all across the maturity structure; all three sets of Treasury assets paid lower returns than they had in 1992 or 1996.

The Real Interest Rate

The interest rate that is relevant for investment spending decisions is not the nominal but the real interest rate. The nominal price a business charges rises with inflation. If a business is willing to invest when the interest rate is 5 percent and inflation is 2 percent per year (and so the real interest rate is 3 percent per year), then the business should also be willing to invest when the interest rate is 10 percent and inflation is 7 percent per year (and so the real interest rate is still 3 percent per year). Figure 10.3 on page 286 shows both nominal and real interest rates in the United States. There is a big difference between the two.

The Risky Interest Rate

Lending money to a business always carries an element of risk. Perhaps the borrower will go bankrupt before the loan is due. Perhaps the creditors will find themselves last, or nearly last, in line as a small amount of leftover postbankruptcy assets are divided up. Financial institutions lending money are keenly interested in the financial health of those to whom they lend. The riskier they believe the loan is — the larger the possibility of a bankruptcy or a debt rescheduling appears to be — the higher is the interest rate that lenders will demand to compensate them for risk.

The interest rate that a firm faces is the interest rate charged to risky borrowers, not the interest rate charged to safe borrowers (like the U.S. government) to

---

[1]Why was the term premium so high in 1992 and 2003? Two reasons. First, in both cases the Federal Reserve had aggressively pushed interest rates down in the recent past to try to boost investment and employment, so short-term interest rates were depressed below their normal levels, and markets were expecting the Federal Reserve to reverse itself as soon as employment returned to normal levels. As the appendix shows, the term premium is likely to be high when interest rates are expected to rise. Second, savers and investors in both 1992 and 2003 could look forward to a future in which there were large budget deficits that the government seemed to have no plans for reducing. In the flexible-price model, high budget deficits produce higher than normal interest rates. And so investors were expecting interest rates to soon be not just at normal but at higher than normal runaway-deficit levels.

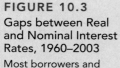

FIGURE 10.3

Gaps between Real and Nominal Interest Rates, 1960–2003

Most borrowers and lenders care not about the nominal interest rate — the interest rate in terms of money — but about the real interest rate on loans — the interest rate in terms of goods. The difference between the nominal and the real interest rates is the inflation rate.

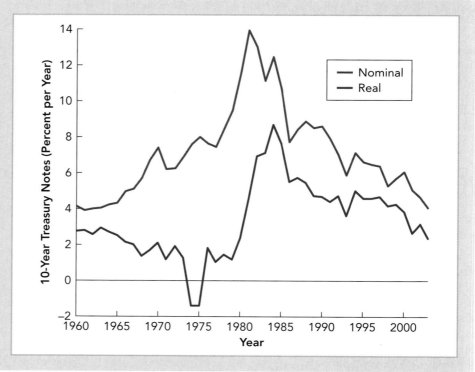

Source: Authors' calculations and 2004 edition of *The Economic Report of the President* (Washington, DC: Government Printing Office).

risky interest rate

The interest rate on assets where there is some chance the debtor will default.

safe interest rate

The interest rate on assets where there is no significant probability of default.

whom people lend when they want to sleep easily at night. The premium that lenders charge for loans to companies rather than to safe government borrowers is called the risk premium. (See Figure 10.4.) Financial and economic disturbances, like the default of the Russian government in August 1998, can cause large and swift moves in the risk premium. The **risky interest rate** does not always move in step with the **safe interest rate**.

Thus — bringing this all together — to determine the level of investment spending, take the baseline level of investment I_0 (determined by businesses' optimism, expected economic growth, and a bunch of other factors for which the level of the stock market serves as a convenient thermometer). Subtract from this baseline level the interest sensitivity of investment parameter I_r times the relevant interest rate r expressed in decimal form, so an interest rate of 3 percent is expressed as 0.03. The relevant interest rate must be long-term because most investments are long-term. The relevant interest rate must be real because investment projects are real assets: Their values rise with inflation. And the relevant interest rate must be risky because businesses borrowing to invest may go bankrupt. In the investment function

$$I = I_0 - I_r r$$

the relevant interest rate r is the long-term, real, risky interest rate, as is plotted in Figure 10.5. The nominal interest rate can be directly observed: It is what the newspapers print every day in their analyses of the *bond market*. The real interest rate is just the nominal interest rate minus the expected rate of

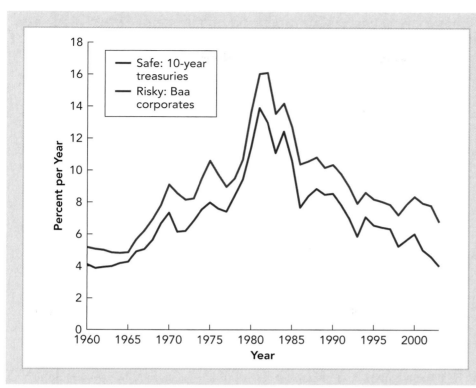

FIGURE 10.4

The Risk Premium: Safe and Risky Interest Rates, 1960–2003

Loans that are not made to the U.S. government are risky: Lenders charge a risk premium that depends both on their tolerance for risk and on the amount of risk involved when they lend to other organizations. This risk premium is not constant but varies over time.

Source: The 2004 edition of *The Economic Report of the President* (Washington, DC: Government Printing Office).

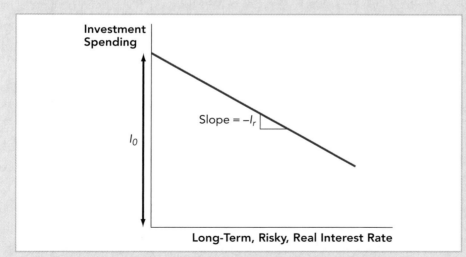

FIGURE 10.5

Investment as a Decreasing Function of the Long-Term, Real, Risky Interest Rate

The baseline level of investment I_0 tells us what the level of investment would be if the real interest rate were zero. The interest rate sensitivity parameter I_r tells us how much investment is discouraged by a 1-unit increase in the long-term, real, risky interest rate.

inflation. But can we find an easy way to observe the rest of the determinants of investment spending — all of those that are packed into the baseline level of investment spending I_0? Box 10.1 tells us that we can, by looking at the stock market.

THE STOCK MARKET AS AN INDICATOR OF FUTURE INVESTMENT: SOME TOOLS

Recall from Chapter 2 that if investors in the stock market are acting rationally, the level of the stock market P^s will be equal to

$$P^s = E^a\left(\frac{E^s}{E^a}\right)\left(\frac{1}{r + \sigma^s}\right)$$

where

- E^a is the accounting earnings corporations report.
- E^s/E^a is the ratio of the long-run "permanent" earnings investors expect to today's accounting earnings. It is a measure of optimism, of expected future growth.
- r is the long-term real interest rate on bonds.
- σ^s is the risk premium investors require to invest in stocks rather than in less risky assets.

Thus the stock market sums up — in one easy-to-find number, reported daily — the real interest rate r plus the same important influences — profitability, expected growth, and attitudes toward risk — that determine the baseline level of investment I_0.

Think of it this way: An investor deciding whether or not to commit his or her portfolio to stocks (rather than bonds) is making more or less the same decision as that made by a business's investment committee deciding whether to build a factory. The purchase of a share of stock gives you title to a share in the ownership of past investments — factories, buildings, inventories, and organizations — that have been undertaken by one company. The same things that determine whether it is a good idea to undertake the construction of a new factory also determine whether it is a good idea to spend money to acquire title to a share of an old factory. And the conclusions reached by investors in the stock market, which we observe every day in stock price fluctuations, are likely to be much the same as the conclusions reached by businesses' investment committees.

The higher the stock market, the higher is the likely future level of investment spending.

Exports and Autonomous Spending

Investment spending is not the only component of autonomous spending that is affected by the real interest rate. In the total-expenditure function

$$PE = A + MPE \cdot Y$$

autonomous spending A — spending that does not depend upon income Y — includes not just baseline consumption, investment, and government purchases, but gross exports as well:

$$A = C_0 + I + G + GX$$

As we saw in Chapter 6, gross exports depend on foreign total income Y^f and the real exchange rate ε. So we can expand the determinants of gross exports in the expression for autonomous spending:

$$A = C_0 + (I_0 - I_r r) + G + (X_f Y^f + X_\varepsilon \varepsilon)$$

As we also saw in Chapter 6, the real exchange rate ε depends on the domestic real interest rate r as well as on foreign exchange speculators' opinions of fundamentals ε_0 and foreign interest rates r^f:

$$\varepsilon = \varepsilon_0 - \varepsilon_r(r - r^f)$$

Substituting this equation for the determinants of the exchange rate into the autonomous spending equation

$$A = C_0 + (I_0 - I_r r) + G + (X_f Y^f + X_\varepsilon \varepsilon_0 - X_\varepsilon \varepsilon_r r + X_\varepsilon \varepsilon_r r^f)$$

we can see that there are two components of autonomous spending affected by changes in the real interest rate. A higher real interest rate reduces autonomous spending by reducing exports (the $-X_\varepsilon \varepsilon_r r$ term) as well as by reducing investment (the $-I_r r$ term). Figure 10.6 provides a graphical summary of how changes in the real interest rate affect exports and thus autonomous spending.

Why does a higher domestic interest rate reduce exports? A higher real interest rate makes purchasing financial assets in the home country more attractive: Foreign exchange speculators try to take advantage of this opportunity to earn higher returns by shifting their portfolio holdings to include more home-currency-denominated assets. This increase in demand for home-currency-denominated

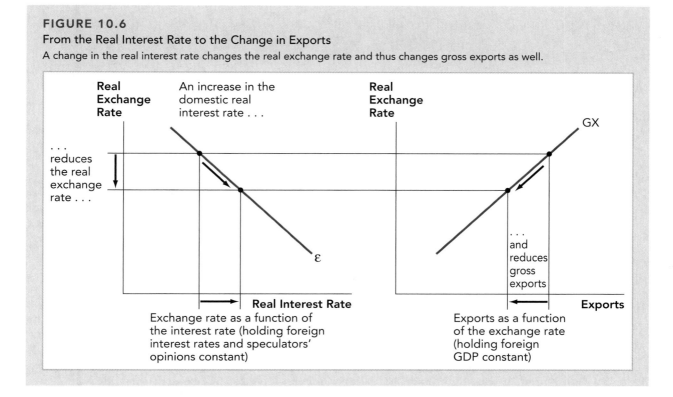

FIGURE 10.6

From the Real Interest Rate to the Change in Exports

A change in the real interest rate changes the real exchange rate and thus changes gross exports as well.

assets and decrease in demand for foreign-currency-denominated assets drives down the exchange rate, which is the value of foreign currency.

A lower value of foreign currency makes our exports more expensive to foreigners: Their currency buys less here because it is less valuable. This diminishes their ability to purchase our exports. Since exports are a part of autonomous spending, a rise in the real interest rate diminishes autonomous spending through this channel as well. Thus a change in interest rates has a bigger effect on output than one would think from the effect of interest rates on investment alone.

RECAP   INTEREST RATES AND PLANNED TOTAL EXPENDITURE

The investment function in the sticky-price model looks the same as it does in the flexible-price model, but it plays a very different role. In the flexible-price model the real interest rate is a market-clearing price. Supply and demand in the loanable funds market determine the interest rate. The level of saving determines the level of investment, and the strength of investment demand determines the interest rate. In the sticky-price model, the interest rate is not set in the loanable funds market but is set directly by the central bank or indirectly by the combination of the stock of money and the liquidity preferences of households and businesses. The interest rate then determines the level of investment, which plays a key role in autonomous spending. Together, autonomous spending and the multiplier determine the level of output. In a sticky-price model the fact that businesses match the quantity they produce to planned expenditure *automatically* creates balance in the financial market, no matter what the interest rate. Any interest rate can be an equilibrium interest rate because the inventory-adjustment process always forces saving equal to investment.

10.2 THE IS CURVE

Autonomous Spending and the Real Interest Rate

If we rearrange the equation for autonomous spending to put the two terms that depend on the interest rate together

$$A = [C_0 + I_0 + G + (X_f Y^f + X_\varepsilon \varepsilon_0 + X_\varepsilon \varepsilon_r r^f)] - (I_r + X_\varepsilon \varepsilon_r)r$$

we see that an increase in interest rates of 1 (an increase of 100 percentage points) reduces autonomous spending by an amount $-(I_r + X_\varepsilon \varepsilon_r)$. A 1 percentage-point increase in r ($\Delta r = 0.01$) will therefore decrease A by $0.01(I_r + X_\varepsilon \varepsilon_r)$. Think back to the income-expenditure diagram of Chapter 9. Recall that the equilibrium level of real GDP depended on the level of autonomous spending:

$$Y = \frac{A}{1 - MPE}$$

Because a change in the real interest rate r changes autonomous spending A by changing investment I and exports GX, it will change the equilibrium level of real GDP. If we graph — as Figure 10.7 does — the real interest rate on the vertical axis and the level of autonomous spending on the horizontal axis, we see a downward-sloping relationship between interest rates and autonomous spending.

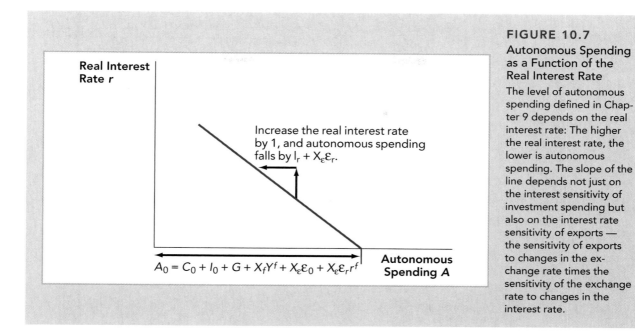

FIGURE 10.7

Autonomous Spending as a Function of the Real Interest Rate

The level of autonomous spending defined in Chapter 9 depends on the real interest rate: The higher the real interest rate, the lower is autonomous spending. The slope of the line depends not just on the interest sensitivity of investment spending but also on the interest rate sensitivity of exports — the sensitivity of exports to changes in the exchange rate times the sensitivity of the exchange rate to changes in the interest rate.

From the Interest Rate to Investment to Planned Total Expenditure

By how much does a change in the interest rate change equilibrium real GDP? By an amount equal to the change in r times the interest sensitivity of autonomous spending $(I_r + X_\varepsilon \varepsilon_r)$ times the multiplier of Chapter 9. The change in the interest rate will change autonomous spending. And the whole point of the multiplier discussion in Chapter 9 was that changes in autonomous spending have multiplied effects on total expenditure. This relationship between the level of the real interest rate and the equilibrium level of real GDP has a name that was coined by economist John Hicks more than 60 years ago: the "**IS curve**," where IS stands for "investment-saving." The IS curve is a workhorse tool that macroeconomists and macroeconomics courses use very, very frequently.

To construct the IS curve, we must first draw a diagram with equilibrium real GDP on the horizontal axis and the real interest rate on the vertical axis, as in Figure 10.8 on page 292. We begin by picking a value for the real interest rate and then determine the level of autonomous spending at that real interest rate. Then we plug the corresponding level of autonomous spending into an income-expenditure diagram and draw the resulting planned-expenditure line. The point where the planned-expenditure line crosses the 45-degree line is the point at which planned expenditure equals national income. That is the value of equilibrium real GDP corresponding to our initial choice of the real interest rate.

The interest rate we started with and the real GDP level we ended with make up a single point on the IS curve. We repeat the process for as many different possible interest rates as we need. Plotting the points on the IS diagram and connecting them produces the IS curve.

The algebra of the IS curve is straightforward, if a little crowded and complicated. We separate the determinants of autonomous spending into those that don't

IS curve

The downward-sloping relationship between the (real, long-term) interest rate and the equilibrium level of national product and aggregate demand.

FIGURE 10.8
The IS Curve

For each possible value of the real interest rate, there is a different level of autonomous spending. For each level of autonomous spending, the income-expenditure process generates a different equilibrium level of real GDP. The IS curve tells us what equilibrium level of real GDP corresponds to each possible value of the real interest rate.

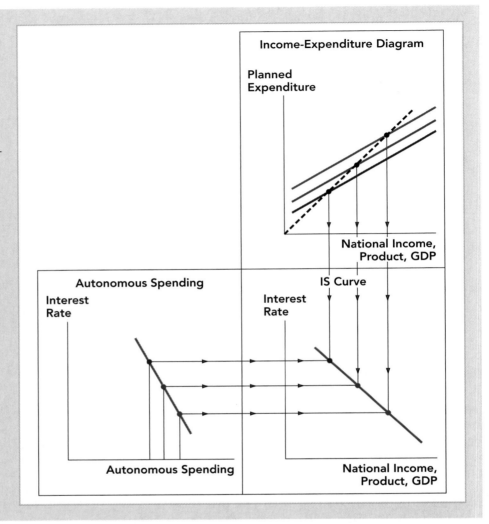

baseline autonomous spending

Written A_0. Those components of autonomous spending that are independent of the level of the interest rate.

depend on the interest rate and those that do, calling the first set of determinants "**baseline autonomous spending**," or A_0:

$$A_0 = C_0 + I_0 + G + (X_f Y^f + X_\varepsilon \varepsilon_0 + X_\varepsilon \varepsilon_r r^f)$$

And we write that total autonomous spending is equal to baseline autonomous spending A_0 minus the long-term risky real interest rate r times the sensitivity of autonomous spending to interest rates $I_r + X_\varepsilon \varepsilon_r$:

$$A = A_0 - (I_r + X_\varepsilon \varepsilon_r)r$$

We then turn back to the income-expenditure analysis in Chapter 9, and remember that real GDP is equal to autonomous spending A divided by 1 minus the MPE, or autonomous spending times the multiplier:

$$Y = \frac{A}{1 - MPE}$$

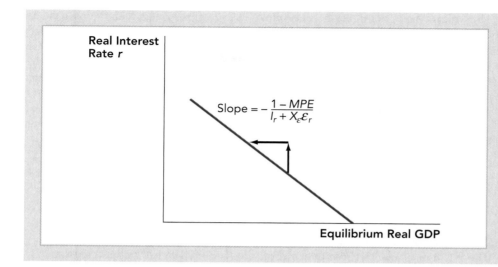

FIGURE 10.9
The IS Curve

The position of the IS curve summarizes all the determinants of equilibrium real GDP and how the level of equilibrium real GDP changes in response to changes in the interest rate.

And we get our expression for the IS curve: Real GDP Y is

$$Y = \frac{A_0}{1 - MPE} - \left(\frac{I_r + X_\varepsilon \varepsilon_r}{1 - MPE}\right) r$$

where baseline autonomous spending A_0 is equal to

$$A_0 = C_0 + I_0 + G + (X_f Y^f + X_\varepsilon \varepsilon_0 + X_\varepsilon \varepsilon_r r^f)$$

and, from Chapter 9, the marginal propensity to expend, the MPE, is

$$MPE = C_y(1 - t) - IM_y$$

In this IS curve equation, the first set of terms gives the horizontal intercept of the IS curve: the value that real GDP would attain if the real interest rate were zero. The second set of terms determines the slope of the IS curve: the responsiveness of equilibrium real GDP to changes in the long-term, risky, real interest rate, as in Figure 10.9.

The Slope and Position of the IS Curve

The Slope of the IS Curve

The slope of the IS curve depends on four factors. Anything that affects the multiplier will change the slope of the IS curve. Anything that affects the responsiveness of investment to a change in real interest rates will change the slope of the IS curve. Anything that affects how sensitive exports are to the real exchange rate will change the slope of the IS curve. And anything that changes how large a swing in real exchange rates is induced by a change in interest rates will change the slope of the IS curve.

These changes are all clearly visible in the term that multiplies the interest rate in the IS curve equation (which is the reciprocal of the slope of the IS curve):

$$-\left(\frac{1}{1 - MPE}\right)(I_r + X_\varepsilon \varepsilon_r)$$

The first of these factors is the multiplier: $1/(1 - MPE)$. The larger the multiplier, the larger is the impact on planned expenditure set in motion by a given change in investment spending and gross exports, and so the flatter is the IS curve. The second factor is the interest sensitivity of investment: the I_r term. The larger is I_r, the larger is the impact on investment due to a change in the real interest rate, and so the flatter is the IS curve. The third factor is how large a change in exports is generated by a change in the real interest rate: the $X_\varepsilon\varepsilon_r$ term, which is the product of the exchange rate sensitivity of exports and the interest rate sensitivity of the exchange rate. The larger is $X_\varepsilon\varepsilon_r$, the larger is the impact on gross exports due to a change in the real interest rate, and so the flatter is the IS curve.

All this means that a great many shocks to the economy change the slope of the IS curve. Thus in analyzing events, the correct calculation of the slope of the IS curve is important. Box 10.2 shows how to do this.

The Position of the IS Curve

The position of the IS curve depends on the baseline level of autonomous spending A_0 times the multiplier $1/(1 - MPE)$. To see how many factors can change the position of the IS curve, let's for the moment expand A_0 and MPE and write them

BOX 10.2

CALCULATING THE DEPENDENCE OF PLANNED EXPENDITURE ON THE INTEREST RATE: AN EXAMPLE

To calculate how much a change in the interest rate will shift the equilibrium level of planned expenditure, you need to know four things:

- The marginal propensity to spend *(MPE)*, and thus the multiplier $1/(1 - MPE)$.
- The interest sensitivity of investment I_r.
- How much a change in the interest rate will affect the real exchange rate ε_r.
- How much a change in the exchange rate will affect exports X_r.

Suppose that you know that the marginal propensity to expend is 0.5 and the interest sensitivity of investment is 10,000, that is, a 1-percentage-point rise in the annual interest rate $(\Delta r = 0.01)$ decreases annual investment by \$100 billion. Then the direct effects of interest rates on investment coupled with the multiplier would lead you to conclude that a 1-percentage-point increase in the interest rate would decrease equilibrium planned expenditure by \$200 billion, acting through the investment channel alone.

However, there is another channel through which interest rates affect planned expenditure — the export channel. If a 1-percentage-point increase in the interest rate $(\Delta r = 0.01)$ reduces the value of the exchange rate by 1,000 units, and if each 1-unit reduction in the exchange rate reduces exports by \$5 billion, then there would be an additional decrease of $2 \cdot (5) \cdot (10) = \$100$ billion in planned expenditure through the exports channel.

Thus the total decline in equilibrium annual planned expenditure from a 1-percentage-point increase in the interest rate $(\Delta r = 0.01)$ would be \$300 billion. The slope of the IS curve would be $\Delta r/\Delta Y$ or $-1/30,000$.

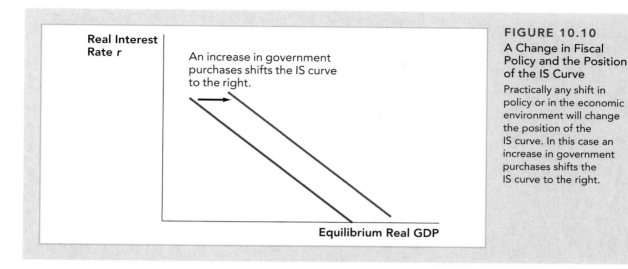

FIGURE 10.10

A Change in Fiscal Policy and the Position of the IS Curve

Practically any shift in policy or in the economic environment will change the position of the IS curve. In this case an increase in government purchases shifts the IS curve to the right.

in terms of their more fundamental determinants:

$$\frac{A_0}{1 - MPE} = \frac{C_0 + I_0 + G + (X_f Y^f + X_\varepsilon \varepsilon_0 + X_\varepsilon \varepsilon_r r^f)}{1 - [C_y(1 - t) - IM_y]}$$

Anything that changes any of the non-interest-dependent components of autonomous spending will shift the position of the IS curve. An increase in government spending G will shift the IS curve to the right and raise the equilibrium level of real GDP for any fixed value of the real interest rate, as Figure 10.10 shows. An increase in the baseline level of investment spending I_0 or consumption spending C_0 will do the same. Other events that shift the IS curve to the right include increases in foreign income Y^f, increases in foreign exchange speculators' expectations ε_0, and increases in foreign interest rates r^f. In analyzing almost any change in the economic environment or in the government's *fiscal policy,* the position of the IS curve will shift.

Moving the Economy to the IS Curve

What happens if the current level of real GDP and the interest rate is not on the IS curve? If the economy is above the IS curve on the diagram, then real GDP is higher than planned expenditure. Inventories are rising rapidly and unexpectedly. So businesses cut back production. Employment, real GDP, and national income fall. If the economy is below the IS curve, planned expenditure is higher than total production. Inventories fall. Firms try to expand production in order to meet unexpectedly high demand. As they do, real GDP, employment, and national income rise, as Figure 10.11 on page 296 shows.

The process that pulls the economy back to the IS curve works relatively slowly, over months and quarters. Firms respond to increases in inventories by contracting (and to decreases in inventories by raising) production. As was noted in Chapter 9, the economy can stay away from its equilibrium on the income-expenditure diagram for a substantial time, all the while with inventories building up or falling. And if the economy is away from its equilibrium level of real GDP on the income-expenditure diagram, it is not on the IS curve either.

FIGURE 10.11

Off of the IS Curve

The economy's position does not have to correspond to a point on the IS curve. But if the economy is not on the IS curve, then powerful forces will push it toward the IS curve.

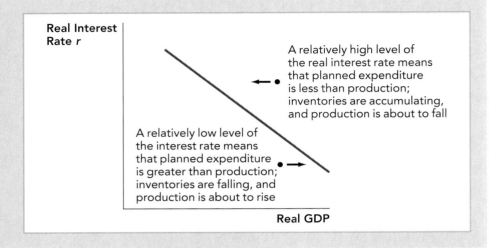

Real Interest Rate r

A relatively high level of the real interest rate means that planned expenditure is less than production; inventories are accumulating, and production is about to fall

A relatively low level of the interest rate means that planned expenditure is greater than production; inventories are falling, and production is about to rise

Real GDP

RECAP   THE IS CURVE

The higher the real interest rate, the lower are the investment spending and exports components of autonomous spending and the lower is real GDP in the sticky-price model. The relationship between the real interest rate and real GDP is called the IS relationship. When plotted on a graph with real GDP on the horizontal axis and the real interest rate on the vertical axis, it is called the IS curve. The IS curve is downward-sloping. Its horizontal intercept is equal to baseline autonomous spending — what autonomous spending A would be if the real interest rate were zero — times the multiplier. Its slope is equal to the reciprocal of the multiplier $1/(1 - MPE)$ times the sum of two terms: (1) the interest sensitivity of investment spending I_r, and (2) the product of the exchange rate sensitivity of gross exports and the interest sensitivity of the exchange rate $X_\varepsilon \varepsilon_r$. The slope of the IS curve is $\dfrac{-(1 - MPE)}{I_r + X_\varepsilon \varepsilon_r}$.

10.3 USING THE IS CURVE TO UNDERSTAND THE ECONOMY

Shifting the IS Curve

We have seen that anything that affects the non-interest-dependent components of autonomous spending shifts the position of the IS curve. Changes that increase baseline autonomous spending shift the IS curve to the right and raise equilibrium real GDP (if interest rates are constant). Changes that reduce baseline autonomous spending shift the IS curve to the left and reduce equilibrium real GDP (if interest rates are held constant).

For example, two kinds of changes in government fiscal policy directly affect the position of the IS curve. A shift in tax rates changes both the position and the

A GOVERNMENT SPENDING INCREASE AND THE IS CURVE: AN EXAMPLE

Calculating the effect on the equilibrium level of real GDP of an increase in a component of baseline autonomous spending such as government purchases is straightforward. For example, suppose that in the economy the initial MPE is equal to 0.5, the baseline level of autonomous spending is $5,000 billion, a 1-percentage-point decline in the real interest rate $(\Delta r = -0.01)$ raises investment spending by $110 billion and exports by $15 billion, and the real interest rate is fixed at 4 percent $(r = 0.04)$. Then the initial equilibrium level of annual real GDP is

$$Y = \frac{A_0}{1 - MPE} - \frac{I_r + X_\varepsilon\varepsilon_r}{1 - MPE}(r) = \frac{\$5,000}{1 - 0.5} - \frac{\$11,000 + \$1,500}{1 - 0.5}(0.04)$$

$$= \$10,000 - \$25,000(0.04) = \$9,000 \text{ billion}$$

And suppose that annual government purchases are then raised by $\Delta G = \$200$ billion.

Since government purchases are a component of baseline autonomous spending A_0, the increase in the equilibrium level of real GDP is straightforward to calculate as long as the central bank does not change the real interest rate r:

$$\Delta Y = \frac{\Delta A_0}{1 - MPE} - \frac{I_r + X_\varepsilon\varepsilon_r}{1 - MPE}(\Delta r)$$

$$= \frac{\$200}{1 - 0.5} - \frac{\$11,000 + \$1,500}{1 - 0.5}(0) = \$400 \text{ billion}$$

Real equilibrium aggregate demand rises by $400 billion.

slope of the IS curve. And a change in the level of government purchases changes the position but not the slope of the IS curve; it shifts the IS curve to the right or the left. The government's fiscal policy thus increases or decreases the equilibrium level of real GDP associated with each possible level of the real interest rate. (See Box 10.3.)

Moving along the IS Curve

Changes in the level of the real interest rate r will move the economy either left and upward or right and downward along the IS curve. A higher real interest rate will produce a lower level of planned expenditure. A lower real interest rate will produce a higher level of planned expenditure and equilibrium real GDP. The Federal Reserve can control — target — interest rates to a considerable degree. Such an **interest-rate-targeting** central bank can stimulate the economy by cutting interest rates (see Box 10.4 and Figure 10.12 on page 298) and can contract the economy by raising interest rates.

How does the Federal Reserve control interest rates? It does so by buying and selling short-term government bonds for cash in open-market operations, so called because they are carried out in the "open market" and the Federal Reserve really does not care whom it buys from or sells to. Whenever the Federal Reserve buys government bonds in return for cash, it increases the total amount of cash in the hands of the public and reserves in the hands of the banking system, as

interest rate targeting

A process whereby a central bank focuses its policies on controlling — i.e., targeting — interest rates.

MOVING ALONG THE IS CURVE: AN EXAMPLE

Suppose that the staff projections of the Federal Reserve predict that if current policies are continued, real GDP will be only $9 trillion at a time for which estimates of potential output are $9.5 trillion. The Federal Open Market Committee (FOMC) might well decide that it is time to lower interest rates to close such a "deflationary gap."

Suppose further that the staff estimates that the marginal propensity to spend is 0.5, that a 1-percentage-point fall in the real interest rate ($\Delta r = -0.01$) generates an extra $110 billion in annual investment spending and a 5-point rise in the real exchange rate. And that each 1-point rise in the real exchange rate — the value of foreign currency — raises exports by $3 billion.

Such estimates of the structure of the economy imply that the slope of the IS curve is

$$\text{IS slope} = -\frac{(1 - MPE)}{I_r + X_\varepsilon \varepsilon_r} = -\frac{1 - 0.5}{\$11,000 + (500)(\$3)} = -\frac{1}{\$25,000}$$

So to boost equilibrium real GDP by $500 billion by moving the economy along the IS curve, the real interest rate has to be reduced by 0.02 — by 2 percentage points.

Figure 10.13 shows. Banks with the extra reserves use them to try to increase their deposits. Thus such an expansionary open-market operation increases the economy's stock of money: It increases the quantity of assets — checking account deposits and cash — that are readily spendable purchasing power.

Banks, businesses, and households take a look at the larger quantity of money — wealth in the form of readily spendable purchasing power — that they hold. At the previous level of interest rates this is more money than they want to hold in their

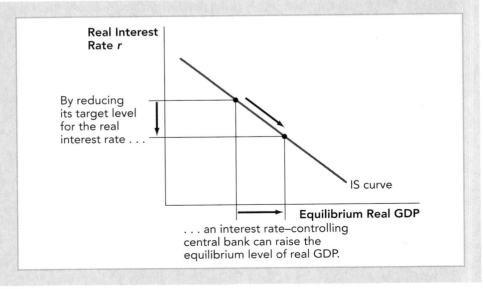

FIGURE 10.12

Cutting Target Interest Rates and Raising Real GDP

The IS curve shows us what happens to real GDP when the central bank changes the real interest rate.

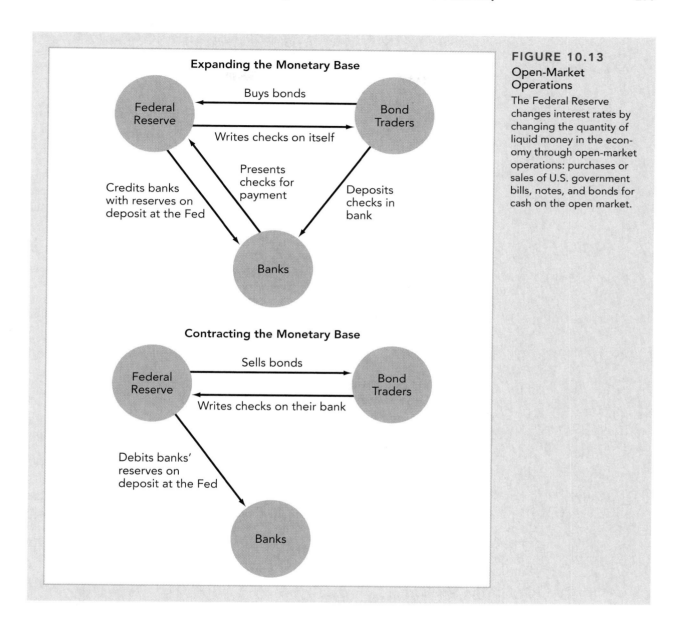

FIGURE 10.13
Open-Market Operations
The Federal Reserve changes interest rates by changing the quantity of liquid money in the economy through open-market operations: purchases or sales of U.S. government bills, notes, and bonds for cash on the open market.

portfolios. So households, businesses, and banks try to use this money to buy assets, such as bonds, that pay higher yields than cash. As they do so, they push the price of bonds up and the interest rate down. Thus an expansionary open-market operation reduces interest rates in the economy. The same process works in reverse to push interest rates up when the Federal Reserve sells bonds for cash on the open market. Box 10.4 shows how central bankers would go about trying to calculate the size of the change in interest rates needed to properly manage the economy.

Difficulties

Attempts to control planned expenditure by manipulating interest rates encounter certain difficulties. First, our knowledge of the structure of the economy is imperfect.

Perhaps at any particular moment the slope of the IS curve is half what the Federal Reserve staff believes or is twice what the Federal Reserve staff believes. Second, even when policies do have their expected effects, these effects do not necessarily arrive on schedule. As economist Milton Friedman often says, economic policy works with long and *variable lags*.

Moreover, the interest rates that the Federal Reserve can control are short-term, nominal, safe interest rates. The interest rate that determines where the economy is in equilibrium on the IS curve is the long-term, real, risky interest rate. Even if the government and central bank attain their target interest rate and even if the effects of changes in the interest rate are exactly as predicted and arrive exactly on schedule, there is a lot of potential slippage: Changes in the term premium between short and long interest rates, changes in the rate of inflation, and changes in the risk premium will each carry the economy to a point on the IS curve other than the point that the Federal Reserve wanted.

What determines the value of the term premium — the gap between short-term and long-term interest rates? Appendix 10a shows that the major determinant is expectations of future *monetary policy*. Long-term interest rates will be high relative to short-term interest rates if people expect short-term interest rates to be raised in the future; long-term interest rates will be low relative to short-term interest rates if people expect short-term rates to be lowered in the future.

Economic Fluctuations in the United States: The IS Curve as a Lens

How useful is the IS curve in understanding economic fluctuations in the United States over the past generation or so? If we plot on a graph the points corresponding to the long-term real interest rate and output relative to potential attained by the U.S. economy since 1960, we see that the economy has been all over the map — or at least all over the diagram (see Figure 10.14). Yet we can make sense of what has happened using shifts in and movements along the IS curve. That in fact is what the IS curve is for. It is a useful tool, which is why we have spent so many pages developing it. In the following five subsections we will apply the IS curve to gain insight into business-cycle fluctuations in each of the past four decades as well as the current decade.

The 1960s

The 1960s saw a substantial rightward shift of the IS curve. Increased optimism on the part of businesses, the Kennedy-Johnson cut in income taxes, and the extra government expenditures needed to fight the Vietnam War all increased planned expenditure. The IS curve shifted rightward by perhaps 3 percent of potential output in the 1960s, as Figure 10.15 shows.

The late 1960s also saw a movement downward and to the right along the IS curve, as real interest rates declined. In large part real interest rates declined by accident. The Federal Reserve did not fully gauge the amount by which inflation was rising. Rising inflation increased the gap between the nominal interest rates directly controlled by monetary policy and the real interest rates that determine planned expenditure. The Federal Reserve did not recognize this as it was happening and thus allowed real interest rates to drift downward.

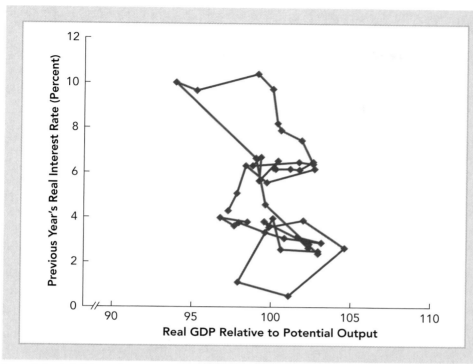

FIGURE 10.14
Real GDP and the Interest Rate, 1960–2004

Much of what has happened to the U.S. economy since 1960 can be understood by thinking of events as either shifts of or movements along the IS curve, though you can't tell by looking at one graph with all 45 years of data.

Source: Authors' calculations and 2004 edition of *The Economic Report of the President* (Washington, DC: Government Printing Office).

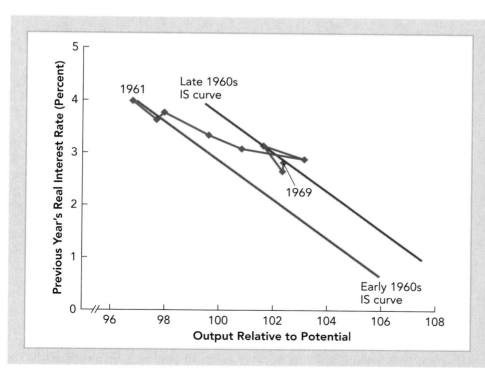

FIGURE 10.15
Shifting Out and Moving along the IS Curve, 1960s

The Vietnam War, the Kennedy-Johnson tax cut, and an increase in business optimism about the future all shifted the IS curve to the right between the start of the 1960s and the second half of the decade.

Source: Authors' calculations and 2004 edition of *The Economic Report of the President* (Washington, DC: Government Printing Office).

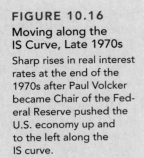

FIGURE 10.16

Moving along the IS Curve, Late 1970s

Sharp rises in real interest rates at the end of the 1970s after Paul Volcker became Chair of the Federal Reserve pushed the U.S. economy up and to the left along the IS curve.

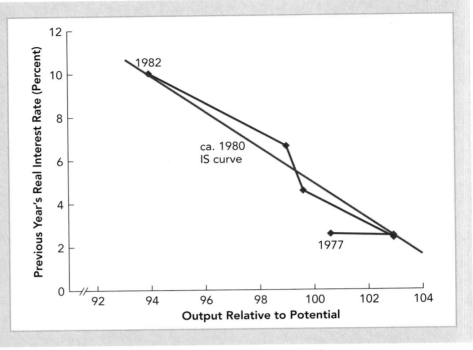

Source: Authors' calculations and 2004 edition of *The Economic Report of the President* (Washington, DC: Government Printing Office).

The 1970s

The end of the 1970s saw the level of real GDP in the United States near the level of potential output. As Figure 10.16 shows, from 1977 to 1979 the U.S. economy moved down and to the right along the IS curve. However, the expansion of output beyond potential was accompanied by unexpectedly high and rising inflation. This rise in inflation was further fueled by a supply shock: the sudden rise in oil prices triggered by the Iranian revolution.

A sudden shift in Federal Reserve policy occurred in 1979 when *Paul Volcker* became chair of the Federal Reserve, replacing G. William Miller. Under Miller fighting inflation had been a relatively low priority. Under Volcker fighting inflation became the highest priority of all. The Federal Reserve raised annual real interest rates step-by-step from 1979 to 1982 up to over 10 percent. The increase in real interest rates moved the economy up and to the left along the end-of-the-1970s position of the IS curve: The unemployment rate reached nearly 10 percent in 1982, and real GDP fell to only 94 percent of the economy's potential output.

The 1980s

The election of Ronald Reagan in 1980 was followed by a massive fiscal expansion. Military spending was increased and income taxes were cut in a series of steps that became effective between 1982 and 1985. The result of these increases in government purchases and cuts in taxes was an enormous government deficit and an outward shift in the IS curve. A simultaneous increase in *investor optimism* triggered by falling inflation combined with the government's fiscal stimulus to

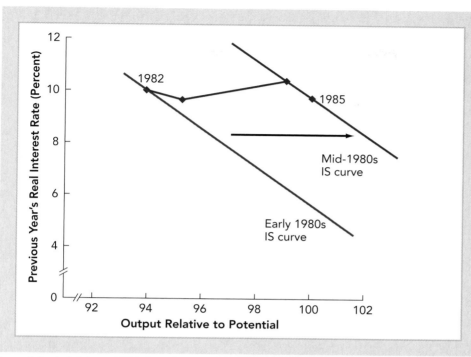

FIGURE 10.17

Shifting the IS Curve Out, Early 1980s

The Reagan budget deficits of the 1980s shifted the economy's IS curve to the right.

Source: Authors' calculations and 2004 edition of *The Economic Report of the President* (Washington, DC: Government Printing Office).

shift the IS curve outward relative to potential output by at least 4 percent. (See Figure 10.17.)

The Federal Reserve responded to this outward shift in the IS curve by maintaining high real interest rates. It sought in the first half of the 1980s to ensure that the success it had achieved in reducing inflation did not unravel. The Federal Reserve feared that a rapid return of real GDP to potential GDP would put upward pressure on inflation once more — hence the maintenance of high real interest rates to make sure that the large Reagan-era fiscal expansion did not have too great an effect.

As inflation remained low throughout the mid and late 1980s, Federal Reserve policy makers gained confidence. They became increasingly optimistic that higher real GDP levels relative to potential would not reignite inflation. Between 1985 and 1990 successive step-by-step reductions in real interest rates carried the U.S. economy back to full employment, and carried it down and to the right along the IS curve. (See Figure 10.18 on page 304.)

The 1990s

The principal maker of economic policy since the late 1980s has been Federal Reserve Chair Alan Greenspan, appointed and reappointed by four successive presidents: Reagan, George H. W. Bush, Clinton, and George W. Bush. Greenspan is somewhat of a paradox: a Federal Reserve chair whom all trust to be a ferocious inflation fighter, yet one who — in the policies that he has chosen — frequently seemed willing to risk higher inflation in order to achieve higher economic growth or to avoid a recession.

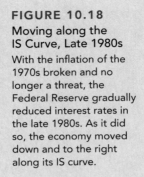

FIGURE 10.18

Moving along the IS Curve, Late 1980s

With the inflation of the 1970s broken and no longer a threat, the Federal Reserve gradually reduced interest rates in the late 1980s. As it did so, the economy moved down and to the right along its IS curve.

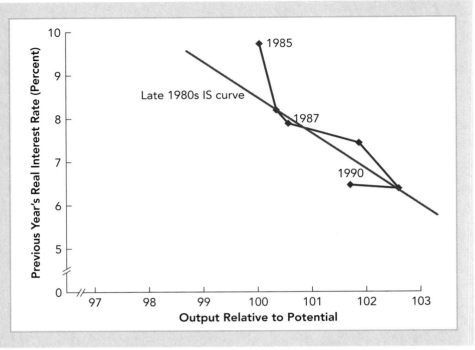

Source: Authors' calculations and 2004 edition of *The Economic Report of the President* (Washington, DC: Government Printing Office).

Immediately after taking office Greenspan faced a challenge: the sudden stock market crash of October 1987. How large an effect would this crash have on planned expenditure? What would it do to investment spending? Would a leftward shift in the IS curve be generated by the sudden change in investors' expectations about the future that triggered the stock market crash? No one knew. If the crash turned out to be the harbinger of a large leftward shift in the IS curve, then an unchanging monetary policy would lead to a significant recession. So the Greenspan-led FOMC lowered interest rates and expanded the monetary base, hoping that this shift in monetary policy would offset any leftward shift in the IS curve and avoid a recession.

In point of fact, the stock market crash of 1987 had next to no effect on investment spending or planned expenditure. Economists have still not come up with a convincing story for why its effects were so small. The two years after 1987 saw higher output relative to potential and saw lower unemployment rates. The years between 1987 and 1990 did not see real interest rates rising — as they usually do in the latter stages of an expansion — but real interest rates that were stable or falling.

As the unemployment rate fell, inflation accelerated. In 1988 and 1989, inflation moved up from 3 to 4 percent. The Federal Reserve found that it had successfully avoided any chance of a (big) recession in 1988 in the aftermath of the stock market crash, but only at the price of letting inflation rise above 4 percent per year. In the second half of 1990 there came a sudden leftward shift in the IS curve: The Iraqi invasion of Kuwait served as a trigger for firms to reduce investment, as they waited to see whether the world economy was about to experience another

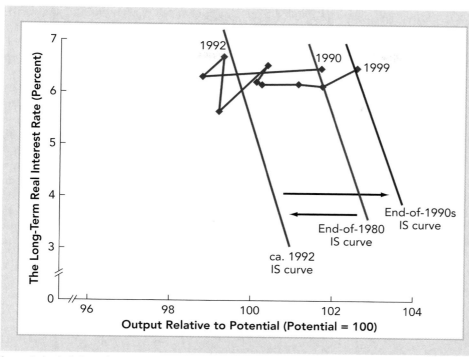

FIGURE 10.19
The 1990s

A sharp inward shift in the IS curve triggered a recession at the beginning of the 1990s. Subsequent increases in autonomous investment shifted the IS curve to the right again.

Source: Authors' calculations from the 2004 edition of the *Economic Report of the President* (Washington, DC: Government Printing Office).

long-run upward spike in oil prices. The U.S. economy slid into recession at the end of 1990. The Federal Reserve, worried about the upward creep in inflation in the late 1980s, took no steps to reduce real interest rates as the economy slid into the recession. (See Figure 10.19.)

During the recession, inflation fell to 2½ percent. Unemployment rose to a peak of 7.6 percent — in the late spring of 1992, just in time to be salient for the 1992 presidential election. Recovery began in mid-1992.

Soon thereafter Greenspan made another decision to risk higher inflation in order to accomplish other goals. In 1993 he signaled that if Congress and the president took significant steps to reduce the budget deficit, then the Federal Reserve would try as best as it could to maintain lower interest rates — a shift in the policy mix that would keep the target level of production and employment unchanged but that with lower interest rates would promise higher investment and faster productivity growth: an "investment-led recovery."

This time the gamble turned out extremely well. As fiscal policy tightened in 1994 and beyond, interest rates remained significantly lower than they had been in the 1980s even though output recovered to potential. Moreover, this time there was no significant acceleration of inflation, even though by the end of the 1990s unemployment had fallen to the lowest level in a generation.

The 2000s

The end of the 1990s saw the end of the dot-com bubble. The crash of the stock market in 2000 was both cause and consequence of the recognition that investors and businesses had been overly optimistic not about the technology and productivity benefits of the computer revolution, but about the ability of businesses to make profits off of the computer boom. Investment fell sharply in 2000 and 2001, carrying real GDP relative to potential down with it. The recession was given a further impetus by the uncertainty created by the terror attack of September 11, 2001. While real GDP had been some 3 percent *above* potential output in 1999, by 2001 it was 1 percent *below* potential.

The executive branch — the administration of George W. Bush — responded by proposing tax cuts that were poorly crafted to stimulate demand: The bulk of the money went to households for which the marginal propensity to consume was low. Fiscal policy thus did little to move the IS curve back to the right and expand output. The Federal Reserve responded by cutting interest rates severely. Observers even began to fear that the Federal Reserve would run out of room to cut interest rates further, since short-term nominal interest rates cannot fall below zero. But during 2002 and 2003 the Federal Reserve's easy-money policies were neutralized by further falls in business and investor confidence and a further move to the left in the IS curve. In spite of remarkably expansionary monetary policy, it was only after 2004 that there were signs that the economy was beginning to close the output gap. (See Figure 10.20.)

FIGURE 10.20

The 2000s

The collapse of the dot-com stock-market bubble in 2000 and the September 11, 2001, attacks were large shocks to the U.S. economy: Output fell from about 3 percent above to perhaps 1 percent below potential in response. The Federal Reserve waited to respond, believing that the economy in 2000 had been running at a rate unsustainable without rising inflation. But when the Federal Reserve did move, it moved rapidly to reduce interest rates. Before 2004, however, few signs suggested that the reduction in interest rates and concomitant stimulative budget deficits had done much to keep output from falling even further below potential.

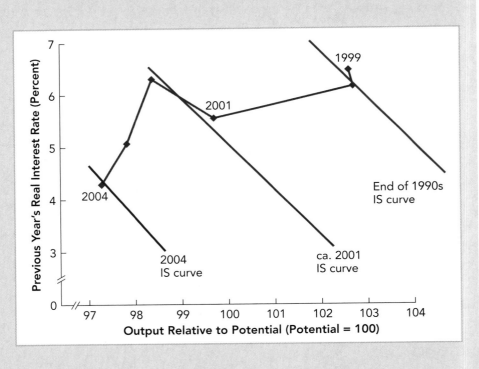

Source: Authors' calculations from the 2005 edition of the *Economic Report of the President* (Washington, DC: Government Printing Office).

> **RECAP USING THE IS CURVE TO UNDERSTAND THE ECONOMY**
>
> We have seen that anything that affects the non-interest-dependent components of autonomous spending shifts the position of the IS curve. Changes that increase baseline autonomous spending shift the IS curve to the right and raise equilibrium real GDP. Changes that reduce baseline autonomous spending shift the IS curve to the left and reduce real GDP.
>
> Changes in the size of the multiplier, the interest sensitivity of investment or gross exports, and the responsiveness of the real exchange rate to changes in the interest rate change the slope of the IS curve. Changes in the level of the real interest rate will move the economy either left and upward or right and downward along the IS curve: A higher real interest rate will produce a lower level of planned expenditure. A lower real interest rate will produce a higher level of planned expenditure and equilibrium real GDP. The Federal Reserve can control — target — interest rates to a considerable degree. Such an interest rate–targeting central bank can stimulate the economy by cutting interest rates and can contract the economy by raising interest rates.

Chapter Summary

1. In the sticky-price model the investment function is the same as in the flexible-price model. But in the flexible-price model the level of saving determines investment, and the investment function determines the real interest rate. In the sticky-price model the real interest rate is determined outside the IS framework, and the level of the real interest rate powerfully affects the level of real GDP.

2. The international sector of the sticky-price model is essentially the same as the international sector of the flexible-price model.

3. The income-expenditure diagram takes autonomous spending as given and then determines the equilibrium level of real GDP, planned expenditure, and national income as functions of autonomous spending and the marginal propensity to spend.

4. The IS curve incorporates the effect of changing interest rates on autonomous spending and adds this effect to the income-expenditure diagram.

5. The IS curve slopes downward because a higher interest rate lowers both investment and exports, and these reductions in autonomous spending in turn lower planned expenditure and equilibrium real GDP.

6. When the central bank targets the real interest rate, then the position of the IS curve and the central bank's interest rate target together determine the equilibrium level of planned expenditure and real GDP.

Key Terms

long-term interest rate (p. 284)

short-term interest rate (p. 284)

risky interest rate (p. 286)

safe interest rate (p. 286)

IS curve (p. 291)

baseline autonomous spending (p. 292)

interest rate targeting (p. 297)

Analytical Exercises

1. Why does an expansion of government purchases have an amplified impact on the equilibrium level of real GDP? Suppose that the central bank does not target interest rates but instead keeps the money stock constant. Is it still the case that an expansion of government purchases will cause a greater than one-for-one increase in the equilibrium level of real GDP?

2. Explain why the IS curve slopes downward. Is its slope steeper in a closed economy with no international trade, or in an open economy?

3. For each of the following, decide whether the IS curve shifts in and to the left, shifts out and to the right, or stays unchanged:
   a. The tax rate decreases.
   b. Foreign interest rates rise.
   c. Businesses become more optimistic about future demand.

   d. Consumers desire to save a greater proportion of their income for the future.
   e. The central bank lowers the short-term nominal interest rate it controls.
   f. The term premium rises.
   g. Foreign exchange speculators become more pessimistic about the long-run value of domestic currency.

4. Suppose that the government and central bank together want to keep GDP constant but raise the rate of investment. What policies can they follow to achieve this?

5. Suppose that the level of investment spending does not depend at all on the interest rate. Does this mean that the IS curve is vertical? If not, how can it be that central-bank changes in the real interest rate affect the equilibrium level of real GDP?

Policy Exercises

1. Suppose that the consumption, investment, net exports, and exchange rate functions are

$$C = C_0 + C_y(1 - t)Y = \$3,000 + 0.5(1 - 0.4)Y$$

$$I = I_0 - I_r r = \$1,200 - \$10,000r$$

$$GX = X_f Y^f + X_\varepsilon \varepsilon = 0.1Y^f + \$4\varepsilon$$

$$IM = IM_y Y = 0.2Y$$

$$NX = GX - IM$$

$$\varepsilon = 100 - 1,000(r - r^f)$$

Derive the IS curve for this economy: real GDP as a function of all the unspecified variables in the economy. Suppose that the foreign interest rate r^f is 5 percent ($r^f = 0.05$), that total foreign income Y^f is $10,000, and that government spending G is $3,000. What then is equilibrium annual real GDP if the central bank sets the real interest rate at 3 percent ($r = 0.03$)? At 5 percent? At 7 percent?

2. Suppose that the economy is the same as in problem 1 except for the fact that it is a closed economy. There are no imports and no exports: $IM_y = 0$, $X_f = 0$, and $X_\varepsilon = 0$. Derive the IS curve for this economy. What is equilibrium annual real GDP if the central bank

sets the interest rate at 3 percent? At 5 percent? At 7 percent?

3. In which of the two economies — the open economy of problem 1 or the closed economy of problem 2 — do you think that changes in interest rates have larger effects on the equilibrium level of real GDP? Explain your answer.

4. Suppose that the short-term nominal interest rate — the one the central bank actually controls — is 3 percent. But also suppose that the inflation rate is zero, that the term premium is 4 percent, and that the risk premium is 3 percent.
   a. What is the real interest rate relevant for the IS curve?
   b. Suppose that the IS equation of the economy is $Y = \$10,000 - 30,000r$. What is the equilibrium level of real GDP?
   c. Suppose that the central bank wants to use monetary policy to raise Y to $9,000. Can it do so by open-market operations that lower the short-term nominal interest rate? Explain why or why not. What other policy steps can you think of that the government and central bank could take to raise equilibrium real GDP to $9,000?

5. Suppose that the consumption, investment, net exports, and exchange rate functions are

$$C = C_0 + C_y(1 - t)Y = \$3,000 + 0.5(1 - 0.4)Y$$

$$I = I_0 - I_r r = \$1,200 - \$10,000r$$

$$GX = X_f Y^f + X_\varepsilon \varepsilon = 0.1Y^f + \$4\varepsilon$$

$$IM = IM_y Y = 0.2Y$$

$$NX = GX - IM$$

$$\varepsilon = 100 - 1,000(r - r^f)$$

Suppose further that the government follows a balanced-budget rule: Government purchases G are equal to government tax collections tY. Derive the IS for this economy: real GDP as a function of all the unspecified variables in the economy. Is the level of real GDP along the IS curve more or less sensitive to changes in interest rates than it was in problem 1? Why?

The Term Premium and Expected Future Interest Rates

APPENDIX $10a$

What determines the value of the *term premium* — the gap between short-term and long-term interest rates? To start thinking about this question, consider once again a simple two-period model in which the periods are "now" and "the future." Bankers make long-term loans that fall due in two periods. Bond traders buy and sell long-term bonds that fall due in two periods. The real interest rate paid on these long-term loans and bonds is the long-term real interest rate r. Bankers also make short-term loans (and bond traders also buy and sell short-term bonds) that mature in just one period.

Someone thinking about buying a long-term bond (or making a long-term loan) knows that for each real dollar invested in such financial instruments today, he or she will after two periods have

$$\text{Gross return} = 1 + r + r$$

Each period they will receive the long-term real interest rate on their investment, r.

Someone thinking about buying a short-term bond today (or making a short-term loan) knows that for each real dollar invested in such financial instruments today, she or he will after the end of the first period (the one that is going on "now") have $1 + r_n^s$: r for the real interest rate, s because it is the rate paid on a short-term loan, and n because it is the interest rate paid in the "now" period. But the person's capital will then, at the start of the second period (the one that will happen in the future), be lying idle. The natural thing to do then will be to invest it again in another short-term bond (or make another short-term loan — this time at the short-term interest rate that will prevail in the future, r_f^s.

So after two periods someone who chooses today to invest money in short-term securities will have

$$\text{Gross return} = 1 + r_n^s + r_f^s$$

for each real dollar that she or he invested at the start of the first period.

What will a flint-eyed money-maximizing rational bond trader do? The first complication is that he or she doesn't know today what the future short-term real interest rate r_f^s will be when the time to reinvest the principal arrives. The best he or she can do is form an expectation now — E_n — of what the future short-term real interest rate will be: $E_n(r_f^s)$.

Thus the bond trader has to decide whether to invest for the long term or for the short term (and then, later, to reinvest). The returns from investing for the long term will be greater if

$$\text{Long-term gross return} = 1 + 2r > 1 + r_n^s + E_n(r_f^s) = \text{short-term return}$$

Or, defining $E_n(\Delta r^s)$, the expected change in the short-term real interest rate, as the difference between expected future short rates $E_n(r_f^s)$ and current short rates r_n^s

$$\text{Expected change in short rates, } E_n(\Delta r^s) = E_n(r_f^s) - r_n^s$$

The returns from investing for the long term will be greater if

$$r - r_n^s > \frac{E_n(\Delta r^s)}{2}$$

and the bond trader will probably decide to invest for the long term. If

$$r - r_n^s < \frac{E_n(\Delta r^s)}{2}$$

then the returns from investing for the short term will be greater, and the trader will probably decide to invest for the short term.

In equilibrium there are *both* short-term and long-term bonds held and short-term and long-term loans made. So in equilibrium the typical bond trader and bank loan officer must think that the expected returns from long-term and short-term financial investments are roughly equal. In equilibrium,

$$r - r_n^s = \frac{E_n(\Delta r^s)}{2}$$

The term premium $r - r_n^s$ is equal to the expected change in short-term interest rates over the life span of the loan, weighted by the proportion of the loan's time span over which the changed short-term interest rate will apply. In other words, *the term premium tells you how bond traders expect short-term interest rates to move in the future.*

If financiers are buying two-year bonds at, say, 5.75 percent — when they could instead buy three-month T-bills every quarter for two years — then they must believe that either portfolio strategy will average out to about 5.75 percent over two years, or else they would all be crowding into one security or the other. Demand for the one would rise; demand for the other would fall. And the interest rates on them and on loans of that duration would change until once more it looked to bond traders that the two strategies were equally attractive. Similarly, if bond traders are buying three-month T-bills at, say, 4 percent when they could instead buy two-year bonds at 5.75 percent, then they must expect that higher short-term rates a year and a half in the future — say, 7.5 percent — will balance out today's low rates to average out to 5.75 percent.

This is the *expectations theory of the term structure:* The long-term interest rate is the average of what bond traders expect future short-term rates to be for the duration of the long-term loan. The term premium tells us how much bond traders are expecting the average short-term interest rate to rise (or fall) over the duration of the long-term loan.

From the standpoint of governments that seek to control interest rates, this dependence of today's long-term interest rate on expectations of what the short-term interest rate will be tomorrow is very inconvenient. All the changes in today's interest rate that the central bank can undertake today will have only a limited effect on long-term interest rates unless bond traders are convinced that policies once adopted will be continued. Thus central banks guard their reputation for credibility and consistency above everything else. They can preserve their ability to move the economy along the IS curve by changing interest rates only if bond traders' expectations of the future, and thus today's long-term interest rates, react predictably to changes in interest rate policy.

CHAPTER 11

The Money Market and the LM Curve

QUESTIONS

What do we mean by "money-market equilibrium"?

What is the LM — liquidity-money — curve?

What is the IS-LM framework?

How is the equilibrium level of real GDP determined when the money stock is constant?

What is an IS shock to the economy? An LM shock?

What is the aggregate demand — AD — curve? The aggregate supply — AS — curve?

The IS curve we built up in Chapter 10 gives us enough theory to think about business cycles — as long as the central bank uses open-market operations to control the real interest rate and keep it pegged to its preferred chosen value. But not all central banks peg interest rates. Not all central banks that peg interest rates today pegged them in the past. And not all economies even today have central banks with the power to peg interest rates.

Thus the analysis of Chapter 10 is fine, comprehensive, and complete only as long as we restrict our view to large postindustrial economies — the United States, western Europe, and Japan — today. If you are willing to do that, fine; stop reading this chapter now, and go to the start of Chapter 12. This is an optional chapter for those with the time and inclination to dig a little deeper into the operations of the money market.

But if you do have time, and if your professor does want to dig deeper into the operations of the money market, then keep reading. For you, extending the analysis in a different direction to consider how the economy behaves when what is fixed is not the real interest rate but instead the economy's money stock — the amount of liquid assets, of wealth held in the form of readily spendable purchasing power — is worthwhile.

In this chapter we derive what economists John Hicks and Alvin Hansen were the first to call an LM — a liquidity-money — curve. The LM curve serves as a sibling to the IS curve, and tells us how interest rates adjust when the stock of liquid money is fixed. The LM curve joins the IS curve in what is called the IS-LM model, which provides our analysis of the determinants of real GDP and the interest rate when the money stock is fixed.

The very end of this chapter begins the process of understanding what determines the price level and the inflation rate in the sticky-price macroeconomic model. We use all the previous chapters of Part 4 to construct the aggregate demand (AD) relationship, which tells how planned expenditure varies in the short run as the price level changes. We combine this with a simple model of short-run *aggregate supply* (AS). Putting these two together generates the AS-AD framework, which allows us not just to analyze what the level of real GDP is but also to begin to analyze how changes in real GDP affect the price level.

11.1 THE MONEY MARKET AND THE MONEY STOCK

Wealth, Bonds, and the Demand for Money

Think about a household or a business trying to figure out in what form to hold its wealth. The household can hold its wealth in the form of interest-bearing or other return-earning assets like real estate, stocks, and bonds — let's lump all of these together and call them "bonds," for bonds are a very typical way that wealth is held. Or the household can hold its wealth in the form of "money," which we call M — where money is shorthand for assets that are liquid, can be readily spent, can be easily used to buy things. Households and businesses can and do move their wealth back and forth between these two forms of assets.

Wealth held in the form of money earns little or no interest. Wealth held in the form of bonds earns interest at the nominal interest rate i. Wealth held in the form of bonds cannot be readily spent: To transform it into a form in which you can use it to buy things takes some time, and so if too great a proportion of wealth is held in bonds, you may miss opportunities to buy goods and services. Wealth held in the form of money is liquid, and it can be easily spent — that's the defining characteristic of money.

There are three important facts about the quantity of money that businesses and households demand to hold, which we will call M^d, with the d superscript there to remind ourselves that this is a demand:

- **Money demand** has a time trend, the result of slow changes in banking-sector structure and technology.
- Money demand is proportional to total income, which by the circular flow principle is the same as total spending and the same as GDP.
- Money demand is inversely related to the nominal interest rate — when nominal interest rates go up, demand for money goes down.

Why does the quantity of money demanded M^d go up when total income — or total spending, or GDP, for they are synonymous — Y goes up? Think of it this way: How much wealth you want to hold in readily spendable form depends on how large are the purchases you typically make in a unit of time. And the higher the flow of total income, the greater the flow of purchases an average household or business wants to make.

Why does the quantity of money demanded M^d go down when the nominal interest rate i goes up? Think of it this way: The nominal interest rate is the opportunity cost of holding money. That part of your wealth which you hold as money — in the form of deposits in your checking account or cash in your pocket — earns zero nominal interest. By contrast, if you were to shift the wealth you hold in the form of money into less liquid but more lucrative investments like bonds, it would earn the prevailing market nominal interest rate i. The difference between the expected return on holding wealth in the liquid form of money and on holding wealth in bonds is thus the nominal interest rate. The nominal interest rate i is the opportunity cost of holding money. You want to hold money because not having liquid assets you can use to buy commodities is very inconvenient. But holding wealth in the form of money means that you are giving up the interest you could otherwise earn. Hence the quantity of money demanded falls when the nominal interest rate i rises.

Notice that money demand depends *not* on the real interest rate r but on the nominal interest rate i. The difference between them is the expected inflation rate π^e: $i = r + \pi^e$.

Economists try to fit these insights into their model by writing down a demand-for-money function:

$$\frac{M^d}{P} = M_y Y - M_i i$$

where M^d is the nominal quantity of money that households and businesses want to hold. It is divided by the overall price level P because what households and businesses really care about is not how many pieces of paper with George Washington's face they have, but how much in the way of goods and services their money holdings can buy. The parameter M_y tells how much in the way of extra **real money balances** people demand when total income — which, you remember, the circular flow principle tells us we can also think of as total spending or GDP — Y goes up. Over long periods of time M_y tends to fall as

money demand

How much wealth in the form of readily spendable purchasing power — money — households and businesses wish to hold at the given levels of national income and nominal interest rates.

real money balances

The total stock of nominal money balances in the economy divided by the price level.

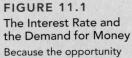

FIGURE 11.1

The Interest Rate and the Demand for Money

Because the opportunity cost of holding wealth in the liquid, readily spendable form of money depends on the nominal interest rate, demand for money falls when the nominal interest rate rises.

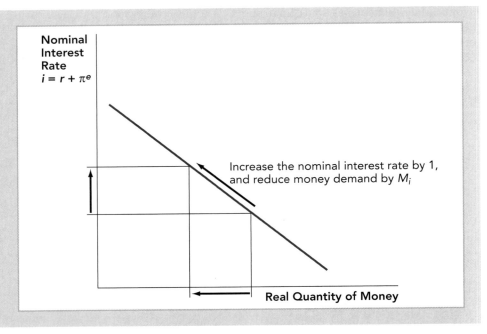

the financial system becomes more sophisticated, the time required for checks to clear falls, and credit card balance limits rise. The parameter M_i tells how much households and businesses shrink the amount of wealth they want to hold in the liquid form of money when the nominal interest rate i goes up, as is shown in Figure 11.1. Box 11.1 explains why we are not using the money demand model of Chapter 8: to keep things simple.

Money Supply and Money Demand

In a sticky-price model — and this is the sticky-price section of this textbook — the price level P is predetermined. In a sticky-price model, the price level cannot jump instantly and substantially. Back in the flexible-price model covered in Chapter 8, the price level could and did jump instantly and substantially. Back in Chapter 8, the level of *bank reserves* and the banking system together determined the supply of money: the amount of liquid readily spendable assets in the economy. Given this supply of money M, the price level back in Chapter 8 jumped to make the economy's level of real money balances M/P such that the money market was in **equilibrium** and to make the real *money supply* equal to the real *money demand*.

But this is not flexible-price Chapter 8; this is sticky-price Chapter 11. In this chapter, the price level cannot move instantly to keep the money market in equilibrium. What, then, makes money supply equal to money demand? The answer is that the nominal interest rate must adjust instead.

The price level P is predetermined. As we saw back in Chapter 8, the nominal money supply M is the result of the interaction of the level of reserves in the economy with the structure of the banking system. For the moment let's assume

money market equilibrium

When the money demand by consumers and firms equals the money supply which the Federal Reserve has allowed the banking system to make available.

MONEY DEMAND AND THE QUANTITY THEORY: DETAILS

Back in Chapter 8 we had a different model of money demand. There the key equation was the so-called quantity theory of money equation:

$$MV = PY$$

which, if you solve for M/P, is

$$\frac{M}{P} = \frac{Y}{V}$$

instead of

$$\frac{M^d}{P} = M_y Y - M_i i$$

The two equations are the same if $M_i = 0$ and if $M_y = 1/V$, and not otherwise. Why start over with this new and different money demand equation, rather than building on the quantity equation taught in Chapter 8? The answer is that we seek simplicity: The equations and formulas later in this chapter are simpler this way, and the equations and formulas in Chapter 8 were simpler with the quantity theory equation. After all, the differences between the two approaches are not that great; no important points of theory depend on them. And so in each case we take whatever starting point makes the end of the argument clearest and simplest.

that we know the level of total income Y. We know that when the money market is in equilibrium, the quantity of money M supplied by the banking system will be equal to the quantity of money demanded M^d by households and businesses:

$$M = M^d$$

And we know the money demand equation

$$\frac{M^d}{P} = M_y Y - M_i i$$

We can solve these two by substituting M for M^d and subtracting $M_y Y$ from both sides:

$$\frac{M}{P} - M_y Y = -M_i i$$

Then we divide by $-M_i$ to solve for i:

$$i = \frac{M_y Y - \left(\dfrac{M}{P}\right)}{M_i}$$

This level of the nominal interest rate i is the equilibrium level of the interest rate. It is the level at which the *money supply* and *money demand curves* cross.

A higher level of total spending and income Y increases the equilibrium interest rate i: With more spending, people find it more urgent to hold wealth in the form of money and are willing to pay a higher opportunity cost to do so. A higher real money stock M/P reduces the equilibrium value of i: With more money in the economy people are happy holding the larger quantity of liquid assets in their portfolios only if the opportunity cost of doing so is lower.

Note that a higher level of M_i — more sensitivity of money demand to the interest rate — means that changes in M/P and in Y would have smaller effects on the equilibrium interest rate i. Note also that a smaller value of M_y — and M_y does tend to shrink over time — also means that changes in Y will have smaller effects on the equilibrium interest rate i.

Adjustment to Equilibrium

Suppose money supply is less than money demand, so that households and businesses want to hold more liquid money balances than exist. Businesses and households sell bonds to boost their cash holdings. The price of bonds falls — and, as is explained in Box 11.2, a fall in the price of bonds is equivalent to a rise in the nominal interest rate. And as the nominal interest rate rises, the quantity of money demanded by households and businesses falls as well: The opportunity cost of holding money has risen.

When the nominal interest rate has risen far enough that the quantity of money demanded has fallen until it equals the money supply, and households and businesses are no longer trying to increase their liquid money balances, there is no more upward pressure on the nominal interest rate.

Now suppose instead that money supply is greater than money demand, so that businesses and households are holding more liquid money balances than they want. They take these extra liquid money balances and buy bonds with them. The price of bonds rises, which means that the nominal interest rate falls. As the nominal interest rate falls, the quantity of money demanded rises because the opportunity cost of holding money has fallen. When the nominal interest rate has fallen enough so that the quantity of money demanded is equal to the money supply, there is no more downward pressure on the nominal interest rate.

BOND PRICES AND INTEREST RATES: DETAILS

Suppose that we have a very long lived bond that pays its holder $1 in interest every year. The interest rate earned by the bondholder depends on the price of the bond. Suppose the price of the bond is $10. Then the bondholder is earning $1 per year on a financial asset whose price is $10, for a rate of return — an interest rate — of 10 percent. Now, what happens if the price of the bond rises? Suppose the price of the bond goes up to $20. Then the rate of return — the interest rate — earned by the bondholder will be just 5 percent, because $1 in interest income is 5 percent of the bond's $20 value. The bond's price is

$$\text{Price of bond} = \frac{1}{i}$$

Thus we see that the nominal interest rate i moves inversely with the price of bonds: The higher the price of bonds, the lower the nominal interest rate; the lower the price of bonds, the higher the nominal interest rate.

> **RECAP**   **THE MONEY MARKET AND THE MONEY STOCK**
>
> Households and businesses want to hold some of their wealth in the form of money: a liquid form in which they can easily spend it. Wealth held in the form of money earns little or no interest, hence the higher the nominal interest rate i, the lower is the demand for money. And the value of holding wealth in readily spendable form depends on the flow of income, hence the higher total income Y, the greater is the demand for money. For given values of the real supply of money M/P and the level of total income Y, supply and demand in the money market produce an equilibrium value of the nominal interest rate i. The higher the real supply of money M/P, the lower is the interest rate i. The higher the flow of total income Y, the higher is the interest rate i.

11.2 THE LM CURVE

Interest Rates and Total Income

We have assumed that the money supply M and the price level P are constant. And we have found that under this assumption the equilibrium nominal interest rate i depends on three other things: the parameter M_y, which tells us how much in the way of money balances households and businesses typically demand per dollar of income (and which is a function of the sophistication of the banking and payments system); the parameter M_i, which tells us how sensitive consumers' and businesses' demand for money is to changes in the interest rate; and the level of total income Y.

This dependence on total income Y means that fully capturing the money market in a single diagram with the quantity of money on the horizontal axis and the nominal interest rate on the vertical axis is impossible. We try to draw such a diagram in Figure 11.2 on page 320, but we find that there is a different curve for real money demand M/P as a function of the nominal interest rate i for each different possible value of income Y. And each of these different curves for each different value of Y generates a different equilibrium nominal interest rate i.

When total income and spending Y rises and the money supply M does not, the nominal interest rate i will rise to keep the money market in equilibrium. With higher incomes, households and businesses want to hold more money. But if the money supply does not increase, then in aggregate their money holdings cannot grow. Households and businesses sell bonds as they try to increase their money holdings — efforts that are futile in the aggregate but successful for individual households and businesses — and these bond sales push down the price of bonds, which is the same thing as pushing up the nominal interest rate i. As the interest rate i rises, the opportunity cost of holding money increases, so money demand M^d falls. The nominal interest rate will rise until the resulting drop in money demand has fully offset the increase in money demand that resulted from the higher income and spending.

Drawing the LM Curve

How are we going to capture these complexities and still manage to draw simple diagrams? Consider placing the nominal interest rate i on the vertical axis and total

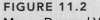

FIGURE 11.2

Money Demand Varies as Total Income Varies

The higher the level of total income Y, the higher the quantity of money demanded for any given interest rate, and (for a fixed money stock) the higher the equilibrium interest rate.

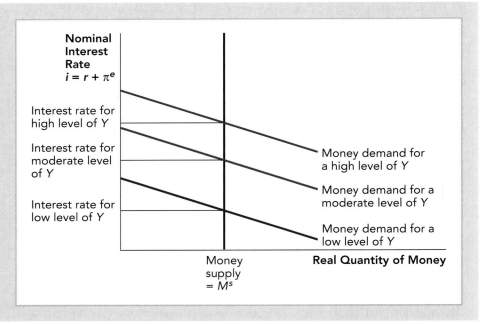

LM curve

The positive relationship between real GDP or total income and the real interest rate that emerges from considering a whole family of money demand–money supply diagrams.

income Y on the horizontal axis. For each possible value of Y on the horizontal axis, plot the point whose vertical axis value is the interest rate that produces equilibrium in the money market. The result is shown in Figure 11.3. This result is called the "LM curve" — the combinations of total income Y and nominal interest rates i that produce money market equilibrium. The LM curve slopes upward: At a higher level of real GDP Y, the equilibrium nominal interest rate is higher.

The equation for the LM curve is one step removed from the money demand function:

$$i = \frac{M_y Y - \left(\dfrac{M}{P}\right)}{M_i}$$

We simply rewrite and transform this equation to put the level of total income Y all by itself on the left side:

$$Y = \frac{\left(\dfrac{M}{P}\right) + M_i i}{M_y}$$

The location of the LM curve depends on the economy's current level of the real money stock M/P. Change M/P, and you change the position of the LM curve. Thus a change in monetary policy that increased the money supply M would shift the LM curve to the right in Figure 11.3: The same equilibrium nominal interest rate i would then correspond to a higher level of total income Y. A shift in monetary policy that decreased the nominal money supply M would shift the LM curve to the left. Similarly, a decline in the price level P would boost the real money supply (M/P), and so shift the LM curve to the right in Figure 11.3. A rise in the

FIGURE 11.3

From Money Demand to the LM Curve The LM curve on the right tells us what the nominal interest rate will be for each value of total income Y.

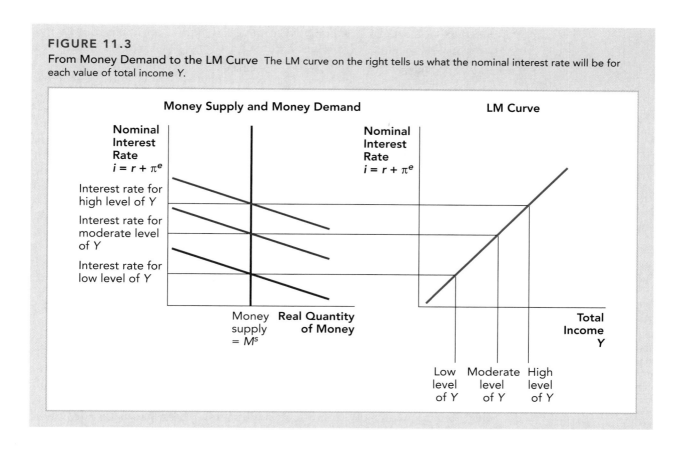

price level *P* would decrease the real money supply (*M/P*) and shift the LM curve to the left.

11.3 THE IS-LM FRAMEWORK

The IS-LM Diagram

If we knew the level of total income *Y*, we could use the LM curve to figure out the nominal interest rate *i*. If we knew the level of the real interest rate *r*, we could use the IS curve from Chapter 10 to figure out the level of real GDP *Y*. The *Y* that is total income in the LM curve is the same as the *Y* that is real GDP in the

IS curve — the circular flow principle guarantees it. But we can't figure out Y without knowing r, and can't figure out r without knowing i, and we can't figure out i without knowing Y.

But we are not at an impasse. The level of total income Y and the nominal interest rate i appear in the LM curve. Total income Y is the same thing as real GDP Y. The nominal interest rate i is equal to the real interest rate r plus the expected inflation rate π^e. The real interest rate r and real GDP Y appear in the IS curve.

Since the nominal interest rate is equal to the real interest rate plus the expected inflation rate, we can plot the IS and LM curves on the same set of axes as long as we know what the expected inflation rate is. And if the inflation rate is and has been constant for some time, we can reasonably assume the expected inflation rate π^e equals the actual inflation rate π. If the inflation rate is 2 percent, then a 3 percent real interest rate is a 5 percent nominal interest rate and a 6 percent real interest rate is an 8 percent nominal interest rate. If the inflation rate is 4 percent, then a 3 percent real interest rate is a 7 percent nominal interest rate and a 6 percent real interest rate is a 10 percent nominal interest rate. As long as we know what the expected inflation rate is, there is no problem with using the vertical axis for both the IS curve's real interest rate r and the LM curve's nominal interest rate i.

Figure 11.4 is called the **IS-LM diagram**. It allows us to figure out what the equilibrium levels of real GDP and of the interest rate are: The equilibrium values are at the point where the IS curve and the LM curve cross. At that level of real GDP and total income Y and the real interest rate r, the economy is in equilibrium in both the goods market and the money market. Planned expenditure is equal to total production, so inventories are stable (that's what the IS curve indicates); and money demand is equal to money supply (that's what the LM curve indicates).

IS-LM diagram

A diagram used to determine what values of the interest rate and of total income together produce equilibrium in the money market — supply of money equal to money demand — and equilibrium in the goods market — planned expenditure equal to real GDP.

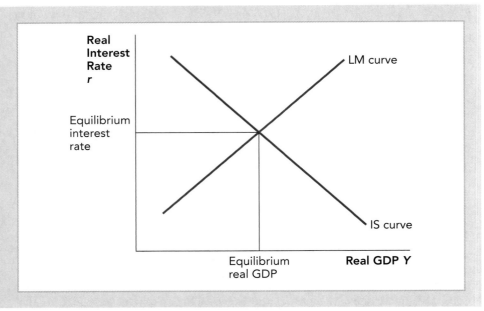

FIGURE 11.4
The IS-LM Diagram
What is the economy's equilibrium? It is the point at which the IS and LM curves cross. Along the IS curve, total production is equal to planned expenditure. Along the LM curve, the quantity of money demanded by households and businesses is equal to the money stock. Where the curves cross, both the goods market and the money market are in balance.

Box 11.3 shows how to calculate the economy's equilibrium position for some specific parameter values of the sticky-price model.

IS Shocks

Any change in economic policy or the economic environment that increases autonomous spending, such as an increase in government purchases, shifts the IS curve to the right. If the money stock is constant, it moves the economy up and to the right along the LM curve on the IS-LM diagram, as Figure 11.6 at the bottom of page 324 shows. The new equilibrium will have both a higher level of real interest rates and a higher equilibrium level of real GDP.

Exactly how the total effect of an expansionary shift in the IS curve is divided between increased interest rates and increased real GDP depends on the slopes of

---

IS-LM EQUILIBRIUM: AN EXAMPLE

BOX 11.3

Suppose that the economy's marginal propensity to expend (MPE) is 0.5, that the initial baseline level of autonomous spending A_0 is $5,000 billion, and that a 1-percentage-point increase in the real interest rate r (an increase, say, from 4 percent to 5 percent — from $r = 0.04$ to $r = 0.05$) will reduce the sum of investment and gross exports by $100 billion. Then, from Chapter 10, the economy's IS curve is (in billions)

$$Y = \frac{A_0}{1 - MPE} - \left(\frac{I_r + X_\varepsilon\varepsilon_r}{1 - MPE}\right)r = \frac{\$5,000}{1 - 0.5} - \left(\frac{\$10,000}{1 - 0.5}\right)r = \$10,000 - \$20,000r$$

Suppose further that the inflation rate π is constant at 3 percent per year — $\pi = \pi^e = 0.03$ — and that the economy's initial LM curve is (in billions)

$$Y = \$1,000 + \$100,000i$$

where i is the economy's nominal interest rate, the sum of the real interest rate r and the expected inflation rate π^e.

The equilibrium point for this economy will be the point at which total income and real GDP Y and the real interest rate r and the nominal interest rate i are at their values where the IS and LM curves cross. Remember that the nominal interest rate i is the real interest rate r plus the expected inflation rate π^e.

$$Y = \$1,000 + \$100,000(r + \pi^e)$$

Set the right-hand sides of the LM and IS curve equations equal to each other:

$$\$1,000 + \$100,000(r + \pi^e) = \$10,000 - \$20,000r$$

Substitute in 0.03 for the expected inflation rate π^e:

$$\$1,000 + \$100,000(r + 0.03) = \$10,000 - \$20,000r$$

And solve for the real interest rate r:

$$\$120,000r = \$6,000$$

$$r = 0.05 = 5\%$$

The equilibrium real interest rate r is 5 percent per year. And from this it is straightforward to solve that real GDP Y is $9,000 billion, as Figure 11.5 shows.

FIGURE 11.5
IS-LM Equilibrium Example

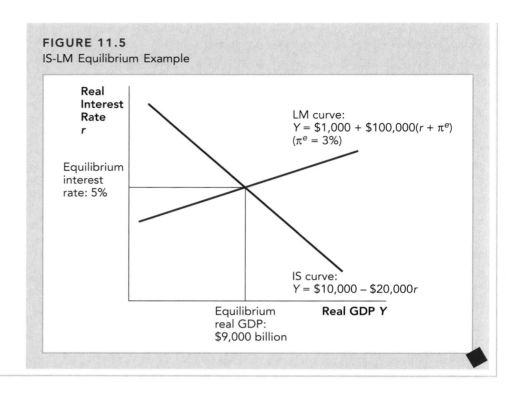

FIGURE 11.6

Effect of a Positive IS Shock

An expansionary shift in the IS curve raises both real GDP Y and the real interest rate r.

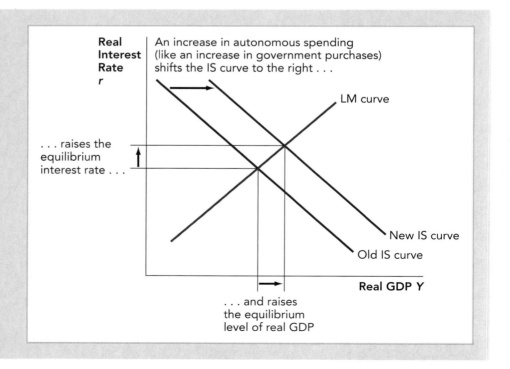

the IS and LM curves. Box 11.4 provides an example of how to calculate exactly what the effects are.

AN INVESTMENT SHOCK IN THE IS-LM MODEL: AN EXAMPLE

Suppose that, as in Box 11.3, the economy's marginal propensity to expend (MPE) is 0.5, that the initial level of baseline autonomous spending A_0 is $5,000 billion, and that a 1-percentage-point increase in the real interest rate r (an increase, say, from 4 percent to 5 percent — from $r = 0.04$ to $r = 0.05$) will reduce the sum of investment and gross exports by $100 billion. Then, as in Box 11.3, the economy's IS curve is (in billions)

$$Y = \frac{A_0}{1 - MPE} - \left(\frac{I_r + X_\varepsilon \varepsilon_r}{1 - MPE}\right) r = \frac{\$5,000}{1 - 0.5} - \left(\frac{\$10,000}{1 - 0.5}\right) r = \$10,000 - \$20,000r$$

And suppose further, as in Box 11.3, that the inflation rate π is constant at 3 percent per year so $\pi = \pi^e = 0.03$, and that the economy's initial LM curve is (in billions)

$$Y = \$1,000 + \$100,000i = \$1,000 + \$100,000 (r + \pi^e)$$

where i is the economy's nominal interest rate, the sum of the real interest rate r and the expected inflation rate π^e.

   Then the initial equilibrium point for this economy is

$$r = 0.05 = 5\% \text{ per year}$$

and

$$Y = \$9,000 \text{ billion}$$

Now suppose there is a positive real shock to demand: Enthusiasm about new technologies leads to an increase in baseline investment I_0 (and thus also in baseline autonomous spending A_0) of $150 billion. What is the economy's new equilibrium?

   The answer is that the IS curve now, because of the increase in baseline autonomous spending, is

$$Y = \frac{A_0 + \Delta I_0}{1 - MPE} - \left(\frac{I_r + X_\varepsilon \varepsilon_r}{1 - MPE}\right) r = \frac{\$5,150}{1 - 0.5} - \left(\frac{\$10,000}{1 - 0.5}\right) r = \$10,300 - \$20,000r$$

The IS curve shifts out and to the right by $300 billion — the value of the increase in autonomous spending $150 billion times the multiplier $1/(1 - MPE)$, which in this economy is equal to 2. The LM curve remains unchanged.

   Set the right-hand sides of the LM and the new IS curve equal to each other:

$$\$1,000 + \$100,000 (r + \pi^e) = \$10,300 - \$20,000r$$

Substitute 0.03 for the expected inflation rate π^e:

$$\$1,000 + \$100,000 (r + 0.03) = \$10,300 - \$20,000r$$

and solve for the real interest rate r:

$$\$120,000r = \$6,300$$

$$r = 0.0525 = 5.25\%$$

The equilibrium real interest rate r is 5.25 percent per year. And from this it is straightforward to solve that real GDP Y is $9,250 billion, as Figure 11.7 shows.

Although the IS curve has shifted outward by $300 billion, real GDP has risen by only $250 billion. Why? Higher income has increased the demand for money. Stronger demand for money has pushed the real interest rate r up to 5.25 percent per year (and has pushed the nominal interest rate i up to 8.25 percent per year). And the increase in interest rates has had a depressing effect on investment, which has crowded out some $50 billion of real GDP that would have been present had interest rates remained unchanged. Figure 11.7 shows how these curves shift.

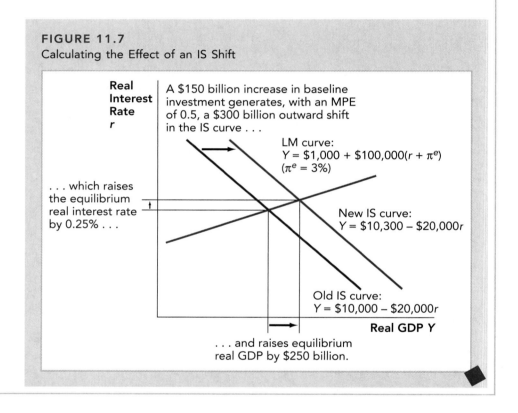

FIGURE 11.7
Calculating the Effect of an IS Shift

A $150 billion increase in baseline investment generates, with an MPE of 0.5, a $300 billion outward shift in the IS curve . . .

LM curve:
$Y = \$1{,}000 + \$100{,}000(r + \pi^e)$
$(\pi^e = 3\%)$

. . . which raises the equilibrium real interest rate by 0.25% . . .

New IS curve:
$Y = \$10{,}300 - \$20{,}000r$

Old IS curve:
$Y = \$10{,}000 - \$20{,}000r$

Real GDP Y

Real Interest Rate r

. . . and raises equilibrium real GDP by $250 billion.

If the LM curve is nearly horizontal, interest rates will show little increase. The increase in equilibrium real GDP will be nearly the same magnitude as the outward shift in the IS curve. If the LM curve is very steeply sloped, there will be a big effect on interest rates and little effect on real GDP. The LM curve will be steeply sloped when M_i is very small — when, that is, demand for money is extremely interest-inelastic. When M_i is small, a large change in interest rates is needed to cause a small change in households' and businesses' desired holdings of money. The LM curve will also be steeply sloped when M_y is large — when, that is, demand for money is extremely income-elastic. Here again, only a large change in interest rates will offset the effects of a small change in income.

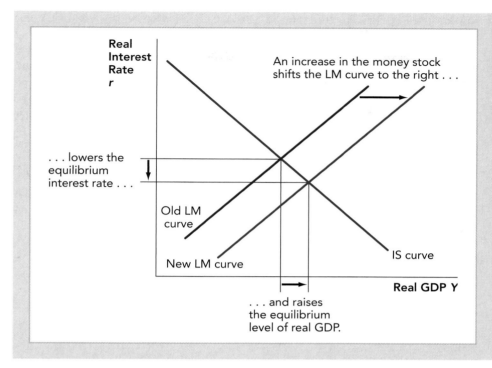

FIGURE 11.8

Effect of an Expansionary LM Shock

An expansionary shift in the LM curve raises real GDP Y and lowers the equilibrium interest rate r.

LM Shocks

An increase in the nominal money stock M will shift the LM curve to the right. The larger money supply means that any given level of real GDP will be associated with a lower equilibrium nominal interest rate. Such an expansionary LM shift will shift the equilibrium position of the economy down and to the right along the IS curve, as Figure 11.8 shows. The new equilibrium position will have a higher level of equilibrium real GDP and a lower interest rate. Box 11.5 provides an illustrative example of such an expansionary LM shift.

CALCULATING THE EFFECTS OF AN LM SHOCK: AN EXAMPLE

Suppose that, as in Boxes 11.3 and 11.4, the economy's IS curve is

$$Y = \frac{A_0}{1 - MPE} - \left(\frac{I_r + X_\varepsilon \varepsilon_r}{1 - MPE}\right)r = \frac{\$5,000}{1 - 0.5} - \left(\frac{\$10,000}{1 - 0.5}\right)r = \$10,000 - \$20,000r$$

that the inflation rate π is constant at 3 percent per year — $\pi = \pi^e = 0.03$ — and that the economy's initial LM curve is (in billions)

$$Y = \$1,000 + \$100,000i$$

where i is the economy's nominal interest rate, the sum of the real interest rate r and the expected inflation rate π^e.

Now suppose that the central bank buys bonds for cash, expanding the economy's money supply, and shifting the LM curve to

$$Y = \$2,200 + \$100,000i$$

shifting the LM curve to the right by $1,200 billion. What will be the new equilibrium for the economy?

Substitute the sum of the real interest rate r and the expected inflation rate π^e for the nominal interest rate i in the LM curve equation, and set the right-hand sides of the LM and IS equations equal to each other:

$$\$2,200 + \$100,000(r + \pi^e) = \$10,000 - \$20,000r$$

Substitute in 0.03 for the expected inflation rate π^e, and solve for r:

$$\$120,000r = \$4,800$$

$$r = 0.04 = 4\% \text{ per year}$$

The real interest rate falls to 4 percent per year (and, with constant expected inflation, the nominal interest rate falls to 7 percent per year). We can then use the IS curve to calculate that total income and output must be

$$Y = \$9,200 \text{ billion}$$

The expansionary monetary policy has succeeded in raising output and incomes. Figure 11.9 shows, graphically, how the LM curve shifts in this example.

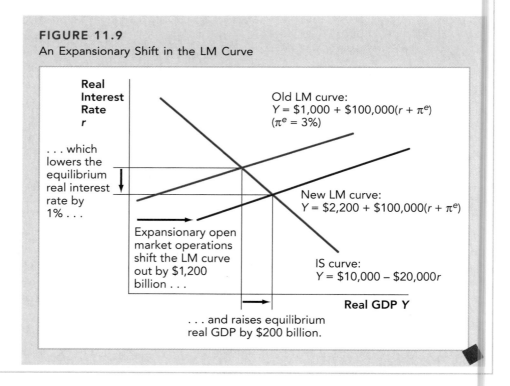

FIGURE 11.9
An Expansionary Shift in the LM Curve

Conversely, a decrease in the money supply or any other contractionary LM shock that shifts the LM curve in and to the left will shift the economy up and to the left along the IS curve, resulting in higher equilibrium interest rates and a lower equilibrium value of real GDP.

Note the difference between how the money market works in this sticky-price model and in the flexible-price model presented in Part 3. In the flexible-price model, the real interest rate balanced the supply and demand for loanable funds flowing through the financial markets. Changes in the money stock had no effect on either the real interest rate or real GDP. Instead, the price level adjusted upward or downward to keep the quantity of money demanded equal to the money supply.

Here in the sticky-price model the price level is . . . sticky. It cannot adjust instantly upward or downward. So an imbalance in money demand and money supply does not cause an immediate change in the price level. Instead, it causes an immediate change in the nominal interest rate.

Classifying Economic Disturbances

The IS-LM framework allows economists to classify shifts in the economic environment and changes in economic policy into four basic categories, two that affect the LM curve and two that affect the IS curve. A surprisingly large number of economic disturbances can be fitted into the IS-LM framework.

Changes That Affect the LM Curve

The LM curve is a relationship between the short-run nominal interest rate i and the level of total income and real GDP Y at a given, fixed level of the real money supply for given, fixed parameters of the money demand function. This means, first, that any change in the nominal money stock or in the price level will shift the LM curve. Second, any change in the parameters of the money demand function — in how sensitive money demand is to changes in the nominal interest rate i or in total income Y — will shift the LM curve.

Moreover, the IS-LM diagram is drawn with the real interest rate — the long-term, risky, real interest rate — on the vertical axis. This has important consequences. As long as the spread between the short-term, safe, nominal interest rate i in the LM equation and the long-term, risky, real interest rate r in the IS equation is constant, the LM curve can be drawn on the same diagram as the IS curve with no complications. But what if the expected rate of inflation π^e, the risk premium, or the term premium between short- and long-term interest rates changes? Then the position of the LM curve on the IS-LM diagram shifts either upward (if expected inflation falls, or if the risk premium rises, or if the term premium rises) or downward (if expected inflation rises, or if the risk premium falls, or if the term premium falls). Figure 11.10 on page 330 illustrates what happens to the position of the LM curve if the expected inflation rate rises.

Thus changes in financial market expectations of future Federal Reserve policy or of future inflation rates or simply changes in the risk tolerance of bond traders shift the LM curve. The IS-LM equilibrium is affected not only by disturbances in the money market but by broader shifts in the financial markets that alter the relationship between the nominal interest rates on short-term safe bonds and the real interest rate paid by corporations undertaking long-term risky investments.

Changes That Affect the IS Curve

Shifts in the IS curve are probably more frequent than shifts in the LM curve, for more types of changes in the economic environment and economic policy affect planned expenditure than affect the supply and demand for money. Any change in the sensitivity of investment to the real interest rate changes the slope of the IS curve.

FIGURE 11.10

An Increase in Expected Inflation Moves the LM Curve Downward

The fact that the interest rate relevant to the IS curve is a real rate and the interest rate relevant to the LM curve is a nominal rate is a source of complications: A rise in expected inflation lowers the real interest rate that corresponds to any given nominal interest rate, and so shifts the LM curve down on the IS-LM diagram.

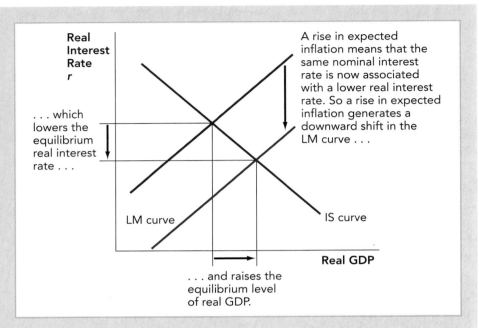

A rise in expected inflation means that the same nominal interest rate is now associated with a lower real interest rate. So a rise in expected inflation generates a downward shift in the LM curve . . .

. . . which lowers the equilibrium real interest rate . . .

LM curve

IS curve

Real GDP

. . . and raises the equilibrium level of real GDP.

So will any change in either the sensitivity of exports to the exchange rate or the sensitivity of the level of the exchange rate to the level of domestic interest rates.

Furthermore, anything that affects the marginal propensity to spend — the MPE — will change the slope of the IS curve and the position of the IS curve as well. Any shift in the marginal propensity to consume C_y will change the MPE. Thus if households decide that income changes are more likely to be permanent (raising the marginal propensity to consume) or more likely to be transitory (lowering the marginal propensity to consume), that will raise or lower the MPE. Changes in tax rates have a direct effect on the MPE. So do changes in the propensity to import. Thus, for example, the imposition (or removal) of a tariff on imports to discourage (or encourage) imports will affect the position and slope of the IS curve.

Finally, changes in the economic environment and in economic policy that shift the level of baseline autonomous spending shift the IS curve. Anything that affects the baseline level of consumption C_0 affects autonomous spending — whether it is a change in demography that changes desired saving behavior, a change in optimism about future levels of income, or any other cause of a shift in consumer behavior. Anything that affects the baseline level of investment I_0 affects autonomous spending — whether it is a wave of innovation that increases expected future profits and desired investment, a wave of irrational overoptimism or overpessimism, a change in tax policy that affects not the level of revenue collected but the incentives to invest, or any other cause. Changes in government purchases affect autonomous spending.

In sum, almost anything can affect the equilibrium level of planned expenditure on the IS-LM diagram. Pretty much everything does affect it at one time or another. One of the principal merits of the IS-LM diagram is its use in sorting and classifying the determinants of equilibrium output and interest rates.

THE IS-LM FRAMEWORK

For a constant value of inflation π and thus of the expected inflation rate π^e, we can think of the LM curve as a relationship between real GDP Y and the real interest rate r, and we can draw it on the same axes as the IS curve to make the IS-LM diagram. The IS-LM diagram shows us how to analyze any of a huge number of shocks to the economy when the central bank sets the money supply. In general, shocks to the IS curve cause real GDP Y and interest rates r to move in the same direction, whereas shocks to the LM curve cause real GDP Y and interest rates r to move in opposite directions.

11.4 AGGREGATE DEMAND AND AGGREGATE SUPPLY

The Price Level and Aggregate Demand

What happens to real GDP as the price level rises? If the nominal money supply is fixed, then an increase in the price level reduces real money balances and shifts the LM curve to the left. The equilibrium real interest rate rises, and the equilibrium level of real GDP falls, as the top panel of Figure 11.11 shows.

Suppose we draw a second diagram, this time with the price level on the vertical axis and the level of real GDP on the horizontal axis. We use this second diagram to plot what the equilibrium level of real GDP is for each possible value of the price level. For each value of the price level, we calculate the LM curve and use the IS-LM diagram to calculate the equilibrium level of real GDP. As the bottom panel of Figure 11.11 shows, we find — if the nominal money supply is fixed — a downward-sloping relationship between the price level and real GDP. With the nominal money stock held fixed, a rise in the price level decreases the real money stock and shifts the LM curve to the left because the position of the LM curve depends on the value of the real money stock.

A leftward shift in the LM curve reduces the equilibrium level of real GDP and increases the interest rate. The lower the price level, the higher real money balances are, the lower the interest rate is, the higher aggregate demand is, and the higher the equilibrium level of real GDP is. Economists call this curve — according to which a lower price level means higher aggregate demand — the **aggregate demand (AD) curve.**

The Price Level and Aggregate Supply

Inflation is an increase in the general, overall price level. An increase in the price of any one particular good — even a large increase in the price of any one particular good — is not inflation. Inflation, then, is an increase in the price of just about everything. Together, the prices of all or nearly all goods and incomes rise by approximately the same proportional amount.

Note — and this is important — that in the sticky-price model prices are sticky, not stuck. They do move over time. They just don't move fast enough to get us to the flexible-price model situation of Chapters 6–8 immediately. (See Box 11.6 on page 333.) Up until this point, paying little or no attention to the fact that prices are not stuck fast in the sticky-price model has been convenient. But from this point on, we

aggregate demand (AD) curve

A downward-sloping relationship between planned expenditure and the price level, produced because a higher price level means a lower real money stock, higher real interest rates, lower investment spending, and lower planned expenditure.

manufacturers will pay any price for brake assemblies if they are in short supply. Such high prices signal to the market that the bottleneck industry should expand and trigger investment that in the end boosts productive capacity. But developing bottlenecks lead to prices that increase faster than expected, thus to accelerating inflation and a higher price level.

Note that here it is not important to distinguish between inflation and the price level. Inflation is, after all, the proportional change between last year's price level and this year's price level. Thus a high price level relative to what was previously expected is a high inflation rate (relative to what was previously expected), and vice versa. When we draw aggregate supply curves on graphs, we won't care too much about whether what is on the vertical axis of the graph is the price level or the inflation rate: They move together.

Note also that expectations play a key role. What calls forth higher (or lower) production is that prices and inflation are higher (or lower) than people had been expecting.

The AS-AD Diagram

We combine the aggregate supply curve with the aggregate demand curve by drawing them both on the same set of axes — the **AS-AD diagram**. Now we can see not just the equilibrium level of real GDP but also the equilibrium price level (and inflation rate), as shown in Figure 11.12. The AS curve slopes upward because an unexpectedly high price level — a relatively high inflation rate between last year and this year — calls forth the more intensive use of resources and thus a higher level of production. A higher price level reduces the real money stock (if the nominal money supply is constant) and thus increases interest rates. Where aggregate supply and aggregate demand are equal — where the two curves cross — is the current level of real GDP and the price level (and inflation rate).

Now for the first time we have an integrated story of business-cycle fluctuations not just in production but in the overall level of prices as well. Suppose the

FIGURE 11.12
Aggregate Supply and Aggregate Demand

Where aggregate supply equals aggregate demand determines not just real GDP but also the price level and the inflation rate.

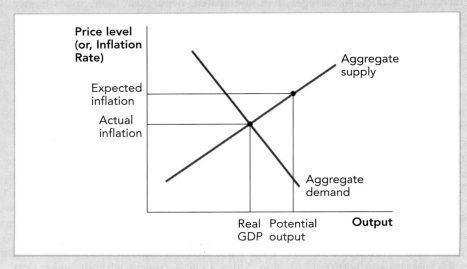

A SHOCK TO AGGREGATE DEMAND: DETAILS

In late 1987, newly inaugurated Federal Reserve Chair Alan Greenspan and the rest of the Board of Governors, Federal Reserve Bank presidents, and staff of the Federal Reserve system faced a dilemma. The stock market had just crashed. Did this mean that investors were getting discouraged — that their baseline level of investment spending I_0 was about to fall and that recession was on the way? They weren't sure, but they did not want to take the chance. Late 1988 and 1989 saw low interest rates and expansionary monetary policy to try to keep production from declining.

The policies were successful. Real GDP rose by a healthy 4.1 percent in 1988 and 3.5 percent in 1989. But inflation, which had been under 4 percent between 1983 and 1987, began to rise. Between December 1989 and December 1990 consumer prices rose by 6.1 percent.

The best way to understand this uses the AS-AD diagram. (See Figure 11.13.) The Federal Reserve's late 1987 resort to expansionary monetary policy shifted the AD curve up and to the right. Production rose, and prices and inflation rates rose too as higher-than-expected demand produced higher-than-anticipated price levels and inflation rates.

The Federal Reserve thus guarded against the possibility of a recession in 1988 and 1989, but at the price of stirring up a different kind of macroeconomic trouble for the future.

FIGURE 11.13

Using the AS-AD Diagram The late 1980s shift to more expansionary monetary policy brought higher output, but also higher prices and inflation as expanding demand pushed the economy up and to the right along the AS curve.

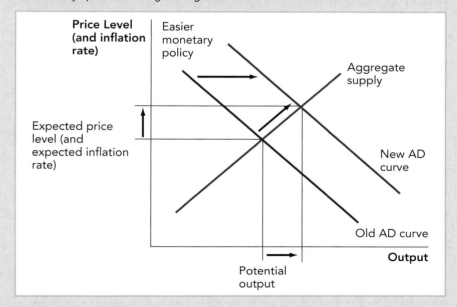

government enacts a tax cut — something that shifts the IS curve out to the right and shifts the point of intersection of the IS and LM curves up and to the right, producing higher equilibrium values of real GDP and interest rates for each possible value of the price level. In the AS-AD framework, such a tax cut shifts the AD curve out and to the right as well. The result in the AS-AD framework sees output expand — real GDP rise — and the price level rise as well.

The AS-AD framework allows us to see why the rapid oil price rises of the 1970s caused recessions. The oil price shocks shifted the AS curve upward, and so moved the economy's AS-AD equilibrium up and to the left: a lower value of real GDP accompanied by a higher price level, which in the 1970s was called *"stagflation."*

RECAP   AGGREGATE DEMAND AND AGGREGATE SUPPLY

As the price level rises, the real value of a fixed money stock falls, interest rates rise, and so planned expenditure falls; the aggregate demand curve slopes downward. As the amount of output produced rises relative to potential, prices and inflation rise above their anticipated levels; the aggregate supply curve slopes upward. Combining the AD and AS curves gives us the AS-AD diagram. For an economy with a fixed money stock, the AS-AD diagram is useful for analyzing the effects on the aggregate price level and output of changes in monetary policy, changes in fiscal policy, and supply shocks such as the 1970s rise of oil prices.

Chapter Summary

1. The money market is in equilibrium when the level of total income and of the short-term nominal interest rate makes households and businesses want to hold all the real money balances that exist in the economy.

2. When the central bank's policy keeps the money stock fixed — or when there is no central bank — the LM curve consists of those combinations of interest rates and real GDP levels at which money demand equals money supply.

3. When the central bank's policy keeps the money stock fixed — or when there is no central bank — the point at which the IS and LM curves cross determines the equilibrium level of real GDP and the real interest rate r.

4. The IS-LM framework consists of two equilibrium conditions: The IS curve shows those combinations of interest rates and real GDP levels at which planned expenditure is equal to total production; the LM curve shows those combinations of interest rates and real GDP levels at which money demand is equal to money supply. Both equilibrium conditions must be satisfied.

5. An IS shock is any shock to the level of total spending as a function of the domestic real interest rate. An IS shock

shifts the position of the IS curve. An expansionary IS shock raises real GDP and the real interest rate.

6. An LM shock is a shock to money demand or money supply. An LM shock shifts the position of the LM curve. An expansionary LM shock raises real GDP and lowers the interest rate.

7. The aggregate demand relationship arises because changes in the price level and inflation rate cause shifts in the level of planned expenditure as changes in the price level change the real money stock and thus interest rates.

8. The aggregate supply curve captures the relationship between aggregate supply and the price level. The higher real GDP, the higher the price level and the inflation rate are likely to be and vice versa: The higher the price level and the inflation rate, the higher real GDP is likely to be.

9. Together the aggregate supply and aggregate demand curves make up the AS-AD framework, which allows us to analyze the impact of changes in economic policy and the economic environment not just on real GDP but also on the price level and the inflation rate.

Key Terms

money demand (p. 315)

real money balances (p. 315)

money market equilibrium (p. 316)

LM curve (p. 320)

IS-LM diagram (p. 322)

aggregate demand (AD) curve (p. 331)

aggregate supply (AS) curve (p. 332)

AS-AD diagram (p. 334)

Analytical Exercises

1. What are the qualitative effects, in the IS-LM model, of each of the following changes?
   a. An increase in firms' optimism about future profits.
   b. A sudden improvement in banking technology that makes checks clear two days faster.
   c. A wave of credit card fraud that leads people to use cash for purchases more often.
   d. A banking crisis that diminishes banks' willingness to accept deposits.
   e. A sudden increase in military spending.

2. What are the qualitative effects of an increase in real GDP on the rate of inflation?

3. Suppose that the expected rate of inflation suddenly jumped. What would happen — with no other changes in the economic environment — to the IS-LM equilibrium? Would equilibrium real GDP go up or down? Would the equilibrium real interest rate go up or down?

4. Suppose that the *term premium* — the gap between short-term and long-term interest rates — suddenly went up. With no other changes in the economic environment, what would happen to the IS-LM equilibrium? Would equilibrium real GDP go up or down? Would the equilibrium real interest rate in the IS curve go up or down?

5. In what directions would you advise a government to change its fiscal and monetary policies if it wanted to make sure that net exports were positive — that it was running a trade surplus?

Policy Exercises

1. Between 1980 and 1986 U.S. net exports shifted from +$10 billion (in 1992 dollars) to −$164 billion. The unemployment rates in 1980 and 1986 were almost identical. Almost all observers agreed that this shift in the trade deficit was driven by shifts in the U.S. domestic condition. Which of the following do you think happened between 1980 and 1986? Why?
   a. The LM curve shifted right and the IS curve shifted right.
   b. The LM curve shifted right and the IS curve shifted left.
   c. The LM curve shifted left and the IS curve shifted right.
   d. The LM curve shifted left and the IS curve shifted left.

2. Rank each of the following pairs by which is likely to have large, medium, or small positive or negative effects on equilibrium output:
   a. A substantial increase in the money stock when demand for money is interest-inelastic versus a substantial increase in the money stock when demand for money is very interest-elastic.
   b. A jump in business willingness to invest when the LM curve is steep versus a jump in business willingness to invest when the LM curve is flat.
   c. A sudden cutback in consumer spending when investment and exports vary little with changes in the interest rate versus a sudden cutback in consumer spending when investment and exports vary a lot with changes in the interest rate.
   d. A sudden increase in the velocity of money when investment is responsive to the interest rate versus a sudden increase in the velocity of money when investment is unresponsive to the interest rate.
   e. A jump in businesses' willingness to invest when money demand does not depend on the interest rate versus a jump in businesses' willingness to invest when the LM curve is flat.
   f. A boost to government spending when the IS curve is flat versus a boost to government spending when the IS curve is steep.

3. Suppose that money demand is interest-insensitive. That is, suppose that the money demand function is

$$\frac{M^d}{P} = M_y Y - M_i i$$

with M_i equal to 0 so that there is no dependence on the interest rate at all. What, then, is the LM curve for this economy? What effect does an increase in government purchases have on the level of real interest rates and the equilibrium level of annual real GDP?

4. Suppose that the economy's LM curve is given by the equation

$$Y = \$1,000 + \$100,000(r + \pi^e)$$

and that the expected inflation rate π^e is constant at 3 percent per year. Suppose further that the economy's marginal propensity to expend (MPE) is 0.6, that the marginal propensity to import IM_y is 0.25, that the initial level of baseline autonomous spending A_0 is \$5,000 billion, that a 1-percentage-point increase in the real interest rate reduces investment spending by \$40 billion and reduces the value of the exchange rate by 10 percent, and that each 1 percent increase in the exchange rate increases net exports by \$6 billion.

What is the effect on the domestic economy's equilibrium of a sudden 30 percent increase in the exchange rate as foreign exchange speculators lose confidence in the economy?

12

The Phillips Curve, Expectations, and Monetary Policy

QUESTIONS

What can shift the Phillips curve?

What is the Monetary Policy Reaction Function? What determines its slope?

What is the natural rate of unemployment? How has its value changed?

What are static expectations of inflation? Adaptive? Rational?

How has the expected rate of inflation changed?

How do we use the Phillips curve, the Monetary Policy Reaction Function, and the way in which expectations of inflation are determined to analyze the economy?

How do we connect the sticky-price model of Part 4 with the flexible-price model of Part 3?

This is the most important chapter in the book. It draws together the flexible-price business cycle model of Part 3 and the sticky-price business cycle model of Part 4. It provides a bird's-eye overview of demand, monetary policy, and inflation. Chapter 9 analyzed demand and the multiplier. Chapter 10 added interest rates and their effect on investment and exports. In this chapter we build on those two and add unemployment, inflation, and monetary policy — how the Federal Reserve makes its decisions.

When you finish this chapter, you will have a comprehensive view of how business cycles and demand management work. The Federal Reserve responds to unemployment and inflation by choosing a monetary policy that aims at *price stability* and full employment with the first goal taking priority. That monetary policy then — through the mechanisms of Chapter 10 — determines investment and exports and — through the mechanisms of Chapter 9 — the level of production. The level of production relative to potential output itself feeds back and generates unexpected rises and declines in inflation relative to what was previously anticipated.

But that is not all this chapter does. It also analyzes expectations — how the previous anticipations of prices and inflation are formed. Expectations are key, for they provide the linkage between the sticky-price model of Part 4 and the flexible-price model of Part 3.

That is how this chapter accomplishes its two major goals: to complete the construction of the sticky-price model begun in Chapter 9 and to link the sticky-price macroeconomic model analysis of Part 4 with the flexible-price macroeconomic model analysis of Part 3. The key to accomplishing both of these is an analytical tool called the Phillips curve. The Phillips curve describes the relationship between inflation and unemployment, according to which a higher rate of unemployment is associated with a lower rate of inflation.

The plan of this chapter is to first examine aggregate supply and the Phillips curve: Why is there — in the short run of our sticky-price model — a positive relationship between production Y on the one hand and the price level P and the inflation rate π on the other (and thus also a negative relationship between unemployment and inflation)? This leads into an analysis of how the existence of the aggregate supply relationship and the Phillips curve affects modern central banks' conduct of monetary policy and the important concept of the Monetary Policy Reaction Function. Then it is time to put all the pieces together by bringing into the picture the key elements of the determinants of the natural rate of unemployment and the three kinds of expectations — static, adaptive, and rational — that play an overwhelmingly important role in determining how modern economies behave.

12.1 AGGREGATE SUPPLY AND THE PHILLIPS CURVE

Unemployment

So far in this book one of our six key economic variables, the unemployment rate, has been largely absent. In Part 2, the long-run growth section, unemployment was not a significant factor. In Part 3, the flexible-price macroeconomic model section, there were no fluctuations in unemployment. Wages and prices were flexible, and so labor supply balanced labor demand.

Now it is time to bring unemployment to center stage. Back in Chapter 2 we showed that there is generally an inverse relationship between the unemployment rate u and the **output gap** — the level of real GDP relative to potential output Y^*. This relationship is called **Okun's law** (see Box 12.1). Because of Okun's law, we do not have to conduct separate analyses of real GDP and unemployment: We know that when one is high the other is low, and vice versa.

When output Y is equal to potential output Y^*, then the unemployment rate is equal to what Milton Friedman in 1966 was among the first to call the **natural rate of unemployment** — let's call it u^* — and the labor market is putting neither upward nor downward pressure on the rate of inflation. When output Y is above potential output Y^*, the unemployment rate u is below the natural rate of unemployment u^* and there is upward pressure on the rate of inflation. When output Y is below potential output Y^*, the unemployment rate u is above u^* and there is typically downward pressure on the rate of inflation.

In this chapter we spend most of our time analyzing the behavior of the unemployment rate. The unemployment rate is of special interest because a high unemployment rate means low social welfare (see Box 12.2). But with only one additional step we could turn that analysis into an analysis of the output gap — of real GDP relative to potential output.

output gap

The difference between the actual and potential levels of output, $Y - Y^*$.

Okun's law

Periods of low (or high) national production relative to potential output correspond to periods of high (or low) unemployment relative to the natural rate.

natural rate of unemployment

The rate of unemployment where actual and expected inflation are equal, and there is no downward or upward pressure on inflation.

FORMS OF OKUN'S LAW: DETAILS

Okun's law relates the unemployment rate u (relative to the natural rate of unemployment u^*) to real GDP Y (relative to potential output Y^*). When Y is equal to Y^*, then the unemployment rate u is equal to the natural rate of unemployment u^*. When real GDP Y is different from Y^*, the unemployment rate u will be different from the natural rate of unemployment u^* by an amount described by the equation

$$u - u^* = -0.4\left(\frac{Y - Y^*}{Y^*}\right)$$

When real GDP is above potential output, unemployment will be below the natural rate of unemployment. When real GDP is below potential output, unemployment will be above the natural rate. And the percentage-point gap between unemployment and its natural rate is two-fifths the magnitude of the percentage gap between real GDP and potential output. For example, if real GDP is 10 percent below potential output $[(Y - Y^*)/Y^* = -0.10]$, then the unemployment rate will be 4 percentage points above the natural rate of unemployment: If the natural rate of unemployment u^* is 5 percent ($u^* = 0.05$), then the unemployment rate u will be 9 percent $[u = 0.05 - 0.4(-0.10) = 0.09]$.

Since 2000 the quantitative form of Okun's law has shifted. Between 2000 and 2004, a 1-percentage-point gap between real GDP and potential output generated a much smaller gap between unemployment and the natural rate of unemployment than we had seen in previous decades. We are not yet sure whether Okun's law will return to its old pattern, or, if it does not, whether the new quantitative relationship between unemployment and the output gap will remain at its 2000–2004 level. Many economists think that the relatively stagnant employment levels seen between 2000 and 2004 have led a great many people who would seek jobs in normal times to drop out of the labor force, and so artificially and temporarily lowered the unemployment rate. If they are right, then Okun's law will once again return to its traditional level soon, with a 1-percentage-point gap between output and potential output corresponding to a 0.4-percentage-point gap between the unemployment rate and the natural rate of unemployment.

But whatever happens with the quantitative relationship, we are still sure about the qualitative relationship: Higher real GDP Y (relative to potential output Y^*) means lower unemployment u (relative to the natural rate u^*) and vice versa.

COSTS OF HIGH UNEMPLOYMENT: POLICY

In a typical U.S. recession, unemployment rises by 2 percentage points. By Okun's law, that means that the output gap — real GDP relative to potential output — falls by some 5 percent. Five percent is about four years' worth of growth in output per worker. Moreover, recessions are not permanent; with rare exceptions, they are over in a year or two and are followed by periods of rapid growth that return real GDP to its prerecession growth trend. Even the steepest post–World War II recession raised the unemployment rate by only 4 percentage points, and it took only three years after the recession trough for unemployment to fall back to a normal level.

These considerations make it somewhat of a puzzle that people fear recessions so much. People fear a deep recession much more than they appear to value an extra four years' worth of economic growth. For example, the memory of the 1982 recession substantially altered Americans' perceptions of how the economy works, how much they dare risk in the search for higher wages, and how confident they can be that their jobs are secure.

Why do episodes of recession and high unemployment have such a large psychological impact? The most likely answer is that recessions are feared because their impact is not distributed equally. Workers who keep their jobs are only lightly affected, whereas those who lose their jobs suffer a near-total loss of income. People fear a 2 percent chance of losing *half* of their income much more than they fear a *certain* loss of just 1 percent of income. So it is much worse for 2 percent of the people to each lose half of their income than for everyone to lose 1 percent. Thus the unequal distribution of the costs of recessions is what makes them so feared — and makes voters so anxious to elect economic policy makers who will successfully avoid them.

Aggregate Supply

sticky prices

When wages and prices do not move smoothly and immediately to keep supply equal to demand in the labor and goods markets.

In our **sticky-price** model prices are sticky, not stuck. (Forget the difference? See Box 11.6 for an example.) They do move over time. They just don't move fast enough to get us to the flexible-price situation of Chapters 6–8 immediately. Up until now we have paid next to no attention to the fact that prices are not stuck fast in the sticky-price model. But now this will change as we start to analyze what the price level P and the inflation rate π are in our sticky-price model.

In the short run, we find that whenever real GDP Y is higher than potential output Y^*, the inflation rate π and the price level P are likely to be higher than people had previously anticipated. There are many reasons for this. One is that whenever demand for products is stronger than anticipated, firms raise their prices higher than they had previously planned. When planned expenditure is higher than potential output, demand is strong in nearly every industry. Nearly all firms raise prices and hire more workers. High demand gives workers extra bargaining power. Unions threaten to strike, knowing that firms will have a hard time finding replacement workers. Individuals quit, knowing they can find better jobs elsewhere. Such a high-pressure economy generates wages that rise faster than anticipated. Rapid wage growth is passed along to consumers in higher prices and accelerating inflation. Thus high real GDP Y relative to potential output Y^* generates a higher price level P and a higher inflation rate π than people had previously expected.

A second reason is that when planned expenditure is higher than potential output, individual economic sectors and industries in the economy quickly reach the limits of capacity: Bottlenecks emerge. Since a building cannot be built without cement, construction companies will pay nearly any price for cement if it is in short supply. Such high prices signal to the market that the bottleneck industry should expand and eventually trigger investment that in the end boosts productive capacity. But in the meantime, developing bottlenecks lead to prices that increase faster than expected, thus to accelerating inflation and a higher price level.

Note that expectations play a key role. What calls forth higher (or lower) production in the bottleneck industries is that prices and inflation turn out to be higher (or lower) than people had been counting on because demand is so high. It's not high prices but higher-than-expected prices and inflation that are associated with high output. Economists call this correlation between real GDP Y (relative to potential output Y^*) and the price level P and the rate of inflation π (relative to their previously expected values) the short-run Aggregate Supply (AS) curve.

Note also that there is little reason to distinguish between inflation and the price level. Inflation is the change between last year's and this year's price level. A high price level relative to what was previously expected is a high inflation rate (relative to what was previously expected), and vice versa. So we can think of Aggregate Supply as an upward-sloping positive relationship between the price *level* P (relative to the previously expected price level) and the *level* of real GDP Y (relative to potential output). Or we can think of it as an upward-sloping positive relationship between the inflation *rate* π (relative to the previously expected inflation rate) and the *level* of real GDP Y (relative to potential output). Or we can think of it in yet a third way, using Okun's law. Because high real GDP Y means low unemployment u, we can think of aggregate supply as a relationship between the inflation rate π (relative to the value that people had previously expected inflation to be π^e) and the unemployment rate u (relative to the natural rate u^*).

This third form of the relationship is the modern **Phillips curve:**

$$\pi = \pi^e - \beta(u - u^*)$$

where we once again use π^e to stand for previously **expected inflation**, with the e reminding us that it is an expectation. This equation tells us that inflation π is higher than it was previously expected to be when unemployment u is lower than its natural rate u^*. By how much? That depends on the parameter β, the slope of this relationship. And it is this relationship that is called the Phillips curve, after the New Zealand economist A. W. Phillips, who first wrote back in the 1950s of the relationship between unemployment and the rate of change of prices.

Phillips curve

The downward-sloping relationship between unemployment and inflation: The higher expected inflation, the higher the unemployment rate needed to keep inflation at any particular level.

expected inflation

The rate at which the inflation rate was expected to increase. Today's expected inflation rate is yesterday's guess about today's inflation rate.

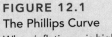

FIGURE 12.1
The Phillips Curve
When inflation π is higher than expected inflation and production is higher than potential output, the unemployment rate u will be lower than the natural rate of unemployment. There is an inverse relationship in the short run between inflation and unemployment.

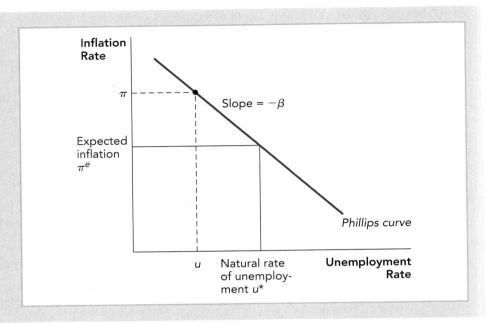

Since Phillips's time, economic events have led economists to change the Phillips curve slightly to take account of shocks that can affect the inflation rate. So we add an extra term to the Phillips curve:

$$\pi = \pi^e - \beta(u - u^*) + ss$$

where ss stands for large sudden *"supply shocks"* — like the 1973 oil price increase — that can affect the rate of inflation by changing prices directly, without first changing the unemployment rate and so putting pressure on wage levels.

Figure 12.1 sketches the Phillips curve on a graph with the unemployment rate on the horizontal axis and the inflation rate on the vertical axis. Figure 12.2 shows the Phillips curve along with the other two possible ways of thinking about aggregate supply. The underlying economic meaning is the same no matter which form — real GDP–price level, real GDP–inflation, or unemployment–inflation — you use. From this point on, however, we will always use the unemployment–inflation Phillips curve form simply for convenience.

The Phillips Curve Examined

The slope of the Phillips curve depends on how sticky wages and prices are. The stickier are wages and prices, the smaller is the parameter β and the flatter is the Phillips curve. The parameter β varies widely from country to country and era to era. In the United States today it is about 0.5. When the Phillips curve is flat, even large movements in the unemployment rate have little effect on the inflation rate. When wages and prices are less sticky, the Phillips curve is nearly vertical. Then even small movements in the unemployment

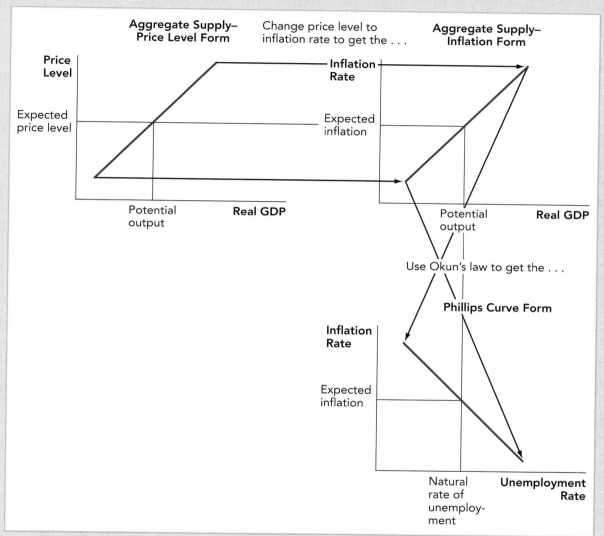

FIGURE 12.2

Three Faces of Aggregate Supply You can think of aggregate supply as a relationship between production (relative to potential output) and the price level, between production (relative to potential output) and the inflation rate, or between unemployment (relative to the natural rate of unemployment) and the inflation rate. These are three different views of what remains the same single relationship.

rate have the potential to cause large changes in the inflation rate, as seen in Figure 12.3 on page 346.

Whenever unemployment is equal to its natural rate u^* and there are no supply shocks, inflation is equal to expected inflation π^e. Thus we can determine the position of the Phillips curve if we know the natural rate of unemployment and

FIGURE 12.3

The Slope of the Phillips Curve When wages and prices are very sticky, β is small and the Phillips curve is flat, so a large change in the unemployment rate — say, from u^* to u_1 in the left panel — results in a relatively small change in the inflation rate. But when wages and prices are less sticky, β is large and the Phillips curve is steep, so even a small change in the unemployment rate — say, from u^* to u_2 in the right panel — results in a relatively large change in the inflation rate.

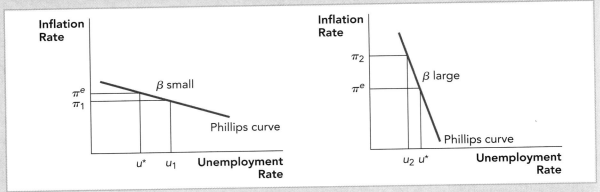

the expected rate of inflation. A higher natural rate shifts the Phillips curve right. Lower expected inflation shifts the Phillips curve down.

If the past 45 years have made anything clear, it is, as Figure 12.4 shows, that the Phillips curve shifts around substantially as *both* expected inflation and the natural rate change. Neither is a constant. Neither is known precisely. That is one of the things that makes the Federal Reserve's job of trying to stabilize the macroeconomy

FIGURE 12.4

Shifts in the Phillips Curve When the natural rate of unemployment or expected inflation changes, the position of the Phillips curve changes too.

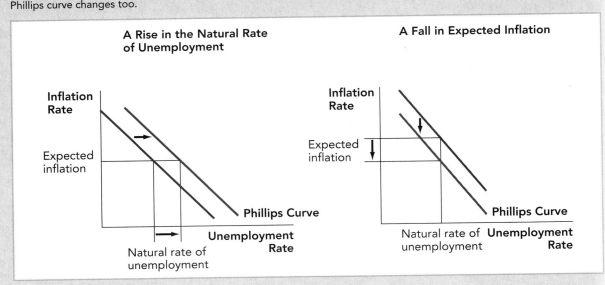

so hard, and so interesting. In America today the current natural rate of unemployment u^* is thought to be near 5 percent. The current rate of expected inflation π^e is about 2 or 2.5 percent per year. But both have been different in the past and will be different in the future.

RECAP   THE PHILLIPS CURVE

The Phillips curve is an inverse relationship between inflation and unemployment. It is the most convenient form of the aggregate supply relationship, so it is the one that we use. The Phillips curve tells us that when unemployment is below its natural rate, inflation is higher than expected inflation; conversely, when unemployment is above its natural rate, inflation is lower than expected inflation. The stickier wages and prices are, the flatter the Phillips curve is. When the Phillips curve is flat, even large movements in the unemployment rate have little effect on the inflation rate. When wages and prices are less sticky, the Phillips curve is nearly vertical. Then even small movements in the unemployment rate have the potential to cause large changes in the inflation rate. When the natural rate of unemployment rises (falls), the Phillips curve shifts to the right (left). When the expected inflation rate falls (rises), the Phillips curve shifts down (up).

12.2 MONETARY POLICY, AGGREGATE DEMAND, AND INFLATION

The Reaction of Monetary Policy to Inflation

Modern central banks do not sit by and passively watch the business cycle. They play a very active role in managing the macroeconomy. Monetary policy of modern central banks reacts to the macroeconomy's condition. And when the central bank reacts to the economy's condition, the action it takes is to change the real interest rate.

How do central banks decide what value the interest rate should be? Stanford University and Treasury Department economist John Taylor proposed a simple model of how central banks act. Modern central banks pay a great deal of attention to the inflation rate. So Taylor said: think of the central bank as having a target value for the inflation rate π^t (t for "target") and having a belief about the **"normal" baseline value r_0 of the real interest rate**.[1] If inflation is higher than the central bank's target value, the central bank raises the real interest rate r above what it considers to be the real interest rate's "normal" baseline value r_0. If inflation is lower than its target value, the central bank reduces the real interest rate r below r_0. We write the **Taylor rule** in the form of an equation as

$$r = r_0 + r_\pi (\pi - \pi^t)$$

where the parameter r_π tells us how much the central bank changes the real interest rate r in reaction to a gap between the actual and target inflation rates. If the central

"normal" baseline real rate of interest

The real interest rate that the central bank would set if the inflation rate were equal to the central bank's target inflation rate.

Taylor rule

A description of how the real interest rate that the central bank sets depends on the gap between the current inflation rate and the central bank's target inflation rate.

---

[1] A more complete version of the Taylor rule would have the central bank responding not just to inflation but also to deviations of the actual unemployment rate from the bank's target unemployment rate.

bankers believe the cost of fighting inflation — increased unemployment due to the higher real interest rate — is too great, r_π will be low and little will be done to fight inflation. If they believe the costs of inflation outweigh the cost of increased unemployment, r_π will be high. Social, political, and economic factors all influence the central bankers' value of r_π.

Unless r_π equals zero, inflation above the central bank's target level of inflation prompts the central bank to raise the real interest rate. A higher real interest rate leads, through the IS curve relationship, to a lower level of real GDP Y relative to potential output Y^*. Chapter 10 showed us the steps: A higher real interest rate dampens planned expenditure — particularly investment and gross export spending — and, through the multiplier, lowers total demand. Real GDP, relative to potential output Y^*, falls. And Okun's law reminds us that reducing output Y relative to potential output Y^* raises the unemployment rate. So the Taylor rule describing how the central bank's monetary policy reacts to inflation, together with the behavior of planned expenditure, and the Okun's law relationship between unemployment and output produce a direct relationship between the inflation rate π and the unemployment rate u. When the inflation rate rises, the central bank raises the real interest rate, which increases unemployment. When the inflation rate falls, the central bank lowers the real interest rate, which decreases unemployment. We call this relationship the **Monetary Policy Reaction Function (MPRF)**. Its derivation is shown in Figure 12.5. A numerical example is in Box 12.3.

The MPRF captures all of the linkages — from inflation to the real interest rate to planned expenditure to output to unemployment — at once. It tells us how the central bank's reactions to inflation π will affect unemployment. We write this monetary policy reaction function — this MPRF — as the equation

$$u = u_0 + \phi(\pi - \pi^t)$$

where

- u_0 is the value of the unemployment rate when the central bank has set the real interest rate to what the central bank thinks is the "normal" baseline value r_0.
- π^t is the central bank's target value for inflation.
- π is the current inflation rate to which the central bank is reacting.
- u is the resulting unemployment rate.
- And ϕ is a parameter that tells us how much unemployment rises when the central bank raises the real interest rate r because it thinks that inflation is too high and needs to be reduced.

This parameter ϕ is itself determined by three different factors:

- The extent of the central bank's distaste for inflation — how much the central bank typically raises interest rates in response to an acceleration in inflation.
- The slope of the IS curve — how much real GDP changes in response to a change in the real interest rate.
- The Okun's law coefficient — how large a change in unemployment is produced by a change in real GDP.

When will the parameter ϕ be large: When will a small increase in inflation above its target level call forth a reaction from the central bank that will push

monetary policy reaction function (MPRF)

An upward-sloping relationship between the inflation rate and the unemployment rate. When the inflation rate rises, a central bank wishing to fight inflation will raise interest rates to reduce output and thus increase the unemployment rate.

FIGURE 12.5

The Monetary Policy Reaction Function (MPRF) The MPRF summarizes a great deal of information in one curve. Inflation π_2 above the central bank's target level π^t leads the central bank to increase the real interest rate above r_0 (Taylor rule), which decreases planned expenditure and real output (IS curve), increasing unemployment (Okun's law).

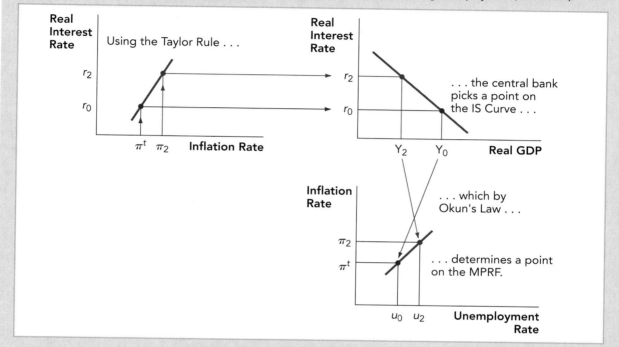

THE MONETARY POLICY REACTION FUNCTION: AN EXAMPLE

The monetary policy reaction function brings together three relationships at once:

1. Taylor rule:

$$r = r_0 + r_\pi (\pi - \pi^t)$$

2. IS curve:

$$Y = \frac{A_0}{1 - MPE} - \left(\frac{I_r + X_\varepsilon \varepsilon_r}{1 - MPE}\right) r$$

3. Okun's law:

$$u = u^* - 0.4\left(\frac{Y - Y^*}{Y^*}\right)$$

Suppose

$$\pi^t = 2\%$$

$$\pi = 5\%$$

$$r_\pi = 1/3$$

$$r_0 = 2.5\%$$

Then by the Taylor rule

$$r = 0.025 + \frac{1}{3}(0.05 - 0.02)$$

$$r = 0.025 + \frac{1}{3}(0.03) = 0.025 + 0.01 = 0.035$$

The central bank will conduct monetary policy so that the real interest rate equals 3.5 percent.

Suppose further that

$$\text{MPE} = 0.5$$

$$A_0 = \$2{,}150 \text{ billion}$$

$$I_r = 8{,}000$$

$$X_\varepsilon \varepsilon_r = 2{,}000$$

Then the IS curve tells us that with an interest rate of 3.5 percent

$$Y = \frac{2{,}150}{1 - 0.5} - \left(\frac{8{,}000 + 2{,}000}{1 - 0.5}\right)(0.035)$$

$$Y = 4{,}300 - 20{,}000(0.035) = 4{,}300 - 700 = \$3{,}600 \text{ billion}$$

Planned expenditure will equal real GDP when total output is $3,600 billion.

Finally, suppose that

$$u^* = 5\%$$

$$Y^* = \$4{,}000 \text{ billion}$$

Then Okun's law tells us that when output is $3,600 billion

$$u = 0.05 - 0.4\left(\frac{3{,}600 - 4{,}000}{4{,}000}\right)$$

$$u = 0.05 - 0.4\left(\frac{-400}{4{,}000}\right) = 0.05 + 0.04 = 0.09$$

The unemployment rate will be 9 percent.

When the inflation rate is 5 percent rather than the central bank's target of 2 percent, the central bank will raise the real interest rate from its normal baseline rate of 2.5 percent to 3.5 percent, which will cause output to fall to $3,600 billion and generate an unemployment rate of 9 percent.

What is the unemployment rate when the inflation rate π equals the central bank's target inflation rate π^t? In this case, the central bank will set the real interest rate to its normal baseline level r_0, which in this example is 2.5 percent. Using the IS curve, we find that output Y is $3,800 billion:

$$Y = \frac{2{,}150}{1 - 0.5} - \left(\frac{8{,}000 + 2{,}000}{1 - 0.5}\right)(0.025)$$

$$Y = 4{,}300 - 20{,}000(0.025) = 4{,}300 - 500 = \$3{,}800 \text{ billion}$$

From Okun's law, we then see that when the interest rate is 2.5 percent, the unemployment rate equals 7 percent:

$$u = 0.05 - 0.4\left(\frac{-200}{4,000}\right) = 0.05 + 0.02 = 0.07$$

We use u_0 to stand for the rate of unemployment when $r = r_0$.

The MPRF for this economy is illustrated in Figure 12.6.

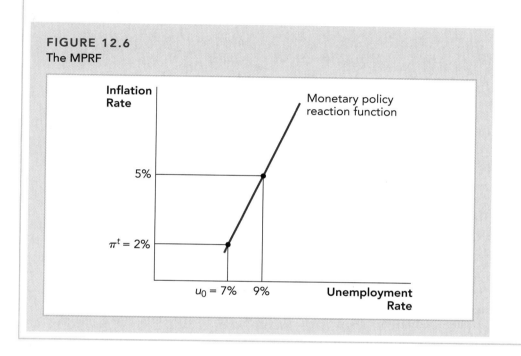

FIGURE 12.6
The MPRF

unemployment up significantly? The parameter will be large — and the MPRF will be relatively flat — if the central bank cares strongly about keeping inflation close to its target, or if investment and export spending are very sensitive to the interest rate, or if the multiplier is relatively large, or if the Okun's law coefficient is large. The parameter will be small — and the MPRF will be steep — if the central bank is not that concerned about keeping inflation close to its target all the time, and if investment and export spending are not very sensitive to the interest rate, and if the multiplier is small, and if the Okun's law coefficient is small. (See Figure 12.7.) Boxes 12.4 and 12.5 illustrate two ways to determine the value of the parameter ϕ and the slope of the MPRF.

Equilibrium: The MPRF and the Phillips Curve

Together, the MPRF relationship

$$u = u_0 + \phi(\pi - \pi^t)$$

and the Phillips curve equation

$$\pi = \pi^e - \beta(u - u^*) + ss$$

FIGURE 12.7

The Slope of the Monetary Policy Reaction Function The slope of the MPRF is $1/\phi$. When the central bank's reaction to a high inflation rate results in very little change in the unemployment rate, as in the left panel, the MPRF is steep. When the central bank's reaction to inflation results in a relatively large change in the unemployment rate, as in the right panel, the MPRF is flat.

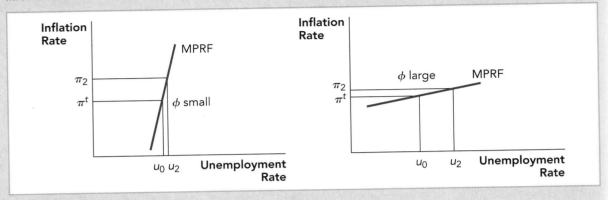

THE SLOPE OF THE MPRF: AN EXAMPLE

In Box 12.3 we found two combinations of inflation and unemployment that were on the MPRF: (1) when the inflation rate was 5 percent, the central bank set the real interest rate at 3.5 percent and the resulting unemployment rate was 9 percent; and (2) when the inflation rate was at its target level of 2 percent and the real interest rate was set at its "normal" baseline rate of 2.5 percent, the resulting unemployment rate was 7 percent.

The equation for the MPRF is $u = u_0 + \phi(\pi - \pi^t)$. The value of the parameter ϕ is simply the change in unemployment for a 1-unit change in the inflation rate. In our example, then

$$\phi = \frac{\Delta u}{\Delta \pi} = \frac{0.09 - 0.07}{0.05 - 0.02} = \frac{2}{3} = 0.67$$

The slope of the MPRF line — where the inflation rate is on the vertical axis (the rise) and the unemployment rate is on the horizontal axis (the run) — is "rise over run," or the change in inflation over the change in the unemployment rate. So the slope of the MPRF is $\Delta \pi / \Delta u$, which is simply $1/\phi$, or, in our example, 1.5.

FROM INCOME EXPENDITURE TO THE MPRF: SOME DETAILS

Whole chapters' worth of detail underpin the parameter ϕ that governs the slope of the MPRF:

$$u = u_0 + \phi(\pi - \pi^t)$$

If we want to look at these details, we can do so by writing the determinants of ϕ as four different factors multiplied together:

$$\phi = r_\pi(I_r + X_\varepsilon \varepsilon_r)\left(\frac{1}{1 - MPE}\right)\left(\frac{0.4}{Y^*}\right)$$

The first term

$$r_\pi$$

comes from central bankers' distaste for inflation. It is the amount by which central bankers raise the real interest rate when inflation is 1 unit higher.

The second term

$$I_r + X_\varepsilon \varepsilon_r$$

comes from Chapter 10. It is the interest sensitivity of autonomous spending. It incorporates both the effect of interest rates on investment spending and the effect of interest rates on the exchange rate and hence on exports spending too.

The third term

$$\frac{1}{1 - MPE}$$

comes from Chapter 9. It is the multiplier, which tells us how much real GDP changes when there is a change in autonomous spending.

The last term

$$\frac{0.4}{Y^*}$$

comes from Okun's law. It tells us the change in the unemployment rate produced by a change in real GDP relative to potential output Y^*.

Thus there is a sense in which much of the work of Chapters 9 and 10 is encapsulated in this single parameter ϕ.

In the example in Box 12.3, we had

$$r_\pi = \frac{1}{3}$$

$$I_r + X_\varepsilon \varepsilon_r = 8,000 + 2,000 = 10,000$$

$$MPE = 0.5$$

$$Y^* = 4,000$$

So in that example, our parameter ϕ equals

$$\phi = r_\pi (I_r + X_\varepsilon \varepsilon_r) \left(\frac{1}{1 - MPE} \right) \left(\frac{0.4}{Y^*} \right) = \left(\frac{1}{3} \right) (10,000) \left(\frac{1}{1 - 0.5} \right) \left(\frac{0.4}{4,000} \right)$$

$$= \frac{4,000}{6,000} = \frac{2}{3} = 0.67$$

The same result we obtained in Box 12.4!

let us find out what the inflation rate π and the unemployment rate u will be in the economy. The MPRF determines the unemployment rate as a function of the inflation rate as the central bank reacts to changes in inflation by using its monetary policy control over interest rates to manipulate planned expenditure. The Phillips curve determines inflation as a function of the unemployment rate. Both must be satisfied for this system of equations to be in equilibrium. The

FIGURE 12.8

Equilibrium Levels of Unemployment and Inflation

The equilibrium levels of unemployment and inflation occur where the MPRF and Phillips curve cross. In the short run, equilibrium inflation can be different from the central bank's target inflation rate π^t and from the expected rate of inflation π^e. In the short run, equilibrium unemployment can be different from the natural rate of unemployment u^* and from the unemployment rate when the central bank sets the interest rate at its normal baseline value u_0.

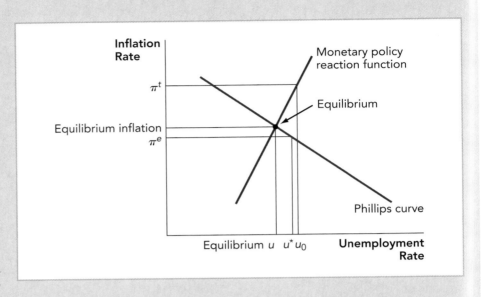

economy's equilibrium is where the curves cross, as Figure 12.8 shows. Box 12.6 shows how to determine the values of the unemployment and inflation rates in equilibrium.

Equilibrium occurs when the unemployment and inflation rates are not changing. Why is the point where the curves cross the only equilibrium? To see the answer, let's choose any unemployment rate along the horizontal axis. The Phillips curve tells us what inflation rate the resulting wage and price bargaining in input markets will generate. But unless that unemployment rate and inflation rate combination from the Phillips curve is also on the MPRF, the central bank will react to that inflation rate by changing the real interest rate. And a change in the real interest rate will ultimately change the unemployment rate, moving us to yet another point on the Phillips curve!

At what combination of unemployment and inflation rates will the supply-side forces that determine inflation be in concert with the central bank's monetary policy and resulting demand for output? Only a combination of unemployment and inflation rates that is on *both* the Phillips curve and the MPRF will accomplish this. Any other combination of u and π is not an equilibrium combination because the central bank's reaction to inflation will change the unemployment rate (move us along the MPRF), which in turn will change the inflation rate (move us along the Phillips curve). The economy will be in equilibrium at that unemployment rate and inflation rate where the Phillips curve and the MPRF cross.

How can the level of inflation be different in the short run from both expected inflation π^e and the central bank's target inflation rate π^t? And how can this equilibrium level of unemployment u be different in the short run from both the natural rate of unemployment u^* and from the level of unemployment u_0 when the

SOLVING FOR EQUILIBRIUM: AN EXAMPLE

How do we actually figure out what the economy's inflation and unemployment rates are? If we have the equations for the Phillips curve and the MPRF, we can solve those equations jointly to determine the equilibrium inflation and unemployment rates.

In our example in Boxes 12.3 and 12.4, we derived the MPRF

$$\text{MPRF:} \qquad u = u_0 + \phi(\pi - \pi^t) = 0.07 + \frac{2}{3}(\pi - 0.02)$$

Suppose the parameter β in the Phillips curve equation is $\frac{1}{2}$, that expected inflation π^e is 4 percent, there are no supply shocks, and as in Boxes 12.3 and 12.4 the natural rate of unemployment u^* is 5 percent. Then the Phillips curve is

$$\text{Phillips curve:} \qquad \pi = \pi^e - \beta(u - u^*) = 0.04 - \frac{1}{2}(u - 0.05)$$

To solve for the equilibrium value of the unemployment rate we can substitute the Phillips curve equation for π into the MPRF equation and solve for the unemployment rate:

$$u = 0.07 + \frac{2}{3}(\pi - 0.02) = 0.07 + \frac{2}{3}\left\{\left[0.04 - \frac{1}{2}(u - 0.05)\right] - 0.02\right\}$$

$$u = 0.07 + \frac{2}{3}\left(0.045 - \frac{1}{2}u\right) = 0.10 - \frac{1}{3}u$$

$$\frac{4}{3}u = 0.10$$

$$u = 0.075$$

Now to solve for the equilibrium value of the inflation rate, we just substitute $u = 0.075$ into the Phillips curve equation:

$$\pi = 0.04 - \frac{1}{2}(u - 0.05) = 0.04 - \frac{1}{2}(0.075 - 0.05) = 0.0275$$

In equilibrium in our example from Box 12.3, the unemployment rate will be 7.5 percent and the inflation rate will be 2.75 percent.

central bank sets the interest rate at what it thinks is the interest rate's normal baseline value r_0?

Actual inflation π can be different from expected inflation π^e because economic decisions have to be made in advance, and people update their expectations only with a time lag. Workers, firms, investors, and financiers would have to have super-human powers of observation and analysis for actual inflation to be — except occasionally and luckily — exactly equal to expected inflation.

Actual inflation π can be different from the central bank's target π^t because the central bank has other things to worry about as well as inflation. If all the central bank worried about was keeping inflation at its target, it could do so: The MPRF would then be flat, at the target level π^t. But the parameter r_π is not infinitely large, which it would need to be to create a completely flat MPRF. Central banks do not want to cause the financial upset that would result from the large rapid swings in interest rates needed to create a flat MPRF.

Unemployment will in general not be equal to the central bank's view of normal unemployment u_0 because inflation will rarely be exactly equal to its target. Unemployment is the central bank's inflation-fighting tool. So the central bank will want to push unemployment above or below its view of normal in order to reduce or increase inflation.

In a good world, with a perfect central bank, the central bank's idea of what the normal unemployment is would be equal to the natural rate of unemployment, and the central bank's target inflation rate would be equal to expected inflation. Then inflation and unemployment would be stable, and the business cycle would be a nonevent. But changes and shocks to the economy — and misperceptions by the central bank and by the economy's workers, firms, investors, and financiers — will keep that from being the case except for moments of exceptional good luck.

Using the MPRF–Phillips Curve Model

We can use this framework to analyze the effects of a shift in policy on the economy's equilibrium. For example, consider a depression abroad that lowers demand for exports. This change in the economic environment causes a decrease in planned expenditure — a shift left of the IS curve — and leads to a rise in the unemployment rate. The Monetary Policy Reaction Function has shifted to the right, as Figure 12.9 shows, and the economy's equilibrium has moved down and

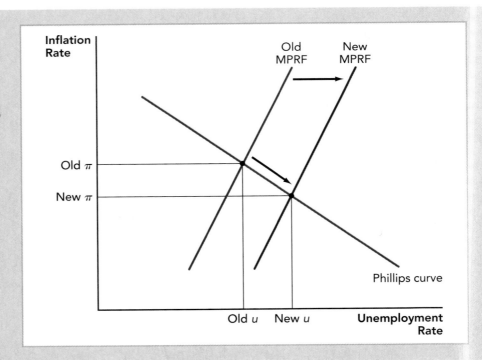

FIGURE 12.9
Effects of a Fall in Exports
A fall in exports with no countervailing change in the central bank's view of the normal interest rate r_0 shifts the MPRF right, raises the equilibrium unemployment rate, and lowers the inflation rate.

to the right along the Phillips curve. The unemployment rate rises. The inflation rate falls.

Consider instead an expansion of government purchases at home. We would show this as a shift to the right of the IS curve of Chapter 10, which shifts the MPRF curve in and to the left. If the central bank does not change its notion of the normal baseline interest rate r_0, and expected inflation does not change, the unemployment rate will fall and the inflation rate will rise.

What if there is no aggressive central bank acting to stabilize the economy by raising interest rates when inflation rises? Does the economy spin out of control? No. Those curious about why not need to look to Chapter 11, which analyzes how the money market works in the sticky-price model when there is no central bank actively managing the economy. It provides the answer to this question in the discussion of aggregate demand and aggregate supply that comes at its end. Without a central bank to control interest rates, inflation itself sets in motion forces that raise interest rates and so "cool off" the economy and raise unemployment. Inflation raises the price level. A higher price level makes the nominal money supply in the economy worth less. A smaller real money stock means higher interest rates. With a fixed money stock, the aggregate demand curve of Chapter 11 can perform the same economy-stabilizing function automatically that modern central banks accomplish through their active control over interest rates.

What about a negative — costly — supply shock such as the oil price hikes in the 1970s? We would show this as a rightward shift in the Phillips curve. The unemployment rate would rise and the inflation rate would rise as well. The MPRF-Phillips curve model is deceptively simple but satisfyingly powerful. It can help us to understand the short-run effects on inflation and unemployment of any number of macroeconomic events.

> ### RECAP   MONETARY POLICY REACTION FUNCTION AND THE PHILLIPS CURVE
>
> Central banks respond to higher-than-desired inflation rates by raising interest rates to "cool off" the economy, thus lowering real GDP Y and raising the unemployment rate u. We model this facet of central bank behavior by a monetary policy reaction function — MPRF — that is an upward-sloping relationship between inflation π and unemployment u. We combine this with our Phillips curve — a downward-sloping relationship between inflation π and unemployment u — to determine the equilibrium levels of the unemployment rate and inflation rate in our sticky-price economy. We can use the MPRF and the Phillips curve to analyze the effects of economic policy.

12.3 THE NATURAL RATE OF UNEMPLOYMENT

In English, the word "natural" carries strong positive connotations of normal and desirable, but a high natural rate of unemployment u^* is a bad thing. Unemployment cannot be reduced below its natural rate without accelerating inflation, so a high natural rate means that expansionary fiscal policy and expansionary monetary policy are largely ineffective as tools to reduce unemployment.

FIGURE 12.10
Fluctuations in Unemployment and the Natural Rate
The natural rate of unemployment is not fixed. It varies substantially from decade to decade. Moreover, variations in the natural rate in the United States have been much smaller than variations in the natural rate in other countries.

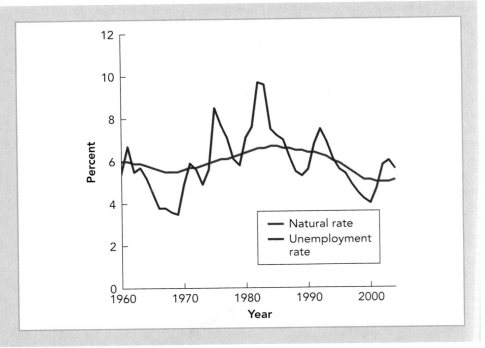

Source: Authors' calculations and 2004 edition of *The Economic Report of the President* (Washington, DC: Government Printing Office).

Today, most estimates of the current U.S. "natural" rate of unemployment are around 5 percent, although uncertainty about the level of the natural rate is substantial. And the natural rate has fluctuated substantially over the past two generations, as shown in Figure 12.10. Broadly, four sets of factors have powerful influence over the natural rate.

Demography and the Natural Rate

First, the natural rate changes as the relative age and educational distribution of the labor force changes. Teenagers have higher unemployment rates than adults; thus an economy with a lot of teenagers will have a higher natural rate. Looking for a job is easier for more experienced and more skilled workers. They need less time to find a new job when they leave an old one, so the natural rate of unemployment will fall when the labor force becomes more experienced and more skilled. Women formerly had higher unemployment rates than men, although this is no longer true in the United States. The more educated tend to have lower rates of unemployment than the less well educated. African-Americans and Hispanic-Americans have higher unemployment rates than whites.

A large part of the estimated rise in the natural rate from 5 percent or so in the 1960s to 6 or 7 percent by the end of the 1970s was due to changing demography. Some component of the decline in the natural rate since then derives from the increasing experience at searching for jobs of the very large baby-boom cohort. But the exact, quantitative relationship between demography and the natural rate is not well understood.

Institutions and the Natural Rate

Second, institutions have a powerful influence over the natural rate. Some economies have strong *labor unions;* other economies have weak ones. Some unions sacrifice employment in their industry for higher wages; others settle for lower wages in return for employment guarantees. Some economies lack apprenticeship programs that make the transition from education to employment relatively straightforward; others make the school-to-work transition easy. In each pair, the first increases and the second reduces the natural rate of unemployment. Barriers to worker mobility raise the natural rate, whether the barrier be subsidized housing that workers lose if they move (as in Britain in the 1970s and the 1980s), or high taxes that a firm must pay to hire a worker (as in France from the 1970s to today).

However, the link between economic institutions and the natural rate is neither simple nor straightforward. The institutional features many observers today point to as a source of high European unemployment now were also present in the European economies in the 1970s—when European unemployment was low. Once again the quantitative relationships are not well understood.

Productivity Growth and the Natural Rate

Third, in recent years the rate of productivity growth has become increasingly implicated as a major determinant of the natural rate. The era of slow productivity growth from the mid-1970s to the mid-1990s saw a relatively high natural rate. By contrast, rapid productivity growth before 1973 and after 1995 seems to have generated a relatively low natural rate.

Why should a productivity growth slowdown generate a high natural rate? A higher rate of productivity growth allows firms to pay higher real wage increases and still remain profitable. If workers' aspirations for real wage growth depend on the rate of unemployment, then a slowdown in productivity growth will increase the natural rate as indicated in Figure 12.11. If real wages grow faster than productivity for an extended period of time, profits will disappear. Long before that point is reached businesses will begin to fire workers, and unemployment will rise. Thus if productivity growth slows, unemployment will rise. Unemployment will keep rising until workers' real wage aspirations fall to a rate consistent with current productivity growth.

The Past Level of Unemployment and the Natural Rate

Fourth and last, the natural rate will be high if unemployment has been high. Before 1980 western European economies had unemployment rates lower than the 5 percent to 6 percent that the United States averaged back then. But the mid-1970s brought recessions. European unemployment rose, but it did not fall back much in subsequent recoveries. Workers unemployed for two or three years lost their skills, lost their willingness to show up on time, and became so discouraged that they lost their interest in even looking for new jobs. Thus the natural rate rose sharply in Europe with each business cycle. By the late-1990s European unemployment averaged 8 percent, as depicted in Figure 12.12, and inflation was stable.

FIGURE 12.11

Real Wage Growth Aspirations and Productivity

Workers aspire to earn higher real wages. How much workers demand in the way of increases in the average real wage is a function of unemployment: The higher unemployment is, the lower workers' aspirations for real wage growth are. But in the long run real wages can grow no faster than productivity. Hence the natural rate of unemployment is whatever rate of unemployment curbs real wage demands so that they are consistent with productivity growth.

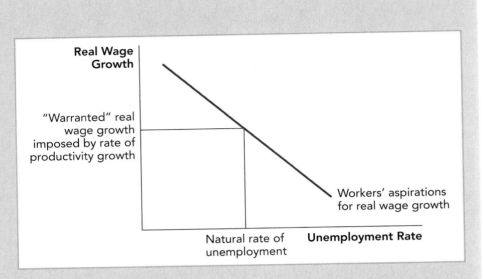

FIGURE 12.12

The Rise in European Unemployment

Unemployment in western European countries grew between 1975 and 2004 as their natural rates of unemployment increased.

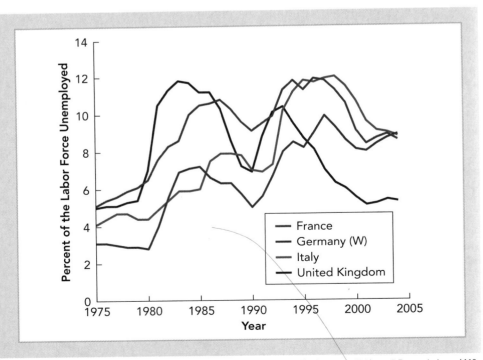

Source: Olivier Blanchard and Justin Wolfers, "The Role of Shocks and Institutions in the Rise of European Unemployment: The Aggregate Evidence," *Economic Journal* 110 (March 2000); extended by the authors.

Conclusion: The Fluctuating Natural Rate

This laundry list of factors affecting the natural rate is incomplete. Do not think that economists understand much about why the natural rate is what it is. Almost every economist was surprised by the large rise in the natural rate in western Europe over the past quarter century. Almost every economist was surprised by the sharp fall in America's natural rate in the 1990s. And economists cannot confidently account for these shifts even in retrospect.

RECAP THE NATURAL RATE OF UNEMPLOYMENT

The natural rate of unemployment is not a constant. It has fluctuated substantially over the past two generations, and it will continue to fluctuate. Four sets of factors drive fluctuations in the natural rate of unemployment. First, the natural rate changes as the relative age and educational distribution of the labor force changes. Second, countries with inflexible labor markets are likely to have high natural rates of unemployment. Third, faster productivity growth brings a lower natural rate with it. Fourth, the natural rate will be high if unemployment has been high in the past and large numbers of workers have become discouraged.

12.4 EXPECTED INFLATION

The natural rate of unemployment and expected inflation together determine the location of the Phillips curve because it passes through the point where inflation is equal to expected inflation and unemployment is equal to its natural rate. This is how the Phillips curve is defined: When inflation π is equal to its expected value π^e, then that tells us that the labor market is in rough balance — that unemployment u is equal to its natural rate u^*. Thus higher expected inflation shifts the Phillips curve upward. But who does the expecting? And when do people form expectations relevant for this year's Phillips curve?

Economists work with three basic scenarios for how managers, workers, and investors go about forecasting the future and forming their expectations:

- **Static expectations** of inflation prevail when people ignore the fact that inflation can change.
- **Adaptive expectations** prevail when people assume the future will be like the recent past.
- **Rational expectations** prevail when people use all the information they have as best they can.

The Phillips curve behaves very differently under each of these three scenarios.

The Phillips Curve under Static Expectations

If inflation expectations are *static*, expected inflation never changes. People just don't think about inflation. There will be some years in which unemployment is relatively low; in those years inflation will be relatively high. There will be other

static expectations

Visions of the future that do not change at all in response to changes in the current economic situation.

adaptive expectations

Expectations of the future formed by assuming the future will be like the past.

rational expectations

Expectations about the future formed by using all information about the structure of the economy and the likely course of government policy.

FIGURE 12.13

Static Expectations of Inflation

If inflation expectations are static, the economy moves up and to the left and down and to the right along a Phillips curve that does not change its position so long as there are no supply shocks and the natural rate of unemployment is constant.

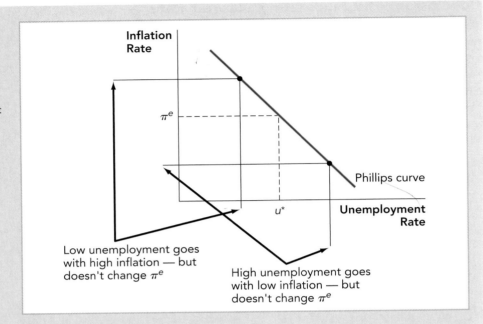

years in which unemployment is higher, and then inflation will be lower. But as long as expectations of inflation remain static (and there are no supply shocks, and the natural rate of unemployment is unchanged), the trade-off between inflation and unemployment — the position of the Phillips curve — will not change from year to year. (See Figure 12.13.)

If inflation has been low and stable, businesses will probably hold static inflation expectations. Why? Because the art of managing a business is complex enough as it is. Managers have a lot of things to worry about: what their customers are doing, what their competitors are doing, whether their technology is adequate, and how applicable technology is changing. When inflation has been low or stable, everyone has better things to focus their attention on than the rate of inflation. The 1960s were an era of static expectations (see Box 12.7).

The Phillips Curve under Adaptive Expectations

Suppose that the inflation rate varies too much for workers and businesses to ignore it completely. What then? As long as inflation last year is a good guide to inflation this year, workers, investors, and managers are likely to hold *adaptive* expectations and forecast inflation by assuming that this year will be like last year. Adaptive forecasts are good forecasts as long as inflation changes only slowly and adaptive expectations do not absorb a lot of time and energy that can be better used thinking about other issues.

Under such adaptive inflation expectations, the Phillips curve can be written with t subscripts to denote time (not "target"):

$$\pi_t = \pi_{t-1} - \beta(u_t - u_t^*) + ss_t$$

STATIC EXPECTATIONS OF INFLATION IN THE 1960s: AN EXAMPLE
The standard example of static expectations is expectations of inflation in the 1960s. When unemployment was above 5.5 percent, inflation was below 1.5 percent. When unemployment was below 4 percent, inflation was above 2.5 percent. This Phillips curve, shown in Figure 12.14, did not shift up or down in response to changes in expected inflation during the decade. Instead, the economy moved along a stable Phillips curve.

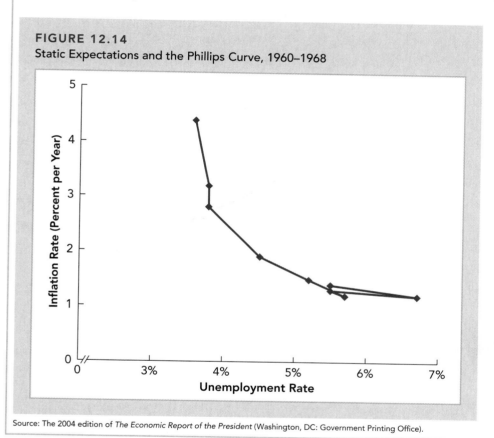

FIGURE 12.14
Static Expectations and the Phillips Curve, 1960–1968

Source: The 2004 edition of *The Economic Report of the President* (Washington, DC: Government Printing Office).

where π_{t-1}, which is just what inflation was last year, stands in place for π_t^e. Why? Because we have assumed that expected inflation is just equal to last year's inflation rate. Under such a set of *adaptive expectations*, the Phillips curve will shift up or down depending on whether last year's inflation was higher or lower than the previous year's (see Box 12.8). Under adaptive expectations, inflation accelerates when unemployment is less than the natural unemployment rate and decelerates when unemployment is more than the natural rate. The 1980s were such an era (see Box 12.9).

The Phillips Curve under Rational Expectations

What happens when government policy and the economic environment are changing rapidly enough that adaptive expectations lead to significant errors and are no

A HIGH-PRESSURE ECONOMY UNDER ADAPTIVE EXPECTATIONS: AN EXAMPLE

Suppose the central bank tries to keep unemployment below the natural rate for a long time in an economy with adaptive expectations. Then year after year inflation will be higher than expected inflation, and so year after year expected inflation will rise. Suppose that the government pushes the economy's unemployment rate down 2 percentage points below the natural rate, that the β parameter in the Phillips curve is 1/2, that last year's inflation rate was 4 percent, and that there are no supply shocks. Then, because each year's expected inflation rate is last year's actual inflation rate, and because

$$\pi_t = \pi_{t-1} - \frac{1}{2}(-0.02) + 0$$

this year's inflation rate will be

$$0.04 - \frac{1}{2}(-0.02) = 0.05$$

next year's inflation rate will be

$$0.05 - \frac{1}{2}(-0.02) = 0.06$$

the following year's inflation rate will be

$$0.06 - \frac{1}{2}(-0.02) = 0.07$$

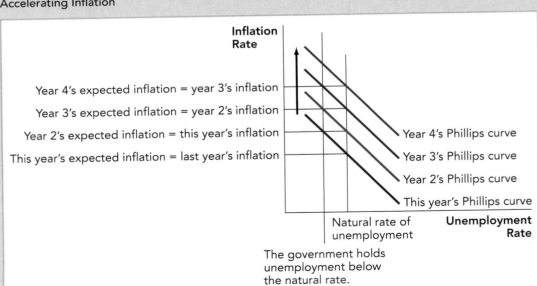

FIGURE 12.15
Accelerating Inflation

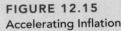

and the year after that's inflation rate will be

$$0.07 - \frac{1}{2}(-0.02) = 0.08$$

as shown in Figure 12.15.

When inflation increases, expected inflation increases. And as expected inflation increases, the Phillips curve shifts up.

ADAPTIVE EXPECTATIONS AND THE VOLCKER DISINFLATION: ECONOMIC POLICY

At the end of the 1970s the high level of expected inflation gave the United States an unfavorable short-run Phillips curve trade-off. Between 1979 and the mid-1980s, the Federal Reserve under Chair Paul Volcker reduced inflation in the United States from 9 percent per year to about 3 percent.

Because inflation expectations were adaptive, the fall in actual inflation in the early 1980s triggered a fall in expected inflation as well. The early 1980s therefore saw a downward shift in the short-run Phillips curve, a downward shift that gave the United States a much more favorable short-run inflation-unemployment trade-off by the mid-1980s than it had had in the late 1970s, as shown in Figure 12.16.

FIGURE 12.16
The Phillips Curve before and after the Volcker Disinflation

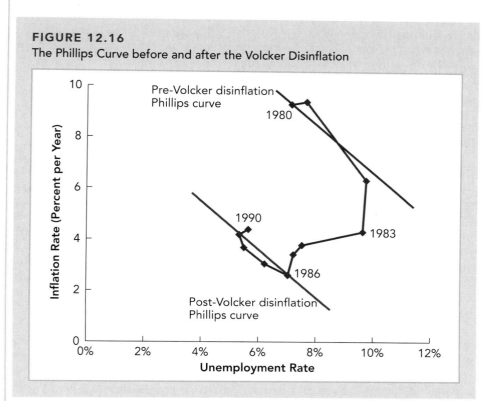

Source: The 2004 edition of *The Economic Report of the President* (Washington, DC: Government Printing Office).

To accomplish this goal of reducing expected inflation, the Federal Reserve raised interest rates sharply, discouraging investment, reducing aggregate demand, and pushing the economy to the right along the Phillips curve. Unemployment rose, and inflation fell. Reducing annual inflation by 6 percentage points required "sacrifice": During the disinflation, unemployment averaged some 1.5 percentage points above the natural rate for the seven years between 1980 and 1986. Ten percentage-point-years of excess unemployment above the natural rate — that was the cost of reducing inflation from near 10 percent to below 5 percent.

longer good enough for managers or workers? Then the economy will shift to *rational* expectations. Under rational expectations, people form their forecasts of future inflation not by looking backward at what inflation was, but by looking forward. They look at what current and expected future government policies tell us about what inflation will be.

Economic Policy under Rational Expectations

Under rational expectations the Phillips curve shifts as rapidly as, or faster than, changes in economic policy that affect the level of aggregate demand. This has an interesting consequence: Anticipated changes in economic policy turn out to have no effect on the level of production or employment.

Consider an economy where the central bank's target inflation π^t rate is equal to the current value of expected inflation π^e and where u_0, the unemployment rate when the real interest rate is at its normal value, is equal to the natural rate of unemployment u^*. In such an economy, the initial equilibrium has unemployment equal to its natural rate and inflation equal to expected inflation.

Suppose that workers, managers, savers, and investors have rational expectations. Suppose further that the government takes steps to stimulate the economy: It cuts taxes and increases government spending in order to reduce unemployment below the natural rate, and so reduces the value of u_0. What is likely to happen to the economy?

If the government's policy comes as a *surprise* — if the expectations of inflation that matter for this year's Phillips curve have already been set, in the sense that the contracts have been written, the orders have been made, and the standard operating procedures have been identified — then the economy moves up and to the left along the Phillips curve in response to the shift in aggregate demand produced by the change in government policy: Unemployment falls and the inflation rate rises, as shown in Figure 12.17.

But if the government's policy is *anticipated* — if the expectations of inflation that matter for this year's Phillips curve are formed after the decision to stimulate the economy is made and becomes public — then workers, managers, savers, and investors will take the stimulative policy into account when they form their expectations of inflation. The inward shift in the MPRF will be accompanied, under rational expectations, by an upward shift in the Phillips curve as well. (See Figure 12.18.) How large is the upward shift? The increase in expected inflation has to be large enough to keep expected inflation after the demand shift equal to actual inflation. Otherwise people are not forming their expectations rationally.

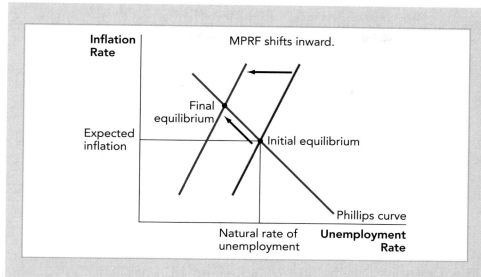

FIGURE 12.17
Results if the Shift in Policy Comes as a Surprise

A government pursuing an expansionary economic policy shifts the MPRF. An increase in production is associated with a reduction in unemployment, so an expansionary shift is a shift to the left in the MPRF. A surprise expansionary policy moves the economy along the Phillips curve, raising inflation and lowering unemployment (and raising production) in the short run.

Thus an anticipated increase in aggregate demand has, under rational expectations, no effect on the unemployment rate or on real GDP. Unemployment does not change; it remains at the natural rate of unemployment because the shift in the Phillips curve has neutralized in advance any impact of changing inflation on unemployment. It will, however, have a large effect on the rate of inflation. Economists will sometimes say that under rational expectations "anticipated policy is irrelevant." But this is not the best way to express it. Policy is very relevant indeed for the inflation rate. It is only the effects of policy on real GDP and the unemployment rate — effects that are associated with a divergence between expected inflation and actual inflation — that are "irrelevant."

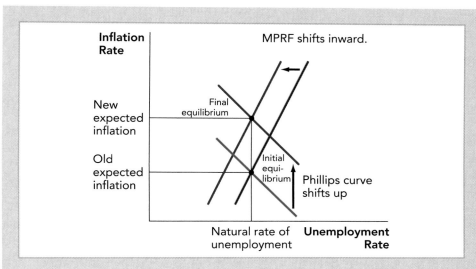

FIGURE 12.18
Results if the Shift in Policy Is Anticipated

If the expansionary policy is anticipated, workers, consumers, and managers will build the policy effects into their expectations: The Phillips curve will shift up as the MPRF shifts in, and so the expansionary policy will raise inflation without having any impact on unemployment (or production).

When have we seen examples of rational inflation expectations? The standard case is that of France immediately after the election of Socialist President François Mitterand in 1981. Throughout his campaign Mitterand had promised a rapid expansion of demand and production to reduce unemployment. Thus when he took office French businesses and unions were ready to mark up their prices and wages in anticipation of the expansionary policies they expected. The result? From mid-1981 to mid-1983 France saw a significant acceleration of inflation, but no reduction in unemployment. The Phillips curve had shifted upward fast enough to keep expansionary policies from having any effect on production and employment.

What Kind of Expectations Do We Have?

If inflation is low and stable, expectations are probably static: Even thinking about what one's expectations should be is not worth anyone's while. If inflation is moderate and fluctuates, but slowly, expectations are probably adaptive: To assume that the future will be like the recent past — which is what adaptive expectations are — is likely to be a good, simple to implement, rule of thumb.

When shifts in inflation are clearly related to changes in monetary policy, swift to occur, and are large enough to seriously affect profitability, then people are likely to have rational expectations. When the stakes are high — when people think, "Had I known inflation was going to jump, I would not have taken that contract" — then every economic decision becomes a speculation on the future of monetary policy. Because their bottom lines and their livelihoods are at risk, people will turn all their skill and insight into generating inflation forecasts.

Thus the kind of expectations likely to be found in the economy at any moment depends on what has been and is going on. A period during which inflation is low and stable will lead people to stop consciously making, and stop paying attention to, inflation forecasts — and tend to cause expectations of inflation to revert to static expectations. A period during which inflation is high, volatile, and linked to visible shifts in economic policy will see expectations of inflation become more rational. An intermediate period of substantial but slow variability is likely to see many managers and workers adopt the rule of thumb of adaptive expectations.

Persistent Contracts

The ways that people make contracts and form and execute plans for their economic activity are likely to make an economy behave *as if* expectations are less "rational" than expectations in fact are. People do not wait until December 31 to factor next year's expected inflation into their decisions and contracts. They make decisions about the future, sign contracts, and undertake projects all the time. Some of those steps govern what the company does for a day. Others govern decisions for years or even for a decade or more.

Thus the "expected inflation" that determines the location of the short-run Phillips curve has components that were formed just as the old year ended, but also components that were formed two, three, five, ten, or more years ago. People buying houses form forecasts of what inflation will be over the next 30 years — but once the house is bought, that decision is a piece of economic activity (imputed rent on owner-occupied housing) as long as they own the house, no matter what they subsequently learn about future inflation. Such lags in decision making tend to produce *"price inertia."* They tend to make the economy behave as if inflation expectations were more adaptive than they in fact are. There will always be a large number of projects and commitments already under way that cannot easily adjust to changing prices. It is important to take this price inertia into account when thinking about the dynamics of inflation, output, and unemployment.

RECAP   EXPECTED INFLATION

The dynamics of how expectations evolve are key to understanding the economy. Economists work with three basic scenarios for how managers, workers, and investors go about forecasting the future and forming their expectations: *Static expectations* of inflation prevail when people ignore the fact that inflation can change. *Adaptive expectations* prevail when people assume the future will be like the recent past. *Rational expectations* prevail when people use all the information they have as best they can.

The Phillips curve behaves very differently under each of these three scenarios. Under static expectations the Phillips curve doesn't shift, so changes in policy have powerful effects on unemployment and real GDP. Under rational expectations the Phillips curve shifts immediately and drastically in response to policies so that anticipated changes in policy have powerful effects on inflation, but not on unemployment and real GDP. And adaptive expectations are in the middle.

12.5 FROM THE SHORT RUN TO THE LONG RUN

Rational Expectations

Our picture of the determination of real GDP and unemployment under sticky prices is now complete. We have a comprehensive framework to understand how the aggregate price level and inflation rate move and adjust over time in response to changes in aggregate demand, production relative to potential output, and unemployment relative to its natural rate. There is, however, one loose end. How does one get from the short-run sticky-price patterns of behavior covered in Part 4 to the long-run flexible-price patterns of behavior that were laid out in Part 3? How do you get from the short run to the long run?

In the case of an anticipated shift in economic policy under rational expectations, the answer is straightforward: You don't have to get from the short run to the long run; the long run is now. An inward (or outward) shift in the monetary policy reaction function on the Phillips curve diagram caused by an *expansionary* (or *contractionary*) change in economic policy or the economic environment sets in motion an offsetting shift in the Phillips curve. If expectations are rational, if changes in economic policy are foreseen, and if there are no supply shocks, then expected inflation will be equal to actual inflation:

$$\pi = \pi^e$$

FIGURE 12.19

Rational Expectations: The Long Run Is Now

Under rational expectations there simply is no short run, unless changes in policy come as a complete surprise.

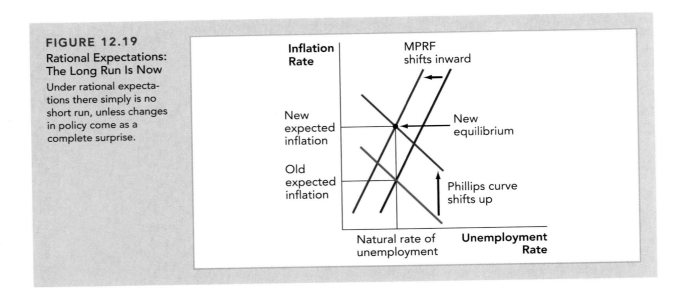

which means that the unemployment rate is equal to the natural rate, as shown in Figure 12.19. The economy is at full employment. All the analysis of Chapters 6, 7, and 8 holds immediately.

Back in the early 1920s the British economist John Maynard Keynes wrote that it was not enough to do just a long-run analysis, because by the time the long run rolled around we would all be dead. But if everyone in the economy has rational expectations, then Keynes was wrong: The long run comes immediately.

Adaptive Expectations

If expectations are and remain adaptive, then the economy approaches the long-run equilibrium laid out in Chapter 7 gradually, as is shown in Figure 12.20. An expansionary initial shock increases planned expenditure and shifts the monetary policy reaction function inward, generating a fall in unemployment, an increase in real GDP, and a rise in inflation. Call this stage 1. Stage 1 takes place before anyone has had any chance to adjust his or her expectations of inflation.

Then comes stage 2. Workers, managers, investors, and others look at what inflation was in stage 1 and raise their expectations of inflation. The Phillips curve shifts up by the difference between actual and expected inflation in stage 1. The central bank begins to fight inflation by increasing the real interest rate, which increases unemployment. Between stage 1 and stage 2 unemployment rises, real GDP falls, and inflation rises.

Then comes stage 3. Workers, managers, investors, and others look at what inflation was in stage 2 and raise their expectations of inflation again. The Phillips curve shifts up by the difference between actual and expected inflation in stage 2. As inflation rises further, the central bank ratchets up its fight against inflation, increasing the real interest rate yet again and thus increasing unemployment. Between stage 2 and stage 3 unemployment rises further, real GDP falls again, and inflation again rises. As time passes the gaps between actual and expected inflation, between real GDP and potential output, and between unemployment and its

FIGURE 12.20

Adaptive Expectations Converge to the Long Run Under adaptive expectations, shifts in policy have strong initial effects on unemployment and production, but those effects slowly die off.

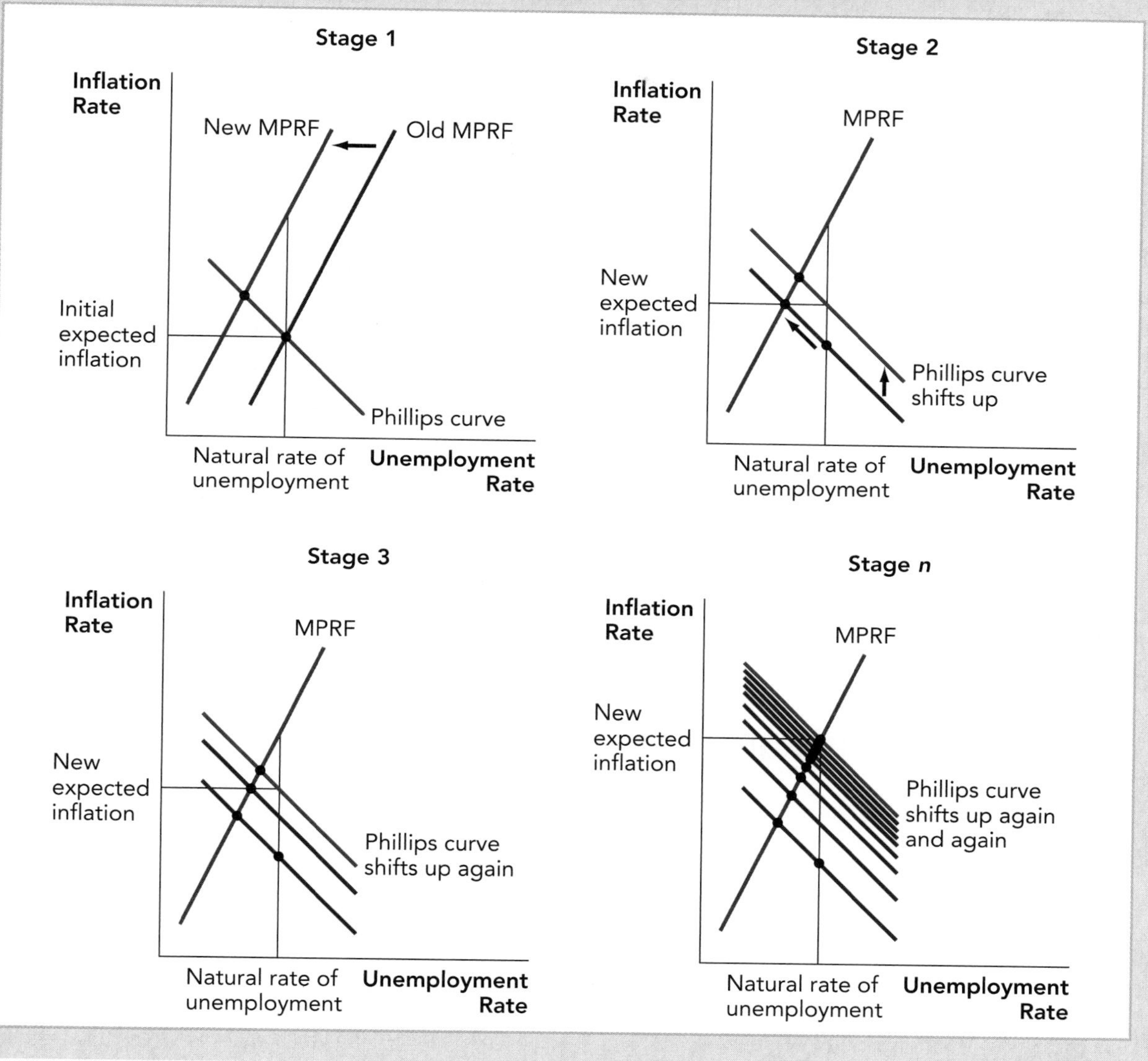

natural rate shrink toward zero. Eventually unemployment returns to the natural rate of unemployment and the only lasting effect of the increase in spending is an increase in the inflation rate.

Under adaptive expectations, people's forecasts become closer and closer to being accurate as more and more time passes. Thus the "long run" arrives gradually. Each year the portion of the change in demand that is not implicitly incorporated in people's adaptive forecasts becomes smaller and smaller. Thus a larger and larger proportion of the shift is "long run, " and a smaller and smaller proportion is "short run."

Static Expectations

Under static expectations, the long run never arrives, and thus the flexible-price analysis of Chapters 6 to 8 never becomes relevant. Under static expectations, the gap between expected inflation and actual inflation can grow arbitrarily large as different shocks affect the economy. And if the gap between expected inflation and actual inflation becomes large, workers, managers, investors, and consumers will not remain so foolish as to retain static expectations.

Under rational expectations, the long run is now. The analysis we did in Chapters 6 to 8 is always relevant. Adaptive expectations provide an intermediate case; as time passes, the analysis of Chapters 9 and 10 becomes less relevant and that of Chapters 6 to 8 becomes more relevant.

> **RECAP**   **FROM THE SHORT RUN TO THE LONG RUN**
>
> The amount of time that must pass before the relevant framework shifts from the sticky-price models of Part 4 to the flexible-price models of Part 3 depends on the kind of inflation expectations held in the economy. If workers, bosses, savers, and investors hold static expectations and never update them, then the flexible-price models never become relevant. If the expectations are adaptive, the shift from Part 4 to Part 3 takes place slowly and gradually. But if expectations are rational, then the shift to Part 3 takes place very quickly indeed — as soon as policy changes are announced or recognized.

Chapter Summary

1. The location of the Phillips curve is determined by the expected rate of inflation and the natural rate of unemployment (and possibly by current, active supply shocks). In the absence of supply shocks, the Phillips curve passes through the point at which inflation is its expected value and unemployment is its natural rate.

2. The slope of the Phillips curve is determined by the degree of price stickiness in the economy. The more sticky are prices, the flatter is the Phillips curve.

3. Modern central banks respond to higher-than-desired inflation by raising interest rates, thus reducing output and raising unemployment. This monetary policy reaction function (MPRF) is a powerful stabilizing factor in modern economies.

4. The MPRF and Phillips curve can be used to analyze the effect of changes in economic policy on the economy's inflation and unemployment rates.

5. The natural rate of unemployment in the United States has exhibited moderate swings in the past two generations, from perhaps 4.5 percent at the end of the 1950s to perhaps 7 percent at the start of the 1980s, and now down to about 5 percent. Changes in the natural rate of unemployment shift the Phillips curve to the left or right.

6. The principal determinant of the expected rate of inflation is the past behavior of inflation. If inflation has been low and steady, expectations are probably static and the expected inflation rate is very low and unchanging. If inflation has been variable but moderate, expectations are probably adaptive and expected inflation is probably simply equal to last year's inflation. If inflation has been high or moderate but has varied extremely rapidly, then expectations are probably rational and expected inflation is likely to be households' and businesses' best guesses of where economic policy is taking the economy. Changes in inflation expectations shift the Phillips curve up or down.

7. The best way to gauge how expectations of inflation are formed is to consider the past history of inflation. Would adaptive expectations have provided a significant edge

over static ones? If yes, then inflation expectations are probably adaptive. Would rational expectations have provided a significant edge over adaptive ones? If yes, then inflation expectations are probably rational.

8. How fast the flexible-price model becomes relevant depends on the type of inflation expectations in the economy. Under static expectations, the flexible-price model never becomes relevant. Under adaptive expectations, the flexible-price model becomes relevant gradually, in the long run. Under rational expectations the long run is now; the flexible-price model analysis is relevant always and immediately.

Key Terms

output gap (p. 341)

Okun's law (p. 341)

natural rate of unemployment (p. 341)

sticky prices (p. 342)

Phillips curve (p. 343)

expected inflation (p. 343)

"normal" baseline real rate of interest (p. 347)

Taylor rule (p. 347)

monetary policy reaction function (p. 348)

static expectations (p. 361)

adaptive expectations (p. 361)

rational expectations (p. 361)

Analytical Exercises

1. What is the relationship between the three views of aggregate supply? Why do economists tend to focus on the Phillips curve to the exclusion of the other two views?

2. Under what circumstances will a government expansionary fiscal or monetary policy do nothing to raise GDP or lower unemployment?

3. Under the circumstances in which an expansionary government policy fails to raise GDP or lower unemployment, what would the policy manage to do?

4. If expectations of inflation are adaptive, is there any way to reduce inflation without suffering unemployment higher than the natural rate? What would you advise a central bank that sought to reduce inflation without provoking high unemployment to do?

5. What do you think a central bank should do in response to an adverse supply shock? How does your answer depend on the way in which expectations of inflation are being formed in the economy?

Policy Exercises

1. In 2004 the unemployment rate averaged 5.6 percent. Back in 2000 it averaged 4.1 percent. Real GDP in 2004 stood some 10.3 percent above real GDP in 2000. Assuming that the natural rate of unemployment remained unchanged between 2000 and 2004, how much growth in real GDP over those 4 years was due to increases in potential output? What was the effect of "cyclical" factors — fluctuations in unemployment?

2. What factors do you think have led the natural rate of unemployment to be so high in Europe today?

3. What factors do you think have led the natural rate of unemployment to be so low in the United States today?

4. Do you think that inflation expectations in the United States today are static, adaptive, or rational? Why?

5. Suppose that the economy has a Phillips curve

$$\pi = \pi^e - \beta(u - u^*)$$

with the parameter $\beta = 0.5$ and the natural rate of unemployment u^* equal to 6 percent. And suppose that the central bank's reaction to inflation, the IS curve, and Okun's law together mean that the unemployment rate is given by

$$u = u_0 + \phi(\pi - \pi^t)$$

with the central bank's target level of inflation π^t equal to 2 percent, with the parameter ϕ equal to 0.4, and with the normal baseline real interest rate level of aggregate demand corresponding to a value of u_0 of 6 percent. Suppose that initially — this year, in the year 0 — expected inflation is equal to actual inflation.

a. What is the initial level of unemployment?

b. Suppose that the government announces that in year 1 and in every year thereafter its expansionary policies will reduce u_0 to 4 percent, that this announcement is credible, and that the economy has *rational expectations* of inflation. What will unemployment and inflation be in year 1? What will they be thereafter?

c. Suppose that the government announces that in year 1 and in every year thereafter its expansionary policies will reduce u_0 to 4 percent, that this announcement is credible, and that the economy has *adaptive expectations* of inflation. What will unemployment and inflation be in year 1? What will they be thereafter?

d. Suppose that the government announces that in year 1 and in every year thereafter its expansionary policies will reduce u_0 to 4 percent, that this announcement is credible, and that the economy has *static expectations* of inflation. What will unemployment and inflation be in year 1? What will they be thereafter?

6. Suppose that the economy has a Phillips curve

$$\pi = \pi^e - \beta(u - u^*)$$

with the parameter $\beta = 0.5$ and the natural rate of unemployment u^* equal to 6 percent. And suppose that the central bank's reaction to inflation, the IS curve, and Okun's law together mean that the unemployment rate is given by

$$u = u_0 + \phi(\pi - \pi^t)$$

with the central bank's target level of inflation π^t equal to 2 percent, with the parameter ϕ equal to 0.4, and with the normal baseline real interest rate level of aggregate demand corresponding to a value of u_0 of 6 percent. Suppose that initially — this year, in the year 0 — expected inflation is equal to actual inflation.

a. What is the initial level of unemployment?

b. Suppose that the central bank raises its target inflation rate for next year — year 1 — to 4 percent, and announces this change. Suppose the economy has *rational expectations* of inflation. What will happen to unemployment and inflation in year 1? What will happen thereafter?

c. Suppose that the central bank raises its target inflation rate for next year — year 1 — to 4 percent, and announces this change. Suppose the economy has *adaptive expectations* of inflation. What will happen to unemployment and inflation in year 1? What will happen thereafter?

d. Suppose that the central bank raises its target inflation rate for next year — year 1 — to 4 percent, and announces this change. Suppose the economy has *static expectations* of inflation. What will happen to unemployment and inflation in year one? What will happen thereafter?

7. Suppose that the economy has a Phillips curve

$$\pi = \pi^e - \beta(u - u^*)$$

with the parameter $\beta = 0.5$ and the natural rate of unemployment u^* equal to 6 percent. And suppose that the central bank's reaction to inflation, the IS curve, and Okun's law together mean that the unemployment rate is given by

$$u = u_0 + \phi(\pi - \pi^t)$$

with the central bank's target level of inflation π^t equal to 2 percent, with the parameter ϕ equal to 0.4, and with the normal baseline real interest rate level of aggregate demand corresponding to a value of u_0 of 6 percent. Suppose that initially — this year, in the year 0 — expected inflation is equal to actual inflation.

a. What is the initial level of unemployment?

b. Suppose that the natural rate of unemployment u^* falls to 4 percent in year 1 and remains at that level indefinitely. And suppose that this fall in the natural rate of unemployment does not come as a surprise. Suppose the economy has *rational expectations* of inflation. What will happen to unemployment and inflation in year 1? What will happen thereafter?

c. Suppose that the natural rate of unemployment u^* falls to 4 percent in year 1 and remains at that level indefinitely. And suppose that this fall in the natural rate of unemployment does not come as a surprise. Suppose the economy has *adaptive expectations* of inflation. What will happen to unemployment and inflation in year 1? What will happen thereafter?

d. Suppose that the natural rate of unemployment u^* falls to 4 percent in year 1 and remains at that level indefinitely. And suppose that this fall in the natural rate of unemployment does not come as a surprise. Suppose the economy has *static expectations* of inflation. What will happen to unemployment and inflation in year 1? What will happen thereafter?

Equilibrium Inflation and Unemployment: Some Details

APPENDIX 12a

The position of the Phillips curve depends on the natural rate of unemployment u^*, the expected rate of inflation π^e, and whether there are any current supply shocks affecting inflation, ss. The position of the MPRF depends on the level of unemployment u_0 when the real interest rate r is at what the central bank thinks of as its normal baseline rate r_0, and the central bank's target level of inflation π^t. All five of these factors together, along with the parameters ϕ and β — the slopes of the monetary policy reaction function and of the Phillips curve — determine the economy's equilibrium inflation and unemployment rates.

From our MPRF

$$u = u_0 + \phi(\pi - \pi^t)$$

and our Phillips curve

$$\pi = \pi^e - \beta(u - u^*) + ss$$

it is straightforward but tedious to obtain an algebraic solution for what the economy's unemployment rate and inflation rate are. Simply substitute the Phillips curve equation into the monetary policy reaction function and solve for the unemployment rate:

$$u = \left(\frac{1}{1 + \phi\beta}u_0 + \frac{\phi\beta}{1 + \phi\beta}u^*\right) + \frac{\phi}{1 + \phi\beta}(\pi^e - \pi^t) + \frac{\phi}{1 + \phi\beta}ss$$

and substitute the monetary policy reaction function equation into the Phillips curve equation and solve for the inflation rate:

$$\pi = \left(\frac{1}{1 + \phi\beta}\pi^e + \frac{\phi\beta}{1 + \phi\beta}\pi^t\right) + \frac{\beta}{1 + \phi\beta}(u^* - u_0) + \frac{1}{1 + \phi\beta}ss$$

We could use these equations together with the values from Boxes 12.3 and 12.6 to again determine that in equilibrium in our example, the unemployment rate u is 7.5 percent and the inflation rate π is 2.75 percent.

In general, we see that the unemployment rate is equal to

- A weighted average of the unemployment rate u_0 when the central bank has set the real interest rate to its normal baseline value r_0 and the natural rate of unemployment u^* (the greater the product of the slope parameters ϕ and β, the higher the relative weight on the natural rate u^*).
- A term that depends on the difference between the expected rate of inflation π^e and the central bank's target rate of inflation π^t (when the expected inflation rate is higher than the central bank's target rate, unemployment is higher because the central bank has raised interest rates to fight inflation).
- A term that depends on current supply shocks ss.

We see that the inflation rate is equal to

- A weighted average of the expected rate of inflation π^e and the central bank's target rate of inflation π^t (the greater the product of the slope parameters ϕ and β, the higher the relative weight on the target rate π^t).
- A term that depends on the difference between the natural rate of unemployment u^* and unemployment rate u_0 when the central bank has set the real interest rate to its normal baseline value r_0. When the natural rate of unemployment is higher than u_0, inflation is higher because there is an inflationary bias to demand.
- A term that depends on current supply shocks ss.

We can use this framework to analyze the effects of a shift in policy on the economy's equilibrium. For example, consider a depression abroad that lowers demand for exports. This change in the economic environment causes a decrease in planned expenditure, which leads to a rise in u_0, the unemployment rate when the real interest rate is at its normal baseline value r_0, by an amount Δu_0. Since none of the other parameters of the inflation-unemployment framework change, the effect on the equilibrium levels of unemployment and inflation can be calculated immediately as

$$\Delta u = \frac{1}{1 + \phi\beta}\Delta u_0$$

and

$$\Delta\pi = \frac{-\beta}{1 + \phi\beta}\Delta u_0$$

Macroeconomic Policy

We now have all the tools we need to understand business cycles: Part 3 showed how to analyze business cycles in a flexible-price macroeconomy. Part 4 showed how to analyze business cycles in a sticky-price macroeconomy, and how to understand when the flexible-price model and when the sticky-price model is the best one to use.

Part 5 uses the tools built up earlier in this book to conduct a guided tour of the major issues in modern macroeconomic policy. Chapter 13 considers stabilization policy: how the government attempts to keep unemployment low, growth steady, inflation low, and recessions shallow. Chapter 14 moves on to consider fiscal policy and the effect of the government's taxes, spending, and national debt on the level of investment and long-run growth. Chapter 15 focuses on the international economy: how a government should try to manage its interconnections with the other economies of the world.

After these first three chapters of Part 5, the two that follow step back and take an even broader view. Chapter 16 discusses how the macroeconomy has changed over the past century, and how the changes in the macroeconomy have affected macroeconomic policy. Chapter 17 considers the discipline of macroeconomics: How has it changed in the past, and how is it likely to change in the future?

13

Stabilization Policy

QUESTIONS

How does the Federal Reserve work?

How does the budget process work?

What are the goals of stabilization policy?

How has the practice of stabilization policy evolved?

What aspects of stabilization policy do economists argue about today?

How does uncertainty affect stabilization policy?

How long are the lags associated with stabilization policy?

Part 4 of this book set out the last of our major models, the sticky-price model of the economy, in which short-run changes in real GDP, unemployment, interest rates, and inflation are all driven by changes in the economic environment and by shifts in two kinds of government policy: fiscal policy and monetary policy. Changes in fiscal policy shift the MPRF curve. Central-bank-driven changes in interest rates — monetary policy — move the economy along the MPRF, changing real GDP as well as unemployment and inflation rates.

These policies and the economic environment together set the level of planned expenditure. They move the economy along the Phillips curve, raising and lowering inflation and unemployment. Changes in expectations of inflation, changes in the natural rate of unemployment, and supply shocks shift the position of the short-run Phillips curve, and thus play a powerful role in determining the options open to the government and the central bank.

This is the context in which the government tries to manage the macroeconomy, controlling to a certain extent unemployment and inflation. It attempts to stabilize the macroeconomy by minimizing the impact of the shocks that cause business cycles. The first part of this chapter looks at the institutions that make macroeconomic policy: the Federal Reserve, which makes monetary policy, and the Congress, which makes fiscal policy (subject to the president's veto). After looking at the institutions we will look at how macroeconomic policy is actually made and how well it works.

13.1 MONETARY POLICY INSTITUTIONS

The Federal Reserve Board

Monetary policy in the United States is made by the Federal Reserve, which is our central bank. (In other countries the central bank bears a different name, most frequently the name of its country: The central bank of country X is probably called the Bank of X.)

Today the Federal Reserve is and for more than two decades past the Federal Reserve has been the most important organization making American macroeconomic policy. Because monetary policy is the most powerful tool for stabilizing the economy, the Federal Reserve has the power to play the leading role in stabilization policy. Because the Federal Reserve is effectively independent of its political superiors, the Federal Reserve has the discretion to play the leading role in stabilization policy. And it does. These days fiscal policy — the decisions about spending levels and tax rates made by the president and the Congress — plays a distinctly second fiddle. And these days the president and the Congress, who could order the Federal Reserve around, do not like to do so. That's why White House press releases talking about monetary policy almost always begin: "The Federal Reserve is an independent agency, charged with the mission of maintaining price stability, full employment, and maximum purchasing power . . ."

This institutional division of labor is probably the correct one. Over the past 50 years in the United States, monetary policy has proved to be more powerful, faster acting, and more reliable than fiscal policy.

The Federal Reserve has a central office and 12 regional offices. Its central office is the Board of Governors, composed of a chair, a vice chair, and five governors, all of them nominated by the president and confirmed by the Senate. The Board of Governors' offices are in Washington, DC. The Federal Reserve's 12 regional offices are the 12 Federal Reserve banks. They are scattered around the country in San Francisco, Minneapolis, Dallas, Kansas City, St. Louis, Chicago, Cleveland, Atlanta, Richmond, Philadelphia, New York, and Boston.

The Federal Open Market Committee

The principal policy-making body of the Federal Reserve system is its Federal Open Market Committee (FOMC). The FOMC lowers and raises interest rates, which increases and decreases the money supply. The *Federal Reserve's Board of Governors* can alter bank regulations and can raise or lower the interest rate at which the Federal Reserve itself lends to banks and businesses. But most of the time the FOMC plays the leading role within the Federal Reserve.

The members of the Board of Governors and the presidents of the 12 regional Federal Reserve banks together make up the Federal Open Market Committee (see Figure 13.1). The chair, the vice chair, the other five governors, and the president of the Federal Reserve Bank of New York are always voting members of the FOMC. The 11 presidents of the other Federal Reserve banks alternate. At any moment four are voting members and seven are nonvoting members of the FOMC (see Figure 13.2 on page 382).

The History of the Federal Reserve

The Federal Reserve was created just before World War I. Its congressional architects feared that a unitary central bank based in Manhattan would pay too much attention to the interests of bankers and financiers and not enough attention to the interests of merchants and producers. A near century of experience, however, suggests that they were wrong: Bankers in St. Louis think like bankers in New York.

The Federal Reserve failed to handle its first great crisis, the Great Depression that started in 1929. Depending on whom you believe, the Federal Reserve either

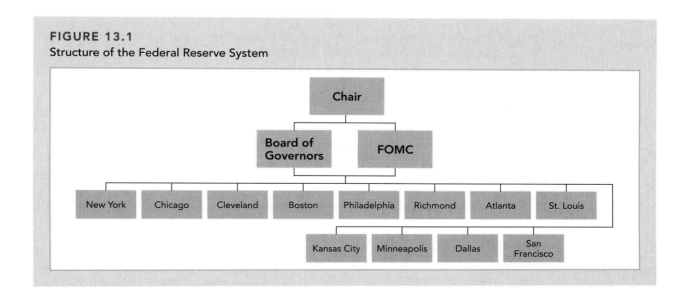

FIGURE 13.1
Structure of the Federal Reserve System

FIGURE 13.2

Composition of the Federal Open Market Committee (FOMC)

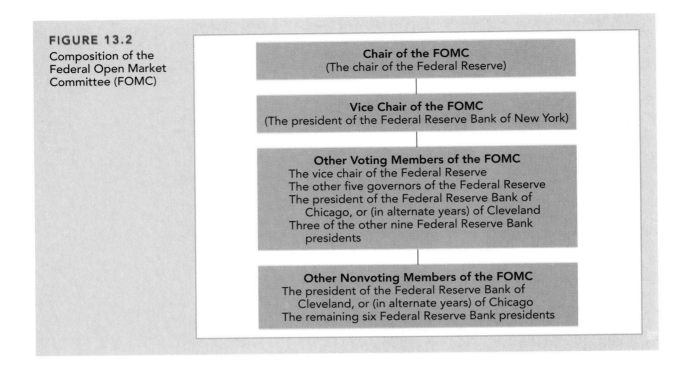

did nothing to help cure the Great Depression, or it made things much worse and played a major role in causing the Great Depression. Since World War II, however, the Federal Reserve has done a much better job: There has been no repeat of the Great Depression.

The Federal Reserve's performance in the 1970s is generally regarded as inadequate. The 1970s were a decade of rising inflation and relatively high unemployment. Today, after two straight decades in the 1980s and 1990s of very successful monetary stabilization policy, the prestige of the Federal Reserve is high. It has almost unlimited freedom to conduct monetary policy as it wishes. Few outside the organization want to challenge its judgments or decisions.

How the Federal Reserve Operates

The FOMC meets about every six weeks to set interest rates. It can and frequently does delegate power to the chair of the Federal Reserve to alter interest rates between meetings if circumstances require. And it can hold emergency meetings on short notice.

The FOMC tries to reach its decisions by consensus. If a consensus cannot be achieved, the members of the FOMC are more likely to postpone the issue than to make a decision that a substantial minority of its members oppose. But a substantial minority almost never opposes. The chair has only one vote of twelve, but almost invariably the FOMC does what the chair wishes. These days questions and dissents from the chair's view of the economy and proposed path for interest rates are much more likely to be voiced in private in the chair's office before an FOMC meeting than in the meeting itself. Alan Greenspan and Paul

Volcker — and, before them, Arthur Burns and William McChesney Martin — have been very strong chairs.[1]

However, once the FOMC decides on a change in policy, that change is implemented immediately. Interest rates shift within minutes in response to FOMC decisions. Indeed, interest rates often change in advance of the actual FOMC meeting as speculators attempt to make money by betting on what they believe the Federal Reserve will do.

The chair of the Federal Reserve Board is the chair of the FOMC. Alan Greenspan was confirmed to another four-year term as chair of the Federal Reserve Board in the summer of 2004. The president of the Federal Reserve Bank of New York is the vice chair of the FOMC; Tim Geithner currently holds the post.

The FOMC changes interest rates by carrying out open-market operations. In an expansionary open-market operation, the Federal Reserve buys government bonds. Such a transaction reduces the amount of interest-bearing government bonds available for financial investors to hold. This reduction in publicly available supply raises the price of short-term government bonds, and as we saw in Box 11.2, an increase in the price of a bond is a decline in its interest rate. When the Federal Reserve buys government bonds it pays for them by crediting the purchasers with deposits at the regional Federal Reserve banks. Commercial banks use these deposits to satisfy the reserve requirements imposed on them by bank regulators. The more reserves a bank has, the more deposits it can accept and the more loans it can make. With more banks trying to make more loans, the interest rates that banks charge on loans drop. Thus purchases of government bonds by the Federal Reserve are expansionary open-market operations, which reduce interest rates. Contractionary open-market operations work in reverse, raising interest rates.

Open-market operations are not the only policy tools the Federal Reserve has. The Board of Governors can alter legally required bank reserves, and it can lend money directly to financial institutions. It can restrict the types of loans that the financial institutions it regulates can make. But these tools are used very rarely. Almost always the FOMC can use open-market operations to set interest rates at whatever it wants them to be. Note the qualifier "almost always." The Federal Reserve's power to set interest rates is subject to only one important restriction: The Federal Reserve cannot reduce the nominal interest rate on any Treasury securities below zero. If a Treasury bill carried an interest rate less than zero, then no one would want to buy it, since simply holding cash would be more profitable.

This inability of the Federal Reserve to push nominal interest rates below zero has potentially destructive consequences. If prices are expected to fall — during a time of anticipated deflation, for example, when the expected inflation rate is negative — a nominal interest rate that is close to but not less than zero may still be a relatively high real interest rate, because the real interest rate r is the difference between the nominal interest rate i and the expected inflation rate π^e:

$$r = i - \pi^e$$

If the expected inflation rate is sufficiently far below zero, the real interest rate will be high, and investment low, no matter what the FOMC does. In 2002 and 2003, a faltering economy led the Federal Reserve to lower short-term nominal

---

[1]Between Burns and Volcker, G. William Miller was chair for a short period of time. He was not a strong chair.

interest rates down to 1 percent per year. Some observers feared that the United States might be teetering on the edge of price deflation. Deflation was feared because it would drive up real interest rates at just the time the Federal Reserve needed to reduce them to stimulate the economy. Yet with nominal interest rates near their minimum of zero, the Federal Reserve's hands would have been tied and stimulative reductions in the real interest rate would have been impossible. But by the middle of 2004 the danger (if indeed it was a danger) had passed, and the FOMC was arguing about how fast and how far to *raise* interest rates to keep inflation from accelerating over the next several years. (However, as Box 13.1 discusses, the inability to push nominal interest rates below zero is relevant to Japan's economic stagnation over the past decade.)

JAPAN'S LIQUIDITY TRAP: POLICY

The possibility that monetary policy might lose its power because expected deflation kept *real* interest rates high used to be dismissed as a theoretical curiosity irrelevant to the real world. But since the mid-1990s the Japanese economy has looked very much as though it might be caught in such a "liquidity trap." Real GDP has been far below potential output. Nominal interest rates on short-term government bonds have at times fallen to 0.04 percent — that is four-hundredths of 1 percent a year; the annual interest on $100 invested at such an interest rate would be four cents. (See Figure 13.3.) But a combination of expected deflation,

FIGURE 13.3

Japan's Liquidity Trap, 1990–2004: Nominal Safe Interest Rates The graph shows the official discount rate of the Bank of Japan. Despite a decade of extremely low interest rates on government bonds in Japan, investment has not boomed. Why not? Because risk premiums and expected deflation have made businesses believe that the real interest rates at which they can borrow remain high.

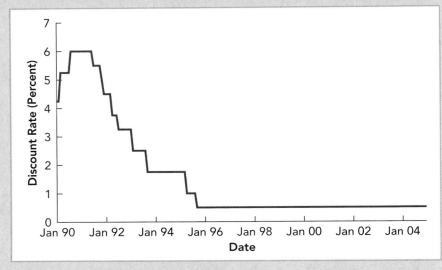

Source: Bank of Japan.

high risk premiums, and steep term premiums meant that businesses found that the real interest rate they had to pay to borrow money was quite high.

This situation continues today. From banks' perspective there are few creditworthy borrowers. Yet from businesses' perspective there is little affordable capital. Japan's stagnation has dragged on for nearly a decade.

What is to be done? Two obvious policies might improve matters. The first is fiscal expansion: Cut taxes or increase spending to shift the IS curve to the right and the MPRF to the left, raising the level of planned spending even if real interest rates are relatively high. The second is to create expectations of inflation by announcing that monetary policy will be expansionary not just now but for the indefinite future.

> **RECAP   MONETARY POLICY INSTITUTIONS**
>
> The most important kind of stabilization policy is monetary policy, carried out by the Federal Reserve, the United States' central bank. The principal policy-making body of the Federal Reserve is the Federal Open Market Committee — the FOMC. The FOMC decides what the level of short-term safe nominal interest rates will be, and how fast the money stock will grow. The head of and the most important decision maker in the Federal Reserve is the chair. Alan Greenspan was reappointed to another four-year term as chair of the Federal Reserve in the summer of 2004.

13.2 FISCAL POLICY INSTITUTIONS

The Budget Cycle in Theory

Fiscal policy in the United States today is managed by Congress (subject to the veto of the president). Congress passes laws which the president then signs (or vetoes — and Congress then overrides or fails to override the vetoes). Congress's tax laws determine the taxes imposed by the federal government. Congress's spending bills determine the level of government purchases. Together these taxes and government purchases make up the government's fiscal policy.

Tax and spending levels are set in a combined bureaucratic-legislative process called the budget cycle, outlined in Figure 13.4 on page 386. The federal government's year for budget purposes — its fiscal year — runs from October 1 of one year to September 30 of the next. The budget period from October 1, 2005, to September 30, 2006, for example, is called "fiscal 2006."

Some broad classes of expenditure, called "mandatory," are the result of open-ended long-term government commitments, and they continue whether or not Congress explicitly appropriates money for them in the current year. Social Security, Medicare, Medicaid, unemployment insurance, food stamps, and so forth fall into this category of so-called mandatory spending. Other broad classes of expenditure, called "discretionary," must be explicitly appropriated by Congress in each fiscal year. Defense spending, the National Park Service, NASA, the National Institutes

FIGURE 13.4

The Budget Process The process by which Congress and the president make fiscal policy is arcane and byzantine.

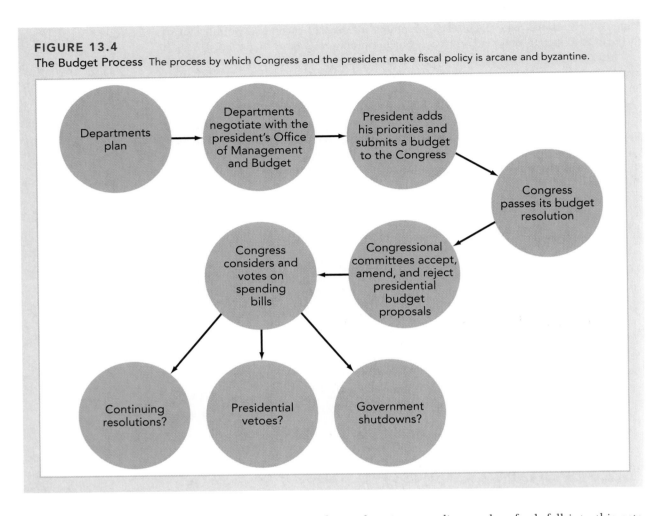

of Health, highway spending, education spending, and so forth fall into this category of so-called discretionary spending. Figure 13.5 shows major areas of spending relative to GDP over the last four decades. Figure 13.6 on page 388 details nondefense discretionary spending.

Early in one fiscal year the executive branch departments and agencies that administer federal programs begin planning for the next. Throughout the fall they negotiate with the president's Executive Office — the Office of Management and Budget. The result of these negotiations, modified by the president's own priorities, becomes the president's budget submission to Congress in January.

Congress considers the president's budget request, conducts its own internal debates, and by the end of April is supposed to have passed a budget resolution giving spending targets for broad classes of expenditure. Using the budget resolution as a guide, Congress alters and amends the laws that control mandatory spending, alters and amends the tax code, and passes the appropriations bills necessary for discretionary spending. By the end of September all of the appropriations bills are supposed to have been passed, so that the new fiscal year can begin with the pieces of the government knowing how much should be spent and on what over the next 12 months.

FIGURE 13.5

Major Federal Government Expenditures by Category, 1965–2003 The past four decades have seen the level of federal government spending as a share of GDP remain roughly constant, but the composition of federal spending has changed remarkably. Spending on national defense and international affairs has fallen from nearly 10 to between 3 and 4 percent of GDP. Spending on Medicare and Medicaid and Social Security has risen from about 2.5 to over 8 percent of GDP. Net interest, which comprises most other "mandatory" spending, rose sharply from 1 to 3 percent of GDP as a result of the deficits of the 1980s, declined in the 1990s, but recently began to climb again. Other social insurance — unemployment insurance, welfare, and so forth — rose from just under 2 percent of GDP in the 1960s to 3.5 percent by the deep recession years of the early 1980s, and has been cut since. And domestic "discretionary" spending — everything else the government does, from the FBI to the National Park Service, the National Institutes of Health, and the interstate highway system — rose from 3 to 5 percent of GDP between 1965 and 1980, and has since been cut back to about 3 percent.

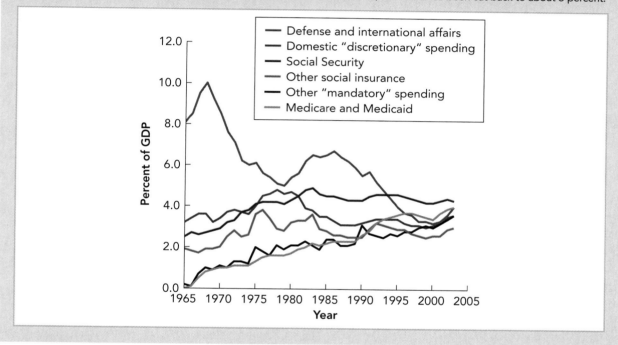

Source: Congressional Budget Office.

The Budget Cycle in Practice

More often than not, however, Congress fails to pass or the president vetoes one or more appropriations bills. In that case the government continues more or less on autopilot if Congress passes and the president signs a continuing resolution until the appropriations bill is passed. If they don't, the government "shuts down." Discretionary spending is cut back to the bone. Nonessential employees are sent home. The Washington Monument and other major tourist attractions are closed. Government office buildings are inhabited by only a skeleton crew of key functionaries and unpaid interns until Congress and the president reach agreement and pass and sign the appropriations bills necessary for the government's discretionary spending programs to go forward.

However, even during a so-called government shutdown, most of what the government does continues. Mandatory spending does not have to be explicitly appropriated every year, and it continues even if there is total gridlock in Washington.

FIGURE 13.6

Federal Government Domestic Discretionary Spending, 2000

Every year Congress and the president must sign appropriations bills for those categories of spending that are not mandated by long-run open-ended enabling statutes (like Social Security, Medicare, and unemployment insurance) or required by the Constitution (like net interest). Of this "discretionary" spending, defense takes about half. The rest is spread out among a wide variety of activities.

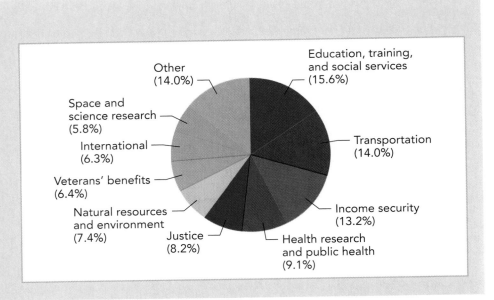

Source: Congressional Budget Office.

inside lag

The lapse of time between the moment that a shock begins to affect the economy and the moment that economic policy is altered in response to the shock.

The lesson to draw from this overview is that making fiscal policy in the United States is complicated, baroque, and time-consuming. The **inside lag** — the time between when an economic shock occurs and when a policy proposal becomes effective — for fiscal policy is measured in years. By contrast, the inside lag associated with FOMC-decided changes in monetary policy is measured in days, weeks, or at most two months. The FOMC can turn on a dime. Congress and the president cannot. This is a key advantage that makes the Federal Reserve more effective at undertaking stabilization policy to manage unemployment and inflation.

> **RECAP   FISCAL POLICY INSTITUTIONS**
>
> Fiscal policy in the United States is conducted by Congress, which passes laws, and the president, who signs — or vetoes — them. Most government spending is "mandatory" and takes place each year regardless of whether Congress acts. Other spending is "discretionary," subject to the whims of politics, lobbying, and, occasionally, economics. Discretionary spending is well less than half of government spending. Defense spending is about half of discretionary spending.

13.3 THE HISTORY OF STABILIZATION POLICY

The Employment Act of 1946

The United States government did not always see itself as responsible for stabilizing the economy and taming the business cycle. It accepted this responsibility in the Employment Act of 1946, which did the following:

- Established Congress's Joint Economic Committee.
- Established the president's Council of Economic Advisers.

- Called on the president to estimate and forecast the current and future level of economic activity in the United States.

- Announced that it was the "continuing policy and responsibility" of the federal government to "coordinate and utilize all its plans, functions, and resources . . . to foster and promote free competitive enterprise and the general welfare; conditions under which there will be afforded useful employment for those able, willing, and seeking to work; and to promote maximum employment, production, and purchasing power."

Passage of the Employment Act marked the rout of the belief that the government could not stabilize the economy and should not try to do so. In the old view, common at the beginning of the twentieth century, monetary and fiscal policies to fight recessions would keep workers and firms producing in unsustainable lines of business and levels of capital intensity, thus making the depression less deep only at the price of making it longer.

This doctrine that in the long run even deep recessions like the Great Depression would turn out to have been "good medicine" for the economy drew anguished cries of dissent even before World War II. John Maynard Keynes tried to ridicule this "crime and punishment" view of business cycles, concluding that he did not see how "universal bankruptcy could do us any good or bring us any nearer to prosperity." Indeed, it was largely due to Keynes's writings, especially his *General Theory of Employment, Interest and Money,* that economists and politicians became convinced that the government could halt depressions and smooth out the business cycle. But Keynes was not alone. For example, Ralph Hawtrey, an adviser to the British Treasury and the Bank of England, called worry about government action the equivalent of "crying, 'Fire! Fire!' in Noah's flood." By the end of the Great Depression there was near universal consensus that the government *had* to take steps to moderate the business cycle to make sure nothing like the Great Depression ever happened again.

Keynesian Overoptimism and the Monetarist Correction

The high-water mark of confidence that the government could and would manage to use its macroeconomic policy tools to stabilize the economy came in the 1960s. In that decade President Lyndon Johnson's chief economic adviser, Walter Heller, wrote of the "New Dimensions of Political Economy" that had been opened by the Keynesian revolution. The Department of Commerce changed the title of its *Business Cycle Digest* to the *Business Conditions Digest* — because, after all, the business cycle was dead.

The 1970s, however, erased that confidence. Economists Milton Friedman and Edward Phelps had warned that attempts to keep the economy at the upper left corner of the Phillips curve would inevitably cause an upward shift in inflation expectations — that even if expectations had truly been static during the 1950s and early 1960s, they would become adaptive if unemployment were pushed too low for too long.

Friedman and Phelps were correct: The 1970s saw a sharp upward shift in the Phillips curve as people lost confidence in the commitment of the Federal Reserve to keep inflation low and raised their expectations of inflation. (See Figure 13.7.) The result was stagflation: a combination of relatively high unemployment and relatively high inflation. The lesson learned was that attempts to keep unemployment low and the level of output stable were counterproductive if they tried to keep

FIGURE 13.7

The U.S. Phillips Curves, 1955–1980 Between the mid-1950s and the late 1960s, unemployment and inflation in the United States were low and stable, and productivity growth was rapid. Economists in government and their politician bosses thought that the new tools of economic policy had licked the business cycle. They were wrong. Between 1967 and 1975 expected inflation nearly tripled, the natural rate of unemployment rose by 2 percentage points, and stagflation set in.

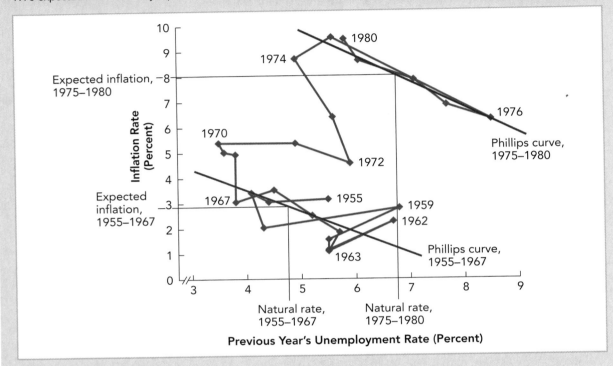

Source: The 2004 edition of *The Economic Report of the President* (Washington, DC: Government Printing Office).

unemployment below the natural rate and so eroded public confidence in the central bank's commitment to keep inflation low and prices stable.

Monetary Management in the 1980s and Beyond

The 1970s ended with many economists convinced that "activist" monetary policy did more harm than good, and that the United States might be better off with an "automatic" monetary policy that fixed some control variable like the money stock on a stable long-run growth path. But the sharp instability of monetary velocity since the start of the 1980s (see Figure 13.8) greatly reduced the number of advocates of an automatic central bank that lets the money stock grow by a fixed proportional amount every year.

Thus today the Federal Reserve acts as outlined in Chapters 10 and 12. As in Chapter 10, the Federal Reserve estimates what level of real GDP will correspond to full employment and where the IS curve will be in a year to a year and a half, and it tries to set a real interest rate today that will produce an appropriate level of output, of capacity utilization, and of the unemployment rate. What is an

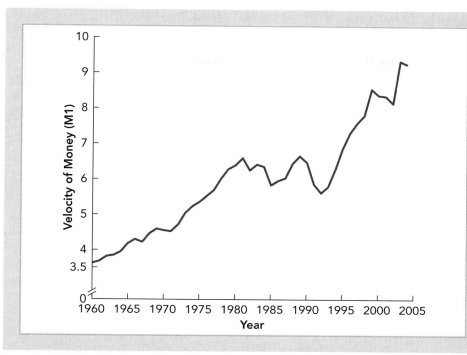

FIGURE 13.8
The Velocity of Money
Before 1980 monetarists argued that the velocity of money was stable and predictable. It had a constant upward trend as new technology was introduced into the banking system, and nearly no other fluctuations. Keep the money supply growing smoothly, they argued, and the smooth trend of velocity will keep the economy stable. They too were wrong. After 1980 the velocity of money became unstable indeed.

Source: The 2004 edition of *The Economic Report of the President* (Washington, DC: Government Printing Office).

"appropriate level"? That is where Chapter 12 comes in. When inflation is above the Federal Reserve's target for where it should be, the appropriate level of demand has a certain amount of economic slack built into it to produce downward pressure on inflation. When inflation is below the Federal Reserve's target, it aims for a level of output above potential, all according to the Taylor rule and monetary policy reaction function (MPRF) of Chapter 12. This is the operating procedure that the Federal Reserve has been following for more than two decades. And it is widely judged to have been highly successful.

RECAP   THE HISTORY OF STABILIZATION POLICY

Before the Great Depression, the government viewed the business cycle much like people today view hurricanes and tornadoes: They are catastrophes, and the government should help those who suffer, but it makes no sense to ask the government to prevent or manage them. Largely as a result of the writings of the British economist John Maynard Keynes, this attitude vanished during the Great Depression and World War II. After World War II, economists and politicians believed that the government could and should prevent great depressions and smooth out the business cycle. Overconfidence in the government's ability to manage the macroeconomy vanished in the 1970s, a decade of both relatively high unemployment and relatively high inflation. Today we have a more limited confidence in the government's ability to stabilize and manage the business cycle.

13.4 THE POWER AND LIMITS OF STABILIZATION POLICY

Economists' Disagreements

Economists today arrange themselves along a line with respect to their views as to how the central bank (the Federal Reserve) and fiscal authorities (the president and Congress) should manage the economy. At one end are economists like Milton Friedman, who holds that activist attempts to manage the economy are likely to do more harm than good. Government should settle on a policy that does not produce disaster no matter what the pattern of shocks or the structure of the economy. This end of the spectrum holds that most of the large business cycles and macroeconomic disturbances experienced in the past century were the result of well-intentioned but destructive economic policy decisions based on faulty models of the economy (see Box 13.2).

THE STRUCTURE OF THE ECONOMY AND THE LUCAS CRITIQUE: THE DETAILS

Economist *Robert Lucas* has argued that most of what economists thought they knew about the structure of the economy was false. Expectations of the future have major effects on decision making in the present: Workers' nominal wage demands, managers' investment decisions, households' consumption decisions, and practically every other economic decision hinge, in one way or another, on what is expected to happen in the future. And expectations depend on many things — including the policies followed by the government. Change the policies followed by the government, and you change the structure of the economy as well.

Thus, Lucas argued, the use of economic models to forecast how the economy would respond to changes in government policy is an incoherent and mistaken exercise. Changes in policy would induce changes in the structure of the economy and its patterns of behavior that would invalidate the forecasting exercise. Economic forecasts based on a period in which inflation expectations were adaptive would turn out to be grossly in error if applied to a period in which inflation expectations were rational. Forecasts of consumption spending based on estimates of the marginal propensity to consume when changes in national income were permanent would lead policy makers astray if used to forecast the effects of policies that cause transitory changes in national income.

This **Lucas critique** is an important enough insight that for it Robert Lucas was awarded the Nobel Prize in 1995.

Lucas critique

The assertion that much analysis of the effects of economic policy is badly flawed because it does not take proper account of how changes in policies induce changes in people's expectations and thus in their behavior.

At the other end of the spectrum are those who hold that shocks to the economy are frequent and substantial. They believe that appropriate government policy can do a lot to stabilize the economy — to avoid both high unemployment and high inflation.

This economic policy debate has been going on for generations. It will never be resolved, for the differences are inevitably differences of emphasis rather than sharp lines of division. Even the most "activist" economists recognize the limits imposed on stabilization policy by uncertainty about the structure of the economy and the difficulties of forecasting. Even the greatest believer in the natural stability of the economy — Milton Friedman — believes that the economy is naturally stable only if government policy follows the proper policy of ensuring the smooth growth of the money stock.

The Implications of Uncertainty

Because economic policy works with long and variable *lags,* stabilization policy requires that we first know where the economy is and where it is going. If future conditions cannot be predicted, policies initiated today are as likely to have destructive as constructive effects when they affect the economy 18 months or two years from now.

In general, economists take two approaches in trying to forecast the near-term future of the economy. The first approach is to use large-scale macroeconometric models — more complicated versions of the models of this book. The second approach is to search for **leading indicators:** one or a few economic variables not necessarily noted in this book that experience tells us are strongly correlated with future movements in real GDP or inflation. Taking over a former U.S. government task, a private economics research group called the Conference Board now publishes a monthly index of leading economic indicators — 10 factors averaged together that many economists believe provide a good guide to economic activity nine or so months in the future.

Of the components that go into the index of leading indicators (see Box 13.3), perhaps the most broadly watched is the stock market. The level of the stock

leading indicators

A number of variables correlated with future movements in real GDP or inflation.

WHAT ARE LEADING INDICATORS? THE DETAILS

The index of leading indicators contains 10 different components. The index used to be constructed by the Commerce Department's Bureau of Economic Analysis. As a cost-saving move, it was privatized: It is now compiled and reported by the Conference Board, a nonprofit economic research group. The Conference Board weights all 10 of these components to try to create the best possible index of leading indicators. The current weighting factors applied to the components of the index are shown in Table 13.1.

BOX 13.3

TABLE 13.1
Components of the Leading Indicators Index

Code	Component	Weighting
BCI-1	Average weekly hours, manufacturing	0.195
BCI-5	Average weekly initial claims for unemployment insurance	0.027
BCI-8	Manufacturers' new orders, consumer goods and materials	0.050
BCI-32	Vendor performance, slower deliveries diffusion index	0.030
BCI-27	Manufacturers' new orders, nondefense capital goods	0.014
BCI-29	Building permits, new private housing units	0.020
BCI-19	Stock prices, 500 common stocks	0.031
BCI-106	Money supply, M2	0.278
BCI-129	Interest rate spread, 10-year Treasury bonds minus federal funds	0.336
BCI-83	Index of consumer expectations	0.019

Source: www.conferenceboard.org.

market is a good indicator of the future of investment spending because the same factors that make corporate investment committees likely to approve investment projects — optimism about future profits, cheap sources of financing, willingness to accept risks — make investors eager to buy stocks and to buy stocks at higher prices. We can read likely future decisions of corporate investment committees from the current value of the stock market. But the stock market is far from perfect as a leading indicator: As economist Paul Samuelson likes to say, the stock market has predicted nine of the past five recessions.

The Money Supply as a Leading Indicator

A second leading indicator that has been closely watched is the money supply. Before the instability of the 1980s monetarists used to claim that the appropriate measure of the money stock was the only leading indicator worth watching. If the central bank can guide the money stock to the appropriate level through open-market operations, then success at managing the economy will immediately and automatically follow.

As we saw in Chapter 8, no sharp, bright line separates assets that are easy to spend from other assets. A dollar bill is clearly "money" in economists' sense of being readily spendable purchasing power. But what about a 90-day certificate of deposit with an interest penalty if it is cashed in before it matures? Each place you draw the line gives you a particular total dollar amount of the assets that make up the economy's "money" — a different monetary aggregate. In order from the smallest to the largest, with each a superset of the one before, the most frequently used measures are called by the shorthand names M1, M2, and M3.

These monetary aggregates do not behave the same. At the start of the 1990s the Federal Reserve faced an especially fierce conundrum. During 1992, for example, M1 — the narrow measure — grew by more than 14 percent while M3, the broad measure, grew by only 0.3 percent, as shown in Figure 13.9.

Different measures of the money stock say different things about monetary policy. Republican Party critics of Alan Greenspan continue to blame his tight money policies for George H. W. Bush's defeat in the presidential election of 1992, with op-ed columnists like Robert Novak and Fred Barnes being the least forgiving of Greenspan, pointing to 1992's M3 growth of only 0.3 percent. The Federal Reserve was keeping M3 stable, pushing up interest rates and deepening the 1990–1992 recession. What Novak and Barnes do not tell you — and what supporters of Greenspan do — is 1992 also saw extraordinarily rapid growth of M1 (and short-term real interest rates of less than zero). While those looking at M3 call 1992's monetary policy extraordinarily contractionary, those looking at M1 take its 14 percent growth rate as evidence of a recession-fighting monetary policy that was strongly stimulative.

To say that the money stock is the single most important leading indicator is not helpful if different measures of "the" money stock say different things. And 1992 is not alone. In 2000 — as the stock market reached its peak and started rapidly down — M3 grew by 8.6 percent and M1 shrank by 3.3 percent. In 1996 M3 grew by 7.5 percent and M1 shrank by 4.3 percent. Easy money or tight money?

All in all, being a monetary economist is much harder than it used to be (see Box 13.4).

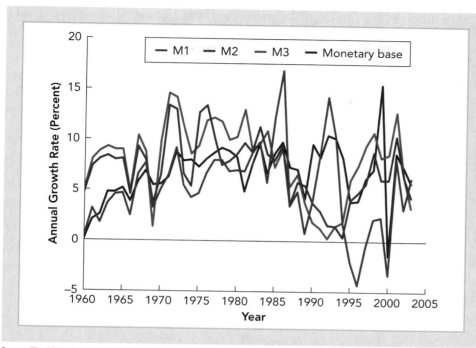

FIGURE 13.9
Different Measures of the Money Stock Behave Differently
The graph shows the annual growth rates of different money stock measures. Since 1980 these different measures have ceased to move together. A year like 1996 in which M1 falls can also see M3 grow, with a difference between the two of more than 10 percentage points per year.

Source: The 2004 edition of *The Economic Report of the President* (Washington, DC: Government Printing Office).

THE MONEY MULTIPLIER: DETAILS

The Federal Reserve's open-market operations change the monetary base: One more dollar's worth of Treasury bills sold to the public means one dollar of cash or reserve deposits fewer in the hands of the public. The effects of Federal Reserve open-market operations on the money supply are less direct, and less certain. Changes in the monetary base cause amplified changes in the money supply through a process called the money multiplier process.

When someone deposits $100 in cash in a bank, the Federal Reserve requires the bank to set aside some portion of that deposit as a reserve to satisfy the Fed that the bank is liquid and can meet its daily demands for funds. Suppose — for simplicity's sake — that the current reserve requirement is 10 percent, so the bank takes $10 of the newly deposited cash and itself deposits it in the nearest regional Federal Reserve Bank as a reserve deposit. The bank then loans out the remaining $90 to collect interest. The borrower receiving the $90 loan typically redeposits it into some other banks. That second wave of banks set aside 10 percent of what they have received — $9 — as their reserves, and loan out the remaining $81. This cycle repeats over and over.

In the end, the Federal Reserve's 10 percent reserve requirement means that an initial injection of $100 in cash into the banking system leads to an increase in total banking systemwide deposits of $100/10% = $1,000, and an increase in banks' own reserve deposits at the Federal Reserve of $100. Thus if the Federal Reserve injects, say, $10 billion into the economy in an open-market operation — by purchasing bonds for cash — it triggers a potential increase of as much as $100 billion in the total money supply. We then say that the economy has a *money multiplier* of 10.

In practice, the increase in the money supply will be less. Borrowing households and businesses who seek to keep a fixed *currency-to-deposits ratio* will keep some of the money in cash, so not all money loaned out by banks in one wave will be redeposited in the next. And banks will keep some excess reserves — not all that they could legally lend will be. The money multiplier depends on three factors: the reserve requirements the Federal Reserve imposes on banks, the proportional amount of excess reserves to deposits that banks seek to keep, and the ratio of currency to deposits in which households and businesses prefer to hold their money. If you know these three factors, then you can calculate that the money multiplier μ is

$$\mu = \frac{(\text{curr/dep}) + 1}{(\text{curr/dep}) + (\text{req/dep}) + (\text{exc/dep})}$$

where (curr/dep) is households' and businesses' desired ratio of currency-to-deposits, (req/dep) is the ratio of required reserves imposed by the Fed, and (exc/dep) is the ratio of excess reserves that banks desire to hold to total deposits.

Once you know the money multiplier, you can calculate the economywide stock of liquid money assets M by multiplying the monetary base B directly controlled by the Fed by the money multiplier μ:

$$M = B \times \mu$$

FIGURE 13.10
Changes in the Currency-to-Deposits Ratio The currency-to-deposits ratio was fairly stable up until the late 1970s. Since then it has first risen and then fallen substantially. Its sharp increase and decrease mean that changes in the money stock are not highly correlated with changes in the monetary base produced by Federal Reserve open-market operations.

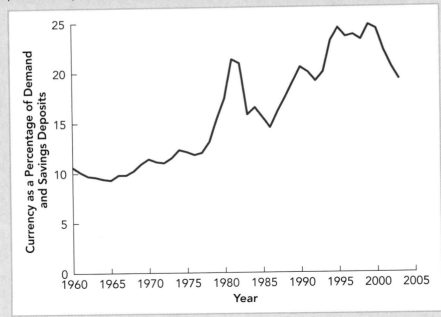

Source: The 2004 edition of *The Economic Report of the President* (Washington, DC: Government Printing Office).

If any of the three factors determining the money multiplier changes, the money multiplier will change as well — and the money supply will change even if the Federal Reserve has not undertaken any open-market operations and has left the monetary base completely alone:

$$\Delta M = B \times \Delta \mu$$

Do the factors determining the money multiplier shift? Yes, they do. Figure 13.10 shows how one of these three factors — the currency-to-deposits ratio — has varied since 1960.

Long Lags and Variable Effects

Even if economists have good, reliable forecasts, changes in macroeconomic policy affect the economy with long lags and have variable effects. Estimates of the slope of the IS curve are imprecise: This isn't rocket science, after all. Economists are estimating the reactions of human beings to changes in the incentives to undertake different courses of action. They are not calculating the motions of particles that obey invariant and precisely known physical laws.

Moreover, changes in interest rates take time to affect the level of planned expenditure and real GDP. It takes time for corporate investment committees to meet and evaluate how changes in interest rates change the investment projects they wish to undertake. It takes time for changes in the decisions of corporate investment committees to affect the amount of work being done that builds up the country's capital stock. It takes time for the changes in employment and income generated by changes in investment to feed through the multiplier process and have their full effect on equilibrium aggregate demand. Thus the level of total product now is determined not by what long-term real risky interest rates are now, but by what they were more than a year and a half ago.

As more than one member of the FOMC has said, making monetary policy is like driving a car that has had its windshield painted black. You guess which way you want to go by looking in the rearview mirror at the landscape behind. Box 13.5 gives an example of how hard driving then becomes.

THE LIMITS OF STABILIZATION POLICY: ECONOMIC POLICY

Suppose that the target level of real GDP that the central bank hopes to attain is $10,000 billion, but that the central bank staff forecasts that if interest rates are kept at their current levels the real GDP will be only $9,500 billion. Reducing the interest rate will boost real GDP. But how far it will be boosted is uncertain. Suppose that there is one chance in four that a 1-percentage-point reduction in the interest rate will not boost real GDP at all, one chance in two that a 1-percentage-point reduction in the interest rate will boost real GDP by $200 billion, and one chance in four that a 1-percentage-point reduction in the interest rate will boost real GDP by $400 billion.

What should the central bank do? In this particular example, the answer is that it should do only about half as much as it would if there were no uncertainty about the effects of its policies. The point is general: If the effects of policy are uncertain, do less than you otherwise would, and be cautious.

Assume that the central bank tries to make the expected value (in billions) of $(Y - \$10{,}000)^2$ as small as possible: The best situation is to actually have real GDP equal to \$10,000 billion, and bigger deviations are proportionately worse. Then we can solve the central bank's problem. We can calculate the amount Δr by which it should reduce the real interest rate.

If the central bank reduces the real interest rate by Δr, there is

- One chance in four that $Y = \$9{,}500$.
- One chance in two that $Y = \$9{,}500 + \$20{,}000(\Delta r)$.
- One chance in four that $Y = \$9{,}500 + \$40{,}000(\Delta r)$.

In the first case, the squared deviation of Y from \$10,000 is

$$(-\$500)^2 = \$250{,}000$$

In the second case, the squared deviation of Y from \$10,000 is

$$[\$20{,}000(\Delta r) - \$500]^2 = 250{,}000 - 20{,}000{,}000(\Delta r) + [400{,}000{,}000(\Delta r)^2]$$

In the third case, the squared deviation of Y from \$10,000 is

$$[\$40{,}000(\Delta r) - \$500]^2 = 250{,}000 - 40{,}000{,}000(\Delta r) + [1{,}600{,}000{,}000(\Delta r)^2]$$

Since there is one chance in four of each of the first and third cases, and one chance in two of the second case, the total expected value (in billions) of $(Y - \$10{,}000)^2$ is

$$0.25(250{,}000) +$$

$$0.50\{250{,}000 - 20{,}000{,}000(\Delta r) + [400{,}000{,}000(\Delta r)^2]\} +$$

$$0.25\{250{,}000 - 40{,}000{,}000(\Delta r) + [1{,}600{,}000{,}000(\Delta r)^2]\} =$$

$$250{,}000 - 20{,}000{,}000(\Delta r) + [600{,}000{,}000(\Delta r)^2]$$

When Δr equals 0, this expected value of $(Y - \$10{,}000)^2$ is \$250,000. When Δr equals 1 percent ($\Delta r = 0.01$), this expected value of $(Y - \$10{,}000)^2$ is \$110,000. When Δr equals 1.5 percent, this expected value of $(Y - \$10{,}000)^2$ is \$85,000. And when Δr equals 2 percent, this expected value of $(Y - \$10{,}000)^2$ is \$90,000. The minimum value of the expected square of the deviation of Y from \$10,000 billion comes for a value of Δr equal to 1.67 percent, which makes the expected square of the deviation of Y from \$10,000 billion equal to \$83,000 billion.

Suppose that we didn't take any account of uncertainty. Suppose that we simply said that the expected value of the increase in real GDP produced by a 1-percentage-point cut in interest rates is \$200 billion, and that we have a \$500 billion output gap to close. Then we would have set Δr at 2.5 percent — a larger change in the interest rate than the 1.67 percent that turned out to be the best a central bank trying to get real GDP as close as possible to \$10,000 billion could do.

Why the difference once one recognizes the uncertainty in the effects of policy? Because active policy to close the output gap has the additional effect of adding yet more variation to real GDP. The stronger the shift in policy, the more uncertain are its effects and the more likely it is that the policy will be counterproductive. This extra risk is the reason that the best thing for the central bank to do in this example is to cut interest rates not by 2.5 percent but by only 1.67 percent.

The point, however, is quite general. When the effects of your policies are uncertain, do less, and be cautious about undertaking bold policy moves.

> **RECAP** **THE POWER AND LIMITS OF STABILIZATION POLICY**
>
> Economists and policy makers have recognized that the ability of the government to successfully conduct stabilization policy is limited. Uncertainty about the actual state of the economy combined with the long and variable lags with which economic policies take effect means that monetary and fiscal policy must be slow to respond to sudden falls in production and rises in unemployment. Beyond that, because economic policies have uncertain effects, policies to aggressively fight recessions may well wind up being counterproductive. Good policy makers must be cautious policy makers.

13.5 MONETARY VERSUS FISCAL POLICY

Relative Power

At the end of the World War II era, most economists and policy makers believed that the principal stabilization policy tool would be fiscal policy. Monetary policy had proved to be of little use during the Great Depression: Risk premiums and term premiums were too high and too unstable for changes in the short-term nominal safe interest rates controlled by central banks to have reliable effects on production and employment. In contrast, changes in government spending and in taxes were seen as having rapid and reliable effects on aggregate demand. But over the past 50 years opinion has shifted. Today the overwhelming consensus is that monetary policy has proved itself faster acting and more reliable than discretionary fiscal policy.

When Congress tries to stabilize the economy by fiscal policy — by passing laws to change levels of taxes and spending — it cannot realistically hope to see changes in the level of output and employment in less than two years after the bill is first introduced into Congress. It takes time for the bill to move through the House of Representatives. It takes more time for the bill to move through the Senate, and for the conference committee to reconcile the different versions. Yet more time must pass before the operating departments in the executive branch of government can change actual spending or write new rules for administering the tax system once Congress has authorized the fiscal change. And it takes more time for the change in government purchases or in net taxes to have its full effect through the multiplier process.

Monetary policy lags are shorter. The FOMC can move rapidly; once its decisions are made they affect long-term real interest rates on the same day. Substantial lags occur between an interest rate change and output reaching its new equilibrium value: Monetary policy still takes more than a year to work. But **monetary policy lags** are shorter than those associated with **discretionary fiscal policy**.

The fact that the Federal Reserve's decision and action cycle is shorter than that of the president and Congress means that the Federal Reserve can, if it wishes, neutralize the effects of any change in fiscal policy on planned expenditure. As a rule, today's Federal Reserve does routinely neutralize the effects of changes in fiscal policy. Swings in the budget deficit produced by changes in tax laws and spending appropriations have little impact on real GDP unless the Federal Reserve wishes them to.

A recent partial exception is provided by the George W. Bush tax cuts of 2001 and 2003. Because the Federal Reserve had already cut interest rates so low, it would have been unable to keep demand stable by lowering interest rates if those

monetary policy lags

The time between when a monetary policy proposal is made and when it becomes effective in changing the economy in some way.

discretionary fiscal policy

Discretionary fiscal policy is made by Congress's and the president's decisions to change levels of spending and of taxes. It is policy that is not automatic in the sense that automatic stabilizers swing into action without anyone making an explicit decision.

TAX CUTS AND ECONOMIC STIMULUS: POLICY

Proponents of discretionary fiscal policy claim the 1964 Kennedy-Johnson tax cut as a success: It stimulated consumption spending and the economy. It was widely perceived as a permanent tax cut that would raise everyone's permanent income. But critics see it as a fiscal policy failure. Discussed in 1961 and proposed in 1962, it was not enacted until 1964 and had little effect on the economy until 1965–1967.

In 1961–1962 the unemployment rate was in the range of 5.5 to 6.7 percent. Maybe there was a case for thinking that unemployment was above its natural rate. But by 1965–1966 the unemployment rate was in the range of 3.8 to 4.5 percent, inflation was about to become a serious problem, and Johnson's advisers were already calling for tax increases to try to reduce aggregate demand and control inflation.

What about the Reagan tax cuts? The deficits that followed the 1981 Reagan tax cut certainly shifted out the IS curve. But did they raise the level of national product? Almost surely not. The Federal Reserve did not want to see national product expanding so fast as to set inflation rising again. Thus the Reagan deficits led to tighter monetary policy, higher interest rates, and lower investment — not to higher employment and total product. The rule that prevails today and probably will prevail for the next generation is that the Federal Reserve offsets shifts in aggregate demand created by the changing government deficit.

There is, however, one exception. Stanford's Michael Boskin argues that the George W. Bush tax cuts of the early 2000s hit the economy at exactly the right moment to cushion the shock to business confidence generated by the September 11, 2001, terror attack on the World Trade Center and the Pentagon. It was not by design — it was by luck — but it was very good luck to have the tax cut taking effect at that exact moment.

tax cuts had not taken place. Near the edge of such a liquidity trap — when the Federal Reserve runs out of room to cut interest rates further — fiscal policy can have powerful effects. But, as Box 13.6 sets out, that is not the rule but the exception.

Fiscal Policy: Automatic Stabilizers

One kind of fiscal policy works rapidly enough to be important. The so-called fiscal **automatic stabilizers** swing into action within three months to dampen business cycle–driven swings in disposable income and so moderate the business cycle.

Whenever the economy enters a recession or a boom, the government's budget surplus or deficit begins to swing in the opposite direction. As the economy enters a boom, tax collections and withholdings automatically rise because incomes rise. Spending on social welfare programs like food stamps falls because higher employment and higher wages mean that fewer people are poor. Thus the government budget moves toward surplus, without Congress passing or the president signing a single bill. And if the economy enters a recession, tax collections fall, social welfare spending rises, and the government's budget swings into deficit.

As unemployment rises and national income falls, taxes fall by about 30 cents for every dollar fall in national product. Government spending rises by about 7

automatic stabilizers

Due to changes in tax revenues and in social insurance spending, the government budget automatically swings toward a deficit, providing a stimulus to aggregate demand, whenever private demand drops. Similarly, it automatically swings toward a surplus, reducing aggregate demand, whenever private demand rises.

cents for every dollar fall in national product. As a result, a $1 fall in national product produces a fall of only 63 cents in consumers' disposable income. Thus automatic stabilizers provide more than $1's worth of boost to planned expenditure for every $3 fall in production.

Such fiscal automatic stabilizers would be large enough to reduce the marginal propensity to spend from about 0.6 to about 0.4. This would imply a reduction in the size of the multiplier from about 2.5 to about 1.67. Business cycles could be considerably larger if these automatic stabilizers did not exist, if the Federal Reserve found itself unable to compensate for their disappearance, and if their disappearance did not lead to counteracting changes in the marginal propensity to spend.

How Monetary Policy Works

For monetary policy to work, the Federal Open Market Committee must first recognize that there is a problem. It takes three to six months for statistical agencies to collect and process the data, for the Federal Reserve to recognize the state of the economy, and for it to conclude that action is needed. To this *recognition lag* add a policy *formulation lag*. The FOMC is a committee that moves by consensus. Members who have taken positions out on various limbs need time to climb down. More than six months can elapse between the start of a recession and decisive FOMC action to lower interest rates to try to increase planned expenditure.

Once the Federal Reserve acts, the response of financial markets is immediate. At the latest, interest rates shift the very day the trading desk at the *New York Federal Reserve Bank* receives new instructions. Often interest rates change in advance of the policy change. Because the Federal Reserve moves by consensus, traders can often guess what it is going to do beforehand. However, for changes in interest rates to change real GDP and unemployment takes more than a year. This means that the Federal Reserve is essentially powerless to smooth out fluctuations in less than a year. The average recession in the post–World War II United States has lasted less than 18 months. This means that by the time monetary policy changes initiated at the beginning of the recession and aimed at reducing its size have their effect on the economy, the recession is likely to be nearly over (see Box 13.7).

MONETARY POLICY INSTRUMENTS: POLICY

Today the Federal Reserve focuses on controlling interest rates. In the past it occasionally let interest rates be more volatile and focused on controlling the rate of growth of the money supply — also called the money stock — which is the economy's total supply of liquid assets.

Should the Federal Reserve target real interest rates — try to keep them stable, perhaps allowing them to climb when inflation threatens and to fall during a recession? Or should it focus on keeping the money stock growing smoothly because the money stock is a good leading indicator and stabilizing the growth path of this indicator is a good way to stabilize the economy as a whole?

It depends.

If the principal instability in the economy is found in a shifting IS curve, then targeting interest rates will do little or nothing to reduce the magnitude of shocks to the economy. Better to have the growth of the money supply react to leading indicators and outcomes. But if the instability lies instead in the relationship between the money stock and real output (the result of volatile money demand) or in a shifting relationship between the monetary base and the money supply (because the currency-to-deposits and *reserves-to-deposits ratios* vary), then targeting interest rates is wiser.

In recent years instability has been primarily in the velocity of money and the size of the money multiplier. The money multiplier fluctuated unexpectedly and widely in the 1980s and 1990s, chiefly because of unexpected fluctuations in the currency-to-deposits ratio. Since 1980, the Federal Reserve's control over the monetary base has not been enough to allow the Federal Reserve to exercise control over the money supply. And the velocity of money has fluctuated as well. By contrast, the position of the IS curve has been relatively stable.

Thus in the past quarter century the Federal Reserve has been more successful targeting the level of interest rates than the growth of the money supply.

RECAP   MONETARY VERSUS FISCAL POLICY

Policy affects the economy with a lag. Months or often years elapse from the time a problem occurs, to when policy makers recognize the problem exists, to when they finally reach agreement on a policy solution, to when the solution is put into place, to when the policy solution actually solves the problem. Monetary policy lags are shorter than fiscal policy lags, and that is why economists typically believe monetary policy solves macroeconomic problems better than does fiscal policy. But one type of fiscal policy does work rapidly: automatic stabilizers.

rules

Fixed rules that a central bank must follow for how fast they will allow the money supply to grow.

authorities

Central bank authorities with the discretion to respond to specific circumstances as they see fit. Contrasted with rules in a debate over the best way to conduct policy.

discretion

Leaving policies to be made and adjusted by appointed bodies of experts with discretion to respond to circumstances.

13.6 MAKING GOOD STABILIZATION POLICY: RULES VERSUS AUTHORITIES

In the late 1940s Chicago School economist Henry Simons set the terms for a debate over macroeconomic policy that continues to this day. He asked, Should macroeconomic policy be conducted "automatically," according to **rules** that would be followed no matter what? Or should macroeconomic policy be left to **authorities** — bodies of appointed officials — provided with wide **discretion** over how to use their power and given general guidance as to what goals to pursue?

Competence and Objectives

The first reason for automatic rules is that we fear that the people appointed to authorities will be incompetent. If people are appointed because of friendships from the past, or because of their ability to rally campaign contributions for a particular cause, there is little reason to think that they will be skilled judges of the situation or insightful analysts. Better then to constrain them by automatic rules. Even if those appointed to authorities are well intentioned, they may fail to find good solutions to macroeconomic problems. The stream of public discourse about macroeconomics is polluted by a large quantity of misinformation.

A second reason for fixed rules is that authorities might not have the right objectives. To institute a good rule it is only necessary for the political process to make the right decision once — at the moment the rule is settled. But an authority making decisions every day may start pursuing objectives that conflict with the long-run public interest. The state of the economy at the moment of the election is a powerful influence on citizens' votes. Thus politicians in office have a powerful personal incentive to pursue policies that will sacrifice the health of the economy in the future in order to obtain good reported economic numbers during the election year, thus creating a **political business cycle** (see Box 13.8).

political business cycle

Movements in unemployment and inflation resulting from discretionary policy timed to enhance the political fortunes of an incumbent president.

THE POLITICAL BUSINESS CYCLE AND RICHARD NIXON: POLICY

The most famous example of the political business cycle at work comes from the American politician Richard Nixon's episodic autobiography, *Six Crises*, published in 1962. Looking back on his defeat in the 1960 presidential election by John F. Kennedy, Nixon wrote:

"Two other developments [that] occurred before the [Republican Party C]onvention . . . [had] far more effect on the election outcome. . . .

"Early in March [1960], Dr. Arthur Burns. . . called on me. . . . [He] expressed great concern about the way the economy was then acting. . . . Burns' conclusion was that unless some decisive government action were taken, and taken soon, we were heading for another economic dip, which would hit its low point in October, just before the elections. He urged strongly that everything possible be done to avert this development . . . by loosening up on credit and . . . increasing spending for national security. The next time I saw the President, I discussed Burns' proposals with him, and he in turn put the subject on the agenda for the next cabinet meeting.

"The matter was thoroughly discussed by the Cabinet. . . . [S]everal of the Administration's economic experts who attended the meeting did not share [Burns'] bearish prognosis. . . . [T]here was strong sentiment against using the spending and credit powers of the Federal Government to affect the economy, unless and until conditions clearly indicated a major recession in prospect.

"In supporting Burns' point of view, I must admit that I was more sensitive politically than some of the others around the cabinet table. I knew from bitter experience how, in both 1954 and 1958, slumps which hit bottom early in October contributed to substantial Republican losses in the House and Senate. . . .

"Unfortunately, Arthur Burns turned out to be a good prophet. The bottom of the 1960 dip did come in October. . . . In October. . . . the jobless rolls increased by 452,000. All the speeches, television broadcasts, and precinct work in the world could not counteract that one hard fact."

By 1972 Richard Nixon was president, and he had appointed Arthur Burns to be chair of the Federal Reserve. The year 1972 saw very good economic statistics — at the price of a sharp acceleration of inflation in subsequent years. Given the smoking gun provided by Nixon in *Six Crises,* many have diligently searched for evidence that the Federal Reserve made economic policy in 1971 and 1972 not in the public interest but to enhance the private political interest of Richard Nixon.

However, things are more complicated. Economist Herbert Stein pointed out that Nixon administration economic policy was in fact less expansionary than many Democratic politicians and economic advisers wished: The claim that Burns was leaning to the expansionary side of the center of gravity of opinion is simply not correct. And once Arthur Burns had become chair of the Federal Reserve, Nixon administration officials found him to be truly and annoyingly independent.

The verdict is that Richard Nixon dearly wished for the Federal Reserve to tune economic policies in a way that would enhance his reelection chances, but that the institutional independence of the Federal Reserve worked. White House political pressure in 1971–1972 led to little if any change in Federal Reserve policy.

The substitution of technocratic authorities — like the Federal Reserve — in the place of presidents, prime ministers, and finance ministers provides some insulation. The fear that politicians will have objectives different from the long-run public interest has led many to advocate that monetary policy be made by independent central banks. If stabilization policy is to be made by authorities, it should be made by authorities placed at least one remove from partisan politics (see Box 13.9). And there is reason to think that the more independent, the better (see Box 13.10 on page 406).

BOX 13.9

IS THERE A POLITICAL BUSINESS CYCLE? THE DETAILS

Few would dispute that politicians seek to tune the macroeconomy to their political advantage. The George H. W. Bush administration tried to persuade Federal Reserve Chair Alan Greenspan to pursue a more expansionary monetary policy in 1991 to produce better economic numbers for the George H. W. Bush reelection campaign in 1992, going so far as threatening not to nominate Greenspan for a second term as Federal Reserve chair. But it was unsuccessful. Richard Nixon certainly believed when he appointed Arthur Burns to be Fed chair that Burns would still be the loyal partisan supporter he had been in 1960 — contemplating this appointment, Nixon referred to the "myth of the autonomous Fed" and laughed.

But how successful are governments at manipulating the political business cycle? It is not clear. It is true that in the United States since 1948, the fourth year of a president's term — the presidential election year — has seen annual real GDP growth average 0.6 percent more than the average of nonpresidential election years. But there is a 15 percent probability that at least that large a difference would emerge from random chance and sampling variation alone. Faster growth in presidential election years is suggestive, but not conclusive.

Moreover, other ways of looking at the data deliver even less evidence. Out of 13 post-1948 presidential terms, fully six — Johnson, Nixon-Ford, Carter, Reagan II,

Bush 41, and Clinton I — saw slower economic growth in the politically relevant second half of the term than in the first half of the term. This alternative way of looking at the data provides not even a suggestion of evidence one way or another. And it is important when analyzing any situation not to choose to look at the data in only the way that makes one's preferred conclusion appear the strongest.

There is, however, stronger evidence not of a politically *motivated* component to the business cycle but of a politically *influenced* component to the business cycle. In seven of the last eight post-WWII presidential terms in which Republicans occupied the White House, growth in the second year of a presidential term has been lower than average real GDP growth over that term. By contrast, in only one of the six terms in which Democrats occupied the White House has second-year growth been lower than average, as shown in Figure 13.11.

The odds against this pattern happening are astronomical: There is less than one chance in a thousand that it could be the result of random sampling variation.

Economists Alberto Alesina and Nouriel Roubini interpret this pattern as showing that the political parties have — or had, for Clinton is the Democratic president

FIGURE 13.11

The Politically Influenced Business Cycle: Relative Growth in the Second Year of Presidential Terms Economic growth (real GDP) tends to be relatively rapid in the second year of the term of a Democratic president. Economic growth tends to be relatively slow — or negative — in the second year of the term of a Republican president.

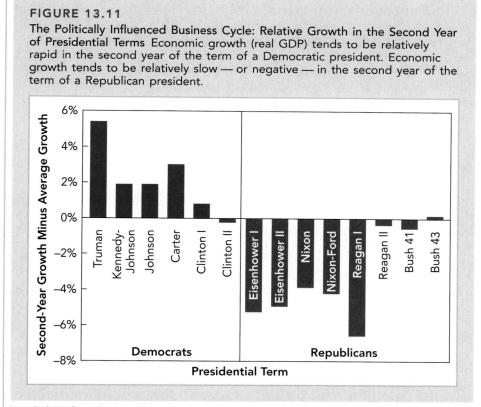

Note: Bush 41 refers to George H. W. Bush, the 41st president of the United States. Bush 43 refers to his son, George W. Bush, the 43rd president.

Source: Authors' calculations based on data from the 2004 edition of *The Economic Report of the President* (Washington, DC: Government Printing Office); replicating an analysis conducted by Alberto Alesina and Nouriel Roubini, "Political Business Cycles in OECD Economies" (NBER: Working Paper 3478, 1990), subsequently published in the *Review of Economic Studies* 59, October 1992, pp. 663–688.

for whom the pattern of growth fits the Republican model and George W. Bush is the Republican president for whom the pattern fits the Democratic model — different views of the relative costs of unemployment and inflation. Republicans have more tolerance for unemployment and less tolerance for inflation than Democrats do. Hence when Republicans come into office the Federal Reserve feels freer to try to push inflation down to a lower level. Because a considerable portion of inflation expectations relevant for the second year of a presidential term were formed back before the result of the election was known, actual inflation in the second year of a term is less than expected inflation and so economic growth is relatively low.

Credibility and Commitment

A central bank is always tempted to pursue a more expansionary monetary policy: More expansionary policy raises national product and reduces the unemployment rate. Moreover, it has little impact on inflation in the short run in which expectations of inflation are more or less fixed. In the short run, expansionary monetary policy always seems to be a central bank's best option.

Suppose firms and unions agree on large nominal wage and price increases. Then the best short-run policy for the central bank is to accommodate inflation and expand the money supply. To fight inflation by raising interest rates would generate a recession, and inflation would continue anyway. Suppose instead that firms and unions decide on wage and price restraint. Expansionary monetary policy is still better — inflation will be low, and the economy will boom. In either case, pursuing a more expansionary monetary policy produces a better short-run outcome.

BOX 13.10

CENTRAL BANK INDEPENDENCE: POLICY

A number of economists have investigated the relationship between macroeconomic performance and the degree to which central banks are insulated from partisan politics. They have examined the legal and institutional framework within which central banks in different countries operate, and constructed indexes of the extent to which their central banks are independent.

Alberto Alesina and Lawrence Summers concluded that the more independent a central bank, the better its inflation performance. More independent central banks presided over lower average inflation and less variable inflation. Moreover, countries with independent central banks did not pay any penalty. Countries with independent central banks did not have higher unemployment, lower real GDP growth, or larger business cycles.

Interpreting this correlation is not straightforward. Perhaps the factors that lead countries to have independent central banks lead them to have low inflation. Perhaps independent central banks do reduce economic growth, but only countries likely to have high economic growth for other reasons are likely to have independent central banks. Nevertheless, at least the post-1950 experience of the industrialized countries strongly suggests that insulating central banks from partisan politics delivers low inflation without any visible macroeconomic cost (see Figure 13.12).

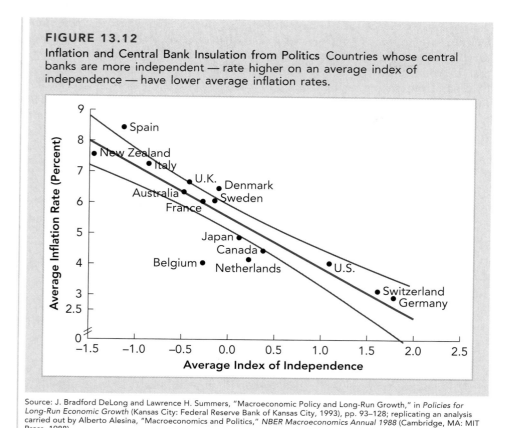

FIGURE 13.12

Inflation and Central Bank Insulation from Politics Countries whose central banks are more independent — rate higher on an average index of independence — have lower average inflation rates.

Source: J. Bradford DeLong and Lawrence H. Summers, "Macroeconomic Policy and Long-Run Growth," in *Policies for Long-Run Economic Growth* (Kansas City: Federal Reserve Bank of Kansas City, 1993), pp. 93–128; replicating an analysis carried out by Alberto Alesina, "Macroeconomics and Politics," *NBER Macroeconomics Annual 1988* (Cambridge, MA: MIT Press, 1988).

At the same time, announcing that monetary policy will be more *restrictive* in the near future produces a better short-run outcome as well, for by announcing that fighting inflation is job one, the central bank may influence the expectations of workers, managers, investors, and households.

But why — given the obvious short-run benefits of a more expansionary monetary policy — should anyone ever believe that a central bank will actually implement restrictive monetary policy and aim for low inflation? Because, in the long run, a central bank is wiser to keep low inflation as its top priority. Central banks benefit if workers, firms, and investors all believe that future inflation will be low. A central bank that succumbs to the temptation to make inflation higher than expected loses its **credibility**. All will soon recognize that the central bank's talk is cheap, and that it has a strong incentive once expectations for a period are formed to make inflation and money growth higher than expected. So the central bank will find that its words about future policy are ignored in the process of setting expectations. And expectations of inflation will be sky-high.

Economists give this conflict the awkward name "**dynamic inconsistency**": What it is good to have workers, managers, investors, and employers believe that you will do in the future is not what seems best to do when the future becomes

credibility

The degree to which the public believes in the policy action taken by some institution of government (e.g., the Fed, Congress, or the president).

dynamic inconsistency

A situation where a central bank succumbs to the temptation to make inflation higher than expected and thereby loses its credibility.

the present. Many economists have argued that this dynamic inconsistency problem is a strong point on the side of rules rather than authorities: You don't have
to worry about a rule breaking its word. Others have pointed out that central banks
that are concerned with their long-term reputation and credibility appear to have
little problem resisting the temptation to make inflation and money growth higher
than the firms and workers in the economy had expected. And they have little
problem acquiring credibility if they really want to do so, which they do in many
ways, including

- Complaining that inflation may be rising.
- Refusing to admit even the possibility that monetary expansion might reduce
  unemployment.
- Repeatedly declaring that price stability is the primary objective.

The most important way to acquire credibility is to possess a history of past successful control of inflation.

Modern Monetary Policy

Whether monetary policy is guided by strict and rigid rules or made by authorities using their discretion to come up with the best policy for the particular —
unique — situation, one question remains: What sort of rule should be adopted,
or how should the authority behave? What sort of guidelines for monetary policy
should those who set the rules or those who staff the authorities follow?

Economists believe that one set of rules to avoid are those that command the
central bank to attain values for real economic variables, like the rate of growth of
real GDP or the level of the unemployment rate. The rate of growth of real GDP
is limited in the long run by the rate of growth of potential output. The level of
the unemployment rate is controlled in the long run by the natural rate of unemployment. A central-bank target of too high a rate of real GDP growth, or too low
a level of the unemployment rate, is likely to end in upward-spiraling inflation. A
policy that targets nominal variables — like the nominal money stock, or nominal
GDP, or the inflation rate — is robust, in the sense that it does not run the risk of
leading to disaster if our assessment of the macroeconomic structure of the economy turns out to be wrong.

Stanford University macroeconomist John Taylor has put forward his Taylor rule
as a description of how the Federal Reserve has typically operated, and as a way
of adding some structure and order to the process by which the Federal Reserve
discusses and makes monetary policy. The Federal Reserve picks a target for inflation. Whenever inflation is higher than the target (and perhaps when unemployment is lower than the Fed's judgment of the natural rate), it raises interest rates
to levels above their normal values to diminish output and employment and put
downward pressure on inflation. Whenever inflation is lower than the target (and
perhaps when unemployment is higher than its judgment of the natural rate), it
lowers interest rates to levels below their normal values to boost output and
employment.

We've seen this before: It is the MPRF from Chapter 12

$$u = u_0 + \phi(\pi - \pi^t)$$

which assumed that the Fed set interest rates according to the Taylor rule

$$r = r_0 + r_\pi(\pi - \pi^t)$$

This is a version of the Taylor rule for interest rates (one that has the central bank reacting only to the inflation rate; in other versions it reacts to unemployment as well).

Former Federal Reserve Vice Chair Alan Blinder said he found the framework set out by John Taylor to be extremely helpful in making monetary policy. Taylor did not intend for the rule to be followed exactly. For example, if fiscal policy is unusually tight (or loose) then the federal funds rate should be lower (or higher) than the Taylor rule prescribes. The Taylor rule provides a way to think about how strongly the Federal Reserve should move to counter shocks to the economy. Do you believe that the Federal Reserve should act more aggressively to boost the economy when unemployment is high? Then you are arguing for a larger parameter r_π in the Taylor rule. Do you believe that the Federal Reserve reacts too strongly to cool the economy when inflation rises? Then you are arguing for a smaller parameter r_π in the Taylor rule.

> ## RECAP   MAKING GOOD STABILIZATION POLICY
>
> Economists disagree over whether the central bank should be tightly constrained by policy rules. Automatic rules are favored by those who believe the authorities are incompetent or misguided. In the United States, the central bank is at least somewhat removed from partisan politics and is given wide discretion. A central bank which, at its discretion, pursues a goal of long-run price stability will have more credibility than one that succumbs to pressure to use short-run expansionary monetary policy to boost employment. The Taylor rule describes how the Federal Reserve typically operates. Despite its name, the Taylor rule is not a rule that the FOMC must follow but a framework for understanding the choices made by monetary authorities operating with discretion.

13.7 FINANCIAL CRISES

But perhaps the most important policy tools of central banks are those that we almost never see used. A huge danger to economies is the possibility of a large-scale financial crisis — like those the U.S. suffered in 1933, 1929, 1907, 1893, 1884, and 1873; like that East Asia suffered in 1997–1998; like that Mexico suffered in 1994–1995. For nearly 400 years market economies have undergone financial crises — episodes when the prices of stocks or of other assets crash, everyone tries to move their wealth into safer forms at once, and the consequent panic among investors can lead to a prolonged and serious depression. Managing such financial crises has been one of the responsibilities of monetary policy makers for more than a century and a half.

A financial crisis sees investors as a group suddenly (and often not very rationally) become convinced that their investments have become overly risky. As a result, they try to exchange their investments for high-quality bonds and cash. But as everyone tries to do this at once, they create the risk that they hoped to avoid: Stock and real estate prices crash, and interest rates spike upward as investors try to increase their holdings of relatively safe, *liquid assets*.

The sharp rise in real interest rates that occurs in a financial crisis can severely reduce investment, sending the economy into a deep depression. Moreover, once the crisis gathers force, the ability of monetary policy tools to boost investment may well be limited. Financial crises are accompanied by steep rises in risk premiums. They are often accompanied by sharp rises in term premiums as well, as investors decide that they want to hold their wealth in as liquid a form as possible. And financial crises frequently generate deflation as well.

All of these drive a large wedge between the short-term nominal safe interest rates that the central bank controls and the long-term real risky interest rate relevant for the determination of investment and planned expenditure. The central bank may have done all it can via open-market operations to reduce short-term safe nominal interest rates to their lowest possible level, but it may not be enough: Long-term real risky interest rates may well remain very high indeed.

But central banks have powerful (albeit rarely visibly used) tools to stem financial crises. They can make direct loans to institutions in trouble — act as what MIT economist Charles Kindleberger called a *"lender of last resort"* in order to restore confidence that making new loans even in a time of crisis is not unduly risky. And since the Great Depression governments have provided *deposit insurance* to keep savers from pulling their money out of the financial system in a crisis, thus generating a collapse of the banking and payments system for no reason other than their fear that the banking and payments system might collapse.

Lenders of Last Resort

What can a central bank do in a financial crisis? In such a situation a central bank can do a lot of good easily by rapidly expanding the money supply, so that the increase in the demand for liquid assets to hold doesn't lead to a spike in interest rates and a crash in other asset prices.

It can also do a lot more good by lending directly to institutions that are fundamentally solvent — that will, if the crisis is stemmed and resolved rapidly, be able to function profitably — but that are temporarily illiquid in the sense that no one is willing to lend to them because no one is confident that the crisis will be resolved. Such a lender of last resort can rapidly reduce risk and term premiums as it reduces safe short-term nominal interest rates, and it can end the financial crisis.

The problem is that a central bank can also do a lot of harm if it bails out institutions that have gone bankrupt, by encouraging others in the future to take excessive risks hoping that the central bank will bail them out. Thus the central bank has to (1) expand the money supply and lend freely to institutions that are merely illiquid — that is, caught short of cash but fundamentally sound — while (2) forcibly liquidating institutions that are insolvent, those that could never repay what they owe even if the panic were stemmed immediately. This is a neat trick, to save one without saving the other.

A central bank can take institutional steps in advance to reduce the chance that the economy will suffer a financial crisis and reduce the damage that a *financial panic* will do. The first and most obvious step is to do a good job as a supervising regulator over the banking system. Depositors will panic and pull their money out of a bank when they fear that it is bankrupt — that it no longer has enough capital, and that the capital plus the value of the loans that it has made are together lower than the value of the money it owes to its depositors. If banks are kept well capitalized, and if banks that fail to meet standards for capital adequacy are rapidly taken over and closed down, then the risk of a full-fledged financial panic is small.

The potential problem with this strategy of supervision and surveillance is that it may be politically difficult to carry out. Bankers are, after all, often wealthy and influential people with substantial political connections. Bank regulators are midlevel civil servants, subject to pressure and influence from politicians.

Deposit Insurance and Moral Hazard

The most recent major financial crisis in the United States was long ago. It took place during the Great Depression, and it was not only the last major but also the most destructive financial crisis the United States ever saw.

Banks closed; at the beginning of 1933, more than one in three of the banks that had existed in 1929 had closed its doors. When banks failed, people who had their money in them were out of luck; years might pass before any portion of their deposits would be returned. Hence fear of bank failure led to an immediate increase in households' and businesses' holdings of currency relative to deposits. In the Great Depression this flight from banks reduced the money supply.

With 6,000 banks failing in the first three years of the Depression, more and more people felt that putting their money in a bank was not much better than throwing it away. Since a rise in the currency-to-deposits ratio carries with it a fall in the money multiplier, fear of bank failures shrank the money stock. That only deepened the Depression. Something had to be done to prop up depositors' confidence.

One of the reforms of President Franklin D. Roosevelt's *New Deal* program in the 1930s was the institution of deposit insurance provided by the Federal Deposit Insurance Corporation — the FDIC. If your bank failed, the government would make sure your deposits did not disappear. The aim was to diminish monetary instability by eliminating bank failure–driven swings in the money supply and interest rates.

Since the 1930s, federal deposit insurance has acted as a *monetary automatic stabilizer.* A financial panic gathers force when investors conclude that they need to pull their money out of banks and mutual funds because such investments are too risky. Deposit insurance eliminates the risk of keeping your money in a bank — even if the bank goes belly-up, your deposit is still secure. Thus there is no reason to seek to move your money to any safer place. Deposit insurance has broken one of the important links in the chain of transmission that used to make financial panics so severe.

The availability of deposit insurance and the potential existence of a lender of last resort do not come for free. These institutions create potential problems of their own — problems that economists discuss under the heading of *moral hazard.* If depositors know that the Federal Deposit Insurance Corporation has guaranteed their deposits, they will not inquire into the kinds of loans that their bank is making. Bank owners and managers may decide to make deliberately risky high-interest loans. If the economy booms and the loans are repaid, then they make a fortune. If the economy goes into recession and the risky firms to which they have loaned go bankrupt, they declare bankruptcy too and leave the FDIC to deal with the depositors. It becomes a classic game of heads-I-win–tails-you-lose.

The principal way to guard against moral hazard is to make certain that decision makers have substantial amounts of their own money at risk. Making risky loans using government-guaranteed deposits as your source of funding is a lot less attractive if your personal wealth is the first thing that is taken to pay off depositors if the loans go bad. Hence deposit insurance and lenders of last resort function well only if there is adequate supervision and surveillance: only if the central bank and the other bank regulatory authorities are keeping close watch on banks, and making sure that every bank has adequate capital, so that it is the shareholders' and the managers' funds, rather than those of the FDIC, that are at risk if the loans made go bad.

> **RECAP   FINANCIAL CRISES**
>
> In the extreme situations of financial crises, economic policy makers face a choice between large-scale bankruptcy, the possible unraveling of the financial system, and deep depression on the one hand; and rewarding those who have made overspeculative and overleveraged bets on the other.

Chapter Summary

1. Macroeconomic policy should attempt to stabilize the economy: to avoid extremes of high unemployment and also of high and rising inflation.

2. Long and variable lags make successful stabilization policy difficult.

3. Economists arrange themselves along a spectrum, with some advocating more aggressive management of the economy and others concentrating on establishing a stable framework and economic environment. But compared to differences of opinion among economists in the past, differences of opinion today are minor.

4. In today's environment, monetary policy is the stabilization policy tool of choice, largely because it operates with shorter lags than does discretionary fiscal policy.

5. Nevertheless, the fiscal "automatic stabilizers" built into the tax system play an important role in reducing the size of the multiplier.

6. Uncertainty about the structure of the economy or the effectiveness of policy should lead policy makers to be cautious: Blunt policy tools should be used carefully and cautiously lest they do more harm than good.

7. The advantage of having economic policy made by an authority is that the authority can use judgment to devise the best response to a changing — and usually unforeseen — situation.

8. The advantages of having economic policy made by a rule are threefold: First, rules do not assume competence in authorities where it may not exist; second, rules reduce the possibility that policy will be made not in the public interest but in some special interest; third, rules make it easier to avoid so-called dynamic inconsistency.

9. Dynamic inconsistency arises whenever a central bank finds that it wishes to change its previously announced policy in an inflationary direction: It is always in the central bank's short-term interest to have money growth be higher, interest rates lower, and inflation a little higher than had been previously expected.

10. Today, however, central banks are by and large successful in taking a long-term view. They pay great attention to establishing and maintaining the credibility of their policy commitments.

11. Monetary authorities are vitally important during a financial crisis. They can expand the money supply or serve as a lender of last resort. But they must be wise, for a bluntly applied policy can hurt as readily as it helps during a financial crisis.

Key Terms

inside lag (p. 388)

Lucas critique (p. 392)

leading indicators (p. 393)

monetary policy lags (p. 399)

discretionary fiscal policy (p. 399)

automatic stabilizers (p. 400)

rules (p. 402)

authorities (p. 402)

discretion (p. 402)

political business cycle (p. 403)

credibility (p. 407)

dynamic inconsistency (p. 407)

Analytical Exercises

1. What is the Lucas critique? How would the Lucas critique suggest that you should design a policy to try to reduce annual inflation from 10 percent to 2 percent?

2. What is "dynamic inconsistency"? Why does dynamic inconsistency strengthen the case for having policy rules rather than having authorities with discretionary power over economic policy?

3. Under what circumstances do you think that the Federal Reserve should shift from targeting the interest rate to targeting the money stock growth rate?

4. What would be the economic advantages and disadvantages of eliminating federal deposit insurance?

5. Why do economic policy makers think it important to get the best available forecasts?

Policy Exercises

1. Suppose that the economy's Phillips curve is given by

$$\pi = \pi^e - \beta(u - u^*)$$

with β equal to 0.4 and u^* equal to 0.06 (6 percent). Suppose that the economy has for a long time had a constant inflation rate equal to 3 percent per year. Suddenly the government announces a new policy: It will use fiscal policy to boost real GDP by 5 percent relative to potential — enough by Okun's law to push the unemployment rate down by 2 percent — and it will keep that expanded fiscal policy in place indefinitely. Suppose that agents in the economy have adaptive expectations of inflation, so that this year's expected inflation is equal to last year's actual inflation. What will be the course of inflation and unemployment in this economy in the years after the shift in fiscal policy? Track the economy out 20 years, assuming that no additional shocks occur.

2. Suppose that all conditions given in question 1 are the case. In addition, suppose that for each 1 percentage point that the inflation rate rises above 3 percent, the central bank raises real interest rates by 2 percentage points — and that each 1-percentage-point increase in real interest rates moves the economy along the IS curve sufficiently to shrink real GDP by 1 percent. As in question 1, suppose that agents in the economy have adaptive expectations of inflation, so that this year's expected

inflation is equal to last year's actual inflation. What will be the course of inflation and unemployment in this economy in the years after the shift in fiscal policy? Track the economy out 20 years, assuming that no additional shocks occur.

3. Suppose that all conditions in question 2 are the case, except that β equals 0.5 and that for each 1 percentage point the inflation rate rises above 3 percent, the central bank raises real interest rates by only 1 percentage point. Again, suppose that each 1-percentage-point increase in real interest rates moves the economy along the IS curve sufficiently to shrink real GDP by 1 percent. Finally, suppose that agents in the economy have rational expectations of inflation, so that this year's expected inflation is what an economist knowing the structure of the economy and proposed economic policies would calculate actual inflation was likely to be. What will be the course of inflation and unemployment in this economy in the years after the shift in fiscal policy? Track the economy out 20 years, assuming that no additional shocks occur.

4. Why do economists today tend to believe that monetary policy is superior to discretionary fiscal policy as a stabilization policy tool? In what circumstances that you can imagine would this belief be reversed?

14

Budget Balance, National Debt, and Investment

QUESTIONS

What is the best measure of the government's budget balance for analyzing short-run stabilization policy? For analyzing the effect of changes in the national debt on long-run growth?

What is the typical pattern that the U.S. national debt follows over time?

How has experience in the past generation deviated from this traditional pattern of debt behavior?

Why should we worry about a rising national debt?

Why shouldn't we worry too much?

government deficit

The difference between government spending and the government's revenue when the first is larger than the second.

national debt

The sum total of all past deficits less all past surpluses the government has run.

government surplus

The difference between the government's spending and the government's revenues when the second is larger than the first.

A government spending more than it collects in taxes (including the inflation tax noted in Chapter 8) must borrow the difference to finance its spending. The amount borrowed this year is this year's **government deficit**. A government borrows by selling its citizens and foreigners bonds: promises that the government will repay the principal it borrows with interest. These accumulated promises to pay make up the **national debt**. In a year when government spending is less than tax collections, the difference is the **government surplus**. The national debt shrinks by the amount of the surplus.

Call the *debt* D and the deficit *d* (and recognize that a surplus is a negative value of *d*). Then the relationship between the debt and the deficit is simple:

$$\Delta D = d$$

The change in the debt from year to year ΔD is equal to the deficit *d*.

Economists are interested in the debt and the deficit for two reasons. First, the deficit is a convenient and often handy — though sometimes treacherous — measure of fiscal policy's role in stabilization policy. It is an index of how government spending and tax plans affect the position of the IS curve of Chapter 10. The central bank will in general adjust its stance to try to offset the effects of the deficit on planned expenditure so that deficits do not upset the monetary policy reaction function (MPRF) of Chapter 12.

Second, the debt and deficit are closely connected with national saving and investment. A rising debt — a deficit — tends to depress capital formation. It lowers the economy's long-run balanced-growth path and reduces the balanced-growth GDP per worker of Chapter 4. Moreover, a high national debt means that taxes in the future will be higher to pay higher interest charges. Such higher taxes are likely to further discourage economic activity and reduce economic welfare.

What to do about the national debt is one of the current flashpoints of American politics. The United States ran its national debt up by an enormous amount during the high-deficit Reagan and Bush 41 (George H. W. Bush was the 41st president) administrations from 1981 to 1992. This pattern of large deficits and rapidly growing debt was restored beginning in 2001 under the Bush 43 administration (George W. Bush is the 43rd president): This self-generated problem is one of the biggest economic problems that will confront the United States in the second half of this decade.

One of the main questions facing American voters and politicians now is: What (if anything) should be done to deal with the large future rise in the debt that is currently being forecast? Should the government accept large deficits? Should it try to stabilize the government debt-to-GDP ratio, and if so at what level? Should the government aim for large surpluses in order to push the debt down to its late-1970s level (or even lower) share of GDP? At the moment this issue hangs in the balance.

14.1 THE BUDGET DEFICIT AND STABILIZATION POLICY

The Budget Deficit and the IS Curve

An increase in government purchases increases planned expenditure. It shifts the IS curve out and to the right, increasing the level of real GDP for each possible value of the interest rate. The increase in government purchases shifts the MPRF in and to the left, decreasing the unemployment rate at each level of inflation.

FIGURE 14.1

An Increase in the Full-Employment Deficit Shifts the IS Curve Outward and the MPRF Inward An increase in government purchases or a decrease in net taxes when employment is held at full employment shifts the IS curve to the right and shifts the MPRF to the left. To keep track of the impact of government tax and spending policy on the position of the IS curve, we need to look at the difference between the two when the economy is at full employment — the full-employment government deficit (or surplus).

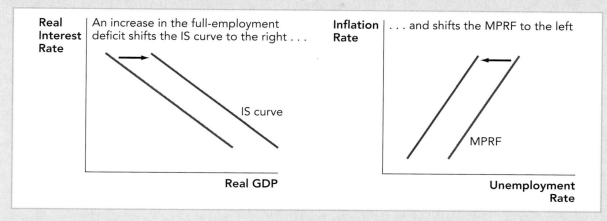

A decrease in government tax collections also increases planned expenditure. If the decrease in tax collections is due to a drop in income, we simply move along an IS curve. But if a change in tax policy made tax collections fall, this change also shifts the IS curve out and the MPRF in: Unless the Federal Reserve changes the rule it uses to set interest rates, it will find that the fiscal stimulus is making unemployment lower than it expected and desired given the current rate of inflation.

The government's budget deficit is equal to purchases minus net taxes. Must we bother with two measures of fiscal policy — purchases and net taxes — when we can just keep track of their difference? No. Our drive for simplification is the reason for focusing on the government's budget balance as a measure of fiscal policy.

But it turns out, as Figure 14.1 shows, that the right measure of budget balance is not the government's actual deficit (or surplus). Instead, the right measure of fiscal policy is the **full-employment or cyclically adjusted deficit** (or surplus): what the government's budget balance would be if the economy were at full employment.

full-employment cyclically adjusted deficit

An estimate of what the budget deficit would be if national product were at potential output. This measure removes shifts in the budget deficit that are due to the operation of the economy's automatic stabilizers.

THE BUSH TAX CUT OF 2001: POLICY

It is extremely rare in the United States that a tax cut legislated by the Congress and signed by the president takes effect at the right moment to offset a recession. Most tax cuts that have their origin in a desire to fight a recession do not take effect until long after the need has passed. The most recent such example is the so-called stimulus package proposed in the aftermath of the September 11, 2001, terrorist attacks on the World Trade Center and the Pentagon. Squabbling between the houses of Congress and between the Congress and the president kept it from being enacted until the consensus of economists and the Federal Reserve was that the recession of 2001 had already ended.

However, one tax cut — the Bush tax cut of 2001 — did, largely by accident, take effect right at the moment that consumer confidence was depressed by the destruction of the World Trade Center. According to Morgan Stanley's economic analysis staff, the tax cut enacted in 2001 boosted household disposable income in the first quarter of 2002 by an amount equal to approximately $100 billion a year, well over 1 percent of GDP. This boost to household disposable income was very welcome and kept the recession of 2001 from being longer and deeper than would otherwise have been the case.

What of the standard argument that fiscal policy — tax cuts and spending increases — should not be used to manage the business cycle? This argument hinges on the belief that the Federal Reserve (1) is more competent than the Congress and the president, (2) is more efficient than the Congress and the president, and (3) has sufficient room to maneuver to stabilize the economy near full employment. Although the quality of the Federal Reserve staff analysis certainly is higher than that of the Congress, and although the long and variable "inside" lags associated with legislation make discretionary fiscal policy erratic, nevertheless, by the end of 2001 the Federal Reserve found that it had cut interest rates almost as far as they could go: The short-term federal funds interest rate was down to 1.75 percent per year, and in its internal discussions the Federal Reserve was beginning to worry that with "short-term interest rates . . . already . . . very low," if "the economy were to deteriorate substantially . . . it might be impossible to ease monetary policy sufficiently through the usual interest rate process" to keep the economy near full employment. In this context, the extra boost to planned expenditure provided by the arrival of the stimulative effects of the Bush 2001 tax cut was very welcome.

In 2003 an even stronger argument could be made for using fiscal policy to try to stimulate demand. The U.S. recovery had stalled in late 2002, and the Federal Reserve had run out of room to lower short-term interest rates further without risking damage to the ability of important financial institutions to survive. A further boost to demand at that time would have been very welcome as well. Unfortunately, the tax cut proposed and passed by the Bush administration was one that channeled most of the tax relief to those with relatively low marginal propensities to consume, and the effectiveness of the 2003 tax reduction as a short-run stabilization policy is questionable.

Does fiscal policy therefore have a stable place as an important stabilization policy tool? This seems unlikely. Recall that the beneficial effects of the 2001 Bush tax cut came about as a result of an unexpected and lucky chance. It is still the case that — as long as full employment does not require that the Federal Reserve push short-term safe nominal interest rates below zero — monetary policy is a faster acting and more flexible stabilization policy tool than discretionary fiscal policy. And situations like those of 2003, when the Federal Reserve found itself in the position of having already reduced interest rates almost as far as they could go, are very unusual.

However, in a low-inflation world like that in which we live today, the fact that the Federal Reserve cannot push short-term safe nominal interest rates below zero places limits on the effectiveness of monetary policy as well.

Measuring the Budget Balance

Unfortunately, the government budget bottom line reported in the newspapers is not the full-employment budget balance. It is either the "unified cash" balance or the balance excluding Social Security. The first of these bottom lines is the difference

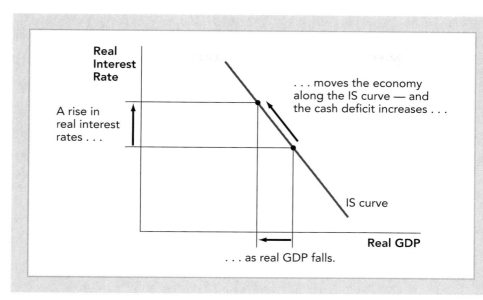

FIGURE 14.2
A Fall in Real GDP
The cash budget balance is not a good indicator of the position of the IS curve.

between the money that the government actually spends in a year and the money that it takes in. This balance is called "unified" because it unifies all of the government's accounts and trust funds (including Social Security). This balance is called "cash" because it does not take account of either changes in the value of government-owned assets or the future liabilities owed by the government: It is just cash in minus cash out. The second of these bottom lines is equal to the unified cash balance minus the revenues and plus the expenditures of the Social Security program. It takes the Social Security system "off budget."

Why is the full-employment budget balance a better index than either of the more frequently mentioned **cash budget balance** measures? Consider a situation in which the government does not change either its purchases or its tax rates, and so there is no change in government fiscal policy. But suppose that monetary policy tightens: Real interest rates are raised, and so the economy moves up and to the left along a stable IS curve (see Figure 14.2). As the economy moves along the IS curve, real GDP falls and tax collections fall too. The government's cash deficit increases, even though there has been no change in government policy to shift the IS curve. The full-employment budget balance, however, remains constant. The fact that the cash budget balance changes as the economy moves along a constant IS curve means that it is not a good indicator of how the government's fiscal policy is affecting the location of the IS curve: The full-employment budget balance is better.

To turn the cash balance into the full-employment balance, we must adjust the budget deficit (or surplus) for the automatic reaction of taxes and spending to the business cycle, as is done in Figure 14.3. When unemployment is high, taxes are low and social welfare spending high. The budget balance swings toward deficit. When unemployment is low, taxes are high and the budget balance swings toward surplus.

However, the cyclically adjusted budget deficit is not a perfect measure of the effect of taxing and spending on the position of the IS curve. And the standard budget deficit you see reported in the newspapers is not even a good measure of the effect of taxing and spending on the position of the IS curve. More adjustments are needed.

cash budget balance

A way of measuring the government's budget balance called "cash" because it does not take account of changes in the value of government-owned assets or of the future liabilities owed by the government.

FIGURE 14.3

The Full-Employment and the Cash Budget Deficits

The difference between the actual cash budget balance and the full-employment balance can be substantial when the economy is either suffering from a recession as in the early 1990s or undergoing an uplifting boom as in the late 1990s.

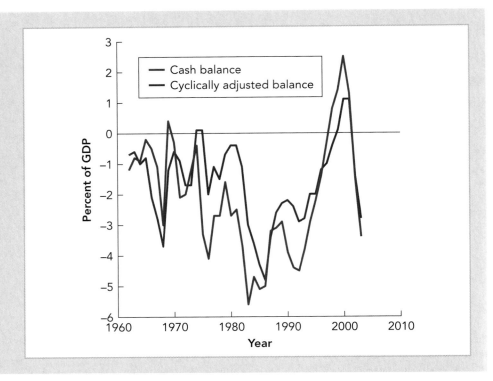

Source: Congressional Budget Office.

RECAP   **THE BUDGET DEFICIT AND STABILIZATION POLICY**

The cyclically adjusted budget deficit is a good measure of the impact of the government's taxing and spending on aggregate demand. When the cyclically adjusted budget deficit rises, the IS curve shifts right as government policy becomes more stimulative. When the cyclically adjusted budget deficit falls, the IS curve shifts left as government policy becomes more contractionary.

14.2 MEASURING THE DEBT AND THE DEFICIT

In addition to cyclical adjustment, we should consider making three other adjustments to the reported cash budget balance. These adjustments matter, as Figure 14.4 shows.

Inflation

One adjustment economists make is to correct the officially reported cash budget balance for the effects of inflation. A portion of the debt interest paid out by the government to its bondholders merely compensates them for inflation's erosion of the value of their principal.

A good measure of the deficit should be a measure of whether the government is spending more in the way of resources than it is taking in: a measure

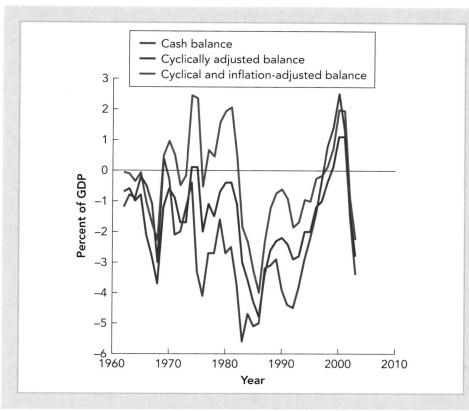

Source: Congressional Budget Office.

FIGURE 14.4

The Cash Balance and the Inflation-Adjusted Budget Balance

Large differences between officially reported and economically relevant measures of budget balance emerge as more adjustments are made. Adjusted for both the state of the business cycle and inflation, the federal budget was in rough balance or even in surplus (save for the peak of the Vietnam War) until the 1980s.

of the change in the real debt that the government owes. At the end of the year the debt principal plus this inflation component of debt interest are together equal — in their power to purchase useful goods and services — to what the debt principal was at the start of the year. So the real interest that the government has paid on its debt is not equal to the nominal interest rate times the debt, iD, but to the real interest rate times debt, rD. The difference between the nominal and the real interest rate is the expected rate of inflation, which we'll assume here equals the inflation rate π. Hence the real deficit d^r is related to the cash deficit d^c by

$$d^r = d^c - \pi D$$

Almost everyone who analyzes economic and budget policy prefers to work with these inflation-adjusted measures of the deficit and debt.

Public Investment

Yet another adjustment corrects for an asymmetry between the treatment of private and public assets. Private spending on long-lived capital goods is called "investment." A business with total sales of $100 million, costs of goods sold of $90 million, and $20 million spending on enlarging its capital stock reports a profit of $10 million — not a deficit of $10 million. Standard and sensible accounting treatment of long-lived valuable assets in the private sector is definitely not to count their entire cost as a charge at the time of initial purchase, but instead to spread the cost out — a process called "amortization" — over the useful life of the asset. The government should do its accounting the same way, like a business, and amortize rather than expense its spending on long-lived assets.

Calls for reforming the federal government budget to use capital budgeting are heard periodically. But few people use numbers based on capital budgeting. The principal reason that capital budgeting is resisted is political. Which government expenditures are capital expenditures? Aircraft carriers and nuclear weapons? The interstate highway system? Improvements to trails in the national parks? Head Start expenditures — money spent on educating poor children? (After all, this is an investment in their future.)

From a political point of view, a dividing line between government investment and government consumption expenditures is unlikely to stand for long when subjected to pressure from Congress eager to justify expenditures by calling them "investments," and possessing the legal power to direct estimating agencies like the Congressional Budget Office and the Office of Management and Budget to do so. Thus critics regard capital budgeting as simply too difficult to implement in a helpful way. Supporters, however, point out that not doing capital budgeting at all is, in a sense, worse than even the least helpful implementation.

The fact that the numbers usually reported do not correct for public investment should be kept in mind: The reported numbers tend to overestimate the real value of the outstanding national debt and overstate the magnitude of the current deficit.

Future Government Liabilities and Generational Accounting

All of the issues surrounding capital budgeting appear again whenever the long-run future of the government's budget is considered. Back when Brad worked at the Treasury Department, some $10,000 a year was set aside for him in his Treasury pension account. It is as if his income had been $10,000 a year higher, and he had invested that extra $10,000 in U.S. government bonds. Bonds issued by the government appear on the books as part of the government's debt. But pension fund liabilities that the government owes to former workers do not.

Thus in a sense the right way to count the government's debt is to look not just at the bonds that it has issued but at all of the promises to pay money in the future that it has made. Indeed, a large chunk of the government's expenditures — those by the Medicare and Social Security trust funds, for example — are presented to the public in just this way. The Social Security deficit reported by the trustees of the Social Security system every spring is not the difference between Social Security taxes paid in and Social Security benefits paid out, but is instead the long-run, 75-year balance between the estimated value of the commitments to pay benefits that the Social Security system has made and will make and the estimated value of the taxes that will be paid into the Social Security trust funds.

But the Social Security trustees' report covers just one program — albeit a big program. And great confusion is created by the fact that the Social Security system's expenditures and revenues are also included within the unified budget balance.

Wouldn't it be better to bring all of taxation and spending within a long-run system like that currently used by Social Security?

Economists Laurence Kotlikoff and Alan Auerbach say an emphatic yes. They propose that instead of the year-by-year budget balances, the U.S. government shift to a system of "**generational accounting**." Generational accounting would examine the lifetime impact of taxes and spending programs on individuals born in specific years and provide a final balance that could be used for long-term planning. Auerbach and Kotlikoff clearly have a strong case. Yet few analysts of the budget use their generational accounting measures, and at the moment these issues are not often dealt with in macroeconomics classes, but are reserved for public finance classes.

Generational accounting is thus not part of the present state of macroeconomics, but it should become part of its future, for the issues involved are the biggest ones facing the domestic American government today. For example, in the fall of 2004 Brookings Institution economists William Gale and Peter Orszag projected that current U.S. government policies would produce cash deficits averaging 3.5 percent of GDP over the next decade as shown in Figure 14.5. Compared to a *balanced budget,* they argued, such deficits would reduce annual GDP a decade from now by 1 to 2 percent — that is, $1,500 to $3,000 per household. And that, they said, was the "good part of the story." The bad part lay further in the future in the liabilities the government was assuming through its big social-insurance programs: Medicare, Medicaid, and Social Security. Over the next 75 years, as Figure 14.6 on page 424 shows, the nation's fiscal gap would amount to about 7 percent of GDP. At some point taxes must be raised substantially or benefits paid to Social Security, Medicaid, and Medicare recipients need to be cut well below currently projected levels. The fact that budget accounting does not include generational accounting reduces politicians' incentives to try to tackle these problems today.

generational accounting

A way of looking at the government's tax and spending plans that attempts to set out the total lifetime impact of government policy on an individual's resources and obligations.

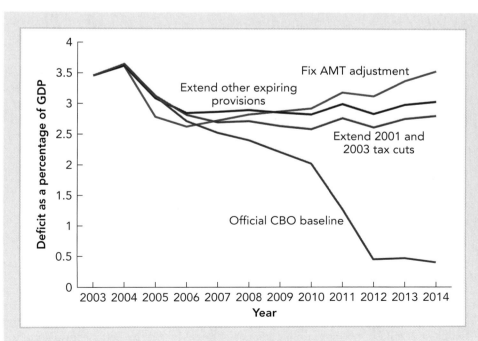

FIGURE 14.5

Budget Deficit Projections over the Next 10 Years

The Bush administration, newly reelected in 2004, is committed to (1) making permanent the 2001 and 2003 tax cuts, (2) extending the standard list of other expiring tax preferences, and (3) keeping the Alternative Minimum Tax (AMT) from becoming the effective tax system. These commitments mean that the deficit is unlikely to decline as a share of the economy.

Source: William Gale and Peter Orszag, Tax Policy Center, www.taxpolicycenter.org.

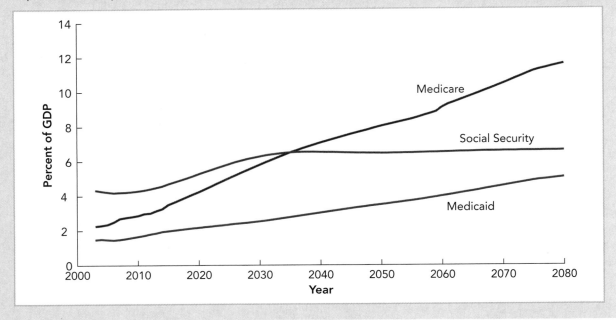

FIGURE 14.6
Projected Entitlement Costs as a Percentage of GDP As America's population ages and medical care costs continue to rise, the costs of federal "entitlement" programs are projected to rise enormously. From today's level of 8.5 percent of GDP, the three big programs — Medicare, Medicaid, and Social Security — are projected under current law to rise to 23 percent of GDP by 2080.

Source: William Gale and Peter Orszag, Tax Policy Center, www.taxpolicycenter.org.

RECAP   MEASURING THE DEBT AND THE DEFICIT

Measuring the debt in an economically relevant way requires — in addition to a cyclical adjustment — three further adjustments to the reported cash government budget balance. Adjusting for inflation's effect on debt interest produces the real deficit. Adjusting for public spending on investment goods — a political hot potato — is capital budgeting. Adjusting for taxes we are strapping our kids and grandkids with — an even hotter political potato — is generational accounting. In practice, the reported government deficit includes none of these adjustments.

14.3 ANALYZING THE DEBT AND THE DEFICIT

Sustainability

The first question to ask about a government that is running a persistent deficit is: "Can it go on?" Is it possible for the government to continue running its current deficit indefinitely, or must policy change — possibly for the better, but also quite possibly for the worse?

The Equilibrium Debt-to-GDP Ratio

The variable to look at to assess whether the government's current fiscal policy is sustainable is the time path of the ratio of the government's total debt to GDP, or the debt-to-GDP ratio, D/Y. Fiscal policy is sustainable if the debt-to-GDP ratio is heading for a constant value; that is, a balanced growth equilibrium.

As in Chapters 4 and 5, we can analyze the debt-to-GDP ratio D/Y by looking to see if it heads for some constant equilibrium value. At that value, both the numerator D (the debt) and the denominator Y (GDP) will be growing at the same proportional rate — there will be balanced growth of debt and GDP. We know that real GDP grows in the long run at a proportional annual rate $n + g$, where n is the annual growth rate of the labor force and g is the annual growth rate of the efficiency of labor.

What is the proportional growth rate of the debt, D? Adding time subscripts to keep things clear, the real debt next year will be equal to

$$D_{t+1} = (1 - \pi)D_t + d_t$$

The real value of the debt shrinks by a proportional amount π as inflation erodes away the real value of the debt principal owed by the government and grows by an amount equal to the officially reported cash deficit d. As the economy grows, tax revenues grow roughly in proportion to real GDP and spending grows in proportion to real GDP too. So it makes sense to focus not on the deficit itself but on the deficit as a share of GDP, d/Y.

Then the proportional growth rate of the debt is

$$\frac{D_{t+1} - D_t}{D_t} = -\pi + \left(\frac{d}{Y}\right)\left(\frac{Y}{D}\right)$$

The debt-to-GDP ratio will be stable when these two proportional growth rates — of GDP and of the debt — are equal to each other:

$$n + g = -\pi + \left(\frac{d}{Y}\right)\left(\frac{Y}{D}\right)$$

which happens when

$$\frac{D}{Y} = \frac{d/Y}{n + g + \pi}$$

This is the level toward which the debt-to-GDP ratio will head; Box 14.2 provides an example of how to calculate this long-run value of the debt-to-GDP ratio. This is the level consistent with a constant cash-balance deficit of d/Y percent of GDP in an economy with long-run inflation rate π and with long-run real GDP growth rate $n + g$.

Is the Equilibrium Debt-to-GDP Ratio Possible?

Why then do economists talk about deficit levels as being "unsustainable"? For any deficit as a share of GDP (d/Y), the debt-to-GDP ratio heads for its well-defined value ($d/Y)/(n + g + \pi$). The reason is that this calculation is at most half the story. The ratio of the debt to GDP that the government wants to issue heads for a stable value, yes. But are there enough investors in the world willing to hold that amount of debt? The higher the debt-to-GDP ratio, the riskier an investment financiers judge the debt of a country to be, and the less willing they are to buy and hold that debt.

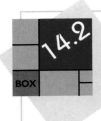

BOX

THE EQUILIBRIUM DEBT-TO-GDP RATIO: AN EXAMPLE

Suppose that the economy is running a constant budget deficit of 4 percent of GDP year after year. Suppose further that the growth rate of the labor force is 2 percent per year, the growth rate of output per worker is 1 percent per year, and the inflation rate is 5 percent per year. What then will be this economy's **equilibrium ratio of government debt to GDP?**

To determine the answer, simply plug the parameter values into the formula

$$\frac{D}{Y} = \frac{d/Y}{n + g + \pi} = \frac{0.04}{0.02 + 0.01 + 0.05} = \frac{1}{2}$$

The equilibrium debt-to-GDP ratio will be ½. If the current debt-to-GDP ratio is less than ½, the debt-to-GDP ratio will grow. If the current debt-to-GDP ratio is greater than ½, the debt-to-GDP ratio will fall.

Notice a similarity to the analysis of the equilibrium capital-output ratio way back in Chapter 4? The mathematical tools and models are the same, even though the phenomena in the world to which they apply are very different. Such recycling of a formal model in a different context is yet another trick economists use to try to keep their discipline and their models simple.

---

equilibrium debt-to-GDP ratio

The constant ratio of government debt to GDP when both real government debt and real GDP are growing at the same rate.

A higher debt-to-GDP ratio makes investment in the debt issued by a government more risky for two reasons. First, revolutions — or other, more peaceful changes of government — happen. One of the things a new government must decide is whether it is going to honor the debt issued by previous governments. Are these debts the commitments of the nation, which, as an honorable entity, honors its commitments? Or are these debts the reckless mistakes made by and obligations of a gang of thugs, unrepresentative of the nation, to whom investors should have known better than to lend money for the thugs to steal? The holders of a government's debt anxiously await every new government's decision on this issue. The higher the debt-to-GDP ratio, the greater the temptation for a new government to repudiate debt issued by its predecessor, hence the riskier it is to buy and hold a portion of that country's national debt.

Second, a government can control the real size of the debt it owes by controlling the rate of inflation. The (nominal) interest rate to be paid on government debt is fixed by the terms of the bond issued. The real interest rate paid on the debt is equal to the nominal interest rate minus the rate of inflation — and the government controls the rate of inflation.

Thus a government that seeks to redistribute wealth away from its bondholders to its taxpayers can do so by increasing the rate of inflation. The more inflation, the less the government's debt is worth and the lower the real taxes that have to be imposed to pay off the interest and principal on the debt. Whether a government is likely to increase the rate of inflation depends on the costs and benefits — and raising the rate of inflation does have significant political costs. But the higher the debt-to-GDP ratio, the greater the benefits to taxpayers of a sudden burst of inflation. When the debt-to-GDP ratio is equal to 2, a sudden 10 percent rise in the price level reduces the real wealth of the government's creditors and increases the real wealth of taxpayers by an amount equal to 20 percent of a year's GDP. By contrast, when the debt-to-GDP ratio is equal to 0.2, the same rise in the price level redistributes wealth equal to only 2 percent of a year's GDP.

Thus the government's potential creditors must calculate that the greater the debt-to-GDP ratio, the greater the benefits to the government of inflation as a way of writing down the value of its debt. The higher the debt-to-GDP ratio, the more likely the government is to resort to inflation. Thus the higher the debt-to-GDP ratio, the riskier it is to invest in a government's debt.

A deficit is sustainable only if the associated debt-to-GDP ratio is low enough that investors judge the debt safe enough to be willing to hold it. Think of each government as having a debt capacity — a maximum debt-to-GDP ratio at which investors are willing to hold the debt issued at reasonable interest rates. If this debt capacity is exceeded, then the interest rates that the government must pay on its debt spike upward. The government is faced with a much larger deficit than planned (as a result of higher interest costs). Either the government must raise taxes, or it must resort to high inflation or hyperinflation to write the real value of the debt down.

Economic Effects of Deficits

Even if a given deficit as a share of GDP is sustainable, it still may have three types of significant effects on the economy. It may affect the political equilibrium that determines the government's tax and spending levels. It may, if the central bank allows it, affect the level of real GDP in the short run. And it will (except in very special cases) affect the level of real GDP in the long run.

The U.S. national debt today, however, is below the level at which economists begin to watch the debt with anxious concern. There were fears during the 1980s that the United States had put itself on a course for national disaster through a mounting national debt. These fears have been renewed as the surpluses of the late 1990s have been replaced by the return of large deficits. But the United States is still far from the edge of the precipice.

The typical pattern the United States has followed is one of sharp spikes in the debt-to-GDP ratio during wartime, followed by paying off the national debt as a share of GDP during peacetime. Why governments usually run up large debts during wartime is easily explained. Their survival, and perhaps the survival of their nation and their civilization, is at stake. So during major wars, governments use all the tools they have to gain control of resources for their fleets, armies, and air forces. And one of those tools is a substantial dose of government borrowing.

The great peaks in U.S. government debt as a share of total domestic product all came after the three major wars in which the United States was engaged: the Civil War, World War I, and World War II. The minor peaks were mostly wartime peaks too: the initial level of debt as the federal government took over responsibility for state borrowing during the Revolutionary War, the uptick during the War of 1812, and a tiny uptick during the Spanish-American War at the end of the nineteenth century. (See Box 14.3 on page 428 for some details.)

There have been only three upward movements in the debt as a share of GDP not connected to wars: the rise in the national debt during the Great Depression of the

THE U.S. DEBT-TO-GDP RATIO: DATA

The United States ended the Revolutionary War with what was then thought of as a considerable national debt given the limited taxing capacity of late-eighteenth-century governments. The first secretary of the treasury, Alexander Hamilton, pressed hard and won congressional approval for the federal government to assume and pay the debts the individual states had incurred to fight the Revolutionary War. Hamilton believed that this assumption of the debt would make it easier for the federal government to borrow in the future. Moreover, he believed that if the government owed people money, there would be a strong interest group in favor of the continuation of the United States of America: Bondholders would like to be paid.

By the presidency of Andrew Jackson, however, virtually the entire debt run up first in the Revolutionary War and then in the War of 1812 had been repaid (see Figure 14.7). The Union debt run up during the Civil War was also repaid within a few decades. But then in quick succession came World War I, the Great Depression, and World War II, which together drove the U.S. national debt up to more than a year's GDP. Thereafter the growth of the economy, inflation, and more-or-less balanced budgets saw the debt fall relative to GDP until the coming of the 1980s with the Reagan tax cut and the resulting deficits and rapid increase in the debt once again.

FIGURE 14.7
U.S. Debt-to-GDP Ratio since the Revolutionary War

Source: J. Bradford DeLong, "Keynesianism, Pennsylvania-Avenue Style: Some Economic Consequences of the 1946 Employment Act," *Journal of Economic Perspectives* 10 (Summer 1996), pp. 41–53; as updated by the author.

1930s, the rise in the national debt during the Reagan and Bush 41 presidencies of the 1980s, and the rise during the Bush 43 presidency (see Figure 14.8).

The reason that during peacetime the size of the government debt as a share of GDP typically falls is also straightforward. Economic growth raises real GDP and inflation provides an additional boost to nominal GDP. As long as the government's tax

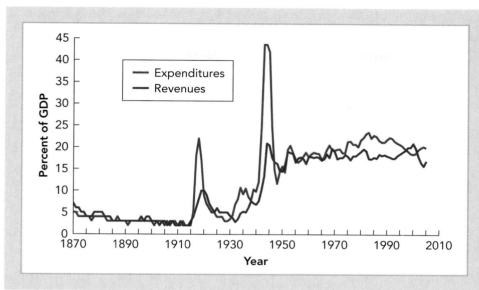

FIGURE 14.8

Federal Revenues and Expenditures as Shares of GDP

Since the Civil War U.S. government expenditures have significantly outrun revenues on five occasions: World War I, World War II, the Great Depression, the Reagan/Bush 41 deficits of the 1980s, and the Bush 43 deficit.

Source: J. Bradford DeLong, "Keynesianism, Pennsylvania-Avenue Style: Some Economic Consequences of the 1946 Employment Act," *Journal of Economic Perspectives* 10 (Summer 1996), pp. 41–53; as updated by the author.

and spending programs are not grossly out of whack, in peacetime government debt tends to fall as a share of GDP. Before 1930 the government's tax and spending programs could not get out of whack in peacetime: There was barely any peacetime federal government. Since 1930, however, the peacetime federal government has increased its share of the economy. Thus to see the emergence of substantial peacetime government budget deficits and a rising national debt-to-GDP ratio first in the 1980s and then again in the 2000s was a great surprise.

Partly because of higher spending on defense and other programs in the 1980s, partly because of substantial tax cuts, and partly because the productivity slow-down led real GDP growth to be smaller than previous forecasts, the Reagan presidency set in motion a series of deficits that ended by nearly doubling the burden of the federal government debt as a share of GDP. The rise in the debt was brought to an end by three factors:

- President George H. W. Bush's (Bush 41) economic advisers and the Democratic and Republican congressional leaders who persuaded him to go back on his campaign pledge of "read my lips, no new taxes" and to negotiate a serious deficit-reduction program including major reforms in congressional budget procedures in 1990.

- President Clinton, his economic advisers, and the Democratic members of Congress who made deficit reduction the highest priority of his administration in 1993.

- A healthy dose of good macroeconomic luck.

A fair but rough assignment of credit would give 40 percent to those who planned the 1990 deficit-reduction program, 30 percent to those who planned the 1993 deficit-reduction program, and 30 percent to sheer dumb good luck.

However, the early 2000s saw a return of the U.S. budget deficit to levels like those of the Reagan and first Bush administrations. It was the deficit-reduction program of the 1990s that appears to have been the anomaly. The big deficits of the 1980s and 2000s appear to have become the rule.

How important is the near doubling of the debt as a share of GDP that took place in the last quarter century, and the further doubling that we can look forward to under current policies over the next generation? One view, held by a majority of economists, is that such large government deficits have three sets of effects. First, they have uncertain but probably destructive effects on the formulation of government spending and tax plans. Second, they have the potential to have expansionary effects on the economy in the short run. Third, they have contractionary effects on the economy in the long run by reducing investment and capital formation, and putting the economy on a less prosperous long-run balanced-growth path. The most important effect is probably the third. How big? The rule of thumb set out by economists Gregory Mankiw and Douglas Elmendorf is that $1 of extra debt reduces long-run real GDP by about seven cents.

Political Effects of Deficits

One thread of political economic analysis holds that deficits have destructive political consequences: The possibility of financing government spending through borrowing makes the government less effective at advancing the public welfare. Electoral politics suffers from a form of institutional **voter myopia**: The benefits from higher government spending now are clear and visible to voters, and the costs of the higher taxes later that will be needed to finance the debt built up via deficit spending are distant, fuzzy, and excessively discounted. Moreover, the unborn and underage do not vote: Many of those who will be obligated to pay taxes to make interest payments on tomorrow's national debt do not vote today. The principle of "no taxation without representation" would seem to call for no long-term national debt — or, rather, for a national debt that is not larger than the government's capital stock.

Thus economists like Nobel Prize–winner James Buchanan have argued for a stringent balanced-budget rule. In Buchanan's view, only if political dialogue must simultaneously confront both the benefits of spending and the pain of the taxes needed to finance that spending can we expect a democratic political system to adequately and effectively weigh the costs and benefits of proposed programs.

Since the start of the 1980s, another argument has appeared: an argument for deficits created by tax cuts. The political system, its proponents argue, delivers steadily rising government spending unless it is placed under immediate and dire pressure to reduce the deficit. Therefore the only way to avoid an ever-growing inefficient government share of GDP is to run a constant deficit that politicians feel impelled to try to reduce. And should they ever succeed, the appropriate response is to pass another tax cut to create a new deficit. Only by starving the beast Leviathan that is government can it be kept from indefinite expansion.

The U.S. experience of the past quarter century tends to support James Buchanan's position, and to count against the alternative position. Few today are satisfied with the decisions about government spending and tax policy made in the 1980s and 1990s. Moreover, the deficits of the 1980s and of today do not seem to have put downward pressure on federal spending. Program spending fell, but total spending rose because of the hike in interest payments created by the series of deficits in the 1980s. Because interest payments are part of government spending, modern deficits appear to put not downward but upward pressure on the size of government.

voter myopia

The theory that voters react to the immediate economic situation, rather than to what happened in the further past or what is likely to happen in the future.

Effects of Deficits on Planned Expenditure

In the short run, the income-expenditure diagram of Chapter 9 tells us that a deficit produced by a tax cut stimulates consumer spending and thus indirectly increases planned expenditure. A deficit produced instead by an increase in government purchases directly increases planned expenditure. Either way, the deficit shifts the IS curve out and to the right: Any given interest rate is associated with a higher equilibrium value of production and employment.

If the money stock is unchanged — if the LM curve of Chapter 11 does not shift — then output and employment rise in response to the tax cut. A deficit is expansionary in the short run.

If monetary policy is set by the Taylor rule of Chapter 12, the MPRF shifts in and to the left. Unless expectations are rational — which they likely are not — unemployment falls and inflation rises. Again, a deficit is expansionary in the short run.

Of course, the belief that deficits are expansionary — that they increase production and employment — in the short run hinges not only on how we form our expectations but also on the Federal Reserve's response to the rise in the deficit. If the Federal Reserve does not want inflation to rise at all — if its r_π is very large — it will respond to the rightward expansionary shift in the IS curve by tightening monetary policy and raising interest rates, neutralizing at least part of the expansionary effect of the deficit. The MPRF will then be very flat. Because the decision-making and policy implementation cycle for monetary policy is significantly shorter than the decision-making and policy implementation cycle for discretionary fiscal policy, the central bank can keep legislative actions to change the deficit from affecting the level of production and unemployment. The question is whether it will. The answer is, most of the time, yes. The central bank is trying its best to guide the economy along a narrow path without excess unemployment and without *accelerating inflation*. It has made its best guess as to what level of planned expenditure leads us along that path. In all likelihood its senior officials are uninterested in seeing the economy pushed away from that path by the fiscal policy decisions of legislators.

International Effects of Deficits

An increase in the government's budget deficit also leads to an increase in the *trade deficit*. The outward shift in the IS curve and inward shift of the MPRF push up interest rates. Higher interest rates mean an appreciated dollar — a lower value of the exchange rate and of foreign currency — and therefore net exports fall. Up to now we have implicitly assumed that the composition of planned expenditure has no effect on the productivity of industry. Businesses have been implicitly assumed to be equally happy and equally productive whether they are producing consumption goods, investment goods for domestic use, goods and services that the government will purchase, or goods for the export market. Yet this is unlikely to be true. Recall from your microeconomics courses that the point of international trade is to trade goods that your economy is especially productive at making for goods that your economy is relatively unproductive at making.

As large deficits that increase interest rates lower the value of the exchange rate, export industries — likely to be highly productive — shrink as exports shrink. This presumably reduces total productivity. Nobody, however, has a very sound estimate of how large these effects might be.

FIGURE 14.9
Higher Full-Employment Deficits Reduce Investment

In the long run, higher budget deficits are not expansionary. Instead, increased interest rates reduce investment spending and lower the economy's balanced-growth path of real GDP per worker.

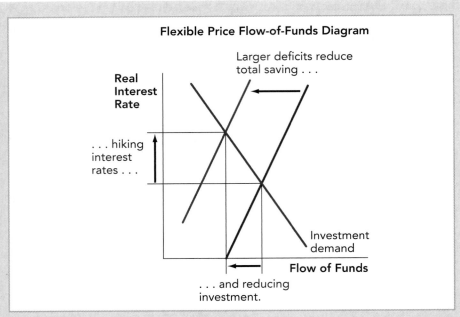

Deficits and Long-Run Economic Growth

Higher full-employment deficits lead to low investment. Higher deficits lower government saving. In any run long enough for the full-employment flexible-price model of Chapter 7 to be relevant, large full-employment deficits lead to lower total saving, higher real interest rates, and, as shown in Figure 14.9, lower investment.

In the flexible-price context the analysis of persistent deficits is straightforward. Such deficits reduce government saving. Flow-of-funds equilibrium thus requires higher real interest rates and lower levels of investment spending and net exports.

Even in a sticky-price context it may well be that higher deficits reduce investment and net exports. The central bank can, and probably will, change monetary policy to neutralize at least part of the effect of the higher deficit on real GDP. The central bank chose its baseline monetary policy in order to try to strike the optimum balance between the risk of higher-than-necessary unemployment and the risk of rising inflation. The central bank does not want this balance disturbed by shifts in the IS curve, so it is highly likely to use monetary policy to offset at least partially the effect of the deficit-driven shift in the IS curve on the level of real GDP and employment. The IS curve shifts out, but interest rates rise, leaving investment lowered. Will the central bank raise interest rates high enough to create a dollar-for-dollar swap between government purchases on one hand and investment plus gross exports on the other? In the long run, it will. But in the short run it may or may not. If the central bank's responsiveness to a rise in inflation — the central bank's r_π — is infinitely large, then it will fully offset the increase in government purchases. Or if the central bank shifts its interest rate rule in order to keep the location of the MPRF unchanged in spite of the fiscal stimulus, then again it will fully offset the increase. In other cases, in the short run, the central bank will allow some of the increase in government purchases to boost the economy.

Low investment reduces capital accumulation and productivity growth, putting the country on a trajectory to a lower balanced-growth path. Since the early 1960s, economists have argued that economic growth is fastest and the economy is best off when the **policy mix** pursued by the government and the central bank is one of tight fiscal policy (a government surplus) and loose monetary policy (a relatively low interest rate). Together this policy mix can produce full employment, high investment, and relatively rapid economic growth.

Over time, the U.S. government has appeared to have the opposite bias. Certainly for a period of two and a half decades now, beginning with the Reagan tax cuts of the early 1980s and interrupted only by Clinton's second term in office, the U.S. economy has had loose fiscal policy and tight monetary policy. If the current deficits continue for long, they will begin to have an effect on the economy's capital intensity. The reduction in national saving as a share of GDP will reduce the economy's balanced-growth capital-output ratio. A lower balanced-growth capital-output ratio implies a lower level of output per worker along the balanced-growth path for any given level of the efficiency of labor. Thus a policy of persistent deficits will — as long as the rise in the deficit reduces national saving — reduce the long-run level of output per worker below what it would otherwise have been. By how much? As mentioned earlier, Mankiw and Elmendorf's rule of thumb says that an extra dollar of debt reduces real GDP by seven cents. (This, at least, is the conventional analysis of the interaction between deficits and long-run growth. It has been challenged by a group of professors centered on Harvard's Robert Barro — as discussed later in this book.)

policy mix

The combination of monetary and fiscal policies being followed by a country's government and central bank.

Debt Service, Taxation, and Real GDP

But there are still more long-term effects. A higher deficit means a higher debt, which means that the government owes more in the way of interest payments to bondholders. Over time — even if the level of the deficit is kept constant — the increase in interest payments will require tax increases. And these tax increases will discourage entrepreneurship and economic activity. In addition to the reduction in output per worker resulting from the lower capital-output ratio, there will be an additional reduction in output per worker: The increased taxes needed to finance the interest owed on the national debt will have negative supply-side effects on production.

The interaction of macroeconomic policy, tax policy, incentives for production, and the level of real GDP deserves more space. No discussion of fiscal policy could be complete without noting, for example, a possible drawback of the progressive tax rates that create strong fiscal automatic stabilizers. The higher the marginal tax rate, the greater the danger that at the margin taxes will discourage economic activity — leading either to hordes of lawyers wasting social time executing negative-sum tax-avoidance strategies, to a shift away from aggressive entrepreneurship toward more cautious, less growth-promoting activities taxed at lower rates, or to a depreciated exchange rate (and thus less power to purchase imports) as capital flows across national borders to jurisdictions that have lower tax rates at the margin.

Thinking through these issues is complicated. Are government expenditures on infrastructure, basic research, and other public goods themselves productive? Do they raise total output by more than the increased tax rates threaten to reduce it? And what is the government's objective? After all, maximizing measured total output is the same thing as maximizing social welfare only if externalities are absent, and only if the distribution of total wealth corresponds to the weight individuals have in the social welfare function — with the tastes and desires of the rich being given more weight.

These topics are traditionally reserved for public finance courses, and are not covered in macroeconomics courses. But no one should think that an analysis of fiscal policy can start and end with the effects of discretionary fiscal policy and automatic stabilizers on the business cycle and the effects of persistent deficits on national saving. There is much more to be thought about.

> ### RECAP   ANALYZING THE DEBT AND THE DEFICIT
>
> A high government budget deficit has three types of significant effects on the economy. First, it will tend to swell the absolute size of the government in relation to GDP. Myopic voters will see the benefits of spending increases and not count the costs of future tax increases to finance them. Higher national debt levels increase interest payments, and the government must eventually raise taxes to make these interest payments. A high government budget deficit may — if the central bank allows it — raise real GDP and lower unemployment in the short run. A high government budget deficit will in the long run slow economic growth and lower real GDP below what it would otherwise have been.

Chapter Summary

1. The United States is usually a moderate-debt country. The level of the national debt with which U.S. politicians and voters are comfortable is not terribly large. Only immediately after major wars does the U.S. national debt reach a high value relative to real GDP.

2. The last quarter century, however, saw steep rises in the national debt — unprecedented rises in peacetime — interrupted by only a few brief and temporary years of budget surpluses at the end of the 1990s.

3. Nevertheless, the U.S. national debt is still significantly below the level at which economists begin seriously worrying about the consequences of the debt for the health of the economy.

4. From the standpoint of analyzing stabilization policy, the best measure of the government's stance is the full-employment deficit. The full-employment deficit is not a bad measure of the net effect of government policy on the location of the IS curve and the MPRF.

5. From the standpoint of analyzing the effect of changes in the national debt on long-run growth, the debt and deficit need to be adjusted for inflation and government investment. A third adjustment — for outstanding government liabilities — has been proposed and has some attractive features, but it is not usually used.

6. Persistent deficits — a rising national debt — threaten to diminish national saving, reduce the level of output per worker along the economy's balanced-growth path, and retard economic growth.

7. Past deficits — which produce a high ratio of current debt to GDP — threaten to reduce national prosperity because the higher taxes required to service the national debt act as a drag on economic activity.

Key Terms

government deficit (p. 416)

national debt (p. 416)

government surplus (p. 416)

full-employment cyclically adjusted deficit (p. 417)

cash budget balance (p. 419)

generational accounting (p. 423)

equilibrium debt-to-GDP ratio (p. 426)

voter myopia (p. 430)

policy mix (p. 433)

Analytical Exercises

1. What is the typical pattern followed by the debt-to-GDP ratio in the United States over time?

2. How does the experience of the past quarter century differ from the typical U.S. pattern as far as the debt-to-GDP ratio is concerned?

3. Why are the deficits of the 1980s generally seen to have been a bad thing? What are the arguments that the deficits of the 1980s were a good thing?

4. Suppose someone asks you which measure of the government budget balance is best to look at. How does your answer depend on the purpose for which this person wishes to use the budget balance?

5. Why might there be a long-run link between government budget deficits on the one hand and the inflation rate on the other?

Policy Exercises

1. Why might it make sense for a government to finance roads and other investments in public infrastructure through borrowing rather than through taxing today's taxpayers?

2. What effect in today's world do changes in tax and spending programs legislated by Congress and the president have on the level of real GDP in the short run?

3. What are likely to be the long-run effects of a fiscal policy that involves ever-present large budget deficits?

4. Politicians sometimes call for the government to exclude Social Security spending and taxes from the federal government budget. They argue that Social Security moneys should not be used to avoid recognizing the fact of possible deficits in other programs. What arguments can you think of to support the claim that the non–Social Security budget balance is the more interesting and relevant measure? What arguments support the claim that the unified budget balance is the more interesting and relevant measure?

5. Suppose that in a debate you claim that large deficits lead to high interest rates and lowered investment spending, but your opponent claims that it is not fiscal policy that leads to high interest rates — it is too-tight monetary policy on the part of the central bank. How would you respond?

CHAPTER 15

International Economic Policy

QUESTIONS

How has the world organized its international monetary system?

What is a fixed exchange rate system? A floating exchange rate system?

What are the costs and benefits of fixed exchange rates vis-à-vis floating exchange rates?

Why do most countries today have floating exchange rates?

Why does western Europe now have a common currency, the euro, and thus fixed exchange rates within western Europe?

What caused the major currency crises of the 1990s?

floating exchange rates

A system of international monetary arrangements by which central banks let exchange rates be decided by supply and demand, so that they "float" against one another as supplies and demands vary.

Up to this point we have assumed that the economy's exchange rate is a **floating exchange rate**, one that rises and falls freely as supply balances demand in the market for foreign exchange. This chapter changes the focus and considers alternative international monetary arrangements. How do such alternative arrangements — chiefly fixed exchange rate systems — work? What are the relative costs and benefits of fixed versus floating exchange rates? How did we arrive at our current system of largely floating exchange rates? And what difference does having this system make?

Our current system is unusual: For most of the past century the dominant regime for international exchange rates has been one of fixed, not floating, exchange rates. This chapter begins by sketching the economic history of the international monetary system in order to understand how we got here from there. It then analyzes how the economy works when the government fixes the exchange rate. The chapter concludes by analyzing some of the major international shocks to the world economy in the 1990s. Three separate major international financial crises (and a host of lesser crises) struck during that decade: the European crisis of 1992, the Mexican crisis of 1995, the *East Asian crisis* of 1997–1998. The years since 1998 have been more quiescent. There have been crises in Brazil, Turkey, Argentina, and elsewhere, and there is the threat of a future crisis involving the United States, but nothing of the magnitude of the decade before. Yet.

15.1 THE HISTORY OF EXCHANGE RATES

The Classical Gold Standard

What the Gold Standard Is

fixed exchange rates

A system of international monetary arrangements by which central banks buy and sell in foreign exchange markets so as to keep their relative exchange rates fixed.

gold standard

A system by which central banks preserve fixed exchange rates by always being willing to buy or sell their currencies at fixed rates in terms of the precious metal gold.

In the generation before World War I nearly all of the world economy was on a particular **fixed exchange rate** system: the **gold standard**. A government would define a unit of its currency as worth such-and-such an amount of gold. It would stand ready to buy or sell its currency for gold at that price at any time, in any amount. Such a currency was convertible, for it could be converted into gold freely (and gold could be converted into it freely). The currency's price in terms of gold was its parity.

When two countries were on the gold standard, their nominal exchange rate was fixed at the ratio of their gold parities. People wishing to turn British currency — pounds sterling — into U.S. currency — American dollars — could begin by taking British currency to the Bank of England and exchanging it for gold at the pound's parity. They would then ship the gold across the Atlantic to New York, take it to the U.S. Treasury office in New York, and exchange it for dollars.

At the post–World War II parities of the Bretton Woods "gold exchange" standard, the U.S. dollar was defined as equal to 1/35 troy ounce of gold, and the British pound sterling was set equal to 1/14.58333 ounce of gold. Thus the exchange rate of the dollar for the pound was £1.00 = $2.40. At the parities that had prevailed from 1879 to 1931 (with an interruption for World War I), the dollar-pound exchange rate was £1.00 = $4.86.

Suppose that supply and demand in the market for foreign exchange in 1910 had balanced not at £1.00 = $4.86 but at some other value — say £1.00 = $5.00. Someone with an idle pound sterling note could then get $5 for it by selling it on the foreign exchange market. But that $5 could then buy enough gold at the U.S. Treasury to recover the original £1, with 14 cents left over. So if the market exchange rate ever drifted up from £1.00 = $4.86 to £1.00 = $5.00, a huge mass of people selling pounds would enter the market and drive the exchange rate back to £1.00 = $4.86 as they attempted to carry out this **currency arbitrage**. Thus under the gold standard, nominal exchange rates were fixed at the ratio of countries' gold parities, as Box 15.1 explains. The gold standard was thus a fixed exchange rate system.

This gold-standard system grew up gradually. It originated when Sir Isaac Newton, in his government job as master of the mint in Britain, fixed the gold parity of the British pound sterling. Because the industrial revolution began in Britain, Britain became the largest trading nation in the world in the nineteenth century. Other countries' governments sought easy access to the British market for the products made by their citizens. A fixed gold parity meant the prices their countries' producers charged would appear stable to British customers. It also meant that

currency arbitrage

A situation, operating under the gold standard, whereby people buying or selling one currency at any price other than the ratio of the two gold parities would find themselves facing an unlimited demand, and would soon find themselves losing a nearly unlimited amount of money.

CURRENCY ARBITRAGE UNDER THE GOLD STANDARD: AN EXAMPLE

As long as central banks or treasuries stood ready to keep their currencies convertible at their gold parities, the ratio of two gold parities determined the nominal exchange rate. Why? Because of currency arbitrage. People buying or selling one currency at any price other than the ratio of the two gold parities would find themselves facing an unlimited demand, and would soon find themselves losing a nearly unlimited amount of money.

Suppose — as originally envisioned under the Bretton Woods system — that the U.S. Treasury stood ready to buy or sell gold from qualified parties at the price of $35 an ounce, that the British Treasury stood ready to buy or sell gold from qualified parties at the price of £14.58333 an ounce, but that the pound sterling was trading in the foreign exchange market not for the $2.40 that was the ratio of the gold parities, but instead for 10 percent more — $2.64.

Then someone with an ounce of gold could

- Trade it to the British Treasury for £14.58333.
- Then trade those pounds sterling for dollars in the foreign exchange market and wind up with $38.50.
- Trade that $38.50 to the U.S. Treasury for 1.1 ounces of gold.
- Repeat the process as rapidly as possible, making a 10 percent profit each time the circle was completed.

Figure 15.1 on page 440 shows these steps. Note that those who sell dollars for pounds at the rate of $2.64 = £1.00 are losing 10 percent of their value each time the circle is completed. The only things hindering this round-trip "arbitrage" process — as long as currencies remain convertible and parities remain fixed — are the costs of transporting and insuring the gold. Thus there can be very small fluctuations of exchange rates within the "gold points," but gold is cheap to transport and straightforward to insure: These fluctuations are minor indeed.

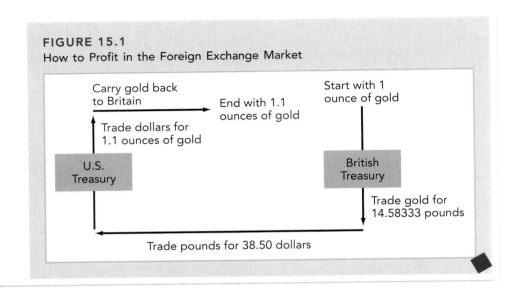

FIGURE 15.1
How to Profit in the Foreign Exchange Market

British investors would not fear that depreciation and *devaluation* would erode the value of the principal that they had lent. Throughout the late nineteenth century, country after country joined the gold standard, as Figure 15.2 shows. By the eve of World War I the overwhelming fraction of world commerce and investment flowed between countries on the gold standard.

A Gold Standard Tends to Produce Contractionary Policies

Even in its turn-of-the-century heyday around 1900 the gold standard had already manifested certain serious weaknesses as an international monetary system. The most important of these weaknesses was that the gold standard tended to be contractionary. In some circumstances it pushed countries to raise their interest rates to reduce production and raise unemployment. And it never provided a countervailing push to other countries to lower their interest rates to raise production and to lower unemployment. To see why, we need to digress for a moment into the role played under a gold standard by a country's gold and other **foreign exchange reserves.** If the exchange rate is floating in country A, foreigners' earnings in currency A must be used to buy A's exports or be invested in country A: Nothing else can be done with them. Under a floating-rate system a country's net exports NX plus net investment from abroad NIA must add up to zero:

$$NX + NIA = 0$$

The exchange rate moves up or down in response to the supply and demand for foreign exchange in order to make this so.

Under a gold standard things are different. There is an extra participant in the market: the country's treasury or central bank. One can do something else with foreign-currency earnings besides using them to buy imports or make investments abroad: Take them to the foreign country's treasury, turn them into gold, ship the gold back home, take the gold to the treasury there, and turn the gold into real spendable cash. Under a gold standard it is net exports plus net investment from

foreign exchange reserves

Foreign currency–denominated assets held by a country's central bank or treasury to use in foreign exchange interventions.

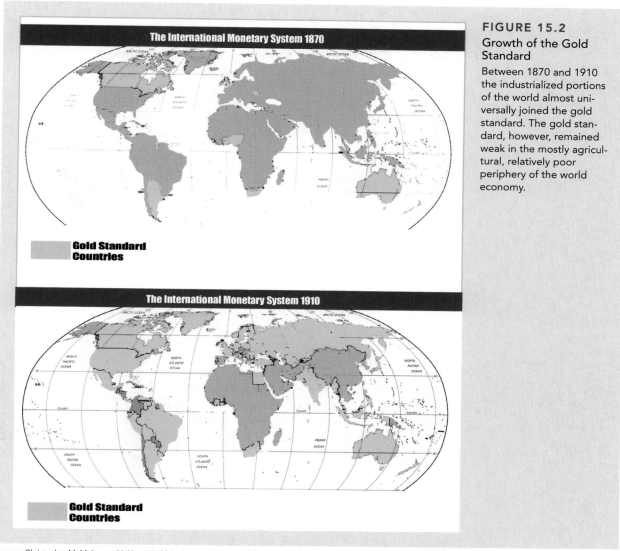

Source: Christopher M. Meissner, "A New World Order: Explaining the Diffusion of the Classical Gold Standard, 1870–1913" *Journal of International Economics,* 2005; and Niall Ferguson and Moritz Schularick, "The Empire Effect: The Determinants of Country Risk in the First Age of Globalization, 1880–1913," mimeo, New York University, 2004.

abroad minus the flow of gold into your country — *FG* — that together add up to zero:

$$NX + NIA - FG = 0$$

What happens if a country finds that net exports plus net investment from abroad are less than zero? Its treasury will find itself losing gold, as a long line of foreigners come into its office, demand gold in exchange for currency, and then ship the gold out of the country. With each such transaction the country's gold reserves shrink. Eventually the government's gold reserves are gone.

   At this point the country has a choice. One option is to abandon the fixed exchange rate system. It "closes the gold window," announces that the country will no longer buy back its currency at the established gold parity, abandons its fixed exchange rate, and lets the exchange rate float. The only other option is to solve its gold-outflow problem by attracting more foreigners to invest. The way to increase net investment from abroad is to raise domestic interest rates. If net investment from abroad rises enough, gold will no longer flow out.

Thus under a gold standard, countries that run persistent *balance-of-payments* deficits — losing gold — must eventually raise interest rates to stay on the gold standard. However, surplus countries — those gaining gold — face no symmetrical crisis in which they must lower interest to stay on the gold standard. Their central banks can lower interest rates if they wish. But if they do not so wish, they can keep interest rates constant and watch their gold reserves grow.

This asymmetry means that a fixed exchange rate system like the gold standard puts periodic contractionary pressure on the world economy. Such pressure turned the interwar period into a disaster; the gold standard's contractionary pressure on countries to raise interest rates played a major role in generating the worldwide Great Depression of the 1930s.

The Collapse of the Gold Standard

The international gold standard was suspended when World War I began in 1914. Every country used inflation to help finance its massive war expenditures. Inflation was inconsistent with the gold standard. Under the gold standard attempted inflation simply leads everyone to immediately trade their currency for solid gold.

After World War I was over, politicians and central bankers sought to restore the gold standard. They believed that the pre–World War I system of a fixed exchange rate based on the gold standard had been a success. They saw restoring it as an important step to restoring general economic prosperity. The gold standard had, after all, delivered 40 years of more rapid economic and industrial growth than the world had ever seen before.

More than half a decade was needed to fully restore the gold standard. But the revived gold standard did not produce prosperity. Instead, in less than half a decade the Great Depression began, and the restored gold standard broke apart. The consensus of economic historians today is that the Great Depression had its principal origin in the United States, where for reasons not fully understood some combination of small shocks set off a downward spiral of destabilizing deflation. But a combination of mistaken policies and flaws in the functioning of the post–World War I gold standard then quickly amplified the Great Depression and propagated it around the world.

Economists Barry Eichengreen and Ben Bernanke argue that four factors made the post–World War I gold standard a much less secure monetary system than the pre–World War I gold standard:

- Everyone knew that governments could abandon their gold parities in an emergency. After all, they had done so during World War I. Thus everyone was eager to turn currency holdings into gold at the first sign of trouble. This meant countries had to maintain much larger gold reserves in order to keep the gold standard functioning.

- Everyone knew that governments had taken on the additional responsibility of trying to keep interest rates low enough to produce full employment.

- After World War I countries held their reserves not in gold but in foreign currencies. This was fine in normal times, but it meant that at the first sign of trouble not only would citizens show up trying to turn their currency into gold, but foreign central banks would do so too, greatly multiplying the magnitude of the gold outflow.

- The post–World War I surplus economies, the United States and France, did not lower their interest rates as gold flowed in.

These factors meant that as soon as a recession set in and gold drains began from countries with weak currencies, their governments found themselves under immediate and massive pressure to raise interest rates and lower output further if they were to stay on the gold standard. If they stayed on the gold standard, they guaranteed themselves high real interest rates and deep depression. If they abandoned the gold standard, they went against all the advice of bankers and gold standard advocates.

There was a clear divergence in the 1930s between those countries that abandoned the gold standard early in the Depression and those that stubbornly clung to gold, as shown in Figure 15.3. Those that clung to their gold parities found themselves forced to raise interest rates and contract their money supplies in order to avoid large gold losses that would rapidly exhaust their reserves. Those that abandoned the gold bloc and floated their exchange rates could avoid deflation,

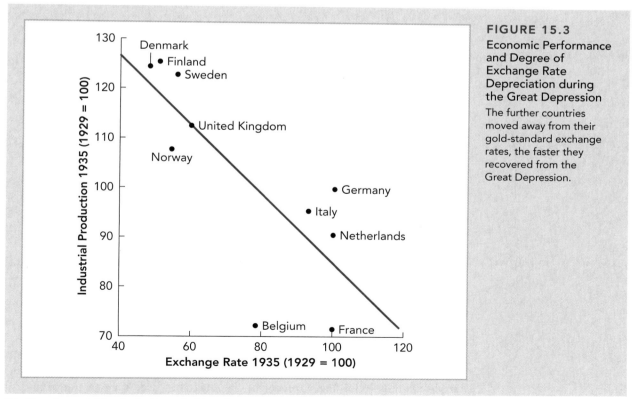

FIGURE 15.3

Economic Performance and Degree of Exchange Rate Depreciation during the Great Depression

The further countries moved away from their gold-standard exchange rates, the faster they recovered from the Great Depression.

Note: The exchange rate is in units of gold per unit of domestic currency.

Source: Barry Eichengreen and Jeffrey Sachs, "Exchange Rates and Economic Recovery in the 1930s," *Journal of Economic History* (December 1985), pp. 925–946.

and avoid the worst of the Great Depression. By the middle of the 1930s the Great Depression was in full swing, and the gold standard was over.

The Bretton Woods System

After World War II, economists took careful note of what they thought had gone wrong after World War I. Led by Harry Dexter White for the United States and John Maynard Keynes for Great Britain, governments tried to set up an international monetary system that would have all the advantages and none of the drawbacks of the gold standard. The system they set up came to be called the "Bretton Woods system," after a New Hampshire mountain resort town that was the location in late 1944 of a key international monetary conference.

Three principles guided this first post–World War II international monetary system:

- In ordinary times, exchange rates should be fixed: Fixed exchange rates encourage international trade by making the prices of goods made in a foreign country predictable, and so have powerful advantages.
- In extraordinary times — whenever a country found itself in recession with a significantly overvalued currency that discouraged its exports, or found itself suffering from inflation because an undervalued currency raised the prices of imports and stimulated export demand — exchange rates should be changed. Such "fundamental disequilibrium" could and should be corrected by revaluing or devaluing the currency.
- An institution was needed — the International Monetary Fund — to watch over the international financial system. The IMF would make bridge loans to countries that were adjusting their economic policies. It would ensure that countries did not abuse their privilege of changing exchange rates. Exchange rate devaluation and *revaluation* would remain an exceptional measure for times of "fundamental disequilibrium," rather than becoming a standard tool of economic policy.

Our Current Floating-Rate System

The Bretton Woods system in its turn broke down in the early 1970s. The United States saw inflation accelerate in the 1960s. It found itself with an overvalued exchange rate and a significant trade deficit at the end of the 1960s. The United States sought to devalue its currency: to reduce the value of the dollar in terms of other currencies, so that exports would rise and imports would fall.

Policy makers in other countries thought that the United States should instead raise interest rates. Higher U.S. interest rates would make foreigners more willing to invest in the United States. The foreign currency committed to those investments could then be used to finance the excess of imports over exports that was the U.S. trade deficit. In the end the deadlock was broken by unilateral American action, and the Bretton Woods system fell apart.

Since the early 1970s the exchange rates at which the currencies of the major industrial powers trade against each other have been "floating" rates. The exchange rate is announced by the government but fluctuates according to the balance of demand and supply on that day in the foreign exchange market. There seem to be few if any prospects for a restoration of a global system of fixed exchange rates over the next generation. Thus this book has assumed as its standard case that exchange rates are free to float and are set by market forces.

Nevertheless, the older system is worth studying for three reasons. First, understanding the functioning of a fixed-rate system sheds light on how a floating-rate system works. Second, economic policy makers still debate the costs and benefits of a fixed-rate system relative to our current floating-rate system. Third, perhaps the pendulum will swing back in a generation and we will find ourselves once more in a fixed exchange rate system.

RECAP **HISTORY OF EXCHANGE RATES**

In the generation before World War I nearly all of the world economy was on a fixed exchange rate system called the gold standard, under which nominal exchange rates were equal to the ratio of currencies' gold parities. The international gold standard was suspended when World War I began in 1914. After World War I attempts to rebuild the gold standard created a system vulnerable to shocks that played a key role in causing the Great Depression. Therefore, after World War II economists built a fixed exchange rate system — the Bretton Woods system — that they hoped would combine the advantages of fixed- and floating-rate systems. But this system collapsed in the early 1970s, and was replaced by our current floating exchange rate system.

15.2 HOW A FIXED EXCHANGE RATE SYSTEM WORKS

We begin by distinguishing between two different economic environments in which a fixed exchange rate system works. The first is an environment of very high *capital mobility*, like the situation the advanced industrial countries face today. Foreign exchange speculators buy and sell bonds denominated in different currencies with a few presses on a keyboard. Hot money — funds that speculators can shift from country to country as fast as they can press the "enter" key — flows around the world nearly instantaneously in response to differences in expected rates of return. Governments find themselves in large part dancing to the tune called by international currency speculators.

The second is an environment of lower capital mobility. The ability of individuals in one country to invest their money in a second is low and limited. Flows of capital out of one country into another are limited. And governments that are willing to do so can shift the exchange rate for a time by using their foreign exchange reserves to intervene in the foreign exchange market.

A fixed exchange rate is a commitment by a country to buy and sell its currency at fixed, unchanging prices in terms of other currencies. To carry out this commitment, the country's central bank and treasury must maintain foreign exchange reserves. If people come to your central bank or treasury under a fixed exchange rate system wanting to exchange your currency for pounds sterling or gold bars, the central bank or treasury must have the pounds sterling or the gold bars to trade to them.

But the foreign exchange reserves of a country are limited. With today's high degree of capital mobility the world has a great many potential foreign exchange speculators. All of them are seeking to make sure that their wealth is invested in the place that offers the highest expected return. Their decisions about where to invest their money are the result of a delicate balance between greed and fear, and all the foreign exchange reserves a government has cannot materially alter the balance of foreign exchange supply and demand for more than a day or two.

High Capital Mobility

Under high capital mobility, countries' foreign exchange reserves are all but irrelevant. The real exchange rate is set by the same exchange rate equation we have seen before, as greed balances fear in the mind of the typical foreign exchange speculator:

$$\varepsilon = \varepsilon_0 - \varepsilon_r(r - r^f)$$

Remember, in this equation ε_0 is foreign exchange speculators' belief about the long-run fundamental value of the real exchange rate; $r - r^f$ is the difference between home and foreign real interest rates; and ε_r is a parameter that tells at what point fear balances greed: It tells how much speculators would be willing to bid up the value of dollar-denominated assets if those assets had an extra 1 unit (100 percentage points) per year interest rate differential. The higher the interest rate differential in favor of the home country, the lower the real exchange rate (which, remember, is defined as the value of foreign currency). (See Figure 15.4.)

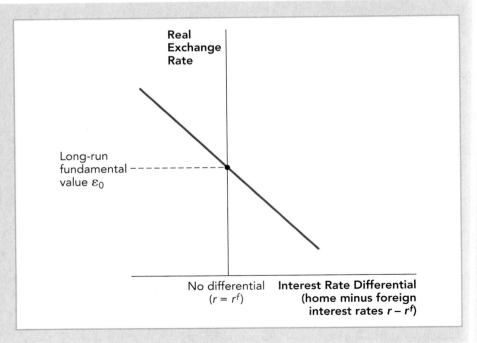

FIGURE 15.4

The Real Exchange Rate, Long-Run Expectations, and Interest Rate Differentials

When there is no differential between home and foreign real interest rates, the value of the real exchange rate is ε_0: what foreign exchange speculators believe and expect the long-run equilibrium value of the exchange rate to be. When home interest rates are higher than foreign interest rates, the value of the exchange rate is lower. When home interest rates are lower than foreign interest rates, the value of the exchange rate is higher.

Why must this equation for the exchange rate hold? Suppose that the government sets a fixed parity such that the fixed value of foreign currency ε^* is lower than given by the equation above. Foreign exchange speculators see foreign currency as a bargain. The extra interest return and potential capital gain from appreciation they get from investing their money in foreign currency–denominated assets more than offsets any risks. So foreign exchange speculators come to the government to sell it the (overvalued) home currency and buy from it the (undervalued) foreign currency at the fixed exchange rate parity. The government spends down its reserves, buying its own currency in exchange for its stocks of other countries' currencies and of gold: It is a fixed exchange rate system after all.

The next day — or hour, or minute — the foreign exchange speculators do it again. And again. And again. The government rapidly runs out of reserves. When its reserves are gone, it can no longer buy and sell foreign currency for domestic currency at the fixed exchange rate parity because it no longer has any foreign currency — or gold — to sell. How long does this process take? Under high capital mobility, hours or days. There are lots of potential foreign exchange speculators. They are all eager to profit by betting against a central bank, especially a central bank that is carrying out its exchange transactions not for economic but for political reasons.

Thus if the government wants to keep the exchange rate at ε^*, its central bank must set interest rates so that the equilibrium value of the exchange rate produced by the equation

$$\varepsilon = \varepsilon_0 - \varepsilon_r(r - r^f)$$

corresponds to the desired fixed exchange rate value ε^*.

For this equation to hold, the central bank must set the domestic real interest rate r at

$$r = r^f + \frac{\varepsilon_0 - \varepsilon^*}{\varepsilon_r}$$

Monetary policy no longer can play a role in domestic stabilization: You cannot ask the central bank to lower interest rates to fight unemployment or raise interest rates to fight inflation because the interest rate is already devoted to maintaining the fixed exchange rate system, as Figure 15.5 on page 448 shows. There is no monetary policy reaction function — no MPRF. Under a fixed exchange rate system with high capital mobility, not macroeconomic policy makers but international currency speculators determine the interest rate.

This means that international financial shocks coming from abroad are immediately transmitted to the domestic economy:

- An increase in foreign interest rates r^f requires an immediate, point-for-point increase in domestic interest rates — and a move up and to the left along the IS curve.

- An increase in foreign exchange speculators' view of the long-run fundamental value of the exchange rate ε_0 requires an immediate increase in domestic interest rates of $(\Delta\varepsilon_0)/\varepsilon_r$.

Figure 15.6 on page 448 shows these effects.

Countries on fixed exchange rate systems find their interest rates tightly linked. This led John Maynard Keynes to warn in the 1920s against an attempt by Britain

FIGURE 15.5

Domestic Interest Rates Are Set by Foreign Exchange Speculators and the Exchange Rate Target

Under high capital mobility, maintaining a fixed exchange rate requires that the central bank ignore domestic conditions and focus on the exchange rate alone in setting interest rates.

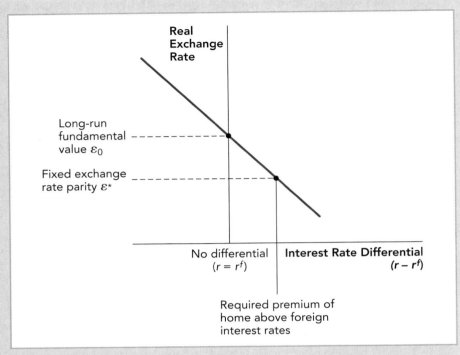

FIGURE 15.6

Effect of Foreign Shocks under Fixed Exchange Rates

If the exchange rate is fixed and if capital mobility is high, external shifts in foreign exchange speculators' opinions or foreign interest rates have direct and immediate effects on domestic interest rates and on domestic output.

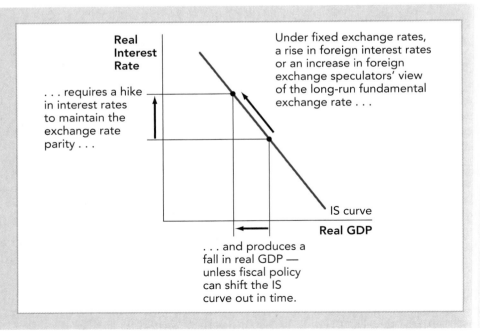

to return to the fixed exchange rate gold standard. It would, Keynes warned, force Britain to receive the full force of interest rate shocks delivered by the unstable U.S. economy. Earlier, when Britain was the leading industrial power before World War I, people expressed it differently: "When [the] London [money market] catches cold," they said, "Buenos Aires [or New York or Sydney] catches pneumonia."

Barriers to Capital Mobility

Now turn to the case of lower, as opposed to higher, capital mobility. Suppose that existing barriers to international financial flows are sufficient to make it difficult and costly to move money across national borders. Thus the government's foreign exchange reserves are sizable relative to flows of capital. Capital mobility today is limited for many developing countries with "thin" financial markets. Capital mobility was limited for all countries only a few decades in the past. It may be limited in the future as well, either as future governments impose explicit controls on types of transactions or as small taxes on international transactions levied by future governments put sand in the wheels of international finance.

If capital mobility is low, the rate at which the government buys or sells its currency for foreign exchange has an impact on foreign exchange supply and demand and thus on the current exchange rate. The exchange rate is determined by foreign currency speculators' expectations, interest rate differentials, and also the speed at which the government is accumulating or spending its foreign exchange reserves R:

$$\varepsilon = \varepsilon_0 - \varepsilon_r(r - r^f) + \varepsilon_R \Delta R$$

A change ΔR in foreign exchange reserves raises the value of the exchange rate by an amount equal to a parameter ε_R times the change in reserves. When the government is accumulating reserves, the value of foreign currency is higher than it would otherwise be: The government is in there buying foreign currency, raising the demand. When the government is spending reserves, the value of foreign currency is lower than it would otherwise be.

Under such barriers to capital mobility, the central bank regains some freedom of action to use monetary policy for domestic uses. It does not have to directly and immediately transmit adverse shocks due to foreign exchange speculator confidence or foreign interest rates to the domestic economy in the form of higher interest rates and a recession. As long as it has reserves, it can choose to let them run down for a while rather than raising domestic interest rates (see Figure 15.7 on page 450). The domestic interest rate r is now

$$r = r^f + \frac{\varepsilon_0 - \varepsilon^*}{\varepsilon_r} + \frac{\varepsilon_R}{\varepsilon_r}(\Delta R)$$

But the amount of freedom of action for monetary policy is limited by (1) the sensitivity of exchange rates to the magnitude of foreign exchange market interventions performed by the central bank and (2) the amount of reserves. The level of foreign exchange reserves must be positive. Policies that spend reserves cannot be continued forever, because once the government's foreign exchange reserves have fallen to zero it can no longer finance interventions in the foreign exchange market. (Note, however, that reserves can be replenished if they drop dangerously close to zero. That is what loans from the IMF, or from other major economy central banks, are for.)

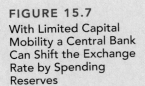

FIGURE 15.7

With Limited Capital Mobility a Central Bank Can Shift the Exchange Rate by Spending Reserves

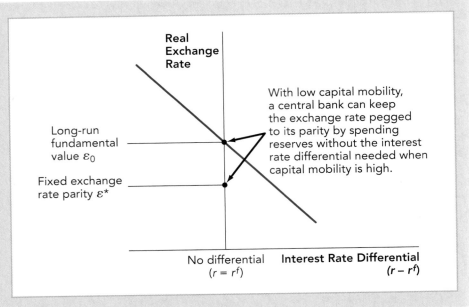

Long-run fundamental value ε_0

Fixed exchange rate parity ε^*

With low capital mobility, a central bank can keep the exchange rate pegged to its parity by spending reserves without the interest rate differential needed when capital mobility is high.

No differential
$(r = r^f)$

Interest Rate Differential
$(r - r^f)$

Real Exchange Rate

RECAP   HOW A FIXED EXCHANGE RATE SYSTEM WORKS

In an environment of very high capital mobility, monetary policy no longer can play a role in domestic stabilization if you have a fixed exchange rate: International currency speculators rather than macroeconomic policy makers determine the value of your domestic interest rate. In an environment of low capital mobility, central banks have some freedom of action to set domestic interest rates to help the domestic economy, but their freedom of action is limited and is constrained by foreign exchange speculators and by limited foreign exchange reserves.

15.3 THE CHOICE OF EXCHANGE RATE SYSTEMS

Economists either applaud or deplore the breakdown of the Bretton Woods system and the resort to floating exchange rates, depending on their underlying philosophy. For some, like Nobel Prize–winner Milton Friedman, the exchange rate is a price. Economic freedom and efficiency require that prices be set by market supply and demand. They should not be set by the decrees of governments. Thus the replacement of the fixed exchange rate, administered-price Bretton Woods system by the floating exchange rate, market-price system of today is a very positive change.

For others, like Nobel Prize–winner Robert Mundell, the exchange rate is the value that the government promises that the currency it issues will have. A stable exchange rate means that the government is keeping the contract it has made with investors in foreign countries. To let the exchange rate float is to break this contract — and everyone knows that markets work only if people do not break their contracts. Thus the replacement of the fixed exchange rate, administered-price Bretton Woods system by the floating exchange rate, market-price system of today is a very negative change.

What's the right answer? "It depends." Philosophy is all very well, but what should really matter are the details of how the choice of an exchange rate regime affects the economy.

Benefits of Fixed Exchange Rates

Under a floating exchange rate system, exporters and firms whose products compete with imported goods never know what their competitors' costs are going to be. Exchange rate–driven fluctuations in the costs to their foreign competitors are an extra source of risk, and businesses do not like unnecessary risks. The fact that exchange rates fluctuate discourages international trade and makes the *international division of labor* less sophisticated than it would otherwise be. Fixed exchange rate systems avoid these costs and encourage international trade by reducing exchange rate fluctuations as a source of risk. They avoid the churning of industrial structure — the pointless and inefficient shift of resources into and out of tradable goods sectors — as the exchange rate fluctuates around its fundamental value. That is an important advantage. That advantage was behind the decision of nearly all western European countries at the start of 1999 to form a monetary union: to fix their exchange rates against each other irrevocably, so that even their national currencies will eventually disappear.

Fixed exchange rate systems avoid some political vulnerabilities as well. Large exchange rate swings are a powerful source of political turmoil. This political turmoil is avoided by fixed exchange rate systems.

Costs of Fixed Exchange Rates

Under fixed exchange rates, monetary policy is tightly constrained by the requirement of maintaining the exchange rate at its fixed parity. Interest rates that are too low for too long exhaust foreign exchange reserves, and are followed either by a sharp tightening of monetary policy or by an abandonment of the fixed exchange rate. A floating exchange rate allows monetary policy to concentrate on maintaining full employment and low inflation at home — on attaining what economists call **internal balance**. By contrast, under a fixed exchange rate system the level of interest rates must be devoted to maintaining **external balance** — the fixed exchange rate. And fixed exchange rates have the disadvantage of rapidly transmitting monetary or confidence shocks: Interest rates move in tandem all across the world in response to shocks. The central bank must respond to any shift in international investors' expectations of future profitability or future monetary policy by shifting short-term interest rates.

This is the cost-benefit calculation facing those who have to choose between fixed and floating exchange rates. Is it more important to preserve the ability to use monetary policy to stabilize the domestic economy, rather than dedicating monetary policy to maintaining a constant exchange rate? Or is it more important to preserve the constancy of international prices, and thus expand the volume of trade and the scope of the international division of labor?

Canadian economist Robert Mundell set out the terms under which fixed exchange rates would work better than floating ones with his concept of an

internal balance

When unemployment is equal to its natural rate, inflation is unchanging, and GDP is equal to potential output.

external balance

When the trade surplus (or deficit) of a country is equal to the value of investors' new long-term investments abroad (or foreigners' new long-term investments here).

"optimal currency area." Mundell said the major reason not to have fixed exchange rates is that floating exchange rates allow adjustment to shocks that affect two countries differently. This benefit would be worth little if two countries suffer the same shocks, and react to them in the same way. It would also be worth little if factors of production possessed high mobility: Then the effects of shocks would be transient because labor and capital would rapidly adjust, and the benefits from different policy reactions to economic shocks would be small. (See Box 15.2.)

BOX

ARE WESTERN EUROPE AND THE UNITED STATES OPTIMAL CURRENCY AREAS? AN EXAMPLE

Today the two largest economic regions within which exchange rates are fixed are the United States and western Europe's "euro zone." California, for example, does not have a separate exchange rate vis-à-vis the rest of the United States. Almost all of the countries of western Europe are now committed to their common currency, the euro. Does this make economic sense? Or should there be a separate "California dollar" to allow California to have a different monetary policy than the rest of America?

Few economists today would maintain that western Europe's euro zone meets Robert Mundell's criteria for an optimal currency area. Shocks to the economy of Portugal are very different from shocks to the economy of western Germany. Southern Italy has few similarities in economic structure with Denmark. Vulnerability to different shocks would be relatively unimportant if factors of production were mobile. But the fact that different European countries have different languages means there is little chance that a boom in Denmark and a bust in Portugal will see large-scale migration to compensate.

Why then has western Europe embarked on monetary union? One reason is that some economists and policy makers hope that the benefits from economic integration are very large indeed — large enough to offset even substantial costs from adopting a common currency. But the main reason is that European monetary unification is not so much an economic as a political project: an attempt to knit Europe together as a single entity whether or not monetary union makes narrow economic sense.

Practically all economists today believe, by contrast, that the United States is an optimal currency area, although the U.S. economy's regions are no more subject to common shocks than western Europe's countries are. The mid-1980s saw the high dollar decimate midwestern manufacturing while leaving most of the rest of the country much less affected. The health of the economies of Texas and Oklahoma still depend substantially on the price of oil. Southern California's defense-industry boom and bust of the 1980s and early 1990s and northern California's high-tech boom and bust of the 1990s make it clear that California is so big a state that its component parts experience very different economic shocks. But even though the United States' component parts experience different shocks, factor mobility across the United States is remarkably high. Capital and workers move to where returns and wages are high with remarkable speed — fast enough that it is hard to believe that different parts of the United States could gain substantially from following the different monetary policies that separate currencies and floating exchange rates would allow.

As far as the United States, western Europe, and Japan are concerned, the issue of fixed versus floating exchange rates appears to have been decided: None of these three powers is willing to sacrifice its freedom of action in monetary policy. Within western Europe the answer also appears clear: Monetary union means that there is now one pan-European monetary policy, and Italy, for example, no longer retains the ability to use monetary policy to lower interest rates in Milan when unemployment is relatively high. Elsewhere in the world, the question is still under debate.

Moreover, fixed exchange rate systems have one more major disadvantage: They seem to make large-scale currency crises more likely. The decade of the 1990s saw three major large-scale currency crises, all of which threatened prosperity in the immediately affected countries, and all of which raised fears (initially at least) of their much wider spread to the world economy as a whole.

RECAP   THE CHOICE OF EXCHANGE RATE SYSTEMS

Fixed exchange rate systems encourage international trade by reducing exchange rate fluctuations as a source of risk, but they also tightly constrain monetary policy. Is it more important to preserve the ability to use monetary policy to stabilize the domestic economy, or to reduce risk by eliminating exchange rate fluctuations? That is the question — the reason that central bankers and finance ministers get paid the big bucks.

15.4 CURRENCY CRISES

The European Crisis of 1992

The first of the three major financial crises that hit the world economy in the 1990s came in the fall of 1992. In 1990 West German Chancellor Helmut Kohl reunified Germany, a country that had been divided since the end of World War II first into zones of occupation — French, British, American, and Russian — and then into two separate countries — East Germany and West Germany.

The two parts of Germany had very similar levels of economic development and economic structures before World War II. But since World War II they had diverged. West Germany had become one of the richest and most developed economies on Earth, while East Germany had turned into a standard communist economy with dirty industry, inefficient factories, and inadequate infrastructure. Chancellor Kohl undertook a program of massive public investment to try to bring East Germany up to the West German standard as quickly as possible.

The expansion of German government purchases shifted the German IS curve to the right in the years after 1990. The German central bank, the Bundesbank, responded by raising real interest rates in order to keep real GDP in the range thought to be consistent with the Bundesbank's inflation targets (see Figure 15.8).

The rise in the real interest rate generated a rise in the German exchange rate vis-à-vis the dollar and the yen, and a sharp fall in German net exports as financial capital flowed into Germany. The other countries of western Europe had then fixed their exchange rates relative to the German mark as part of the European Exchange Rate Mechanism (ERM). Britain, France, Italy, and other countries found

FIGURE 15.8

German Fiscal Policy and Monetary Response in the Early 1990s

The reunification of Germany led to a large outward shift in the IS curve and a large increase in real interest rates as Germany's central bank, the Bundesbank, fought to keep real GDP from rising too far above its planned targets.

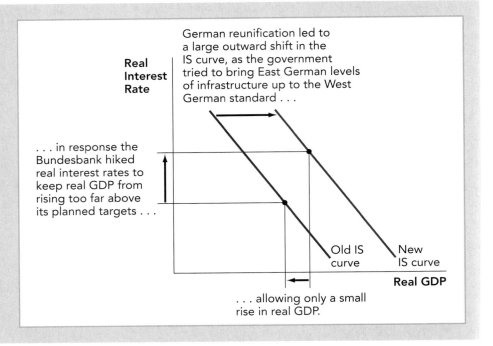

German reunification led to a large outward shift in the IS curve, as the government tried to bring East German levels of infrastructure up to the West German standard . . .

. . . in response the Bundesbank hiked real interest rates to keep real GDP from rising too far above its planned targets . . .

Real Interest Rate

Old IS curve

New IS curve

Real GDP

. . . allowing only a small rise in real GDP.

themselves trapped: The rise in interest rates in Germany required that they too increase interest rates because r^f had risen in the equation

$$r = r^f + \frac{\varepsilon_0 - \varepsilon^*}{\varepsilon_r}$$

and r had to rise in response if the ERM was to be maintained. Without the surge of spending found in Germany and without the ability or desire to rapidly shift policy to run large deficits, such increases in interest rates threatened to send the other European economies into recession (see Figure 15.9).

Politicians in other European countries — Britain, Sweden, Italy, France, and elsewhere — promised that their commitment to their fixed exchange rate parity was absolute. They promised that high interest rates and the risk of a domestic recession were prices worth paying for the benefits of a fixed exchange rate system within western Europe itself. But foreign exchange speculators did not believe they would keep their promise to maintain the fixed exchange rate parity when unemployment began to rise.

Thus foreign exchange speculators' expectations of the long-run fundamental value of the real exchange rate, ε_0, rose as well. This expectation that other European currencies would lose value vis-à-vis the German mark in the long run put their values under pressure in the short run as well.

The domestic real interest rate required to maintain the exchange rate parity, given by

$$r = r^f + \frac{\varepsilon_0 - \varepsilon^*}{\varepsilon_r}$$

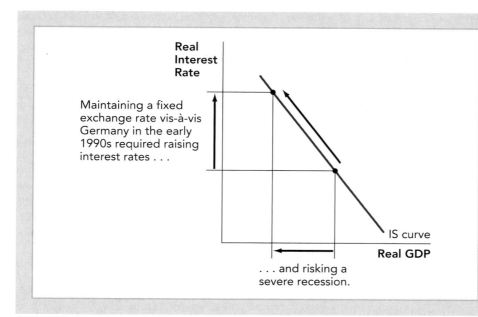

Maintaining a fixed exchange rate vis-à-vis Germany in the early 1990s required raising interest rates . . .

Real Interest Rate

IS curve

Real GDP

. . . and risking a severe recession.

FIGURE 15.9
Effect of German Policy on Other European Countries
At the start of the 1990s governments in other western European countries were raising interest rates and contracting their economies, risking a recession, in order to maintain the parities of ERM exchange rates.

was rising not just because of higher real interest rates in Germany but also because of foreign exchange speculators' more pessimistic expectations. The governments of much of western Europe found themselves in a trap. Different governments undertook different strategies:

- Some tried to avoid the consequences of the shift in expectations. They spent reserves like water in the hope that a demonstrated commitment to maintain the parity would reverse the shift in speculator expectations. All this did was give international currency traders like George Soros the opportunity to make profits measured in the billions by betting on the abandonment of the fixed exchange rate. Economists Maurice Obstfeld and Ken Rogoff report that the British government may have lost $7 billion in a few hours during the September 1992 speculative attack on the pound.

- Some tried to demonstrate that they would defend the parity no matter how high the interest rate required to keep the exchange rate fixed. The Swedish government raised its overnight interest rate to 500 percent per year for a brief time. But all this did was reinforce speculators' opinion that the political and economic cost of keeping the exchange rate parity was too high for governments that sought to win reelection.

- Finally, some abandoned their parity against the German mark and let their currencies float as for a while they turned monetary policy to setting interest rates consistent with internal balance.

In less than two months what had seemed a durable framework of fixed exchange rates in western Europe had collapsed into a floating-rate system.

But governments interested in long-run exchange stability within Europe regrouped. They proposed to try again to fix their exchange rates, with the European Monetary Union that began in January 1999. This time, however, they decided not to peg their exchange rates while keeping their national currencies (thus retaining at least the possibility of someday changing parities), but to eliminate their separate national currencies entirely: not fixed exchange rates, but monetary union. The hope was to eliminate once and for all any fear or expectation that exchange rates might ever change again.

The Mexican Crisis of 1994–1995

currency crisis

A situation where a country's currency is in serious trouble relative to the exchange rates of other countries.

In the winter of 1994–1995 the second of the major **currency crises** of the 1990s hit the world economy. The Mexican peso crisis came as a shock to economists and to economic policy makers. Previous speculative attacks on and collapses in the value of currencies had occurred for one of two reasons. In situations of limited capital mobility, governments with overvalued exchange rates and large inflation-financed budget deficits had suffered speculative attacks. And in cases like western Europe in 1992, currencies had suffered speculative attacks when speculators judged that the policies needed to maintain fixed exchange rates had become inconsistent with the government's political survival.

Mexico, however, fit neither of these two cases. The government's budget was balanced, so an outbreak of renewed inflation was not generally expected. The government's willingness to raise interest rates was not in question: In the end the government of Mexico raised real interest rates to 40 percent per year during the crisis. The Mexican peso was not clearly overvalued: In the winter of 1993–1994 the Mexican government had conducted large exchange rate interventions and had eased monetary policy to try to keep the value of the peso from rising. Yet the Mexican peso lost half of its value in four months starting in December 1994. The peso fell from about 3.5 to about 7 to the U.S. dollar before recovering somewhat in the summer of 1995 (see Figure 15.10).

The sudden reversal of investor expectations about the long-run fundamental value of the Mexican peso was startling. At the start of 1994 Mexico had just joined the world's club of industrialized countries, the Organization for Economic Cooperation and Development (OECD). It had just entered into the North American Free Trade Agreement (NAFTA), which granted Mexico tariff-free markets for its products in North America. Expectations were that the Mexican peso would strengthen in real terms in the future, and that the profits from investing in Mexico were high.

Optimism eroded in 1994. At the start of the year a guerrilla uprising in the poor southern Mexican province of Chiapas cast doubt on political stability. Further doubt was cast by a wave of assassinations killing, among others, Luis Donaldo Colosio, the presidential candidate of the ruling Party of the Revolution (Institutionalized) (PRI). During the presidential election year of 1994 itself, the central bank raised the money supply, causing some international investors to worry that macroeconomic policy was more political and less "technocratic" than they had thought. All of these events plus a wave of pessimism reduced foreign exchange speculators' estimates of the long-run value of the Mexican peso and raised their assessment of the long-run fundamental value of the exchange rate, ε_0.

During 1994 the Mexican government spent $50 billion in foreign exchange reserves supporting the peso, believing at each moment that the adverse shift in expectations had to turn around. It did not. By the end of 1994 the Mexican government was out of foreign exchange reserves. And so it devalued the peso and let it float against the dollar.

The devaluation of the peso had destructive consequences, however. First, a great many — naive — investors in New York and elsewhere had believed the

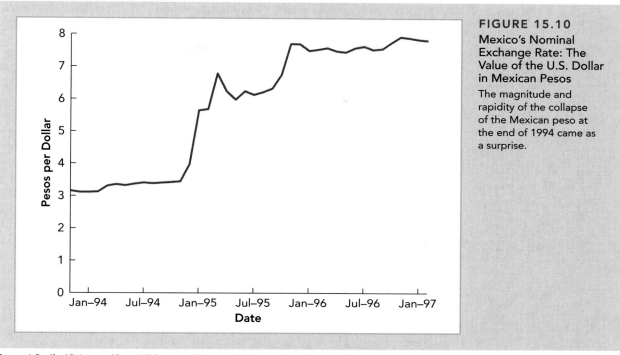

FIGURE 15.10

Mexico's Nominal Exchange Rate: The Value of the U.S. Dollar in Mexican Pesos

The magnitude and rapidity of the collapse of the Mexican peso at the end of 1994 came as a surprise.

Source: J. Bradford DeLong and Barry J. Eichengreen, "Between Meltdown and Moral Hazard: Clinton Administration International Monetary and Financial Policy," in Jeffrey Frankel and Peter Orszag, eds., *American Economic Policy in the 1990s* (Cambridge, MA: MIT Press, 2002), pp. 191–254.

Mexican government when it said that it would do whatever was necessary to defend the value of the peso. The increase in the value of the Mexican exchange rate ε led to a further fall in the perceived fundamental value of the peso — a rise in ε_0 — which added pressure for further depreciation and a further rise in the exchange rate ε. A more serious problem soon became clear: Much of the Mexican government's debt was indexed to the dollar in the form of securities called tesebonos. Each depreciation of the peso raised the peso value of the Mexican government's debt, increasing the temptation for the Mexican government to default on its debt, and the resulting financial distress led to further rises in foreign exchange speculators' opinions of ε_0.

The Mexican government seemed faced with a horrible choice. The first option was to raise interest rates to defend the peso, but adverse movements in foreign exchange speculator expectations meant that the level of interest rates that would be required by the formula

$$r = r^f + \frac{\varepsilon_0 - \varepsilon^*}{\varepsilon_r}$$

was a level that would produce a Great Depression in Mexico. This first option would produce catastrophe.

The second option was to keep interest rates low and let the value of foreign currency rise much further. This would mean that Mexican companies — and the Mexican government — would be unable to pay their dollar-denominated and dollar-interest debts. Companies would declare bankruptcy. The government would default on its debt. Mexican exports would fall because foreign creditors would try to seize Mexican goods as soon as they left the country. Mexican imports would fall because foreign creditors would try to seize goods purchased by Mexico before they entered the country.

The result would be to delink Mexico from the world economy. Mexico's *foreign trade* would fall drastically. Meanwhile, international committees of lenders and creditors would thrash out a settlement of the bankruptcies with Mexican companies and the default with the Mexican government. This second option would produce catastrophe too. The Mexican government of Presidents Carlos Salinas and Ernesto Zedillo had bet Mexico's economic future on increased integration with the world economy and the use of foreign capital to finance domestic industrialization.

The U.S. government and the IMF tried to give the Mexican government more options. The Clinton administration proposed loan guarantees to Mexico. But these guarantees fell through because neither then–Speaker of the House Newt Gingrich nor then–Majority Leader of the Senate Robert Dole nor other congressional leaders were willing to spend political capital on the issues. The administration then made direct loans to Mexico out of the U.S. Treasury's Exchange Stabilization Fund. These built Mexico's foreign exchange reserves back to a level where they could support the peso to some degree without pushing domestic interest rates to Great Depression–causing levels.

These loans allowed the Mexican government to refinance its debt and helped restore confidence that the Mexican government would not be forced into hyperinflation or resort to default. As time passed, Wall Street investors calmed down too. They recognized that Mexico was still the same country with relatively bright economic growth prospects, with promises of financial support if necessary from the U.S. Treasury and the IMF, and with NAFTA-guaranteed tariff-free access to North America, the largest market in the world. Thus the Mexican economic meltdown of 1994–1995 was a short, sharp recession that reduced Mexican real GDP by about 6 percent, but that was then followed by resumed economic growth.

The central lessons were two. First, the views of foreign exchange speculators could change radically with extraordinary speed. Second, developing countries that had not carefully prepared beforehand were extremely vulnerable to the shocks that such changes in international expectations could deliver.

The East Asian Crisis of 1997–1998

Two and a half years after the beginning of the Mexican crisis, the third international financial crisis of the 1990s hit the world economy. For 20 years before 1997 the economies of the Asian Pacific rim had been the fastest-growing economies the world had ever seen. But in mid-1997 foreign investors began to worry about the long-run sustainability of the East Asian miracle and the growing overhang of nonperforming loans in East Asian economies. They began to change their opinions of the fundamental long-term value ε_0 of East Asia's exchange rates.

In Thailand, Malaysia, South Korea, and Indonesia the values of domestic currency fell, and once again falling currency values caused a further swing in foreign exchange speculators' expectations of ε_0. Indonesia was hit worst: Real GDP fell by one-sixth in 1998; the Indonesian currency, the rupiah, lost three-quarters of its nominal value against the dollar; and short-term real interest rates rose to 30 percent and nominal interest rates to 60 percent. Figure 15.11 shows the shock to two other currencies' exchange rates.

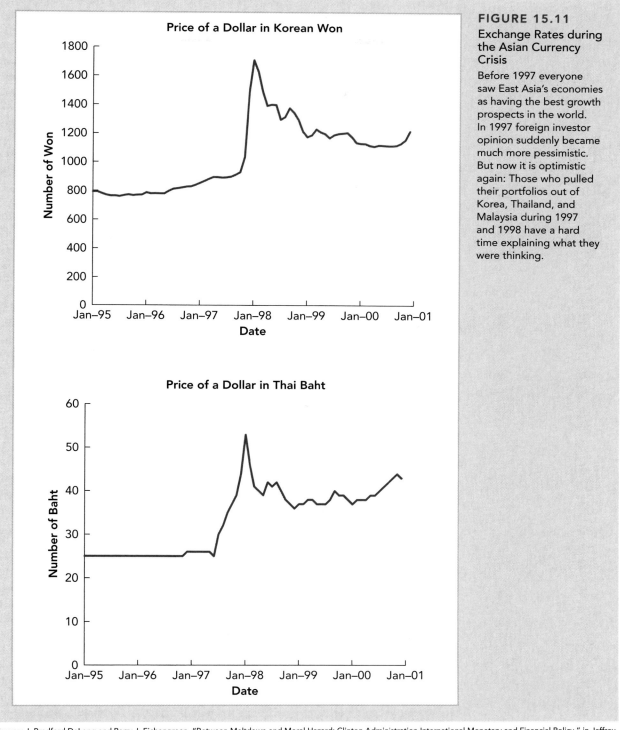

FIGURE 15.11
Exchange Rates during the Asian Currency Crisis
Before 1997 everyone saw East Asia's economies as having the best growth prospects in the world. In 1997 foreign investor opinion suddenly became much more pessimistic. But now it is optimistic again: Those who pulled their portfolios out of Korea, Thailand, and Malaysia during 1997 and 1998 have a hard time explaining what they were thinking.

Source: J. Bradford DeLong and Barry J. Eichengreen, "Between Meltdown and Moral Hazard: Clinton Administration International Monetary and Financial Policy," in Jeffrey Frankel and Peter Orszag, eds., *American Economic Policy in the 1990s* (Cambridge, MA: MIT Press, 2002), pp. 191–254.

Once foreign exchange speculators began lowering their estimates of the long-run value of investments in East Asia, other, deeper problems in the Asian economies became apparent and were magnified. As East Asian exchange rates fell, it became clear that many of East Asia's banks and companies had borrowed heavily abroad in amounts denominated in dollars or yen. They had used those borrowings to make loans to the politically well connected, or to make investments that turned out not to be profitable in the long run.

The fact that East Asia's financial system was based on close links between governments, banks, and businesses — and that it was very difficult to obtain financial accounts from any East Asian organization — increased fear that more East Asian banks and companies were bankrupt than had been thought. This caused a further increase in foreign exchange speculators' views of the long-run fundamental value of the exchange rate.

The vicious circle continued. Each loss of value in the exchange rate increased the burden of foreign-denominated debt and increased the likelihood of general bankruptcy. Each increase in the perceived burden of foreign-denominated debt caused a further loss of value in the exchange rate. Poor bank regulation had created a situation in which a small initial shock to exchange rate confidence could produce a major crisis. The shorter term the debt held by a country and its citizens, the more easily capital can flee — and the larger is the impact of the crisis.

As the Asian crisis developed, the IMF stepped in with substantial loans to boost foreign exchange reserves, made in return for promises to improve bank regulation and reform the financial system. The hope was that short-term loans would allow East Asian economies to avoid catastrophe until the pendulum of Wall Street expectations began to swing back. The hope proved sound. Since mid-1998, investors in New York and elsewhere have remembered that East Asia's economies had been the fastest-growing in the world in the previous generation, and were in all likelihood good places to invest.

The Dollar in the 2000s

Where is the next currency crisis going to occur? One possibility is that it will occur in the United States. Since 1998 U.S. exports have stagnated and imports have grown so that at the start of 2005 the U.S. imports half again as much as it exports — a trade deficit of more than $600 billion a year, as Figure 15.12 shows. Will foreigners be willing on net to invest some $600 billion of their wealth in the United States each year, every year, without ever drawing down their wealth? Almost surely not. What will happen if foreigners' desired annual net investments in the United States fall to, say, $200 billion a year? The dollar will fall in value, and on the rule of thumb that a 1 percent fall in the value of the dollar raises annual net exports in the long run by about $10 billion, the fall in the dollar would have to be on the order of 40 percent.

Logically, currency speculators should want to be compensated for this risk — so interest rates in the United States would be above interest rates elsewhere — but they are not. This means one of two things: First, perhaps international economists' expectation of a decline in the U.S. trade deficit and a large fall in the dollar are wrong — something else is going to happen. Second, perhaps investors and speculators do not have rational expectations.

If the second possibility is the correct one, then a dollar crisis in the second half of the decade of the 2000s is a serious possibility. At some point speculators' expectations

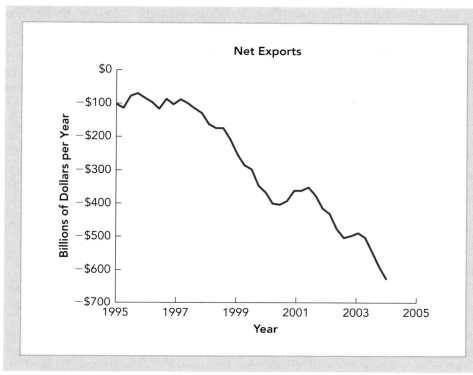

FIGURE 15.12
The U.S. Current-Account Deficit
The U.S. trade deficit began to grow in the late 1990s as foreigners took some of their earnings from U.S. imports and spent them investing in the dot-com bubble. The deficit continued to grow to extraordinary size in the 2000s, in large part as we would expect from the model of Chapter 7: a cut in taxes produces a fall in net exports.

Source: http://www.economagic.com.

will begin to factor in the possibility of a large decline in the dollar, and that factoring-in will produce a steep fall in the dollar and a rise in U.S. interest rates. However, a dollar crisis — should it happen — would not be as serious an event as all these other financial crises we have seen over the past decade and more. In other countries — because so much of their foreign debt was denominated in dollars — a fall in the value of the currency raised the burden of international debt and worsened the crisis. In the United States — because so much of its foreign debt is denominated in dollars — a fall in the value of the dollar will lower the burden of international debt and ease the crisis.

French President Charles de Gaulle complained more than 40 years ago about the "exorbitant privilege" the United States had because of the key role played by the dollar as the currency in which contracts were written and which everybody wanted to hold as their reserves. This exorbitant privilege is still operating, making the United States less vulnerable to international monetary disturbances than other countries are.

Managing Crises

We can see the real exchange rate equation

$$\varepsilon = \varepsilon_0 - \varepsilon_r(r - r^f)$$

as offering a country a menu of choices for the value of foreign currency ε and the value of the domestic real interest rate r. The higher the domestic real interest rate r, the more appreciated is the exchange rate and the lower is the value of ε.

If for any of a number of reasons speculators lose confidence in the future of the economy, their assessment of the fundamental price of foreign goods and currency, ε_0, suddenly and massively shifts. The menu of choices that a country has for its combination interest rate r and the exchange rate ε suddenly deteriorates. If the interest rate r is to remain unchanged, the value ε of the real home currency price of foreign exchange must rise a good deal. If the exchange rate ε is to remain unchanged, then the domestic real interest rate r must rise a good deal. Raising interest rates appears unattractive because it will create a recession. No domestic purpose would be served by such a recession; it is just the result of foreign investors' change of opinion. Thus, letting the exchange rate depreciate would seem to be the natural, inevitable policy choice. A sudden panic by foreign exchange speculators is a sudden fall in demand for your country's products: International investors are no longer willing to hold your country's bonds at prices and interest rates that they were happy with last month. What does a business do when all of a sudden demand for the products it makes falls? The firm cuts its price. Perhaps a country faced with a sudden fall in demand for the products it makes should do the same — cut its price. And the easiest way for a *country* to "cut its price" is to let the home-currency value of foreign currency and goods rise.

Yet throughout the 1990s, whenever international investors suddenly turned pessimistic about investing in a country, observers reacted with shock and horror when the value of foreign currency rose. This was the story in the collapse of the European Monetary System in 1992, the collapse of the Mexican peso in 1994–1995, and the East Asian financial crisis of 1997–1998. In all these cases the trigger of the crisis was a sudden change of heart on the part of investors in the world economy's industrial core — in New York, Frankfurt, London, and Tokyo.

Economists will long argue whether it was the relative optimism of investors before the crisis or the relative pessimism of international investors after the crisis that was the irrational speculative wave. The right answer is probably "yes"; financial markets were excessively enthusiastic before the crisis and were excessively pessimistic afterwards. But why did such changes in international investor sentiment cause a crisis rather than an embarrassment? Why not let the exchange rate depreciate — the value of foreign currency rise — and keep domestic monetary and fiscal policy aimed at maintaining internal balance?

The answer appears to be that letting the value of foreign currency rise is dangerous if banks, businesses, and governments have borrowed massively abroad in foreign currencies. Then a depreciation of the exchange rate bankrupts the economy: The foreign-currency value of all the foreign-currency and business assets is brought down by the depreciation, while the home-currency value of their liabilities is unchanged. Such an interlinked chain of general bankruptcies destroys the economy's ability to transform household saving into investment and shifts the IS curve far and fast back to the left. Such chains of bankruptcies are the stuff of which Great Depressions are made.

Some specific steps should have been taken to reduce vulnerability to a crisis. Strongly discourage — that is, tax — borrowers from borrowing in foreign currencies. If you are going to accept free international capital flows (in an attempt to use foreign financing for your industrial revolution), then be sure that your exchange rate can float without causing trouble for the domestic economy. If your exchange rate must stay fixed (to fight inflation or for other reasons), then recognize that an important part of keeping it fixed is controls over capital movements.

But once the crisis has hit, good options are rare. Is there a possible path to safety? Can you raise interest rates enough to keep the depreciation from triggering bankruptcy and hyperinflation while still avoiding a high-interest-rate-generated recession? Can you depreciate the exchange rate far enough to restore demand for home-produced goods without depreciating it so far as to bankrupt local businesses and banks?

Maybe.

The dilemmas are real. It is economic policy malpractice to claim that it is obvious that in a financial crisis interest rates should not be raised and the exchange rate should be allowed to find its own panicked-market level even if banks and firms have large foreign-currency debts. It is also economic policy malpractice to claim that in a financial crisis interest rates should be raised high enough to keep the exchange rate from falling at all. It's not that simple. So if sudden changes of opinion by international investors cause so much trouble, shouldn't we keep such sudden changes of opinion from having destructive effects? Shouldn't we use capital controls and other devices to keep international flows of investment small, manageable, and firmly corralled?

Once again, maybe.

The first generation of post–World War II economists — John Maynard Keynes, Harry Dexter White, and their students — would have said, "Yes." Sudden changes of opinion on the part of international investors can cause enormous damage to countries that allow free movement of capital. Such sudden changes of opinion are a frequent fact of life. Therefore, make it illegal, or at least very difficult, to borrow from and lend to, invest in, or withdraw investments from foreign countries. The second and third generations of post–World War II economists had a different view. They regretted that capital controls kept people with money to lend in the industrial core away from people who could make good use of the money to expand economic growth. The balance of opinion shifted to the view that too much was sacrificed in economic growth at the periphery for whatever reduction in instability capital controls produced. Moreover, a regime of capital controls encouraged corruption. Often it was the cousin of the wife of the vice minister of finance who received permission to borrow abroad. Thus, capital controls paved the way to kleptocracy: rule by the thieves.

So today we have the benefits of free international flows of capital. The ability to borrow from abroad does promise to give successful emerging market economies the power to cut a decade or two off the time needed for them to industrialize. It promises to give investors in the world economy's industrial core the opportunity to earn higher rates of return. But this free flow of financial capital also is giving us a major international financial crisis every three years or so.

What is to be done will be one of the major economic policy debates of the next decade. Should we try to move toward a system in which capital is even more mobile than it is today, but in which international financial crises may become an even more common occurrence? Or should we try to move toward a system in which capital is less mobile — more controlled — and in which some of the benefits of international investment are traded for less vulnerability to financial crises? We don't have to have a global economy as vulnerable to currency crises as the economy of the 1990s was.

THE ARGENTINEAN CRISIS OF 2001: AN EXAMPLE

During the 1990s, some economists argued that the reason that economies such as Mexico, Korea, Thailand, Malaysia, Indonesia, and Brazil were subject to such sharp financial crises was that their exchange rates were not fixed enough. When a crisis developed, the fact that the government *could* change the exchange rate meant that financiers feared that the government *would* change the exchange rate. The result was large-scale *capital flight,* which triggered the devaluation financiers had feared, and the devaluation of the home currency set off the chain of threatened bankruptcies that turned an adjustment of international prices into a full-blown crisis. If, some economists argued, the government lacked the power to change the exchange rate, no one would fear devaluation, capital flight would be avoided, and the crisis would never occur.

Thus, in the aftermath of all these other crises, the Argentinean government of the 1990s believed that it had arrived at an institutional setup that would guarantee the credibility of its currency and eliminate any possibility of a crisis. It set up an independent *currency board* to manage its exchange rate, fixed its currency to the dollar, and obligated the currency board by law to make sure that the supply of cash money in the economy was no greater than the currency board's foreign exchange reserves. With one Argentinean peso equal to one dollar, and with the currency board having more dollars in its asset holdings than there were cash pesos in the Argentinean economy, the theory was that confidence in the fixed exchange rate would be complete. If people did begin to doubt the peg, they would trade their cash pesos for dollars at the currency board. The cash money supply would thus fall because the currency board would not spend but would retire the cash pesos it was offered. A falling money stock would raise the value of the peso. And as pesos became scarce and more valuable, confidence would return.

That was the theory.

The collapse of the Argentinean economy at the end of 2001 provides a test case for this theory. And the answer appears to be, "No." Even if — as the Argentinean government did — the government delegates control over the exchange rate to an external authority, a "currency board," and assigns the currency board the mission of keeping the exchange rate fixed, a large-scale financial crisis is still possible. And Argentina has had one: The peso collapsed at the end of 2001, and Argentinean GDP declined by 15 percent in 2002.

What happened? In practice, things worked differently than in theory. Argentina's federal and state governments did not balance their budgets. As long as the Argentinean economy was growing, the fiscal deficits were of little concern. But internal inflation made Argentina's exports noncompetitive. The fear that the currency board might someday end made Argentina's interest rates higher than those elsewhere. High interest rates tended to discourage investment. The resulting decline in real aggregate demand meant recession. Recession meant larger fiscal deficits.

In the end, a government deficit must lead to one of three things: Taxes must be raised, inflation must take hold and expropriate the debt holders, or the government must formally default. The failure of Argentina's government to effectively collect the taxes due it under law meant that as 2000 and 2001 proceeded, confidence that taxes would be raised diminished.

The currency board was a creature of the government. Would the government continue to let the currency board exist if the consequences were (1) a recession and (2) a sharp cutback in government spending as the government's sources of borrowing dried up and as the currency board refused to print more money to cover the government's deficit? Faced with a growing national debt, the currency board no longer served as a source of confidence — that the government lacked the power to change the exchange rate was no longer reassuring. And so the same process of large-scale capital flight that had produced the earlier crises was set in motion in Argentina at the end of 2001 as well. Currency speculators bet "No" on the future of the currency board. They were right. And Argentina at the end of 2001 suffered the first big currency crash of the third millennium.

The lesson from Argentina is that the formal structure of institutions matters less than the spirit of the political and economic system that supports them. Argentina's currency board of the 1990s was sound in theory, but not in practice.

RECAP CURRENCY CRISES

Three major (and many more minor) financial crises hit the world economy in the 1990s. The western European crisis of 1992 came about because foreign exchange speculators (correctly) doubted the commitment of other European countries to maintain their fixed parity with Germany as German interest rates rose. The Mexican crisis of 1994–1995 came about because foreign exchange speculators (incorrectly) doubted the commitment of the Mexican government to low inflation and economic reform, and because the fact that Mexico's government had borrowed heavily in dollars meant that a reduction in the value of the peso destabilized Mexico's finances. The East Asian crisis of 1997–1998 came about because foreign exchange speculators (correctly) feared that much recent investment in East Asia had been unproductive and (incorrectly) feared that the age of fast growth in East Asia was over, and because heavy dollar borrowings by East Asian companies meant that a reduction in the value of their currencies threatened to send much of East Asia's manufacturing and financial corporations into bankruptcy.

Chapter Summary

1. For most of the past century, the world has operated with fixed exchange rates — not, as today, with floating exchange rates.

2. Under fixed exchange rates, monetary policy has only very limited freedom to respond to domestic conditions. Instead, the main goal of monetary policy is to adjust interest rates to maintain the fixed exchange rate.

3. Why would a country adopt fixed exchange rates? To make it easier to trade by making foreign prices more predictable and less volatile. Fixed exchange rate systems increase the volume of trade and encourage the international division of labor.

4. Nevertheless, in the past generation countries usually concluded that freedom to set their own monetary

policies to satisfy domestic concerns is more important than the international integration benefits of fixed exchange rates.

5. An exception is western Europe, which has permanently and irrevocably fixed its exchange rates via a monetary union.

6. Wide swings in foreign exchange speculators' views of countries' future prospects caused three major currency crises in the 1990s.

7. Such currency crises, although triggered by speculative changes in opinion, were greatly worsened by poor bank regulation and other policies that threatened to send economies subject to capital flight into a vicious spiral ending in depression and hyperinflation.

Key Terms

floating exchange rates (p. 438)

fixed exchange rates (p. 438)

gold standard (p. 438)

currency arbitrage (p. 439)

foreign exchange reserves (p. 440)

internal balance (p. 451)

external balance (p. 451)

currency crisis (p. 456)

Analytical Exercises

1. Why does a country's fixing the value of its currency in terms of gold also fix its nominal exchange rate?

2. Why do many economists think that a gold standard tends to put contractionary and deflationary pressure on economies that adhere to it?

3. What are the principal benefits of fixed exchange rates?

4. What are the principal costs of fixed exchange rates?

5. Why did the 1990s see so many international financial crises?

Policy Exercises

1. Suppose that foreign exchange speculators' believed value for the long-run fundamental value of the real exchange rate suddenly rises by 30 percent, from 100 to 130. How does the interest rate increase required to keep the exchange rate constant in the face of this shift depend on the interest sensitivity of the exchange rate parameter ε_r? Under what circumstances would you think that the parameter ε_r would be large? Under what circumstances would it be small?

2. Look in the back of the book for the annual values of the U.S. real exchange rate. Suppose that the parameter ε_r is 1,000; then a swing of 1 percentage point in domestic real interest rates is associated with a 10-point change in the exchange rate. By how much (and in which direction) would interest rates have to have changed in 1985 to push the real value of the U.S. exchange rate to the value it reached in 1990? By how much (and in which direction) would interest rates have to change today to push the real value of the exchange rate back to the value it reached in 1990? Would either of these shifts improve the condition of the domestic economy?

3. Suppose that a developing country with low capital mobility finds that foreign exchange speculators' views of the long-run fundamental value of its currency have

suddenly shifted upward to 130, but that it wishes to maintain its pegged exchange rate ε^* of 100 and also keep domestic interest rates from rising above foreign interest rates. In the formula

$$r = r^f + \frac{\varepsilon_0 - \varepsilon^*}{\varepsilon_r} + \frac{\varepsilon_R}{\varepsilon_r}(\Delta R)$$

if $\varepsilon_R = 1{,}000$, $\varepsilon_r = 1{,}000$, and the relevant period of time is one month, how fast will the country lose reserves if it tries to maintain both its pegged exchange rate and the (relatively) low real interest rate? How high would it have to raise the domestic real interest rate above foreign rates to stop its loss of reserves?

4. Suppose you are asked to analyze whether Europe's monetary union was a mistake. What kinds of evidence would you look for to try to make up your mind?

5. Suppose you are asked whether some small Latin American country should dollarize — that is, fix its exchange rate with the United States once and for all by adopting the U.S. dollar as its own internal currency. What kinds of evidence would you look for to try to determine whether such dollarization is a good idea or not?

CHAPTER 16

Changes in the Macroeconomy and Changes in Macroeconomic Policy

QUESTIONS

How has the structure of employment and production changed over the past century? How has the business cycle changed? How has economic policy changed?

What are future prospects for successful management of the business cycle?

Why does unemployment in Europe remain so high?

Why has growth in Japan been so slow for the past decade and a half?

16.1 CHANGES IN THE MACROECONOMY

The Past

Back in Chapters 4 and 5 we analyzed economic growth as a process of rising capital stocks, productivity levels, and living standards. We gave short shrift to the fact that economic growth is also a process of structural change — of shifts among occupations, industries, and forms of business activity. And these changes mean that the patterns of aggregate economic activity called business cycles that are studied in macroeconomics change too. Consumers' opportunities and spending patterns change, industries grow and shrink, the role of international trade steadily expands. The role of the government changes too, rising sharply during the New Deal era of the 1930s and the Great Society era of the late 1960s and early 1970s. It would be surprising indeed if the patterns of macroeconomic fluctuations remained unchanged as all these factors that underpin the macroeconomy change.

Over the past century the structure of modern industrial economies has changed, by some measures at least, more than in the entire previous millennium. Between the year 1100 and the start of the U.S. Civil War in 1860 the share of the labor force engaged in agriculture fell from perhaps 80 percent to perhaps 50 percent. But between the Civil War of the 1860s and the end of the twentieth century the share of the U.S. labor force engaged in agriculture fell from 50 percent to 2 percent, as shown in Figure 16.1. Today in America gardeners, groundskeepers, and producers and distributors of ornamental plants outnumber farmers and farm laborers.

The decline of agriculture is not the only major shift in the economy's occupational and industrial distribution. A century ago perhaps 40 percent of the labor force was engaged in mining, manufacturing, and construction — the nonagricultural industries that still required heavy lifting. Today perhaps 25 percent of the labor force is so engaged. The fall in relative employment in these industries has been offset by a rise in service-sector employment — both traditional services and what one might call information-intensive services.

Moreover, a hundred years ago the government's social insurance state was barely in embryo: We had the remnants of the Civil War pension system and the start of health and safety and economic regulation, but little else of the large edifice that is the twenty-first century social insurance state. A hundred years ago the tax system was not at all progressive. A hundred years ago nearly all households found it very difficult to borrow in order to see themselves through a year of low income and of unemployment.

Today, by contrast, the American financial system lends immense amounts of money to all kinds of consumers. In standard economic theory, this should allow them to smooth their consumption spending. Households should be able to greatly reduce the impact of changes in their incomes on changes in consumption, and so reduce the marginal propensity to consume. Such reductions in the marginal propensity to consume should carry along with them a substantial reduction in the size of the multiplier. The same holds true for the fiscal automatic stabilizers of progressive taxes and social insurance, which appear to exert a powerful stabilizing force on the economy. They were not present a century ago.

financial automatic stabilizers

Features of the financial system, such as deposit insurance, that help to prevent stress on the financial system from culminating in total collapse.

The past century has also seen the rise of **financial automatic stabilizers** — the most important of which is deposit insurance. One major factor making depressions (most notably the Great Depression) larger in the distant past was the fear that banks might fail, which induced people to pull money out of banks and hide

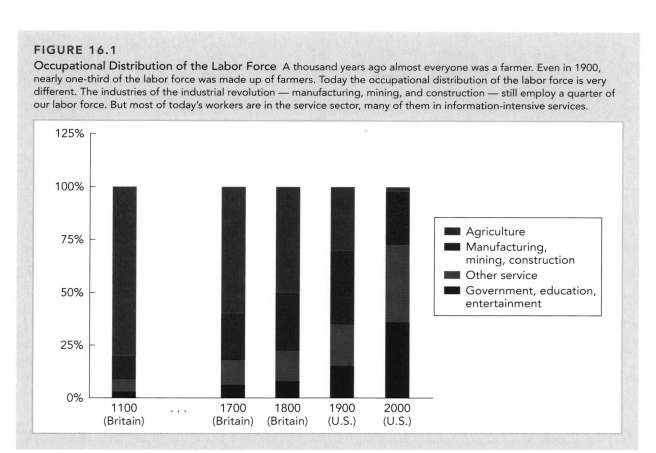

FIGURE 16.1

Occupational Distribution of the Labor Force A thousand years ago almost everyone was a farmer. Even in 1900, nearly one-third of the labor force was made up of farmers. Today the occupational distribution of the labor force is very different. The industries of the industrial revolution — manufacturing, mining, and construction — still employ a quarter of our labor force. But most of today's workers are in the service sector, many of them in information-intensive services.

Source: Authors' calculations from *Historical Statistics of the United States* and other sources.

it under their mattresses. Such sudden increases in the demand for cash during financial panics caused interest rates to spike, investment to fall, and production to decline. Today the existence of a large deposit insurance system has all but eliminated this fear.

Still another change has come in the pace and direction of material progress. Back in the late nineteenth century the bulk of improvements in labor productivity came from *capital deepening:* the buildup of the infrastructure and the factories of the country. In the twentieth century the bulk of improvements in labor productivity came from improvements in the efficiency of labor as a result of improvements in science and technology: inventions and innovations in materials production, materials handling, and organization.

The share of economic activity oriented toward the future increased as well. Research and development became not a casual by-product of the rest of economic activity, but an organized branch of industry and a key component of investment. At least partly as a result, labor efficiency growth in the twentieth century proceeded at twice the pace of labor efficiency growth of the nineteenth century. And few if any signs suggest that the pace of growth in the early twenty-first century will be slower.

TABLE 16.1
Business Cycle Patterns

Period	Typical Swing in Unemployment	Typical Swing in Nonfarm Unemployment	Proportion of Time Spent in Recession
1870–1910	2.3%	4.4%	NA
1886–1915	2.9	4.8	22%
1901–1930	1.4	1.9	30
1916–1945	7.2	8.7	28
1931–1945	8.1	10.1	18
1946–1975	1.2	1.3	19
1976–1998	1.3	1.3	11
1946–1998	1.5	1.5	15

Source: Authors' calculations from estimates provided by Christina Romer, "Spurious Volatility in Historical Unemployment Estimates," *Journal of Political Economy* 94, no. 1 (February 1986), pp. 1–37; and from *Historical Statistics of the United States* (Washington, DC: Government Printing Office, 1975).

Yet in spite of all of these changes in the structure of the economy, the U.S. economy's business cycle has continued. The patterns of the business cycle we see today would seem familiar to those who watched business cycles late in the nineteenth century. As Table 16.1 shows, there are some signs that fluctuations in unemployment have become smaller in recent years (and many signs that the Great Depression of the 1930s involved an extraordinarily violent business cycle). But in spite of a number of structural changes that would seem likely to change the size and duration of the business cycle, business cycles today are surprisingly similar to those of a century ago. Different changing factors appear to have largely offset each other.

The Future

We should not imagine that economic structural change is over: It will continue. We can already see some of the future changes that will transform the macroeconomy, for they are already under way.

For example, the past two generations have seen a great easing in credit — an increase in **financial flexibility** that allows more consumers to borrow more on less collateral. This will continue, diminishing the importance of liquidity constraints and making consumption spending less dependent on income as consumers are better able to plan for the future.

The increase in financial flexibility will also make interpretation of financial markets more difficult — and is thus likely to make monetary policy somewhat more difficult to conduct. International trade will continue to expand. The odds are that international investments will become easier to make, and so the speed at which capital flows across national borders will increase. And labor markets are likely to continue to change as well.

Consumption

Already **liquidity constraints** — the inability to borrow and the consequent fact that consumption spending is limited by income — play a relatively small role

financial flexibility

A situation in which a large number of different financial instruments are traded on thick and liquid markets.

liquidity constraints

An inability to borrow.

in determining consumption spending in America. They certainly play a much smaller role than at the beginning of the twentieth century, or even early in the post–World War II period. Economists' theories tell us that if liquidity constraints are absent, then the marginal propensity to consume should be very low. The level of consumption should depend on one's estimate of one's lifetime resources, and it should be affected by changes in current income only to the extent that changes in current income change one's estimate of lifetime resources.

Now economists' standard theories may overstate the case. Tying your current level of spending to your current level of income is a simple, reasonable rule of thumb for managing your affairs. The time needed to do better than you would by using simple, reasonable rules of thumb may simply not be worth spending. And as economist Chris Carroll of Johns Hopkins has pointed out, reasonably strong evidence indicates that American households are both *impatient* (i.e., wish to shift more consumption from the future into the present) and *prudent* (i.e., unwilling to take a significant chance of seeing their future standard of living fall substantially). If true, then such households' patterns of behavior would look very much like the simple consumption functions on Chapters 6 and 9 even if there were no hindrances to borrowing.

Thus the marginal propensity to consume may remain at some constant fraction significantly greater than zero. The increasing ease of borrowing may not lead the multiplier to completely disappear. Nevertheless, the multiplier is likely to grow still smaller over time. It will surely play a smaller role in the economy (and in economic policy, and in economics textbooks) in the future than it has in the past.

Globalization

Globalization has, from one perspective, been going on for centuries. But it continues to accelerate. The future is likely to see international trade continue to expand even more rapidly. The growth in trade, depicted in Figure 16.2, will also lower the multiplier: A greater portion of changes in domestic spending will show up as changes in demand for foreign-made goods. So the economy at home will be even less vulnerable to domestic shocks that disturb employment and output. However, increased international integration means that the domestic economy is

globalization

The ongoing process by which barriers to the free flow of commodities, capital, and information across countries are reduced.

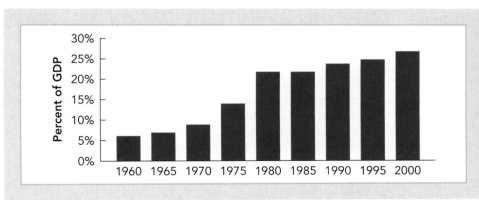

FIGURE 16.2

Globalization: Merchandise Imports as a Share of Total Goods Production

Since 1960 the share of merchandise imports has quadrupled relative to total production of goods.

Source: The 2004 edition of *The Economic Report of the President* (Washington, DC: Government Printing Office).

more vulnerable to foreign shocks: Recession abroad that lowers demand for exports will have repercussions at home.

Accompanying the increase in international trade will be an increase in the magnitude of international financial flows. The odds are that international investments will become easier to make. And the odds are — as means of international communication increase — that investors in one country will become much more confident in making investments in another. So the speed with which capital flows across national borders will increase.

Yet in Chapter 15 we saw that increased flow of capital across national borders is a potential source of financial crisis and macroeconomic volatility. In the East Asian crisis of 1997–1998 a sudden shift in investors' expectations meant that $100 billion a year in international capital flows that had financed investment in East Asia was no longer there. That $100 billion a year had financed the employment of 20 million people working in investment industries — digging sewer lines, building roads, erecting buildings, and installing machines — as both domestic and foreign investors bet that there was lots of money to be made in East Asia's industrial revolution. These 20 million East Asian workers had to find new jobs outside of industries engaged in construction and making capital goods. The fall in the value of East Asian currencies went a long way to bringing the supply of and demand for foreign exchange back into balance. Falling exchange rates made East Asian goods more attractive to European and American purchasers, pushing East Asia's economies back to rapid growth.

But what caused the sudden sharp shift in investment patterns? Unfortunately for economists, unfortunately for economics as a social science, unfortunately for the people of East Asia, and unfortunately for others who live in countries at risk of financial crisis, we cannot find any convincing disturbing cause proportional to the large effect. The shift in Wall Street's desires to invest in East Asia appears to have been impelled much more by the trend-chasing and herd instincts of Wall Streeters — a community of people who talk to each other too much, and whose opinions often reflect not judgments about the world but simply guesses about what average opinion expects average opinion to be — than by any transformation in the fundamentals of East Asian economic development.

Here we have reached the limits of economics. Economists are good at analyzing how asset markets work if they are populated by far-sighted investors with accurate models of the world and long horizons. Economists are even good at pointing out that such asset markets can be subject to multiple equilibria — situations in which it is rational to be optimistic and rational investors are optimistic if they think that everyone else is optimistic, and in which it is also rational to be pessimistic and rational investors are pessimistic if they think that everyone else is pessimistic. But that is all they can say.

Note that the process of international investment may still be worth supporting. It does promise powerful benefits: faster industrialization on the developing periphery and higher rates of return for investors from the industrial core, as well as diversification to reduce risk. These benefits may well outweigh the costs of international financial crises. Nevertheless, the next generation of business cycles will likely be judged to have gone well or ill depending on whether the financial crises generated by cross-border financial flows are handled well or badly.

Monetary Policy

The increase in financial flexibility that reduces the multiplier will also make it more difficult to read the financial markets, and probably to conduct monetary policy. Monetary policy works, after all, because the central bank's open-market operations change interest rates. These operations have large effects on interest rates because the assets traded — Treasury bills, on the one hand, and reserve deposits at regional Federal Reserve banks, on the other hand — play key roles in finance. Few substitute assets can serve the functions that they serve.

But as financial flexibility increases, any one kind of asset will become less and less of a bottleneck. There will be more ways of structuring transactions, and more kinds of financial instruments will be traded. Thus in the future, changes in the supply of Treasury bills likely will have less effect on interest rates than they do today. Open-market operations are likely to become somewhat less effective, and monetary policy somewhat more difficult to conduct, in the future.

Will this make much of a difference? Nobody knows. But monetary policy today is very effective at controlling production, employment, and prices — albeit with long and variable lags. Even a considerable reduction in the power of open-market operations would still leave central bankers with more-than-ample tools to carry out whatever kinds of policies they wished. The fear that increases in financial instability will rob central banks of their power to control economies is at least a generation in the future.

Will these ongoing and future changes in the structure of the macroeconomy have as little effect on the relative size of the business cycle as past changes appear to have had? To answer that question we need to look at the history of macroeconomic fluctuations, which we do in the next section.

Inventories

Fourth and last of the changes that we can foresee is that improvements in information technology will improve businesses' ability to control their inventories. Mismatches between production and demand — unanticipated large-scale inventory accumulation or drawdowns — have been a principal source of fluctuations in unemployment and output over the past century. Better information technology may well reduce this component of macroeconomic instability. But how large this reduction will be is, once again, something that nobody knows.

RECAP   CHANGES IN THE MACROECONOMY

The future is likely to bring a continued increase in the liquidity of the economy and a relaxation of borrowing constraints. People will find borrowing easier and easier, hence their spending will be less closely tied to their current income, and the marginal propensity to consume will fall. International trade and financial markets are likely to become increasingly integrated, but at least as far as financial markets are concerned it is not clear that this is a good thing. Over time, the power and effectiveness of monetary policy will likely decline as increased financial options erode the key role played by commercial bank deposits in finance. And firms will probably become better at managing their inventories, so that inventory fluctuation–driven business cycles will become largely a thing of the past.

16.2 THE HISTORY OF MACROECONOMIC FLUCTUATIONS

Estimating Long-Run Changes in Cyclical Volatility

Assessing changes in the size of the overall business cycle turns out to be harder than it looks. The obvious thing to do is to compare the cyclical behavior of real GDP and unemployment over the last century. But good-quality data exist only for the post–World War II period. The pre–World War II data are much spottier. The Federal Reserve Board index of industrial production begins only in 1919. The Commerce Department GDP series begins only in 1929. The Bureau of Labor Statistics unemployment rate series begins only in 1940. And there is good reason to think that pre-1950 data are less reliable than post-1950 data.

Professor Christina Romer of the University of California–Berkeley has demonstrated that the procedures used to construct pre-1950 data tended to artificially inflate the **cyclical volatility** of the data. If you simply use the estimates reported in *Historical Statistics of the United States,* you will be comparing pre–World War II apples to post–World War II oranges. On the other hand, a consistent division of the past century-plus into recessions and expansions, as used in Table 16.2, shows little difference in the size of recessions. The average pre–World War I recession was about two weeks shorter than the average post–World War II recession.

cyclical volatility

The amount of variation in the size of swings from peak to trough over time.

TABLE 16.2

Length of Recessions and Expansions since 1886

Pre–World War I recessions (months to trough) are almost exactly the same length as post–World War II recessions. Post–World War II expansions (months from trough to peak), however, are half again as long as pre–World War I expansions.

1886–1916			1920–1940			1948–Present		
Year of Peak	Months to Trough	Months from Trough to Next Peak	Year of Peak	Months to Trough	Months from Trough to Next Peak	Year of Peak	Months to Trough	Months from Trough to Next Peak
1887	5	66	1920	14	26	1948	11	45
1893	13	23	1923	14	32	1953	10	39
1896	12	39	1927	9	21	1957	8	24
1900	8	31	1929	34	61	1960	10	106
1903	8	40	1937	10	18	1969	11	36
1907	11	19	1939	3		1973	16	58
1910	16	37				1980	6	12
1914	6	17				1981	16	98
1916	8					1990	8	119
						2001	7	
Avg.	9.7	34.0		14.0	31.6		10.1	53.7

Source: Christina Romer, "Remeasuring Business Cycles" (NBER Working Paper 4150), http://papers.nber.org/W4150, published subsequently in *Journal of Economic History* 54 (September 1994), pp. 573–609; and authors' calculations.

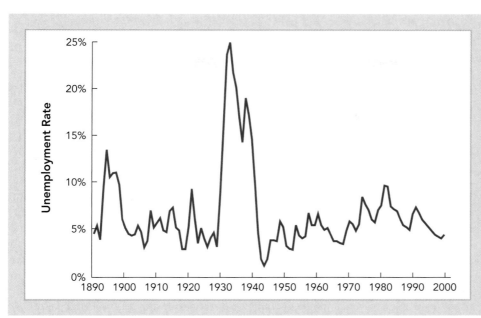

Source: The 2004 edition of *The Economic Report of the President* (Washington, DC: Government Printing Office); *Historical Statistics of the United States* (Washington, DC: Government Printing Office); and Christina Romer, "Spurious Volatility in Historical Unemployment Estimates," *Journal of Economic History* 94, no. 1 (February 1986), pp. 1–37.

FIGURE 16.3

The Great Depression Relative to Other Business Cycles: U.S. Unemployment

Calculating fluctuations in unemployment according to a methodology consistent with the post–World War II data reveals that past unemployment estimates contained in *Historical Statistics of the United States* overstated the size of the depression of the 1890s.

We can reach a few solid conclusions about the changing cyclical volatility of the American economy. The first and most obvious fact is the extraordinarily large size of the business cycle during the interwar period — the 1920–1940 period that came after World War I and before World War II. The Great Depression that began in 1929 was only the largest of three interwar business cycles. Other major contractions in economic activity took place in 1920–1922 and 1937–1938 (see Figure 16.3).

A second clear conclusion is that in the post–World War II era the business cycle, measured relative to the size of the economy, has been a little bit but not much smaller than before World War I. The shrinkage in the business cycle appears to be between 25 and 30 percent. The postwar business cycle is a somewhat smaller animal, but it would seem to be of the same species.

Thus many of the changes in the economy since 1900 must have roughly canceled each other out. The decline of agriculture as a share of employment and production (as a rule not very susceptible to the industrial business cycle) has been offset by the rise in importance of relatively acyclical services (also not very susceptible to the business cycle). An increase in the life span of capital equipment built with more durable materials might seem likely to increase cyclical volatility because more economic activity takes the form of long-term bets on the future. But this has apparently been offset by faster technological obsolescence, which reduces the effective economic life of investments in fixed capital. A smaller multiplier due to reduced liquidity constraints on households has presumably had some effect. But perhaps keeping spending proportional to income remains a useful rule of thumb even as credit becomes widely available, and so perhaps credit availability has not done as much to reduce the multiplier as economists' theories claim.

Economic Policy

How Economic Policy Has Worked

Yet if we look a little deeper, we see that business cycles today are not the same animals that they were before the Great Depression. The fall in the multiplier, the arrival of automatic stabilizers, and the increasing power of central banks have allowed monetary policy to offset many of the kinds of shocks that generated pre-Depression business cycles. The absence of significant stabilization springs from the fact that the increasing power of central banks has created a new class of shocks to the economy: recessions deliberately induced by monetary authorities to curb rising inflation. The post–World War II economy appears to have had fewer small recessions caused by shocks to the IS and LM curves. **Stabilization policy** has worked, in that it allows the central bank working in combination with automatic stabilizers to react when the economy threatens to turn down into recession because of any sudden shock.

stabilization policy

Policy aimed at avoiding recessions and undue inflation by keeping total aggregate demand growing smoothly.

Before 1916 it was impossible for the U.S. government to have any effect on planned expenditure. Government purchases and net taxes were so small relative to economic activity that no fiscal policy variation short of fighting a major war could materially shift the IS curve and change equilibrium real GDP. The pre–World War I government also lacked, until the founding of the Federal Reserve in 1914, the ability to affect the level of interest rates. Neither fiscal stabilization policy nor monetary stabilization policy as we know them today was possible before World War I.

By the end of World War II the power of stabilization policy and the government's commitment to manage aggregate demand were both firmly established. The war left the United States with a federal government that annually spent about one-fifth of GDP, and a government committed to countercyclical fiscal policy. Before World War II it had been a commonplace of political and policy-making discourse that taxes should be raised and spending cut to try to balance the budget in a recession. By the 1950s this doctrine was dead; the automatic stabilizers of the federal budget were in place.

The emergence of a significant progressive income tax made government revenues substantially procyclical. The emergence of unemployment compensation, food stamps, and welfare led government spending to have a substantial automatic countercyclical component. By the 1960s the federal government believed that it ought to be undertaking countercyclical discretionary fiscal policy as well (even though it has never been able to succeed in doing so). In monetary policy a similar shift had been accomplished near the beginning of the post–World War II period. By the early 1950s the U.S. Treasury and the Federal Reserve had agreed — in their Accord of 1951 — that the principal task of the Federal Reserve was to use monetary policy to stabilize the economy.

Since then the Federal Reserve has attempted to use monetary policy, within the limits placed on it by long and variable lags, to stabilize the economy and to moderate recessions. Both overall survey studies and detailed studies of cases like the interest rate cuts that followed the stock market crash of 1987 teach the lesson that the Federal Reserve has had considerable success in cutting short recessions and in accelerating growth in the early stages of the subsequent economic expansion.

Automatic stabilizers as well have clearly played a role in moderating the business cycle. Yet a third innovation in economic policy — deposit insurance — has had effects that are harder to quantify. However, as Christina Romer observes, "The obvious starting point is the observation that financial panics were ubiquitous before World War I and almost nonexistent since World War II . . . there were major panics in 1890, 1893, 1899, 1901, 1903, and 1907 — all of them the source of substantial contractionary pressure on real GDP." Perhaps the effects of deposit insurance have been large as well; we are not really sure.

How Economic Policy Has Not Worked

But if economic policy since World War II has prevented or moderated many recessions, it has caused recessions as well. The existence of **policy-induced recessions** like those of 1981–1982 and 1990–1992 is what explains why there has not been a more dramatic reduction in the size of the business cycle over time. At least four times in the United States since World War II the Federal Reserve has engineered a recession, or has willingly accepted a substantial risk of a recession, in order to accomplish its policy goal of curbing inflation. It has had to curb an inflation rate that has crept upward into an uncomfortably high range.

policy-induced recessions
Recessions started not by swings in consumer or investor confidence, but by contractionary monetary policy.

If the prewar boom-and-bust business cycle was driven by, in John Maynard Keynes's phrase, the "animal spirits" of investors' shifts from optimism to pessimism and back again (and by financial panics), the post–World War II boom-and-bust business cycle has been driven by economic policies that have allowed rises in inflation, followed by the development of a consensus within the Federal Reserve that the rise in inflation must be reversed.

Why have economic policy makers in the post–World War II era found themselves repeatedly driven to risk recession in order to fight inflation? In the late 1940s inflation was allowed to accelerate because the Federal Reserve had adopted the mission of keeping interest rates low to reduce the cost of financing the huge national debt incurred during World War II. The Federal Reserve was not satisfied with this mission, and in fact negotiated the Treasury–Federal Reserve Accord of 1951 to remove it from its list of policy objectives.

In the 1960s and 1970s inflation was allowed to accelerate for reasons that economists still debate. Berkeley economist DeLong has stressed historical accidents and the lingering memory of the Great Depression. Stanford economist John Taylor stresses mistaken economic theories held in the early 1960s — in particular, the Phillips curve model of Samuelson and Solow constructed under the assumption that inflation expectations were and would remain static. Political scientists like Edward Tufte stress political business-cycle considerations.

At the first, surface level, the United States had an unstable macroeconomy in the 1970s because no influential policy makers — until Paul Volcker chaired the Federal Reserve in the 1980s — would place a sufficiently high priority on keeping inflation from rising. As long as inflation remained relatively low, it was not seen as a crisis, and so other goals took precedence among every group of economic policy makers. Thus presidents, members of Congress, and members of the Federal Open Market Committee were willing to accept the risk of increasing inflation to achieve other goals. Only after inflation had risen — only after it had reached the level of a political crisis — did a consensus develop that priorities needed to be changed, and steps were taken to reduce inflation.

Under this interpretation, the United States after World War II had a boom-bust, stop-go business cycle because the political system could pay attention to only one phenomenon at a time: When inflation wasn't a crisis, it wasn't an issue.

Only with the acceleration of inflation toward the end of the 1970s did political sentiment begin to shift. For rising inflation did become a severe political problem in 1979. Paul Volcker was then nominated and confirmed as chair of the Federal Reserve in a political environment in which controlling inflation — rather than reducing the unemployment rate — was the highest priority for economic policy. The Volcker-led Federal Reserve quickly signaled its intention to place first priority on controlling inflation by shifting its operating procedures to place a greater emphasis on money supply targets.

At a second, deeper level, the United States had a burst of inflation in the 1970s that required a painful recession cure in the 1980s because economic policy makers during the 1960s had dealt their successors a bad hand: an unfavorable Phillips curve. Thus the policies of the 1960s left economic policy makers of the 1970s with a painful dilemma: either higher-than-usual inflation or higher-than-usual unemployment. Bad cards coupled with bad luck made inflation in the 1970s worse than anyone expected it might be. And unsuccessful attempts to find a way out of this dilemma gave the economy the boom-bust cycle of the 1970s.

And at a third, deepest level, the truest cause of the inflation of the 1970s was the memory of the Great Depression. The Great Depression made it impossible for a while to believe that the business cycle was a fluctuation *around* rather than a shortfall *below* potential output and potential employment. The memory of the Great Depression made everyone skeptical of taking the average level of capacity utilization or the unemployment rate as a measure of the economy's sustainable productive potential.

Only after the experiences of the 1970s were economic policy makers persuaded that the flaws and frictions in American labor markets made it unwise to try to use stimulative macroeconomic policies without limit. Only after the experiences of the 1970s were policy makers persuaded that the minimum sustainable rate of unemployment attainable by macroeconomic policy was relatively high, and that the costs — at least the political costs — of even moderately high one-digit inflation were high as well.

That the post–World War II gains from stabilization policy appear to have been relatively small is somewhat depressing. Nearly 50 years ago Milton Friedman warned that stabilization policy, if pursued overly aggressively by policy makers who did not understand its limits, could easily turn into destabilization policy. His gloomy warning appears very close to being correct. Yet important lessons may have been learned.

RECAP   THE HISTORY OF MACROECONOMIC FLUCTUATIONS

The pre–World War II boom-and-bust business cycle was driven by investors' shifts from optimism to pessimism and back again. The post–World War II boom-and-bust business cycle has been driven by economic policies that have allowed rises in inflation, followed by a Federal Reserve–caused recession to reverse the rise in inflation. There is reason to hope that the modern Federal Reserve has learned how to eliminate or at least reduce the size of these inflation-fighting recessions.

16.3 UNDERSTANDING THE GREAT DEPRESSION

But if the business cycle has remained in spite of — and in part because of — active macroeconomic policy, it is important to remember that active macroeconomic policy has made a disaster on the order of magnitude of the Great Depression nearly inconceivable. To see how bad things could get in an extreme situation when economic policy does not do its job, we need only to look back 75 years at the Great Depression.

The Magnitude of the Great Depression

The speed and magnitude of the economy's collapse during the first stages of the Great Depression were unprecedented. Nothing like it had been seen before, and nothing like it has been seen since. From full employment in 1929, real GDP fell until it was nearly 40 percent below potential output by 1933 (see Figure 16.4). Investment collapsed: By 1932 real investment spending was less than one-ninth what it had been three years before. And by 1933 unemployment had reached a quarter of the labor force.

In our analytical framework, understanding why investment and real GDP fell so far so fast between 1929 and 1933 is straightforward. They did so because of an extraordinary rise in real interest rates. Real interest rates that had been 4 percent in 1929 spiked to nearly 13 percent by 1931 and stayed high throughout 1932 (see Figure 16.5 on page 480). With such high real interest rates, investment spending naturally fell off.

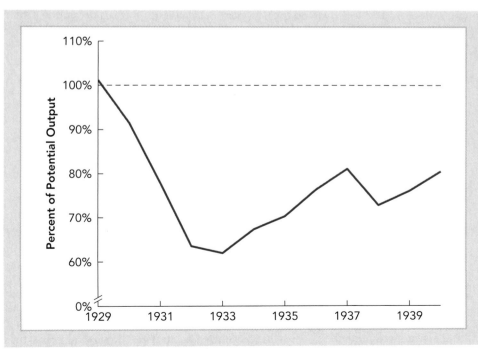

FIGURE 16.4
Real GDP Relative to Potential Output during the Great Depression
The Great Depression saw the steepest fall ever in real GDP relative to potential output.

Source: Authors' calculations from *Historical Statistics of the United States* (Washington, DC: Government Printing Office, 1975).

FIGURE 16.5

Movement along the IS Curve: The Great Contraction, 1929–1932

Sharp rises in expected real interest rates due to deflation and rising risk premiums pushed the economy far up the IS curve between 1929 and 1932.

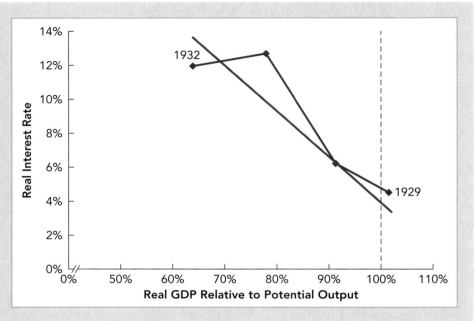

Source: Authors' calculations from *Historical Statistics of the United States* (Washington, DC: Government Printing Office, 1975).

After 1932 investment spending remained low, averaging less than half its 1929 value for the rest of the Great Depression decade even though real interest rates returned to more normal values. Why didn't the return of real interest rates to normal values cause a revival of investment? Because the magnitude of the Great Depression itself caused businesses to put off expanding their capacity. In 1933, with real GDP less than two-thirds of potential output, practically every business in the United States had excess capacity and hence no immediate incentive to invest at all. The very depth of the Great Depression caused a steep fall in baseline investment I_0 in the investment equation

$$I = I_0 - I_r r$$

Thus even a restoration of real interest rates to normal levels was not sufficient to restore the economy to full employment.

Deflation and High Real Interest Rates

So why did real interest rates rise so high between 1929 and 1932? The immediate, proximate cause of high real interest rates was rapid deflation: rapid sustained falls in prices that, when combined with moderate nominal interest rates, produced very high real interest rates, as shown in Figure 16.6.

What caused the deflation? The first thing was the depth of the Great Depression itself: Falling production, employment, and demand produced steep falls in prices, which caused high real interest rates that reduced demand, production, and employment still further. But saying that the Great Depression caused itself makes little sense. An initial shock must have occurred to start the downward spiral that was the Great Depression.

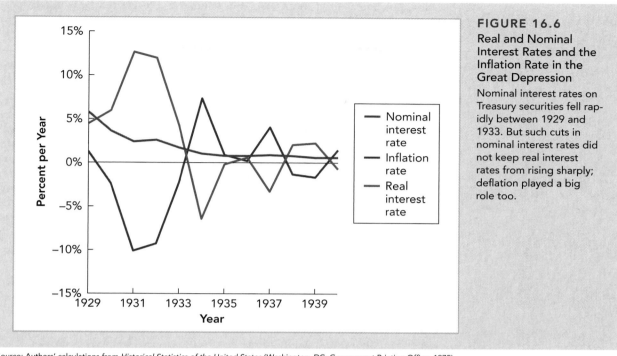

FIGURE 16.6

Real and Nominal Interest Rates and the Inflation Rate in the Great Depression

Nominal interest rates on Treasury securities fell rapidly between 1929 and 1933. But such cuts in nominal interest rates did not keep real interest rates from rising sharply; deflation played a big role too.

Source: Authors' calculations from *Historical Statistics of the United States* (Washington, DC: Government Printing Office, 1975).

The Initial Shock

Economists have proposed many candidates for the shock that triggered the Great Depression. Perhaps the stock market crash of 1929 reduced wealth and increased uncertainty, causing a downward shift in the baseline level of consumption. Perhaps the availability of consumer credit in the 1920s caused a consumption spending boom that then came to a natural end. Perhaps there was excessive residential investment in the 1920s because builders failed to realize how the restrictions on immigration put into place in the mid-1920s would affect housing demand in the long run. Perhaps the recognition that the housing stock was too large triggered a downward shift in the baseline level of investment. Perhaps the Federal Reserve's 1928 increases in interest rates, an attempt to reduce stock market speculation, triggered the initial slump.

Practically any analyst soon reaches the conclusion that the response was disproportionate to the initial shock. Somehow the American economy at the end of the 1920s was very vulnerable in the sense that a small shock could cause a big depression. It is this disproportion between the hard-to-find initial shock and the subsequent depression that makes many economists fear that the economy will be unstable if not managed by appropriate government policies.

Consequences of the Price Level Decline

Economists have reached a consensus that a sufficiently aggressive and activist monetary policy could have stemmed the price decline, and so ended the Great Depression much earlier if undertaken rapidly and aggressively enough. Policies of massive federal deficits funded by money-printing, coupled with aggressive open-market operations to increase the monetary base, could have, if carried far enough, produced inflation. And without the high real interest rates produced by deflation in the early 1930s, it is hard to see how there could have been a Great Depression.

Falling price levels reduce real GDP through two separate channels. The first is the real interest rate channel that we saw above: The real interest rate is the nominal interest rate minus the expected inflation rate, so deflation that is expected to continue leads to high real interest rates, to a move up and to the left along the IS curve, and to falling real GDP and employment.

But there is a second channel as well. Unexpected falls in the price level redistribute wealth from debtors to creditors. Those businesses that are heavily in debt find that they cannot pay, and so they go bankrupt. Those financial institutions that have loaned to heavily indebted businesses find that their loans are worthless, and so they go bankrupt as well. Deflation destroys the web of credit that channels funds from savers through banks and other financial institutions to businesses wanting to invest. More than one-third of U.S. banks failed in the first years of the Great Depression. And without the web of financial intermediaries to channel investment through the financial markets, maintaining or restoring the flow of investment becomes very difficult.

These effects of deflation are long-lasting. Even after real interest rates have returned to normal, the deflation-driven destruction of the web of financial intermediation will continue to depress investment. So it was in the Great Depression. Only with the cleaning-up of the insolvent parts of the banking system and rises in prices after the abandonment of the gold standard did recovery begin.

The memory of the Great Depression was an important factor that made the Federal Reserve unwilling to raise interest rates during the dot-com stock market bubble of the 1990s and eager to lower interest rates far and fast after the stock market began to decline. Heading off any possibility of a deflationary spiral of bankruptcy like the one that happened in the 1930s was the Federal Reserve's highest priority in the early 2000s. Prominent economists — monetarist Milton Friedman, and former Council of Economic Advisers Chair Michael Boskin among them — made much of the structural similarities between 1929–1934 and 1999–2004. In their view, economic policy makers deserve extremely high marks in the early 2000s for having learned the lessons taught by the Great Depression, and for applying them.

RECAP   THE GREAT DEPRESSION

The Great Depression was the largest macroeconomic disaster in history. The greatness of the Great Depression was the result of economic policy makers' failure to stem the tide of deflation that the stock market crash of 1929 and the initial recession set in motion. As prices declined, firms and banks became insolvent, and the entire network of financial intermediation that finances investment broke down. Recovery could not come until rising prices diminished the fear of future bankruptcies and until creditors and investors in financial markets could determine which banks and firms were still solvent and thus creditworthy. This required, first, the cleaning-up of the insolvent parts of the banking system and, second, the rises in the general price level that followed Roosevelt's abandonment of the gold standard.

16.4 MACROECONOMIC POLICY: LESSONS LEARNED

Stabilization

For almost all of your lives — "you" being the typical reader of this textbook — the business cycle has been relatively quiescent. Even the recession of 2001 was small, as recessions go. It was nothing like 1982 or 1975, let alone 1933. A substantial difference in business-cycle behavior can be seen if we divide the post–World War II era into two periods, with the breakpoint chosen at the end of the Volcker disinflation in the early 1980s. The pre-1984 years show much more business-cycle volatility than do the post-1983 years, as Table 16.3 indicates.

One possibility is that the period since 1984 has been the result of good luck — that business-cycle macroeconomic performance has been good because shocks have been few and rarely had large effects on the economy. But as time passes and as the volatility of output and inflation remain relatively low, the notion that the recently stable U.S. macroeconomy is just the result of good luck becomes less and less likely.

Learning

Thus we look at the second possibility: that lessons have truly been learned from the experience of the 1960s and 1970s. The late 1980s through the middle of the first decade of the 2000s was not only an era of relatively stable economic growth but also an era of low inflation. Recessions have been few and growth relatively steady since the early 1980s, in large part because inflation has been firmly under control: A lack of inflation has meant that the Federal Reserve has not had to risk a recession to control inflation.

This leads to the hope that the monetary policy authorities have gained sufficient experience and expertise at using their policy tools to successfully carry out stabilization policy. Perhaps the first three decades of the post–World War II era saw little stabilization of the business cycle because of repeated policy mistakes:

TABLE 16.3

Post-Volcker Stabilization of the U.S. Economy: Standard Deviation of Percentage Changes

Since the mid-1980s the U.S. economy has been astonishingly, remarkably stable. Typical business-cycle movements in the unemployment rate or in real GDP have been half the size they were from 1948 to 1984.

Series	1948–1984	1985–Present
Industrial production	5.7%	2.0%
GNP	2.8	1.1
Commodity output	5.3	3.2
Unemployment rate	1.2	0.5

Source: Christina Romer, "Changes in Business Cycles: Evidence and Explanations" *Journal of Economic Perspectives* 13 (Spring 1999), pp. 23–44; and authors' calculations.

overoptimism with respect to the possible sustainable rate of economic growth, followed by recessions to demonstrate that the central bank was, after all, serious about controlling inflation.

Prospects

Perhaps the more recent era shows how much more stable our economic system can be with successful institutions that understand the limits of their power. But whether the growth of aggregate demand has been smoother because economic policy makers have recognized the limits of what they can achieve, because of the skill of Paul Volcker and Alan Greenspan, because of better economic theories to guide policy — or simply because of good luck — is not clear. Clearly, however, every time in the past a "new era" or a "new economy" has been proclaimed, the same old business cycle has soon returned.

The expansion of the 1920s led economists to hope that the newly constructed Federal Reserve had learned how to stabilize output by eliminating the fluctuations in interest rates that caused financial crises. Irving Fisher, the most prominent monetarist of his day, went so far as to claim on the eve of the 1929 crash that stock prices had reached a "permanent and high plateau." The prolonged expansion of the 1960s led the Department of Commerce to change the name of its *Business Cycle Digest* to the *Business Conditions Digest,* for it seemed silly to have a publication named after a phenomenon that no longer existed. Both President Eisenhower's and President Johnson's Council of Economic Advisers chairs, Arthur Burns and Walter Heller, agreed that substantial progress in economic science and policy making toward economic stability had opened up new dimensions of political economy.

One can be optimistic about the future of macroeconomic policy, counting up all the lessons that economists and policy makers successfully learned over the course of the twentieth century. One can be especially optimistic from the perspective of the United States today. From that perspective macroeconomic policy appears remarkably successful. Unemployment is very low, at levels that have rarely been seen in a generation. Inflation is also low, at consistently low levels that have not been seen in a generation either. And in recent years measured productivity growth has been very rapid, as a result primarily of the technological revolutions in information and communications technology and secondarily — for a few years anyway — as a result of the Clinton administration bet in the early 1990s that deficit reduction would lead to a high-investment, high-productivity-growth, high-income-growth recovery.

RECAP　MACROECONOMIC POLICY: LESSONS LEARNED

The extraordinary stability of the U.S. economy since the mid-1980s suggests that the Federal Reserve has learned important lessons about how to conduct monetary policy: make sure its commitment to fighting long-run inflation is ironclad and credible; look far ahead in estimating the effects of policies; do not be afraid to take preemptive action against dangers — whether rising inflation or rising unemployment — that are not yet visible but that the Federal Reserve's forecasting models suggest are imminent.

16.5 MACROECONOMIC POLICY: LESSONS UN- OR HALF-LEARNED

One can also be pessimistic about the future of macroeconomic policy. One can count up all the lessons that economists and policy makers did not learn, or half-learned, or learned and then forgot over the course of the twentieth century. Certainly a look outside the United States, either at Japan, or at the financial-crisis-ridden emerging economies, or at Europe with its stubbornly high unemployment, does not lend strength to the claim that traditional business-cycle patterns have come to an end.

Lessons Unlearned: High European Unemployment

Europe currently is not in a Great Depression. Nevertheless, unemployment rates in western Europe are dangerously, disturbingly high. Until very recently unemployment has averaged nearly 10 percent in the zone of countries that now share the common currency of the euro (see Figure 16.7).

Up until the end of the 1970s, unemployment in western Europe had been lower — sometimes substantially lower — than unemployment in the United States. But starting in the 1970s European unemployment began to ratchet upward. Unemployment rose during recessions, yet it did not fall during economic expansions. During the recession of the Volcker disinflation at the start of the 1980s, western European and U.S. unemployment rates were about equal. But during the later 1980s and 1990s the trend of U.S. unemployment was down; the trend of European unemployment was stable or upward.

In the United States the comovements of unemployment and inflation over 1960–2004 can be understood by using the standard Phillips curve. The Phillips

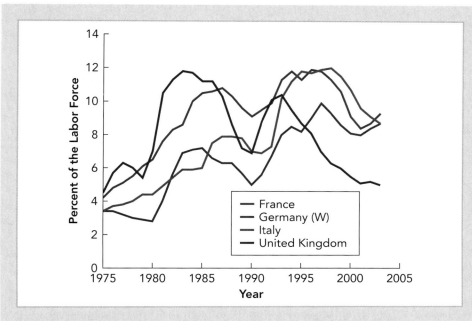

FIGURE 16.7

European Unemployment

The growth of unemployment in the four largest western European countries between 1975 and 2003 is of concern to economists and policy makers.

Source: The 2004 edition of *The Economic Report of the President* (Washington, DC: Government Printing Office).

curve shifts out in the 1970s as everyone begins to expect higher inflation and demographic factors cause the natural rate of unemployment to rise. The Phillips curve shifts back in the 1980s and 1990s as people regain confidence in the Federal Reserve's commitment to low inflation and as changing demographic factors cause the natural rate of unemployment to fall. The story does not fit badly. Movements in the expected rate of inflation reflect changes in the economic policy environment. Movements in the natural rate of unemployment are relatively small, and can be linked to plausible factors.

In western Europe, by contrast, this standard Phillips curve never fit the historical experience very well. Each policy episode from 1970 on — supply shocks, the Volcker disinflation, the recession of the early 1990s — seemed to shift the Phillips curve further out, and to further raise the natural rate of unemployment. It seemed as if this year's natural rate of unemployment was equal to whatever unemployment had happened to be last year.

The dominant view expressed in Europe since the early 1990s has been that high European unemployment was the result of labor market rigidities. Europe possessed laws, restrictions, and regulations that made it too difficult for firms to hire new workers cheaply at a relatively low wage, and too difficult for firms to fire workers (and thus forward-looking firms were reluctant to hire workers). Thus it was too expensive to conduct a labor-intensive business in Europe or to adjust to changes in the economic environment.

classical unemployment

When unemployment arises not because aggregate demand is too low, but because government regulations or market power keep the labor market from clearing and keep labor demand by firms below labor supply.

According to this dominant view, high unemployment in Europe is an equilibrium level that is what economists call **classical unemployment**: It arises not from any deficiency of aggregate demand, but simply from the fact that the state's regulations keep the labor market from clearing. The state's regulations boost the cost of employing the marginal worker far above the extra revenue the typical firm would gain from employing an extra worker.

But the "rigidities" in the European labor market were stronger in the 1960s — when European unemployment was very low — than they are today. It is not that the natural rate of unemployment in Europe has always been high; it is that each additional adverse shock that increases unemployment seems to increase the natural rate as well. Thus many economists who have examined European unemployment dissent from the conventional wisdom of the editorial writers and the politicians. They tend to see western Europe not as locked into high unemployment, but as in a reversible situation. Just as increases in unemployment in the 1970s and 1980s raised the natural rate of unemployment in Europe, so decreases in the rate of unemployment in the late 2000s would in all likelihood lower the natural rate of unemployment in Europe.

A Grand Bargain?

Economists' views of western European unemployment thus suggest there is potential for much improvement. Central bankers and governments could shift to a more expansionary monetary policy. As demand expands, people will find that the natural rate of unemployment is falling. The falling natural rate of unemployment will create still further room for demand expansion and for further unemployment rate reduction.

Central bankers may fear that the economists' view is wrong and that the conventional wisdom is right — that attempts to expand demand and reduce unemployment a little bit will lead to accelerating inflation as unemployment falls below its (high) current natural rate. Therefore begin the process with some steps to eliminate labor-market rigidities: Reduce employers' contributions to social security, reduce severance costs, transfer unemployment insurance money from the payment of benefits to assistance with job searching, and allow the minimum wage to fall. These steps should leave central bankers confident that there is room to expand demand in the context of a falling natural rate of unemployment.

But governments find that such steps to initiate the process of demand expansion can be portrayed as an attack on the standard of living of the unemployed — as an antiworker, antihuman policy. Only if governments are confident that reform of the social insurance system will be accompanied by stronger demand and higher employment will they be willing to undertake their part of the grand bargain. Otherwise they will fear that — with high interest rates and slow demand growth — social insurance system reform will merely change high classical unemployment to high Keynesian unemployment, and in the process create mass poverty. And only if central banks are confident that their expansionary monetary policies will be accompanied by social insurance system reform would it make sense for them to risk lower interest rates and a change in monetary policy.

Even if the conventional wisdom is right, such a grand bargain promises to make everyone — the currently unemployed, the currently employed who pay taxes to support the social insurance system, politicians dealing with high unemployment, central bankers accused of being out of touch with human experience — better off. And if the economists' view is right — if the principal determinant of a high natural rate of unemployment in Europe is the fact that unemployment has been high in Europe for a long time — then the benefits to such a grand bargain are overwhelmingly large.

Yet European politicians and central bankers have been unable to learn how to deal with their high, stubborn rates of unemployment. The current macroeconomic policy near gridlock has been ongoing for nearly two decades, with no end in sight.

Lessons Half-Learned: Japanese Stagnation

The End of the Bubble Economy

The standard analysis of how the Japanese economy entered its present period of stagnation is straightforward. The Japanese stock market and real estate market rose far and fast in the 1980s, to unsustainable "bubble" levels. And eventually the market turned, and both the real estate and stock markets collapsed.

When stock and real estate prices collapsed, it was discovered by creditors that lots of enterprises and individuals had borrowed heavily against their real estate and security holdings, putting up their real estate and their stocks as collateral. After the collapse, not only were those who had borrowed heavily bankrupt, but the banks and other institutions that had loaned them money were bankrupt as well: The value of the collateral they had accepted was no longer enough to repay the lenders' creditors.

One problem was that no one was exactly sure which institutions were bankrupt — which institutions had liabilities in excess of their assets. Thus no one was eager to lend money to anyone: You might well never see your money again if the organization you loaned it to was one of those that had extended itself during the **bubble economy** of the late 1980s. A second problem was regulatory forbearance: the belief that the best way to solve the problem was to pretend that it did not exist, try to let business go on as usual, and hope that a few good years would allow all of the institutions that were "underwater" to make enough in profits to repay their debts even given the low value of the collateral that they had accepted.

bubble economy

When a country's stock and real estate markets have risen far and fast to unsustainable "bubble" levels that cannot be justified on the basis of fundamental values.

These two problems together meant that investment spending was depressed. Financial institutions exist to channel money from savers with purchasing power to businesses that can use that purchasing power to expand their capital. But in the aftermath of the collapse of the bubble, no one really wanted to lend — knowing whether the organization wanted the money to invest or to try to paper over some of its previous losses was impossible.

The situation was analogous to the collapse of investment spending in the Great Depression, when the chain of deflation and bankruptcies had similar effects. The collapse of the Japanese financial bubble of the 1980s depressed consumption and investment spending. Banks' and other institutions' large bets on the real estate market meant that the collapse of the bubble put them underwater — with assets and lines of business that were worth less than the debt they already owed that they had borrowed to speculate in real estate. Who will invest in a business — or a bank — if they fear that their money will be used not to boost profitability but instead to pay back earlier creditors?

Thus Japan has fallen into more than a decade of economic stagnation. Growth since 1990 has been almost zero, as Figure 16.8 shows. Unemployment has risen to levels previously unheard-of in Japan. The IS curve has shifted far to the left. And nothing seems to correct it: Even extremely low nominal interest rates are not sufficient to boost investment and aggregate demand.

What should economic policy makers do in such a situation? The answer to what you should do to recover from such a state of depressed aggregate demand is "everything." You should have the government run a substantial deficit (although, as E. Cary Brown of MIT pointed out in the 1950s, it requires truly awesome deficit spending — on the order of deficit spending in World War II — to reverse a Great Depression like that in the United States in the 1930s or a Great

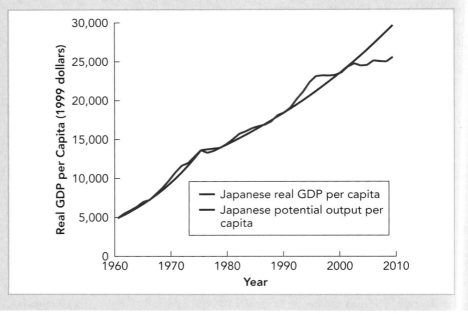

FIGURE 16.8

The Japanese Bubble Economy

Japan's output per capita outstripped potential output during the late 1980s bubble. But the bubble burst with the Japanese stock market crash at the beginning of the 1990s, and Japanese economic growth has since been extremely slow. What was the fastest growing of the major industrial economies has become the slowest growing.

Source: Organization for Economic Cooperation and Development; and authors' calculations.

Stagnation like that in Japan today). You should have the central bank push the interest rate it charges close to zero (to make it very easy and cheap to borrow money).

If that isn't enough, you should try to deliberately engineer moderate inflation. If demand is depressed because people think investing in corporations is too risky, change their minds by making the alternative to investment spending even more risky. If the alternative is hoarding your money in cash, then eat away a share of its real purchasing power every year with inflation.

So far Japan has changed its fiscal policy to run big deficits (but, as any student of the Great Depression would suspect, they haven't been big enough). Japan has lowered its short-term safe nominal interest rates to within kissing distance of zero, and has convinced the markets that this low–interest rate policy will not be easily or quickly reversed. As of the beginning of 2005, many forecasters have turned optimistic about the future of the Japanese economy. But the fact of a decade and a half of near stagnation remains. The lessons of the Great Depression have been only half-learned.

Lessons Half-Learned: Moral Hazard

Even in the United States, some of the lessons on economic policy taught by the past century of experience seem to have been only half-learned. Consider the problem of dealing with financial crises: those moments when large and highly leveraged financial institutions have failed or are about to, and when people genuinely fear that a chain of bankruptcies is about to be triggered.

In such a situation the fear that the organization to which one might lend will fail greatly retards lending. The flow of funds through financial markets will slow to a trickle, as savers conclude that keeping their wealth close at hand in safe forms is a much better opportunity than lending it to organizations that are probably bankrupt. Thus such a financial crisis is likely to see the IS curve shift far and fast to the left as the level of investment spending collapses. If this leftward shift in the IS curve is not stemmed, there will be a recession and the financial crisis will rapidly become worse as businesses that were solvent at normal levels of production and sales find that the falloff in demand has bankrupted them.

What to do in such a situation was first outlined a century and a quarter ago by Walter Bagehot, editor of *The Economist* in the mid-1800s and one of the most influential economic journalists of his time. The government needs to rapidly close down and liquidate those organizations that are fundamentally bankrupt. If they would be bankrupt even if production and demand were at normal levels relative to potential, then they should be closed. The government needs to lend money — albeit at a high, unpleasant, penalty rate — to organizations that would be solvent if production and demand were at normal levels, but that nevertheless suffer a cash crunch now. The key is twofold: Government support is necessary to prevent a deep meltdown of the entire financial system, but government assistance must be offered on terms unpleasant enough and expensive enough to prevent people from wishing in advance to get into a situation in which they need to draw on it. Moreover, the government must accept that its ability to distinguish between the two classes of institutions is imperfect, and that it will inevitably make mistakes.

Yet more and more in the political discussion over economic policy one hears the claim that government provision of liquidity and support in a financial crisis is dangerous — that it causes "**moral hazard**" because organizations place

moral hazard

The danger of imprudent, improper, or dishonest behavior in economic situations where actions are not easily or routinely monitored.

riskier and riskier bets counting on government support to bail them out if things go wrong. The right policy in a financial crisis, those who fear moral hazard say, is a completely hands-off one. A century and a quarter of experience suggests that this is only a half-truth. Moral hazard is a problem, but so is a Great Depression. The balancing point is hard to determine: Bank and financial regulators must impose rules that restrict the growth of moral hazard, assistance in times of financial crisis must be expensive and painful to the organization drawing on the government, and yet the worst outcome — a freezing-up of the financial system and a severe recession — must be guarded against. To focus on only one of these three rather than balancing between them is to recommend bad economic policy.

Yet the U.S. government seems to have a hard time performing this balancing act. As of the beginning of 2005, the big worry was the status of the large mortgage finance institutions — Fannie Mae and Freddie Mac. Did the government maintain the proper balance between providing assurances of system stability and guarding against moral hazard? Almost all economists would say, "No." And all remembered that fifteen years earlier similar problems had blown up the *savings-and-loan* institutions sector of the American banking system.

The Ultimate Lesson

It is strange that neither European nor Japanese governments appear to have learned the lessons that macroeconomists have to teach. It is also strange that fundamentals of crisis policy that seemed settled more than a century ago are still up for grabs in America's political debate. The principal lesson is that it seems very hard to learn the lessons of history.

Thus the future of economic policy seems likely to be similar to the past. Gross mistakes will be made, historical analogies will be misapplied, and economists and other observers after the fact (and sometimes during the fact) will find major policy mistakes made by governments and central banks to be inexplicable: We will genuinely be unable to figure out just what the people who made the decisions were thinking.

So do not mistake the steady hand on the monetary policy tiller and the relatively placid business cycle that the United States has experienced since the mid-1980s for the way things will be in the future.

> ### RECAP   MACROECONOMIC POLICY: LESSONS UN- OR HALF-LEARNED
>
> Western Europeans have not learned how to combine policies to gain structural flexibility with policies to expand demand, and so western Europe remains trapped with inflexible labor markets and slack demand. Japanese policy makers have finally learned the importance of cleaning up the banking system in the aftermath of a financial crisis in order to restore possibilities for growth, but they needed fifteen years to do so. American policy makers continue to struggle with the dilemmas of deposit insurance and moral hazard. If many lessons taught by history about how to conduct macroeconomic policy have been successfully learned, many have not.

Chapter Summary

1. The structure of the economy has undergone mammoth changes over the past century, yet these changes appear to have had relatively little impact on the size of the business cycle.

2. Stabilization policy as we know it was impossible a hundred years ago; yet it is now performed routinely and aggressively.

3. Since World War II, stabilization policy has had successes and failures. Its principal failure has been that it has generated recessions to fight inflation, and these policy-induced recessions have kept policy from successfully stabilizing the economy to a greater degree.

4. In the past two decades, stabilization policy in the United States has been very successful. Is this just good luck, or is it a pattern? We shall see.

5. Certainly from the U.S. perspective there is every reason to be optimistic about the future of macroeconomic policy and of the macroeconomy.

6. From a European perspective there is less reason to be optimistic: European governments and central banks have not learned how to deal with their high levels of unemployment.

7. From a Japanese perspective there is a little more reason to be optimistic: After 15 years, the Japanese government seems to have finally learned how to deal with its financial meltdown.

8. Even from a U.S. perspective, it seems to be hard to learn the lesson that good economic policy during an economic crisis is not a matter of clinging to one principle, but of balancing the conflicting requirements of several valid principles.

Key Terms

financial automatic stabilizers (p. 468)

financial flexibility (p. 470)

liquidity constraints (p. 470)

globalization (p. 471)

cyclical volatility (p. 474)

stabilization policy (p. 476)

policy-induced recessions (p. 477)

classical unemployment (p. 486)

bubble economy (p. 487)

moral hazard (p. 489)

Analytical Exercises

1. What changing factors since the start of the twentieth century would make one expect business cycles to become larger?

2. What changing factors since the start of the twentieth century would make one expect business cycles to become smaller?

3. As the macroeconomy continues to change in the twenty-first century, do you expect business cycles to become larger or smaller?

4. Why has production become more stable in the United States since the early 1980s?

5. Why does unemployment remain high in Europe today?

Policy Exercises

1. How, in your view, is the way the Federal Reserve conducts monetary policy likely to change over the next generation?

2. If the government's share of GDP in spending shrinks over the next generation, what in your view is likely to happen to the size of the business cycle?

3. How, in your view, will increased ease of international trade and increased international capital mobility change the workings of the macroeconomy over the next generation?

4. What steps would you take to try to reduce European unemployment, and how might those steps backfire?

5. What steps would you have taken to end Japan's current depression, and how might those steps have backfired?

17

The Future of
Macroeconomics

QUESTIONS

What might the future of macroeconomics bring? How might the macroeconomics taught two decades from now differ from what is taught today?

What have been the principal changes in the way macroeconomics is taught over the past quarter century?

What changes had taken place in the 20 years previous to that?

What direction will macroeconomics take if the real-business-cycle research program proves more successful? If the new Keynesian research program proves more successful?

How will economists in the future understand the foundations behind the power of monetary policy?

The past 16 chapters of this book have given a historically informed, long-run, growth-stressing, largely new-Keynesian view of macroeconomics. But that is not all of macroeconomics — there are other currents of thought and other live research programs. What is the past, and what might be the future of macroeconomics? This chapter takes a look back at the history of macroeconomics, and then looks forward and sketches a few outlines of what the future of macroeconomics might be.

If one thing is certain, it is that we will know different (and, we hope, know more about) macroeconomics in a decade than we do today. What will be taught in macroeconomics courses in 20 years will not be the same as what is taught today.

17.1 THE PAST OF MACROECONOMICS

The Age of John Maynard Keynes

Macroeconomics as a discipline is to a remarkable extent the creation of John Maynard Keynes. His 1936 book *The General Theory of Employment, Interest, and Money* shifted economic research and macroeconomic thought into new and different directions that have led us where we are today. The *General Theory's* extraordinary impact was in large part a result of the then-ongoing Great Depression. Other and previous approaches to understanding business cycles had little useful to say about it. Keynes had a lot to say.

Keynes's book emphasized (1) the role of expectations of future profits in determining investment, (2) the volatility of expectations of future profits, (3) the power of the government to affect the economy through fiscal and monetary policy, and (4) the multiplier process, which amplified the effects of both private-sector shocks and public-sector policies on aggregate demand. It swept the intellectual field and shaped modern macroeconomics.

By a decade or so after World War II much of the analytical apparatus used in this textbook was already in place. The IS-LM model was developed by economists John Hicks and Alvin Hansen. Other economists developed the approaches used in this textbook to understanding consumption (Milton Friedman and Franco Modigliani), investment (Dale Jorgenson, James Tobin, and many others), and the relationship between interest rates and the money supply (James Tobin once again, along with many others). The difference between the behavior of the macroeconomy in the flexible-price long run and the fixed-price short run was clarified by many economists (here Franco Modigliani was again a major contributor). The Solow growth model that is the workhorse of Chapters 4 and 5 was developed by — no surprise — Robert Solow.

This is not to say that the bulk of this textbook stands as it would have been written back in 1960. Macroeconomics textbooks in 1960 had next to no discussion of the relationship between production and inflation. They had little discussion of expectations. The short run was seen as lasting for decades, and analysis of the long-run flexible-price model was rarely included in undergraduate courses. Textbooks in 1960 also downplayed monetary policy and emphasized fiscal policy: Investment was seen as responding little to changes in interest rates, and estimates of the multiplier were much higher than we believe today to be correct for now or for then.

The Age of Milton Friedman and Robert Lucas

Between 1960 and 1980 a good deal of the rest of the meat of this textbook was added to macroeconomic views. Powerful critiques of the then-established conventional wisdom of macroeconomics were made first by Milton Friedman and then by Robert Lucas, both of whom made their intellectual home at the University of Chicago.

Milton Friedman's critique of the then-dominant tradition in macroeconomics had four major parts. The first was that the standard models of the time greatly overestimated the government's ability to manage and control the economy. Great uncertainty, long lags, and variable effects of policy actions placed extremely tight limits on the ability of the government to smooth out recessions and avoid periods of high unemployment. The second was that the standard models greatly overestimated the power of fiscal policy and greatly underestimated the power of monetary policy. The third was that the measurement of the money supply told you most of what you needed to know about how economic policy was working.

The fourth was the idea of the natural rate of unemployment, developed by Friedman and Edward Phelps in the second half of the 1960s. To the extent that macroeconomists in the early 1960s talked about aggregate supply and inflation at all, they tended to follow the lead of economists who took the location of the short-run Phillips curve to be fixed. A given level of unemployment would produce a fixed, unchanging rate of inflation with no feedback of past inflation on expected inflation and no shifts in the natural rate of unemployment. Friedman and Phelps argued that high past inflation would raise expected inflation, and that if unemployment were kept below its natural rate, then the Phillips curve would shift upward over time, generating higher and higher inflation.

The "stagflation" of the 1970s proved Friedman and Phelps to be completely correct on their fourth point. In less than a decade the economics profession shifted to the *"accelerationist" Phillips curve* that we use today. Friedman's first and second points also became part of the received wisdom. Only the claim that the money supply was the sole important variable for understanding macroeconomic policy failed to win broad acceptance.

But Milton Friedman's **"monetarist"** critique was only the first half of the successful revisionist challenge to the doctrines of the post–World War II **Keynesians.** The "rational-expectations" macroeconomists — Robert Lucas, Thomas Sargent, Robert Barro, Finn Kydland, Edward Prescott, and others — argued that Keynesian economics had systematically failed to think through the importance of expectations.

The rational-expectations economists assumed that people were doing the best they could to figure out the structure of the economy in which they lived. Because standard Keynesian models did not pay enough attention to expectations, the models failed to recognize that systematic changes in economic policy would change the parameters of the consumption and investment functions as well as the location of the Phillips curve. Thus macroeconomic models that took estimated consumption functions, investment functions, and Phillips curves as building blocks would blow up in the face of policy makers.

Once again the critique was incorporated into the mainstream quite rapidly. As MIT economist Olivier Blanchard puts it, the "idea that rational expectations was the right working assumption gained wide acceptance . . . not . . . because all macroeconomists believe that people, firms, and participants . . . always form

monetarism

The theory, very popular in the 1970s and the early 1980s, that fluctuations in interest rates had little impact on money demand, so that stabilizing national product and employment could be carried out in a smooth and straightforward fashion by stabilizing the rate of growth of the money stock.

Keynesianism

The school of thought, developed from the ideas of John Maynard Keynes, that emphasizes (1) the role of expectations of future profits in determining investment; (2) the volatility of expectations of future profits; (3) the power of the government to affect the economy through fiscal and monetary policy; and (4) the multiplier process, which amplifies the effects of both private-sector shocks and public-sector policies on aggregate demand.

expectations rationally . . . [but because] rational expectations appears to be a natural benchmark, at least until economists have made progress . . . understanding . . . actual expectations." By the mid-1980s the intellectual structure of the version of modern macroeconomics presented in this book was largely complete.

And since? The late 1980s and 1990s were a time of idea generation and exploration, as macroeconomists explored and tested a large number of different ideas and models. It was an age in which the set of possible approaches expanded, but in which the mainstream policy-analytic position of macroeconomists did not shift much. If the past is any guide, such a period of exploration and experimentation will eventually be followed by another period of successful critique, during which the mainstream of macroeconomics will once again change substantially and rapidly as it did in the 1970s and early 1980s.

What might the future of macroeconomics bring?

> **RECAP   THE PAST OF MACROECONOMICS**
>
> John Maynard Keynes's 1936 book *The General Theory of Employment, Interest, and Money* swept the intellectual field, shaped modern macroeconomics, and set the groundwork on which the analytical apparatus used in this textbook was built. Milton Friedman's critique in the 1960s established that the then-standard models greatly overestimated the government's ability to manage and control the economy. Friedman's critique was reinforced by a further critique led by Robert Lucas that established that Keynesian economists had failed to think through the importance of expectations. Since the Lucas critique a lot of ideas have been generated and explored in macroeconomics, but the views held on economic policy issues today are as they were shaped by Keynes, Friedman, and Lucas.

17.2 THE FUTURE OF MACROECONOMICS: "REAL" BUSINESS CYCLES

One Possible Road

real business cycles

A boom generated when rapid technological innovation opens up new industries and new possibilities for investment. An adverse supply shock can generate a real-business-cycle recession.

One place where the future of macroeconomics might lie is in the theory of **"real" business cycles.** The fundamental premise of this line of thinking is that all the other macroeconomists took a wrong turn a long time ago. It is more than half a century since economists turned away from this line of analysis — the brainchild of Austrian economist Joseph Schumpeter — and toward that of the monetarists and Keynesians. One possibility is that this was, in the long run, a mistake.

John Maynard Keynes, Irving Fisher, Milton Friedman, Paul Samuelson, and all of the economists working in both Keynesian and monetarist traditions believe that there are two key elements to understanding business cycles. First, you need to understand the determinants of nominal aggregate demand. Second, you need to understand the division of changes in nominal aggregate demand into changes in production (and employment) on the one hand and changes in prices (inflation or deflation) on the other. Thus Keynesians and monetarists think about the velocity of money, the determinants of investment spending, the multiplier, crowding out, the natural rate of unemployment, the rate of expected inflation, the Phillips curve, and other related topics.

To real-business-cycle economists in the Schumpeterian tradition like Edward Prescott, most of this is a waste of time. There are changes in nominal aggregate demand, but their impact falls mostly on prices and only a little on output and employment. To understand the roots of real fluctuations — fluctuations in the real economy — you need to follow a different road.

The theory of real business cycles begins with the fundamental assumption that the same theory that determines what happens in the long run — the theory of economic growth — should also be applied to explain fluctuations in production and employment in the short run. It is not that real-business-cycle theorists assume that prices are never rigid, or that markets always clear, or that every price paid for every good balances supply and demand at that moment. Instead, real-business-cycle theorists assume that the price rigidities and patterns of sluggish adjustment that Keynesians and monetarists see are simply not very relevant. They assume that a reasonable first approximation is to suppose that the money supply and the level of potential output determine the price level, and that the level of potential output at any moment is more or less equal to actual real GDP. They believe strongly in the classical dichotomy: Real fundamentals effectively determine the values of real quantities like GDP even in the short run, and nominal variables (like the money stock) determine the values of nominal quantities (like the price level).

The Unevenness of Economic Growth

Some years there are adverse cost shocks — the tripling of world oil prices in 1973, for example. In such years it makes no sense to produce at what had been the normal level of economic output. The normal level balances social benefits and social costs: When social costs increase, the last 1 percent of output produced is certainly no longer worth the resources in people's time, used-up capital, depleted natural resources, and so on, that it consumes. So when an adverse cost shock hits the economy, a recession ought to follow and people ought to spend less time working: That's what an efficient economy would look like. Conversely, when a favorable cost shock hits the economy, it is advantageous to produce as much as possible: Because goods and services can then be produced at low cost, workers should work extra shifts and heavy demands should be placed on other resources.

But these are not the only "real" shocks to the economy's production possibilities that happen. Entrepreneurs have to guess at the future of technological development and the value of new investment. At moments when rapid technological innovation opens up new industries and new possibilities for investment, the stock market will be high and the returns to investment large; thus investment spending will be high and an efficient economy will be in a boom even though the new technologies have not yet increased real output. Current productivity is not especially high. But putting much new capital in place is uniquely profitable.

At other moments entrepreneurs will realize that they and those who came before them have been overly optimistic. Branches of industry that have been built up turn out to be unpromising. The socially optimal thing to do is not to invest, but instead to retrench: to cut back on investment spending and scrap capital until emerging opportunities for profitable large-scale investment become clear. Most of the work on real-business-cycle theory has concentrated on the effect of cost — supply — and productivity shocks on output. But shocks to future technologies are just as "real" in that they involve changes in the economy's long-run production possibilities. And they are large: Just look at the technology section of your newspaper, or visit Silicon Valley.

Supply Shocks (Oil Prices, for Example)

In some episodes, real-business-cycle theory is clearly right. The Keynesian tradition assumes that business cycles are produced by *demand* shocks that have no effect on potential output. But some short-run shocks to the economy have had powerful effects on potential output by reducing — or increasing — aggregate *supply*. Supply shocks like the 1973 tripling of world oil prices reduce potential output. Inventions and innovations can be positive productivity shocks that increase the level of potential output.

In 1973, as a side effect of that year's Arab–Israeli war, the world price of oil tripled. The Organization of Petroleum Exporting Countries exerted its market power to restrict the worldwide supply of oil and raise the price. Capital- and energy-intensive production processes that had made economic sense and been profitable with oil costing less than $3 a barrel became unproductive and unprofitable with oil costing $10 a barrel. Thus potential output fell because it was now more profitable to use technologies that economized on oil by intensively using other factors of production such as labor. The efficiency of labor E in the production function fell.

Such an adverse supply shock lowers the level of potential output and current GDP, raises inflation, and is also likely to generate an increase in the domestic real interest rate. Why? Because a fall in GDP due to an oil price increase or some other adverse supply shock reduces income and so reduces the flow of private saving into financial markets. The supply shock of 1973 was the most powerful disturbance to the American economy in the 1970s.

Analyzing Real Business Cycles

It is easy to see how uneven invention and innovation patterns might be a powerful source of large real business cycles — business cycles driven by the fundamental technological dynamic of the economy. Suppose that the most common shifts in technology involve (1) a sudden step up in the efficiency of labor, accompanied by (2) a sudden rise in investment demand as it becomes more profitable for a business to enlarge its capital stock. Such a shock has a supply component — an increase in this year's potential output — and an investment demand component — an increase in this year's investment demand. How does the economy's full-employment equilibrium shift in response to such a combined shock? We add together the effects of a positive supply shock — the reverse of the oil price decline — and the effects of an investment boom driven by investors' increasing optimism.

In the flexible-price model we built in Chapter 7, the increased profitability of investment expands investment demand, shifting the investment demand curve to the right. But the positive technology shock does more than just make investment more profitable: It boosts the current efficiency of labor as well. Higher productivity means higher income, which means more saving, which shifts the total saving line to the right as well. The increase in investment demand tends to raise the interest rate; the increase in saving caused by higher income tends to lower it.

Which dominates? Suppose that the investment demand condition dominates. Then this positive-technology shock to both the efficiency of labor and the profitability of investment has produced

- A rise in output.
- A sharp rise in investment.
- A decline in the exchange rate: a decrease in the value of foreign currency and an increase in the value of domestic currency.
- A decrease in net exports and an increase in foreign saving: an increase in the flow of foreign capital into the country to finance domestic investment.

These shifts in the economy are typically found in a business-cycle boom. Perhaps these Schumpeterian forces are the principal cause of the booms and recessions that we see in our economy.

Is this theory of real business cycles a promising theory of short-run economic fluctuations? Economists disagree. Perhaps fewer economists think that real-business-cycle theory is a progressive research program this year than thought so a decade ago, but that could change — and probably has, with the award of the 2004 Economics Nobel Prize to Finn Kydland and Edward Prescott for their work on real-business-cycle theory.

Whether you think that real-business-cycle theory is promising depends on answers to three questions:

- Should the fact that a reduction in work hours shows up as some people becoming wholly unemployed change one's interpretation of what causes a decline in total hours worked?
- Should the fact that many wages and prices are not flexible lead one to assign a prominent role to monetary factors as causes of real fluctuations in output and employment?
- How large are technology shocks to the economy, anyway?

Problems of Real-Business-Cycle Theory

Unemployment

Real-business-cycle theory assumes that the total number of hours worked at any moment is largely determined by how many hours it makes sense for people to work. The supply of hours worked is set at the point where the marginal displeasure of working an extra hour is just about equal to the marginal social product of an extra hour's work, given the marginal value of extra goods for consumption or for investment purposes.

When the marginal social product of labor is high — when labor is more than usually productive or when an increase in work hours, and thus of total product, can take advantage of extremely valuable opportunities to invest — workers are willing to work more hours. When labor is relatively unproductive, or when highly valuable investment opportunities are scarce, it makes sense for total work hours to fall. Instead of spending extra time on the job producing output of relatively little marginal value, take a week or two off and go on an extra vacation, or spend some extra time with the kids.

Such a willingness to work more hours when the incentive to work is relatively high and fewer hours when the incentive to work is relatively low is called an intertemporal substitution of labor. As an example, consider a student who needs to (1) take classes and (2) earn money to save toward some goal. Taking classes and earning money at the same time is hard, so the choice is between either working in the summer and taking classes in the winter or working in the winter and taking classes in the summer. If the student works in the summer and gets paid at the end of the summer, then at the end of the winter the student will have $W_S(1 + r/2)$ dollars — the sum of his or her summer wage and the interest for half a year that he or she would earn by banking that money until it is needed at the end of the winter. If the student works in the winter, then at the end of the winter the student would have W_W dollars.

The real relative wage between the summer and the winter is thus equal to

$$\frac{W_S(1 + r/2)}{W_W}$$

The higher this quantity, the more likely the student is to choose summer rather than winter work. Thus the incentive to work hard now — accept lots of overtime, say — depends on three things: the wage now, the wage expected in the future, and the real interest rate. Increases in the first and the third tend to lead people to postpone recreation and other nonwork uses of time to the future. Increases in the second tend to lead people to cut back on work effort now. If people are highly willing to shift their hours of work from season to season or from year to year, then one would expect fluctuations in current productivity and technological opportunities to lead to substantial fluctuations in employment.

But critics of real-business-cycle theory think that analyzing the total amount of hours worked in the economy as if it were like the decisions of a representative worker makes little sense. They point out that people change their weekly work hours by relatively little. People in the labor force want to work. Total work hours fall not because people have chosen to work shorter shifts and avoid overtime, but because people have lost their jobs. The unemployment rate fluctuates substantially over the business cycle. And high unemployment in a recession is not a market-clearing phenomenon: People don't say they are "taking an extra vacation" or "out of the labor force because wages will be higher next year"; people say they are "unemployed."

Advocates of real-business-cycle theory say that this critique misses the point. People stay unemployed because they would rather spend more time searching for a better job that matches their skills and pays more than the job they could get today. And the job they could get today pays relatively little either because labor productivity is not high or because there are no extremely valuable uses in investment or consumption for the good produced by an extra amount of work.

Technology and Real Business Cycles

According to real-business-cycle theories, production fluctuates because of the changing value of output and the changing productivity of the economy. When production technology improves, more is produced. When unique opportunities for investment open, more is produced. Perhaps recessions are times in which increases in costs — the tripling of oil prices in 1973, say — make it socially inefficient to run factories near capacity. Perhaps recessions are times in which everyone recognizes that too much has been invested, and that it is better to cut back on investment than to continue to build up capital that adds little to the economy's productive capacity.

The part of the theory that explains booms — rapid rises in output — as the result of the rapid diffusion of technology and a sharp increase in the efficiency of labor is highly plausible. But how can it describe recessions or depressions, during which production does not grow at all but declines? Does the efficiency of labor decline because of technological regress? Are we supposed to believe that production was lower in 1991 than in 1990 because businesses had forgotten how to use their most productive modes of operation? This seems unlikely. Thus the Schumpeterian approach may well provide a correct theory of booms — or at least some booms. But how this approach could provide an accurate account of recessions and depressions or of the high levels of cyclical unemployment found in times of recession and depression is difficult to see.

Critics of real-business-cycle theory concentrate their fire on the claim that the economy experiences large negative shocks to productivity. They claim that increases in costs like the 1973 oil shock are the exception rather than the rule. Critics tend to be silent on whether downturns in investment are to be understood as rational reactions to news about future growth and productivity, and have little to offer as alternative explanations of why investment fluctuates so much.

Money and Real Business Cycles

Real-business-cycle theorists tend to argue that monetary policy has little impact on production and employment, and that fluctuations in the money stock and interest rates are mostly reactions to changes already taking place in output and employment. But the Federal Reserve certainly believes that it makes decisions about the level of interest rates, that it affects the level of the money supply, and that its decisions cause changes in the level of production and output. Either everyone in the Federal Reserve's conference room is hopelessly deluded (and what they think are their decisions are instead the result of fluctuations in real activity that they do not consciously know about at the time they make their votes) or monetary policy has a powerful impact on production and employment.

Assessment

If we thought this line of research is truly the future of macroeconomics, we would have written a different book. Nevertheless these theorists make important points, especially those in what could be termed the Schumpeterian wing of the real-business-cycle tradition. Economic growth is *not* smooth. It *does* proceed sector by sector. Shifts in investment — big backward-and-forward moves in the position of the IS curve — do arise out of changing beliefs about the current productivity of the economy and the future value of new investment.

The existence of real-business-cycle theory is a call for all economists to spend more time thinking about the determinants of investment fluctuations: either tying them to changes in productivity and the value of investment or developing useful social-psychological theories of the shifts in animal spirits that cause such large movements in investment over time. Our guess is that a lot of what is now called real-business-cycle analysis will be incorporated into mainstream macroeconomics over the next two decades as the theory of growth is integrated with the theory of business cycles and as economists make progress in understanding why investment is so volatile.

> **RECAP** **THE FUTURE OF MACROECONOMICS:**
> **"REAL" BUSINESS CYCLES**
>
> Real-business-cycle theorists see booms as generated when rapid technological innovation opens up new industries and new possibilities for investment. At such moments the stock market will be high and the returns to investment large, so investment spending will be high. Real-business-cycle theorists see recessions as generated when entrepreneurs conclude that those who came before them have been overly optimistic. The socially optimal thing to do is not to invest, but instead to retrench: to cut back on investment spending and scrap capital until it becomes clear where there will be opportunities for profitable large-scale investment.

17.3 THE FUTURE OF MACROECONOMICS: NEW KEYNESIAN ECONOMICS

The second possible future for macroeconomics sees the continued development of the mainstream research program, as its weaknesses and incoherencies are slowly repaired.

Certainly the area of modern macroeconomics that is in least satisfactory shape is the area of aggregate supply. Why do changes in nominal aggregate demand show up as changes in the level of production and employment, and not just as changes in the level of prices? Since at least the 1930s, the mainstream of macroeconomics has attributed the sluggishness of aggregate supply — the fact that the Phillips curve has a slope, and is not vertical — to stickiness in wages and prices. Thus fluctuations in the nominal level of aggregate demand cause fluctuations in output and employment. But where does this stickiness and slow adjustment of wages and prices come from? After all, business cycles appear to be so unpleasant and costly to society as a whole that by now we should have found a way to greatly reduce the harmful macroeconomic consequences of **price stickiness**.

Thus a possible future direction for macroeconomics is a deep investigation into the sources of sluggish wage and price adjustment and of aggregate supply. This research program has gained the name new Keynesian economics.

price stickiness

A condition that exists when wages and prices do not move smoothly and immediately to keep supply equal to demand in the labor and goods markets.

Menu Costs

Prices do not adjust immediately and completely in the short run because changing them is costly. A restaurant must print up a new menu; a mail-order firm must send out a new catalog. Economists call these costs of changing prices **menu costs**. They are what lead firms to adjust prices once in a while — not, with a few exceptions, every second. In most cases such menu costs are small: The cost a firm incurs to change its prices is not much. But "small" does not mean "unimportant." As macroeconomists George Akerlof, Janet Yellen, and Greg Mankiw have stressed, small menu costs at the level of an individual firm, in theory at least, can have large effects on the economy as a whole.

A price adjustment or a failure to adjust prices on the part of one firm affects other firms. Whenever one particular business lowers its price, it frees up a little bit of nominal purchasing power. The extra nominal purchasing power that would

menu costs

The costs to a firm of changing the price(s) of a good(s) or service(s).

have been spent buying that particular firm's product (but that wasn't spent because the price was lowered) is instead free to be spent on products made by other firms. As long as total nominal spending remains constant, a decline in one firm's price slightly increases demand for other firms' products. New Keynesian economists call this phenomenon an aggregate demand externality.

Because of such aggregate demand externalities, as long as total nominal demand is fixed, the economy as a whole benefits more by one firm's reduction in price than that one firm does. But the firm decides whether to cut its price depending on whether the benefit to the firm from cutting its price exceeds the menu costs the firm must pay. Thus the economy can get stuck in a situation in which no firm reduces its price—because no firm can see a private benefit in excess of its menu cost—even though the economy as a whole would benefit by vastly more than the sum of menu costs if all businesses were to reduce their prices.

Staggered Prices and Coordination Failures

Even if menu costs are not important, the fact that one firm's best choice for its price depends on the prices that other firms are charging may lead to sluggish adjustment in wages and prices even though individual prices are theoretically free to move without hindrance.

Macroeconomist John Taylor was the first to consider an economy in which large groups of workers sign multiyear labor contracts. Those who negotiate their wages in years divisible by three will look forward at what demand and supply on the labor market is likely to be, but they will also look sideways, at firms that negotiated their labor contracts one or two years ago. Thus the wage negotiated this year will depend not just on what will happen but on what people one or two years ago—when the last set of contracts were signed—thought was likely to happen. The aggregate wage and price levels will thus exhibit inertia even without barriers to price flexibility when renegotiations occur, just because of the institutional structure of the economy.

Are such **coordination failures** caused by the fact that agents in the economy do not all make long-run decisions at the same time or are unable to commit to deciding in similar ways important causes of business cycles? Two decades ago economists thought that the answer was almost surely yes. Many studies were written comparing the U.S. system of wage negotiation with other, more centralized systems found in Germany and Japan that seemed less likely to lead to coordination failures.

Today, because of the relatively good macroeconomic performance of the U.S. economy, theories that point out structural flaws in U.S. macroeconomic institutions receive little attention. The theoretical point, however, remains unsettled.

coordination failures

Failures of firms to change prices to respond quickly to the marketplace or in concert with other firms.

Assessment

At the moment these ideas about the microfoundations of price stickiness are at the stage of just-so stories: plausible and possible mechanisms, but only that. There are no convincing quantitative analyses of just how much sluggishness in wage and price adjustment is contributed by each possible cause. There are no tests of one theory against another, and no predictions of the magnitude of price inertia that should emerge from any of the possible theoretical causes. In this sense, the theory of aggregate supply today is in a position roughly analogous to the position of the theory of aggregate demand just before John Maynard Keynes.

We have no doubt that the mechanisms of business cycles should be a large part of the future of macroeconomics. We should be able to learn a lot about which models of business cycles are potentially useful by turning theories loose on perhaps the greatest macroeconomic laboratory available: the extant record of macroeconomic historical statistics. A robust and useful theory of business cycles should be able to account for the patterns seen in the long-run data for many countries.

The historical evidence suggests that business-cycle models that do not put monetary economics at the center of their analysis are inconsistent with the evidence on the behavior of real interest rates. Events like the comparative pattern of national recoveries from the Great Depression cannot be understood without placing prices that are sticky at the center of the analysis as well. Thus we think that the new Keynesian research program is likely to play a stronger role in the future of macroeconomics than the real-business-cycle research program. But then again, we could be wrong.

> **RECAP**   **THE FUTURE OF MACROECONOMICS: NEW KEYNESIAN ECONOMICS**
>
> Why do changes in nominal aggregate demand show up as changes in the level of production and employment, and not just as changes in the level of prices? The mainstream of macroeconomics has attributed this to stickiness in wages and prices. But where does this stickiness come from? One possibility is that small costs of changing prices on the part of individual firms have large effects because a price adjustment or a failure to adjust prices on the part of one firm affects other firms through aggregate demand externalities. Another possibility is that prices and wages are sticky because agents in the economy do not all make long-run decisions at the same time.

17.4 DEBTS AND DEFICITS, CONSUMPTION AND SAVING

Debts and Deficits: Ricardian Equivalence

Chapter 14 detailed economists' standard view of debts and deficits. Fiscal deficits stimulate the economy in the short run as long as the central bank does not take action to neutralize the fiscal stimulus. In the long run, however, debts and deficits crowd out investment and shift the economy to a less favorable steady-state growth path.

But this standard view has been subject to a powerful challenge that may become an important part of the future of economics. Whether it is successful or not, this challenge is likely to change the way we think about how the government's budget affects the economy. This alternative view of the long-run (and also the short-run) effects of debts and deficits is called "**Ricardian equivalence**," after David Ricardo, who does not seem to have held the view; it should be called "Barrovian equivalence," after its most effective and powerful advocate, Harvard macroeconomist Robert Barro.

Ricardian equivalence

The hypothesis that households will cut consumption whenever they see a government deficit, anticipating higher future taxes that will be raised to pay off that deficit.

Robert Barro's View

Think of it this way: The government is, in a sense, our agent. It buys things for us (government purchases) and it collects money from us to pay for the things it buys on our behalf. The moneys it collects from us are called taxes. Sometimes the government collects as much from us as it buys on our behalf: Then the government budget is balanced. Sometimes the government collects less from us than it spends on our behalf: Then the government budget is in deficit, and the government makes up the deficit by borrowing money now and implicitly committing to raise taxes to repay the debt (interest and principal) at some time in the future.

Suppose that the government spends an extra $1,000 on your behalf and at the same time raises your taxes by $1,000. Because your after-tax income has gone down by $1,000, you cut back on consumption spending. Now suppose that the government spends an extra $1,000 on your behalf, but doesn't raise taxes—instead it borrows the $1,000 for one year, and announces that it is going to raise taxes next year to repay the debt.

What is the difference between these two situations? In one case, the government has collected an extra $1,000 in taxes from you this year. In the other case, the government has announced that it will collect an extra $1,000 in taxes from you next year. In either case you are poorer. In the first case you cut back on your consumption. Shouldn't you cut back on your consumption in the second case too—set aside a reserve to pay the extra taxes next year, and invest it, perhaps in the bonds that the government has issued? After all, the effect of the government policy on your personal private wealth is identical in the two cases.

Robert Barro would say yes. He would say that what matters for the determination of consumption spending is not what taxes are levied on you this year, but what all of the changes in government policy tell you about the value of the total stream of taxes this year, next year, and on into the future. Government policy thus ought to affect consumption only to the extent that it tells you how much the government is going to spend—and thus what will be the total lifetime tax bill levied on your wealth.

Counterarguments

Many economists point out that the theoretical elegance of Barro's view is broken by a number of different considerations, including the following:

- **Myopia.** Perhaps people are not far-sighted enough to fully work out what an increased deficit in the present implies for their future taxes.

- **Liquidity constraints.** Barro's argument implicitly assumes that people can borrow and lend readily. If a good many people can't borrow and lend—they would spend more if only they could borrow on reasonable terms—then you would expect consumers to react to tax cuts by increasing consumption spending even if they knew full well that the government was going to recapture those tax cuts with tax increases later.

- *Beneficiaries and payers differ.* I am the beneficiary from increased spending this year, but the extra taxes that the government will exact two decades hence may well not be paid by me but by someone who isn't even in the labor force today.

But are any of these—or all of them together—really enough to make us confident that changes in the timing of taxes (holding government spending patterns constant) will have a big effect on overall consumption? Even if Barro's challenge

myopia

Short-sightedness. A failure to look far enough ahead into the future.

liquidity constraints

An inability to borrow.

to the conventional wisdom is unsuccessful, it will become clear that his challenge is unsuccessful only when we have a much better understanding of how and why people divide their income between consumption and saving.

Consumption and Saving

In the early part of the twentieth century, justifying a relatively high marginal propensity to consume was relatively easy. Most households had little if any savings. Most households found themselves unable to borrow. Hence they were liquidity-constrained: They wished to spend more today, but they could not find anyone to lend them the liquid wealth to enable them to do so. Thus one would expect a boost to income to generate a large rise in consumption spending. Add to this the fact that buying consumer durables is in a sense as valid a way of saving for the future as putting money in the bank; then a high marginal propensity to consume and a strong multiplier process seem easy to understand.

The past 50 years, however, have seen steady and large increases in the flexibility of the financial system. Few Americans today are without the ability to borrow to increase current consumption should they so wish. Those Americans whose liquidity is constrained today receive a very small portion of total income, and a small portion of increases in total income. Thus economists' theories would predict that in the aggregate the marginal propensity to consume would have dropped far by today, and that the multiplier process would be more or less irrelevant to aggregate demand. Nevertheless, consumption still declines significantly when the economy goes into recession.

This consumption puzzle is another substantial hole in today's current macroeconomic knowledge. Many economists are trying to close it. Some, like Johns Hopkins macroeconomist Chris Carroll, argue that typical consumers are both impatient and prudent. Prudence makes them unwilling to borrow. Impatience makes them eager to spend increases in income. Thus the fact that improvements in financial flexibility mean that consumers *could* borrow doesn't mean that they *will*. Other economists focus on the persistence of income changes and say that current income is a good proxy for permanent income and hence should be a strong determinant of consumption. Still others — led by Chicago economist Richard Thaler — argue that the time has come for economists to throw the simpleminded psychological theory of utility maximization overboard and to take seriously what psychologists have to say about how humans reason.

How this hole in macroeconomists' understanding of consumption and saving will be resolved is unclear. But the resolution will clearly have a powerful impact on the debate over debts and deficits.

17.5 DOES MONETARY POLICY HAVE A LONG-RUN FUTURE?

When the Federal Reserve uses open-market operations to affect interest rates, it does so because its purchases or sales of Treasury bills raise or lower the supply of bank reserves in the economy, and so make it easier or harder for businesses to borrow money. But total commercial bank reserves in the United States amount to less than 0.5 percent of GDP. A typical open-market operation is a few billion dollars.

In the context of an economy in which annual GDP is more than $11 trillion and in which total wealth is something like $40 trillion, how is it that a swap of one government promise to pay (a Treasury bill) for another (a dollar bill) can cause big changes in the cost of borrowing money, and ultimately in the level and composition of economic activity? This question has not been asked often enough in the past hundred years. Economists have tended to assume that monetary policy is powerful and that the reasons for its power are relatively uninteresting. They have by and large ignored the fact that to shift from an extremely tight monetary policy in which long-run nominal GDP growth is zero to a loose one in which long-run nominal GDP growth is 10 percent per year requires that the Federal Reserve increase purchases of Treasury bills by an average of only some $20 million a day.

Monetary policy is certainly powerful. But in at least one of the potential futures of macroeconomics the reasons for its power become very interesting indeed. For it is at least possible that the future evolution of the financial system might undermine the sources of influence that monetary policy today possesses.

The reasons that monetary policy has power today that economists usually bring forward rest on what Harvard macroeconomist Benjamin Friedman calls — politely — "a series of . . . familiar fictions: Households and firms need currency to purchase goods . . . nonbank financial institutions [cannot] create credit . . . [and] so on."

The standard explanation is that open-market purchases of Treasury bills increase the reserve balances held by the banks where the sellers of the Treasury bills receive payment. Thus the total volume of reserves in the banking system as a whole rises, and the banking system responds to this increase in reserves by increasing total credit in the economy by more than 10 times the reserve increase. Because commercial banks must hold reserves, and because only the Federal Reserve can change the total amount of reserves, it has a uniquely strong ability to affect interest rates. In the standard story the central bank's power is further boosted because everyone in financial markets takes its actions today as a powerful signal of what its actions will be in the entire future.

This Federal Reserve power, however, would be of little use if nobody much cared about keeping deposits at commercial banks, and nobody used reserve-backed commercial *bank deposits* as transactions balances. Looking to the future, it's likely that more and more transactions will be carried out not through cash or check but through credit cards, debit cards, smart cash cards now used in Europe, or other forms of electronic funds transfer at points of sale.

Will the future hold a gradual weakening of central bank power? Macroeconomists know that central banks today are powerful and are likely to remain so for at least a generation. But forecasting beyond that point requires a deeper knowledge and better models of the sources of central bank power than macroeconomists currently possess. This is thus another area in which the macroeconomics taught in the future is likely to be substantially different from the macroeconomics taught in the past.

Chapter Summary

1. Modern macroeconomics has its origin in the Keynesian theories of the Great Depression and the immediate post–World War II era.

2. Modern macroeconomics was reforged by the monetarists under Milton Friedman in the 1960s and 1970s and by the rational-expectations economists led by Robert Lucas in the 1970s and 1980s.

3. Perhaps the focus on aggregate demand will turn out in the long run to have been a false road. Perhaps a better theory of the macroeconomy can be built up out of the theory of real business cycles in the Schumpeterian tradition.

4. Perhaps the future of macroeconomics lies in a more detailed investigation of aggregate supply. Perhaps uncovering the reasons that prices are sticky will lead to the next wave of progress in macroeconomics.

5. The entire conventional analysis of debts and deficits is under challenge by Robert Barro, who argues that individuals are far-sighted and closely linked, and that they take action to neutralize the effects of many government policies.

6. The conventional analysis of consumption — the permanent income hypothesis — is also under challenge by more psychological approaches to understanding consumption.

7. The other possible interesting direction in which macroeconomics might evolve relates to the future of monetary policy. How will the coming of the "new economy" and the changing institutional framework of transactions and settlements affect the power of monetary policy?

Key Terms

monetarism (p. 495)

Keynesianism (p. 495)

real business cycles (p. 496)

price stickiness (p. 502)

menu costs (p. 502)

coordination failures (p. 503)

Ricardian equivalence (p. 504)

myopia (p. 505)

liquidity constraints (p. 505)

Analytical Exercises

1. What are the principal pieces of real-business-cycle theory?

2. Why is it possible that real-business-cycle theory will play a much larger role in macroeconomics courses in the future than in the present?

3. In what areas do new Keynesian economists concentrate their research?

4. What is Ricardian equivalence? Why might it not be a good approximation to the way individuals actually behave?

5. Why do some economists fear that monetary policy is going to lose its effectiveness?

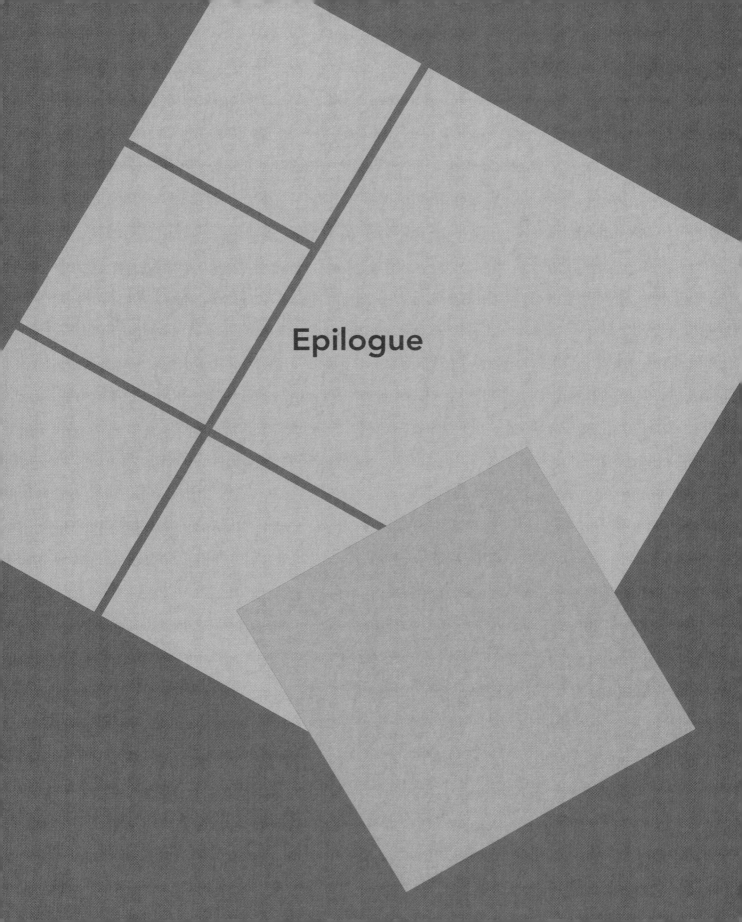

Epilogue

Macroeconomics is not now and never will be "complete." Physicists talk about someday arriving at a "Theory of Everything," after which there will be no more fundamental physics — just materials science and applied physics and physical chemistry and chemistry and biochemistry and biology. Nothing like that will ever happen to macroeconomics. Macroeconomics will not become "complete" in our lifetime. It will not become "complete" in your lifetime.

There are several reasons for this. The first is that the subject is complicated. The economy is complicated. The fact that markets do not work perfectly, and that market imperfections are macroeconomically important, makes it complicated. The unique role of expectations — and the fact that the (expected) future can influence and "cause" the past — makes it complicated.

A second reason that macroeconomics will never be complete is that macro-economists are pursuing an ever-changing and ever-moving target: As the economy changes, its macroeconomic behavior changes as well. Four centuries ago (if there had been a macroeconomics course then) the macroeconomics of harvest failures would have been a big topic. Today it isn't. Back when John Maynard Keynes wrote, unions were of first-order importance in understanding the macroeconomy. Today that is no longer the case. In the first few post–World War II decades, foreign trade simply wasn't that important for the U.S. macroeconomy. Now it is.

Many of what we see as important topics today will be dismissed as irrelevant a generation or a century from now. And much of what those societies will need answers to is unimportant to us, or unknown to us.

Here at the end of the book is a very convenient place to quickly look back over the entire text. There are a great many things that macroeconomists do know. And this is the place to summarize them, before going on to discuss what macroeconomists don't know, and what we believe macroeconomists will never know.

WHAT ECONOMISTS KNOW . . .

. . . About the Current State of the Economy

A great deal of what economists know, they know because they can rely on the statistics collected by governments. Thus economists know what is an astonishing amount about the current state of the economy. Economists have good estimates of the scope of economic activity. Economists have good estimates of the level of potential output. Economists have good estimates of the current real wage level, of the amount of unemployment, and of the general state of the labor market. They have good estimates of the rate of inflation.

Economists' knowledge of the long-run pace of economic growth is, however, much more partial and incomplete. As we discussed in Chapter 5, the size and extent of the biases inevitably present in the national income and product accounts remain elusive. Moreover, economists' knowledge of the current state of the economy comes with a substantial lag: Economists know much more about the state of the economy last year than they do about the state of the economy today.

All in all, the NIPA system — and the other largely government-collected economic statistics — gives us a remarkable amount of knowledge. Certainly the amount of easily and publicly available information about the state of the American macro-economy today dwarfs the knowledge that even the best-informed in previous centuries had, or even the knowledge that the leaders presiding over the centrally planned economies of the twentieth century had of the real state of affairs.

. . . About Long-Run Economic Growth

Economists also know a surprising amount about the preconditions for successful long-run growth. We understand demography: Malthus, the population explosion, the demographic revolution, and the importance of education. We know that back before the Industrial Revolution living standards were very low because in the race among human fertility, diminishing returns, and technological development, the third — technological development — lost. We know that once human populations pass a threshold level of material prosperity and literacy, population growth rates slow down drastically — the experience of western Europe suggests that negative population growth may be in humanity's future after the middle of the next century. And we know that once through the demographic transition technological progress and technology transfer make for an economic future that looks very bright indeed, at least judged by the yardstick of the average generation since the invention of agriculture.

Economists understand the importance of a high rate of investment for achieving successful economic growth — both because capital goods amplify our skills and capabilities and because much of modern technology that increases total factor productivity works only if it is accompanied by, embodied in, the right kinds of capital goods. A high rate of investment is key to a rapidly growing and relatively prosperous economy.

Economists also know that better technology — understood in both a broad and a narrow sense — is the single most important key to sustained progress in material standards of living. And here economists have fallen down on the job: Macroeconomists know much less about the development and diffusion of this truly important source of growth, technology, than we should. But it is completely clear that a high rate of investment to generate a high capital-output ratio, a strong commitment to education to create a skilled and literate workforce (and a low rate of population growth), and better technology are the goals of economic policy as far as the long run is concerned.

Economists do know some important things about how to achieve these goals of economic policy: The role of the government in economic development has become increasingly clear over the past generation. Clearly, achieving successful long-run growth by relying on the market system to coordinate economic activity is much easier than relying on central planning and central commands. Market economies appear to function well only if they are coupled with strong legal and institutional protections for private property. Overly mighty governments — governments that regard other people's things as the government's property — appear to be very bad for economic growth.

Clearly, too, government policy needs to provide the market economy with the right incentives and signals if it is to function: Activities with negative externalities like pollution need to be penalized; activities with positive externalities like research and development need to be encouraged. Thus a government that protects property rights, promotes education, and promotes innovation seems important as a precondition for successful economic growth.

But our knowledge of economic growth is incomplete. The links between different kinds of investment and rates of total factor productivity growth and the mechanisms underlying the transfer of technology from rich countries to poor countries remain elusive.

. . . About Business Cycles, Unemployment, and Inflation in the Long Run

Economists know that market economies are robust things. In the long run — and exceptional circumstances like the Great Depression aside — the market economy does tend to return to a position of nearly full employment. Markets for goods and for labor do — absent large blockages — reach something like a supply-and-demand equilibrium. In a recession it is safe to predict that the next five years will bring a boom. In a gigantic boom it is safe to predict that the next five years will bring a slowdown.

Thus economists know that shifts in government spending will crowd out (or crowd in) consumption and investment. They know that shortfalls of national saving or booms in investment will bring inflows of capital and the trade deficits needed to finance them. They know that the central bank's policy is in the long run the absolutely crucial determinant of the price level and the inflation rate.

. . . About Business Cycles, Unemployment, and Inflation in the Short Run

Economists know that the basic Keynesian sticky-price model still provides a good guide to the basic determinants of the level of planned expenditure. And the Phillips curve diagram still provides a guide — not necessarily a good guide, but the best one we have — to the relationship between the level of real GDP and the rate of price increase.

Because planned expenditure is the principal determinant of the level of GDP in the short run, anything that affects planned expenditure affects employment and output: fiscal policy, monetary policy, expectations, shocks to components of demand, shocks to the financial markets, changes in the international environment — all of these produce shifts in the equilibrium level of output. And economists have a pretty good grasp of how and why.

Economists know that aggregate demand interacts with aggregate supply — the Phillips curve — to generate the inflation rate. And economists know that the Phillips curve is extremely volatile. The natural rate of unemployment can undergo substantial shifts much more rapidly than the changing composition of the labor force would suggest is possible. The expected rate of inflation depends critically on expectations of the central bank's competence and commitment to price stability.

. . . About the Making of Macroeconomic Policy

Thus governments attempting to stabilize the economy face a hard task of damping out many kinds of shocks. Their task is made harder because shifts in economic policy have uncertain and delayed effects on spending: Policy affects output and prices with long and variable lags. Perhaps the first lesson of stabilization policy is that governments should not overestimate their power and attempt to do too much. The second lesson is that monetary policy is the most useful discretionary stabilization policy tool. And the third lesson is that automatic stabilizers — the fiscal automatic stabilizers in the government's budget and the financial automatic stabilizers of deposit insurance — are important factors that help limit the need for discretionary stabilization policy.

Economists have learned over the past two decades that peacetime inflation at a level high enough that it becomes an important part of voters' consciousness — inflation at a rate of even 10 percent per year — is politically unacceptable in modern industrial democracies. Voters appear to hate and loathe politicians who preside over such episodes of inflation. Why even moderate inflation should be viewed so negatively is somewhat of a mystery: Economists' attempts to model costs of inflation have a difficult time coming up with costs that justify the high political value of low inflation. It may be that people simply dislike the greater uncertainty that inflation generates. It may be that people are simply making a mistake — that they should not dislike inflation as much as they do. But for whatever reason, in any modern democracy, successful control of inflation clearly must be a very high priority for public policy.

At the root, the ultimate determinant of inflation is growth in the money supply. Control the rate of growth of the money supply, and you control inflation. A central bank that loses sight of this goal will find itself unable to control inflation. But that is not all that economists know about controlling inflation. We also know that controlling inflation is easy — can be accomplished at low cost — if and only if investors, managers, and workers have confidence in the central bank's commitment to control inflation. Central bank credibility is the most important asset in order to make control of inflation easy and cheap. Central bank credibility is the most valuable thing a central bank can have — and is the most costly thing to regain once it is lost.

Economists know that in the short run the level of GDP and of employment depends on the level of planned expenditure for goods and services. Thus a good macroeconomic policy that seeks to avoid unnecessary unemployment and inflation must walk a fine line. Planned expenditure must be high enough to eliminate unnecessary unemployment, but not high enough to generate accelerating inflation or (worst of all) to call into question the central bank's commitment to low inflation.

WHAT ECONOMISTS DON'T KNOW — BUT COULD LEARN . . .

. . . About the Long-Run Relationship between Kinds of Investment and Productivity Growth

The list of what macroeconomists don't know is, unfortunately, longer than the list of things they do know. First, large chunks of the process of long-run economic growth remain a mystery. Macroeconomists cannot prescribe to poor countries the policy mix that would enable them to duplicate the rapid convergence of Japan or Italy to industrial-core status that we have seen since World War II. Macroeconomists cannot prescribe to rich countries how to maximize their rates of economic growth and appropriately discounted levels of economic welfare. Macroeconomists do not know what is the right degree of "openness" for the world economy. They do not know at what point we would get the most benefits from international trade and investment flows while suffering the lowest costs from international financial market–generated economic instability.

But in these areas, at least, macroeconomists can learn. The history of the world over the past century provides a lot of lessons about the sources of long-run growth and stagnation. And the future will continue to provide more such lessons. As long as economists are willing to take fresh looks at the world and revise their beliefs in response to new information, macroeconomists in a generation will know much more about long-run growth than we do today.

...About the Short-Run Determinants of Investment

Ultimately the key issue dividing the new Keynesian and the real-business-cycle schools of macroeconomists is the sources of shifts in investment. The most common large-scale macroeconomic shock hitting a modern industrial market economy is, in Keynesian language, an inward (or outward) shift in the IS curve caused by an investment slump (or boom) accompanied by a fall (or a swift rise) in the stock market. The most common large-scale macroeconomic shock hitting a modern industrial market economy is, in real-business-cycle language, an upward (or downward) shift in expected future productivity that would lead a rational and benevolent social planner to increase (or decrease) investment, and a well-functioning market economy mimics the decisions that would be made by a social-welfare-maximizing benevolent social planner.

Which of these descriptions is correct? Are the big shocks to investment that we see better thought of as optimal responses of the market to news about future profits and technological opportunities? If so, then the real-business-cycle research program will be the most fruitful over the next generation. Is this shock more accurately seen as one of the less-than-rational shifts in social-psychological opinion that John Maynard Keynes referred to as "animal spirits"? If so, then the new Keynesian research program is likely to pay the highest dividends over the next generation.

This question of the most important determinants of domestic investment booms is closely tied to the key issues in international finance. Why are international financial markets so vulnerable to financial crises? They have been so over the past century. And what is the appropriate response to constrain governments from engaging in disturbing policies that set the stage for such policies? Is it to reduce the magnitude of cross-border trade and financial flows, or to adopt more aggressive policies to intervene to support countries afflicted by financial crises?

As of the start of 2005, these questions are acquiring extra urgency for the United States, where a financial crisis has gone from being an unthinkable event five years ago to a quite possible event as of the beginning of 2005.

The only true answer is that macroeconomists today do not know. This area will be one of the major political flashpoints of the next generation. It will also be one of the major battlegrounds — and hopefully areas of the progress of knowledge — for macroeconomic theory over the next generation.

...About the Impact of Government Policy on the Economy

A lot is still not known about how and why government policy affects the economy. Macroeconomists still argue about the relative roles played in generating short-run business cycles of "monetary" shocks and "real" shocks. Macroeconomists for the most part feel that eliminating noise in the price system ought to yield powerful benefits. But these gains from achieving low and stable inflation have not hitherto been demonstrated. And why voters seem so averse to inflation when its measured economic costs appear relatively low remains a mystery.

Thus many fundamental questions about government policy remain up for grabs. How aggressively should central bankers pursue stabilization policy? The answer to that question depends on the solutions to the mysteries noted in the paragraph above. How much should we worry about large government deficits? The answer turns on whether or not Ricardian equivalence is roughly correct, and that depends in turn on the determinants and motivations of households' consumption and saving decisions.

. . . About the Microfoundations of Macroeconomics

Thus we come to the final set of things that economists do not know — but might someday find out. Macroeconomists do not understand aggregate consumption and saving decisions in the economy. They do not understand what determines the large shifts in the natural rate of unemployment seen over the past 30 years. Nor do they understand what can be done to constructively lower the natural rate of unemployment, or even what the natural rate of unemployment should be. Clearly it is worthwhile for the average worker who loses a job to spend some time unemployed searching for a new job. But how much?

And last, what are the underlying reasons that wages and prices are slow to respond to shifts in aggregate demand?

These questions about the "microfoundations of macroeconomics" have been at the top of the agenda for economic research at least since the end of World War II. Looking back, we should be somewhat depressed to realize how little progress has been made, and how much the live microfoundational issues of today are those that economists like Franco Modigliani were worrying about immediately after World War II.

WHAT ECONOMISTS WILL NEVER KNOW . . .
. . . Chasing an Ever-Moving Target

The natural sciences are characterized by a strong sense of progress toward a goal: Knowledge advances, and the amount of unknowns left to be understood shrinks. The social sciences are not as able to show progress. More is known, yes. But we are chasing an ever-moving target: One economist's joke is that you can give the same exam every 20 years, as long as you remember that the right answers will change.

Macroeconomics is a science of what might be called emergent phenomena. The marginal propensity to consume, the slope of the IS curve, the velocity of money — these are not basic, unchanging, fundamental quantities that can be measured and described once and for all. They are, instead, summary rule-of-thumb characterizations of phenomena that emerge from the billions of economic decisions made by hundreds of millions of workers, consumers, and firms. Thus we should expect macroeconomic "truth" to change over time as our economy changes.

So if there is a final lesson, it is this: Keep an open mind. Recognize that some of the things taught in this book will turn out to be wrong or incomplete. And recognize that the questions that people want macroeconomics to answer will change in the future as well, both because the economy will change and because macroeconomics is the handmaiden of policy, which is a subbranch of politics. And as politics changes, the questions that policy makers will ask of macroeconomists will change as well.

Glossary

A

accelerating inflation When inflation is rising yearly, so that this year's inflation is greater than last year's inflation, which is greater than inflation in the year before. Not only are prices rising, but they are rising at an increasing proportional rate. Accelerating inflation is typically found when the unemployment rate is lower than the natural rate of unemployment, or when the economy is hit by an adverse supply shock like a sharp oil price increase.

accelerationist Phillips curve Found when inflation expectations are adaptive, that is, the expected rate of inflation that determines the position of the Phillips curve is equal to last year's rate of inflation. Each extra percentage point rise in expectations of inflation shifts the entire Phillips curve upward by 1 percentage point. Thus if unemployment falls and remains below the natural rate, inflation will accelerate.

accommodation A strategy for economic policy in which the central bank does not counteract but reinforces the consequences of a shock. For example, consider an adverse supply shock that boosts inflation. A policy of accommodation would not increase real interest rates to fight inflation, but would instead allow real interest rates to fall and so further boost inflation.

adaptive expectations Expectations of the future formed by assuming the future will be like the past. Usually applied to expectations of inflation: Adaptive inflation expectations forecast future inflation by assuming it will be equal to inflation in the recent past. Adaptive expectations of inflation are one of the three cases economists typically analyze; the other two are static inflation expectations and rational inflation expectations.

AD-AS diagram *See* AS-AD diagram.

aggregate demand Also called planned expenditure. Total spending — by consumers, investing firms, the government, and the international sector — on final goods and services. When the details of national income accounting are considered, differences between aggregate demand, national product, GDP, and national income are caused by differences in their exact definitions. At the eagle's-eye level of analysis used in most of this book, however, the circular flow principle means that aggregate demand, national product, GDP, and national income are all equal.

aggregate demand (AD) curve A downward-sloping relationship between planned expenditure and the price level, plotted on the AS-AD (or aggregate supply–aggregate demand) diagram. This inverse relationship is produced because a higher price level means a lower real money stock, higher interest rates, lower investment spending, and gross exports and lower planned expenditure.

aggregate demand–aggregate supply diagram *See* AS-AD diagram.

aggregate demand line Usually called the planned expenditure line. Found on the income-expenditure (or Keynesian cross) diagram, which shows planned expenditure on the vertical and national income on the horizontal axis. An important part of the sticky-price, short-run business-cycle model. The planned expenditure line shows total spending — aggregate demand — as a function of the level of national income. The slope of the planned expenditure line is the MPE — the marginal propensity to expend income on domestic goods. The intercept of the planned expenditure line is the level of autonomous spending.

aggregate supply The quantity of final goods and services that firms produce given their existing stocks of plant, equipment, and other capital, and given the prevailing wage and price levels. In the flexible-price business-cycle model of Chapters 6 through 8 (and in the growth model of Chapters 4 and 5), wages and prices adjust so that in equilibrium, aggregate supply is equal to the economy's potential output. In the sticky-price model of Chapters 9 through 12, aggregate supply in the short run is an increasing function of the inflation rate (and thus of the price level).

aggregate supply (AS) curve The curve on the AS-AD (aggregate supply–aggregate demand) diagram that shows the dependence of firms' production on the inflation rate (and thus on the price level): the higher the inflation rate, the more goods and services are produced. The aggregate supply curve and the Phillips curve are different ways of expressing the same economic relationship.

analytic geometry The idea that graphs and equations are two different ways of expressing the same concepts. It allows lines and curves on a graph to represent algebraic equations — and algebraic equations to represent lines and curves on a graph. In economics, it is the use of graphs and diagrams as an alternative to equations and arithmetic for expressing economic relationships. In mathematics, it is the branch of mathematics that relates geometry and algebra. Often called Cartesian geometry because much of it was invented by René Descartes.

animal spirits Waves of optimism and pessimism — perhaps irrational or self-confirming — about the future of the economy that affect investment spending. Shifts in animal spirits push stock market and other asset prices up and down, and they lead businesses to increase and decrease how much they spend on investment. A term often used by John Maynard Keynes as part of his argument that private investment spending was inherently unstable and that strong stabilizing monetary and fiscal policies were needed to control the natural fluctuations of the business cycle.

anticipated monetary policy Found when workers, managers, and investors have rational expectations of inflation. Anticipated monetary policy is then those shifts in the money stock or interest rates that they had anticipated in advance. Under rational expectations, anticipated changes in monetary policy have no effect on production or unemployment, but they do have powerful effects on prices.

appreciation An increase in value, usually on the part of a currency. The opposite of depreciation. When an appreciation is sudden and is the result of an explicit change in policy by a government, it is called a revaluation. An appreciation of foreign currency is an increase in the value of the exchange rate. By contrast, an appreciation of the dollar is a fall in the value of the exchange rate.

arbitrage Earning profits by buying a good or an asset in one place (or time) and selling it in another place (or time) where its price is higher. In this book, arbitrage is used to derive equilibrium conditions in financial markets: In equilibrium, no arbitrage opportunities are left for financiers to exploit. Thus, for example, any differential in interest rates paid on investments at home and investments abroad must be offset by an expected change in the exchange rate.

AS-AD diagram It plots real GDP (relative to potential output) on the horizontal axis and the price level (or the inflation rate) on the vertical axis. On this diagram the aggregate demand curve shows how planned expenditure varies with the price level (or the inflation rate); the aggregate supply curve shows how firms' total production varies with the price level (or the inflation rate). Equilibrium is where the curves cross, and thus where production is equal to sales, inventories are stable, and there is neither upward nor downward pressure on production or prices.

authorities Central bank authorities with the discretion to respond to specific circumstances as they see fit. Contrasted with rules in a debate over the best way to conduct monetary policy.

automatic stabilizers In a recession, tax revenues automatically decline as incomes fall, and social insurance spending automatically rises as more people qualify for food stamps, unemployment insurance, and other social welfare expenditures. The government budget automatically swings toward a deficit, providing a stimulus to aggregate demand, whenever private demand drops. Similarly, it automatically swings toward a surplus, reducing aggregate demand, whenever private demand rises. The structure of the government's tax and spending programs thus automatically provides a degree of stabilization to aggregate demand. These fiscal automatic stabilizers are the only form of fiscal policy in the United States that works rapidly and effectively to reduce the size of the business cycle.

autonomous consumption Written C_0. That component of consumption spending that is independent of the level of national income.

autonomous spending Written A. Those components of planned expenditure that are independent of the level of national income. A higher level of autonomous spending is an upward shift in the planned expenditure line on the income-expenditure diagram. A higher level of autonomous spending increases equilibrium planned expenditure by an amount equal to the boost in autonomous spending times the multiplier. Autonomous spending A is equal to autonomous consumption C_0, plus investment I, government purchases G, and gross exports GX: $A = C_0 + I + G + GX$.

B

bads The opposite of "goods." Elements produced by an economy that diminish consumers' welfare, and that would constitute a subtraction from GDP in some better, future system of social accounts to measure economic welfare. Bads include congestion (waiting in traffic jams), pollution, increases in crime (which increase measured GDP to the extent that they trigger greater expenditures on security), and the depletion of valuable resources (which are thus removed from the wealth of future generations).

Bagehot rule The principle that in a financial crisis the government needs to keep functioning those financial institutions and other businesses that are fundamentally sound and to — rapidly — close down and liquidate those organizations that are fundamentally bankrupt. If they would be bankrupt even if production and demand were at normal levels relative to potential, then they should be closed. If they would be solvent if production, demand, and asset prices were at their normal levels, the government needs to lend them as much money as they need to keep functioning through the crisis — albeit at a high, penalty rate.

balance of payments account The accounting system used to measure and comprehend a country's economic relations with the rest of the world. The balance of payments account has three parts: The current account tracks a country's imports and exports of goods and services; the capital account tracks a country's gross investment of capital abroad and foreigners' gross investment of capital at home; and, under a fixed exchange rate system, the official settlements account tracks changes in governments' exchange reserves.

balanced budget When the government's tax receipts equal its spending. Since there are many possible ways of accounting for tax receipts and for spending, the concept of a balanced budget is a fuzzy one.

balanced growth When a country has converged to its long-run balanced-growth path, and has a capital-output ratio equal to its equilibrium value $(K/Y)^*$, which is found by dividing the country's saving-investment rate s by the sum of the labor force growth rate n, the efficiency-of-labor growth rate g, and the capital depreciation rate δ: $(K/Y)^* = s/(n + g + \delta)$.

balanced-growth equilibrium capital-output ratio The value of the capital-output ratio to which an economy with constant saving, depreciation, labor-force growth, and efficiency growth rates converges over time. Sometimes called the steady-state capital-output ratio. The balanced-growth capital-output ratio is calculated by dividing the investment share of national product by the sum of the labor-force growth, technology growth, and depreciation rates.

balanced-growth path The path toward which national product per worker tends to converge as the capital-output ratio converges to its balanced-growth equilibrium value. In analyzing long-run growth it is often easiest to first calculate an economy's balanced-growth path, and then to use the fact that the economy tends to converge to that path.

bank assets The sum of a bank's reserves and the loans it has made (and thus that people owe it). Bank assets are equal to the sum of a bank's liabilities — its deposits and its borrowings — and shareholders' net worth.

bank deposits Sums of money that people and organizations have taken to and placed in the bank for convenience, safe-keeping, and profit. Deposits are usually classified as either checking-account deposits (which can be transferred to others by writing checks) and saving-account deposits (which must be withdrawn or transferred into some other form before they can be spent). But there are other forms as well: certificates of deposit or money market account deposits, for example.

bank liabilities How much a bank owes to other people and organizations. The sum of the deposits that people have made in the bank, any direct borrowings that the bank itself has undertaken, and any bonds that the bank itself has issued.

bank reserves Cash held in bank vaults, or money that banks have on deposit at the local branch of the Federal Reserve. A bank's reserves are the amount of money it can pay out to depositors easily and immediately, without selling less than perfectly liquid assets, calling in loans, or borrowing itself. Bank regulators require that banks maintain a specified level of reserves in proportion to the total deposits that they have accepted. Changing reserve requirements is a way that the Federal Reserve affects the money supply.

bank run Before deposit insurance, when the depositors in a bank fear that it is insolvent, and so all at once demand that the bank liquidate their deposits for cash.

base year In the construction of an index, the year from which the weights assigned to the different components of the index are drawn. It is conventional to set the value of an index in its base year equal to 100.

baseline autonomous spending Written A_0. Those components of autonomous spending that are independent of the level of the interest rate.

behavioral relationship One of the two key kinds of equations that appear in economic models. (The "equilibrium condition" is the other kind.) A connection between economic variables that is the result of people's actions — how consumers change their spending in response to changes in income, how businesses change employment in response to changes in inventories, how foreign exchange speculators assess the length of time that interest rates in the United States will remain higher than interest rates abroad, and so forth.

bond A tradable financial instrument that is a promise by a business or a government to repay money that it has borrowed. A discount bond is a short-term promise to pay a fixed sum on the date that the bond matures. A coupon bond is a promise to periodically pay out coupon interest payments until the bond matures, and then to repay the bond's principal value at maturity.

bond market The set of places and communication links along which governments and others bid for, offer, and trade bonds. Economists often say that interest rates are determined by supply and demand in the bond market. These days the bond market is largely a computer network — numbers on bond traders' computer screens, and electronic offers to buy and sell.

bond rating Some financial information services rate bonds, thus telling investors how safe and secure an investment a particular bond is. The highest-rated bonds are rated AAA.

boom A situation in which production is above long-run trend and has been growing rapidly, in which employment is high and unemployment is low, and in which nearly everyone is optimistic about the future of the economy.

bubble economy When a country's stock and real estate markets have risen far and fast to unsustainable "bubble" levels that cannot be justified on the basis of fundamental values. Bubbles are driven by investors' belief in the "greater fool" theory: Even though they may be fools for buying stocks and bonds at overvalued prices, somewhere out there is a greater fool who will soon buy the securities from them at even higher prices. At some point, however, the greater fool theory turns out to be false, the markets turn, and values on the stock and real estate markets crash. Today when economists refer to the bubble economy, they are typically referring to Japan in the late 1980s.

budget balance The net state of the government's finances. When government spending equals tax receipts, economists say that the budget is in balance or that the budget balance is zero. When spending exceeds taxes, the government's budget is in deficit. When taxes exceed spending, the government's budget is in surplus.

budget deficit The difference between government spending and taxes when the first is larger than the second. In sticky-price short-run models, a budget deficit raises aggregate demand: The government's purchases of goods and services inject more spending power into the economy than the government's net taxes are withdrawing from the economy. In flexible-price models, a budget deficit lowers national saving and investment: Money that would otherwise have been borrowed by businesses and used to finance investment in new plant and equipment is borrowed by the government instead.

budget surplus The difference between the government's spending and the government's revenues when the second is larger than the first. In sticky-price short-run models, an increase in a budget surplus lowers aggregate demand: The government's purchases of goods and services inject less spending power into the economy than the government's net taxes are withdrawing from the economy. In flexible-price models, an increase in a budget surplus raises national saving and investment: The government's retirement of its debt injects purchasing power into financial markets that is then borrowed by businesses and used to finance investment in new plant and equipment.

Bureau of Economic Analysis A bureau in the U.S. Department of Commerce charged with estimating macroeconomic data. The Bureau of Economic Analysis maintains the national income and product accounts, the NIPA.

Bureau of Labor Statistics A bureau of the U.S. Department of Labor charged with keeping track of key labor market and living standard data. The Bureau of Labor Statistics calculates the unemployment rate and the consumer price index (CPI).

Burns, Arthur Chair of the Federal Reserve Board from 1970 to 1978. Before that, he had been a senior member of Richard Nixon's White House staff, chair of Dwight Eisenhower's Council of Economic Advisers, and president of the National Bureau of Economic Research. One of Nixon's relatively few long-time friends.

business cycle A short-run fluctuation in the output, income, and employment of an economy. A political business cycle is one produced by policy actions implemented for political gain. A real business cycle is a boom generated not by stimulative monetary or fiscal policies or by the irrational animal spirits of investors, but by rapid technological innovation opening up new industries and new possibilities for investment.

business structures One of the components of investment spending. The construction of buildings, railroad tracks, bridges, or other things that are not machines, not inventory, yet improve the productive capacity of businesses.

C

capital Produced goods, like machines, buildings, transportation infrastructure, or inventories, that amplify the economy's productive potential.

capital account That part of the international balance of payments that covers investment flows from one country to another. When gross investment in foreign countries by domestic citizens is greater than gross investment in the home country by foreigners, economists say that there is a capital outflow. When gross investment in foreign countries by domestic citizens is less than gross investment in the home country by foreigners, we say there is a capital inflow. The capital account and the current account must match: When there is a capital inflow, the current account must show a trade deficit — an excess of imports over exports — of equal magnitude; when there is a capital outflow, the current account must show a trade surplus — an excess of exports over imports — of equal magnitude.

capital accumulation Increases in a country's capital stock when gross investment is greater than depreciation.

capital deepening Increases in an economy's capital-labor ratio.

capital flight When a collapse of confidence in a country's economic policy leads investors to try to pull their investments out of a country and invest them somewhere else. Capital flight is associated with a sharp depreciation in the value of the currency and poses very difficult economic policy choices.

capital flows Net investment by the citizens of one country in another — the "flow" of financial capital from one country to another. When there is a net outflow of capital from a country, the outflow is equal to its trade surplus — net exports. When there is a net inflow of capital into a country, the inflow is equal to its trade deficit — imports minus exports.

capital inflow Net investment by the citizens of one country in another — the "flow" of financial capital from one country to another.

capital intensity The ratio of the capital stock to total potential output (K/Y) which describes the extent to which capital, as opposed to labor, is used to produce goods and services.

capital mobility The extent to which it is easy for investors to place their wealth in or pull their wealth out of other countries.

capital-output ratio The economy's capital stock divided by potential output. In the economic growth chapters, Chapters 4 and 5, the capital-output ratio is the key variable in the economic growth model. Over time, economies converge to balanced-growth paths along which the capital-output ratio is at a constant, equilibrium level. The equilibrium capital-output ratio is equal to the share of national product that is saved and invested, divided by the sum of the depreciation, labor-force growth, and labor efficiency growth rates.

capital share The share of national income that is received as income by the owners of capital: the sum of profits, rent, and net interest divided by total national income. If the economy is competitive — without monopolies — and there are no major external benefits to investment in the economic growth process, then in equilibrium the capital share of an economy will be equal to the diminishing-returns-to-investment parameter of its aggregate production function.

capital stock The economy's, or sometimes a firm's, total accumulated stock of buildings, roads, other infrastructure, machines, and inventories. The greater the capital stock, the more productive the average worker. A substantial chunk of long-run economic growth is due to increases in the capital stock.

cash budget balance A way of measuring the government's budget balance called "cash" because it does not take account of changes in the value of government-owned assets or of the future liabilities owed by the government. It is just cash paid in minus cash paid out.

cash flow The difference between a business's revenues and its immediate cost of doing business. Cash flow is available for the business to return to its shareholders in dividends, use to buy back its stock or its bonds on the financial market, or spend on increasing its capital stock through investment.

CBO *See* Congressional Budget Office.

central bank The arm of a national government that controls the money supply and the credit pattern of an economy, and usually oversees and regulates the banking system as well. The Federal Reserve system — the Board of Governors in Washington, DC, and the 12 regional Federal Reserve banks in Boston, New York, Philadelphia, Cleveland, Richmond, Atlanta, Chicago, Kansas City, St. Louis, Dallas, Minneapolis, and San Francisco — is the United States' central bank.

certificate of deposit A type of bank account that is one step less liquid, and thus one step less moneylike, than a savings account. You give your money to the bank. In return it gives you a "certificate of deposit" that you can redeem after a fixed period of time to get your money back with interest. However, if you try to cash in your certificate of deposit early, you will suffer, as the advertisements all say, "substantial penalties for early withdrawal."

chain-weighted index An index constructed not by choosing one particular year as the base year and calculating the index value for every year using the base-year weights, but by "chaining" together year-to-year changes. That is, each year-to-year change in the index is calculated using that particular year as the base year. These calculated changes in the index are then linked together to create the index level values. Chain-weighted indexes avoid problems that fixed-weight indexes develop as time passes and the base-year weights used to construct the index become less and less relevant.

checking account deposits Often called "demand deposits" because the bank pays them out whenever the depositor demands (usually by writing a check that the check recipient's bank then presents to the depositor's bank). Because it is so easy to use checking account balances to pay for goods and services, checking account deposits are included in every possible measure of the money stock.

circular flow The central, dominant metaphor in macroeconomics, and the way of looking at the macroeconomy that underlies the national income and product accounts. Every economic transaction is made up of a flow of goods or services and of an offsetting flow of purchasing power in the opposite direction. Every economic agent has an income and an expenditure, and the two must match. Thus purchasing power flows from businesses to households and back in a circular fashion.

classical assumption The assumption that wages and prices are flexible.

classical dichotomy When real variables (like real GDP, real investment spending, or the real exchange rate) can be analyzed and calculated without thinking about nominal variables (like the price level or the nominal money stock). If the classical dichotomy holds, then economists also say that money is neutral: Changes in the money stock do not affect the real variables — income, production, and employment in the economy. They also say that money is a veil — a covering that does not affect the shape of the face underneath.

classical unemployment When unemployment arises not because aggregate demand is too low, but because government regulations or market power keep the labor market from clearing and keep labor demand by firms below labor supply.

closed economy An economy in which international trade is so small a share of national product that exports and imports can be ignored. Contrast with an open economy, in which trade and capital flows have important effects on real GDP and other economic variables.

commodity futures A contract that allows you to "lock in" today the price at which you will buy or sell a commodity in the future. The contract can then itself be traded, and depending on how prices move a contract that allows you to buy a commodity — euros, say — at a low price can itself be very valuable. Businesses and investors can use such commodity futures contracts to avoid bearing various forms of risk. Other businesses and investors use such commodity futures to gamble.

comparative statics A method of analysis to determine the effect on the economy of some particular shift in the environment or policy. First look at the initial equilibrium position of the economy without the shift; then look at the equilibrium position of the economy with the shift; and finally see the difference in the two equilibrium positions as the response to the shift.

Congressional Budget Office Abbreviated CBO. The place to go to look for forecasts of the government's tax and spending programs, and what they mean for the economy.

consumer confidence How optimistic or pessimistic are consumers about the economy? The University of Michigan and the Conference Board conduct surveys of consumer confidence. The more confident consumers are, the higher consumption is likely to be for any given level of GDP. Consumer confidence is a powerful determinant of autonomous consumption.

consumer price index Abbreviated CPI. The most commonly used measure of the cost of living. It measures the cost of a slowly changing basket of consumer goods. The change in the CPI is the most frequently used measure of inflation. Because of difficulties in getting good measurements of components of the cost of living, the CPI probably contains a slight bias. A plurality of economists believe that the CPI overstates true changes in the cost of living by between 0.5 and 1.0 percentage point per year.

consumer prices The average prices paid by households for the goods they buy as consumers. Consumer prices are distinguished from investment-goods prices, the prices paid by the government, and export prices.

consumption function The dependence of aggregate consumption spending on baseline consumption C_0, the marginal propensity to consume C_y, and disposable income Y^D: $C = C_0 + C_y Y^D$.

consumption per worker A measure of the consumption of the workforce — the consumption component of GDP divided by the labor force for the national economy.

consumption spending Spending on goods and services purchased and used by consumers. Consumption spending is the major component of national product, equal to about two-thirds of the total. Consumption spending does not include purchases of existing houses or the construction of new houses. The purchase of an existing house is an asset. Housing construction is counted in investment.

contractionary policy The opposite of expansionary policy: shifts in government spending, taxation, or monetary policy that reduce aggregate demand and tend to reduce national product, income, employment, and inflation. A contractionary fiscal policy increases net taxes or reduces government spending. A contractionary monetary policy is usually an open-market operation by which the Federal Reserve sells bonds for cash, thus reducing the money supply and raising short-term interest rates.

convergence Applied to a set of countries, the tendency for productivity and real wage levels to draw together. Applied to one country, the tendency for it to approach a balanced-growth path with a constant capital-output ratio determined by the country's investment, technology, population growth, and depreciation rates.

coordination failures Failures of firms to change prices to respond quickly to the marketplace or in concert with other firms. Such things as long-term price and labor contracts produce a kind of inertia.

cost-of-living escalators Provisions in contracts that automatically raise wages or prices as official price indexes rise.

countercyclical Something that moves in the opposite direction from the business cycle; something that is low when national product is above potential output, and vice versa. The unemployment rate is countercyclical, as is the government's budget balance.

coupon bond A bond that pays its holder not only its principal value at maturity but also a periodic interest payment called a "coupon."

CPI *See* consumer price index.

CPS *See* Current Population Survey.

credibility The degree to which the public believes in the policy action taken by some institution of government (e.g., the Fed, Congress, or the president). As long as people in an economy believe that the central bank will act to keep inflation low, it is possible that the economy will be able to have both relatively full employment and relative price stability. But if the central bank does not have this credibility, either unemployment will be high or inflation will be high — or both.

crowding out Decreases in investment spending caused by a drop in government saving that leads to higher real interest rates.

currency The sum of paper money and coins. Currency is one of the major components of the money stock. It is the form of money that is easiest to use to buy goods and services.

currency arbitrage A situation, operating under the gold standard, whereby people buying or selling one currency at any price other than the ratio of the two gold parities would find themselves facing an unlimited demand, and would soon find themselves losing a nearly unlimited amount of money.

currency board An exchange rate system in which the central bank gives up its power to conduct domestic open-market operations and commits to buying and selling foreign currency at the official exchange rate only. Under a currency board, a country's stock of high-powered money is equal to its foreign exchange reserves. Establishing a currency board system is a way that a central bank can gain credibility: It not only fixes its exchange rate in terms of foreign currency, but it abandons the key lever — open-market operations — that it would use should it wish to begin a policy of inflation.

currency confidence The condition where people have faith in the continuing value of one country's currency relative to one or more other currencies.

currency crisis A situation where a country's currency is in serious trouble relative to the exchange rates of other countries. The most common problems facing that country are the prospect of hyperinflation or the need for significant devaluation.

currency-to-deposits ratio How much individuals and firms wish to hold in currency for every dollar that they hold in bank deposits. When people are nervous about the banking system, the currency-to-deposits ratio will rise, pushing the money multiplier and the money stock down and perhaps causing a recession.

current account In the balance of payments, the account that keeps track of a country's exports and imports. When exports exceed imports, economists say that there is a current account or trade surplus. When imports exceed exports, economists say that there is a current account or trade deficit. The current account and the capital account must match: Whenever there is a capital inflow, the current account must show a trade deficit — an excess of imports over exports — of equal magnitude; whenever there is a capital outflow, the current account must show a trade surplus — an excess of exports over imports — of equal magnitude.

Current Population Survey Abbreviated CPS. The survey undertaken by the Labor Department's Bureau of Labor Statistics to estimate the unemployment rate.

cyclical unemployment The difference between the current unemployment rate and the natural rate of unemployment. Cyclical unemployment is associated with deviations of national product from potential output.

cyclical volatility The amount of variation in the size of swings from peak to trough over time.

cyclically adjusted The value of an economic variable if unemployment were at its average rate and the business cycle were in neither a boom nor a depressed state.

cyclically adjusted budget deficit Also called the high-employment budget deficit. An estimate of what the budget deficit would be if national product were at potential output and unemployment were equal to the natural rate. This measure removes shifts in the budget deficit that are due to the operation of the economy's automatic stabilizers.

D

debt The national debt of a country is the sum total of all past deficits less all past surpluses the government has run. The government owes interest on the national debt — thus to avoid piling up even more debt, taxes must be higher when the debt is higher. And the fact that investors hold the bonds issued by the government that are the national debt means that they have less to finance private investment that boosts the country's capital stock.

deficit The amount by which government spending on goods, services, and transfer payments exceeds tax revenues in a given year. A national debt is created when the government borrows to cover the shortfall.

deflation When the price level falls for some substantial period of time. The opposite of inflation. Deflation is rarely seen today, but the deflation of 1929–1933 was a major factor contributing to the depth of the Great Depression: The falling price level bankrupted firms and banks that were in debt, and so reduced total aggregate demand.

demand deposits Checking account deposits. Called demand deposits because the bank pays them out whenever the depositor demands (usually by writing a check). Checking account deposits are part of what economists call the money stock because it is so easy to use checking account balances to pay for goods and services.

demographic transition A period in history which sees a rise in birth rates and a sharp fall in death rates as material standards of living increase above "subsistence" levels. (But after a while birth rates start to decline rapidly too. The end of the demographic transition sees both birth and death rates at a relatively low level, and the population nearly stable.)

dependent variable The variable alone on the left-hand side of an equation. The variable whose value is determined by the values of the variables on the right-hand side, and that changes when the variables on the right-hand side change.

deposit insurance A promise by the government or the central bank that bank failures will not freeze consumers' or firms' bank deposits and thus their ability to spend. Deposit insurance in the United States was instituted by Franklin Roosevelt's New Deal and has reduced the risk of a classic financial crisis. (But it also obligated U.S. taxpayers to bail out many bankrupt savings and loan associations in the late 1980s.)

depreciation (of capital) The difference between gross and net investment in capital; the amount by which the capital stock wears out, becomes obsolete, or is scrapped over a year.

depreciation (of currency) A decrease in the value of a currency. Depreciation of the dollar is a rise in the value of the exchange rate.

depreciation rate The rate at which capital wears out, rusts, or becomes obsolete and is scrapped. Because of depreciation, the economy's capital stock does not grow by the full value of gross investment. It grows by the amount of net investment — the difference between gross investment and depreciation.

depression The word used for an economic downturn, a fall in national product and a rise in unemployment, before "recession" was coined as a euphemism. Today the meaning of "depression" is a very severe downturn.

devaluation In a fixed exchange rate system, a reduction in the value of a country's currency so that it takes more units of the home country's currency to purchase one unit of foreign currency. An action taken by a central bank or treasury to decrease the official price of a country's currency relative to the price of other currencies — or in terms of gold. (Revaluation is the opposite action.)

diminishing returns Doubling the number of workers on a farm, or doubling the value of the capital each employee uses in a factory, does not generally increase production by the same amount each time. As more factors are added, smaller and smaller increases in production are generated. Such diminishing returns prompted nineteenth-century essayist Thomas Carlyle to call economics "the dismal science."

discounting Figuring out how much money you would have to put aside today and invest at the prevailing interest rate in order to obtain a specified sum at some particular point in the future. We calculate the profitability of investments by discounting future profits from investment and comparing the discounted present value to the cost of the investment.

discouraged workers Potential workers who have left the labor force because they do not believe they can find worthwhile jobs. Discouraged workers return to the labor force when the labor market tightens. Many think that official unemployment rates understate the unemployment problem because of the existence of discouraged workers.

discretion Leaving policies to be made and adjusted by appointed bodies of experts with discretion to respond to circumstances.

discretionary policy Policy that is not automatic in the sense that automatic stabilizers swing into action without anyone making an explicit decision. Discretionary monetary policy is made by the FOMC's decisions to change interest rates. Discretionary fiscal policy is made by Congress's and the president's decisions to change levels of spending and of taxes.

disinflation A reduction in inflation, a reduction in the rate at which prices are increasing — but not so great a reduction as to cause deflation. Usually seen in the context of the Volcker disinflation, the 1979–1984 fall in the U.S. inflation rate carried out by the Federal Reserve during the term of Chair Paul Volcker.

disposable income What is left of income after taxes have been paid and transfer payments received. The difference between national income and net taxes. Even when national income is unchanged, changes in the government's tax and transfer programs change disposable income and so are likely to change consumption spending. Disposable income $Y^D = Y - T$ where Y is total income and T is net taxes. If taxes are proportional to income, $T = tY$ where t is the tax rate, and then $Y^D = (1 - t)Y$.

divergence The tendency for a per capita measurement (e.g., incomes or standards of living) in various countries to become less equal over a period of time.

dividends Payments by a corporation to its shareholders on a regular, periodic basis. Dividends are the primary way that a firm rewards those who have invested in its common stock by returning a portion of the firm's profits to its investors.

domestic investment The same as "investment" in the national income and product accounts. Distinguished from foreign investment, which is investment by one country's citizens in the economy of another country.

durable manufacturing That part of the economy's manufacturing sector that makes durable goods — long-lived goods like refrigerators, large turbine generators, structural steel, and washing machines.

dynamic inconsistency A situation where a central bank succumbs to the temptation to make inflation higher than expected and thereby loses its credibility. That central bank will find that its words about future policy are ignored in the process of setting expectations, and expectations of inflation will be sky-high.

E

East Asian crisis The remarkably deep and sudden financial crisis that hit East Asian economies in 1997 and 1998. The East Asian crisis came with the least warning of any financial crisis in the 1990s. In other crises — Britain's, Brazil's, or Mexico's — some observers at least had pointed out fundamental problems that made that economy vulnerable to a crisis. The East Asian crisis appeared to come out of a blue sky.

East Asian miracle Since the mid-1960s the economies of East Asia have grown more rapidly than any other group of economies, anywhere, anytime.

economic expansion A sustained increase in GDP bracketed on either side by a period of recession.

economic growth The process by which productivity, living standards, and output increase.

Economic Report of the President A "book" prepared once a year (in February) by the president's Council of Economic Advisers. It gives their view of the economy's accomplishments, problems, and opportunities.

efficiency of labor The skills and education of the labor force, the ability of the labor force to handle modern technologies, and the efficiency with which the economy's businesses and markets function. The efficiency of labor is very closely linked to an economy's total factor productivity.

elasticity The proportional response of one quantity to a proportional change in another quantity. If a 1 percent change in one variable generates a 1 percent change in the other, the elasticity is one. If a 1 percent change in one generates a 2 percent change in the other, the elasticity is two.

equilibrium Short-run equilibrium is a state of balance between supply and demand in a particular market or in the economy as a whole. Long-run equilibrium requires that markets balance and also that expectations of inflation and other quantities be correct.

equilibrium capital-output ratio In the economic growth chapters, Chapters 4 and 5, the equilibrium capital-output ratio is the key to understanding where the economy is headed: what its long-run dynamic trajectory will be. Over time, the economy will converge to its balanced-growth path along which the capital-output ratio is constant at its equilibrium level. This equilibrium capital-output ratio is equal to the share of national product that is saved and invested, divided by the sum of the depreciation, labor-force growth, and labor-efficiency growth rates.

equilibrium condition A relationship between two economic quantities that holds not because any one actor or group in the economy makes it hold, but because the operation of the system as a whole pushes the economy to a state in which the relationship holds. The requirement that planned expenditure equal total output on the income-expenditure diagram is an equilibrium condition: If it does not hold, then inventories are either rising or falling and so businesses are either cutting back or raising production, and thus total output is either rising or falling toward planned expenditure.

equilibrium debt-to-GDP ratio The constant ratio of government debt to GDP when both real government debt and real GDP are growing at the same rate.

establishment survey A survey of businesses and how many employees they have that is carried out by the Bureau of Labor Statistics. The establishment survey is not used to calculate the unemployment rate.

excess bank reserves Bank reserves held over and above those mandated by law because banks are not confident that they would be paid back if they made additional loans, or because banks believe that some loans they have already made are about to go into default, or because they believe depositors are about to withdraw deposits.

exchange rate The nominal exchange rate is the rate at which one country's money can be turned into another's. The real exchange rate is the rate at which goods produced in one country can be bought or sold for another's. The definition of the exchange rate is either the value of home currency or the price of foreign currency, depending on the textbook. In this book, the nominal exchange rate is the price of foreign currency.

expansion A period when real GDP is growing.

expansionary policy Increases in government spending, decreases in net taxes, or increases in the money stock that lower interest rates. Expansionary policies raise aggregate demand, national product, employment, and inflation.

expectations Everyone in the economy makes plans about what to do that depend on what they think the future will be like. Economists focus on this dependence of behavior on beliefs about the future: Investors', consumers', employers', and workers' expectations are a principal determinant of economic behavior. As a shorthand, economists usually collapse the range of different and conflicting expectations held by people into a single average number — for example, expectations of inflation.

expectations theory of the term structure The theory that the long-term interest rate is an average of today's short-term interest rate and of the short-term interest rates that are expected to prevail in the future, plus a term premium.

expected inflation rate The rate at which prices were expected to increase. Today's expected inflation rate is yesterday's guess about today's inflation rate.

expenditure side That part of the national income and product accounts made up of total expenditure — on consumption spending, investment, net exports, and government purchases.

exports Total goods and services produced at home and sold to purchasers in foreign countries. Exports are an addition to aggregate demand for home-produced products.

external balance When the trade surplus (or deficit) of a country is equal to the value of investors' new long-term investments abroad (or foreigners' new long-term investments here). A lack of external balance means that something — usually the exchange rate, but possibly interest rates or the level of GDP — is about to change.

F

Federal Open Market Committee Abbreviated FOMC. The principal decision-making body of the Federal Reserve. The FOMC meets roughly every other month, decides on the level of short-term interest rates, and directs the open-market operations that the New York Federal Reserve Bank carries out on behalf of the Federal Reserve system.

Federal Reserve The United States' central bank. The institution conducts monetary policy and regulates banks. Its open-market operations change the money stock and peg short-term nominal interest rates. The Federal Reserve consists of a Board of Governors (seven, one of whom is chair) and 12 regional Federal Reserve banks.

Federal Reserve banks The 12 regional banks — located in New York, Chicago, Cleveland, Boston, Philadelphia, Richmond, Atlanta, St. Louis, Kansas City, Dallas, Minneapolis, and San Francisco — that are the local branches of the Federal Reserve system.

Federal Reserve Board The Washington, DC–based head office of the United States' central bank, the Federal Reserve system. The board consists of seven governors, one of whom is chair and one of whom is vice chair. The chair is appointed to a four-year term by the president with the advice and consent of the Senate.

final goods and services Products that are not themselves used by businesses to make other products. Products that are (*a*) bought by consumers, (*b*) bought by firms or individuals as investments that increase their capital stock, (*c*) bought by the government, or (*d*) bought by foreigners (in excess of intermediate goods bought by domestic producers).

financial automatic stabilizers Features of the financial system, such as deposit insurance, that help to prevent stress on the financial system from culminating in total collapse.

financial flexibility A situation in which a large number of different financial instruments are traded on thick and liquid markets. This means that any one kind of asset has less and less potential to become a bottleneck.

financial markets The stock market, the bond market, the short-term borrowing market, plus firms' borrowings from banks. The markets in which the flow of money from savers seeking a return to investors seeking money to finance purchases takes place.

financial panics Sudden falls in stock and bond market prices, and rises in interest rates, driven at least in part by the fear that other people are about to panic and sell.

fine-tuning The hope that the Federal Reserve, Congress, and the president could together adjust fiscal and monetary policy to keep the economy always near full employment — as you tune a radio to get the strongest signal.

fiscal automatic stabilizers In a recession, tax revenues automatically decline as incomes fall, and social insurance spending automatically rises as more people qualify for food stamps, unemployment insurance, and other social welfare expenditures. The government budget automatically swings toward a deficit, providing a stimulus to aggregate demand, whenever private demand drops. Similarly, it automatically swings toward a surplus, reducing aggregate demand, whenever private demand rises. The structure of the government's tax and spending programs thus automatically provides a degree of stabilization to aggregate demand. These fiscal automatic stabilizers are the only form of fiscal policy in the United States that works rapidly and effectively to reduce the size of the business cycle.

fiscal policy Changes in government purchases or in net taxes that affect the level of aggregate demand. Increases in purchases or in transfer payments are expansionary policy; increases in taxes are contractionary policy.

Fisher effect An empirical regularity whereby nominal interest rates typically rise roughly point-for-point with the inflation rate.

fixed exchange rates A system of international monetary arrangements by which central banks buy and sell in foreign exchange markets to keep their relative exchange rates fixed. Before 1971 the industrial world was on a fixed exchange rate system called the Bretton Woods system.

fixed investment Investment to build houses and apartments, infrastructure, offices, stores, and other buildings, plus investment in machinery and equipment. The other important component of investment is inventory investment.

fixed-weight indexes Indexes formed by taking a weighted average of different quantities, where the weights are fixed and unchanging over the span of years for which the index is constructed.

flexible prices When wages and prices in an economy are not sticky, but move smoothly and rapidly to keep supply equal to demand in the labor market and in the goods market. Under flexible prices, real GDP is equal to potential output and unemployment is equal to its natural rate. Under flexible prices, changes in monetary and fiscal policy do not affect the level of real GDP, but they do affect its composition, and they affect the price level as well.

floating exchange rates A system of international monetary arrangements by which central banks let exchange rates be decided by supply and demand, so that they "float" against one another as supplies and demands vary. Floating systems can be "clean" — if central banks truly leave the markets alone — or "dirty" — if central banks try at times to nudge exchange rates in one direction or another.

flow of funds The process by which saving — whether household, government, or foreign — is transformed into purchasing power useful for businesses undertaking investment spending. The flow of funds through financial markets is the center of macroeconomic analysis in the flexible-price full-employment model of Chapters 6 and 7.

flow variable An economic quantity measured as a flow per unit of time. GDP, investment spending, and inflation are examples of flow variables. The unemployment rate, the capital stock, and the price level are not flow variables — they are stock variables.

FOMC *See* Federal Open Market Committee.

foreign currency The money of any country save the one you happen to live in. When domestic exporters earn foreign currency by exporting, they have to figure out what to do with it — it's no good in this country, after all. So they need to trade it either to someone who needs foreign currency to buy imports or to someone who wants foreign currency to make an investment abroad.

foreign exchange market The decentralized trading around the world of assets denominated in one currency for assets denominated in another: euros or dollars, pounds or yen. Exchange rates are set in the foreign exchange market.

foreign exchange reserves Foreign currency–denominated assets held by a country's central bank or treasury to use in foreign exchange interventions. Under a fixed exchange rate system, a government must maintain sufficient foreign exchange reserves so that it can satisfy the people who wish to trade home currency for foreign currency.

foreign saving The net amount of money that foreigners are committing to buying up property and assets in the home country, equal to minus net exports.

foreign trade The purchase of commodities made in other countries. Imports and exports.

formulation lag The lapse of time between the moment that makers of economic policy recognize that a shock has affected the economy and the moment at which their policy response begins to be implemented. The time it takes to formulate policy.

fractional reserve banking A banking system — like the one we have — in which banks hold in their vaults only a portion of deposits they accept as reserves and lend the rest to customers who pay interest.

frictional unemployment The unemployment generated by firms taking time to fill vacancies and workers taking time to find the right job. Frictional unemployment is

the labor market counterpart of goods inventories in the goods market: It boosts output and workers' incomes by giving them the opportunity to find jobs that match their skills.

Friedman, Milton One of the four most influential macroeconomists of the twentieth century (the other three being John Maynard Keynes, Irving Fisher, and Robert Lucas). Leading exponent of monetarism, and one of the first to recognize the dominant role potentially played by the Federal Reserve in stabilization policy.

full-employment cyclically adjusted deficit An estimate of what the budget deficit would be if national product were at potential output. This measure removes shifts in the budget deficit that are due to the operation of the economy's automatic stabilizers.

future value The inverse of present value — the value that a sum of money or a flow of cash would have at some date in the future, if it were invested and compounded at the prevailing rate of interest.

G

GDP *See* gross domestic product.

GDP deflator The ratio of nominal GDP to real GDP. The second most used estimate of the overall price level (the consumer price index is the most-used estimate).

generational accounting A way of looking at the government's tax and spending plans not individual year by individual year, but all at once. Generational accounting attempts to set out the total lifetime impact of government policy on an individual's resources and obligations.

globalization The ongoing process by which barriers to the free flow of commodities, capital, and information across countries are reduced.

GNP *See* gross national product.

gold standard The particular fixed exchange rate system dominant for more than a half century before the Great Depression. A system by which central banks preserve fixed exchange rates by always being willing to buy or sell their currencies at fixed rates in terms of the precious metal gold.

golden rule In growth theory, when an economy's saving rate is equal to its capital share. In such a case the balanced-growth path has a higher level of consumption associated with it than any other balanced-growth path with the same path over time of the efficiency of labor.

goods market Economists sometimes divide the economy into four "markets" — the labor market where firms hire and pay workers; the money market where people buy and sell liquid assets; the bond market where people buy and sell bonds and stocks; and the goods market where people (and firms, and the government) buy and sell final goods and services.

goods market equilibrium In the flexible-price model, when prices have adjusted to make total aggregate demand for goods equal to potential output. In the sticky-price model, when firms have responded to their increasing or decreasing inventories by adjusting production to aggregate demand so that inventories are stable.

government deficit The difference between government spending and taxes when the first is larger than the second.

government purchases Government spending on goods or services (including the wages of government employees). Much government spending is not purchases but is instead transfer payments: payments like Social Security or food stamps that do not buy any good or service for the government.

government saving The government's budget surplus. Government saving is negative when the government runs a budget deficit.

government surplus The difference between the government's spending and taxes when the second is larger than the first.

Great Depression From 1929 to 1941, the deepest depression the United States has ever experienced. At its nadir in 1933, more than a quarter of the labor force was unemployed.

gross domestic product Abbreviated GDP. The most commonly used measure of product, output, and income. The total amount of final goods and services produced. By the circular flow principle, equal to the total income earned through domestically located production. Also equal to total expenditure on domestically produced goods and services.

gross exports Total goods and services produced at home and sold to purchasers in foreign countries.

gross investment Spending on investment goods that includes spending to simply replace worn-out or obsolete pieces of capital, or to keep existing capital in working condition. Subtract depreciation from gross investment to obtain net investment, the net increase in the economy's capital stock.

gross national product Abbreviated GNP. Equal to GDP minus the income earned by foreign-owned factors of production located in the United States, plus income of U.S. factors of production located abroad. GNP formerly was the most frequently used measure of national product, but the government lost confidence in its ability to estimate the difference between GNP and GDP.

growth rate Almost always the annual growth rate of GDP, or of GDP per worker. The amount by which real economic product is increasing from year to year.

H

high-employment budget deficit Also called the cyclically adjusted budget deficit. An estimate of what the government's budget deficit would be if national product were equal to potential output and unemployment were equal to the natural rate. This measure removes shifts in the budget deficit that are due to the operation of the economy's automatic stabilizers.

high-powered money Usually called the monetary base. The sum total of currency and of bank reserves on deposit at the Federal Reserve. The money stock is equal to the monetary base times the money multiplier.

high-pressure economy Another example of hydraulic metaphors: an economy in which the "pressure" of economic activity is high. Unemployment is low, production is often higher than potential output, workers are being pulled into the labor force, and inflation is often rising.

household saving Households' disposable income minus their consumption spending. Note that earnings not paid out but retained by corporations and then reinvested are counted in disposable income. Hence household saving includes both saving done directly by households and saving done on their behalf by firms whose stock they own.

hyperinflation Extremely high inflation, so high that the price mechanism breaks down. Under hyperinflation people are never sure what the true value of their money is, and they spend a great deal of time and energy trying to spend their cash incomes as fast as possible before they lose value. One rule of thumb is that inflation of more than 20 percent per month is hyperinflation.

I

imperfect information The information workers or managers have for decision making when they lack full information about the state of the economy.

implementation lag The time that passes between the completion of a monetary or fiscal policy action by the Federal Reserve or Congress and the onset of that action's effects on real GDP, unemployment, and inflation.

imports Goods and services produced in and purchased from other countries. Imports are a reduction in aggregate demand: Consumption and investment spending that are diverted to imports are not part of aggregate demand for domestically produced goods and services.

imputed rent Some people rent apartments from landlords. Other people own houses or condominiums. National income accountants were worried at the idea that if a tenant bought an apartment or a house from his or her landlord, real GDP would go down. So they invented "imputed rent" — the rent that those who live in owner-occupied housing pay as tenants to themselves as landlords — and include imputed rent in their calculations of GDP.

income-expenditure diagram The tool for figuring out what the equilibrium level of planned expenditure or aggregate demand and national product is. If national product is too low, it is to the left of equilibrium on the income-expenditure diagram and inventories are rapidly being exhausted. If national product is too high, it is to the right of equilibrium and inventories are being involuntarily built up.

income side That part of the national income and product accounts made up of total income — earned by workers, received by investors, paid to landlords — and residual economic profits left for entrepreneurs and risk-bearers.

independent variable A variable often on the right-hand side of an equation. A variable whose value helps determine the value of the dependent variable, and that, when it changes, makes the dependent variable change.

index number A number that isn't a set sum, value, or quantity in well-defined units (like dollars, people, or miles) but that is a quantity relative to a base year given an arbitrary index value of 100. Index numbers are usually weighted averages of a large number of individual components, and the weights can be either fixed or chained.

industrial economies Those economies that have finished the process of industrialization — the United States, Britain, Germany, Japan, France, Canada, Italy, and the smaller economies at roughly the same stage of economic development.

Industrial Revolution The transformation of the British economy between 1750 and 1850 when largely hand-made production was replaced by machine-made production, a change made possible by technological advance. Following the initial British industrial revolution, other countries have in turn undergone their own industrial revolutions.

inflation An increase in the overall level of prices in an economy, usually measured as the annual percentage change in its consumer price index.

inflation rate The annual rate of change of the overall level of prices in the economy.

inflation tax The tax implicitly levied on an economy's private sector by the government's exercise of its power to print more money. Also called "seigniorage."

inside lag The lapse of time between the moment that a shock begins to affect the economy and the moment that economic policy is altered in response to the shock. The inside lag has two parts: the recognition lag, during which makers of economic policy do not yet recognize the shock; and the formulation lag, during which makers of economic policy are designing the policy response.

insider-outsider theory A theory of how cyclical unemployment that persists for too long becomes transformed into structural unemployment. Workers who remain unemployed gradually lose their skills and their attachment to the labor force. And unions bargain to raise the wages of current members, not to find jobs for ex-members.

interest The periodic sums that you pay to "rent" the money that you have borrowed.

interest rate The price, measured in percent per year, paid for borrowing money. Conversely, the return earned by saving, and the relative price at which purchasing power can be transferred from the present to the future.

interest rate targeting A central bank that focuses its policies on controlling — targeting — interest rates.

intermediate goods Goods that are not final goods and services. Goods that are bought by businesses as inputs into some further process of production. Intermediate goods are excluded from product-side counts of GDP: To include them would lead to double counting (counting the same economic product twice), once in the intermediate good and once again in the final good that the intermediate good was used to produce.

internal balance When unemployment is equal to its natural rate, inflation is unchanging, and GDP is equal to potential output. Under a fixed exchange rate system, monetary policy cannot be used to pursue internal balance because the level of interest rates must be devoted to maintaining the fixed exchange rate.

international division of labor Resource-rich countries produce and export natural resources and resource-based products, industrialized economies export capital-intensive high-technology manufactures, and other countries export labor-intensive manufactures. All gain by concentrating their production in those sectors in which their economy is most efficient.

inventory investment A change in the stock of goods that make up firms' inventories: materials and supplies, work in progress, goods in storage, and finished goods that have not yet been sold. Fluctuations in inventory investment are primarily involuntary, the result of quarter-by-quarter differences between national product and aggregate demand.

investment The buildings and goods (both machines and inventories) purchased to add to the economy's stock of capital, plus (sometimes) government creation of infrastructure, plus residential construction.

investment accelerator The dependence of the level of business investment on the level of production. It arises from firms' preference to use internally generated rather than externally raised funds to finance investment, and from other causes. A strong accelerator increases the value of the Keynesian multiplier.

investment function How investment spending depends on the interest rate. Investment considered as a function of the interest rate. The relationship between the baseline level of investment I_0, the real interest rate r, and the responsiveness of investment to a change in real interest rates I_r: $I = I_0 - I_r r$.

investment requirements The share of GDP that must be devoted to investment spending in order to keep an economy's capital-output ratio from falling.

investment spending That portion of total spending (approximately 20 percent) devoted to increasing business capacity and the economy's capital stock.

investor optimism The principal determinant of baseline investment I_0. When investors are optimistic, I_0 is high. Fluctuations in investor optimism — what John Maynard Keynes called investors' "animal spirits" — are a principal cause of the business cycle.

IS curve The downward-sloping relationship between the (real, risky, long-term) interest rate and the equilibrium level of national product and aggregate demand. The IS curve summarizes the information about equilibrium national product in an entire family of income-expenditure diagrams, one for each possible value of the interest rate.

IS-LM diagram A diagram with the interest rate on the vertical axis and the level of national product on the horizontal axis, used to determine what values of the interest rate and of total income together produce equilibrium in the money market — supply of money equal to money demand — and equilibrium in the goods market — planned expenditure equal to real GDP. Whenever the central bank does not set the interest rate but instead sets the money stock, you need to look at the IS-LM diagram to determine the economy's equilibrium.

K

Keynes, John Maynard One of the four most influential macroeconomists of the twentieth century (the other three being Milton Friedman, Irving Fisher, and Robert Lucas). To Keynes we owe the income-expenditure aggregate-demand framework that still dominates intermediate macroeconomics courses and textbooks.

Keynesian cross diagram The income-expenditure diagram by another name. The tool for finding equilibrium planned expenditure and national product. Principally used in the derivation of the multiplier: the amplified response of changes in equilibrium planned expenditure and national product to fluctuations in autonomous spending.

Keynesian multiplier The change in national income and planned expenditure that follows from a one-dollar change in any component of autonomous spending, such as government purchases. To find the value of the multiplier, subtract the economy's marginal propensity to expend from 1, and then take that number's inverse.

Keynesianism The school of thought, developed from the ideas of John Maynard Keynes, that emphasizes (*a*) the role of expectations of future profits in determining investment; (*b*) the volatility of expectations of future profits; (*c*) the power of the government to affect the economy through fiscal and monetary policy; and (*d*) the multiplier process, which amplifies the effects of both private-sector shocks and public-sector policies on aggregate demand.

L

labor force The sum of those who are employed and those who are actively looking for work. The unemployment rate is defined as the number of unemployed divided by the labor force.

labor market The market in which workers are hired by firms.

labor market equilibrium When the only kind of unemployment is "frictional" unemployment, and there is neither cyclical nor structural unemployment. When, save for those in the process of changing jobs, the economy is at full employment.

labor productivity National product divided by the number of workers (or, alternatively, by the total number of hours worked). Such a measure of output per worker is probably the best available measure of long-run economic growth.

labor supply The number of workers who want to work.

labor unions Organizations of workers that attempt to bargain with employers for higher wages and better working conditions by threatening to strike. Multiyear union contracts have been seen as important causes of price inertia.

lags The time between when a policy proposal is made and when it becomes effective in changing the economy in some way. Lags can arise during recognition of a condition, formulation of a policy, or implementation of that policy. The first two are inside lags, because they occur inside the government. The last is sometimes called the outside lag.

leading indicators A number of variables correlated with future movements in real GDP or inflation. Many economists believe these indicators can be relied on as a good guide to economic activity nine or so months ahead. Some key indicators are stock prices, new manufacturing orders, the money supply, and the index of consumer expectations.

lender of last resort When the government steps in and lends money to organizations that are thought to be fundamentally sound, but that are critically short of cash in a financial crisis.

life-cycle consumption Consumption is depressed below income in peak earning years because people are saving for retirement. Before and after peak earning years, consumption is raised above income either as parents pay for upbringing or as retirees spend their savings.

liquid assets Forms of wealth that can be readily and cheaply converted into spendable form. Forms of wealth that can be easily used to finance purchases.

liquidity Applied to assets, whenever they can be easily, quickly, and without cost turned into money.

liquidity constraints An inability to borrow. When consumers suffer from liquidity constraints, their consumption spending is limited by their current income, and the marginal propensity to consume is likely to be high.

liquidity crisis When banks or other institutions cannot make the payments they owe because they lack cash, but when nobody (or few people) doubts that they will be solvent and profitable if the current financial crisis is successfully resolved.

LM curve The positive relationship between national income and the interest rate that emerges from considering a whole family of money demand–money supply diagrams, a different diagram for each possible level of national income. Plotted along with the IS curve on an IS-LM diagram, it determines the levels of national income and of the interest rate consistent with goods-market and money-market equilibriums.

loanable funds The total flow of resources available — household saving, government saving, and foreign saving — to finance investment spending and capital accumulation.

long-run growth The path of economic growth once the business-cycle fluctuations have been removed. The long-run pace of growth of potential output or of potential output per worker.

long-term interest rate The interest rate required if you are going to borrow money not for a short term of months but for a long term of decades.

long-term real interest rate The interest rate required if you are going to borrow money not for a short term of months but for a long term of decades, adjusted for inflation by subtracting the expected inflation rate from the nominal interest rate.

Lucas, Robert One of the four most influential macroeconomists of the twentieth century (the other three being John Maynard Keynes, Irving Fisher, and Milton Friedman). The leader of the rational-expectations school of macroeconomics for nearly two decades.

Lucas critique The assertion that much analysis of the effects of economic policy is badly flawed because it does not take proper account of how changing policies induce changes in people's expectations.

M

M1, M2, M3 Different measures of the money stock — of the total stock of assets in the economy that are liquid enough to be readily used to finance purchases.

macroeconomics The study of business cycles, the determinants of inflation and unemployment, and probably long-run growth and effects of government fiscal policy. Macroeconomics is contrasted with microeconomics — the study of what goes on in individual markets within the economy.

Malthusian age A period in which natural-resource scarcity limits any gains from increases in technology; a larger population becomes poor and malnourished, lowering their standard of living, and ultimately lowering population growth to zero.

marginal product of capital The increase in potential output from a unit increase in the economy's capital stock. Often calculated as equal to $\alpha Y/K$ (α, the share of national income received by owners of capital, divided by the capital-output ratio K/Y).

marginal product of labor (MPL) The increase in potential output from a one-unit increase in the supply of labor to the economy. Often calculated as $(1 - \alpha)Y/L$ (the share of national income received by workers, $1 - \alpha$, times average labor productivity Y/L).

marginal propensity to consume (MPC) The increase in consumption spending resulting from a one-dollar increase in disposable income. The parameter C_y in the consumption function $C = C_0 + C_y(1 - t)Y$, where C_0 is baseline consumption, t is the tax rate, and Y is total national income.

marginal propensity to expend (MPE) The increase in total spending — on consumption goods through the marginal propensity to consume and on net exports — from a one-dollar increase in national income. In the model of Chapters 9–12, $MPE = C_y(1 - t) - IM_y$, where C_y is the marginal propensity to consume, t is the tax rate, and IM_y is the share of income spent on imports. Note, however, that in more complicated models MPE may be different: Changes in national income may have other effects as higher firm profits lead to higher investment spending and as higher household incomes lead to lower social insurance spending.

maturity The date or the number of years in the future at which a bond's interest payments cease and its principal sum is returned to the lender.

median The middle one of something. The value such that half are as large or larger, and half are as small or smaller.

medium of exchange A commodity or an asset that almost everyone will accept as payment for a transaction. The most important function of money.

menu costs The costs to a firm of changing the price of a good or service. They lead firms to adjust their prices infrequently.

microeconomics That field of economics that deals with the behavior of the individual elements in an economy with respect to the price of a single commodity and the behavior of individual households and businesses.

mixed economy An economy in which markets control the allocation of resources and of labor to industries and firms, but in which the government plays a not overwhelming but significant role: providing social insurance and social welfare benefits on a large scale, trying to stabilize the macroeconomy, and enforcing contracts. Post–World War II mixed economies have been extraordinarily successful at generating economic growth.

model A construct that aims to establish relationships — usually quantitative — between and among economic variables. Economists describe the process of reducing the complexity and variation of the real-world economy into a handful of equations as "building a model."

monetarism The theory, very popular in the 1970s and the early 1980s, that fluctuations in interest rates had little impact on money demand, so that stabilizing national product and employment could be carried out in a smooth and straightforward fashion by stabilizing the rate of growth of the money stock.

monetary automatic stabilizers Named by analogy with the fiscal automatic stabilizers produced by the structure of the government's budget. Features of the financial system that tend to cushion and prevent declines in the money stock that would otherwise occur during a financial crisis. For example, deposit insurance is a monetary automatic stabilizer: It prevents bank deposits and the money stock from dropping when people begin to fear that a depression may bankrupt the bank they use.

monetary base Often called high-powered money. The sum total of currency and of bank reserves on deposit at the Federal Reserve. The money stock is equal to the monetary base times the money multiplier.

monetary policy How the supply of money or the interest rate varies with economic conditions like inflation, unemployment, and the exchange rate. The rules of thumb that the Federal Reserve uses to decide what instructions it is going to give the Federal Reserve Bank of New York.

monetary policy lags The time between when a monetary policy proposal is made and when it becomes effective in changing the economy in some way.

monetary policy reaction function An upward-sloping relationship between the inflation rate and the unemployment rate. When the inflation rate rises, a central bank wishing to fight inflation will raise interest rates to reduce output and thus increase the unemployment rate.

monetary transmission mechanism How changes in the money supply or in interest rates affect spending on consumption, investment, and other components of aggregate demand, thus leading to changes in national income and product.

money A word that economists use in a technical sense. To an economist, "money" means only "wealth in the form of readily spendable purchasing power." Cash, plus balances in checking accounts, plus whatever other assets are held primarily as a way to keep purchasing power on hand to spend rather than as long-term investments.

money balances How much money — wealth in the form of readily spendable purchasing power — consumers and firms actually hold at a given moment.

money demand How much money — wealth in the form of readily spendable purchasing power — consumers and firms wish to hold at the given levels of national income and of interest rates.

money demand curve A curve drawn for a given and fixed level of national income showing how consumers' and

firms' demand for money varies with the interest rate: The higher the interest rate, the lower money demand is. On the money demand–money supply diagram, the point where the money demand curve is equal to the supply of money determines the market-clearing interest rate.

money illusion When managers, workers, and others fail to recognize that some of the change in their nominal income and revenue is a result of inflation and is not a change in their real income and revenue.

money market equilibrium When the money demand by consumers and firms equals the money supply which the Federal Reserve has allowed the banking system to make available.

money multiplier The change in the money stock that follows a one-dollar change in the monetary base; the ratio between the money stock and the monetary base. Increases in the reserves-to-deposits ratio or in the currency-to-deposits ratio reduce the money multiplier.

money stock The equilibrium of money supply and money demand. The amount of money the Federal Reserve has allowed the banking system to create.

money supply How much in the amount of liquid assets the Federal Reserve has allowed the banking system to create.

money supply curve The money supply considered as a function of the interest rate. In general the higher the interest rate, the lower are the excess reserves that the banking sector holds and the higher is the money stock.

money supply–money demand diagram The building block of the LM curve, the diagram with the interest rate on the vertical and the quantity of money supplied and demanded on the horizontal axis.

moral hazard The danger of imprudent, improper, or dishonest behavior in economic situations where actions are not easily or routinely monitored. A possible drawback of deposit insurance and of lender of last resort activities.

MPC *See* marginal propensity to consume.

MPE *See* marginal propensity to expend.

MPL *See* marginal product of labor.

multiplier The change in national income and aggregate demand that follows from a one-dollar change in any component of autonomous spending, such as government purchases. To find the value of the multiplier, subtract the economy's marginal propensity to expend from 1, and then take that number's inverse.

myopia Short-sightedness. A failure to look far enough ahead into the future. For example, "voter myopia" is the theory that voters react to the immediate economic situation, rather than to what has happened in the further past or what is likely to happen in the future.

N

NAIRU Acronym for the nonaccelerating inflation rate of unemployment, which is the same as the natural rate of unemployment. The rate of unemployment when inflation is equal to expected inflation. The rate around which unemployment tends to fluctuate, and at which (because actual and expected inflation are equal) there is neither upward nor downward pressure on inflation.

national debt *See* debt.

national income The total income from all work and asset ownership in an economy. Leaving aside differences in accounting definitions, national income is equal to national product (for the only way income can be earned is by producing products) and is equal to total expenditure, or aggregate demand (for all income flowing to individuals must be expended one way or another).

national income and product accounts Abbreviated NIPA. The system that government statisticians use to measure, estimate, and check data on the flow of economic activity.

national income identity The requirement — built into the national income and product accounts — that total income add up to total expenditure, and that both be equal to the total value added produced by businesses: $C + I + G + NX = Y$, where C is consumption spending, I is investment spending, G is government purchases, NX is net exports, and Y is total national income.

national product The total value of all final goods and services produced in an economy. Leaving aside differences in accounting definitions, national product is equal to national income (for the only way products can be produced is by paying people to make them) and is equal to total expenditure, or aggregate demand (for every product is ultimately purchased).

national product per worker A synonym for labor productivity. It is probably the best measure of an economy's development. Other measures — national product per adult or per capita — fail to take account of the changing mix of market and household production, or imply that adults who spend their money on raising children are impoverished compared to adults who buy videos.

national saving The sum of household saving and government saving — or, since the government is usually not saving but running a deficit, household saving minus the government deficit. Domestic investment is equal to national saving plus net investment in this country by foreigners.

national saving identity A consequence of the national income identity: that household saving $(Y - T - C)$ plus the government's budget surplus $(T - G)$ plus the net inflow of capital $-NX$ is equal to investment: $(Y - T - C) + (T - G) - NX = I$, where Y is total national income, T is net taxes, C is consumption

spending, G is government purchases, NX is net exports, and I is investment spending.

natural rate of unemployment A synonym for NAIRU: the rate of unemployment where actual and expected inflation are equal, and there is no downward or upward pressure on inflation. Milton Friedman coined the phrase "natural rate"; those who did not like the hint in the word "natural" that such unemployment was a good thing preferred the colorless acronym NAIRU.

net domestic product Another measure of total production, obtained by subtracting capital depreciation from GDP.

net exports The difference between exports and imports. Net exports have to be added to the sum of consumption, investment, and government purchases in order to arrive at aggregate demand, because exports are an addition to and imports a subtraction from aggregate demand for domestically produced goods and services.

net investment The difference between gross investment and depreciation. Net investment is the increase in the economy's capital stock — the stock of buildings, infrastructure, machines, and inventories that amplify worker productivity.

net national product Abbreviated NNP. Yet another measure of the economy's total output. Net national product subtracts depreciation from gross domestic product, and also subtracts payments that foreigners receive for the use of foreign-owned productive resources located in this country. Net national product is from a conceptual point of view the best estimate of national product.

net taxes The difference between taxes collected by the government and transfer payments received by households and businesses. Net taxes are the impact of the government's fiscal policy on the disposable income of the private sector. A fall in net taxes raises disposable income, and thus consumption spending. Net taxes are the variable T in the models of this book.

New Deal President Franklin D. Roosevelt's programs during 1933 to 1941 to attempt to pull the economy out of the Great Depression. Of mixed success.

New York Federal Reserve Bank The most important of the 12 banks that are the regional branches of the Federal Reserve. The bank that carries out the open-market operations that the Federal Reserve uses to change interest rates.

NIPA *See* national income and product accounts.

NNP *See* net national product.

nominal A quantity that is not adjusted for inflation, or for changes in the price level.

nominal exchange rate The exchange rate not adjusted for the changes in countries' relative price levels over time. The rate at which one country's money can be turned into another's; the cost of a unit of foreign currency in terms of the home currency.

nominal GDP Real GDP times the price level as measured by the GDP deflator. Nominal GDP is the total current-dollar value of final goods and services produced.

nominal interest rate The interest rate measured in terms of money: how many dollars you have to pay in the future in exchange for one dollar borrowed today. The nominal interest rate is equal to the real interest rate plus the expected inflation rate.

nominal wage The average level of money wages paid in an economy; the money cost to an employer of an average worker.

nondurable manufacturing Manufacturing that produces relatively short-lived products. Demand for nondurable manufactures is fairly steady — since they wear out, there is always a stable source of replacement demand.

"normal" baseline real rate of interest The real interest rate that the central bank would set if the inflation rate were equal to the central bank's target inflation rate.

O

OECD *See* Organisation for Economic Co-operation and Development.

official settlements account International transactions that are neither current account transactions (payments for imports or exports) nor capital account transactions (payments for investments in other countries) but the purchase or sale of foreign currency assets by governments, or central banks.

Okun's law A fall in the unemployment rate of 1 percentage point is associated with a 2.5 percent rise in national product relative to potential output. This association is called Okun's law: Periods of high (or low) unemployment relative to the natural rate are the same as periods of low (or high) national product relative to potential output.

100 percent reserve banking A banking system — never seen in the real world, but sometimes used in economics textbooks as a baseline case — in which banks accept deposits but cannot make loans. When they accept deposits they must either (*a*) hold them in cash in their vaults or (*b*) redeposit the money in their own accounts at the central bank.

open economy An economy without substantial tariffs on imports or restrictions on international investments. Alternatively, an economy where imports, exports, and international capital flows are relatively large shares of national product and are important determinants of fluctuations in employment and output.

open-market operation The principal way that central banks affect interest rates; the purchase (or sale) of short-term government bonds to increase (or decrease) the money supply, and push interest rates down (or up). Open-market operations are not the only tool that central banks have to affect money supplies and interest rates, but they are by far the most often used.

opportunity cost The next best opportunity forgone in order to do something else. One of the key concepts in all of economics.

Organisation for Economic Co-operation and Development (OECD) Originally a club of all countries that received Marshall Plan aid from the United States, plus the United States and Canada. Now a club of the industrialized countries that is used to collect data and try to coordinate economic policy.

output gap The difference between the actual and potential levels of output, $Y - Y^*$. Okun's law reminds us that it is changes in the output gap — not just in output — that bring about changes in the unemployment rate.

output per worker The average amount of output produced in a year per worker, Y/L. Equal to the average labor productivity. Used as a proxy for the material standard of living.

P

participation rate The fraction of adults who are in the labor force. The participation rate is procyclical, because discouraged workers drop out of the labor force when unemployment is relatively high. The participation rate has grown steadily over time, as gender roles have changed and the boundary between market and household work has shifted.

patent laws and copyrights Laws designed to encourage invention and innovation by providing the right to exclude anyone else from using a discovery (patent) or intellectual property (copyright) for a period of years.

permanent income The level of income that households regard as likely to persist in the future. Their income minus any transitory windfalls that they do not expect to receive again in the future.

Phillips curve The downward-sloping relationship between unemployment and inflation. The old-fashioned (incorrect) flavor implied unemployment could be permanently reduced at the price of a small (permanent) rise in inflation. The location of the more satisfactory "accelerationist" Phillips curve depends on expectations of inflation: the higher expected inflation, the higher the unemployment rate needed to keep inflation at any particular level.

planned-expenditure function The relationship $PE = C + I + G + NX$ used to build aggregate demand for domestically produced products from the determinants of each of its components: consumption spending C, investment spending I, government purchases G, and net exports NX.

planned total expenditure line Found on the income-expenditure (or Keynesian cross) diagram that shows aggregate demand on the vertical and national income on the horizontal axis. An important part of the sticky-price short-run business-cycle model. The planned expenditure line shows total spending — aggregate demand — as a function of the level of national income. The slope of the planned expenditure line is the MPE — the marginal propensity to expend income on domestic goods. The intercept of the planned expenditure line is the level of autonomous spending.

policy-induced recessions Recessions started not by swings in consumer or investor confidence, but by contractionary monetary policy.

policy mix The combination of monetary and fiscal policies being followed by a country's government and central bank.

political business cycle Movements in unemployment and inflation resulting from discretionary policy timed to enhance the political fortunes of an incumbent president.

potential growth rate The growth rate of potential output. The growth rate at which the economy's unemployment rate is neither rising nor falling.

potential output The level at which national product would be if expectations were correct, and if unemployment were equal to its natural rate. Potential output grows smoothly over time as technology advances, as net investment augments the capital stock, and as the labor force grows.

present value How much money you would have to put aside and invest today (at prevailing interest rates) in order to match a specified sum or pattern of cash flows in the future. Thus the value in today's dollars (calculated using prevailing interest rates) of a sum or sums of money to be received in the future.

price inertia Inflation can be slow to accelerate and also slow to decline because many decisions on changes in prices and wages are made with a long advance lead.

price level The average level of nominal prices in the economy. Changes in the price level are inflation (or deflation). The concept of the price level is meant to abstract from shifts in relative prices like a rise in the relative price of oil or a fall in the relative price of computers, and to capture changes in the value of the unit of account in which goods are priced, workers are paid, and contracts are written.

price stability The goal of central banks. An inflation rate so low that no one worries about it.

price stickiness A condition that exists when wages and prices do not move smoothly and immediately to keep supply equal to demand in the labor and goods markets.

procyclical Varying with the business cycle. A procyclical variable tends to be high when national product is high relative to potential output. Investment, especially investment in inventories, is procyclical; employment is procyclical; and inflation is procyclical. Unemployment is countercyclical.

producers' durable equipment One of the major components of business investment. The machines that

embody the technologies of the industrial revolution bought by businesses: computers, fax machines, large turbine generators, metal presses, and other capital goods that are not structures and not part of inventories.

production function The relation between the total amount of national product produced and the quantities of labor and capital (and the level of technology) used to produce it. The production function tells us how the productive resources of the economy — the labor force, the capital stock, and the level of technology that determines the efficiency of labor — can be used to produce and determine the level of output in the economy. In the Cobb-Douglas form of the production function, $Y^* = (K)^\alpha (L \cdot E)^{1-\alpha}$, potential output Y^* is determined by the size of the labor force L, the economy's capital stock K, the efficiency of labor E, and a parameter α that tells us how fast returns to investment diminish.

productivity Usually a synonym for labor productivity: total national product divided by the number of workers, or by the number of hours worked. Sometimes used for total factor productivity: the amount of national product divided by the number of weighted units of labor and capital used in production.

productivity growth The rate at which the economy's full-employment productivity expands from year to year as technology advances, as human capital increases, and as investment increases the economy's physical capital stock.

productivity growth slowdown Around 1973, the rate of productivity growth in the United States and other economies suddenly slowed. The causes of this slowdown still remain somewhat a mystery. The most likely explanation is bad luck: a number of small negative factors all affecting the economy at once, each with its own separate causes. The productivity slowdown era appears to have come to an end in the mid-1990s.

profits Income earned by entrepreneurs and equity investors. What is left over from the receipts of an enterprise after it has paid for (*a*) intermediate goods and materials, (*b*) wages, salaries, and fringe benefits, (*c*) rent, and (*d*) interest.

purchasing power parity Valuing production in different countries as if the relative exchange rate gave you equal purchasing power in each country; sometimes also used for the theory that exchange rates ought to fluctuate around the values that correspond to purchasing power parity.

Q

quantity theory of money The core belief of monetarism — strongly pushed by Milton Friedman in the 1960s and 1970s — that money demand is insensitive to changes in interest rates and that the velocity of money is nearly constant. If true, then successful stabilization policy would require little more than stabilizing the rate of growth of the money stock.

R

rational expectations Expectations about the future formed by using all information about the structure of the economy and the likely course of government policy. When people in an economy have rational expectations, it is extremely difficult for shifts in economic policy to cause anything other than shifts in the rate of inflation or the price level. Contrasted with static expectations and adaptive expectations.

real Adjusted for inflation; either divided by the price level, or with the inflation rate subtracted from it.

real appreciation A fall in the value of the nominal exchange rate (the price of foreign currency) under a floating-rate system that is greater than the ongoing difference in inflation rates between the home country and other countries. An increase in the relative price of domestic-made goods in terms of foreign-made goods.

real balances The purchasing power of the money — wealth in the form of readily spendable purchasing power — that consumers and firms actually hold at a given moment. Equal to nominal money balances divided by the price level, and thus adjusted for inflation.

real business cycle A boom generated when rapid technological innovation opens up new industries and new possibilities for investment. At such moments the stock market will be high, the returns to investment large, and so investment spending will be high as well. An adverse supply shock — like the sudden and extreme rises in oil prices in the 1970s — can generate a real-business-cycle recession as well.

real depreciation A rise in the value of the nominal exchange rate (the price of foreign currency) under a floating-rate system that is greater than the ongoing difference in inflation rates between the home country and other countries. A reduction in the relative price of domestic-made goods in terms of foreign-made goods.

real devaluation An increase in the value of the nominal exchange rate (the price of foreign currency) under a fixed-rate system that is greater than the ongoing difference in inflation rates between the home country and other countries.

real exchange rate The nominal exchange rate adjusted for changes in relative price levels. The price of foreign-made goods measured relative to the price of domestic-made goods.

real GDP Inflation-adjusted gross domestic product; the most commonly used measure of national product, output, and income. The total income earned through domestically located production. Equal as well to total expenditure on domestically produced goods and services. Real GDP can be calculated by dividing nominal (or money) GDP by the price level.

real interest rate The nominal interest rate minus the expected inflation rate. The real interest rate measures the cost in terms of goods to borrow purchasing power. It answers the question: "How much more power to purchase goods and services in the future must I offer in order to borrow a fixed amount of power to purchase goods and services today?"

real money balances The total stock of nominal money balances in the economy divided by the price level. Money demand is usually thought of as a demand for real money balances: If the price level doubles while interest rates and (real) national income remain the same, then nominal money demand should double as well in order to keep real money demand constant.

real wage The wage paid to the average worker divided by the price level.

real wage growth The change in the wage paid to the average worker divided by the price level. Found by taking the rate of increase of nominal wages, and subtracting the inflation rate.

recession A fall in the level of GDP for at least six months, or two quarters of the year. The National Bureau of Economic Research announces and dates recessions. They sometimes, but rarely, deviate from this simple definition.

recognition lag It takes time for the Bureau of Labor Statistics and the Bureau of Economic Analysis to compile and analyze data about the economy. The recognition lag is the lag between when a process begins and when those making economic policy recognize that it is going on. Recognition lags are on the order of three to six months.

representative agent A simplification often made in macroeconomics that assumes all participants in the economy are the same (i.e., that the differences between businesses and workers do not matter much for the issues under study). Macroeconomists will analyze a situation by examining the decision making of a single representative agent and then generalize to the economy as a whole from what would be his or her decisions.

reserve requirements The amount of money that the central bank requires other banks to maintain either as cash in their vaults or at the central bank for each dollar of deposits that they hold. Reserve requirements are one of the principal determinants of the money multiplier. Their adjustment is a rarely used tool of central banks.

reserves-to-deposits ratio The ratio of bank reserves to bank deposits; partly the result of mandated government regulations, and partly the result of banks' desire to avoid getting caught short and of fear that those they lend to will not pay the money back. One of the two determinants (along with the currency-to-deposits ratio) of the money multiplier.

residential investment New construction of residences, both single-family homes and apartment buildings. An important component of total investment, and the principal nonbusiness component of investment. Fluctuations in residential investment are an important source of the business cycle.

resource scarcity Shortage in natural resources, such as land and water, relative to population.

revaluation When a central bank raises the value of its currency (lowers the nominal price of foreign currency) under a fixed exchange rate system.

Ricardian equivalence The hypothesis that households will cut consumption whenever they see a government deficit, anticipating higher future taxes that will be raised to pay off that deficit. Named for the nineteenth-century economist David Ricardo, but should be named after its principal advocate, the late-twentieth-century economist Robert Barro.

risk averse When individuals and institutions are unwilling to invest in ventures with a reasonable expected return, but also with a substantial probability of disaster.

risk premium The higher interest rate that lenders charge some of their borrowers because they fear that the borrower may not repay their money. Risk premiums are measured relative to the interest rates that the U.S. government can borrow using Treasury bills.

risky interest rate The interest rate on assets where there is some chance the debtor will default.

rules Monetarists believe that central banks should operate by setting fixed rules for how fast they will allow the money supply to grow. Only by setting policy according to fixed rules, they argue, can the central bank minimize uncertainty and let the private sector do its job.

rules versus authorities The debate, started by the early Chicago School economist Henry Simons, over whether macroeconomic policy should be conducted "automatically," according to rules that would be followed no matter what, or determined by authorities with the discretion to respond to specific circumstances as they saw fit.

S

sacrifice ratio The number of percentage points of unemployment in excess of the natural rate times the number of years such excess unemployment must be endured to reduce annual inflation permanently by 1 percentage point.

safe interest rate The interest rate on assets where there is no significant probability of default.

Samuelson, Paul Nobel Prize–winning MIT economist. The person whose late-1940s economics textbook set the mold for the economics textbooks that you use.

saving rate The share of total GDP that an economy saves. Usually calculated as the sum of household, government, and foreign saving divided by total output.

savings-and-loan crisis In the United States in the late 1980s, perhaps $200 billion worth of deposits in savings and loan associations were lost in a run of bad and risky investments, mostly in real estate and in high-yield "junk" bonds.

seasonal adjustment Over a year, employment and production undergo seasonal fluctuations about as large as in a typical business cycle. They build up in the fall in preparation for the Christmas rush. They fall in the summer as vacations are taken. Seasonal adjustment removes these seasonal variations from economic data to give a better idea of the longer-term evolution of the economy.

seignorage The tax implicitly levied on an economy's private sector by the government's exercise of its power to print more money.

services Commodities that are not (or are only incidentally) physical objects but are instead useful processes or pieces of information. Services are contrasted with goods — commodities that are principally useful physical objects.

shareholders Those who own the common stock issued by a company, and so are entitled to vote for its directors and other officers at the company's annual meeting, and to receive dividends (if any).

short-term interest rate The interest rate paid to borrow money for the short term, three to six months.

short-term nominal interest rate The interest rate paid to borrow money for the short term, three to six months. A nominal interest rate is not adjusted for inflation. The short-term nominal interest rate is important because it is the interest rate that has the greatest impact on money demand.

spending multiplier The changes in national income and total expenditure that follow from a one-dollar change in any component of autonomous spending.

stabilization policy Policy aimed at avoiding recessions and undue inflation by keeping total aggregate demand growing smoothly and unemployment near its NAIRU. Stabilization policy is countercyclical policy.

stagflation The coexistence of recession and rising inflation, or of recession and relatively high inflation. Politicians on whose watch economies suffer from stagflation usually lose their jobs at the next election.

static expectations Barely deserve the name of "expectations" at all — visions of the future that do not change at all in response to changes in the current economic situation. Contrasted with adaptive expectations and rational expectations.

statistical discrepancy A fudge factor added to reconcile two measurements of the same quantity that should be equal by definition, but that are not equal as measured.

The national income and product accounts are full of statistical discrepancies. The statistical discrepancy in the international trade sector is often the largest.

sticky prices When wages and prices do not move smoothly and immediately to keep supply equal to demand in the labor and goods markets. With sticky prices, inventory adjustment is the principal determinant of short-run equilibrium.

stock A tradable financial instrument that is a share of ownership of a corporation.

stock market The market on which the shares of common stock that carry ownership of companies are bought and sold. A company's bondholders have a right to be paid their interest and principal out of a company's operating profits. A company's stockholders have the right to elect the company's board of directors and to decide what to do with the rest of its profits. A relatively high stock market indicates optimism about future profits and is likely to be accompanied by a high level of investment.

stock variable An economic quantity or variable that is measured not as a flow over some period of time but as a stock that exists at a single moment in time. For example, the capital stock and the money supply are "stock variables." GDP, consumption, and the government deficit are "flow variables." The capital stock and the money supply can be measured in dollars. But when you speak of GDP, consumption, or the government deficit, you must always be measuring — implicitly or explicitly — in dollars per year.

structural deficit A synonym for cyclically adjusted or high-employment government budget deficit. The government runs a structural deficit when its budget deficit exists not because real GDP is less than potential output, but because taxes are too low or spending too high to balance the budget even when real GDP equals potential output and unemployment is at its natural rate.

structural unemployment Unemployment that is not "cyclical" and not "frictional." Cyclical unemployment goes away when output expands and real GDP reaches the level of potential output. Frictional unemployment serves as the economy's inventory of workers and is part of the normal process of workers changing jobs and finding good matches. Structural unemployment is the result of (a) a real wage level stuck too high for supply to balance demand in the labor market, (b) poor labor-market tax and regulatory policies that drive a large wedge between the earnings that workers receive and the costs firms must pay to employ them, (c) other policies that make it difficult for workers to move to where the jobs are and for jobs to move to where the workers are, or (d) a gross mismatch between the educational and skill levels of the labor force and the levels that employers require. Structural unemployment has been high

in western Europe for two decades, was high in the United States during the Great Depression, and is frequently high in the developing world.

structures Buildings, docks, bridges, and every other component of investment that is neither a piece of machinery and equipment nor a component of inventories. One way of looking at investment is to divide it into spending on machinery and equipment, changes in inventories, and spending on construction and remodeling of structures — residential, business, and government structures.

supply shocks Changes — usually large, sudden changes — in the productivity of the economy. Supply shocks can take the form of a large, sudden change in the price of a key raw material, as happened in the oil shocks of the 1970s. The sudden rise in the price of oil gave businesses a powerful incentive to use less oil and energy and more labor and capital in production; thus the economy's output per worker and its potential output dropped. The sudden rise in the price of oil also set in motion compensating price rises in other sectors, and led to higher inflation. The supply shocks of the 1970s were a major contributing factor to the stagflation of that decade. Rapid changes in technology can be seen as supply shocks as well.

surplus A shortened form of "government surplus." The amount by which the government's taxes exceed its spending.

T

taxes Payments by citizens and other residents to the government. Transfer payments are subtracted from gross taxes to calculate net taxes, or taxes less transfer payments. Net taxes are the measure of how much purchasing power is removed from the private sector by the government's fiscal policies.

taxes less transfers A synonym for "net taxes." The difference between total gross taxes collected by and transfer payments issued by the government. Taxes less transfers is a measure of how much purchasing power the government's fiscal policies remove from private households. Taxes less transfers is the variable T in the models of this book and is here equal to tY, the tax rate t times national income Y.

Taylor rule A description of how the real interest rate that the central bank sets depends on the gap between the current inflation rate and the central bank's target inflation rate.

technological progress Invention and innovation in the broadest sense — including innovations in organization and control — that boost economic productivity over time.

technology transfer The rapid advance in total factor productivity possible in developing countries as they adopt the more productive technologies already well known in the world economy's industrial core. Since most of the difference between productivity levels across countries is due to differences in total factor productivity and the efficiency of labor, successful technology transfer is at the heart of successful economic development.

term structure The relationship between the lifetime — the maturity — of bonds and the interest rates buyers receive from holding bonds until their maturity. "Term structure" is a synonym for "yield curve." The term structure of interest rates usually has an upward slope: The interest rate on long-term bonds is higher than the interest rate on short-term bonds. When the interest rate on short-term bonds is higher, economists say that the term structure is inverted, and an inverted term structure is one sign of a possible future recession.

time inconsistency In macroeconomics, the temptation for central banks to make total nominal spending a little higher than people had expected, for once expectations have been formed, contracts made, and wages and prices set, there appear to be only benefits and no costs to a little more total nominal spending. With total nominal spending a little higher than had been expected, output and employment boom. And since wages and prices have already been set, there is little corresponding increase in inflation. Of course, if a central bank establishes a pattern of always making total spending a little higher than anticipated, people will come to expect such action, and the result will be high and destructive inflation. In the long run the central bank wants to gain and keep a reputation for keeping inflation low. Thus what the central bank would like to do in the short run (boost the economy a bit) is inconsistent with what it needs to do in the long run (maintain its credibility as an inflation fighter).

total factor productivity Total factor productivity is not labor productivity — not real GDP Y divided by the labor force L. Total factor productivity is not capital productivity — not real GDP Y divided by the capital stock K. Instead, total factor productivity is real GDP Y divided by a geometric weighted average of the factors of production, where each factor's weight is the share of national income that is paid to it. Total factor productivity is very closely related to the efficiency of labor E: In the Solow growth model of Chapter 4, total factor productivity is equal to $E^{1-\alpha}$. Total factor productivity is the best measure of the technological level and the overall efficiency of an economy.

total saving Household saving (by businesses and households) plus government saving (the government's surplus, and government saving is negative when the government runs a deficit) plus the capital inflow (the net amount of money that foreigners are committing to buying up property and assets in the home country, equal to minus net exports). Total saving is equal to total investment. Total saving is distinguished from national saving, which is equal to household saving plus the government surplus (leaving out the capital inflow); and total saving is distinguished from household saving, which is just the saving directly undertaken by households plus the business saving undertaken by firms on behalf of the households that are their owners.

trade balance A synonym for net exports, equal to gross exports minus imports.

trade deficit When gross exports are less than imports, and thus when net exports are negative. A country runs a trade deficit when international demand for goods and services it produces is less than home demand for goods and services produced abroad. A trade deficit is a subtraction from aggregate demand for domestically made products. A trade deficit is also necessarily associated with an equal capital inflow: net investment by foreigners in the home country.

trade surplus When gross exports are greater than imports, and thus when net exports are positive. A country runs a trade surplus when international demand for goods and services it produces is greater than home demand for goods and services produced abroad. A trade surplus is a boost to aggregate demand for domestically made products. A trade surplus is also necessarily associated with an equal capital outflow: net investment by home-country citizens in foreign countries.

transfer payments Spending by the government that is not a purchase of goods or services but instead simply a transfer of income from taxpayers to program recipients. Payments to contractors who have built highways or to bureaucrats who have sold their labor time to the government are not transfer payments. Payments to food stamp recipients, Social Security recipients, or unemployment insurance recipients are transfer payments. Transfer payments are included in the NIPA not as government purchases but under the "taxes" category. Transfer payments are subtracted from gross taxes to arrive at net taxes.

transitory income The difference between a household's current income and its permanent income. A household's transitory income is any portion of its current income that is seen as a windfall, and is not expected to continue in the future. Households tend to spend most of changes in their permanent income and to save most of changes in their transitory income. The marginal propensity to consume out of transitory income is much lower than the marginal propensity to consume out of permanent income.

Treasury bill A short-term bond issued by the United States Treasury. A U.S. government bond with a maturity — a period between the date at which the bond is issued and the date at which its principal comes due — of a year or less. A Treasury bill is a discount bond. It has no explicit payment of interest associated with it, and it pays a positive interest rate to investors solely because it is initially sold at a discount to — for less than — its principal value. Federal Reserve monetary policy is carried out almost exclusively by open-market operations in Treasury bills.

Treasury bond A long-term bond issued by the United States Treasury. A U.S. government bond with a maturity — a period between the date at which the bond is issued and the date at which its principal comes due — often years or more. A Treasury bond is a coupon bond: Not only does the government pay the holder the bond's principal at its maturity, but it pays the holder periodic "coupon" interest payments throughout the bond's lifetime.

Treasury note A medium-term bond issued by the United States Treasury. A U.S. government bond with a maturity — a period between the date at which the bond is issued and the date at which its principal comes due — between one and ten years. A Treasury note is a coupon bond: Not only does the government pay the holder the note's principal at its maturity, but it pays the holder periodic "coupon" interest payments throughout the note's lifetime.

twin deficits During the 1980s the U.S. government budget deficits and trade deficits mirrored each other: When one rose, the other rose; when one fell, the other fell; they were "twins." The argument was made that the first was driving the second — that high U.S. trade deficits were the result of large government budget deficits — and that the cure for the trade deficit was for the government to get its fiscal house in order and balance its budget, and not to impose tariffs and import restrictions on goods coming into the United States. In the 1990s the U.S. government budget and trade deficits were no longer twins: By the end of the decade the U.S. government was running a surplus, and the trade deficit was larger than it had ever been before. Why? Because the "twin deficits" doctrine was too simplistic: It would have been more accurate to say that a large trade deficit is the result of a large net capital inflow into the United States, and while a government budget deficit that raises domestic interest rates is one factor that can cause such a capital inflow, there are others as well. In the 1990s the inflow of capital into the United States was driven by investor optimism and high rates of investment in America.

U

unemployment rate The share of the labor force who are looking for but have not found an acceptable job. The labor force is calculated by adding (*a*) the number of people who told the Current Population Survey interviewers that they were at work and (*b*) the number of people who told the CPS interviewers they were looking for

work but had no job. The number of unemployed is calculated as the number of people who told the CPS interviewers they were looking for work but had no job. The unemployment rate is the number of unemployed divided by the labor force. The conventionally measured unemployment rate is usually seen as an underestimate of the amount of unemployment in the economy. The unemployment rate fails to take account of discouraged workers — those who want to work but are not looking for a job now because they don't think they can find one. It also makes no allowance for those who are working part-time for economic reasons — people who want a full-time job, but have found only a part-time one.

unionization rate The share of an economy's workforce that belongs to a labor union. In the United States the unionization rate has been falling slowly but steadily since World War II, so that private-sector unionization rates are now about one-third what they are in western Europe.

unit of account One of the three functions that economists traditionally ascribe to money: Money is a medium of exchange, a store of value, and a unit of account. To say that a form of money — the U.S. dollar, say — is a unit of account is to say that a great many contracts are written promising to exchange such-and-such a good or service for such-and-such a number of dollars. The fact that a form of money is a unit of account means that changes in that form of money's value — inflation or deflation — can have powerful effects on the distribution of income and the level of production. Falling prices — deflation — increase the real wealth of creditors: The amount of money they are owed buys more real goods and services when the price level is lower. Rising prices — inflation — increase the real wealth of debtors: The quantity of real goods they must sell to raise the money to pay off their debt is lower when the price level is higher. As John Maynard Keynes wrote in 1923, "The fact of falling prices injures entrepreneurs; consequently, the fear of falling prices causes [them to] . . . curtail . . . their operations" and leads to reduced production and high unemployment.

V

value added The difference between the material costs a business incurs in production by buying raw materials and intermediate goods and the revenue it earns when it sells its products. Value added is equal to the sum of (*a*) employee compensation (wages, salaries, and benefits), (*b*) capital costs (depreciation and interest), and (*c*) profits.

variable lags Part of a phrase from economist Milton Friedman: "Monetary policy works with long and variable lags." It reflects the idea that shifts in government policy will have powerful effects on aggregate demand, but that the time needed for such policy shifts to have their effects is not fixed but varies from time to time, country to country, and case to case. Because changes in economic policy work with long and variable lags, caution in changing economic policies helps avoid doing more harm than good.

velocity of money The rate at which the economy's money stock "turns over" in an economy, equal to nominal expenditure or income divided by the money stock. If an economy has $1 trillion of monetary assets and annual nominal national income of $10 trillion, economists say that money has an income velocity of ($10 trillion)/ ($1 trillion) = 10. The velocity of money is a measure of how often the average monetary asset is used as a means of payment, and thus changes hands, over the course of a year. The higher the interest rate, the greater the velocity of money. A higher interest rate gives businesses and households an incentive to economize on their use of money — that proportion of their wealth they hold in liquid and readily spendable but low interest–earning form.

Volcker, Paul Chair of the Federal Reserve Board from 1979 to 1987. His tenure saw the highest unemployment rates in post–World War II U.S. history and the reduction of inflation from near 10 percent per year to less than 4 percent per year.

voter myopia The theory that voters react to the immediate economic situation, rather than to what has happened in the further past or what is likely to happen in the future.

W

wage indexation When unions or workers negotiate with managers for wage levels that rise automatically when the price level rises. If (say) a steelworkers' contract provides them with an extra 1 percent increase in wages for each 1 percent rise in the CPI, economists say that their wages are indexed to the CPI. The more prevalent wage indexation is in an economy, the steeper its Phillips curve and the larger the change in inflation produced by any shift in the unemployment rate. When wage indexation is prevalent, changes in prices will immediately and automatically trigger corresponding changes in wages.

Y

yield curve The relationship between the interest rate you earn for lending or are charged for borrowing money and the length of time of the loan contract. "Yield curve" is a synonym for "term structure." A yield curve diagram is drawn with the interest rate for a given risk category of bonds on the vertical axis, and the bonds' maturity — the time until the borrower repays the principal — on the horizontal axis. The yield curve usually slopes upward: You pay a higher interest rate to borrow and earn a higher interest rate to lend for a longer term because longer-term investments bear higher risk. Whenever the yield curve slopes downward — whenever short-term interest rates are higher than long-term rates — economists say that the yield curve is inverted. An inverted yield curve is a sign of a possible future recession.

yield to maturity The interest rate you will earn over the life span of a bond if you buy it today and hold it until it reaches its maturity and the issuer pays you back the bond's principal. Note that if the bond's current price is different from its face (or principal) value, the yield to maturity will be different from the coupon interest rate. Consider a five-year bond with a principal value of $100 that pays annual coupon interest of 5 percent, or $5 a year. If you paid $100 for this bond, its yield to maturity would be the coupon interest rate of 5 percent per year. But if you buy the bond for $85, its yield to maturity is 8.84 percent. Remember: The lower the price of a bond, the higher the interest rate it pays.

Index

U.S. Macroeconomic Data

Year	Real GDP (billions of chained 2000 dollars)	Real GDP per Worker (chained 2000 dollars)	Inflation (based on GDP deflator, percent per year)	Unemploy-ment (percent)	Long-Term Real Interest Rate (BAA bonds - actual inflation rate)	Real Exchange Rate (dollar value of foreign currency; 1982 = 100)	Real Stock Market Value (S&P composite; 2000 index value)	Consumption (billions of chained 2000 dollars)
1959	2,441.3	35,708	1.2	5.5	3.85		276.48	1,554.6
1960	2,501.8	35,931	1.4	5.5	3.79		265.40	1,597.4
1961	2,560.0	36,333	1.1	6.7	3.98		311.40	1,630.3
1962	2,715.2	38,451	1.4	5.5	3.62		289.17	1,711.1
1963	2,834.0	39,453	1.1	5.7	3.76		320.49	1,781.6
1964	2,998.6	41,026	1.5	5.2	3.33		367.62	1,888.4
1965	3,191.1	42,859	1.8	4.5	3.07		391.21	2,007.7
1966	3,399.1	44,861	2.8	3.8	2.87		367.82	2,121.8
1967	3,484.6	45,052	3.1	3.8	3.13		384.69	2,185.0
1968	3,652.7	46,391	4.3	3.6	2.64		396.13	2,310.5
1969	3,765.4	46,640	5.0	3.5	2.81		374.11	2,396.4
1970	3,771.9	45,570	5.3	4.9	3.81		302.20	2,451.9
1971	3,898.6	46,202	5.0	5.9	3.56		339.92	2,545.5
1972	4,105.0	47,165	4.3	5.6	3.86	102	361.94	2,701.3
1973	4,341.5	48,547	5.6	4.9	2.64	113	337.26	2,833.8
1974	4,319.6	46,978	9.0	5.6	0.50	116	238.62	2,812.3
1975	4,311.2	45,974	9.5	8.5	1.11	122	226.70	2,876.9
1976	4,540.9	47,223	5.8	7.7	3.95	124	253.74	3,035.5
1977	4,750.5	47,980	6.4	7.1	2.57	120	229.66	3,164.1
1978	5,015.0	49,046	7.0	6.1	2.49	133	209.82	3,303.1
1979	5,173.4	49,288	8.3	5.8	2.39	134	207.88	3,383.4
1980	5,161.7	48,267	9.1	7.1	4.57	131	219.71	3,374.1
1981	5,291.7	48,695	9.4	7.6	6.64	111	216.56	3,422.2
1982	5,189.3	47,088	6.1	9.7	10.01	100	190.81	3,470.3
1983	5,423.8	48,622	3.9	9.6	9.65	95	245.97	3,668.6
1984	5,813.6	51,201	3.8	7.5	10.39	89	237.14	3,863.3
1985	6,053.7	52,431	3.0	7.2	9.72	86	267.97	4,064.0
1986	6,263.6	53,156	2.2	7.0	8.19	98	331.62	4,228.9
1987	6,475.1	54,020	2.7	6.2	7.88	107	391.82	4,369.8
1988	6,742.7	55,418	3.4	5.5	7.43	115	351.08	4,546.9
1989	6,981.4	56,361	3.8	5.3	6.38	113	410.90	4,675.0
1990	7,112.5	56,520	3.9	5.6	6.46	115	409.97	4,770.3
1991	7,100.5	56,199	3.5	6.8	6.30	116	445.41	4,778.4
1992	7,336.6	57,270	2.3	7.5	6.68	119	481.17	4,934.8
1993	7,532.7	58,303	2.3	6.9	5.63	117	510.70	5,099.8
1994	7,835.5	59,787	2.1	6.1	6.52	117	510.08	5,290.7
1995	8,031.7	60,706	2.0	5.6	6.20	121	588.09	5,433.5
1996	8,328.9	62,182	1.9	5.4	6.15	118	714.37	5,619.4
1997	8,703.5	63,857	1.7	4.9	6.16	112	915.40	5,831.8
1998	9,066.9	65,858	1.1	4.5	6.12	103	1125.16	6,125.8
1999	9,470.3	67,952	1.4	4.2	6.47	104	1356.25	6,438.6
2000	9,817.0	68,851	2.2	4.0	6.16	100	1427.22	6,739.4
2001	9,890.7	68,813	2.4	4.7	5.55	94	1166.17	6,910.
2002	10,074.8	69,547	1.7	5.8	6.10	94	954.82	7,123
2003	10,381.3	70,857	1.8	6.0	4.97	100	910.57	7,355
2004	10,837.2	73,522	2.1	5.5	4.29	105	1044.18	7,634
2005*	11,216.5	74,977	2.5	5.3	4.39	110	1036.53	7,86

Investment (billions of chained 2000 dollars)	Government Purchases (billions of chained 2000 dollars)	Net Exports (billions of chained 2000 dollars)	Short-Term Nominal Interest Rate (3-month Treasury bills; percent per year)	Long-Term Nominal Interest Rate (BAA bonds)	Price Level (GDP deflator, 2000 = 100)	Government Budget Surplus (percent of GDP; deficit is a negative; fiscal years)	Nominal Stock Prices (S&P composite index)	Labor Force (thousands)
266.7	714.3	−24.7	3 .405	5.05	20.75	−2.6	57.38	68,369
266.6	715.4	−12.7	2 .928	5.19	21.04	0.1	55.85	69,628
264.9	751.3	−11.5	2 .378	5.08	21.28	−0.6	66.27	70,459
298.4	797.6	−18.6	2 .778	5.02	21.57	−1.3	62.38	70,614
318.5	818.1	−14.8	3 .157	4.86	21.80	−0.8	69.87	71,833
344.7	836.1	−9.0	3 .549	4.83	22.13	−0.9	81.37	73,091
393.1	861.3	−18.9	3 .954	4.87	22.54	−0.2	88.17	74,455
427.7	937.1	−31.1	4 .881	5.67	23.18	−0.5	85.26	75,770
408.1	1,008.9	−39.6	4 .321	6.23	23.90	−1.1	91.93	77,347
431.9	1,040.5	−54.6	5 .339	6.94	24.92	−2.9	98.70	78,737
457.1	1,038.0	−58.9	6 .677	7.81	26.15	0.3	97.84	80,734
427.1	1,012.9	−52.0	6 .458	9.11	27.54	−0.3	83.22	82,771
475.7	990.8	−60.6	4 .348	8.56	28.92	−2.1	98.29	84,382
532.1	983.5	−73.5	4 .071	8.16	30.17	−2.0	109.20	87,034
594.4	980.0	−51.9	7 .041	8.24	31.85	−1.1	107.43	89,429
550.6	1,004.7	−29.4	7 .886	9.50	34.72	−3.4	82.85	91,949
453.1	1,027.4	−2.4	5 .838	10.61	38.01	−4.2	86.16	93,775
544.7	1,031.9	−37.0	4 .989	9.75	40.20	−3.2	102.01	96,158
627.0	1,043.3	−61.1	5 .265	8.97	42.76	−2.7	98.20	99,009
702.6	1,074.0	−61.9	7 .221	9.49	45.76	−2.7	96.02	102,251
725.0	1,094.1	−41.0	10 .041	10.69	49.55	−1.6	103.01	104,962
645.3	1,115.4	12.6	11 .506	13.67	54.06	−2.7	118.78	106,940
704.9	1,125.6	8.3	14 .029	16.04	59.13	−2.6	128.05	108,670
606.0	1,145.4	−12.6	10 .686	16.11	62.74	−4.0	119.71	110,204
662.5	1,187.3	−60.2	8 .63	13.55	65.21	−6.0	160.41	111,550
857.7	1,227.0	−122.4	9 .58	14.19	67.66	−4.8	160.46	113,544
849.7	1,312.5	−141.5	7 .48	12.72	69.72	−5.1	186.84	115,461
843.9	1,392.5	−156.3	5 .98	10.39	71.27	−5.0	236.34	117,834
870.0	1,426.7	−148.4	5 .82	10.58	73.20	−3.2	286.83	119,865
890.5	1,445.1	−106.8	6 .69	10.83	75.71	−3.1	265.79	121,669
926.2	1,482.5	−79.2	8 .12	10.18	78.57	−2.8	322.84	123,869
895.1	1,530.0	−54.7	7 .51	10.36	81.61	−3.9	334.59	125,840
822.2	1,547.2	−14.6	5 .42	9.80	84.46	−4.5	376.18	126,346
889.0	1,555.3	−15.9	3 .45	8.98	86.40	−4.7	415.74	128,105
968.3	1,541.1	−52.1	3 .02	7.93	88.39	−3.9	451.41	129,200
1,099.6	1,541.3	−79.4	4 .29	8.62	90.27	−2.9	460.42	131,056
1,134.0	1,549.7	−71.0	5 .51	8.20	92.12	−2.2	541.72	132,304
1,234.3	1,564.9	−79.6	5 .02	8.05	93.86	−1.4	670.50	133,943
1,387.7	1,594.0	−104.6	5 .07	7.86	95.42	−0.3	873.43	136,297
1,524.1	1,624.4	−203.7	4 .81	7.22	96.48	0.8	1085.50	137,673
1,642.6	1,686.9	−296.2	4 .66	7.87	97.87	1.4	1327.33	139,368
1,735.5	1,721.6	−379.5	5 .85	8.36	100.00	2.4	1427.22	142,583
1,598.4	1,780.3	−399.1	3 .45	7.95	102.40	1.3	1194.18	143,734
1,560.7	1,857.9	−472.1	1 .62	7.80	104.10	−1.5	993.94	144,863
1,628.8	1,909.4	−518.5	1 .02	6.77	106.00	−3.5	965.23	146,510
1,839.1	1,946.7	−586.4	1 .38	6.39	108.28	−3.6	1130.65	147,401
1,949.5	2,024.6	−670.6	3 .15	6.89	110.99	−3.5	1150.42	149,600

Notation	Introduced in chapter	Definition
α (alpha)	4	parameter of Cobb–Douglas production function
β (beta)	12	$-\beta$ is the slope of the Phillips curve
δ (delta)	4	depreciation rate of physical capital K
ε (epsilon)	2	real exchange rate
ε^* (epsilon)	15	the government's target real exchange rate
ε_0 (epsilon)	6	baseline level of the real exchange rate
ε_r (epsilon)	6	responsiveness of the real exchange rate to changes in the real interest rate
ε_R (epsilon)	15	responsiveness of the real exchange rate to changes in foreign exchange reserves
μ (mu)	13	money multiplier
π (pi)	7	inflation rate; rate of change of price level P
π^e (pi)	7	expected future inflation rate
π^t (pi)	12	the central bank's target inflation rate
σ^s (sigma)	2	risk premium
ϕ (phi)	12	slope of the monetary policy reaction function
A	9	total autonomous spending; spending not affected by income; $A = C_0 + I + G + GX$
A_0	10	baseline autonomous spending; spending not affected by income nor interest rates
AD	7	aggregate demand: $AD = C + I + G + GX - IM$
B	13	monetary base
C	4	consumption spending by households
C_0	6	baseline level of consumption
C_y	6	marginal propensity to consume, mpc; $C_y = \Delta C / \Delta Y^D$
d	14	government deficit; if $d < 0$, there is a government surplus
D	14	government debt
e	2	nominal exchange rate; domestic price of 1 unit of foreign currency
E	4	efficiency of labor force
FG	15	flow of gold into the domestic economy
g	4	growth rate of labor efficiency E
G	4	government purchases of goods and services
GX	4	gross exports; goods and services sold to foreigners
i	7	nominal interest rate; $i = r + \pi^e$
I	4	investment spending by businesses
I_0	6	baseline level of investment spending
I_r	6	responsiveness of investment spending to changes in the real interest rate
IM	4	imports; goods and services purchased from foreigners
IM_y	6	responsiveness of import spending to a change in real GDP Y
K	3	real physical capital
K/L	4	capital per worker
K/Y	4	capital-output ratio
L	3	size of labor force